Date Due

The Wilson Era

Years of Peace—1910-1917

WOODROW WILSON

An unfinished portrait painted by Sir William Orpen. Now in the home of the
Honorable Bernard M. Baruch, close friend and adviser of Wilson.

The Wilson Era
Years of Peace—1910-1917

BY JOSEPHUS DANIELS

SECRETARY OF THE NAVY, 1913-1921

"These things I saw and part of them I was."
—Virgil

CHAPEL HILL: *The University of North Carolina Press*

1944

TO

MY WIFE, MY BEST COUNSELLOR

ADDIE WORTH BAGLEY DANIELS

"The truest and tenderest and purest wife ever man was blessed with. To have such a love is the one blessing, in comparison of which all earthly joy is of no value; and to think of her is to praise God."

FOREWORD

As the only surviving member of Woodrow Wilson's cabinet during his occupancy of the White House, privileged to be admitted to personal and political friendship, I have felt the compulsion—"looking back to glory"—to record from an inside seat the story of how he won every battle for the domestic reforms embodied in his New Freedom and strengthened international friendships.

I have sought to give the highlights of the Wilson Era from the time he doffed the university cap and gown and entered the arena of politics and official administration, first as Governor of New Jersey (1910) and afterwards in his first four years as President of the United States (1913-17). I have traced with sketchy outlines his course through the tortuous days of neutrality up to the Day of Decision in March, 1917. A subsequent volume will deal with his leadership in the World War, the drafting of the Covenant of the League of Nations, and the years that followed, when, fighting for that chart and compass of world peace, he fell as the great casualty of the World War.

It was from the Navy's Conning Tower that I observed—all of which I saw and part of which I was—the most revealing events of those historic years. Naturally I write of "what me befell" as Secretary of the Navy, of the development toward the two-ocean Navy that came into being in Wilson's day, and of the authorization in 1915-16 of the building of the greatest Navy in the world. I relate incidents that came under my personal and official observation as to measures which were considered at Cabinet meetings and by other agencies of government. I accompany this relation with an appraisement of some of the leaders of that period which was ushered in with Wilson's appeal: "I summon all honest men, all patriotic, all forward-looking men to my side," when he made the pledge he ever held sacred: "God helping me I will not fail them if they will but counsel and sustain me."

Josephus Daniels

CONTENTS

PART FIVE

Resignations and Elections

PART SIX

Portraits

PART SEVEN

Preparation and Neutrality

ILLUSTRATIONS

CARTOONS

Part One

"LET THE PEOPLE IN"

WHEN I FIRST MET WILSON

I REMEMBER the first time I met Woodrow Wilson. I had seen him only once before, and that was in Washington when he delivered the address at the unveiling of a statue of John Witherspoon, in the triangle facing the Church of the Covenant on Connecticut Avenue. I was impressed then by his original style and his just appraisement of Witherspoon—whose signature to the Declaration of Independence had caused Horace Walpole to say, "Cousin America has run off with a Presbyterian parson."

Earlier than 1912, in fact even before George Harvey claimed to have discovered him, I had been impressed by the suggestion of Woodrow Wilson for President. In November, 1907, Joseph Pulitzer, of the New York *World,* had written to Frank Cobb to try to head off Bryan and had suggested that the *World* propose Wilson as a "Southern candidate," saying:

> "Woodrow Wilson was born in the South. His wife was born in the South. What better candidate could they present who would have a better chance to carry New York and New Jersey than anybody I can think of now? He is a statesman and a scholar and a man of extraordinary ability."

I was sitting at my editorial desk in *The News and Observer* office in Raleigh shortly before nine o'clock on the night of January 18, 1909, when I heard a voice asking, "May I invade your sanctum?" I recognized Woodrow Wilson standing at the door and hastened to welcome him. Though this was our first meeting, I felt that he was not a stranger. Letters had passed between us. I knew his father and had once heard him preach, and, of course, I knew that the son was winning fame in the world of letters. I had read some of his books and had a second-hand knowledge of his academic war at Princeton.

I remember vividly when his name was first mentioned to me as a possible President of the United States. It was on the night of August 31, 1886. The date is photographed indelibly on my memory.

It was the night of the "Charleston Earthquake," so called because, although it was felt over a large territory, the chief damage was done in Charleston.

Having finished supper at the Yarborough House, Walter Hines Page and I repaired to my bedroom on the third floor for a chat. He told me about his experiences and observations in the metropolis to which he had gone after he had started the *State Chronicle,* in Raleigh in 1883, a paper of which I became editor in 1885. Page was keen to see this baby he had brought into the world grow and prosper, and he had volunteered the contribution of a weekly letter from New York under the initials "W.H.P." I recall that he wrote these letters with his own hand. The chirography was beautiful—like copper plate. All the Page admirers were tied to my paper by these weekly letters. They were as fresh as a spring morning and as stimulating as his active mind. He was a pioneer columnist and a brilliant one. His style had a quality all its own.

I am not clear how we fell to talking about Woodrow Wilson, but we did. He asked me if I had read Wilson's *Congressional Government: A Study in American Politics,* which had appeared the previous year. He said it was the elaboration of Wilson's thesis for the degree of Doctor of Philosophy at Johns Hopkins University, where he and Page had formed a strong friendship in 1876 as fellow students. I told him I had not read it.

"I will send it to you," he said, "for you cannot fully understand the workings of our government without reading Wilson's book, particularly his comparison with the British system." He added, "Keep your eye on Wilson. His is the best mind in America studying political questions. One day he may be President of the United States."

Hardly had Page uttered the words, "President of the United States," when the hotel began to rock. "My God, Joe," he said. "It's an earthquake! Let's get out!" We bounded down two flights of swaying stairs and mingled with the excited crowd seeking a safe place.

When, on that 18th of January, I looked up from my desk and saw Woodrow Wilson standing at the door, he had come to Raleigh en route to Chapel Hill to speak the next day at the University of North Carolina in commemoration of the one hundredth anniversary of the birthday of Robert E. Lee. As I was a trustee of the University and had become an admirer of Wilson at a distance, I had invited him to be my guest in Raleigh on his way to Chapel Hill. He replied that as his time was limited he must go direct and his route would not enable him to stop in Raleigh. However, when he reached Washington, he discovered that the best way to reach Chapel Hill was to spend the night in Raleigh. He had arrived an hour or so before his call, registered at the hotel, and walked to my office to express thanks for the invitation. As he had already taken a room at the hotel and must leave early next morning, he thought it best not to become my overnight guest, but he would be glad, he said, to visit my home and see my wife. I telephoned her, and we walked about a mile to my house. When he learned that my wife was a niece of David G. Worth and a grandniece of B. G. Worth, both ruling elders in the First Presbyterian Church in Wilmington, of which his father had been pastor for some years, he recalled his father's friendship for them both and his own acquaintance with them during his father's pastorate. This association at once formed a link between him and my wife, and they talked of Wilmington, particularly of his father. A lasting friendship between them was born. He related some incidents of his residence in Wilmington, revealing that sense of veneration and comradeship between father and son which I was later more fully to understand. One incident that I recall was an account of how his father, travelling by horse and buggy to preach in Sampson County, was asked how it happened that his horse was so fat while he himself was so thin. Dr. Wilson, with the ready wit for which he was noted, replied, "Well, you see I feed my horse, but my congregation feeds me."

PRINCETON'S DEMOCRATIC REGENERATION

Turning from reminiscences of his days in North Carolina, I ventured to ask a question about the controversy at Princeton, of which I had read something. I saw that I had struck fire. Wilson was instantly alert and proceeded for more than an hour, sometimes with feeling and sometimes with a dash of humor, to review the issues at Princeton, which were acute at that time.

"I have told the trustees of Princeton that I will not be the president of a country club," he said, "and that unless it is to be an educational institution I cannot continue as its president." He then reviewed the story of his purpose to make Princeton a place free from the snobbery which had crept into American universities. He explained his plans for what was known as the "quad system," outlining it as a plan to bring undergraduates together in residential "quads," in which they should eat as well as lodge together, and in which they would be under the direction of a resident member of the faculty and would regulate their own corporate life by a simple method of self-government. He related how the clubs at Princeton had caused young men to give their enthusiasm to club life and bring tired minds to their studies. He told how freshmen fawned on upper classmen in order to win access to exclusive clubs, preferring such distinctions to scholastic honors. I can never forget his scorn when he denounced the propaganda: "Wilson wants to make a gentleman eat with a mucker," and "What is the world coming to when a man is compelled to submit to dictation as to his table companions?" He dilated upon his resolve to bring democratic regeneration of spirit in the university over which he presided. My wife and I sat enthralled as he lived over something of what was called "The Battle of Princeton." We could not understand how anyone could resist his democratic program.

WILSON SPEAKS AT CHAPEL HILL

The next morning we left on a special train for the University. Governor Kitchin, nearly all the members of the State Legislature then in session in Raleigh, state officials, and prominent citizens were on the train, going to hear the man who was then being spoken of as a possible candidate of the Democratic Party in the coming presidential election. Political sentiment had hardly begun to crystallize, and the North Carolina politicians took advantage of the opportunity to hear Wilson and take his measure. His speech made a profound impression, and if the politicians, educators, and editors present could have voted that day, Woodrow Wilson would have been their choice. He made no reference to politics. If he had come to North Carolina to build fences for 1912, there was no indication of it. However, in his address he used Lee's devotion to principle as the example for public service, saying: "If I did not, after saturating myself in the conceptions upon which this government was formed, express my knowledge of those principles and my belief in them by the way I voted, I would lose my self-respect."

Said President Venable at the dinner following the address, "I think the University has introduced to North Carolina the next Chief

Executive of the United States." I agreed and so did others who heard his remark.

Freed from the absorption that seemed to make him uncommunicative before his address, Wilson was the soul of the company at the dinner in his honor. He told stories and anecdotes, most of them about teachers and the refusal of educational institutions to leave their cloistered atmosphere and serve the needs of the hour. I recall that he spoke with affection of his old teacher, Dr. Charles Phillips, who, when the University was closed after the war of the sixties, became a professor at Davidson when Wilson was a student at that small and good Presbyterian College. "If you were as expert in taking aim at your studies as in hitting the mark with your tobacco juice, you might graduate," he related as the remark Dr. Phillips once made to a student who occupied himself during recitation by spitting through a knothole in a plank that closed the fireplace in the classroom. The recollection of that incident caused much merriment, for Dr. Phillips and his father had both been distinguished professors at the University of North Carolina.

When the dinner ended, Wilson had charmed the entire company. I felt, as he won all at the table by his brilliant conversation, that Wesleyan's college annual, *Olla Podrida,* had appraised him justly when it said he "made everything he touched interesting, and expressed the opinion of the students in these lines:

> "Prof. W - l - n —
> 'A merrier man,
> Within the limit of becoming mirth,
> I never spent an hour's talk withal.'"

The pleasure he manifested in being with his sister's son, Dr. George Howe, head of the Latin Department, was beautiful to see. They were more like boys in a reunion after long separation than like college president and college professor.

This revealing of himself in social life gave me an insight into the man that heightened the enthusiasm which his address had kindled. It showed the softer and more delightful side of one who could turn from the serious purpose of his visit to enjoy and please small circles of new-found friends.

LEE NO PLASTER SAINT

In his address, while he was speaking of Lee, somehow one felt that he was describing himself—and he was, all unconsciously—as the sort of man to whom people ascribe distinction. "When you come into the presence of a leader of men," he said, "you know you have come into the presence of fire,—that it is best not incautiously to touch that man,—that there is something that makes it dangerous to cross him, that if you grapple his mind you will find that you have grappled with flame and fire. You do not want sweetness merely and light in men who lead you."

This seemed to be an aside from an address, delivered without notes, in which he had begun by saying that Lee's "fame is not enhanced, his memory is not lifted to any new place of distinction by any man's words of praise, for he is secure of his place." He envisioned Lee as no plaster saint, as he has so often been described. "There was just as much fire in Lee as there was in Washington," but "he was always well in hand; ... you knew that the man himself was aware that he was driving a mettlesome team, which he had to watch at every moment to avoid sudden runaway."

That estimate of Lee was new to me. I had conceived of him as a man free from the passions that burst forth at times in most men, as having by a supreme control and sweetness and light risen above the temptations of other soldiers.

CRIME IS PERSONAL

If Wilson did not say anything that indicated he might be looking to political preferment, toward the close of his address he touched upon the remedies needed to end corporation evils. He emphasized a doctrine that he had before touched upon, saying that "until you have picked them out [the "malicious" men engaged in handling corporations] and distinguished them for punishment you have not touched the process by which they succeed in doing what they wish." He was here stressing his belief that "crime is personal" and cannot be ended by fining the corporation and letting the individual go free.

Returning to Raleigh that afternoon I observed that the corporation lawyers on the train expressed regret that Wilson had weakened a great oration on Lee by his condemnation of the evils of big business. But these objections were drowned, for the time being, by the plaudits of most of his hearers. Personally he had won me to whole-hearted admiration, and I returned to my editorial desk believing that he should be the next President. Often in the succeeding days I was to express that belief in the columns of my paper. With others whose hearts had been stirred by his eloquence, I began to try to organize sentiment toward Wilson for President.

Shortly after his visit to North Carolina, a small organization, "Wilson for President," opened headquarters in New York. It was headed by William F. McCombs, a New York lawyer, who had been a student of Wilson's at Princeton. This group saw that if Wilson was to win the votes of the West he would have to do so on his "personality as well as upon his public record and his political opinions." He was a new figure in the political world and was unknown to the people of the West. With interest I followed in the papers the reception accorded him on his speaking tour of the West, and as he was returning through the South I got in touch with McCombs and asked him to include Raleigh in Wilson's itinerary.

WILSON REVISITS NORTH CAROLINA

This was done, and on May 30, 1911, Wilson delivered the Commencement address at the University of North Carolina. His subject was "When a Man Comes to Himself." The address increased my admiration. I recall that he said: "I am two kinds of a Democrat— first I was brought up to be one; and, second, because by study and maturing of my judgment, I have become convinced that the Democratic party is in the right." On the previous day he had spoken at the Alumni luncheon on "The Mission of the University in America." He asked why universities "should teach young men to seek to stop the combination between political power and financial organizations or teach young engineers to build a great bridge unless you teach them the great good that shall come of the work in uplifting the moral tone of the nation."

I was in Chapel Hill when Wilson arrived and invited him to be my guest while he was in Raleigh. I communicated with my wife, who invited several score of the leading citizens to meet Wilson at our home the next day. In addition to my happiness in having him as a guest, I wished Raleigh friends to meet him, feeling assured that he would win them and that they would support him for the nomination, which I foresaw would be contested in North Carolina.

After the luncheon, there was a reception at my home attended by hundreds of people. When Dr. R. T. Vann, president of Meredith College, came along the receiving line and was introduced, he halted for a little chat with Wilson and remarked, "Governor Wilson, did you read Mr. Shaw's speech this morning?" Wilson asked, "Do you mean Mr. Leslie M. Shaw, Secretary of the Treasury under Roosevelt?" "Yes," Dr. Vann replied. "No, I have not read Mr. Shaw's speech," said Wilson. "His ways and mine are as far apart as the poles. I have no interest in Mr. Shaw, or any of his doings. He has been repudiated even by his own party." Said Vann, undaunted, "Still, Governor, you must admit Mr. Shaw has the courage of his convictions." "No," retorted Wilson, his eyes flashing, "he has neither courage nor convictions." Vann, somewhat taken aback, walked away.

When there was a lull, Dr. Hubert Royster, who had made the introduction, explained to Wilson that Shaw, on the day before, had delivered the Commencement address at Meredith College, and Vann was merely making conversation; he held no brief for Shaw. Wilson's face relaxed and he asked that Vann be called back. As he approached, Wilson smiled and said,

"Doctor, I am sorry if I unconsciously offended you a moment ago. I did not know that Mr. Leslie M. Shaw had given your Commencement address yesterday, though what he might say to interest the graduates of a woman's college is questionable. My manner in talking to you was incited by the fact that Mr. Shaw has been around lately, as I have been, making speeches, and the same question has been put to me at different places. I had no intention of being rude to you. I offer you my sincere apology, but I do not take back what I said about Mr. Shaw."

Vann accepted the amende in a gracious spirit and soon the two were conversing pleasantly.

When informed that arrangements had been made for him to speak that afternoon to a large crowd in Capitol Square, Wilson rebelled, saying it was impossible for him to speak in the open air. The committee was in desperation. Persuasion did not avail until Dr. Royster as a trump card said to him, "Governor, I have heard that your father trained you to declaim Burke's orations in the woods and I know that you once took voice instruction and that you were a member of the Princeton Glee Club. Your voice will easily carry over the space as arranged, which is skirted by trees." This seemed to change Wilson's attitude, and smiling he said, "I'll try it, if you will have someone in the back of the audience hold up his hand as a sign that he hears me after I have begun to talk." This was done and his words reached the outermost parts of the large crowd, though he never strained his voice.

CHIEF DIFFERENCE IN PARTIES

In his open-air address at Capitol Square, where he was introduced by General Albert L. Cox, a supporter and the next year a Wilson delegate at the Baltimore Convention, Wilson began by saying that whenever he was introduced in such complimentary terms as General Cox had employed, he looked around to see how many Princeton men were present, for, he added, "if I see many of them I feel an uneasiness not unlike that of the lady who went into a sideshow and saw, or thought she saw, a man reading a newspaper through a two-inch board, whereupon, quickly getting up, she said, 'Let me out of here. This is no place for a woman who is wearing no petticoat.'" He said that "the chief difference between the Democratic and Republican parties is that in the Republican Party the reactionaries are in the majority whereas in the Democratic Party they are in the minority." He made this distinction: "A reactionary is a man who looks at public affairs through spectacles of his own; a progressive looks without regard to his own interests, with the purpose and hope that he may be privileged to serve the country by some touch of self-sacrifice, some consideration of those things which are larger and greater and more permanent than himself." Referring to the program of the Democratic Party, he said: "We are not after the rich man or corporations as such." With regard to such monopolies as the oil and tobacco trusts, he declared that he was in favor of prosecuting the men really responsible, not the little fellows, and he added: "An aroused public conscience will pillory them even more than jail sentences." He continued:

"I must say that I have been a great deal amused at the nervousness of certain millionaires whom I have met—they have the look of a person who thinks that somebody is on his trail. ... I have not found the people of the United States wishing to destroy wealth or discourage enterprise, nor make any man feel that there is no place for him ... but have found them in a great passion of resentment against the man who would use his wealth to control the political processes of the country.... There is almost no exaggerating the detail of the plans that have been kept afoot by which politics in this country were to be controlled by wealth, were to be controlled by money."

He made one statement that all who heard him were to remember when, as President, he incarnated his conviction: "The people will forgive a President his mistakes, but they will not forgive him if he declines to lead."

That night Wilson was requested, upon behalf of Henry E. Litchford, who had given a portrait of Stonewall Jackson to the Capital Club in Raleigh, to make the presentation address. This was the fifth time Wilson had been introduced that day. In presenting him, Dr. Royster said: "When the Governor of New Jersey leaves the State tomorrow, he will wish to add another prayer to the Litany: 'From all our traducers and introducers, Good Lord, deliver us.'" Wilson spoke briefly. It was a gem. All who heard it regretted that it had not been taken down by a stenographer and preserved for all time. I can never forget his concluding words: "I do not understand how any man can approach the discharge of responsible duties without faith in the Lord Jesus Christ." It was an unusual place for a confession of faith—a ballroom of a social club. But those who heard him became as reverent as the speaker. He had spoken, not of Jackson's military genius, but of Jackson the Christian, whose faith in God was the dominant force in his life. At his concluding words, a solemn hush fell on the company.

As we were leaving the club, Wilson said to Royster, "That was rather a neat turn to give an introduction. Where did you get it?" Royster answered that he had thought it up while he was entering the ballroom. Wilson replied, "I thought mine up as I ascended the stairs, and it was a good thing there were not over twenty steps or I would have gone over my time."

The speech Wilson had made in the afternoon in Capitol Square was delivered almost on the very spot where Henry Clay in 1844 made his famous and unfortunate declaration on the Mexican question. Up to that meeting, Clay had not defined his position on the all-absorbing Mexican issue. When he failed of election in the fall, it was the general opinion that "the Raleigh speech caused Clay's defeat." No such jinx followed Wilson.

He left Raleigh with the plaudits of those people who sensed that he incarnated the progressive policies then in the air—the reactionaries dissenting. But as we left the Capitol he confided to me his conviction that he had not scored in his address in Capitol Square and it depressed him. He said:

"I lack the voice for out-door speaking and I felt out of place trying to ingratiate myself and my candidacy. The presidency is not worth my trying to do what I was not cut out to do. I went West where the people are radical. I am a radical. I have been interested to see how the conservative South would receive my radical doctrine. Though I was born in the South and spent my youth in it, I have been away so long that I fear it regards me as a Yankee. The love I bear for North Carolina made me desirous, if I must try to commend myself to people anywhere— something that goes against the grain—to come to speak in the capital of North Carolina. I have always been grateful to Davidson College where I studied for a time, to Wilmington where I spent a year getting well, and I'd like Wake Forest College to know I hold it in gratitude because it was the first institution to confer on me the degree of LL.D. as far back as 1887. But the program fixed for me by my friends is about over and I will not go out on a like trip again, no, not for the presidency. The years ahead are going to be critical ones. It daunts me even to contemplate being chosen to lead and I have no stomach to be asking for leadership."

He was thinking aloud to me. He always had to let his feelings out to somebody.

During his visit to North Carolina, so far as I know, Wilson did not speak to any other person about his candidacy. I tried to draw him out about the prospects of carrying the Western States. He said he really did not know—that large crowds had attended his speaking—but he was too much of an amateur in politics to know whether applause of a speech would result in delegates to the convention. He left that to his political friends. Seeming not desirous to talk about prospects, Governor Wilson said:

"Let me tell you of the funniest experience on my Western trip. It was at Denver and the Press Club invited me to a supper at night after the speaking. The journalists were most cordial. One, who had imbibed too freely, was particularly friendly and too affectionate. My train was to leave around midnight and nothing would do but they must escort me to my train. They remained until the train was pulling out of the station. With their adieux they departed—all but my bibulous friend. He put his arm around my shoulders, and then swung off the train, calling back in hic-cough voice in cordial tones: 'God damn, God Damn you, Governor Wilson.' He thought he was saying 'God bless you.' "

After his return to Trenton there came two prized letters—one to my wife and one to me—expressing in his own inimitable gracious style his delight in the visit to our home. I have always regretted that those cherished notes and like words in his own handwriting were burned in a fire that destroyed *The News and Observer* building. They were heart messages couched in choice language.

II

FROM CAMPUS TO HUSTINGS

I N THE WINTER OF 1911 I received a letter from Colonel George Harvey saying he was spending some days at the hunting lodge of Charles H. Mackey near High Point and asking me to visit him and talk over the way to advance Wilson's prospects. I accepted his invitation and we talked far into the night. Rather, he talked, for my knowledge of the situation was limited. He acquainted me with the steps he had taken to secure support for Wilson. He detailed to me the story of how he had resolved to nominate Wilson for Governor of New Jersey as the necessary first step to putting him in the White House.

It was an interesting account of how, against their inclination, he had won the support of James Smith, boss of the Democratic Party, Robert Davis, boss of Jersey City, and James R. Nugent—the big three who were in control of the Democratic machine in New Jersey; how he had hidden Wilson in his room at Trenton until the nomination was made and then had produced him at the psychological moment; and how, all according to the program he had meticulously worked out, Wilson captured the convention by his eloquent speech. Bob Davis had been the first to see the light—so Harvey said.

"Do you think Wilson would make a good governor?" Davis was asked by a gentleman who was discussing the situation.

"How in the hell do I know?" replied Davis. "But I do know he will be a good meal ticket for hungry Democrats. On his coattail hundreds of Democrats will be elected to small offices and the party will win a victory, something it needs if it is to live."

Nothing was lacking in Colonel Harvey's narrative to show that he regarded himself as a twentieth-century Warwick. Discounting his egotism, I knew he had been zealous and active. But I confess that his vanity lessened such admiration as I had entertained for him.

"The first goal reached, the next one is to nominate Wilson for the presidency and then elect him. I know it can be done and how to do it," the self-confident Colonel said. He wanted to know about North Carolina. I told him of the good impression Wilson had made on his visit to the University and said I thought that he would carry a majority of the delegation but that sentiment had not sufficiently crystallized to be certain of what the State would do. Harvey had a table of States and checked them off. He felt sure that Wilson would be nominated if he would follow the right course. I saw that "the right course" was to put himself into the hands of Colonel Harvey.

I surmised that the conflict at Princeton had worked toward sending Wilson to the White House, and that pleased me. The surmise was well founded, for Wilson, who had always had a repressed desire for a political career, was glad to leave the bitterness of university life for the unknown conflicts of the political arena. He would not retire from one fight except to don his fighting clothes for another. In 1885, writing from Bryn Mawr to an old schoolmate (so the papers said when people questioned whether the schoolmaster would doff his cap and gown for the harder political warfare), Wilson had confided that as a young man he had hoped he might enter politics. His father told friends in Wilmington that when a boy in Georgia Wilson printed cards with the words

WOODROW WILSON
UNITED STATES SENATOR FROM GEORGIA

Another early ambition, when he lived in Wilmington and saw the ships come in from all parts of the world, was to become a Naval officer, but his scholastic father felt that the boy was cut out for the collegiate role in which he later distinguished himself.

Though far removed from the scene, I rejoiced when Wilson took the plunge, accepted the nomination, and was elected Governor of New Jersey in 1910 by a majority of 49,000, reversing a Republican majority in the previous election of 82,000. I felt then that he was the hope of the Democratic Party for 1912, and I converted *The News and Observer* into an enthusiastic and persistent advocate of his nomination.

BREAKS WITH MACHINE POLITICIANS

In 1911, when Wilson broke with the New Jersey party leaders and caused the defeat of ex-Senator Jim Smith for the U. S. Senate, the machine politicians of North Carolina and elsewhere believed he had thrown away his chances for nomination to the presidency. I was quite sure that while the machine politicians would be alienated, Wilson's courageous independence would attract the admiration and support of thousands who were not interested in politics for selfish reasons. My paper applauded Wilson's defiance of the machine and expressed gratification in the hope of having a chief executive in the White House who placed devotion to the common weal uppermost.

When I saw Bryan next, I found that Wilson's action had won his commendation, though Bryan could not then forget that Wilson had not supported him in 1896. Moreover, I knew James Smith. I had held a position in the Interior Department in the early days of Cleveland's second administration, and had seen how he and a few other special interest Democratic Senators had emasculated the Wilson-Gorman tariff act in such a way as to draw from Cleveland the denunciation that they were guilty of "party perfidy and party dishonor." That record was known to Wilson, but he based his fight against Smith on the fact that the voters had chosen Martine as the candidate in the primary. Wilson had said: "It is the clear duty of every Democratic legislator who would keep faith with the law of the State, with the avowed principles of his party, to vote for Mr. Martine."

In my paper I hailed Wilson as a modern Andrew Jackson. My admiration was stirred to the highest pitch when he gave this encouragement to all who were weary of machine rule and wished to throw it off:

"Do not allow yourselves to be dismayed. You see where the machine is intrenched, and it looks like a real fortress. It looks as if real men were inside, as if they had real guns. Go and touch it; it is a house of cards. Those are imitation generals. Those are playthings that look like guns. Go and put your shoulder against the thing and it collapses."

In the previous year I had helped to defeat the city machine in my own city of Raleigh and county of Wake. It was not as easy as Wilson's words might indicate, but it proved that with an aroused and determined electorate a selfish organization can be ousted from domination, under militant leadership based upon Wilson's trumpet creed: "God defend me against compromise. I had rather be a knave than a coward." I rejoiced that in a larger field a great leader had appeared to do combat with predatory influences in the political and economic sphere.

Every paper in America followed that bitter fight in New Jersey, and it was as bitter as it was sensational. Wilson won. That was the second rung of the ladder which was to elevate him to the presidency. If Wilson thought when he entered politics he was escaping from conflicts that bred hatred at Princeton, he was destined to a rude awakening. Though the Democratic bosses had favored Wilson's nomination for Governor, he was to receive their hatred and active opposition. How? Although he appointed organization Democrats to most positions, he refused to be controlled in his appointments and policies, as these two incidents illustrate:

James R. Nugent, Chairman of the Democratic State Committee, called by invitation to see Wilson at the Governor's office in Trenton, "to talk things over." Disagreeing about pending legislation which Wilson was urging, Nugent turned to the Governor and said in a loud, insulting tone:

"I know you think you have got the votes. I know how you got them."

"What do you mean?" asked Wilson.

"It is the talk of the State that you got them by patronage," said Nugent.

Pointing to the door, Wilson said, "Good afternoon."

"You are no gentleman," cried back the enraged political boss.

"You are no judge" was Wilson's reply, as the interview was terminated.

A brief time after that, Nugent was dining with some friends in a hotel at Sea Girt, where a party of officers of the New Jersey National Guard were dining. Nugent rose and asked the members of the Guard to join his party in a toast. The diners at both tables rose to their feet. "I give you," he cried "The Governor of the State of New Jersey [all glasses were raised] a liar and an ingrate!" Those who had risen to drink the toast upon his invitation lowered their glasses, stupefied by the toast suggested. Nugent said, "Do I drink alone?" He did, and that was the end of Nugent.

Accounts of these incidents were spread all over the country and influenced machine politicians—some in North Carolina—to oppose the nomination of Wilson for the presidency.

Shortly after my meeting with George Harvey in Mackey's hunting lodge in North Carolina, I went to Washington and had another conference with him. He seemed so confident of Wilson's nomination that he talked mainly about the character of the platform he ought to run on. Harvey had drafted some planks which he read me. He was disturbed about the money plank and how the traditional Democratic tariff doctrine could be harmonized with the desire for protection by the industrial East. I told him that I was satisfied with Wilson's views on the tariff and that a tariff plank should make a clear-cut issue between the Aldrich act and the Democratic doctrine. I pointed out that the excoriation of that act by Dolliver and other Republican progressives would attract the Western farmer to the support of Wilson. He was troubled about Bryan, whom he did not trust and whose opposition to Wilson he took for granted, and said he thought Bryan would try to "upset the apple-cart" by insisting on a free silver declaration. He asked if I believed Watterson would demand a tariff-for-revenue-only plank. I told him that I did not believe Bryan would inject the silver question into the campaign and that he was more concerned to see the party truly progressive than to see any particular candidate nominated. Harvey thought Bryan would wish the nomination for himself. We talked an hour about planks in the coming platform, Harvey assuming that he would write the platform, select the candidate, and run the campaign. He strutted sitting down. Finally I said, "Colonel, I believe we ought to imitate the hunters who refused to discuss the best way of skinning a rabbit until they had caught the rabbit." I had already sensed that Wilson would have a hard road to travel to secure the nomination. "Let the platform wait upon the securing of delegates," I advised. He thought leaders should be thinking about both, to which I agreed, but told him that discussing the platform over a year before the selection of delegates was putting the cart before the horse.

TOM PENCE, PRESS REPRESENTATIVE

The Wilson managers sent out literature during the summer and early fall and I had an occasional letter from McCombs, who reported accessions to the Wilson ranks. Not only was I printing everything that indicated support of Wilson, but Tom Pence, Washington correspondent of *The News and Observer,* had become an ardent advocate of Wilson's nomination. He kept in touch with Burleson, Gore, Henry, Mitchell Palmer, and other members of Congress who were Wilson men, and his dispatches to *The News and Observer* enabled our paper to be among the first to print the real political news from the capital. The Wilson supporters came to rely on Pence. On political trends he was the best informed newspaper man in Washington.

The Wilson organization soon felt the need of a publicity man in Washington, who not only could print favorable news but who could be a recruiting officer for the cause as well. Pence's zeal and capacity and other good qualities had become known to early Wilsonites. They asked him to undertake the task and I advised him to accept. From the day Wilson spoke in Raleigh, Pence had been the main reliance for Wilson publicity. He went to Trenton with McCombs and from the moment he met Wilson he fell under the spell of his charm and Wilson reciprocated with a deep and abiding friendship. Nothing about the contest escaped Pence. He knew every move the Clark and Underwood and Harmon advocates were making, and he gave tips on how to checkmate their moves. During the year before the Baltimore Convention, he was the most helpful and alert of all Wilson's supporters at the national capital. He saw every important Democrat who visited Washington, talked Wilson as the only sure winner, and sent out to the papers hundreds of interviews with those who agreed that Wilson should be the nominee. He had no personal political ambition—seemed to be only a newsgatherer—but to this skill he added a peculiar sense of what issues would appeal to the public. Moreover, he was a sound Democrat at heart, although he talked more about how to win political fights than he did about the formulation of doctrines.

III

THE INGRATE CHARGE DID NOT STICK

I T WAS TOM PENCE who first scented the famous news story that exploded around Christmas, 1911, when Colonel Henry Watterson, who had favored Wilson's nomination, went to Washington boiling with indignation at what he called Governor Wilson's "base ingratitude" to his friend Colonel Harvey. The story had a North Carolina angle. In fact, the news that Wilson had insulted Harvey in the presence of Watterson came out through Major J. C. Hemphill, who was at that time editing the Charlotte (N. C.) *Observer*. Major Hemphill in the Charlotte *Observer* had tried to stem the tide running toward Wilson in North Carolina and was happy in believing that the incident which put Harvey and Watterson in the ranks of the opponents of Wilson would be a death blow to the New Jersey Governor. Hemphill, a South Carolina Democrat who had become an intimate friend of Taft, was well known and well liked in the South. He had a style all his own—of mingled humor and sarcasm. He had invited Harvey to Charleston to speak at the time when Harvey gave mortal offence to South Carolinians. Wishing to please his Palmetto audience, Harvey told how his father, a Vermont Democrat, was a Southern sympathizer and could not be induced to fight against the South. He therefore hired a substitute. Harvey was astounded when this recital received no applause. He learned later that South Carolinians, who fought early and late, had a genuine contempt for a man who hired a substitute in any war. Harvey was to get deeper into Palmetto contempt when on a hunting trip he offered a tip of ten dollars to an aristocratic young Carolinian who volunteered to enable Harvey to carry antlers back home.

Hemphill, having opposed Bryan, early sensed that Wilson was radical in his views and scintillated in the Charlotte *Observer* against "the visionary schoolmaster." The publication of the Wilson-Harvey-Watterson luncheon talk created a greater sensation than had occurred in national politics in a decade. Pence called up and gave me the tip before the news broke so that I could be ready to combat the editorial comment which he felt sure Hemphill would make in the Charlotte *Observer*. According to Hemphill's story, on the occasion of Colonel Watterson's visit to New York, Harvey wished him to call on Governor Wilson. All three lunched at the Manhattan Club. And that was the scene of the plot of "The Great Conspiracy," the name given to it later by the Wilson supporters. "Marse Henry," as Watterson was called, had long been a fiery, and sometimes influential, political leader in the South. His active support was desired by the friends of Wilson.

Pence believed that Harvey, who was Pierpont Morgan's agent in publishing *Harper's Weekly* and other periodicals, realizing that Wilson had shown himself the foe of privileged classes, created the incident in order to kill off his own candidate at the behest of Morgan, who disliked Wilson. Harper and Brothers, controlled by Morgan, had published Wilson's *History of the American People*. Morgan had gone in a special car to Princeton in 1902 when Wilson was inaugurated as president. At that time Wilson was deemed a conservative. He had not voted for Bryan in 1896. He had been outspoken in criticism of free silver. He was the president of a university so conservative that it had harbored no radicalism since Witherspoon had led in the American Revolution. Wilson's inaugural address was a masterpiece, and Morgan, along with all the others who heard it, fell under his spell. If any Democrat was to win, why not a college president who gave no hint of radicalism? Wilson had as yet said nothing that bore resemblance to his later declaration in Oregon for the referendum and the initiative, or to his attacks on monopoly when Governor of New Jersey. Morgan doubtless felt no danger to the big interests in Harvey's placing

"FOR PRESIDENT
WOODROW WILSON"

at the masthead of *Harper's Weekly*. It pleased Harvey and gave an issue to a paper that was dying but did not know it. It was later, on January 10, 1910, to be exact, that Morgan was to learn Wilson was not a conservative. The Princeton president was speaking at a meeting of the bankers of New York City. All the big financiers were there, among them Morgan, who turned red in the face when Wilson said: "You bankers sitting in this provincial community of New York see nothing beyond your own interests and are content to sit at the seat of custom and take tolls of all passers-by." Morgan's wrath blazed as Wilson made this direct appeal: "You should be broader-minded and see what is best for the country in the long run." When Wilson finished, Morgan expressed his dissent. He told Wilson his remarks were "personal" and he resented them. Wilson retracted nothing but said he was making no personal allusions. That may have slightly mollified Morgan for a time, but it was not forgotten. At any rate, it did not at that time affect Harvey's advocacy of Wilson's nomination. Harvey no doubt told Morgan that all men in politics must "take a fling at Wall Street," but that he was sure Wilson as President would never do a thing to lessen its power.

A WALL STREET PLOT

I remember having been impressed by Harvey's article, which appeared in his *North American Review* shortly after our conference at Mackey's hunting lodge in North Carolina. It impressed me so favorably that I wrote enthusiastically of my appreciation to Harvey. The subject was "The Political Predestination of Woodrow Wilson." This extract I can never forget: "The finger of Predestination, guided by Logic, Circumstances, Conditions and History, points unerringly to Woodrow Wilson as the opponent of William H. Taft, Republican, in 1912." I then believed Harvey had the insight of a prophet, even though I did not accept the doctrine of predestination in religion. When Tom Pence was in Raleigh early in the fall (1911) I told him I feared that Harvey's active support and the feeling that he was Wilson's closest friend were causing men who had supported Bryan to distrust Wilson as a true progressive. "It is an open secret in Washington," said Pence "that Pierpont Morgan is bitter in his criticism of Wilson, and he and others who are beginning to fear Wilson as a second Bryan would spend millions to defeat him. In fact, Harvey has told McCombs and others that strong pressure has been brought to bear on him in Wall Street to abandon Wilson."

Shortly after the story of the break between Wilson and Harvey became public, I went to Washington and found two views prevailing in Wilson circles. Tom Pence held the view I had expressed in *The News and Observer*. He said: "It is the best thing that could have happened for Wilson because it proves to the country that Wall Street has no strings tied to him." "The bomb is a dud," said Wilson's friends, but the Clark and Underwood supporters were quite sure it would eliminate Wilson as a successful candidate. They thought the ingrate charge would stick.

"The bitterness against Wilson is due to his courage in defying Wall Street when its help was tendered by Harvey, who had been his earliest supporter among influential editors," declared McCombs, who added in a public statement, prepared by Pence: "It is a put-up job—a Wall Street conspiracy."

That angle greatly incensed Watterson, who was no conspirator. He was a man given to extreme chivalry. When he felt that Wilson had been guilty of a show of ingratitude to his friend, his resentment overpowered all other considerations and he let zeal for a friend warp his judgment. Harvey was different. He had no affection. He had long before, by a process of selfish reasoning, come to the conclusion that 1912 was to be a Democratic year and he hitched his paper to Wilson's kite. When Wilson became a radical, Harvey saw he could no longer support him and retain the patronage of Morgan. He chose to have his bread well buttered. Watterson, all unsuspectingly, was the medium to make the break, idealize Harvey and damn Wilson. It was a well-planned plot and it might have worked if the country had not been persuaded that Morgan was the heavy villain. For that Tom Pence was mainly responsible. I backed him up. Hemphill lambasted me and so did Watterson. Some people, knowing Harvey's connection with Morgan, were asking, "Is Wilson to be controlled by George Harvey?"

STORY OF THE BREAK WITH WILSON

The authentic story of the break with Wilson may be thus summarized: At the end of a luncheon at the Manhattan Club, in the latter part of 1911, Colonel Harvey asked a question. Wilson's answer caused Harvey and Watterson to withdraw their support and become his bitter enemies. There have been many versions of the cause of the break. Perhaps the memorandum written by Harvey conveys as true an account as can be given.

According to Harvey, he asked Wilson: "Is there anything left of that cheap talk during the gubernatorial campaign about my advocating you on behalf of the interests?"

Governor Wilson replied with great positiveness: "Yes, there is. I lunched today with two of the young men in my literary bureau, and they both declared it was having a serious effect in

Upper left, Henry Watterson, journalist and statesman, who out of friendship for Harvey became Wilson's political foe (Brown Brothers). *Upper right,* George Harvey, editor of *Harper's Weekly,* early advocate of Wilson's nomination, who later turned against him (Brown Brothers). *Lower left,* James Pierpont Morgan, financial backer of *Harper's Weekly,* opponent of Wilson (Brown Brothers). *Lower right,* Thomas J. Pence, Washington correspondent of *The News and Observer,* publicity director of the Wilson forces, who exposed the Harvey plot against Wilson.

Upper left, James Bryce, eminent author and statesman, Ambassador from Great Britain to Washington in the early days of the Wilson administration (Brown Brothers). *Upper right,* Winston Churchill, First Lord of the Admiralty of Great Britain, who in 1913 advised a Naval building holiday. *Lower left,* Andrew Carnegie, whose gifts erected the Peace Palace at the Hague and the Pan American Building in Washington, a supporter of Bryan's peace treaties. *Lower right,* William E. Chandler, U. S. Senator and Secretary of the Navy under Arthur.

the West. I didn't ask them for the information. They volunteered it."

Colonel Harvey asked: "Have you thought of any way to
counteract this harmful effect?"

Governor Wilson replied: "I have not. In fact, I am greatly
perplexed to know how to do it. I have been able to satisfy those
I can reach, but there are thousands, of course, whom we cannot
reach—I have not yet been able to devise a way to meet the situation."

Harvey asked: "Is there anything I can do except, of course,
to stop advocating your nomination?"

Governor Wilson answered: "I think not. At least I can't
think of anything."

Harvey said: "Then I will simply sing low."

Wilson made no reply. An embarrassed pause followed, which
Colonel Watterson broke with: "Yes, that is the only thing to do.
The power of Wilson is very great—for myself, too, I shall not
say a word for the present."

A long pause; it must have been icy. Governor Wilson said:
"Good-bye, gentlemen."

The two insulted colonels, Harvey and Watterson, nodded
responses.

W. W. exit.

Governor Wilson left the luncheon with no suspicion that a frank
answer to a frank question from an ardent supporter had given
offense. When he related the conversation to his private secretary
on his return to Trenton, Tumulty sensed that Harvey would be
"deeply wounded." At his suggestion Wilson wrote Harvey saying
that he regretted having answered his question about the *Weekly*
"with never a word of my sincere gratitude to you for all your
generous support, or my hope that it will be continued." He added:
"Forgive me, and forget my manners." Harvey gave out interviews
in support of Wilson's candidacy after the meeting, for which Wilson
wrote him a warm letter, repeating his apologies and saying he
wished he might express, face to face, how grateful he was. Harvey
replied saying that he had no "personal rancor or resentment."
However, in its next issue *Harper's Weekly* quit advocating Wilson,
Harvey saying it did so "in response to a statement made directly to
us by Governor Wilson that our support was affecting his candidacy
injuriously." He added that he had taken this course "in perfect

fairness to Governor Wilson" and "in consideration of self-respect." When the sensational publication broke and Watterson trumpeted a message that "Wilson lied," and that but for Harvey's support Wilson would not be in the running, Tom Pence hastened to get in touch with Senator Tillman (a Wilson supporter) and acquaint him with the situation and the danger to Wilson if it were not handled wisely. Tillman got into action and said that if Watterson had evidence to prove Wilson was an ingrate it was his duty to give it to the public. He used severe Tillmanesque language.

IT LOOKED LIKE A DUEL

There was blood on the moon in the national capital when "Pitch-fork" Senator Tillman, of South Carolina, entered the scene, saying: "I have given Henry Watterson credit for more sense than to try to foist a story like this, with the material facts concealed." Infuriated, the Kentucky editor sent a letter to Tillman by Congressman Swager Sherley, in which he said, "The man who makes a public statement with the material facts concealed is little other than a scoundrel." He demanded: "Upon what warrant of authority have you made this serious accusation against me?" He asked a reply "through my friend, Honorable Swager Sherley." That was the way duels came about. When two Southerners of the old school set themselves down to write sarcastic letters and demand a reply "through a friend," it sounded like a challenge. People began to discuss the character of weapons. As both had suffered the loss of one eye, the contest would have been equal, even if defect of vision might prevent serious consequences.

However, Tillman, known as a fighter who never feared the face of man, was no devotee of the code duello. His reply had no pitch-fork flavor. In his letter the Senator said: "All the leading papers of the country seem to know why Governor Wilson severed relations with Colonel Harvey, and you, as a leading newspaper man and self-confessed expert groomer of presidential candidates, must have known it at the time your statement was published." No "pistols and coffee for two" in that. Watterson's anger cooled off in his next letter, in which, on January 26, he said:

"I have been aware for nearly a week that recognized spokes-men for Governor Wilson were industriously circulating the story that the real reason why Governor Wilson broke with

Colonel Harvey was that Colonel Harvey had tried to bring
Mr. Thomas F. Ryan into the Governor's campaign.... That
story is a lie out of the whole cloth.... I hoped I might induce
him to help. Colonel Harvey had nothing to do with it."

In a later letter, however, Colonel Watterson said he had been
"dragooned—I will not say decoyed—into the service of Governor
Wilson and Colonel Harvey," and he went on to say that the supporters of Wilson were "delighted with the suggestion, but when I
spoke to Governor Wilson about it, he said some uncivil things of
Mr. Ryan, expressing a fear that if the knowledge of such a contribution got abroad it might do more harm than good—an opinion
in which Colonel Harvey promptly concurred." When Wilson was
asked about the statement that he had wished Ryan money, he said:
"So far as I am concerned, the statement that Colonel Watterson was
requested to assist in raising money in my behalf is absolutely without foundation. Neither I nor anyone authorized to represent me
ever made such request of him."

This caused Watterson to reply in vitriolic words, daring Wilson
to ask the publication of his letter to Harvey. Then, going to his
Florida winter home where he did not have a telephone, Watterson
sent to Tillman the last challenge to what turned out to be not a
duel but a fiasco: "I refuse longer to follow a man whose nomination,
in my judgment, will be a disaster and whose election would be a
calamity."

Tillman answered: "If he has other letters let him print them."
Watterson offered to show them to "a court of honor." The controversy ended there. Congressman Burleson, of Texas, afterwards
Postmaster General in Wilson's cabinet, took a hand in the controversy and his statement threw light upon a situation which now
and then makes politics look like war. The Texan said:

"The plan that was fixed up at the Manhattan Club when,
according to the report that has not been denied to date, Colonel
Harvey attempted to persuade Governor Wilson to let Thomas
Fortune Ryan and his Wall Street associates finance the Wilson
candidacy, was of the same character as the Joline letter.* Wall
Street sprang the Joline letter, not because it loves Bryan, but
because it feels it cannot handle Wilson. It looks like there is a

*An account of this letter appears in the following chapter.

whole lot of truth in the saying that every time one of these anti-Wilson explosions is pulled off, you are sure to find the remnants of a Wall Street alarm clock in the wreck."

The Thomas Fortune Ryan here referred to is the man who as an Underwood delegate from Virginia was to be the object of Bryan's famous resolution to deny Ryan and Belmont seats in the Baltimore Convention.

When the break was blazoned on the front page of nearly every daily in the country, and many declared, "Wilson Is Ended," Walter Page wrote Wilson: "The incident is a positive asset," and I printed the following editorial in *The News and Observer*:

"Wilson's Good Luck

"Woodrow Wilson was born to good luck. George Harvey has come out against his nomination. Harvey and his Morgan connections had become a dead weight around the Wilson candidacy. Now that Wilson, from no act of his, has lost that deadly support, the prospect of his nomination has brightened."

For that sharp criticism I incurred the bitter and lasting hostility of Harvey, who made me the butt of ridicule and abuse for eight years, periodically demanding my removal from the Cabinet. His attacks culminated in a long denunciatory article printed as the leading feature of *The North American Review* of April, 1915, and reprinted and circulated by the Republicans in the campaign of 1916. It was headed:

THE RT. HON. SIR JOSEPHUS N.C.B.
OUR FIRST LORD OF THE ADMIRALTY
BY THE EDITOR

The vitriolic article, abounding in sarcasm, closed with:

A VOTE FOR WILSON IS
A VOTE FOR DANIELS

That slogan, in large letters, displayed on billboards, appeared all over the country during the 1916 compaign and was the challenge to the voters echoed by Republican spellbinders.

Result: I am the only man ever elected by the people as Secretary of the Navy. I was appointed to my first term but, according to the Republican posters, I was elected in 1916.

C. K. Berryman, Gridiron Club Souvenir 1916

ONLY SECRETARY OF THE NAVY TO BE ELECTED BY THE PEOPLE

The Republican Campaign Committee told the voters: "A vote for Wilson means a vote for Daniels."

HARVEY SUPPORTS CLARK

Soon after the break, Harvey became an active supporter of Champ Clark and passed out of the scene in which he had strutted for a brief period on the stage as "the discoverer of Woodrow Wilson." He undoubtedly had originated the plan to nominate Wilson for Governor, and his financial backers would have given him leave to advocate Wilson's nomination for the presidency if they had not become convinced that Wilson would smash the trusts and punish the men behind them.

Harvey was at the Baltimore Convention working with Hearst and Jim Smith to compass Wilson's defeat. In 1920 he loomed as the literary luminary of Warren G. Harding and was credited with being his ghost writer. He blossomed out as the chief figure of Harding's kitchen cabinet, being rewarded with the post of Ambassador to Great Britain. In that post, with his knee breeches and his quips, he went down to lasting ignominy when he declared that the Americans did not fight the World War to make the world safe for democracy, but "to save their own skins."

IV

NOT KNOCKED INTO A COCKED HAT

S CARCELY HAD THE EXPLOSION of the Watterson-Harvey bomb died down, when the opposition to Wilson fired what it regarded as a deadly projectile—warranted to kill. It came from the office of the New York *Sun*. That paper printed conspicuously a letter which it said Woodrow Wilson had written on April 29, 1907, to Adrian H. Joline, a railroad lawyer. This letter, written just a year before Bryan's third nomination, contained the following sentence: "Would that we could do something, at once, dignified and effective, to knock Mr. Bryan, once for all, into a cocked hat."

That publication created a sensation in political circles and sent consternation into the hearts of some Wilson leaders. With Wilson extricated from the embrace of Wall Street, they had hoped for the support of the progressives who had followed Bryan. But that hope now seemed to have been shot to pieces by the Wilson demand of a previous year that Bryan be knocked into a cocked hat.

This torpedo was hurled into the Wilson ranks on the eve of the most famous of the Jackson Day dinners at the national capital. Bryan and all the announced candidates for the presidency had been invited, as had also a few "willin' Barkises." The dinner had been heralded as the trying-out race of the political trotters, as in the celebrated Kentucky Derby. The Wilson supporters, knowing the fine impression he had made by his addresses from coast to coast, had looked to this occasion as the hour when Wilson would convert leaders from all over the country who had signified their intention to come and take a look at the entries in the race. But now joy was turned to fear that bordered on panic by the appearance of the Joline letter. They knew Wilson had not voted for Bryan in 1896 and had not favored the free coinage of silver at the ratio of 16 to 1. In their hearts they felt that Wilson could not win if Bryan began warfare, which they feared he would do, to "knock Wilson into a cocked hat." A hasty conference was called. "What will Bryan say when he reads the Joline letter? Will he say that knocking a candidate into a cocked hat is a game that two can play at?" They had no answer to their questions and turned to ways and means to reach Bryan. He had left Nebraska for Washington. That was all his friends in Lincoln knew. "Where is Bryan?" was the unanswered question as the Wilson supporters huddled in an atmosphere of anxiety. Then Tom Pence entered the room, his face wreathed in smiles. "Bryan is in Raleigh," he said, "at the home of Josephus Daniels." A murmur of "Thank God," went up from the group, for, as I was told afterwards, knowing of the close friendship between Bryan and myself and my enthusiasm for Wilson's nomination, all felt that nobody could handle the delicate situation unless I could. Fearful and doubtful, they awaited our coming to Washington.

At Raleigh, when I first read the Joline letter, my heart sank. It was shown me by a fellow journalist who had been instructed by the *Sun* to see Bryan and "get an interview about the Joline letter." I told Bryan about the letter and the desire of the *Sun* to ask what he had to say about it. I ventured to suggest that he had no proof that the letter was genuine. "Why not wait until you reach Washington before saying anything?" I asked, and added: "If anybody is to discuss the Joline letter it is Wilson. Let him speak first." I did not know whether I had made the impression I hoped, even as the correspondent entered my home. He showed Bryan the Joline letter. The Commoner read it slowly as if he had heard nothing about it until that minute. "What have you to say?" the correspondent asked. "You represent the New York *Sun,* do you not?" Bryan asked. When he replied, "Yes," Bryan said, "In that case, you may just say that if Mr. Wilson wanted to knock me into a cocked hat, he and the *Sun* are on the same platform. That's what the *Sun* has been trying to do to me since 1896."

"Is that all you have to say?" asked the reporter.

"Isn't that enough for the *Sun*?" Bryan asked and, turning to read the morning paper, ended the interview.

The next day Bryan and I travelled to Washington together, and talked about many things. I mentioned the Joline letter but once, and that was to say, "I do not think you are the man to speak. It seems it is Wilson's turn to do the talking, if any is to be done. He may say something that will put another light on it."

In that visit to me in Raleigh Bryan and I had talked till late in the night, reviewing our political experiences and coöperation beginning in 1893-95 when he was in Congress and I was Chief Clerk of the Department of the Interior. In the course of the exchange of confidences he said, "Many friends have declared their belief that this is my time to be elected President and have urged me to become a candidate again." He then analyzed the situation from every angle, saying his party had made him its candidate three times and he felt that the honor should go to someone else. He believed he could be elected "except for the opposition of city Democrats in a number of pivotal states in the North." He reviewed his fight for prohibition in Nebraska and the enemies it had brought him, and he concluded by saying that so many Democrats were opposed to prohibition that his advocacy of the cause might prevent his election. He did not regret his espousal of prohibition. He believed he had followed the path of duty, but recognized that it would militate against a Democratic victory, which was dearer to his heart than the highest honor which he had coveted. He spoke of his renunciation quietly and without a tinge of feeling. I was sure he had reached his conclusion after serious reflection. He asked whether I agreed. I told him that the dearest political desire of my life had been for years to see him in the White House, but that I was so familiar with the hostility to prohibition by Democrats in the big cities that I had no illusions about their hostility to any man who wished to close the saloons and stills. The conversation ended. I did not doubt that Bryan, having reached the conclusion he had unfolded to me in the sacred precinct of friendly communion, had given up ambition for the presidency and would not permit the use of his name at the Baltimore Convention.

The station was crowded with Washingtonians as our train pulled in. Bryan drove off quickly with Senator La Follette, but before he got into the automobile with the Wisconsin progressive, the reporters asked him, "What about the Joline letter?" to which Bryan made this Delphic reply:

"I am in the position of the juror who was asked if he had formed an opinion of the case on trial. The juror replied in the negative. The juror was then asked if he felt that he could form an opinion upon the presentation of the evidence. Again the juror replied in the negative. That is my present position relative to the Wilson-Joline correspondence."

I drove at once to the Willard Hotel with Tom Pence to see Wilson and his board of strategy. Pence acquainted me with their disturbed feeling. Arriving at the Wilson headquarters I was bombarded with questions: "What did Bryan say? What is he going to do?" After a brief word of greeting, Governor Wilson asked me, "What did Bryan say?" I answered, "I think it would be better first to ask me what I said to Bryan." Evidencing surprise at my remark, he said, "Well, what did you say to Bryan?" I answered, "I told Bryan we must give these college professors time to catch up with us." Then seriously I related what had passed between Bryan and the newspaper correspondent and said that Bryan would make no statement now about the Joline letter. That relieved Wilson and his associates, but Wilson asked, "What do you think I should do?" Before I could answer he drew me aside and wrote a brief statement about it and asked, "What do you think of my giving this to the press?" After rereading what he had written, he said, "No, that will not do," and tore it up. He wrote another brief statement which did not wholly satisfy him. After handing it to me, he said, "What would you think of giving out no statement, but taking occasion to pay a tribute to Bryan tonight in my speech, which might be satisfactory?" I thought it was a happy idea and said so. Governor Wilson handed me the paper and said: "I think what I shall say tonight will satisfy him, but if not I will give out something like this tomorrow." I told him that I was to have breakfast with Bryan the next morning and would report.

When I broached the subject to Bryan at the breakfast table and handed him the statement Wilson had written in script-like style, he read it and handed it back to me, saying, "I think after last night's speech, nothing further need be said." I agreed and the Joline letter turned out to be a dud so far as any explosion was concerned. I did not preserve Wilson's note, but I recall that he said he had a bad habit of writing freely to friends, that he had voted for Bryan in 1900 without agreeing with all he advocated, and added something to this effect: "Office could not add to the great name and place Mr. Bryan has made for himself in the history of the country—and the loss of it cannot deprive him of his undisputed hold upon the affections and confidence of the people." In his speech at the Jackson Day dinner, speaking of Bryan Wilson said:

"We have differed on measures: it has taken us sixteen years and more to come to any comprehension of our community of thought in regard to what we ought to do. What I want to say is that one of the most striking things in recent years is that with all the rise and fall of particular ideas, with all the ebb and flow of particular proposals, there has been one interesting fixed point in the history of the Democratic Party and that fixed point has been the character and the preaching of William Jennings Bryan. I for my part, wish never to forget this: That while we have differed with Mr. Bryan upon this occasion and that, in regard to the specific things to be done, he has gone serenely on pointing out to a more and more convinced people what it was that was the matter. He has had the steadfast vision all along of what it was that was the matter and he has not, any more than Andrew Jackson did, based his career upon calculation, but has based it upon principle."

The enthusiasm that followed cannot be described. From rapt attention when Wilson began, his hearers rose to such applause as has seldom been given an address. As he closed, Wilson turned to Bryan—it was described as "a really Chesterfieldian gesture"—and said:

"Let us apologize to each other that we ever suspected or antagonized one another; let us join hands once more all around the circle of community of counsel and of interest, which will show us at the last to have been indeed the friends of our country and the friends of mankind—"

The sentence was not ended because of the cheering and applause.

Bryan was moved as I never saw him before or afterwards. He told Judge Hudspeth after the dinner: "It was the greatest speech in American political history." The other speeches were forgotten. "It's 'Wilson—that's all,' " shouted a Jersey man. And that told the story of the Jackson Day dinner of 1912.

V

TAR HEELS FOR A SCHOLAR IN POLITICS

AFTER THE JACKSON DAY DINNER triumph of Wilson, I returned to North Carolina, confident that Woodrow Wilson would be the next President. I tried to transfer my feeling to the people of North Carolina, many of whom already shared it, but I soon found that it would be a Herculean task to secure a Wilson delegation. Most of the politicians of the dominant Simmons machine were against him. Governor Kitchin and Claude Kitchin, powerful leaders, preferred Champ Clark, both having served with him in the House of Representatives, but as Governor Kitchin was a candidate for the Senate they were not active. Aycock publicly applauded Wilson's policies. Senator Simmons, a candidate for reëlection, took no part, though most of his close friends, headed by A. D. Watts and H. B. Varner, were organizing the State for Underwood. They had plenty of money, but found it did little good in securing delegates. In fact, after the Baltimore Convention Senator Bankhead, leader of the Underwood forces, said to me, "North Carolina politicians are the most honest in the world. Do you know that, after the campaign, they returned some of the money we had sent them to promote Underwood's candidacy? I have been in politics all my life and it is the first case of its kind on record."

In April I received a letter from W. G. McAdoo, who had become active in promoting Wilson's candidacy. He deplored the lack of organization and said, "I am sure that if we could have organized everywhere, so that the great popular sentiment for the Governor could have found expression, he would have been irresistible." He said he had made a contribution of $500 for North Carolina, and that he had asked Colonel W. H. Osborne if he would not raise some money in the State. "Can you not take this up?" he asked, and added: "I know how much you are doing in this direction, and I hesitate to suggest that you do more, but we have all got to stand together and meet the demands as far as it is possible to do."

I did not know until I received McAdoo's letter that any money had been sent into the State for Wilson. Though the Underwood managers had a plethoric purse, my plan was to spend nothing, and to make no appeal except through the press and by personal letters and talks to key men. If any money above the $500 was expended to promote the Wilson candidacy in North Carolina I never heard of it and saw no evidence of it. Wilson's triumph was not accelerated by expenditure, but by appeals to those whom money could not influence. His Wilmington friends had a sense of pride in Wilson as a former resident and rallied to him. Members of the Presbyterian church there took the lead, with influential James Sprunt in the forefront, aided by such political leaders as John D. Bellamy, by business men like the MacRaes, McQueens, Taylors, and Worths, and practically the whole city.

The Davidson College alumni all over the State rejoiced in helping to send a fellow alumnus to the White House. This was particularly true in Charlotte, just a few miles from Davidson, under the leadership of Editor Carey Dowd of the *News*. Major Hemphill, editor of the Charlotte *Observer,* who had "spilled the beans" of the Wilson-Harvey-Watterson luncheon break, sought without avail to stem the Wilson tide. Hemphill, did not remain long on the *Observer*. Later he became a staunch supporter of the Wilson administration as a columnist on the New York *Times*. His close association with Harvey and Watterson and his opposition to Wilson doubtless shortened his stay in Charlotte. Practically all the larger towns and cities, except Asheville and Raleigh, were for Wilson.

MONSTER UNDERWOOD MEETING

Not long before the primaries, Honorable Tom Heflin, member of Congress from Alabama and afterwards Senator, came to Raleigh to "whoop it up" for Underwood, whose supporters staged a reception for him, the like of which Raleigh had not known. Heflin's reputation as a good story teller and as a "rousement" speaker preceded him. The local Underwood men, with plenty of money, employed bands and paraded all over the town. They packed the auditorium. It was a dreary night for the Wilson people, and when the great crowd poured into the auditorium and Heflin was received with cheers, partly manufactured and partly spontaneous, it looked as if the whole of Raleigh, Wake County, and the surrounding country would go for Underwood. Undoubtedly the meeting did carry many who were on the fence. It is rare that you can attribute to a single meeting direct effect upon the primary vote, but this meeting, I think, had more effect upon votes for the candidates for President than any I have ever known. Heflin told many good stores. A perfect mimic and master of the Negro dialect, he could tell a Negro story, with all the frills, in a way to delight an audience, particularly a Southern audience. He was at his best that night.

James H. Pou, an astute leader of the Raleigh bar, who had then a sort of Svengali influence, was scheduled to be one of the Underwood electors at large. He had been out of politics since the defeat of the Democrats in 1894, when he was State chairman, and it was now planned for him to make his reëntry. It looked as if he were riding on the top of the wave that night. The News and Observer reporting this meeting said, "James H. Pou is not an Underwood man but a Clark supporter; yet he presented that gentleman in a magnificent speech and was himself one of the most eloquent orators." This was printed as a matter of news, but it was also proof of what The News and Observer had been saying all during the campaign, that it was a fight against Wilson—that in States like North Carolina, the Clark and Harmon people were fighting for Underwood, and in States where Harmon was in the lead the Underwood people were fighting for him, and the supporters of these three candidates were pulling against Wilson. The chairmanship of Pou, a Clark man at an Underwood meeting, was regarded as absolute proof by Wilson people that they were right, as indeed the result at Baltimore proved.

When the meeting adjourned, some Wilson men felt that Underwood would carry the State. I did not attend the meeting. I had known Heflin a long time and we were friendly. The next morning I called upon him at the hotel. He was reading The News and Observer account of the meeting as I entered his room. He said, "Hello, Joe. I have just been reading your paper and I was rather surprised at the report you gave of my speech." "Why?" I asked him. "Well, last night the Underwood boys told me you are such a partisan of Wilson that you would not let anything go in The News and Observer in favor of anybody else and that I would pick up your paper this morning and find myself ridiculed, if I were noticed at all, but that the odds would be that your paper would merely say I 'also spoke'—and here I find several columns of my speech and a very good account and very kind treatment."

"You know, Tom," I said, "when boys get wrought up in a campaign and are themselves very partisan, they cannot do justice to the other side. They attribute the same feeling to others. I am strongly for Wilson, and therefore against Underwood, and I am against every statement you made last night and shall say so editorially, but we are printing a newspaper, and whether we like what a man says or not, if he comes to Raleigh and speaks to a large audience, the paper wouldn't be fit to read if it didn't fairly report what he said and give the color of the meeting."

"You have observed I have no bitterness toward Wilson," he said. As a matter of fact, Heflin never had any great enthusiasm for Underwood. They were on opposite sides in Alabama, and Heflin was for him only because they lived in the same State. From the day Wilson was elected, he had no more faithful supporter in Congress than Heflin. His later attacks on Smith, bitter hostility toward Catholics, and popularity with the Ku Klux Klan lost him standing, and he was defeated for reëlection. He was the most likeable of men and money honest.

When he lost his poise and was retired, old friends missed him. He was not able afterwards to stage a comeback.

Because my ward was controlled by the city ring, I could not carry it for Wilson. The bosses sent word: "Defeat Daniels as a delegate." I did not permit my name to be presented, not wishing to give the opposition the satisfaction they desired of wiring to the papers: "Josephus Daniels, leader of Wilson forces, was defeated for delegate in his own ward."

More than once the majority in my ward, controlled by the city machine and opponents of prohibition, did not select me as a delegate to the State convention. However, usually the Democrats of the township of which Apex was the center named me as one of their delegates, or some other country district, favoring liberal policies, selected me to represent them in the State convention. Banteringly when I was a delegate from Apex, I would say to my neighbors who did not elect me because I opposed the city ring which gave employment to a number of them: "I am on the Apex of the Wake delegation."

WILSON CARRIES RALEIGH DISTRICT

When the Wake County convention met, the Wilson people, with Josiah Bailey as their spokesman, demanded a poll in accordance with Sections 44 and 45 of the plan of organization. The Underwood men fought it bitterly but were defeated, and when the vote was taken, Wake County gave Wilson 103½ and Underwood 59½ and the delegates were instructed in that proportion. The city of Raleigh was 30 for Underwood and 18 for Wilson. The "embattled farmers" saved the day. However, when the Wake County vote was cast in its district convention, all delegates from the country districts not having arrived, the vote was almost reversed. The Underwood candidate, for national delegate, W. B. Jones, was given 50 votes to 30 for Albert Cox, the Wilson candidate. It was a clear violation of instructions. However, in the congressional convention, Cox and three other Wilson delegates were elected. Cox received 164 votes and Jones 100.

The result in the congressional convention depended upon the vote of Johnston County. N. E. Edgerton, leading cotton manufacturer, and Ed Abell, long a State Senator, and most of the other Johnston County people were for Wilson, without instructions. The Underwood folks in Wake County wanted the Johnston delegates to agree to divide the vote half and half, which would have elected the Underwood delegate, W. B. Jones, from Wake County. Congressman Pou favored Wilson but wished to divide Johnston half and half as a matter of comity and amity. Abell desired to try to divide the vote half for Cox and half for Jones, but he was a greater friend of mine than of Wilson or Jones or Cox. I was a member of the national committee and there was some opposition to my reëlection. Abell, thinking to adjust matters, went to Jones and said, "We will agree in Johnston County to divide our vote equally between you and Cox provided you give me your word that if you are elected you will vote for Josephus Daniels for national committeeman." Jones replied, "I will be damned if I will." Then Ed said, "I will be damned if you get a vote from Johnston County." I did not know this until a few minutes before the convention met, when Abell and Edgerton told me not to worry about Johnston County for it would vote for Wilson and against anybody who wasn't for me. The convention was in session for hours and it was a very bitter contest. Josiah Bailey was

NORTH CAROLINA DELEGATES TO THE BALTIMORE CONVENTION

Upper left, Julian S. Carr, captain of industry, philanthropist, and commander of the Confederate veterans. *Upper right,* Carey Dowd, on platform committee of the North Carolina delegation, editor of the *Charlotte News,* speaker of the North Carolina House of Representatives. *Lower left,* W. T. Dortch, member of Congress from the third district. *Lower right,* W. C. Hammer, member of Congress, who won victory for the Wilson forces in the credentials committee.

NORTH CAROLINA DELEGATES TO THE BALTIMORE CONVENTION

Upper left, Angus W. McLean, Assistant Secretary of the Treasury under Wilson, Governor of North Carolina. *Upper right,* R. B. Glenn, Governor of North Carolina. *Lower left,* E. J. Hale, editor of the *Fayetteville Observer* and diplomat. *Lower right,* W. C. Newland, Lieutenant Governor of North Carolina. Another delegate-at-large, pictured elsewhere, was E. J. Justice.

the floor leader for the Wilson forces, and the Wilson supporters elected all four of our Wilson delegates.

SENATOR BANKHEAD TOLD TO GO HOME

On the afternoon before the State convention met, able veteran Senator John H. Bankhead of Alabama, manager for Underwood, by invitation came to Raleigh to direct the Underwood fight for delegates. My paper the next morning had a leading editorial set in twelve-point type, which, if there had been any doubt of what the convention would do, turned the tide strongly against Underwood. The editorial was headed, "Do We Need Senator Bankhead, Underwood's Manager, At Our Convention?" and said that North Carolina people would welcome him at any other time, but never before had the campaign manager of any presidential aspirant assumed to attend a State convention in North Carolina to try to control it. The editorial went on to say:

"But men and brethren, North Carolina is able to attend to its own affairs. Outside men are not needed at its convention and there is no welcome in North Carolina today for Senator Bankhead as the manager of the Underwood campaign, just as there would be no welcome for Mr. McCombs, manager of the Wilson campaign, or Senator Pomerene, manager of the Harmon campaign, or Senators DuBois and Pettigrew (particularly the last), managers of the Clark campaign, if they should elect to come to North Carolina today upon the assembling of the state convention to try to influence the voice of North Carolina in sending its delegates to the Baltimore Convention. . . .

"Never before in the history of North Carolina has a presidential campaign manager visited a state convention while it was in session and spent the day before the convention talking to delegates and seeking to influence the action of the convention. 'Them ain't North Carolina ways' as the old hero in the play 'Esmeralda' put it. We have a habit of tending to our own business in North Carolina. . . .

"Senator Bankhead knows these words are not written about him personally because for twenty-five years the editor of this paper and Senator Bankhead have been on friendly relations and these shall always continue. It is written because the people of North Carolina do not welcome outside help or the idea of doing the pleasure of any man in the world, even though it be Oscar Underwood himself, or Woodrow Wilson, or Judson

Harmon, or Champ Clark, at the time they are performing a great public duty."

After that leader had been written, I spoke about it to a friend. It reached the ears of some of the more cautious Wilson men, and they were afraid it might be a boomerang. Several of them, headed by Crawford Biggs, came down to my office after midnight. They thought the editorial would hurt Wilson and suggested that it be tamed down; that telling a United States Senator to get out of the State didn't seem to be very courteous. I told them it was no time for the taming down processes, that if I knew anything about the temper of North Carolina people it would be worth not less than 50 to 100 votes for Wilson, and that almost everybody who was on the fence (and there were lots of them), would resent the presence of a United States Senator from another State. The editorial, set in blackface type, appeared, and the next morning it was the talk of the town; and the Wilson folks, of course, went through all the delegations spreading it. They denounced Bankhead for attempting to come to Raleigh and apply the lash to the people of North Carolina. The Underwood supporters were furious and called it "rude inhospitality." It created so much indignation that it stampeded the Underwood people utterly, so much so that they advised Senator Bankhead to take the noon train and return to Washington and not be in Raleigh at the time of the holding of the convention. He took their advice.

As I was leaving *The News and Observer* office to attend the convention I met the Senator face to face. He was alone, carrying his bag, and on his way to catch the train. I had known him long, and our wives had been friends from the time when Mrs. Bankhead had shown my wife as a bride in Washington many gracious courtesies.

"Good morning, Senator," I said, forgetting for the nonce my inhospitable editorial. "I am very glad to see you."

His face looked like a thunder-cloud as he replied, "Glad to see me, are you? It doesn't look so according to your editorial ordering me to leave the State."

I was embarrassed, but recovered myself to say, "You know, Senator, I am always glad to see you and we would all welcome you with cordiality at any time except when we are holding our State conventions. We need no outside help in attending to the big task before us." I extended my hand, "Good-bye, give my love to your wife." He hesitated a minute, and then shook hands with ill grace. I would not have blamed him if he had refused.

Later when he was a leader in the Senate during the Wilson administration, though he never admired Wilson, he supported nearly all his policies—sometimes with a wry face. He was a conservative of conservatives, an old-timer, and some of Wilson's liberal ideas were anathema to him, but he had been raised in a school of regularity and believed in it. He regarded a political party as something like an army in which the colonels must follow the lead of the general. He was succeeded in the Senate by his son and namesake, who led in farm relief and other farm legislation in Franklin Roosevelt's administration. Another distinguished son, Honorable William B. Bankhead, became Speaker of the national House of Representatives, dying in his prime, greatly beloved. Another son and a grandson held important positions as commercial attachés. His daughter, Mrs. Marie Bankhead Owen, was made head of the Alabama Historical Commission; a granddaughter, Tallulah Bankhead, became famous as an actress, and other members of the family served their country with honor and distinction, as did the Senator I invited to leave North Carolina.

WILSON MEN SELECT DELEGATES

On the night before the State convention met, the Wilson forces held a meeting, presided over by Major Henry A. London, of Chatham. The attendance was so large that it overflowed the courthouse. It was called to agree upon a Wilson slate for the delegates at large and a program. I wanted binding instructions, but there was strong feeling against instructions. The Edgecombe County delegates, who were strong for Wilson, positively refused to vote for instructions, saying it had been a policy of their county for one hundred years never to instruct delegates. The same was true of some other counties. As we did not know our strength in some counties, it was regarded as dangerous to offer a resolution for instructions which might be voted down. Judge Avery, of Morganton, favored the resolution for instructing introduced by E. J. Justice. He was a strong Wilson man who never knew that the word compromise was in the dictionary. He never entered a fight with any idea of anything but wiping up the enemy or getting wiped up. He vigorously opposed the policy, advocated by Judge Crawford Biggs and others, of a resolution of simple endorsement and of straining every effort to elect all Wilson delegates.*

We agreed upon a set of Wilson delegates to the national convention and later found that, without any thought of how these men stood for United States Senator, we had chosen only one Simmons supporter on our delegation. This came to the ears of A. D. Watts and Henry Varner, who were running the Underwood campaign and who cared more about Simmons than about the presidency. They made the charge that a vote for Wilson was a vote against Simmons. Senator Simmons was not present. We saw then that the senatorial contest might be injected into the presidential fight, something we didn't desire. When we looked at the list of our delegates, none of them political friends of Simmons, we saw we must make some change in the ticket in order to keep the senatorial fight from hurting Wilson. Whereupon Crawford Biggs, who was the Wilson floor manager in the caucus, suggested that we place on our ticket A. W. McLean, afterwards Governor, a warm supporter of Simmons. "Never," said Judge Avery. "He is on the Underwood ticket, placed there by his consent, and why should we vote for an Underwood man?" Biggs said: "Take my word for it. If we elect McLean, he will go with us." "Has he given you any such pledge?" "No," Biggs replied. "How do we know we shall be electing a man who will be with us?" Biggs said, "I am confident he will go for Wilson if we elect him." McLean's name went before the convention on both tickets. At Baltimore McLean supported Wilson earnestly and became one of the most valued officials in the Wilson administration.

Why was Judge Biggs so confident that McLean would be for Wilson at Baltimore and why did I agree to his proposal? I think it was subconsciously because the Presbyterians as a rule, proud that they could support the son of an able divine of their faith who had

* Judge Alphonso Calhoun Avery, whose political ability and freedom from compromise were inherited from his father, who presided over the Charleston Convention in 1860, never forgot, with all his espousal of progressive policies, that the "Calhoun" in his name connoted devotion to State's Rights. He and his brothers were among the first to don the uniform of the gray when Vance called for troops for the Confederate Army as an answer to Lincoln's call for North Carolina to furnish troops for the Federal Army. Avery's brother, Isaac Erwin Avery, won immortality by courage beyond the call of duty in the bloody fighting at Gettysburg. The incorruptible judge, though holding the scales of justice evenly on both the Superior and the Supreme Court Bench, when wearing the ermine, never forgot that he was a Democrat of "the most straitest sect."

long been pastor at Wilmington, North Carolina, had gone all out in support of Wilson delegates. Biggs and I, knowing McLean was a Scotch Presbyterian, banked on the belief that the Tar Heel Presbyterian Elder would back the Presbyterian Elder from Princeton. Inasmuch as Cleveland, the only Democrat elected President since 1860, was a son of the manse, it was a good presumption that McLean would think another son of the manse ought to live in the White House, and he would feel predestined and foreordained to help in that direction.

WILSON CARRIES THE STATE CONVENTION

It was a battle royal in the State convention. *The News and Observer* had claimed, before the convention met, that Wilson had a lead of more than 75 per cent in all the counties. At the beginning, the convention indicated its enthusiasm for Wilson by giving a great demonstration in response to that paragraph in Governor Glenn's speech in which he named Wilson (who had been a schoolmate at Davidson College). It also applauded warmly a statement by Governor Jarvis that the convention should endorse Wilson. Judge Biggs, for the Wilson people, offered the following resolution:

"RESOLVED, that it is the judgment of this convention that Woodrow Wilson should be the candidate of the Democratic Party for president as he is the most available man to lead the Democratic hosts to victory in November and we heartily endorse his candidacy."

This resolution, though not one of positive instruction, was so near it that it was accepted by most of the delegates and by the country as equivalent to instructions. It insured that Wilson would get at least three-fourths of the delegation at first, and, when it was clear that Underwood could not be nominated, would get all the delegates. The convention was in session all night and adjourned at 6:30 in the morning, the Underwood men fighting to the end. The vote for endorsement of Wilson was 520 to 390, but the real test vote was on the motion of the Underwood men at 5:55 in the morning to adjourn without action. It was defeated 543 to 377. The Wilson slate was elected. The delegates at large were the nine State leaders: R. B. Glenn, chairman of the delegation, W. C. Dowd, editor of the Charlotte *News,* A. W. McLean, J. S. Carr, W. C. Newland, E. J. Justice, W. C. Hammer, E. J. Hale, and W. T. Dortch.

As the time for the holding of the Baltimore Convention approached, some politicians sought to prevent my reëlection as national committeeman, a position I had held since 1896. James H. Pou, who resented my criticism of his lobbying for big interests, engineered the movement. He approached Governor Kitchin with a proposition that the Simmons and Kitchin forces, who were very antagonistic, cease their warfare long enough to "eliminate Daniels, who has fought both." He said the Simmons men would coöperate, though he had not talked with the Senator. Nothing came of it. Kitchin refused and Simmons was not consulted. Both were more interested in going to the Senate than in eliminating me, even if they had wished my retirement. The delegates chosen, or a majority of them, were my friends and supporters, stronger for me than for Simmons or Kitchin. The attempt to defeat me "died a-bornin'." I was reëlected easily for the fifth time.

Almost immediately after the convention, I went to Baltimore to attend a meeting of the subcommittee in charge of the convention. When interviewed by the Baltimore *Evening Sun* of June 10, I was quoted as saying Wilson would be nominated and also:

"The Democrats will carry every state in the Union but Utah and Vermont. If the Southern delegates stay bought, Taft will be nominated, but if Perkins puts up more money than brother Charlie, it is Roosevelt. It is just a question between Brother Charlie and Perkins, between Taft, who doesn't do anything to the trusts or tariff, and Roosevelt, who hates Standard Oil and loves United Steel. The Southern delegates would rather stay bought by Brother Charlie and go home like honest men, but if they have to sell out to Roosevelt, go home disgraced and all that, to buy farms and new harness and paint their barns right away; they haven't had any real good pickings for a lot of years and they will be eager to get all there is in sight. They have got the pap hunger."

I was also quoted as saying: "All this talk about Bryan's attempting to secure the nomination is moonshine. He is not and will not be a candidate."

VI

BRYAN STAMPEDES THE CONVENTION FOR WILSON

From the day he was elected Governor of New Jersey, Ruling Elder Woodrow Wilson was preordained and predestinated (so my Presbyterian wife believed) to be nominated in 1912, but there were many hurdles to surmount before his supporters could find realization of the doctrine of election. His tour of the West won him many friends, but when the State conventions were held Wilson carried only Oregon among the Pacific States and only Wisconsin, North Dakota, and a few other votes in the West. He carried no State in the South between Texas and the Carolinas, except parts of Oklahoma and Louisiana. He lost all the border States and the Central West. He picked up Pennsylvania and Delaware along with most of New Jersey in the Middle States, lost New York, and had only a handful of delegates in New England. The outlook was not very promising in the days before the Baltimore Convention. In fact, Colonel Edward M. House, who afterwards was wrongly credited (and he did not dissent) with "making Wilson," was hopeless.

The nomination of Wilson could not have been brought about without the solid and militant support of the Pennsylvania and Texas delegations. They had a large vote and the delegates were men of force and enthusiasm. In Pennsylvania a new type of Democrat was to the front, led by Mitchell Palmer, Vance McCormick, Ambassador Guthrie, Roland Morris, and Joseph Guffey and others quite as active if not so well known. They ended the old alliance between the minority Democratic leaders and the Republican machine and lived to see Pennsylvania a mighty factor in the Wilson administration, with two members in the Cabinet and other positions of importance, and in the Roosevelt era, with a Democratic Governor and a Democratic United States Senator.

All the biographers of Colonel House and many other writers give him the credit for Texas' going for Wilson. One writer, George Sylvester Viereck, says: "Colonel House controlled the Texas delegation to the Baltimore Convention." It is strange how such a report, without foundation, should have been so generally accepted and perpetuated. The truth is that Texans had virtually put Texas in the Wilson column while Colonel House was seeking to promote the nomination of Mayor Gaynor and went to Texas, vainly hoping to advance Gaynor's candidacy. He found the Texans committed to Wilson. Thomas B. Love, afterwards Assistant Secretary of the Treasury, wired Wilson upon his election as Governor: "I am for you for President in 1912," and led in the organization which gave the Texas delegation to Wilson at Baltimore. Wilson wrote Love a letter of warm thanks. With him were Albert Burleson, Postmaster General; Thomas W. Gregory, Attorney General; Cone Johnson, Solicitor of the State Department; Thomas H. Ball, Senator Culberson, Cullen Thomas, and other influential leaders, including four members of Congress— Burleson, Henry, Smith, and Hardy. Upon the invitation of Love and others Wilson went to Texas in October, 1911, made three speeches, and cinched the State's vote before House had ever met Wilson. Love wrote to Wilson advising him to get in touch with House, saying, "I would rather have Colonel House's judgment on a sheer question of political tactics of the right sort than that of any man I know." Two weeks after that, House wrote Love he had talked with Wilson and "am going to support him." House went to Texas, contributed three hundred dollars to the Wilson campaign. He afterwards put himself at Wilson's service and made contacts that he thought would help him. But he did not control a delegate to the Baltimore Convention.

After Wilson lost most of the States in the primaries in the spring of 1912, House gave up, and was in Europe when the critical fight was on at Baltimore. Before sailing he wrote to Senator Culberson (May 1): "It looks to me as if the opposing candidates might again be Bryan and Roosevelt," and wrote to Wilson, "the fight seems to be going against us," adding, "I shall not abate my efforts," though he was abandoning the ship, leaving the country while the contest called for the presence of all Wilson supporters at Baltimore, where the fight was won over great odds by those on the ground. House came back in time to aid in a behind-the-scene way in the campaign.

In his authorized biography of Wilson, Ray Stannard Baker said that "three weeks before the Convention Wilson had practically given up hope of being nominated." If so, it was due to the pessimism of House and McCombs. Neither I nor his leading supporters shared that belief. As the delegates gathered in Baltimore, the Wilson-pledged delegates amounted to only 248 out of the 1,088. However, those of us on the inside knew that Wilson was stronger than appeared. As a matter of fact, on the first ballot he received 324 votes, 76 more than pledged.

FIGHT FOR TEMPORARY CHAIRMANSHIP

The forces began early to try to gain control of the organization of the convention. I was a member of the special committee on the convention as well as the executive committee of the national committee. About a week before the time of the convention, I received a telephone call from National Chairman Mack, who said, "I want you to come to Baltimore tomorrow without fail." I asked, "Why so soon?" He said it was of the highest importance, the other members of the committee would be there, and he wished to see me about a very pressing matter. I left that night. Mack informed me that he and others had been talking about whom the subcommittee should recommend to the full committee for temporary chairman. He proceeded to tell me that as New York would have no candidate for President or Vice-President, the Empire State felt that it should be permitted to name the temporary chairman. That sounded all right to me, and I said I would be glad to support Senator O'Gorman, of New York, who was for Wilson. Mack replied that the New York organization would ask the selection of Alton B. Parker, candidate for President in 1904, and he wanted me to help elect him. My opinion was that those interests in New York pressing for Parker believed that if they could secure the temporary chairmanship they could name the nominees of the convention. They were ready to move heaven and earth to carry their point. Mack said it would be a personal favor and he made the request as an old friend.

I told him I would do anything I could for him, but it would be a mistake to have a back number and reactionary like Parker. I said that as I was supporting Wilson I could make no commitment without conferring with other Wilson men. I added that Bryan would be a power in the convention and suggested he consult Bryan. Mack said that some weeks ago he had offered to place Bryan in nomination, but the Commoner had replied he did not desire to be temporary chairman. I suggested he telephone Bryan. He said, "You sound him out first." I put in a call, and when I informed Bryan of the plan to select Parker, he went up in the air—said it would not do at all—that he would demand a progressive and would fight Parker. Bryan was in Chicago reporting the Republican National Convention for a string of papers. Over the telephone he told me that the nomination of Taft would split the Republican Party and we had an easy road to victory if we could make the country realize that our party had no entangling alliances with the interests. He asked, "What on earth does anybody want Parker for? He would start us off on a reactionary basis that would give the lie to all our progressive declarations. I don't care to be the temporary chairman and have no candidate. I don't care whether a Clark man or a Wilson man is selected, but we ought to have a man the whole country will accept as a real progressive. Parker will not do at all." He telegraphed Chairman Mack: "I have no choice among progressives for temporary chairman, but it would be suicidal to have a reactionary for chairman when four-fifths of the whole country is radically progressive. I cannot believe such criminal folly is possible."

With a disappointed expression, Mack showed me the telegram from Bryan. It troubled Mack greatly, but he had no choice but to stand for Parker or lose reëlection on the national committee and that was his heart's desire. In the afternoon Tom Taggart, influential Indiana committeeman, came to see me and said the only reason he was for Parker was to help Norman Mack. "Confidentially," he said, "Charlie Murphy has told Norman that he must put Parker over. If he fails, Mack will not be reëlected on the national committee." Roger Sullivan, Ed Wood, and other old-timers of the committee made a like appeal "to help Norman." They were the type of man who puts accommodating a personal and political friend first. They could see nothing wrong in "helping Norman." As to what would follow such aid, they did not consider. I have seen such friendships impair great issues. My affection for Mack caused me to wish to help him, but I finally told him I could not vote to organize the convention against my candidate and my progressive principles. The whole matter got into the papers.

The fight over the temporary chairman became the big issue. Should the convention start off with a conservative keynoter? Or should a progressive be named? I declared I would support O'Gorman of New York, or any progressive, but could not stomach Parker. There was a long discussion in the subcommittee. It soon became clear that the Harmon, Clark, and Underwood leaders were for Parker, while the Wilson forces were ready to go for any progressive. During the debate I pointed out that the fight in the Republican convention, resulting in the nomination of Taft, and the probable bolt for Theodore Roosevelt, made it imperative for the Democratic convention to be militantly progressive to win, and that Parker was a dead one—to let him be the keynoter would be to surrender an advantage within our grasp. My designation of Parker as a reactionary and a dead one aroused my good friend Clark Howell, of Georgia, who was an Underwood supporter. He took the floor and argued that Parker was not a reactionary, but a true representative of the progressive democracy. I shook my head. He then turned to me and asked:

"Josephus, do you think I am a progressive?"

I did not think so, but wished to be courteous, and drew laughter from all in the meeting when I replied good-humoredly: "We vaccinated you for it once, Clark but it did not take." The result of the vote in the subcommittee was that our side lost. Norman had been helped; so it went out to the country that Parker was the choice.

BRYAN PUTS THEM ON THE SPOT

Parker's selection aroused Bryan and he put on his fighting clothes. He at once sent telegrams to Clark, Harmon, Underwood, Wilson, and Marshall—the five candidates—telling of the action of the subcommittee and saying that Parker "is in the eyes of the public most conspicuously identified with the reactionary element of the party. I shall be pleased to join you and your friends in opposing his selection." He requested an answer. Wilson telegraphed Bryan: "You are quite right," and did so over the protest of his chairman, McCombs, who advised Wilson to answer: "I have neither the right nor the desire to influence the organization of a convention of which I am not even a member." Without consulting any of the Wilson forces in Baltimore, McCombs assumed to speak for Wilson. McAdoo happened to drop in at headquarters after Bryan's telegram was made public. McCombs informed McAdoo that he had written a telegram which he had advised Wilson to sign. He showed it to McAdoo and asked, "What is wrong with that?" McAdoo replied, "That won't do at all. I think he should unhesitatingly answer that he agrees with Bryan." "If Wilson should do that," said

McCombs, "he will destroy all his chances." McAdoo told me that he hurried to the telephone to urge Wilson to disregard McCombs' advice, and Wilson told him he had just sent Bryan the telegram beginning: "You are quite right."

The majority of the national committee, when they met later, followed Mack and the majority of the subcommittee and approved the selection of Parker, some declaring for Ollie James, of Kentucky, who was a supporter of Clark but had a lifetime record as a militant liberal and a warm friend of Bryan. He had served in the House with his fellow Kentuckian Clark, and was an instructed Clark delegate. When I proposed James for temporary chairman, my friend Urey Woodson, national committeeman from Kentucky, begged me to withdraw it, saying, "Josephus, it will embarrass me to vote against my own Senator and you ought not to place me in that position. I have promised to vote for Parker and must keep my word. What will my friends in Kentucky say if I vote against James?"

"I am trying to honor Kentucky," I said. "Why do you refuse the honor?" He continued to plead in vain. In the end, he voted for Parker. I then felt sure that Clark's managers had made a trade with New York, or were casting an anchor to windward in that direction. Wilson was the only candidate who showed himself ready to fight. Clark and Underwood, as well as Harmon, were angling for New York's vote and knew that if they opposed Parker, they might abandon hope. McCombs also cherished a wish for the New York vote and this made his leadership impossible. Wilson's telegram to Bryan fixed him in the mind of the country as a militant progressive who was not afraid, and that action was a long step towards his nomination.

WASHED OR UNWASHED

"We are for you washed or unwashed," came a telegram to me from Frank Winston of North Carolina on the day before the opening of the Baltimore Convention. The previous morning I had slipped and fallen as I was getting out of the bathtub. It seemed a little matter, and I paid no attention to it. As I was leaving a meeting of the committee, Dr. Hall, member from Nebraska, noticed I was holding my side. He asked me why, and I told him of my fall. He said, "Go to your room by the back stairs and undress and lie down and I will treat you." As I reached my room, my neighbor surgeon from Raleigh, Dr. Hubert Royster, asked, "What's the matter?" He and Dr. Hall put me in bandages not unlike a corset so that, sans bathing, I missed no meeting of the convention. Some of the paragraphers more than hinted I had violated the old Southern practice of waiting until Saturday night to take the weekly bath.

A PYRRHIC VICTORY

In the opening hour of the convention, after the venerable and beloved Cardinal Gibbons had offered the prayer: "Let the light of Thy divine wisdom direct the deliberations of this convention," Chairman Mack announced that he had been directed by the majority of the national committee to submit the name of Alton B. Parker for temporary chairman.

Bryan arose. A great demonstration followed. It continued so long that the band was ordered to play. When quiet was restored, Bryan nominated Senator Kern of Indiana, "a genuine progressive." In the course of his speech, Bryan said: "Let the commencement of this convention be such a commencement that the Democrats of this country may raise their heads among their fellows and say, 'The Democratic Party is true to the people. You cannot frighten it with your Ryans nor buy it with your Belmonts.'" Pandemonium broke loose, for Ryan and Belmont were seated as delegates on the floor. Their delegations and others voiced indignation at the reference to them.

Kern proposed, in the interest of harmony, that he and Parker request to have their names withdrawn. He paused for Parker to speak. But Parker sat silent. Later, Kern, withdrawing his name, nominated Bryan for temporary chairman. When the vote was taken, the leaders of the Clark, Underwood, and Harmon forces stood for Parker, and he was elected. The country was then convinced that Wilson was the progressive. The vote was Parker 579, Bryan 508. Most Wilson delegates had voted for Bryan, and so had others who were already restive under their instructions. The leaders of the other candidates gave Parker enough votes to elect him.

Parker droned through his prepared address in a tone inaudible to most of the people in the Armory where the convention was held. After those who could hear found it platitudinous—not a scintillating sentence or a "forward march" in it—nobody listened.

The reactionaries had won a Pyrrhic victory. They congratulated themselves that, having defeated Bryan, they had rid themselves of any danger that he would upset their plans. They were chiefly intent upon nominating a candidate who would be "safe and sane." By this they meant one who would not interfere with the invisible government pleasing to the Morgans, the Ryans, and the Belmonts. I early became convinced that they preferred Harmon, or Underwood (who had Ryan's support from the beginning), and would take Clark as third choice, but only to beat Wilson. They had maintained relations with the leaders of all three. In other words, it was "anything to beat Wilson," and they believed Bryan was impotent to interfere with their program because he was instructed to vote for Clark. They thought they were sitting pretty.

CONTESTED SEATS WON FOR WILSON

I was deeply interested in the contested seats and thought that the nomination might be determined by the action of the credentials committee. I had suggested in the North Carolina delegation that William C. Hammer be selected on that committee. He was almost as large as Ollie James, a real fighter and a good lawyer. He worsted Senator Pettigrew, a Clark man, in the South Dakota contest and secured the vote of that State for Wilson, over the protests of the Clark and Underwood men on the committee. The big interest was the contest in the Ohio delegation. The State convention, which elected Harmon delegate at large, had sought to bind the nineteen Wilson delegates, elected by districts, to vote for Harmon. The speech of Newton D. Baker, a Wilson district delegate, was a masterpiece. I have never seen a verdict won so completely by eloquence and logic. It shattered the opposition. The Wilson delegates from Ohio were unshackled. That victory added 19 votes needed to ensure Wilson's nomination. I was quick to congratulate Baker, who had by sheer ability extorted support from enough delegates pledged to Clark or Underwood to adopt his report, which denied the right of a State convention to instruct delegates elected in district conventions. Such is the power of oratory at its best.

BRYAN EXPLODES A BOMB

It was early on the second night of the convention that I received a telephone message asking me to come to see Bryan and to go with him to the session. I went to his room and found him in his shirtsleeves busily dictating. "Wait a moment," he said, and then took me into his room where Mrs. Bryan was. "Read that," he said, "while I get my coat." I read the famous resolution against Ryan, Belmont, and Morgan. It was a bomb destined to stir the people. Its detonation was to reverberate from the Chesapeake to the Golden Gate and from the Great Lakes to Key West.

"What do you think of my resolution?" Bryan asked as we were riding to the convention hall.

"I think it is full of dynamite," I replied.

"Whom will it blow up?" he asked.

"It certainly will blow up Ryan and Belmont and Morgan, but it may also flare back and 'kick the owner over.'"

"We shall see," he said as his big jaws closed.

I saw that he was in for a hard fight and told him so. I admired his sheer audacity. I felt that he was taking a great risk but loved his daring. We separated when the Armory was reached. I spoke to nobody about the TNT I knew Bryan concealed in his pocket. I feared and hoped for the explosion and was ready to stand by him no matter what happened. I had a seat on the platform in the rear of the presiding officer. Bryan sat with the Nebraska delegation, the fire of battle in his eye. Soon he arose and addressed the chair, was recognized, and asked consent to offer a resolution for immediate consideration. If its purport had been known, his opponents would have sought to prevent his reading it. As they did not, some delegates cried out, "What is the resolution?"

Quickly Bryan read his resolution in which he asked the convention to declare itself "opposed to the nomination of any candidate who is the representative of or under obligation to J. Pierpont Morgan, Thomas F. Ryan, August Belmont, or any other member of the privilege-hunting and favor-seeking class." The second clause demanded the withdrawal of delegates Belmont and Ryan. I had read about Inferno but had never seen it in action before. Unrestrained madness took possession of the gathering. New York and Virginia delegations, in which Belmont and Ryan sat, surged toward the platform with loud and heated denunciation of the Nebraskan. Some ascended to the platform where Bryan stood near the towering figure of Ollie James, the chairman. He was a master parliamentarian, but he could do nothing with the storm that raged.

THE BALTIMORE TRANSFORMATION

This speaking cartoon tells the story of the rejection of Ryan and reactionaries and the matchless victory of Bryan in the convention of 1912, which nominated Woodrow Wilson for President. (Reproduced by permission from *A Tale of Two Conventions,* by William Jennings Bryan.)

OFFICIALS AT THE BALTIMORE CONVENTION

Upper left, Alton B. Parker, temporary chairman (Brown Brothers). *Upper right,* Ollie James, permanent chairman. *Lower left,* Norman Mack, national chairman (Harris & Ewing). *Lower right,* Mitchell Palmer, floor leader of the Wilson forces, member of Congress from Pennsylvania.

UNSUCCESSFUL CANDIDATES FOR PRESIDENT

Upper left, Oscar Underwood, Representative, Senator, co-author of the Tariff Act of 1913 (Brown Brothers). *Upper right,* Judson Harmon, Attorney General under Cleveland, Governor of Ohio (Brown Brothers). *Below,* Champ Clark, speaker of the House for many years, in friendly handclasp with Woodrow Wilson (Underwood & Underwood).

Delegates, breathing out threats, rushed to the platform. Tall Cone Johnson, with a voice that could be heard above the clamor and Ball, looking like a Viking, both of Texas, I, and other friends hurried forward to stand by Bryan. His foes also gathered around the platform, which was soon crowded. Opponents and partisans of Bryan were ready for anything that might happen. Ollie James, fearing the worst, turned to me and said, "My God, Josephus, what is the matter with Bryan? Does he want to destroy the Democratic Party?"

I answered, "No, Ollie, he is risking his life to save it."

The uproar went on, and every minute I feared Bryan would be killed. Never have I seen such hate. Chairman James, having recovered his equilibrium, stood unmoved amid the storm. When the fury had spent itself, he recognized Bryan, and the delegates had to listen. Bryan declared, "The attempt to sell the Democratic Party into bondage to the predatory interests is the most brazen, the most insolent, the most impudent attempt that has ever been made in the history of American politics." When the rancorous debate finally ended—Bryan's foes having stressed that the convention had no right to unseat a delegate—Bryan, just before the vote was taken, withdrew the second section asking the expulsion of Ryan and Belmont. A "nay" vote on the first section was virtually to declare in favor of the nomination of a candidate supported by the "privilege-hunting and favor-seeking class." Even Charlie Murphy and Tom Martin, backers of Belmont and Ryan, saw that would not do. But 201 delegates voted "no" against 883 who voted for the Bryan resolution. As the vote of New York was recorded for the Bryan resolution, with grim humor Murphy said to Belmont, "Now Augie, listen to yourself vote yourself out of the convention."

BRYAN SWITCHES FROM CLARK TO WILSON

It seemed that nothing more superheated could follow, that the apex of venom and hate had been reached, but greater pandemonium was to break loose later. Clark led in the balloting, and on Friday the climax came when Murphy changed the solid vote of New York to Champ Clark, and Bryan changed his vote from Clark to Wilson. I was not unprepared for the latter. Herbert Daniel, of Omaha, had told me that he and other Nebraska delegates were urging Bryan to change with them. Mrs. Bryan and "Brother Charlie" preferred Wilson to Clark. The New York change gave Champ Clark a clear

majority, and no man in political history had failed to receive the
nomination who had mustered a majority since the convention met
in Baltimore in 1844. The demonstration for Clark was beyond description. His friends believed his nomination was assured. But they
figured without appreciating Bryan's resourcefulness. He was not
present when Clark's majority, thanks to New York's vote, was
recorded, but was snatching a little sleep and rest. He had just begun
to fight. He came in and cried out: "A progressive candidate must
not be smirched by New York's vote! As long as New York's 90
votes are cast for Mr. Clark, I withhold my vote from him and cast
it for Woodrow Wilson." Other Nebraska delegates did likewise.
Again pandemonium broke loose—there was a near riot. The enraged Clark men surged around Bryan and tore down the Nebraska
banner. Violent threats were made by excited men shouting
"traitor!" at the Nebraskan. He stood unmoved in the turbulence.
It was a long time before the storm subsided sufficiently for anyone
to be heard. When some sort of quiet had been restored, the calmer
Clark leader, Senator Stone, confident of victory and wishing harmony, requested the Convention to hear Bryan. Great and continued
applause greeted every utterance. I was never more thrilled, not even
at Chicago, where I heard Bryan deliver his eloquent "Cross of Gold"
speech.

Cardinal Gibbons was captivated by Bryan's eloquence. He later
said:

> "It was the first time I had ever heard him speak. He is, in
> every sense of the word, a great orator, one who can sway crowds
> and hold them. He is a man of courage and determined appear-
> ance, and his speech sparkled with gems of oratory. It was an
> event I shall never forget."

As Bryan had delighted Cardinal Gibbons by his eloquence and
unhorsed those who were blind to the necessity of a militantly progressive candidate on a liberal platform, and had been the central and
dominating figure at every stage of the convention, he "furnished
the last thrill when he mounted the platform the last night to decline
the nomination for vice president," said the Baltimore *Sun*, "When
after declaring that he had never advocated a man except with gladness, and that he had never opposed a man except with sadness, he
declared there was not a human being for whom he felt a hatred,
the whole convention rose to cheer."

Senator Stone wired Wilson to withdraw and thus "vindicate majority rule." Clark hurried to Baltimore to denounce "Bryan's treachery and falsehoods," but fearing that bloodshed might follow, his leaders united with Wilson and Underwood leaders to adjourn the convention over until Monday. If Bryan was just beginning to fight, McCombs was throwing up the sponge. He called up Wilson and asked authority to release his delegates, all hope being gone, and asked which candidate Wilson wished his friends to vote for, suggesting Underwood. Wilson refused to have a preference. If he was out, he was out and would try no long-distance control.

WILSON TOLD HE WOULD WIN

"This is Governor Wilson at the phone," were the first words I heard when I was called to answer the telephone from Sea Girt late Saturday. "How does this situation look to you, Daniels? Some of my friends think that as Clark has a majority I should release my delegates. What do you advise?"

I had not been consulted by McCombs and did not then know he had given up. I replied: "It may take several days but you are sure to be nominated."

With a voice indicating his incredulity, Wilson said, "Since Clark has been gaining and now has a majority how do you make out that I can win?"

My reply was:

"I can well appreciate that at your distance from the scene you can't understand it, but here we know the undercurrents. I personally know a score of delegates instructed for another candidate who wish to vote for you and will do so before the end. Roger Sullivan is for you and will find a way, when he can do so safely, to swing Illinois to your column. Tom Taggart is coming along with Indiana. In most delegations there are men who wish you nominated. Delegates who are instructed for other candidates are getting orders from home to vote for you. Hostility to New York and Tammany is growing and will make itself felt. My experience in politics is that men find a way to do what at heart they desire to do. It will be so with enough delegates in other camps to nominate you."

From Sea Girt came the voice: "I hope you are right. You are very encouraging. Let me tell my wife what you say." Mrs. Wilson sent me a message that my certainty had brought hope and confidence after McCombs' surrender.

TALK WITH CLARK LEADER

Upon adjournment, after Clark had received a majority, Senator Jim Reed said to me, "Josephus, I wish to have a serious talk with you. Can you come to my hotel one hour from now?" I had no engagement and was on hand. We found a quiet place, and he opened up by saying that the last ballot must have convinced me that Wilson could not be nominated. He stressed that no candidate in half a century who had a majority had been denied the nomination.

I replied, "No man will ever fail of a nomination if all the people who are voting for him really wish his nomination. The weakness of Clark is that there are scores of instructed delegates who have been voting for him but who do not now desire his nomination. They will presently find a way to do as Bryan and other Nebraskans have done."

He did not agree and changed the line of discussion, saying, "You and I are old-time Democrats, but these amateurs are trying to defeat old Champ by throwing the vote to a dark horse. It has been a stand-up fight between Wilson and Clark. Now that Wilson cannot win I want you to prevent your associates, who are trying to get revenge by defeating Clark, from carrying out their plans." He continued in that vein. He was referring to the attempt of some leaders who proposed to nominate Mitchell Palmer, leader of the Wilson forces on the floor, as the compromise candidate. I agreed with him that either Wilson or Clark would be the nominee and told him I had high regard for Champ and would be no party to defeating him for revenge. In fact, if Wilson could not win I preferred Clark to anyone in sight. I told him I was sure Palmer would not listen to the suggestion. He said he felt that would be my view. "But," I added, "Wilson is going to be nominated."

He looked at me as if he thought I was out of my head. "He hasn't a chance," said Reed. "Champ will win unless his enemies can get a dark horse." I insisted that Wilson would win, but if he could not I would be for Clark. He told me I was following a will-o'-the-wisp. I replied, "Wait and you will see that Wilson will win before Wednesday night."

PALMER SUGGESTED AS A DARK HORSE

After the convention, it was stated by friends of Mitchell Palmer that enough of the opponents of Wilson offered to make Palmer the nominee if the united Wilson forces would support him and Palmer would accept. I was in several conferences of the Wilson forces at Baltimore—not all of them—but I never heard this matter suggested at any of them or heard that there was any concerted movement in that direction. This, of course, does not mean that there was not such a movement. No doubt men of prominence did approach Palmer and offer to vote for him if Wilson withdrew. Palmer believed the nomination was within his grasp, and, if Mc-Combs' opinion that Wilson could not be nominated, on Saturday, had proved true, who can tell but that some arrangement would have been made for the nomination of Palmer for the presidency? Palmer always thought so. I never did. Always afterward Palmer had an air implying that Wilson owed him a great deal—and he did. Palmer had done much to carry Pennsylvania, without which Wilson could not have been nominated. But Palmer imagined he had waived the sceptre aside and surrendered the place to Wilson. He rarely mentioned it, but once or twice I heard him say that the nomination was offered or tendered him and that, if he had listened to it, he might have been President. They say a man who gets the presidential bee in his bonnet never gets rid of it, and I think it is equally true that a man who in the convention thought the nomination was in his grasp is ever afterward affected by it. Certainly the bee buzzed in Palmer's bonnet thereafter, though of course he did not permit it to influence him until 1920. I had first met Palmer at a Democratic dinner in Baltimore. Handsome, well-groomed, and eloquent, he made a speech which captivated his hearers. I was greatly attracted to him, and we formed a warm friendship which endured until his death.

Saturday afternoon I took part in a conference of Wilson supporters at Mitchell Palmer's and Vance McCormick's quarters, and it was agreed that victory was possible and efforts for his nomination were renewed. Though Palmer believed that if Wilson could not win, he might emerge as the dark horse nominee, to the last he was as true to Wilson as the needle to the pole. As floor leader he was superb. The same was true of the solid Pennsylvania delegation.

In the interval McCombs asked Wilson to let him promise, in order to secure needed support, that if elected he would not have Bryan in his Cabinet; but that proposal, like all McCombs' suggestions, was turned down. "It would be foolish," said Wilson, "for me at this time to decide upon a Cabinet officer, and it would be outrageous to eliminate anybody from consideration now, particularly Mr. Bryan, who has rendered such fine service to the party at all seasons."

TIDE TURNS TOWARD WILSON

The vigorous support of Wilson by the New York *World,* directed by Frank Cobb, the Baltimore *Sun,* directed by Charles H. Grasty, and the Scripps-MacRae papers, with the liberal policies of the elder Scripps—all demanding Wilson's nomination—had a powerful effect. Frank Cobb wrote: "It is too late to talk compromise. Ryanism and Murphyism have created an issue that makes the nomination of Woodrow Wilson a matter of Democratic life or death."

Sunday's tide set so strongly toward Wilson that it was clear he would be nominated. One hundred thousand telegrams came to the delegates from all over the country, particularly from the West and the South, demanding of delegates instructed for Clark that they should no longer support him but should name Wilson as the best hope of carrying the country. The blunder of Clark's managers in hitching him up with Tammany had ruined him with the progressives of the West, and the delegates at Baltimore responded to the call from home. On the first ballot Clark had 440½ votes; Wilson 324; Harmon, 148; Underwood, 117½; Marshall, 31; Baldwin, 22; Sulzer, 1; Bryan, 1½. On the tenth ballot Clark had 556, eleven more than a majority, to Wilson's 350½. On the thirteenth ballot Wilson had 460 and Clark fell to 455. When Monday arrived, although Clark's forces held in the early ballots, the tide set in so strongly toward Wilson that he was nominated on Tuesday on the forty-sixth ballot, receiving 990 votes. Missouri stuck to Clark. Senator Stone moved to make the nomination of Wilson unanimous. It was soon all over but the shouting. Bryan declined the vice-presidential nomination, as did Clark and Underwood. It was given to Marshall, and he proved a good choice, though I was at first inclined to advocate the nomination of John Burke, liberal Catholic Governor of North Dakota, who had been a tower of strength for Wilson and Bryan.

ADMIRATION FOR GENEVIEVE CLARK

One of the stirring and inspiring events of the convention occurred when Miss Genevieve Clark, the beautiful and charming daughter of Champ Clark, was cheered by shouting delegates when her father had received the vote of the majority of the delegates. She had been the center of a group of Clark enthusiasts and had followed every act in the convention with affection for her father and pride in the great support he had won. She was a picture of grace and beauty, radiantly happy, as she was carried on the shoulders of Clark enthusiasts over the convention hall, while all the bands played Missouri's favorite, the Champ Clark "houn' dawg song":

> "I doan keer ef he *is* a houn',
> You gotta quit kickin' my dawg aroun'."

She already saw her father in the White House and lived in anticipation of the great days in store for all the family. I saw her again sitting silently and forlornly on the platform when her White House dream faded. I had liked her and applauded when her joy and happiness beamed at the honor done her father, presaging, as she and many (Woodrow Wilson almost persuaded) thought, that another ballot would make her father President. Rejoicing as I did in the nomination of my choice, I felt admiration and sympathy for her in the hour of her keen disappointment, and I was to have my admiration heightened by better acquaintance in the years ahead, as did my wife, for her and her fine mother.

CLARK NEVER FORGAVE BRYAN

In his *My Quarter Century of American Politics* Clark devoted many pages to charging and undertaking to prove that Bryan "by his amazing insinuations unquestionably prevented my nomination." He declared Bryan "was as bad as a felon." His deep-seated and lasting feeling stands out in such extracts from his book as follow:

"If Bryan had told me on his birthday in 1911 that he was going to be a candidate for President in 1912, I would not have become a candidate because the chief strength of both of us lay in the same region—that is, west of the Alleghanies, and because of his vast acquaintance with the people, especially the Democratic politicians.... Bryan's animus against me at Baltimore grew out of two facts. First, he could not pull me around by the nose in my conduct as Speaker. Second, his ambition to be nominated himself. [Bryan had urged Clark to stand for putting wool on the free list and was critical when he refused to do so.] . . .

"It was on the fourteenth ballot that William Jennings Bryan violated his instructions and by base and false insinuations —to use no uglier word—robbed me of the nomination to which I was entitled by all the rules of decency, justice, honesty, common sense and fair dealing. . . . The two-thirds rule was a device of the pro slavery propagandists to enable them to nominate Democratic candidates for the Presidency in whom they could trust and in whose hands they felt their interests would be safe. It was used in 1912 to gouge me out of the presidential nomination, notwithstanding the fact that I led on 29 ballots and received a clear majority on eight. . . . Bryan was dishonest in his contention that he changed his vote because New York was voting for me. The principal reason he changed his vote, thereby flagrantly violating his instructions and thereby proving that all his prating about the people's rule was hyprocrisy, was that he wanted a deadlock and grab off the nomination for himself."

Clark was a true party man and when Wilson was nominated gave him hearty support, saying, "I never scratched a Democratic ticket or bolted a Democratic nominee in my life. I shall not change the Democratic habit now," adding, "I shall support Governor Wilson."

BRYAN DID NOT WISH NOMINATION

Clark was not the only man who believed that Bryan wished and hoped the nomination would come to him. Nothing was further from his thoughts. If Bryan had desired the nomination for himself, he would have played his cards very differently. From the day he led the fight against Parker and nominated Wilson (for without Bryan's support Wilson could not have been nominated), Bryan had but one dominating purpose: It was to make the Democratic Party militantly Progressive, with a big P, in both its candidates and its platform. He would never have voted for Wilson if Wilson had listened to McCombs and coquetted with Tammany, or had failed to show his progressiveness by brave words and readiness to lose or win for liberalism. It was Bryan's conviction that Wilson was truly progressive and courageous that attracted him and finally made Wilson's nomination possible. That and nothing else. I was in a

OFFICIALS IN THE WILSON CAMPAIGN

Upper left, W. G. McAdoo, vice-chairman of the Democratic Campaign Committee, Secretary of the Treasury under Wilson. *Upper right,* William F. McCombs, chairman of the Campaign Committee. *Lower left,* Rolla Wells, treasurer of the Committee (Brown Brothers). *Lower right,* Joseph E. Davies, secretary of the Committee, chairman of Western Headquarters in 1912 campaign, Ambassador to Russia under Roosevelt (Harris & Ewing).

Upper left, William Jennings Bryan, who changed the course of the Baltimore Convention. *Upper right,* Homer Cummings, member of the Democratic Committee and chairman of the Speakers' Bureau, Attorney General under Roosevelt. *Lower left,* Joseph R. Wilson, brother of Woodrow Wilson, who helped in the publicity campaign in 1912. *Lower right,* Robert W. Woolley, Assistant Director in Wilson's publicity campaign in 1912 and 1916, Director of the Mint.

position to know Bryan's attitude before the convention and at every step during the convention.

Norman Mack, chairman of the national committee, told me before the convention that Bryan had a good chance to obtain the nomination if he "plays his cards right." Asked to explain, Mack said to me:

"If Bryan will let matters take their course, busy himself with the platform, he will be the nominee, and that would please me. I offered to recommend Bryan for temporary chairman several weeks ago. It would have given him the chance to electrify the convention. It was his chance, but he declined, saying that he preferred to be on the floor. He is making a mistake. If he will antagonize nobody, and sit still while Harmon, Champ Clark, Wilson, and Underwood have their fling, they will kill each other's chances, and then some night the convention will nominate Bryan and he will be elected. In fact, New York, while not now for Bryan, would prefer to vote for his nomination than to see Wilson the nominee."

After the convention, Mack said:

"Bryan could have had the nomination. It was in his grasp. He threw it away when he antagonized New York when he should have acquiesced in Parker's selection. That was but a gesture and Bryan made it a big issue. Even so, if he had not introduced the Ryan-Belmont resolution and made Virginia and all conservatives mad, I believe Bryan would have won out when the conservatives saw they must take either Bryan or Wilson. And you know, Josephus, it would have pleased me better to see Bryan the nominee."

Carter Glass thought Bryan was prolonging the contest so as to get the nomination himself. Later he said:

"It was and still is my judgment, proclaimed at the time and frequently repeated since, that Mr. Bryan had not the slightest idea, when he changed the vote of Nebraska, of contributing to the nomination of Wilson. He merely desired to defeat Champ Clark, with the concealed hope and expectation of prolonging the contest and receiving the nomination."

The Virginian was never more mistaken in his life. Bryan was incapable of playing a game. The personality of the nominee did not concern him very much, but his heart was on fire for Wilson after he believed that the Clark managers were accepting the aid of the Ryans, the Belmonts, and Tammany.

THE SINGLE TERM PLANK

Bryan not only secured the nomination of Wilson but dominated the writing of the platform and won such accepted recognition that he was offered the nomination of Vice President. His first great victory was a proposal to reverse a long-standing rule that the platform should be adopted before the candidate was nominated. His argument was that before accepting the nomination the candidate must pledge himself to stand upon the platform adopted, without repudiating the platform to meet his personal views. Bryan won, but the successful candidate was not, as he had planned, required to pledge, while the convention was in session, to carry out all the planks in the platform. Wilson was neither asked nor did he make any such pledge. As told later, he repudiated Bryan's plank as to reëlection.

THE CLARK-BURLESON FEUD

One of the Wilson leaders who came in for Clark's condemnation was Albert Sidney Burleson, afterwards Postmaster General for eight years in the Wilson administration. In his memoirs Clark wrote of Burleson: "His talents run largely to intrigue and who delights in that sort of work." There was an old House of Representatives feud between them. I knew nothing of it until a few months before Burleson's death. When I visited him at Austin he confided to me that Clark had prevented his receiving an important assignment on a House committee to which by all precedents he was entitled. "I went to see Champ," he told me, "and protested that he was about to do me a grievous wrong." He made no effort to prevent the injustice to me. I never forgot it and Clark came later to feel the force of my resentment." And then Burleson, twenty years after, still resentful, quoted these lines:

> "Time at last sets all things even;
> And if we do but wait the hour,
> There never yet was human power
> Which could evade, if unforgiven
> The patient search and vigil long
> Of him who treasures up a wrong."

CLARK-BRYAN HARMONY LUNCHEON

After the inauguration of Wilson, friends of both men desired to bring Clark and Bryan together. For some time Clark peremptorily refused to meet Bryan, "even," as he said, "in the most formal manner," asserting that Bryan "had for his own selfish purpose slandered me out of the nomination and tried to the utmost to blacken my name." However, when insistence came from his friends that the feud should be ended for the good of the party, Clark reluctantly assented, "with the condition precedent that Bryan should in writing retract the base and injurious insinuations he had made against me at Baltimore." Mutual friends found Bryan more than willing to meet Clark half way. He wrote: "I am glad of the opportunity to correct any such impression" (that he had implied Clark was in sympathy with any of the reactionary forces). Clark in his reply said: "Now that Colonel Bryan in his public statement has done what he can to remove the injurious impressions that were created by his Baltimore speeches, I feel that we can all the better coöperate for the good of the administration."

I attended that harmony luncheon given by Clark's friends, Theodore Bell and Ira Bennett. It was so cold that the ice-cream seemed warm by comparison. Bryan radiated friendliness; Clark went through the formalities but did not unbend. However, the luncheon opened the way for coöperation in the advancement of public policies.

VII

THE CAMPAIGN THAT PUT WILSON IN THE WHITE HOUSE

IMMEDIATELY AFTER THE ADJOURNMENT of the Baltimore Convention, the members of the national committee and their wives went to Sea Girt to greet the presidential candidate and effect an organization for conducting the campaign. While we talked with Wilson, my wife and the other ladies were entertained by Mrs. Wilson and her daughters. It was the beginning of an affectionate friendship.

The secretiveness of McCombs, his bad advice at the Baltimore Convention, and his jealousy of McAdoo had cost him Wilson's confidence and created an embarrassing situation. Tom Pence, who knew all the inside news and gossip, told me that Wilson did not wish McCombs to be chairman.

"It would never do to throw McCombs overboard," said Tom, "for people would say that it was an evidence of the charge about Wilson's ingratitude."

"Whom does he want?" I asked.

"McAdoo and his friends have been urging McAdoo's selection. He is the acme of ambition."

I talked with Burleson, Palmer, Gore, and others. I favored McAdoo, but finally we all agreed to recommend McCombs. It was not very willingly that Wilson accepted the recommendation. He made the condition that McAdoo should be vice chairman. When Wilson made known his wish, McCombs resented it. He did not wish McAdoo for vice chairman. In the last month or two of the pre-convention campaign McAdoo had entered the fight and had been influential. He had verve and a knowledge of men which he later demonstrated as Secretary of the Treasury. McCombs felt that with so vibrant a man as vice chairman, he could not run things with a lone hand. The rest of us thought McAdoo's selection fine and approved it. It was a wise action, although it gave me, and others, many hours of trouble in adjustments during the campaign.

I became chairman of publicity, charged with preparing the campaign's textbook, literature, and cartoons, and giving news to the press. I spent most of the summer and fall until the election at New York headquarters. Shortly after I was in harness in New York, Franklin Roosevelt dropped in to renew the Baltimore acquaintance and talk over the situation. He told me he was running for reëlection to the State Senate and might have trouble because he had opposed Sheehan, but he thought the Independents and the Republicans would make up for any loss he might sustain. I was even more attracted by his personality than when I first met him at Baltimore. I did not see him again until after Wilson was elected, for he was soon stricken with fever and Louis Howe carried on his campaign for reëlection successfully.

When I organized the literary and publicity departments and began work on the campaign textbook, I was fortunate to have as assistants Tom Pence, who, however, was more of a liaison between the chairmanship office and the outside public than a worker in the publicity department, and Robert Woolley, who had been secretary of the congressional committee which investigated the steel trust, and of the Pujo committee that uncovered the money trust. He was later to be appointed director of the Mint in the Wilson administration, and was a close friend of McAdoo in his political fights. Woolley had the largest part in preparing the textbook. Among my other assistants was Joseph R. Wilson, a brother of Governor Wilson, an experienced newspaper man, modest to an extraordinary degree, who had long been city editor of the Nashville *Banner*.

My good friend Tom Pence was McCombs' right-hand man, and at first he shared the feeling that McAdoo was trying to horn in and push McCombs out. The truth was that, for a good portion of the campaign, McCombs was an ill man, unable to carry on the duties of chairmanship, and was confined to his room at times and could not come to Democratic headquarters. He resented McAdoo's taking charge during his illness.

I went up one day with Pence to see McCombs while he was ill, and found him in a bad state of mind. He was physically racked with pain and partly under the influence of narcotics. He wanted me to tell him everything that was going on at Democratic headquarters, saying he understood that McAdoo had supplanted him while he was sick and was trying to run the campaign on lines that would humiliate McCombs and elevate McAdoo. He had that obsession all the time he was ill and never recovered from it. I assured him his information was entirely inaccurate, that we had called McAdoo in and he was eager to work, and that the campaign was being carried along on the same lines on which it had been started. We told him that when he was able to return McAdoo would coöperate with him in every way; that it was not any one man's campaign but one in which the lines had been laid down by the committee and neither he nor McAdoo was other than the trusted and active head of a committee which was bent upon bringing about the election of Wilson.

On August 29 Wilson came to New York headquarters for a conference. There were present McAdoo, Daniels, Palmer, Morgenthau, and Crane. There was a division of opinion at this conference as to whether Wilson ought to speak in Maine or Pennsylvania during the campaign. He himself was positive that he ought not to speak in Maine. He said if he were to speak there it would be regarded by the country as a test vote. The Maine Democrats were insistent. The New York *World,* which was a staunch Wilson supporter, had taken the ground that the Democrats ought to fight in Maine. It said that in most elections, when the Republican majority was reduced in September it presaged a Democratic victory in November. But Wilson could not be moved by any of these considerations, and he did not go to Maine.

There was considerable opposition in the committee to his going to Pennsylvania, but A. Mitchell Palmer would not take no. He said the situation in his State was so mixed that it was not beyond the realm of possibility that Wilson would carry it, and even if he didn't, his going would insure the election of a number of Democrats to the House of Representatives, who might be needed in organizing the House. We ragged Palmer about his rainbow-chasing, but Wilson felt he ought to go. He could not have been nominated at Baltimore but for the solid support of the Pennsylvania delegation. He owed them much.

Early in the campaign Champ Clark went to Sea Girt to call upon Wilson, who said the Speaker was "very fine, his position was admirable and generous in every way." He took with him 116 members of the House and made a speech which was effective in lining up all the Clark supporters for Wilson.

WILSON DID NOT SWING AROUND THE CIRCLE

Wilson made very few speeches during the campaign. He didn't like swinging around the circle. He preferred to speak to the country through the published addresses he made at Sea Girt. He would have loved the modern campaigning over the radio. It was hard to persuade him to "go to the country." He had none of Bryan's love for appealing to great gatherings. For one thing, he lacked the carrying voice. For another thing, he wished to write carefully what he said and rewrite and then give time to considering what the effect would be on the voter. So Bryan was the leading spellbinder as in every campaign since 1896, and the most effective America has known. "I honestly believe," he said to me, "that I am more anxious to win this year with Wilson than I was in any campaign when I was the presidential candidate." And I am sure he was sincere.

About the hardest job I had during the campaign was to induce Wilson to make some "canned" speeches. I wrote to him, telling him that this would enable him to speak to the whole country, whereas otherwise he could reach only a few voters. He wrote back that he did not believe in canned speeches and that his statements in the papers and his speeches conveyed his position. When I was at Sea Girt, I pressed it upon him and induced Mrs. Wilson to join in presenting the matter and urging it after I left. She did so. He wrote me he would be in New York on a certain day, ready for execution as I had planned. He went at it as if he were going to the stake. I took him down to the headquarters of the recording company, after having made all the arrangements. He spoke into the machine and made the records and when he came out he said he felt as though he had been offered up. I doubt if he ever heard one of these records. He acted as if Mrs. Wilson and I were his worst enemies and persecutors.

EATING CARROTS MAKES SUCCESSFUL POLITICIANS

During the campaign there was friction not only between the McAdoo contingent and the McCombs contingent at headquarters but also between Eastern and Western headquarters. Shortly after the campaign began, Western headquarters were established at Chicago, and the members of the committee from the Southwest and West were put in charge. The central headquarters were in New

York. The members of the Western committee felt that they were not being given the consideration that the importance of their work deserved and that they were not receiving enough money. The men in Eastern headquarters told them they had everything, including Chicago to the Pacific Ocean, to draw upon and they ought to collect all the money they needed from their own territory. They replied that the average man, contributing to the campaign, would naturally send his contribution to the national chairman's office in New York and that part of that money ought to go to them. There were other differences of opinion. Therefore, Martin J. Wade, of Iowa, later appointed Federal judge by President Wilson, came to New York to discuss the situation. McAdoo and I met Wade and made an appointment to talk with him at luncheon. When we were seated at the table, McAdoo said, "I have ordered lunch," and the waiter then brought it in. It consisted of nothing but carrots—carrots fried, carrots stewed, and carrots baked. McAdoo began a dissertation on carrots, saying there was no food so wholesome and healthful.

"When I took this job," he said, "I was informed that, being an amateur, the only way to learn the political game quickly was to eat carrots. A friend of mine told me a diet of carrots would make a man an astute politician in a few weeks. Therefore, since I have been in politics I have been eating nothing but carrots—carrots for breakfast, carrots for dinner and carrots for supper." He dilated upon the health-giving properties of carrots and upon how they would convert an amateur into a seasoned and successful politician. I saw that Wade was not enthusiastic about a diet of carrots but would have preferred an English chop or a filet mignon. He ate the carrots very sparingly, while McAdoo ate them with seeming great relish, boasting that he was getting to be a great political power from a carrot diet. He said, with a twinkle in his eye, "The reason I had this diet of carrots is because we, in Eastern headquarters, have come to think that you gentlemen in Western headquarters need to learn more about practical politics and I wish to prescribe a diet of carrots for all who engage in campaign work in Chicago." Then, with a wave to the waiter, the carrots were taken off and as nice a filet mignon as I ever tasted was brought in. We had a laugh when it was seen that McAdoo had been playing a practical joke on Wade.

When McAdoo was singing the virtues of carrots, I never dreamed that Miss May Foley, nutritionist at the Massachusetts State College in Amherst, believed that eating carrots would prevent what is called "night blindness," and that anyone contemplating a long night motor drive should eat a carrot or two before starting. Maybe, since a political campaign is called a "drive" and most of the speaking is at night, politicians should eat carrots so that they can see well. After the carrot joke we "got down to our mutton" and discussed the situation. From that time on there was never any friction. Harmony was perfect.

The Western headquarters had to do with electing United States Senators in doubtful States by taking advantage of the division between the Republicans and the Roosevelt Progressives. Illinois had a law by which, in each legislative district, two members of the majority party and one member of the minority party were chosen. Democrats, accustomed to defeat, had not nominated enough men to control the Legislature, even if they should carry the state. Many districts had refused to nominate more than one candidate. It was necessary for the committee to take a hand. Upon Wade's suggestion, the national committee sent word to Illinois, urging all the districts to nominate two Democrats for the Legislature. It was well that course was taken, for, in the division between the Republicans and Rooseveltians, the Legislature of Illinois was closely divided. By that course the Democrats secured the election of James Hamilton Lewis to the Senate, and this gave to the party during the Wilson and Roosevelt administrations a very remarkable Senator.

THE NEW JERSEY SENATORSHIP

The Illinois situation was not the only senatorial election that gave the national committee concern. In fact, its greatest trouble came in New Jersey. A Senator was to be elected from that state. It was generally believed that the Democrats would win if they could unite on one candidate. However, there were three or four candidates, all excellent and able men, the two strongest being John W. Westcott, who had placed Wilson in nomination at Baltimore, and William Hughes, who had been elected several times to the House from New Jersey and who had come up from an employee in a factory in Passaic to leadership in the Democratic Party of the State. There were two or three others in what was known as the Wilson faction. Jim Smith, who had been defeated by Wilson for the Senate two years before, announced himself as a candidate. It was clear that the candidate approved by Wilson would win the nomination over Smith, but that with three or four Wilson men in the race, Smith would be nominated. Each of the candidates went to him and said, "Governor Wilson, I will retire if you say so, and if you will pick out which one of the four men you prefer, we will all support him." Of course, this was putting up to Wilson an impossible situation. He declined to make a choice among his friends. The time of filing in the primary was drawing near. Unless something heroic was done, it was clear that five Wilson candidates would go into the New Jersey primary and that Jim Smith, anti-Wilson man, would receive more votes than any of the Wilson men. But if the Wilson men could unite, one of them could be nominated and elected. Not many days before the time for filing in the primary Wilson went on his Western trip, not having made any selection and leaving the matter up in the air. He said that whatever was done should be done by the party leaders, that he would not take the responsibility of selecting among his supporters.

I thought it was of the utmost importance that we should carry the Senate as well as elect the President, for I had been in Washington long enough to know that a President without a Congress in sympathy with him could do little. No one else taking action, I decided something must be done. After a conference with McAdoo and Senator O'Gorman, I wrote a letter to each of the candidates for the Senate in New Jersey and asked them to come to New York headquarters on a certain day to confer about the situation. They all came and told us exactly what they had said to Wilson—that they were willing to submit the matter to him and have him settle it. I pointed out to them that they ought not to put such a question up to Wilson; that naming a preference might cool the ardor of men whose friendship he valued; that some other way of settlement ought to be found. "It would give a severe blow to the party in the country," I said, "if Senator Jim Smith is nominated. The enemies of Wilson would say that, in order to win the presidency, he was willing to send to the Senate from New Jersey a man he kept out of the Senate two years ago as unworthy. It will negative all our progressive campaign claims and make us look ridiculous."

They all agreed, but it was hard to find a way out. The State committee of New Jersey was not willing to make a selection. I suggested to the candidates that they go back to New Jersey, discuss it with their friends, and each of them appoint two friends with power to act to come back to New York. Then the claims of each one of the Wilson candidates should be presented to a committee composed of McAdoo, O'Gorman, and myself, and we would undertake to say which of the four or five would be the strongest candidate. They agreed.

In the meantime, I took the matter up with the editors of several newspapers supporting Wilson in New Jersey, most of them independent in politics, to ascertain their point of view, among others Mr. Scudder, editor of the leading paper in Newark. His paper was not Democratic but, from the beginning, it had espoused Wilson for Governor and now for President. He advised me that, under the circumstances, while Westcott was a man of great ability, Hughes would make much the stronger candidate; that he had behind him the enthusiastic support of the laboring people and was well esteemed by others. When the time arrived for the decision, we repaired to a restaurant in New York where we could get a private room. The matter was discussed fully. The candidates and their friends, after presenting their cases, withdrew, and the committee of three, McAdoo, O'Gorman, and myself, decided it was the wisest thing for all to withdraw except Hughes. We then called the candidates in and they all accepted the decision. Hughes was elected. During the administration of Wilson, one of his most capable and enthusiastic supporters was Senator Hughes, his loyalty being in marked contrast to the rather pathetic and distressing attitude of Senator Martine who, though owing his election solely to Wilson, gave the President little support.

Early in August I dined at Sea Girt with Wilson and gave him the outline of the campaign and talked to him about the plan I had of what should go into the campaign textbook, of furnishing cartoons to all the independent and Democratic papers and organizing a publicity campaign that would reach every newspaper in the country. I had been there a day or two before Roosevelt was nominated for President by the Progressives. Wilson was confident he would be elected whether Roosevelt was nominated or not. He felt that, as a candidate against Taft, he would receive practically the solid Democratic vote and enough of the dissatisfied Progressive Republicans to elect him, in much the same way that Cleveland was elected in 1892. He believed Roosevelt would divide the Republican

Party. Our only danger was that the Roosevelt Party would be regarded as the Progressive and ours a sort of conservative party standing between the two. "We must be militantly progressive," Wilson said, "and make it clear to every voter that the Democratic Party is the champion of progress and the foe of reaction, and that the only hope of untangling the threads of privilege and permeating the whole country is in a Democratic victory."

Early in the campaign we circulated quite a number of copies of William Bayard Hale's *Woodrow Wilson: The Story of His Life.* It was the *vade mecum* of all Democratic speakers. I had been familiar with the campaign biographies of candidates for a long time and had gone as far back as Nathaniel Hawthorne's *Life of Franklin Pierce,* which was the high-water mark of campaign biography. Usually they are written hastily and are so laudatory and so poorly written that, after the campaign, nobody ever hears of them any more. I had read Hale's life of Wilson before the Baltimore Convention and had drawn upon it. When I reached New York I sent for Hale and arranged to secure copies of his book to send to the Democratic committee and speakers. It was the best story of Wilson, before he became President, that had been written. Hale was later entrusted by Wilson with an important and confidential mission to Mexico in the critical days of "Watchful Waiting."

NO PRINTING BY RAT SHOPS

When I went to New York to take charge of the business of writing the textbook and literary and publicity end of the campaign, I got in touch with Walter Page of the Doubleday Page Publishing Company. *World's Work,* for a year or more, had advocated Wilson's nomination and his election. I asked Page to come to New York to talk about the textbook and the campaign publicity, and he asked me to come over to Garden City and spend the day there, saying that he would be glad to do anything he could. I did so and as I wished to get the textbook out that year in a form different from the regulation style and, as the Doubleday Page Company did much printing, I asked if he could help in the preparation of the book and also do the printing in his plant. He said he would help in any way he could but he was very busy and of course he did not care anything about the printing, but, if desired, his company would print the campaign book in attractive form. He had an artistic eye and shared with me the belief that most campaign textbooks were so uninterestingly gotten up and printed that they had little value.

Just before I left Garden City, he said to me, "I ought to tell you, Joe, that we run what you call a 'rat shop.' We do not employ any union men, and you ought to know that before letting us print the book. The union might get after you." I thanked him and said at once, "We must have this book printed in a union office. All the printing done by the Democratic Party carries the union label and I am myself a union man and it would be politically unwise for us, and might be serious, to have the book printed without this label." His son, who was present, said contemptuously, "And so the Democratic Party is going to be bulldozed by the union." His father said, "We don't care anything about the printing, son, and Joe must do what is best for the Democratic Party," and that ended the matter.

The preparation of the textbook took some time, and it was finished and in the hands of the printer and I had read the proof before I was called to Raleigh by the illness of my two sons in the late summer.

ALL TRUSTS LOOK ALIKE

When Woolley, who was in charge of publicity and getting out the textbook in my temporary visit to Raleigh, delivered a copy to McAdoo, who was then acting chairman, McAdoo said, "My God! Does Daniels know that Cyrus McCormick and Thomas Jones of the Harvester Company are Wilson's closest friends and among the largest contributors to the campaign? I wonder what Governor Wilson will think and say when he sees this book roasting the Harvester Company as belonging to the predatory interests and trusts." He was greatly troubled about it and sent me a message asking whether, under the circumstances, I thought the book ought to be issued without conferring with Wilson about it. I directed Woolley to send the book out as it was, saying that nothing had been put in it about the Harvester Company except what had been sworn to in the anti-trust hearings and that Wilson would be the last man to hold up or suppress any denunciation of the monopolistic features of the Harvester Company, when we were denouncing the steel trust and when Wilson himself was making a campaign, the keynote of which was that the individual officers ought to be held responsible for violations of the law. The book came out unchanged. Some Republican papers played up the fact that the Wilson textbook had denounced Wilson's particular friends, but I never heard a word from Wilson about it and I never spoke to him about it. I was quite sure he would have wished me not to show any favoritism to his friends if they were charged with violating the laws.

MAKES NOISE LIKE A PROGRESSIVE

After I returned to New York, we were issuing cartoons and sending them out, free of charge, to all the papers that would use them. At that time, George Perkins, who had become very rich as a member of the J. P. Morgan firm, was running the Roosevelt campaign and was making a noise like a progressive. Perhaps he was sincere, for he had cut all connections with big business, but I doubted the genuineness of his conversion. Personally he was almost a worshipper of Roosevelt and had thrown himself into the Progressive campaign with enthusiasm. One of our cartoons represented Perkins in a light that reflected upon his sincere advocacy of progressive measures and antitrust laws. When he saw it he was furious and wrote McAdoo a letter, saying that was a blow beneath the belt, and asking him to recall the cartoon before it was printed. I do not know how he had gotten hold of it, for it was sent out to be released on a certain day, but he had. McAdoo directed Woolley to hold up the cartoon, saying there was no need of giving offense to Perkins, a great friend of his.

When I came in and found out about it, I said, "Tell McAdoo that it has gone out and is going to appear; that I have no faith in the Perkins end of the Roosevelt campaign. It is financed by money made when he was in the Morgan firm. We are not hitting him beneath the belt but are treating him like the other men who are trying to fool the people." The cartoon appeared. Perkins was indignant and sent McAdoo a protesting letter, which he showed to me. McAdoo thought it was a mistake to send out cartoons like that, but they continued to go out. I told him I was running the publicity campaign and Wilson was talking against monopoly. If we soft-pedaled on a personal friend who had been connected with trusts, our monopoly talk would lose its effectiveness and I did not believe in any death-bed repentence from George Perkins or others of his kind.

It was my job to circulate widely all the statements made by Independents or Republicans advocating Wilson's nomination, and there were many such. One of the best pieces of literature sent out during the campaign was the statement by Dr. Charles W. Eliot, of Harvard, urging Wilson's election. Probably no document in the campaign had more effect with independent voters. It was more effective because Roosevelt was a Harvard graduate.

Only once during his campaign did Wilson depart from his policy of having nothing to say about his opponents. On October 4 he said, "Roosevelt was incompetent as President; Taft didn't carry out his policy and monopolies flourished under both Roosevelt and Taft." This declaration was a surprise to the Wilson campaign managers because he had before that made no reference to his opponents. He evidently thought he had made an error, for my recollection is that in the balance of the campaign he stuck to his original resolution.

HEARST'S SUPPORT NOT ASKED

In 1908 Hearst had organized a new political party, the Independence League. He nominated, or the League did, John Temple Graves, editor of his New York *American,* as candidate for Vice-President. Mr. Graves canvassed the country, and the Hearst papers were bitterly denunciatory of the two old parties, calling them corrupt. In the election of 1910 the Democrats swept the country, carried the House by a large majority, electing Speaker Clark. Clark and Hearst were good friends, and, after the 1910 election, Hearst wrote a letter saying that, inasmuch as the Democratic Party had returned to its old faith he had decided to return and be an active member of the party and edit his papers in behalf of it. He said, in the present conditions, the only hope for reform and progress lay in the success of that party. This declaration by the editor of a paper having millions of subscribers, particularly when the Democrats did not have very large newspaper support in the big cities, was hailed by many Democratic leaders as a valuable ally. Hearst printed, day after day, letters from most of the leaders of the Democratic Party, rejoicing that he had come back to the party and giving him a cordial welcome. He wished such letters from all Democratic leaders. He received none from Wilson, who had been elected Governor of New

Jersey; and so, after one of his staff had written to Wilson and asked for such a letter as Champ Clark, Underwood, and others, had written, and received no reply, Hearst sent a representative to Trenton to call on Wilson, with instructions to show him the letters written by other Democratic presidential candidates and to ask him, point blank, for a similar letter. Governor Wilson said he could not write such a letter and, when pressed for a reason, declared, "I cannot write it because I am very sorry Mr. Hearst has come back into the Democratic Party. I think it was stronger with him on the outside than on the inside. I do not want him and do not want the support of his paper." This, of course, was not printed in the Hearst papers, but was duly reported to Hearst, who from that time on was Wilson's most bitter antagonist.

When Wilson was nominated, Hearst was in a very embarrassing position. Roosevelt had called on Elihu Root to denounce Hearst as the most malign influence in American politics, in language which, for bitterness of arraignment and contempt had never been equalled in American political annals. Hearst could not support Roosevelt. His papers had been antagonistic to Taft and to the reactionary forces behind him, and so he could not support Taft. He hated Wilson, but Wilson had said nothing about him publicly and was standing for most of the progressive policies which Hearst papers had been advocating for years, including initiative, referendum and primaries, regulation and suppression of trusts, and the like. As soon as the convention adjourned, Hearst, disappointed that Clark had not won, sailed for Europe. Writing of the presidential campaign, his papers said: *"We Are for Wilson."* That was all. His papers took no active part in the campaign. His news columns were quite as friendly to Roosevelt and Taft as to Wilson and some people thought more so. As the campaign wore on, Hearst's managers in New York wished him to get into the campaign. They probably saw that Wilson was going to win, and as they had declared, "We are for Wilson," they wanted Hearst to authorize active support. They felt this was hopeless unless Hearst had an invitation from Wilson or received particular recognition.

When Thomas R. Marshall, candidate for Vice President, came east, John Temple Graves saw me and said he wanted to arrange an interview with Marshall to discuss the campaign, expressing his very earnest interest in Wilson's election and his desire that the

Hearst paper should fall in line enthusiastically. I made the engagement for a conference with Marshall and Graves. A singular incident happened in connection with it. I told Marshall that Graves and I would meet him at my hotel, the Belvedere, at three o'clock on a certain afternoon. I had stopped at the Belvedere in Baltimore during the convention and, absent-mindedly, gave him that name instead of the Martinique, where I was staying in New York. Graves and I repaired to the Martinique at three o'clock and waited for nearly an hour, but no Marshall appeared. Finally, after a long time, a telephone message came and it was from the vice-presidential candidate. "We have been waiting for you an hour," I said, to which he replied, "I will be right up." When he arrived, he informed us he had been driving all over New York and in some of its worst parts, looking for the Belvedere Hotel, which he had finally found over a little saloon in a disreputable part of the city, and when he inquired for me he was told they had never heard of me. Then he laughed and turned to Graves, saying, "They said they had never heard of Daniels, but he is the only man I know in New York, who ever heard of the Belvedere."

Graves made known that he wished Wilson to cable Hearst, asking him to come back from Europe and enter the campaign. I knew Wilson wouldn't do it, but I didn't want to say so. I didn't want the issue raised and so suggested that since Wilson did not know Hearst personally and as Marshall knew him well and was on friendly terms with him, it might be better if Marshall were to send the cable on his own and my behalf and that of others at Democratic headquarters. I said we appreciated the fact that the Hearst papers had said they were for Wilson and hoped his papers would enter heartily into the campaign. Graves did not think much of that, for he did not think it would satisfy Hearst. He wanted Marshall and me to go to see Wilson and ask him to cable Hearst. I told him we would see about it later.

After he left, I told Marshall about Wilson's refusal to say he wanted Hearst in the Democratic Party and I knew Wilson wouldn't send such a telegram. Marshall said that when he ran for office he wanted everybody's support and he had never seen a man he wouldn't welcome in the Democratic Party. He thought it was bad politics, in a campaign, to give the cold shoulder to anybody, particularly one whose papers had such large circulation. But he didn't take the matter up with Wilson and neither did I, and the Hearst papers went on during the campaign, every now and then saying, "We are for Wilson," but giving no real support. The result was that they helped Wilson, for it is the history of Hearst papers that their advocacy of a candidate is not helpful, but they are very effective when they are against a man, using all their powers of opposition. Hearst received no invitation from Wilson and the Hearst papers continued nominally for Wilson but were not active in the fight.

BIG CONTRIBUTIONS DECLINED

During the summer there was investigation of the campaign contributions, which proved the wisdom of Wilson's refusal to permit large contributions. It came out that the Standard Oil Company had given $125,000 to the Republican campaign committee in the previous campaign and the money had gone to Penrose. J. P. Morgan had given $150,000, which he said he gave without expectation of return; but as that company was the steel trust and other trusts, nobody believed the statement. It was pointed out in *The News and Observer* that the Morgan companies were capitalized at seventeen billion dollars and they contained only eight billion dollars of water, which made his contribution of $150,000 an insurance rate of 1,875/1,000,000 of 1 per cent. Archibald, of the Standard Oil Company, had stated that he gave $100,000 to the Roosevelt campaign in 1904, under the impression that Roosevelt knew of it and approved the acceptance of it. Roosevelt vigorously denied this. Perkins lost his head before the committee and got very mad. He denied he had underwritten the financing of Roosevelt's pre-convention campaign or that any money had been contributed by the Harvester Company or United Steel Corporation. He said $126,000 had been spent in the pre-convention campaign and said he almost dropped dead when Senator Beveridge, of Indiana, returned to him $10,000 which he had sent to him for use in Indiana. "This is the only instance I know of," he said, "where a man running for office turned money down after he had his hands on it."

On October 26, after the investigation showing that Cyrus H. McCormick had contributed $2,500 to the Democratic campaign fund, Wilson made the statement that this money was returned to McCormick. The total campaign contributions for Wilson were

$1,159,446. When McCombs made his report, it turned out that he had disregarded Wilson's injunction forbidding the acceptance of any contribution over $5,000 and I think Wilson started out with $1,000—for it was pointed out that Charles R. Crane, the heaviest contributor, gave $40,000, Cleveland Dodge, $35,000, and Herman Ridder $30,000. There were 89,854 separate contributions, all but 1,625 of which were less than $100. The amount spent by the Wilson forces in the pre-convention campaign was $208,000, of which Cleveland Dodge and other Princeton friends, gave $85,000. Included among the friends were Cyrus H. McCormick, Thomas D. Jones, and others of the International Harvester Company. The Harmon forces spent $150,946.45, of which $77,000 was contributed by Thomas Fortune Ryan. Ryan also supplied a large amount of the $52,000 Underwood fund.

Up to October the contributions to the Wilson campaign fund were not large enough to meet the expenses. By that time, however, it was pretty generally believed that Wilson would be elected and the campaign contributions came in large enough to meet the expenditures.

NO SAILING UNDER FALSE COLORS

One day I was sitting in my office in headquarters when Mr. Henry Morgenthau afterwards Ambassador to Turkey, came in and handed me a roll of bills—I think it was about five thousand dollars—and said, "You know our friend Governor Wilson issued a rule that no man should be allowed to make a large campaign contribution. I have given all they would take, but I know that the committee ought to spend more money than Wilson thinks, and I am not only willing to give more but desirous of doing so. Inasmuch, as Wilson will not permit anyone to give more than I have contributed, here is this money. You take it and give it yourself to the campaign fund." Of course I knew that Morgenthau had plenty of money and that he was sincerely interested in the election of Wilson and wanted the committee to have enough money to do larger things than Wilson deemed necessary or the committee had planned. I was unwilling to sail under false colors, and yet I did not wish to offend him, for I liked him very much. So I said to him laughingly, "I would like very much to do it but it is impossible." "Why impossible?" he asked. I replied, "If my creditors in North

Carolina should read in the papers that I had contributed five thousand dollars to the campaign fund, they would send a telegram here to attach it and the committee would never get the money." Of course he saw the point and said no more about it.

The next day Mr. Penfield, Consul in Egypt under Cleveland and later appointed Ambassador to Austria, one of the early Wilson supporters, who had also been willing to make a large contribution and had given all the committee would accept, came to publicity headquarters and said, "I don't think you are putting enough advertisements in the newspapers. I think we ought to have a page in several widely circulated weeklies and if you will get up the advertisements, I will pay for them. It need not go through the regular channels at all. Just see the editors and make arrangements personally and I will pay the bill." It was praiseworthy on his part, but it would have been violating the spirit of Wilson's insistence and would have put him under as much obligation to Penfield as if he had given the money to the committee. I told him I thought the plans the committee had worked out would suffice but, if he wished it, I would take it before the committee and see what they had to say. "Don't do that," he said, "I have already asked the treasurer to take the money and he declined."

By the way, Wilson did not take any chances about the committee's publicly saying one thing and doing something different about contributions. He surprised the whole committee when he said he wished Rolla Wells to be treasurer. Nobody around headquarters knew Wells, although he had been mayor of St. Louis and a prominent Democrat there. He was a Princeton man and Wilson had high regard for him. When he came to headquarters, instead of being a perfunctory treasurer, he gave his whole time to the duty and did it as carefully as he would have his own private business. He showed judgment and was highly respected.

COLONEL ROOSEVELT PRAISED

The middle of October saw the speaking campaign ended for a time. When Roosevelt was speaking at Minneapolis, an attempt was made upon his life. He continued his speech and made light of the wound, but immediately after the meeting the doctors announced that it was more serious than at first believed and he was hurried to a hospital and given antitoxin. For some time, it was feared the wound would be fatal. As soon as the news came, Wilson cancelled all his speaking dates and said he would not speak again until Roosevelt was in shape. He called Roosevelt "that gallant gentleman," and Roosevelt replied that the campaign ought to go on and Wilson ought to continue his speaking—that his wound would not affect the situation. Bryan also said the discussion should go on. Roosevelt issued a statement agreeing with Bryan, and Bryan called it a "manly assertion and just what might be expected from him. It clears the air and permits the renewal of the issues. Speed to his recovery."

In an editorial headed, "Roosevelt In The Crisis," *The News and Observer,* my paper, said, "The ability to go into a crowded auditorium and speak with almost his accustomed vigor, with the knowledge that a bullet had been sent hurtling through his body, required determination and stuff, the possession of which is the secret of Mr. Roosevelt's long continued popularity." It also said the mob would have killed the man who fired the shot if Roosevelt had not saved him.

WILSON'S BOOK PLAGUED HIM

In the pre-convention campaign Wilson had lost nearly all the States for the nomination in which there was a large foreign vote. This was largely due to the attacks made upon him by Hearst, who had read in Wilson's history statements by him to the effect that emigrants from southern Europe, who had come to this country, were not desirable. He said Wilson had referred to "men of the meaner sort from the south of Europe." Such statements by Wilson, in his history, were unfortunate. When they were dug out of the context, made public, and sent by Hearst to the leaders and editors of all the newspapers published in the foreign languages, sentiment was crystallized against Wilson. After he was nominated, the Republicans undertook to use Hearst's publication against his election. Wilson saw it was necessary to answer these attacks, but he did not mention Hearst in explaining his views on immigration. Writing a statement to a Hungarian paper, he spoke of the "vast service done by Hungarians in Europe for the cause of European freedom" and defined his attitude on immigration by saying that it should have "only such regulations and restrictions as will help the health and moral conditions of the United States."

But all during the campaign, what he was alleged to have said about "men of the meaner sort in Europe" came up to plague him. The most difficult job I had was in connection with the foreign language newspapers. It was important to make them understand that, as a historian, Wilson did not refer to those nationalities as a whole but to such men as were unworthy. I was in frequent conference, during the whole campaign, with editors of these foreign newspapers and with other leaders among the people from foreign countries. We had a department devoted to that task, and some very patriotic men tried to erase the impression made against Wilson. We were able to do it only in part; yet enough of these people coming from southern Europe saw that it was not right to judge Wilson in the campaign by what he had written years before, but rather by his present appreciation of the worth of these nationalities and their contribution to American life. Taft and Roosevelt divided with Wilson the vote which he would have received more largely if he had never written a history. One day, speaking to Wilson about the difficult position in which this had placed him, I told him that I felt like saying with the psalmist, with some variation, "Oh, that our candidate had never written a book."

CAP'N BILL MCDONALD GUARDS WILSON

Colonel House was the man of mystery in the campaign. He came in quietly and unheralded to Democratic headquarters and gave his views, which were supposed to reflect Wilson's desires, and for that reason they were given great weight. Toward the close of the campaign Wilson was injured in a night ride. As an attempt had been made to kill Roosevelt, headquarters thought Wilson ought to have a bodyguard. House suggested that the very man was Cap'n Bill McDonald, famous Texas ranger. In answer to a telegram Cap'n Bill wired, "I am a-coming." He never let Wilson get out of his sight, sleeping on a cot outside his bedroom and accompanying him on every trip. I would have been sorry for any man who came within reach of Cap'n Bill's gun. One of Wilson's very first appointments, after he entered the White House, was to make his Texas ranger friend, whom he had come to respect and like, a United States Marshal in the famous Panhandle district of northwestern Texas.

UNOFFICIAL TOWERS OF STRENGTH

There were two or three other men who had large part in the campaign, about whom little was known. One of these was Charles R. Crane of Chicago, a remarkable man to whom I became attached. He had been a lifelong Republican, had been appointed Minister to China by Taft but, while on his way to that post, had been recalled because he had made some statement concerning Chinese affairs (about which he was well informed), which offended the Chinese. Taft cancelled his appointment and he was ordered back home. He was a genuine progressive and had been a Progressive Republican, but he was not of the Teddy type. Before the nominations he had said his first interest was in supporting a real progressive for President and he did not care to what party he belonged—that if the Democrats nominated Wilson and the Progressives nominated La Follette, he would not care much which was elected, but if the Democratic Party nominated Wilson and the Progressive Party did not nominate La Follette, he would support Wilson.

Another man, one destined to occupy a high place, who was regarded in the campaign as a man of mystery, was Bernard M. Baruch. He was a close friend of McAdoo, came now and then to headquarters, and was quietly active in helping to raise money. He was, himself, ready to make any contribution that would be accepted. His father, who had been a distinguished surgeon in the Confederate Army, was a South Carolinian and had moved to New York after the Civil War. Baruch had early gone on the stock exchange, was a successful operator, and had amassed a fortune. He and his father retained the Democracy which they had embraced in South Carolina, and though he had never been active in politics, Wilson's career in New Jersey fired his imagination and evoked his enthusiasm. When Wilson was a candidate for the nomination, he threw himself, in a quiet way, into the fight and was ready to do anything to further Wilson's success, and the same was true in the campaign. He was a Jew and a Southern Jew, with a background of education and business sagacity. Later I was to know him well and to be closely connected with him in World War work, in which he was the resourceful chairman of the War Industries Board and had Wilson's complete confidence.

Several times during the progress of the campaign Wilson's daughters came to New York to get a thrill out of the campaign rallies and parades. Living in quiet classic towns, they had never known what a political campaign was like. They were enthusiastic and I felt as if I were accompanying three little maids let out of school. Nobody recognized them in the crowds and we went from one rally to another until the last lights were out. It was real fun!

PROPHECY THAT CAME TRUE

Not many days before the election, I had a message from Governor Wilson asking me to come down to Sea Girt. He wanted to know the latest news from all the States and to confer about some campaign matters. I spent the afternoon and took dinner with him and his family and went back to New York that night. When I reached the station at Sea Girt, newspaper correspondents, a dozen or more of them, who had remained there for the campaign, asked me for a statement. They said, "You have been with Wilson all the afternoon and people want to know what you have to say." I answered, "You can print tomorrow that Wilson will carry every State except eight." They all wrote that down very quickly, then wanted to know, "Which eight?" I said, "I decline to name them, but you may print it without any doubt that, after a thorough study of the campaign, the Democratic managers know what they are talking about and Wilson will carry forty States, including such great States as New York, and the other eight will be divided between Taft and Roosevelt." "How will they be divided?" they asked, but I boarded the train and left them with that statement.

Next morning there appeared in most of the papers a statement attributed to me, naming the eight particular States which the Democrats had conceded to Roosevelt and Taft. When I picked up the paper and saw I had been so quoted, I was disposed not to deny the quotation, since I was a member of the profession. Before the day was over my desk was piled high with telegrams from members of the national committee and from the chairman and leading Democrats from each of the eight States mentioned. The telegram from the chairman of Utah's State committee asked, "What in the hell do you mean by conceding Utah to the Republicans? Such statements will demoralize our fight and show you as not fit for the job." That was the tenor of the telegrams from such States as Utah and Vermont. Democrats were fighting hard everywhere, and even in such

LEADERS BEHIND THE SCENES

Upper left, Bernard M. Baruch, chairman of War Industries Board under Wilson. *Upper right,* Cleveland Dodge, Princeton classmate and close friend of Wilson (Brown Brothers). *Lower left,* Edward M. House, unofficial adviser in the Wilson campaign of 1912 (Brown Brothers). *Lower right,* Charles R. Crane, globe-trotter and unofficial adviser in the Wilson administration (Harris & Ewing).

WOODROW WILSON AND HIS FAMILY AT SEA GIRT, N. J.

This picture was taken when they heard the news of Wilson's nomination for President of the United States. Seated in front are Eleanor Randolph Wilson, later Mrs. McAdoo (in the large hat), and Margaret Woodrow Wilson. At Mrs. Wilson's right is Jessie Woodrow Wilson, who married Francis B. Sayre, later High Commissioner to the Philippines (Underwood & Underwood).

States they believed the division in the Republican Party would enable them to carry the electoral votes. The Democrats even in Pennsylvania had that expectation. I then telegraphed that I had said Wilson would carry forty States and I had declined to name the eight. The Associated Press had not quoted me as naming any particular eight, but only what I had really said. It raised a storm and the Utah and Vermont Democrats did not forgive me until the election returns showed that Taft had carried those two states and none others.

ON WHICH SIDE—MCADOO OR MCCOMBS

I did not go home to vote, having arranged a pair with a Republican friend. Most officials at headquarters lived in doubtful States. North Carolina was certain. I remained at headquarters. "What are you going to do on election day?" McAdoo asked me the night before the election after the last statements and predictions had gone out.

"I am leaving for Raleigh as soon as we learn the result of the election," I answered, "and as I do not expect to be in this section again soon I have an engagement with Governor Wilson to go to Princeton in the morning to see him and in the afternoon to go with Mayor McGuire to the polls and see how elections are conducted on the Bowery."

"If it is all right, I will take you down in my car," McAdoo said. "I will be happy for you to go," I replied, "but wherever there are two tracks going to a place I go on the train." We arranged to go by rail. I knew McAdoo was a fast and furious driver, and I was not fully automobile "broke" at that time. A few minutes after McAdoo left, Tom Pence came into the office. To his inquiry of what I was planning to do on election day, I told him McAdoo and I were going to Princeton to see the President-elect.

"You should not go with McAdoo," he said with feeling, and added: "During the whole campaign you have kept the rudder even, and the campaign ends with your being on most friendly and cordial terms with both the McAdoo and the McCombs people. Now you have to go to Princeton with McAdoo to spend the day with Governor Wilson and make all the McCombs people feel you have joined the McAdoo forces and it may result in your not being in the Cabinet." He was very insistent that I find some excuse for not going or for not letting McAdoo go with me. I told him I had made the appointment to go with him without any consultation with anybody and that if McCombs had come and asked to go with me, I would have been glad to have him or any other member of the committee; that the fact was that, while I preferred to go alone, where I could talk more freely with Wilson, I was happy to go with McAdoo as I would have been with McCombs or Palmer or anybody else on the committee. Pence was very much worried about it at that time, and when the New York papers began to write me up as being with the McAdoo forces and against McCombs, he was so fond of me and so ambitious for me, that it troubled him.

Toward the end of the year some New York papers had much to say about the break between McCombs and McAdoo. Some of McCombs' super-serviceable friends felt that they had to break McAdoo down in order to uphold McCombs. They resented any member of the national committee's being friendly to McAdoo because they believed that McAdoo was doing everything he could to undermine McCombs. In a Sunday copy of the New York *Herald* there was a news story saying that I had lined up with McAdoo. As proof, it instanced the fact that, on the day of the election, McAdoo and I went together to spend the day with Governor Wilson in Princeton. I was put down as one of the cabal of the McAdoo forces that were trying to control the appointments in the Cabinet and put McCombs in the sidelines. When that appeared I received a letter from Tom Pence, who was still all for McCombs and critical of McAdoo, saying that if I had listened to him and refused to let McAdoo go with me to Princeton, such an article would not have appeared. But he convinced McCombs I was not a partisan of any faction and calmed him down.

There were no other visitors when McAdoo and I reached the Wilson home in Princeton. We went downstairs to enter the well-lighted library and living room. Mrs. Wilson, who was an artist and something of an architect, had made the plans. Most of the time I was in conversation with Wilson, while McAdoo talked to the ladies. I did not imagine then that Eleanor would within a few months become Mrs. McAdoo, and neither did she, but the whole Wilson family liked him.

My purpose in wishing to see Wilson prior to going South was to urge him to make an announcement, immediately or soon after his election, that he would call a special session of Congress to revise and reduce the tariff, with emphasis on the "reduce." I pressed my view as strongly as I could and reinforced it by relating the unfortunate experience of Cleveland, who delayed action on tariff in his second term. I said:

"I was in the Interior Department in Cleveland's second term and was witness to the effect of his sidetracking tariff reduction. He was elected as a tariff reform president. If he had called an extra session and pressed for action in the spring, Congress, fresh from the people, would have gone along with him and would have passed a good measure. Instead, he gave the first place to the repeal of the silver purchase act. Upon the money question the party was divided; upon the tariff in March it was united. Tariff legislation was postponed and he was so disgusted with the final bill he said the Wilson-Gorman act represented 'party perfidy and party dishonor.'

"You will be strong enough to carry any measure through, because you have a large majority in the House and will carry the Senate. You can get a real reform measure if you will let everything else stand aside and do nothing until that measure is adopted. But, if you wait, every little and big interest in the country, local and otherwise, will be urging their congressmen to get them a slice, and when they come to make a tariff law you will have Cleveland's experience. I urge you to announce at once an extra session of Congress for the sole purpose of revising the tariff."

TARIFF REFORM TO COME FIRST

He had said, in the campaign, that the tariff constituted the great issue; that reforms could not come until the favors to private interests were removed. That night, I talked to Ralph Pulitzer of the *World* and detailed to him my conversation with Wilson and said, "Your father had a way of making things that ought to prevail come to pass by iteration and reiteration. If the *World* will come out, as soon as Wilson's election is announced, for an immediate session of Congress, after his inauguration, for tariff revision, the country will take it up and it will strengthen Wilson's hands and make certain that we shall not lose the tariff reform, for which we have fought." He asked me to write a letter about it, which I did. Shortly after that the *World* came out in an old-time Pulitzer sort of editorial (written by Frank Cobb at his best), pointing out that the first thing on the program was an extra session of Congress to revise the tariff, and using the arguments I had made to Wilson and in my letter. It was taken up by the press. A few days after the election, *The News and Observer* had an editorial urging such a session, and on November 16 my paper had an eight-column streamer heading: "Wilson Will Keep The Pledge Of Democracy And Will Call Extra Session Of Congress To Convene Not Later Than April Fifteenth And Says He Will Issue The Call Immediately After The Inauguration," which he did.

I saw at Princeton that the argument for prompt action on the tariff had weight with Wilson, though he said he had not given thought to his course in that respect and added, "I haven't been elected yet." He said he would give my suggestion serious consideration. We talked about other matters and I congratulated him on his coming election. He said it would be best to withhold congratulations, until the votes were cast. His wife and daughters were keyed up, confident and happy.

THE BOWERY ON ELECTION DAY

Returning from Princeton, I went with Mayor James K. McGuire of Syracuse, a delightful companion, to many precincts and Democratic clubs on the East Side. It was interesting to see and talk with the people. I met a number of local leaders. Most of them were Irish and regaled me with stories about how they kept the voters in line. We went into some Jewish wards and watched the balloting. There was no confusion, but voters would be instructed in the clubs how to vote and would go direct to the booth. There were few scratched tickets and most of them were for the Democratic nominees.

"It is too quiet here," said Mayor McGuire. "It is not natural. You ought to come down when there is a regular knock-down and drag-out fight over local candidates." As we passed the more squalid places I walked along streets whose names recalled my reading of "Ragged Dick" when I was a boy. He was a bootblack and though many years had passed I found myself wondering if I could recognize the scenes described in the book which I had avidly read. In our tour, McGuire, who knew the ABC's of politics, regaled me with stories from the days of John Kelly and Samuel J. Tilden.

BACK TO THE SANCTUM

Long before midnight it was conceded that Wilson was elected, for he had carried every State but eight. I said good-bye to my associates, with whom I had been working day and night since the middle of July, and took the train for Raleigh. It was good to get home and to find that the city was rejoicing over the victory and to find two of my boys and my wife, who had been sick, restored to health. It seemed that I had been gone for years. I dropped everything about national politics, falling back into a happy home life, and returned to editing *The News and Observer*. It felt good to be at my old job, which had been interrupted for over half a year in the campaign.

DEMOCRATS MAKE CLEAN SWEEP

Taft carried only two States—Vermont and Utah. Roosevelt bagged five—Michigan, Minnesota (by a hair's breadth), Pennsylvania, South Dakota and Washington. In California Wilson had two electors and Roosevelt eleven. The popular vote was: Wilson, 6,286,-214; Roosevelt, 4,126,020; and Taft, 3,483,922. In addition, the Democrats carried both Houses of Congress, with a majority of six in the Senate and 147 in the House.

The campaign had ended gloriously.

ACCLAIMED A PROPHET

Not long after the election Bryan came to Raleigh on his regular lecture schedule. I introduced him, and in his speech he said, "At last, as a result of the election, I am glad that Josephus Daniels' reputation as a prophet has been redeemed. He has been, for a number of years, prophesying that I would be elected, when I was a candidate. Wilson's election has now put him in the class of the true prophets." He was uncertain whether Wilson would ask him to go into the Cabinet and more uncertain whether he ought to go if he was invited. I told him that he was certain to be asked and that, under no circumstances, must he decline; that Wilson would need him and the country would expect him to aid in the great tasks ahead.

VIII

WILSON GETS READY TO BREAK PRECEDENTS

I N JANUARY, 1913, the citizens of Asheville, North Carolina, decided to make an offer of a summer home to the newly elected
President. They insisted that I go to Trenton to make the tender and
urge acceptance. "Do nothing of the kind," said my best friend,
Honorable Fred A. Woodard, of Wilson. "They have no right to
ask you and you ought not to go, particularly since you are talked
of for a Cabinet position." My Asheville friends insisted, and I made
the arrangement to see Governor Wilson. Before leaving Raleigh
I received a message from William Bayard Hale, a member of the
staff of the *World's Work,* edited by Walter H. Page, saying it was
imperative that he see me at once. I wired him to meet me on the
train as I was leaving Trenton.

At Trenton I found the Governor closeted with McCombs, and
I had a chat with Joseph Tumulty, slated to be private secretary to
the President. He had served as private secretary to Wilson during
the years he was Governor of New Jersey. I had early formed a high
regard for him in our association during the campaign—a friendship
that strengthened during long association in Washington. Wilson
greeted me cordially and asked about my wife, who had won his high
regard. I told him that I had three things I wished to speak to him
about. He listened. First, I asked, "What do you regard as the most
important goal of your administration, certainly in the early years?"

He replied by asking, "What do you think?"

I said that in my judgment the biggest duty and opportunity related to agriculture. I gave some illustrations of how producers were
getting very little for their crops, while consumers were being made
to pay high prices and said that a system of scientific marketing
under government auspices would end the inequitable spread. I
instanced that with all the improved transportation and commerce,
little benefit had come to either the farmer or the consumer. I related that in the previous summer, when I was taking lunch at the
Waldorf-Astoria in New York with Mitchell Palmer, we ordered

half a cantaloupe each. While we were eating, the waiter brought Palmer's mail. He opened it and said, "Look here. I have a letter from the manager of my farm. I raise cantaloupes. He reports that he has received eighty-five cents for a crate of cantaloupes shipped to New York. And now we are paying eighty cents for one cantaloupe at this hotel."

"There is something wrong," I told the newly elected President, "in a situation where a consumer in New York pays eighty cents for one cantaloupe and the grower receives only eighty-five cents for the whole crate. The country cannot prosper unless farmers receive fair prices for their crops, and therefore a practical agriculturist, the man who can do most to secure prosperity, should be Secretary of Agriculture, a man who can reduce the spread between producer and consumer. He is your key man." I was going further when he said:

"I agree with you and the subject has my best thought. Of course that means we must have the best man we can find in the country for Secretary of Agriculture. Whom have you in mind?" He evidently thought I had come to suggest a name. I disabused him promptly of that idea and replied, "I have no one to suggest. I do not know the great agriculturists of the country. I do know that the Secretary of Agriculture should be aware of the needs, and know how to secure the coöperation of the farmers; he should be a good mixer and have ability and initiative. Our future prosperity depends upon a prosperous agriculture and the first step is marketing."

Governor Wilson stopped me. "You have described the very man for the place and I have such a man." I told him that in my opinion this was the best step he could take to make his administration a success. Of course I did not ask him the name of the new Secretary of Agriculture, and he did not volunteer the information. Not long before the inauguration, Walter H. Page, on a visit to relatives in North Carolina, told one of them that Wilson would name, as Secretary of Agriculture, "a man born within one hundred miles of Aberdeen," but would say no more. Speculation followed, and most North Carolinians thought Page was referring to himself, for his name had frequently been mentioned for the position. Others thought he referred to Clarence Poe, of Raleigh, editor of *The Progressive Farmer*, who would have filled the position with ability, but who was not an aspirant. Evidently, Page had received the tip as to David

F. Houston. Afterwards I learned he had been partly responsible for Houston's appointment.

I next conveyed the offer of the summer home at Asheville, which I had been commissioned to present, and started to say something about the climate of Western North Carolina. The Governor interrupted me: "I know it perfectly. There is no more delightful place in the world. My wife and I spent the first weeks after we were married in Haywood County, thirty miles from Asheville, and we were in Asheville a brief time." He was not prepared to think where he would spend the summer if his duties in Washington should afford him a vacation. He asked me to express his thanks and defer an answer.

FOR A DEMOCRATIC SENATE

"I feel, Governor," I said, "that a safe majority in the Senate is of the highest importance, and we should be alert to that objective. Whenever there is a chance, you should throw your influence to elect Democratic Senators." He agreed. I then told him that the deadlock in the Legislature of Delaware threatened the election of a Democrat —that Robert R. Kenney and Willard Salisbury were rivals and the fight was so bitter there was real danger that a Republican might be chosen. "I know Kenney well," I said. "He is a man who should be seen and urged to make a sacrifice for the party." The Governor knew something of the situation in Delaware but did not know Kenney. "I wish you would go to Wilmington and see Kenney and Salisbury and tell both I asked you to say that I as the chosen leader of the party request them to do nothing that will jeopardize the election of a Democrat." I promised to do as he requested and left him to telephone Kenney for an immediate appointment and to take the train for Wilmington.

McCombs was waiting for me and I saw he was anxious to know what I had come to talk to Wilson about. I told him of the Asheville tender of the summer home—nothing else. I did not wish him to put his hand in the Delaware deadlock or to know I had talked of the right kind of man for Secretary of Agriculture. We had a friendly chat. He assumed to know much about the Cabinet—thought Bryan was certain but doubted the wisdom of his selection, said Burleson and Wilson were sure, and probably Palmer. As for himself, he said he had told the Governor he did not wish to be considered, but did

former appraisement of the author of the McKinley bill. As a close friend and supporter of Bryan, whose tariff record was as good as Cleveland's, I told Page that the election of McKinley would result in a return to the rule of the tariff barons. To no effect. These differences of opinion have not altered my friendly feelings, and I did not suppose he either disliked or envied me."

"It may be," said Hale, "that he doesn't want any other North Carolinian except himself close to Wilson."

What Hale said hurt and disturbed me, but the hurt was the worst. Page and I had been warm friends in the old days, and I had supposed our differences were purely political.

"Do you think it possible," Hale asked, "that he became offended when, after you had planned to get his company to print the Democratic textbook, you told him that the printing would have to be done elsewhere because his firm conducted a non-union shop?"

I told him I was sure that could not be the cause, for Page had consented to do the work only at my request and because he was interested in Wilson's election.

Hale did not know exactly what argument Page made against naming me to a Cabinet post. He knew only that Page was determined if possible to prevent it. Colonel House was given as the authority for the statement that when Page went to Trenton determined to prevent my appointment, he was told by Wilson that he "had already tendered me the post and I had accepted." Colonel House was in error. The record shows that Page entered his objection and protest to Wilson in December, 1912. Wilson did not tender me the Navy portfolio until February 23, 1913.

I thanked Hale, but told him that as I had not sought a Cabinet assignment there was nothing to be done—that Governor Wilson knew me well—that he would not be controlled in his choice by anyone opposing or urging any selection. I did not mention Page's unfriendly attitude to anyone, not even to my wife. I knew it would wound her.

SIMMONS WAS SHOCKED

It was on this visit to Trenton that the President-elect asked me, "Did you ever hear of a President's occupying a room in the Capitol called 'the President's Room'?" I told him that it was customary for the President to go to that room adjoining the Senate Chamber on the day Congress adjourns so as to expedite the signing of bills but that at all other times it was used as a reception room where Senators received their visitors.

"What would be thought of it, if, instead of asking Senators with whom I wished to consult to call at the White House, I should occupy that room for such conferences?"

I told him that I thought the Senators would prefer to go to the White House as had long been the practice but I could see no reason why he should not make use of the President's room. The next day in Washington I asked Senator Simmons, of North Carolina, what Senators would think if President-elect Wilson should make use of the President's room for conferences with Senators.

"My God," exclaimed Simmons. "Is Wilson thinking about doing that? Tell him not to do it. It would be resented by the Senators. It would look as if the Chief Executive were coming to the Capitol to tell the Senators what he wanted them to do, and they would not like it."

WOULD ADDRESS CONGRESS IN PERSON

"There's another precedent-breaking idea I am incubating," Wilson said, on that visit, "and I would like to ask your opinion about it. First, were you ever in Congress when a President's message was read?" I replied that I had been there several times. "Did anybody listen?" My answer was that after the first few paragraphs, the reading clerk would drone through it, while the members, already having the message in print on their desks, would engage in writing letters. "That confirms my resolution not to send my messages to be read by the clerk, but to deliver them in person to the joint session of Congress. Am I right?"

I told him that nothing pleased me more than to break precedents, even though in this case he would be running counter to the course pursued by Jefferson, and no President had appeared in person to deliver his message in over a century.

"Yes, I know," he said. "Jefferson thought that for a President to go to Congress in person to deliver his messages would be re-garded as a message "from the throne." Wilson didn't think much of Jefferson's reason and said that, as a matter of fact, unconsciously Jefferson was sending a written message because he knew he could write well but speak indifferently. "I wish to speak *to* Congressmen to try to influence them and not *at* them," he said, and there was the oratorical light in his eye as he made that declaration. I was, therefore, not surprised when he went before Congress in person and delivered his message. It created quite a stir, and Senator John Sharp Williams, a devoted disciple of Jefferson, who became one of Wilson's staunchest supporters, thought the "speech from Wilson was a cheap imitation of the pomposities and cavalcadings of monarchical countries." Some members of the Cabinet had voiced doubts of its wisdom until they heard him. Houston thought he discovered "a sullen look" on the faces of some congressmen while Wilson was speaking. I saw nothing of that kind. In fact, he captured the great concourse on the floor and in the gallery by saying he had embraced the opportunity to verify for himself "the impression that the President of the United States is a person, not a mere department of the government, hailing Congress from some isolated island of jealous power, sending messages, not speaking naturally and with his own voice—that he is a human being trying to coöperate with other human beings in a common service."

Simmons also went up in the air when I told him that Wilson expected to deliver his address to Congress in person. He urged me to advise him not to do it. Of course, I did nothing of the sort, and later when Wilson did deliver the address, Simmons was the first to approve. He had been converted.

Finding that Congress was pleased that he spoke in person, the President followed it up by attending a meeting the next day, in the President's Room, in the Senate, of the Finance Committee that was drafting the new tariff bill.

NO LIMITATION OF PRESIDENTIAL TERM

After Wilson's election, but before his inauguration, the Senate approved an amendment to the Constitution making the presidential term six years and forbidding reëlection. A like bill was introduced in the House and was favorably received. Many Republicans were glad to support such a measure because if it could pass before Wilson's inauguration it would make a second term for him impossible. The Democrats were in a sense committed to it because the Baltimore platform contained a plank calling for a single term. It read:

"TERM OF PRESIDENT".

"We favor a single term and to that end we urge adoption of an amendment to the Constitution making the President of the United States ineligible for reëlection and we pledge the candidate of this Convention to this principle."

It was drawn by Bryan and unanimously adopted. Bryan had long believed that a President ought to have only one term and had instanced the fact that the Southern Confederacy had been wiser than the Federal government in making a six-year term with no reëlection. While I was preparing the campaign textbook and talking to Wilson about what should go into it, I asked him what he thought we ought to say about the plank for a single term for the President. He said he thought it was wise not to say anything about it; and that he was not going to mention it. He did not believe in putting any restrictions on the right of the people to reëlect a man if they wished to do so. He said he had not been consulted about the plank and was embarrassed about its being in the platform. Of course I followed his suggestion. The Republicans did not discuss it. Roosevelt was a candidate and evaded it. Little or nothing was said about it during the campaign.

BRYAN FAVORED SINGLE TERM

When the bill for a single term for the chief executive was introduced in Congress, Bryan's friends favored it. They thought if it became a law, Wilson would have his term and Bryan was young enough to succeed to the presidency, particularly as he would doubtless be Secretary of State under Wilson and as such be premier of the administration. If Wilson had not at that time been so powerful, the measure would have gone through. Evidently having his eye upon a second term even before he had begun the first, Wilson wrote a letter to A. Mitchell Palmer and opposed its passage. Many Democrats, who favored it, did not wish to put themselves in antagonism to the earnest expression of the President-elect. The measure did not pass. I think Bryan felt that the platform ought to be carried out, but he could not press it and become Secretary of State. Some of his friends urged him to do so and they also urged him strongly not to accept a portfolio in the Cabinet. They told him he ought to stay out, that in the first place he could help the administration better if he remained a private citizen, and in the second place that if he took a seat in the Cabinet, he would be bound by a sense of loyalty to support Wilson for reëlection. However, even then he was considering his peace treaties, and he believed that if he could get them through, it would be as important as the Monroe Doctrine and even more far reaching. He was willing to forego ambition to secure peace treaties which he believed would prevent war. That was his supreme desire. Also the opportunity to serve as Secretary of State, an office graced by such men as Thomas Jefferson, James Madison, Daniel Webster, Henry Clay, was most attractive to him.

WILSON CRITICIZED

There was some undercurrent criticism of Wilson for his early going back on the party platform. He placed his opposition on what he called the fundamental right of the people to select their officers, and he pointed out to those who talked to him about the matter that if the people had wished to limit the term of the presidency they would have done so when Washington declined the second term, or when Jackson or Jefferson put it aside when they might have had it. He did not favor any limit on the term, and would not have been averse to a third term for himself if his health had not been impaired. When some of Clark's friends in 1916 advised him to invoke the one-term plank in the 1912 platform and become a candidate, the Speaker said, "If the nomination is worth having, Wilson will get it; if it is an empty honor, nobody else will want it."

IX

"LET THE PEOPLE IN"—THE INAUGURATION

THE INAUGURATION OF WILSON on one of the most perfect March days Washington has ever known was the realization of a cherished dream of Democrats to see a leader of their party in the White House. Only one Democrat had been elected in half a century. As a boy I had stood on the outskirts of the crowd to see Garfield inaugurated on a wintry day, and I had witnessed Cleveland's second inaugural. Now, with many others, I was thrilled as, in a clear voice of authority, the new leader said: "Remove the ropes and let the people in!" He did not wish to speak to the empty spaces from which the expectant people were excluded. The great multitude, moved as by one impulse, acclaimed his low-spoken direction, and, when they filled the spaces that had been roped off, he began his address. It seemed to me that it was symbolic of a new era when the first concern of the new President was to "let the people in."

His voice was clear and steady and rang out, inaugurating a new day. The President said, "It means much more than the success of a party," and declared that the nation was seeking "to square every process of our national life again with the standard we so proudly set up at the beginning and have always carried in our hearts." He characterized our system of government as a model in many respects for those whose citizens would "set labor upon foundations that will endure against fortuitous change, against storm and accident," but he saw that "evil has come with the good and much fine gold has been corroded." He also said, "With riches has come inexcusable waste; we have squandered a great part of what we might have used and have not stopped to conserve the exceeding bounty of nature." He declared that in our pride of industrial achievement the country has not been thoughtful enough to "count the human cost, the cost of lives snuffed out, of engines overtaxed and broken, the fearful physical and spiritual cost to the men, women and children upon whom the dead weight has fallen pitilessly the years through." Here was a prophecy of the eight-hour law, the protection

PRESIDENT-ELECT WILSON VISITING HIS BIRTHPLACE
AT STAUNTON, VIRGINIA, DECEMBER 28, 1912

From left to right, Woodrow Wilson, Mrs. Wilson, Mrs. Mann, Governor Mann, of Virginia, and Chairman McCombs, of the Democratic National Convention Committee (Underwood & Underwood).

PRESIDENT WILSON AND FORMER PRESIDENT TAFT IN THE
INAUGURAL PARADE OF 1913 (Harris & Ewing)

They were the horse-and-buggy days.

of the child, and other humane legislation that distinguished his administration.

He made this indictment of the previous administrations: "The great government we love has too often been made use of for private and selfish purposes and those who used it have forgotten the people. There has been something crude, heartless, and unfeeling in our effort to succeed and be great; our thought has been 'let every man look out for himself; let every generation look out for itself.'"

Amid the applause of the multitude, which hung upon his words, he declared, "Ours is a work of restoration," and he outlined the six important pieces of legislation which were soon to become law. He concluded with these immortal words, which were received with emotions of consecration by those in sympathy with him and which stimulated all Americans who hoped for a better day:

"This is not a day of triumph—it is a day of dedication. Here muster not the forces of party but the forces of humanity. Men's hearts must wait upon us; men's lives hang in the balance; men's hopes call upon us to say what we will do. Who shall live up to the great trust? Who dares to try it? I summon all honest men, all patriotic, all forward-looking men to my side. God helping me, I will not fail them if they will but counsel and sustain me."

VISION OF A NEW DAY

Wilson saw "the vision of a new day." He was the first Southern born President since Abraham Lincoln. Lincoln, born in Kentucky, won the presidency as a citizen of Illinois. Wilson, a native of Virginia, won the presidency as a citizen of New Jersey. The oath of office was administered to the Presbyterian Elder by Chief Justice White, a Roman Catholic, who had served as a soldier in the Confederate Army. A new era had truly arisen, as these circumstances showed.

TWO IMPRESSIVE DEMONSTRATIONS

Apart from the glamour of the inauguration with the inspiring inaugural address and the parade of gold braid—the Annapolis and the West Point youngsters taking the show, the Democratic Club with Tammany Braves carrying banners, the Governors of the States, my own Governor, Locke Craig, looking like the knight he was— two incidents stand out with great distinctness, even after the passage of time. One was the impressive demonstration of the militant suffragists, staging their first battle in Washington, and the other was the loving pride and affection shown Wilson by his Princeton classmates and the alumni. I think the last had a peculiar significance in that it attested then and afterwards the new President's capacity for lasting friendships. The old Princeton friends, whom he had by adoption tried, felt that the whole class and all alumni were being honored. Standing as tall and erect as an Indian in the procession of college mates, towered the figure of Cleveland Dodge, between whom and Wilson there was a lasting love, rarely seen between men, which illuminated their lives. Wilson could have asked nothing of Cleveland Dodge that he would not have been happy to grant. When Wilson informed his friend Dodge that Walter Page, newly appointed Ambassador to Great Britain, was not a rich man, Cleveland Dodge sent a check for $25,000 each year of Page's ambassadorship, so that he would not be financially embarrassed.

X

WILSON SWEATS BLOOD IN HIS CHOICE OF A CABINET

H ARDLY HAD THE RESULT of the election been made known before Cabinet-making had become the uppermost topic of discussion in the press and among leaders of the successful party. Early Wilson had said, "I shall not be acting as a partisan when I pick out progressives and only progressives." Soon after the election, seeking needed rest, he and his family went to Bermuda, Wilson saying, "As soon as I knew I had been sentenced to hard labor, my first thought was to get away to Bermuda and enjoy my liberty while I might." With other members of the press, Tom Pence went to Bermuda and kept me posted as to Cabinet talk. "You and McAdoo are sure to go into the Cabinet," he wrote. I took no steps in the matter, but on their own initiative friends wrote the President-elect recommending my selection.

Seeing much in the papers about the possibility that I would be in the Cabinet, my brother, Judge Frank Daniels, inquired if I had been asked to be a Cabinet member. I told him no. He then strongly advised that if I were asked, I decline, for while it would be a great honor, it would be contrary to all my practice and preaching that an editor ought to keep out of public office, that in the long run it would weaken my influence in North Carolina and weaken the influence of my paper. I told him that I entirely agreed with him and that, if a Cabinet position were offered to me, I ought to decline it, but I said, "I have not the nerve to do it. I never dreamed it possible that I should ever be tendered a place in a Cabinet. I have no assurance that it will be offered now. It is an even chance whether it will be or not. I have asked nobody to recommend me. I have taken no part in it except a passive one, but, if I am asked to take it, I will do it with great pleasure, knowing that I am doing wrong."

Always ambitious for me at heart, I guess, after it was offered, that he would have advised me to take it although we both of us had the feeling that an editor of a newspaper was sacrificing much if he held any public office. Certainly if he aspired to public office and permitted his ambition to influence the policy of his paper, he would be unworthy of the office.

DEMOCRATIC COMMITTEEMEN RECOMMEND

A. W. McLean, afterwards Assistant Secretary of the Treasury and Governor of North Carolina, who had been a delegate at large at Baltimore, wrote to the delegates from North Carolina to unite in asking the President-elect to name me as a member of the Cabinet. They did so. This without suggestion from me. The State Democratic Committee and the members of the electoral college of North Carolina and the North Carolina Press Association did likewise. I learned later that a number of individuals well known to Wilson had written him strongly in my behalf, among the most influential being James Sprunt, of Wilmington, a close friend of Wilson's father. R. E. L. Montcastle, of Tennessee, member of the national committee, wrote me that he had written to all members of the National Democratic Committee suggesting that they endorse me to the President-elect for a Cabinet portfolio. He said most of them had done so and were glad to join him. Montcastle and I had served on the committee and were good friends. I had looked to seeing him called to high station, but he died early in the year. A royal gentleman! Homer Cummings, of Connecticut, afterwards Attorney General in Franklin Roosevelt's administration, with whom I had served on the national committee a long time, wrote Wilson hoping I would be a member of his Cabinet, and Wilson answered, though I never saw the answer until long afterwards: "Anybody who speaks in behalf of Josephus Daniels speaks to my heart as well as to my head. I have a real affection for him as well as a very high opinion of him, and you may be sure that suggestions such as yours carry great weight with me."

NORTH CAROLINA CONGRESSMEN FAVORABLE

My lifetime friend, Honorable Edward W. Pou, member of Congress from my district, wrote me that he had sent to Princeton letters to the President-elect from both Senators and all the Representatives from North Carolina recommending that I be named a member of the Cabinet. Senators Overman and Hoke Smith wrote me they had seen Wilson and personally urged my appointment. Hoke Smith wrote that he told Wilson if the Cabinet choices had been made I would suit him better than anybody else as secretary to the President.

RESOLUTION OF LEGISLATURE

Without my knowledge that it was to be introduced, the Legislature of North Carolina passed a resolution unanimously requesting Wilson to appoint me as a member of his Cabinet. The Republicans joined with the Democrats. In view of the many attacks on *The News and Observer* by Republican members and my paper's critical attitude toward Republican policies, it was gratifying to me that they should unite with Democrats in passing the resolution, which had been presented by Rufus A. Doughton, of Allegheny. Neither he, nor any other friend, said anything to me about it until after the Legislature acted.

At that time, almost everybody who suggested me for a Cabinet position picked out the Postmaster Generalship. I always had an idea, if I were asked to go into the Cabinet it would be as Postmaster General or Secretary of the Interior. Having been Chief Clerk of the Interior Department in the Cleveland Administration I felt I knew more about that department than any other. Nobody thought my having held a clerkship in the Wilson postoffice when I was a boy, at a salary of $75 a year, gave me peculiar fitness for the position of Postmaster General.

The resolution of the North Carolina Legislature adopted January 17, 1913, was as follows:

"Resolved by the House of Representatives, the Senate concurring:

"Section 1. That, as representatives of the whole people of North Carolina, we present to the Honorable Woodrow Wilson, President-elect of the United States, the name of our distinguished fellow citizen, Josephus Daniels, as one eminently qualified in both character and ability for the office of Postmaster-General.

"Sec. 2. That Mr. Daniels has ever been staunch and fearless in the advocacy of all truly progressive measures for the accomplishment of the practical ends of patriotic statesmanship. He has rendered service to all the higher interests of the people of North Carolina, unsurpassed in this generation, and we have faith that, in the cabinet of the nation, he would be in purpose devoted, and in counsel and action helpful to our country's welfare.

"Sec. 3. That a copy of this resolution be transmitted to the President-elect."

SELECTION PREDESTINED

"How did it come about that when the country went Democratic and Presbyterian in 1912, an old-fashioned Methodist like you obtained a place in the Cabinet?" asked the Reverend Martin D. Harden, when I accepted his invitation to make an address in his Presbyterian Church in Chicago.

I replied: "I looked into the future thirty-five years ago and qualified myself by the great good fortune of getting a Presbyterian wife. She, like Wilson, Marshall, and Bryan (three Presbyterian Elders) believes in the doctrine of predestination and election and thinks my selection was foreordained from the foundation of the world. That is the only time I was ever tempted to accept Calvinism. My creed was expressed by Senator Zebulon Vance (a Presbyterian), War Governor of North Carolina in the Confederacy, who was denied a seat in the United States Senate, to which he had been elected by the Legislature, because his disabilities as a Confederate official had not been removed. The next day a Methodist and a Presbyterian preacher, who were debating the question, asked Vance how he stood on the doctrine of election and predestination. He replied, smarting under his rejection, "It doesn't do you a particle of good to be elected if your disabilities have not been removed."

FIRST NEWS OF SELECTION

About the middle of February my wife began to worry about what she should wear in Washington if we were to be there after March Fourth. She said she needed some new clothes anyhow, for we would attend the inauguration whether I was to be a member of the Cabinet or not. She said she was like Flora McFlimsy—"had nothing to wear." To be sure she had given herself to nursing Worth and Frank through typhoid fever in the fall and had caught it from them, and except for a brief sight-seeing trip with the boys to New York, had been nowhere, and her wardrobe needed replenishing. So off she went on a visit to her mother in Washington City, somewhat excited as to whether she was to live the next four years in Washington or in Raleigh. Shortly after her arrival the telephone rang and I heard her cheerful and happy voice over the telephone: "I cannot help smiling to think how you will look standing attention while the officers of the Navy salute you as you are received aboard." She knew the honors the Navy gives to the Secretary of the Navy, and that was the manner she chose to tell me that I had been offered the Navy portfolio. She knew I regarded forms and ceremonials and rituals as more or less frummery and could hardly conceive of me as holding a position where salutes and the like were regarded as very important. "Mitchell Palmer and his wife are here," she said. "He has just returned from Trenton, where he saw Governor Wilson and he is glad we are to be here."

"What about Mitchell?" I asked, because I looked forward to serving with him.

"O, you know we Quakers cannot fight either on land or sea," she said, and then in language which would not let a listener-in understand, conveyed to me that Palmer had been offered and declined the post of Secretary of War. "Palmer says information is most confidential," she added. Palmer had declined, saying no member of the Quaker church could act as Secretary of War.

WILSON TENDERS CABINET PORTFOLIO

The next morning I was to be in Chapel Hill at a meeting of the building committee to decide on plans for building Swain Hall at the University. I had, as a trustee, long pressed the building of a dining hall where students could live cheaply. We had gotten the money and I was on the building committee. The train was to leave early. I rushed to catch it, devoted the day to examining plans. All that day there reposed in my pocket the most important letter ever addressed to me, and I had forgotten I even so much as had any mail in my pocket. As I was returning to Raleigh, I suddenly remembered and took out the letters. I recognized one addressed to me in the well-known handwriting of the President-elect and post-marked Princeton, New Jersey. It was as follows:

"23 February, 1913
"Princeton, New Jersey.

"My dear Friend:
"I have been sweating blood over the cabinet choices, and have decided to beg of you that you will do me the very great service of accepting the Secretaryship of the Navy. I know of no

one I trust more entirely or affectionately; and I am sure you will trust and believe me when I assure you that you will, in my judgment, best serve the party and its new leader by accepting this post. I cannot spare you from my council table.

"Faithfully and affectionately yours,

"WOODROW WILSON

"May this be confidential between us for the present?"

As soon as I had reached my office I sat down and with my own hand made reply as follows:

"Raleigh, North Carolina,
"February 25th, 1913.

"Dear Governor:-

"From the day it was my pleasure to accompany you to Chapel Hill and hear your inspiring address to our University boys, it has been my hope and belief that you would be called to the great work upon which you are to enter next Tuesday.

"The privilege of working with you in last year's campaign to win the people's approval of the principles you incarnate was cherished as an opportunity to render service for a cause dear to us both.

"It is my conviction that your administration, under the blessings of the Almighty, will mark a new era in our Republic. Sharing your faith in the people and sharing your ambition to make easier the path for those who toil and have been forgotten by those in power, I count it an honor to be asked to sit in the councils where the policies for carrying out our pledges will be formulated. More than that; I prize your confidence and esteem as evidenced by your invitation to become Secretary of the Navy. With great doubt as to my ability to measure up to the high duties of that responsible post, I will accept it with the earnest desire that in this portfolio and in the councils my service may be as acceptable as my endeavor will be sincere and patriotic.

"Your expressions of affection are most grateful to me and to my wife, and your letter of friendship will be handed down to my boys. It makes me happy to have come into close relationship with you—a relationship which has sweetened my life. I confidently look forward to a strengthening of friendly ties in the yoke-fellowship in labors during the coming days.

"With warmest regards to your wife and daughters, I am, with life-long sentiments of affectionate regard,

"Faithfully, your friend,

"JOSEPHUS DANIELS."

In his authorized life of Wilson, discussing Wilson's choices of the Cabinet members, Ray Stannard Baker says:

"Though several other prominent leaders were suggested for the Navy, Wilson never seriously considered anyone but Daniels. And in the years that followed—years of stupendous conflict that tested men to their souls—Daniels, though often under attack, never lost the confidence of his chief. And Wilson had no more loyal friend and supporter in his cabinet. . . . McAdoo and Daniels seem to have been practically determined in Wilson's mind before he left for Bermuda, although he had not decided regarding the posts they should fill."

FIVE TAR-HEEL SECRETARIES

Nearly all the newspapers of the country commented favorably upon my appointment, a few wondering humorously if a country editor's training was calculated to give knowledge of commanding Uncle Sam's Navy. I was the fifth North Carolinian to be Secretary of the Navy. They, with their length of service, were:

John Branch, in Jackson's administration, served from March 9, 1829, to May 12, 1831.

William A. Graham, in Fillmore's administration, served from August 2, 1850, to July 25, 1852.

George E. Badger, in Harrison's and Tyler's administration, served from March 6, 1841, to September 11, 1841.

James C. Dobbin, in Pierce's administration, from March 8, 1853, to March 6, 1857.

Josephus Daniels, who served through both terms of Wilson's administration, from March 5, 1913, to March 6, 1921.

WILLIAM JENNINGS BRYAN, PROPHET OF PEACE

Bryan, of Nebraska, the new Secretary of State, long a commanding figure in American politics and statesmanship, was a progressive ahead of his time, eloquent, devoted to the weal of the average man, a prophet of peace, who incarnated the spirit of Christianity. He had the largest personal following in the country. It was Bryan's early, effective preaching of liberal doctrines that sowed the seed of whatever advanced policies distinguished the administration of Theodore Roosevelt and made the Democratic Party militantly progressive.

It was the natural thing for Wilson to invite Bryan to become

Secretary of State. Wilson hoped to signalize his administration by movements looking toward peace and progressive domestic policies. Bryan's devotion to peace was known of all men. He had been, from boyhood, a consistent fighter for genuine tariff reform; Wilson had preached the sound doctrine to thousands of students and in public addresses. Bryan's large following would strengthen popular support of the administration. Moreover, without Bryan's powerful aid Wilson would not have been nominated. That alone would not have caused Wilson to offer Bryan the State portfolio. If he had not known Bryan was sound and in sympathy with him on foreign policies looking toward world peace, on the tariff, and on currency reform, he would not have made the tender. And Bryan would not have accepted it if he had not felt that his mind and Wilson's ran together on the main policies. Wilson had gratitude, no man more, but he did not show gratitude by bestowal of a public appointment upon a man he deemed not qualified for the place. However, between November and March Wilson had to stem a strong current of opposition from detractors who did not wish to see Bryan in any key position in the new administration.

When offered the portfolio of Secretary of State Bryan made it a condition to his acceptance that Wilson would make the Bryan treaties an integral part of his foreign policy. After reading a draft of the proposed treaties, Wilson found they accorded with his own views. Some of Bryan's old friends advised him not to go into the Cabinet. As the Democratic platform had sought to limit its nominee to a single term, they wished him to be free to seek election to the presidency in 1916. They felt that he and Wilson would not see eye to eye and there would come a break. On the other hand, there were anti-Bryan Democrats who hoped Bryan would go in the Cabinet because "he can do less harm on the inside of the administration than he will do on the outside." Before his acceptance Bryan talked to me about his duty. We agreed that the hope for attaining the reforms we had long advocated depended upon the success of the Wilson administration, and, as somewhat responsible for his selection, he owed it to Wilson and to the party to coöperate whole-heartedly and make a solid front. He said, "It does not matter so much who holds the office. It is the reforms that are important." If Bryan had expressed what was in his heart he would have quoted Oliver Wendell Holmes:

"What if another sit beneath the shade
Of the broad elm I planted by the way,—
What if another heed the beacon light
I set upon the rock that wrecked my keel,—
Have I not done my task and served my kind?"

MCADOO FIRST CHOICE

William G. McAdoo had won Wilson's absolute confidence and affection and no other name had been considered for Secretary of the Treasury. He justified Wilson's high estimate—and this independent of the fact that he later married the President's youngest daughter. Among other achievements he had performed the miracle of tunneling under the Hudson river. He was to become one of the greatest Secretaries of the Treasury.

GARRISON—A CONSERVATIVE

Secretary of War Lindley M. Garrison was the last member of the Cabinet to be chosen. Garrison owed his selection to his residence in the President's home State and to his ability as lawyer and jurist. He was what Wilson called "a legalist," a strict constructionist and very conservative. Disagreement with Wilson over progressive and military policies caused his resignation. If I could be a conservative, which God forbid, I should like to be a cheerful and consistent one like Garrison.

MCREYNOLDS BUSTED A TRUST

James C. McReynolds, of Tennessee, was made Attorney General solely by reason of his refusal to acquiesce in a surrender by the Taft administration to the tobacco trust after he had won the suit and secured conviction. He was an ultra-conservative and black-letter lawyer, the soul of honor and consistency. Wilson, having confidence in his ability and integrity "kicked him up stairs," by making him Associate Justice of the Supreme Court, where he lived to be the sole exponent of the archaic rule of law.

BURLESON HONEST AND TRUSTED

Albert Burleson, of Texas, was an early Wilson supporter, who became the liaison officer between the President and Congress. He had won distinction as a member of the House. He was honest and forthright and was esteemed highly by Wilson, who leaned upon him and trusted his loyalty and wisdom. His service was distinguished by ability and efficiency. During his administration of the Post Office Department, many progressive steps were taken, not the least of which was his inauguration of the first use of airplanes to carry the mails.

SCHOLAR AND ECONOMIST

David Franklin Houston, native of North Carolina, mainly owed his selection as Secretary of Agriculture to Walter Page and Colonel House. Missouri, his adopted State, resented the appointment of one little known to the State. A graduate of Harvard, a college president, he had two heroes—Dr. Eliot and Woodrow Wilson. He was an authority on finance as taught at Harvard and was made Secretary of the Treasury when Mr. McAdoo resigned, a position more to his liking. Wilson esteemed him highly and leaned upon his loyal coöperation and his thorough knowledge of economic and world affairs.

LANE—A PROGRESSIVE

Franklin K. Lane, of California, Secretary of the Interior, was easily one of the most gifted and versatile men in public life. He won his spurs in battles for good government and liberal policies in California in days calling for high courage and emprise. He came into the Cabinet with the prestige of successful service as chairman of the Interstate Commerce Commission and initiated many policies that advanced the welfare of the Indians and the development of the West. He had a genius for friendship.

REDFIELD—TARIFF REFORMER

William C. Redfield, of New York, Secretary of Commerce, was named because of his able championship in Congress of tariff reform. Wilson had been greatly impressed by his knowledge of the tariff and he was Wilson's most trusted adviser on tariff during the campaign. To his convictions he was as true as a needle to the pole.

A TOWER OF STRENGTH

William B. Wilson, Secretary of Labor, was the only man considered for the position. A forward-looking member of Congress, he had piloted the bill creating the Cabinet position of Secretary of Labor. He was a tower of strength to the administration. Self-educated, he was well educated and the wisest type of leader of the labor forces.

NO CABINET OF TRADE OR BARTER

The composition of the new Cabinet was well received by press and people. It was called "a Cabinet of Forty-Niners," most of us being around forty-nine. The general sentiment was expressed in a two-column editorial by Frank Cobb in the New York *World,* summing up in these words:

"Whether strong or weak in its various elements, this is a Cabinet of no political trade or barter. It was fashioned by no political boss. It was fashioned to placate neither sordid political interests nor sordid financial interests. Every member stands on his own merits as Woodrow Wilson sees those merits. His only concessions are concessions to locality and geography. It is no Cabinet of corporation lawyers. It is no Cabinet of hack politicians or machine leaders. It is a Cabinet of public servants, appointed to administer the affairs of a vast government and appointed because the President selecting them believes they are qualified for their work."

HOW THE CABINET WAS SELECTED

How was the Wilson Cabinet made? Five of its members—Bryan, McAdoo, Burleson, Daniels, and Wilson had been leaders in the fight to nominate Wilson and in the campaign. They were decided upon immediately after the election. From my diary the following sidelight is thrown upon the selections:

"I had a long talk today with Joseph Tumulty, the President's private secretary. He was reminiscent, particularly about the days when Woodrow Wilson was engrossed in the task of selecting his Cabinet. Once Burleson's name was erased from the list. Some people advised that Daniels was not known and was editor of a small paper. 'The President appreciated your friendship and held and holds you in high regard.' Wilson did not know that Palmer was a Quaker when he asked him to be Secretary of War, but Palmer thought he did. Four days before the inauguration the post of Secretary of War was still open, Palmer having said no Quaker could conscientiously hold the war portfolio. The President tried in vain to overcome Palmer's scruples. 'He then asked me (Tumulty) if I had any suggestion. I told him I thought he ought to have a New Jersey man in the Cabinet.

Various men were discussed. In looking over the Lawyer's Directory I came across the name of Lindley Garrison, Vice Chancellor of the highest court of the State. He had impressed me favorably in the few cases I had tried before him. The President agreed that a Jerseyite should be in the Cabinet. He was familiar with the high reputation of Garrison as a jurist and his high character as a man. The next day by invitation, Garrison was in Trenton; Wilson asked him to be Secretary of War, and Garrison accepted.'"

WHY MCCOMBS WAS NOT IN THE CABINET

It had been expected that McCombs would be a member of the Cabinet. Among the things that troubled Wilson was how to deal with McCombs, who had been chairman of the pre-convention Wilson campaign and afterwards chairman of the national committee. McCombs thought of himself as something of a king-maker and wanted to dish out the offices. I understood that his first ambition was to be Attorney General. Why? "Because I can make such contacts as will insure me a lucrative practice after my term has expired." That eliminated him from consideration. His biographer said he wished to be Secretary of the Treasury. Fortunately for Wilson, McCombs had made a renunciation which enabled Wilson to write in his own hand: "Those who know my admiration and affection for Mr. McCombs will naturally wonder why his name is not on the Cabinet list. Mr. McCombs told me that he did not desire a Cabinet appointment." He offered McCombs the position of Ambassador to France. McCombs thought Wilson wished to get him out of Washington. Maybe he did, for McCombs would have busied himself with patronage. When I urged him to accept the ambassadorship, he railed at me and declared he would "not be banished." He would and he would not for weeks, and finally declined the post with a feeling that he had not been given the consideration he deserved.

XI

COUNTRY EDITOR IN A CONNING TOWER

I MMEDIATELY AFTER I received my appointment, I called at the Navy Department to pay my respects to the Honorable George von Lengerke Meyer, who had been Secretary of the Navy for four years. He received me with dignified courtesy, introduced me to his Council of Aides, and then talked to me about the duties of the office. When the aides had withdrawn, he said, "I do not wish to give you any advice, but merely to suggest to you that you keep the power to direct the Navy *here,*" and he laid his hand with emphasis on the biggest desk in Washington. He said:

"In the Navy Department there is no chief of staff and nothing important is done which does not go over the desk of the Secretary. Through the aide system, which is the best organization that possibly could be effected, the Secretary is kept in touch with everything afloat and ashore about the Navy. I advise you not to permit any change that will take out of the hands of the Secretary the control of the Navy. Many suggestions have been made to that end and you will find that in the Navy there are officers who wish to have an organization like that in the Army or of some foreign Navy. The present organization makes the Secretary of the Navy controller of everything that goes on. Some of the admirals do not like this. You can delegate as much power as you choose under the present system and hold on to all the things that are important."

He discussed the various methods of operating a Navy in this country and abroad and said there was always a desire on the part of some Naval officers to encroach upon the prerogative of the Cabinet officer, who, being held responsible, ought to have the strings in his own hands. I knew little about the Naval administration but what he said interested and impressed me. I was soon to find out what Mr. Meyer meant when the Aide for Operations besieged me to effect an organization of the Navy based on the imperial German plan.

I had made no preparation about taking the oath and did not know the custom. McAdoo was sworn in by Justice Hughes. If I had thought of it in time, I would have requested my brother, Judge Frank Daniels, to come to Washington to administer the oath. The oath was administered by Ralph T. Bartlett, Notary Public in the Navy Department and was recorded in my Bible presented to me in 1899 by Judge James E. Shepherd, who was afterwards promoted to Chief Justice of the Supreme Court of North Carolina. The simple ceremony was graced by the presence of my wife, whose heart was in the Navy, her mother and sisters and my four sons, Bryan, Redfield, the Senators and Representatives in Congress from North Carolina, most of the members of the National Democratic Committee, headed by Chairman Mack, and many other friends who had remained over after the inauguration. I was the only Cabinet minister who was a member of that committee. Quite a number of my fellow journalists were present to see the first editor made "Managing Editor" of the Navy since Gideon Welles took the oath on March 5, 1861.

The visitors and the new Secretary were impressed with the magnificence and beauty of the Secretary's office, by all odds the largest and most beautiful of all the Cabinet offices—"finer than any Minister's office in Europe," said Mr. Balfour, who had been First Lord of the Admiralty in Britain,—a post corresponding to that of the Secretary of the Navy, when he visited me in 1919. It had been constructed as a reception room, but a predecessor had made it his spacious office. There were Naval trophies in cases, a large globe of the world, and the most magnificent chandeliers I had ever seen, with old-fashioned glass pendants that shone brilliantly when the lights were turned on. As they were seldom lighted, visitors saw their scintillation only by day. All visitors were attracted by their stately beauty. Years afterwards, when indirect lighting came into vogue, my modern aide, Captain Byron McCandless, worked out a plan to remove the lovely chandeliers and light the room by what I called "ugly pots" to reflect the light. He and the Chief Clerk had almost made a contract for the new system and the sale of the chandeliers before I knew what they were about. When I threatened to have them shot before sunrise if they removed a single prism, McCandless said, "But the new lighting system is a hundred times better." I replied, "Maybe so, but you destroy the dignity and distinction of this lovely and spacious room. Besides, when I work here at night I have an electric light on my desk and nobody was ever expected to work by the light of the chandeliers. They give a fine glow that illuminates the whole room, and we can keep them as beautiful reminders of a past where utility was not all in life, while men work by the little bulbs which are hardly seen." I preserved the chandeliers and they were treasured as much by General Pershing as by me when that fine office was assigned to him as he became "the General of the Army."

What chiefly interested me and my North Carolina friends in the Secretary's office was a sword presented to John Paul Jones by Willie Jones, the right-hand man of Jefferson in North Carolina, in whose family John Paul Jones lived when he sought a quiet haven after he had killed a man on his ship in the Caribbean. In gratitude for the hospitality of Willie and Allen Jones on their North Carolina plantation in the days when he needed a refuge and friends, John Paul added the name of Jones to the name he bore. He went to North Carolina as John Paul. He emerged as John Paul Jones and was known as "the North Carolina Captain," because he owed his commission in the Navy to Joseph Hewes, of Edenton, North Carolina, a signer of the Declaration, who was Chairman of the Committee on Marine and to whom Jones attributed his opportunity to serve his adopted country in the Navy. I learned that the sword belonged to Admiral Nicholson. When we became good friends and I sent him to Chile on important missions during the World War, I banteringly told the Admiral that as John Paul Jones was known as "the North Carolina Captain," I was minded to confiscate the sword and send it to the North Carolina Hall of History.

The ceremonies over and the inspection ended, my wife and friends withdrew, and in the early twilight I was alone in that long and stately room, with its large mirror, marble fireplace, and scintillating chandeliers, sitting at a desk big enough for half a dozen people. There were the telephone and the pushbuttons to send messages and summon assistants. I felt very small in that big room, somewhat as Howard Chandler Christie had pictured Mr. and Mrs. Pipp in their large dining room with the dignified English butler— only there was no Mrs. Pipp then in the office to keep me company, and no towering butler. Perhaps a better comparison would be to the scene in which Dickens described David Copperfield in the grand

English home of his friend Steerforth, when he sat for the first time at a table where the meal was served in courses by a butler not unlike the one pictured by Christie. The butler's condescending manner to the young schoolboy, who had never seen such opulence, made David very uncomfortable, and he said that every time the butler passed his place at the table he seemed to say to the boy, "You are very small indeed," and somehow to make him feel out of place. Here I was in a grand office, undertaking a great task for which I had received no training, and feeling "very small indeed." The most I knew about the Navy was my inherited fondness for the sea and ships, my forebears having been fishermen and sailors and my father having been a ship carpenter who had bequeathed me his chest of tools, which I never had the skill to use; my close association with my wife's brother, Ensign Worth Bagley, who was killed in action at Cárdenas Bay in the early days of the Spanish-American War, and whose love of the Navy was so contagious that it reached me; my association with my wife's younger brother, now Vice-Admiral David Worth Bagley, who was then a young officer; my enthusiastic interest in the historic trip of the *Oregon* around the tip-end of South America to take part in the Spanish-American war waging in the Caribbean; my admiration for Admiral Dewey, whom I had never expected to know, much less to become his intimate friend; my knowledge that John Paul Jones received his name and commission from North Carolina, and that four predecessors in the office of Secretary of the Navy were North Carolinians, who "did the State some service" in the post to which the President had assigned me.

As all alone I reflected upon the job ahead, realizing I knew nothing of navigation or of Naval technique, I was helped by the thought that I had been able to publish a newspaper without the knowledge of operating a linotype or running a perfecting rotary press. I recalled that the great Naval statesman, Admiral Mahan, had quoted with approval Nelson's biographer who had written of his Naval hero: "He was no seaman. All his energies were turned towards becoming a great Commander." Napoleon's biographer said of the great Corsican: "He had no practical experience in handling troops. What he knew he had picked up from study. He had the undeviating energy of his will." Did a man need to be an expert to direct the Navy? Could a country editor become managing editor of the Navy without mastery of the sea? Years afterwards a newspaper man asked Congressman Madden, Republican leader, "Can a civilian direct the Navy if he has no experience in Naval affairs?" Madden answered, "Daniels did." In the quiet of that self-examination I resolved to give myself unremittingly to learning the job and trying to administer the Navy in such way as to make it the most efficient first line of defense and offense, too, the country had known. And for eight years I devoted every hour and every effort to that dedication.

XII

LOVE AT FIRST SIGHT—F. D. R. AND J. D.

As I entered the Willard Hotel on the morning of Wilson's inauguration, I ran into Franklin Roosevelt. I had not seen him since the election. He was bubbling over with enthusiasm at the incoming of a Democratic administration and keen as a boy to take in the inauguration ceremonies. He greeted me cordially and said, "Your appointment as Secretary of the Navy made me happy. I congratulate you and the President and the country." I responded by asking him, "How would you like to come to Washington as Assistant Secretary of the Navy?" His face beamed his pleasure. He replied, "How would I like it? I'd like it bully well. It would please me better than anything in the world. I'd be glad to be connected with the new administration. All my life I have loved ships and have been a student of the Navy, and the assistant secretaryship is the one place, above all others, I would love to hold." He added that, coming over on the train, McAdoo had asked if he would like to go into the Treasury Department, "but," with enthusiasm he said, "nothing would please me so much as to be with you in the Navy."

I explained that I had not consulted the President, who might have someone in mind, but that if not I would recommend his appointment. The proposal was no sudden impulse. It was in fulfillment of what I had told my wife on the day I received the letter from President Wilson asking me to be a member of his Cabinet. As I finished reading the letter aloud to my partner in all things, I said, "I will ask the President to appoint Franklin Roosevelt as Assistant Secretary."

The first time I saw Franklin Roosevelt was in the Baltimore Convention when Wilson was nominated for President. I had charge of the distribution of tickets for editors, and Roosevelt came to my room with some up-State editors who wished seats in the press section. He was in a gay humor and I thought he was as handsome a figure of an attractive young man as I had ever seen. He was an enthusiastic supporter of Wilson, though, under the majority rule,

PRESIDENT WILSON ADDRESSING CONGRESS

Wilson was the first President to deliver his address to Congress in person since the time of John Adams. Vice-President Marshall and Speaker Champ Clark are presiding.

WOODROW WILSON AND JOSEPH P. TUMULTY

Tumulty was private secretary to Wilson when he was Governor of New Jersey
and secretary to President Wilson, 1913-1921. This picture was taken in the
White House in 1913. Tumulty is author of *Woodrow Wilson As I Know Him*
(Edmonston).

he feared his vote would not be counted. Among the other stories he told was this: "I came down on the train with Kermit and he said that his father [Theodore Roosevelt, then planning to run as a candidate of the Progressive Party] was praying that Champ Clark would be nominated." This story appeared in the press and did not please the Clark supporters because it indicated that Teddy felt it would be easier to defeat Clark than Wilson. It had a tendency to strengthen Wilson's chance for the nomination, for there were not a few Democrats who had faith in T. R.'s political acumen.

At that convention Franklin and I become friends—a case of love at first sight—for when men are attracted to each other there is born a feeling that Mexicans call "simpática," a word that has no counterpart in English. A lasting friendship was born, which has increased with the passing years, not broken even when we were in occasional disagreement upon some men and measures, as sometimes happened. The two most charming and handsomest young men I have known in my life were Herbert W. Jackson, a first cousin of my wife, who became a friend at Chapel Hill and whose friendship was a joy to me as long as he lived, and Franklin Roosevelt. They both possessed a spontaneity and gaiety, as well as good looks, fine bearing, and sterling qualities which made them beloved of all who knew them.

ROOSEVELT'S CAREER AS SENATOR

Before meeting Franklin I had been attracted to him by his brilliant fight as State Senator against the election as United States Senator of William F. Sheehan, a utility lawyer supported by the special interests, and by his opposition to permitting the water power of his State to be given for private exploitation. His brilliant campaign, electioneering in an automobile in horse-and-buggy days, securing election in 1910 in a strong Republican district, had given him a place in the public eye. When he led in the fight to prevent the election to the Senate of a corporation lawyer with no liberal leanings, and secured the election of the most progressive Democrat in the Tammany organization, Judge O'Gorman, I had written an editorial in my Raleigh paper rejoicing in the selection of a United States Senator who owed no obligations to special interests. The fight in the New York Legislature was long-drawn-out and commanded the attention of the country. Perhaps the reason for my rejoicing in a contest in a distant State was that Sheehan had been a close friend of David B. Hill when I, young in politics, had been an enthusiastic supporter of Grover Cleveland and tariff reform and had conceived a distrust of Hill. Time proved my hunch was well founded. The contest lifted young Roosevelt into the "coming man" politics class. It was this background of the young New Yorker that made me feel he would be sympathetic in advancing the policies of the administration whose head incarnated the New Freedom.

WILSON MAKES APPOINTMENT

Two days after the inauguration I had an appointment to see the President. I wished to discuss the selection of the Assistant Secretary. I asked him if he had anyone in view for the position. He said he had not given it consideration. I then said, "If you have no one for the position I would like to make a recommendation." "You are quick on the trigger," he said. "Whom have you in mind?" I told him I would like him to appoint Franklin D. Roosevelt, and the reason I was quick on the trigger was that I knew that there would be a number of applicants and that by filling the position at once, we would not be under the necessity of rejecting any applicant. Moreover, I felt that the sooner the new organization was effected the better. I added, "As I am from the South, I think the Assistant Secretary should come from another section, preferably from New York or New England."

"How well do you know Mr. Roosevelt?" he asked, "and how well is he equipped?"

"I never met him until the Baltimore Convention," I replied, "but I was strongly drawn to him then and more so as I met him during the campaign when I was in New York. I have admired him since the courageous fight he made in the New York State Senate, which resulted in the election of a liberal who had favored your nomination at Baltimore. Besides, I know he has been a Naval enthusiast from his boyhood." I expressed the conviction that he was one of our kind of liberal.

"Very well," he said, "send the nomination over."

I did so, and that night wrote Roosevelt that the President would send his nomination to the Senate and asked him to come to Washington. When he arrived, he said the Senate of New York, of which he was a member, was in session and he would not like to resign until action was taken on some measures relating to agriculture and water power ownership. He was then fighting the grant of water power to private corporations and was interested in plans to advance agriculture. Later, in a larger field, he was to carry out his early policies. I told him it would not be necessary for him to hurry over because Beekman Winthrop, Assistant Secretary under Meyer, was a capable man and was willing to remain until it suited Roosevelt's convenience to come. Roosevelt knew Winthrop well, and while in Washington talked with him about the duties of the office.

SENATORS CONSULTED ABOUT APPOINTMENT

I believed the courteous and proper thing to do before the nomination went to the Senate was to consult the Senators from Roosevelt's State. In response to my request, Senator O'Gorman came to the Navy Department. He said the appointment was agreeable to him and the Senate would confirm it promptly. I expected him to show enthusiasm for the appointment of the young man chiefly responsible for his election to the Senate. The most I gathered was that it was agreeable. Later Senator Root called at my request, and when I told him that the President had in mind naming Franklin Roosevelt as Assistant Secretary, a queer look came on his face. "You know the Roosevelts, don't you?" he asked. "Whenever a Roosevelt rides, he wishes to ride in front." He added, "You know they like to have their own way," and intimated that T. R. and those of the family whom he knew were pretty insistent about being the lead horse in any team. He clearly intimated that the fifth cousin (once removed in political affiliation) might have T. R. qualities. He made reference to the trouble T. R. gave Secretary Long when he was Assistant Secretary of the Navy, at the beginning of the Spanish-American War. "I know the young man very slightly," he added, "but all I know about him is creditable and his appointment will be satisfactory so far as I am concerned, though, of course, being a Republican, I have no right to make any suggestion. I appreciate your courtesy in consulting me." I told the Senator that I would hate to have an assistant who did not have a mind of his own. I told him I wanted an assistant who would help pull the load and I had no fear of a strong man as Assistant Secretary. I would wish no other kind, and I added, "A chief who fears that an assistant will outrank him is not fit to be chief."

HOWE COMES WITH FRANKLIN

The nomination having been promptly confirmed, Roosevelt came to Washington and took the oath. He was accompanied by Louis Howe as his private secretary. They had formed a David and Jonathan friendship when Roosevelt was State Senator and Howe a newspaper correspondent at Albany. During Roosevelt's second campaign for the State Senate he was ill, and Howe directed it to a second victory. Always fertile in resources and suggestions and with a keen sense of public opinion, Howe had boldness in as large measure as his chief. And he could write, having a style that was luminous and convincing. Roosevelt leaned upon Howe, whose devotion made him sensitive to every wind that might affect "Franklin," as he always called him. His chief interest in life was to advance Franklin in his public career. He advised him about everything, suggested policies he should adopt, helped him in data for his speeches, and occasionally gave me suggestions and ideas for my addresses. Always keeping himself in the background, he knew all the tides and eddies in the Navy Department, in the administration, and in the political life of the country. His one and only ambition was to help steer Franklin's course so that he could take the tide at the full. Even in 1913 he expected to see Franklin occupy the White House, and to further that ambition he devoted his every effort. Nobody else counted much with him, and until after Franklin was elected President he kept in the background. Then, with the public made acquainted with his part in Roosevelt's career, Howe was happy to bask in public favor and honor until he was stricken in the height of Roosevelt's success, to which he had made devoted contribution. In his long illness no day passed, no matter how pressing the public demands, that Franklin did not visit Howe in his room in the White House, and the sick man was kept in touch with all the matters that interested them both. It was a beautiful friendship, broken only by death. His widow was appointed Postmaster at her home, Fall River, Massachusetts, after her husband's death, an act characteristic of President Roosevelt's devotion to friends.

LOOKING AT THE WHITE HOUSE

Not long after Roosevelt entered upon the duties of Assistant Secretary, photographers wished to make a picture of the new Secretary and Assistant Secretary. It was taken as we stood by the high pillars on the eastern portico of the State, War, and Navy Building, looking down on the White House. It was about the best picture taken during our service. Roosevelt was just turned thirty-two—was tall, athletic, handsome, happy in his new work. When the photographers brought the proof of the picture (which appears in this volume) for approval, I asked:

"Franklin, why are you grinning from ear to ear, looking as pleased as if the world were yours, while I, satisfied and happy, have no such smile on my face?"

He said he did not know of any particular reason, only that he was trying to look his best.

"I will tell you," I answered. "We are both looking down on the White House and you are saying to yourself, being a New Yorker, 'Some day I will be living in that house'—while I, being from the South, know I must be satisfied with no such ambition."

We both laughed as we returned to our desks. Later, when he was in the White House, he recalled the event, and we both preserve copies of that autographed photograph, taken when we were young and consecrated to a great task.

For seven years and five months, until he resigned to become the candidate of his party for Vice President in 1920, we occupied adjoining offices and labored, at first against odds, to reach the goal attained in the three-year program of 1915, to make the American Navy the strongest in the world. There was nothing in Naval efficiency that did not command his interest, from offering prizes to induce enlisted landlubbers to learn to swim, up to the laying of a mine barrage across the North Sea, the greatest Naval achievement in the World War. He was young then and made some mistakes. Upon reflection, although I was older, I made mistakes too.

TEACHING SAILORS TO SWIM

One day Franklin came into my office and asked me, "Have you observed that a number of sailors lose their lives by drowning? There are said to be many who cannot swim."

"What would you suggest?" I asked. "Would you refuse to accept a recruit unless he could swim?"

Roosevelt doubted whether such rule should be made. Instead he said he would like to present a cup trophy to be awarded to the winner in swimming contests. The "Roosevelt Cup" was eagerly sought after and became permanent, decreasing the number of personnel who were not expert swimmers.

Woodrow Wilson was the first man who suggested that "the hornets be shut up in their nests" as the only insurance against destruction by U-boats. Franklin also had a like view early, and prepared a memorandum of "Proposed measures to close English Channel and North Sea against Submarines by Mine Barrage," and sent a copy to President Wilson.

DESIRED TO ENTER ARMED FORCES

Early in the war Franklin confided to me that he wished to enter the armed forces, and that would require his resignation as Assistant Secretary. I told him that he was rendering a far more important war service than if he put on the uniform in either the Army or the Navy. Around the Department it was said that, inasmuch as his cousin Theodore left the position of Assistant Secretary to become a Rough Rider, later Governor of New York, and then President, and both had served in the Legislature of New York, Franklin thought actual fighting in the war was the necessary step toward reaching the White House. I told the President that Franklin was minded to resign and to enroll in the Navy. He said, "Tell the young man his only and best war service is to stay where he is." And Franklin himself went to see the President who refused to permit him to resign. As a good Navy man he gave the "Aye, aye, Sir," and surrendered his own idea as to where he could serve best. But he still hoped he might go to sea before the war ended. When he sailed for Europe in July, 1918, making the voyage on a destroyer at a time when the U-boats were a menace, his ambition was to return to Europe as a Lieutenant Commander attached to the Naval railway battery of fourteen-inch guns under Admiral Plunkett. That was not to be, for he was stricken with pneumonia as were a number of others on the ship. It was mid-October before he was well enough to return to Washington. Shortly after, he was ill with "flu." I recalled years afterwards, when he was stricken with infantile par-

alysis, that in 1912 he was out of the campaign with typhoid fever
and that in 1917, when Walter Camp was directing the exercise of
officials to make them fit, Franklin fell out for a while from illness.
And yet, so rapidly did he recover each time and so much did he
seem the athlete that I never dreamed the time would come when
I could outrun him.

OVERCOMES PHYSICAL HANDICAPS

Even so, the first time I saw him after the disease had prevented
locomotion for a long time, as I approached his bed, he hauled off
and gave me a blow that caused me nearly to lose my balance. He
said: "You thought you were coming to see an invalid, but I can
knock you out in any bout." It was that stuff—there is no other word
for it—that enabled him to rise superior to any physical or other
handicap. I once told an audience that he owed his success to over-
coming handicaps and defeats. The handicaps of the Groton and
Harvard brand of education did not impair his fundamental democracy; defeat as candidate for the Senate and vice-presidency did not
stand in the way of future victories; and the handicap of infantile
paralysis did not slow down his marathoning to the gubernatorial
mansion at Albany and the White House, breaking the jinx of
reëlection in New York and the third term tradition at Washington.
Quite the contrary.

THE CALL OF POLITICS

Three more times I thought to lose my dynamic assistant. The first
was in 1914. The very ambitious Secretary McAdoo was active early
in the administration to build up in New York a Democratic organization against Tammany. He secured the appointment to Federal
positions of Democrats who began an opposition Democracy. In this
anti-Tammany organization, Franklin Roosevelt was an enthusiastic
ally. He had fought Tammany when a State Senator, and Tammany
did not then love him. Early in the summer Roosevelt confided to
me that McAdoo was urging him to become the anti-Tammany
candidate for United States Senator in the Democratic primary. I
advised Franklin not to yield to the persuasion and told him I had
a hunch he could not win in the primary, and even if he did the
indications were that the Republicans would carry the State. He
spoke of asking Wilson's advice. I never heard that he did so. At

any rate he became a candidate against James W. Gerard, then Ambassador to Germany. Gerard did not come home to make a campaign but won the nomination easily. It hurt Roosevelt, and I refrained from telling him "I told you so," when Gerard defeated him and the Republicans carried New York. It was, perhaps, part of Roosevelt's good luck not to have been nominated that year.

When in 1918 there was a movement to draft him as candidate for Governor of New York, Franklin advised the nomination of Alfred E. Smith, with whom he had served in the General Assembly of New York in 1911-13, but some friends were persistent and planned to have him nominated while he was on a destroyer en route to Europe. He heard they would ask President Wilson to encourage him to accept. On July 8, prior to sailing, he wrote the President, saying, "My duty lies in my present work," adding, "If I were at any time to leave the Assistant Secretaryship it would only be for active service." Smith was nominated and elected and twice Roosevelt supported him for President, making the nomination speech both at New York and at Houston.

At the San Francisco Convention, to which he was a delegate, he was nominated for Vice President. As soon as it was announced, the delegates called for a speech, and, in order not to break a precedent that a candidate must be mum until his official notification and response, Franklin hastily left the auditorium and I pinch-hit for him in congratulating the convention upon the wisdom of the nomination and predicting a brilliant campaign. I immediately sent this telegram:

"Mrs. Franklin D. Roosevelt
"Campobello, Maine

"It would have done your heart good to have seen the spontaneous and enthusiastic tribute paid when Franklin was nominated unanimously for Vice President today. Accept my congratulations and greetings. Will you be good enough to send my congratulations and greetings also to his mother as I do not know her address?

"Josephus Daniels"

There had grown up between my wife and Mrs. Roosevelt the same friendship, increasing with the passing of the years, that existed between their husbands, as is shown by this paragraph in

FRANKLIN D. ROOSEVELT AND JOSEPHUS DANIELS

Standing on the portico of the War, State, and Naval Building, looking toward the White House in 1913 (The National Archives).

Upper left, Mrs. Franklin D. Roosevelt, wife of the Assistant Secretary of the Navy, who with Mrs. Daniels led in the Navy Red Cross in the Wilson Administration. *Upper right,* Louis McHenry Howe, close friend of Franklin D. Roosevelt as Senator in New York, Assistant Secretary of the Navy, and President of the United States (from a drawing by Miss Jacobs). *Below,* Franklin D. Roosevelt in the early days of his Assistant Secretaryship of the Navy.

Mrs. Roosevelt's "My Day" in 1943, upon the passing of my life partner:

A sad loss came to us yesterday in the news that Mrs. Josephus Daniels has passed away. No one could have been kinder to young people than she was to us when Mr. Daniels was Secretary of the Navy and my husband's chief in Washington. She was full of fun and her life was a very rich and useful one. I cannot bear to think of Mr. Daniels and her boys without her. She gave out a great deal to those around her and I think she was always the tactful and unifying influence which someone must be in every big family.

In the war days of 1917-18, my wife as president and Mrs. Roosevelt vice president of the Navy Red Cross, devoted themselves, along with the wives of Navy officers and enlisted men, in the beneficent work of that organization.

I was present and participating when he was nominated for Vice President and at Hyde Park when he accepted the nomination. I was likewise a delegate supporting his nomination for President at Chicago in 1932, at Philadelphia in 1936, at Chicago in 1940 and 1944. By his appointment I was Ambassador to Mexico until the early days of 1942. Our lives of devotion to liberalism, though separated geographically, he in New York and I in North Carolina, have run in almost parallel lines. When he resigned to make the campaign for Vice President, I named Gordon Woodbury of New Hampshire, as fine a man as lived, to fill out the term.

As Assistant Secretary, and as Acting Secretary when duties called me away from Washington, and after the Armistice directing Naval demobilization in Europe, Franklin Roosevelt demonstrated the same high qualities that he evidenced in the presidency. His experience, in the Navy Department, particularly in the war days of 1917-18, was invaluable when he became Commander in Chief in the conduct of World War II.

If I were asked by what rule Franklin Roosevelt has sought to regulate his life—private and public—I would answer that his philosophy is along the line laid down by the Sage of Craigenputtock, old Thomas Carlyle, who wrote: "On the whole, a man must not complain of his 'element', of his 'time' or the like; it is thriftless work doing so. His time is bad: well then, he is there to make it better."

That breathes the same spirit as expressed by William James, who, in difficult eras, counselled that we "redeem our own hearts from atheism and fears."

Let me conclude this chapter with a quotation from my Diary:

"December 25, 1913: My most prized Christmas present was a painting of the U.S.S. *North Carolina* which Franklin Roosevelt had ordered for me. It is the work of a famous artist. Franklin had the record showing that it was the first American line-of-battle ship to cross the Atlantic. She made that voyage in 1825. She returned to New York from her last voyage in 1839, and was finally sold in 1867 for $30,000. She was built at the Philadelphia Navy Yard and launched in September, 1820. In 1825 she visited Europe under the command of Commodore John Rogers, the first to make the voyage. She was the largest and most formidable vessel that had made the Atlantic crossing up to that time. She mounted 102 guns in three tiers, her battery exceeding that of *Lord Nelson* by 304 pounds. The *Lord Nelson* was at that time the heaviest British battleship afloat in commission. For two years she served as flagship of the Mediterranean squadron, and returned to Norfolk July 28, 1827. She made one more cruise, this time to the Pacific in 1837, returning to New York June 28, 1839. There she spent the remainder of her career as a receiving ship. So far as records go, the *North Carolina* was never in North Carolina waters."

A picture of this historic ship hangs in the Office of Naval Records and Library in the Navy Department. Under it are the words:

Struck by lightning in a severe hail Squall off the island of Sardinia on the 15th Jan. 1827

There is much interesting history about the *North Carolina*. Vice Admiral John H. Dayton, on a visit to Port Mahon, where men of the American Navy were buried during the war with Algeria, deciphered, among others, this inscription:

Sacred to the Memory of Henry Jones
Quartermaster on board US Ship NORTH CAROLINA
a native of Boston, America, aged 28 years.
He was unfortunately killed in this port
March——1842
This monument was erected as a tribute by his
messmates:

The Bark is waiting
I must be ready
Charon put off
Steer small and steady

During our administration a giant dreadnaught was given the name *North Carolina*. As a result of the inept Washington Conference that mighty leviathan, though far advanced toward completion, was scrapped in the vain hope that by scrapping its Navy this country could avoid war. But in 1940, a new and greater *North Carolina* dreadnaught, given that honored name by Franklin Roosevelt, was added to the ships of the American Navy. I had expressed to him my desire that the name *North Carolina* be perpetuated in the greater Navy that was being built. One day—when it is not a "military secret"—the distinguished service of the *North Carolina* in World War II will be told. Christened by the wife of Governor Broughton, it has the Tar-Heel fighting spirit.

XIII

CABINET MEMBERS GET ACQUAINTED

O<small>N FRIDAY</small> after the inauguration (Cabinet meetings were held regularly on Tuesday and Friday) the first meeting of the new Cabinet was held. All of us were new at the business and some had never met until the inauguration. Lane had never met Wilson, and walked up to him the day before the inauguration saying, "Mr. President, I am your Secretary of the Interior." I had never met Garrison, McReynolds, Lane, and Houston until March 4.

I of course had never attended a Cabinet meeting, though because of my intimate association with Secretary Hoke Smith in the Cleveland era, he had told me much of the methods of conducting meetings of the Cleveland Cabinet. All of the ten were new at the business. For that matter, so was the President. Neither he nor any member of his family had ever entered the White House until his inauguration. He had, however, a profound knowledge of the business of government and particularly of cabinets, as shown when he wrote his standard books on government and cabinets.

As I took my seat just ahead of Houston, I asked him, "Do you pronounce your name Houston as in *house* or as in *hoose?*"

"You ought to know," he said, "seeing I have relatives in North Carolina of that name, and I was born in Union County."

I replied that of course I knew how the people of that county in North Carolina pronounced the name, but as he had lived long in South Carolina I didn't know but that it was pronounced differently in that State, and called his attention to the differences in pronunciation; as, for example, North Carolina pronounced Beaufort as if spelled Bo-fert, whereas in South Carolina they pronounce it Bu-fert. He said that the old North Carolina way was good enough for him, even though his youth had been spent in South Carolina.

HOW THE CABINET FUNCTIONED

President Wilson, acting as if being chief executive were no new experience to him, said in a matter-of-fact way as he entered the

Cabinet room after the members had arrived and introduced themselves to each other: "Gentlemen, I have asked you to meet unofficially so that we could talk about getting started at once on our way." The room in the Executive Offices building where Cabinet meetings were held was not large or impressive. It was lighted by large windows opening on the White House grounds. It was quiet and with no exposure where people could see the Cabinet in action. There were pictures of Washington and Lincoln, a long mahogany table, with chairs bearing the names of the various departments placed in the order of their rank. The President sat at the head of the table, Bryan, the ranking member, sat on his right, and McAdoo, who ranked second, on his left. The President and Bryan did most of the talking—some stories and discussion of problems ahead.

As President Wilson took his seat at the head of the table, he looked the moderator, fitting into place and power. His plan from the first was to present some matter or matters about which he desired what he was fond of calling "common counsel," and after he had received the reaction of Cabinet members, his practice was to call on each member to present any question that concerned departmental policies, for debate and exchange of news. At one Cabinet meeting he would begin with the Secretary of State, and at the next the Secretary of Labor would be called upon first. It was all like a round-table discussion without formality, with now and then sharp differences of opinion. That method brought light upon the matter under discussion. He never took a vote, pursuing a course, as he often said, more like a Quaker meeting, in which after full discussion the President would say, "It seems to me the sense of the meeting is so and so," and the policy thus ascertained would be the program of the administration. Usually he found himself in harmony with a majority. He wished in all important decisions to know the views of his associates. I do not recall that any important decision was made by the President, after the matter had been freely discussed by all the members, when he was not fully assured of the strong support of the Cabinet.

Though there were sharp divisions among members of Wilson's Cabinet, and occasionally some feeling was injected in the debate, such things were rare. The President was the soul of courtesy and his spirit set the pace. Inasmuch as he had named only Democrats in his Cabinet, though McReynolds had not voted for his colleague

C. K. Berryman, in the *Washington Star*

MEMBERS OF WILSON'S FIRST CABINET

The members are preparing to enter the campaign of 1914, when the Democrats carried Congress.

Bryan, when he was a candidate in 1896, the separations of opinion were more on policies than on opposing principles.

"I TAKE THE RESPONSIBILITY"

There is an old saying in Washington that if the administration was under attack the answer was to "throw some Cabinet member or high ranking official to the wolves." The theory was that the President would escape if the mistakes could be saddled upon some appointee who was removed or permitted to resign under fire. No such practice prevailed in the Wilson administration. Every loyal official knew his chief would stand by him through thick and thin as long as he conscientiously performed his duty. While he did not proclaim the Andrew Jackson slogan, he lived up to the policy of "I take the responsibility."

As an illustration of the loyalty Wilson gave as well as the loyalty he expected, Admiral Watson, U. S. Navy, retired, told me this incident:

"I had called at the White House to talk to the President about a matter on which he wanted some information. As I was leaving the President asked, 'Admiral, do you ever go to the Army and Navy Club?' I answered in the affirmative, whereupon the President said, 'I wish you would inform those Naval officers who spend their time criticizing the Navy that I am behind Daniels 100 per cent and nothing they can say can injure him.'"

Wilson was irritated when some narrow-minded correspondents falsely charged Private Secretary Tumulty with being "an agent of the Pope." He wrote Tumulty, "The attitude of some people about this irritates me more than I can say. It is not only preposterous, but outrageous and of course you know it never makes the slightest impression on me." Wilson's attitude of standing by officials unjustly assailed was well stated by John R. Dunlap, editor of an engineering journal, in these words:

"No president was ever more loyal or determined in his defense of close associates than Wilson. Tumulty had been Wilson's private Secretary when he was Governor of New Jersey and went with him to Washington where he won high place by his courtesy, ability, devotion to reform and loving loyalty to his chief. The letters that passed between them breathed affection."

WILSON ASSUMES LEADERSHIP

"Having been chosen the leader of my party for the time being, I feel it my duty to lead," said Woodrow Wilson in a Cabinet meeting in the summer of 1913, when it looked as if the Senate would debate the Federal Reserve Act indefinitely, and when it appeared that opposing Senators would hang it by the neck until it was dead. He took the reins in his own hands and backed up Senator Owen, who was having a difficult time piloting the measure through the Senate. Wilson went on then to discuss his theory of the place of a President in American government and voiced opinions contained in his writings and lectures of former years. Once when he thought the government was leaderless, Wilson had said, "I can vote for nobody I can depend upon to do anything—no, not if I were to vote for myself."

During the eight years he was in the White House there was no lack of leadership. He was not in the least disturbed at the hue and cry sometime raised that he was usurping functions that belonged to the legislative branch of government and becoming an autocrat. He said:

"There can be no destruction of democracy in our country as long as money bills must pass both Houses of Congress, but there will be stagnation unless the executive in constitutional ways not only makes recommendations but also assumes leadership of the members of his party on measures that are important."

NO SECRETS AT THE CABINET TABLE

At an early Cabinet meeting, Bryan, who sat next to the President, spoke to him in low tone, not audible to the other nine members of the Cabinet. It was embarrassing for the other members to wait while a whispered conversation went on at the head of the table. As Bryan finished, the President turned to us and said, "Mr. Bryan was just telling me," and repeated the conversation between them. It was about a matter that was later discussed by the whole Cabinet and no secrecy was intended. President Wilson added:

"I am repeating the whispered conversation to you all for fear that it might be inferred that the Secretary of State and I have some secrets from our colleagues. I do this in the beginning because I recall the severe criticism in Gideon Welles's *Diary* because, as he said, Secretary Seward would upon occasion lead Lincoln into a corner and they would talk in undertone for minutes while the other members of the Cabinet sat as if they had no part in the important matters that Seward was communicating in the President's ear. There will be no secrets between this President and the Secretary of State and our colleagues at the Cabinet table."

BURLESON CALLED "CARDINAL"

As the Cabinet members at an early meeting were leaving, Wilson asked Burleson to remain, and Garrison created a laugh by saying, "The Cardinal will remain behind to take the confession of the Pope." Some papers had said Burleson looked like a Cardinal. His enemies compared him unjustly with Richelieu. Wilson was influenced in selecting him partly because he was familiar with congressional workings. "Poor Burleson," Wilson wrote, "has the hardest sledding of all." But Burleson loved the political game and almost from maturity to 1921 held public office. To him official position was truly a public trust, and while he believed "deserving Democrats" ought to be given all positions outside the Civil Service, he contributed much to the enlargement of that service.

THE CAMINETTI CASE

One of the early differences of opinion in the Cabinet grew out of a charge brought against young Caminetti, son of the new Commissioner of Immigration, who was charged with violating the Mann Act in taking a young woman across State lines for immoral purposes. The case stirred California. The authorities were charged by the press with readiness to condone the crime. Telegrams poured in upon Wilson urging him to see that because the young man's father held a high position in his administration, the son should not escape punishment. It was charged that instead of vigorous prosecution, young Caminetti was being shielded by officials. When Wilson asked the Attorney General about the matter, McReynolds replied in a way that showed he was treating the matter rather cavalierly. In fact, he sneered at the Mann Act. Not so the President. The telegrams convinced Wilson that vigorous action should be taken, and he directed the Attorney General to engage F. J. Heney, a distinguished lawyer who had supported Theodore Roosevelt, and another lawyer of like standing who had no connection with the administration, to take charge of and press the prosecution.

"I do not agree with you at all," said the President when the Attorney General said too much fuss was being made out of a case of no great importance. His instructions to McReynolds showed he was resolved that a man accused of crime should not escape because his father happened to be a trusted member of the administration. During the discussion, Garrison remarked that the Mann law was a bad law and made possible the blackmailing of men by women who were not forced to immoral practices but willingly accompanied men out of the State. I felt sorry for Secretary Bryan and Secretary Wilson. For a score of years the elder Caminetti had been one of Bryan's closest friends and most ardent supporters. Bryan had recommended his appointment and Secretary Wilson had named him to an important post. Both agreed with the President but they were disturbed because of the distress of their friend. I rejoiced that the President acted with such firmness and vigor to uphold the law and to rid the administration of the charge made in California that it would shield a son of an honored and worthy associate.

"A LEETLE TOO FUR"

At a meeting of the Cabinet after Wilson made his rather famous Jackson Day speech in Indianapolis, Burleson asked the President, "Don't you think you were going 'a leetle too fur' when you said the Republican Party had not had a new idea in thirty years?" Wilson replied,

"I was speaking then not as a politician, but as a historian. Looking back upon the statement, and considering it wholly from the standpoint of history, I am inclined to marvel at my moderation. In the excess of my desire to be fair to the party tied to the apron strings of its grandmothers, I gave them the benefit of twenty years too much. But for my desire always to be more than fair to opponents, I would have said fifty years instead of thirty."

He gave a poser to the inquirer when he asked, "Can you name a single new idea the Republican Party has had in fifty or thirty years?"

He reviewed the big questions that had been under consideration, and stuck to his statement that the Republican Party "is the covert and refuge for those who are afraid, for those who want to consult their grandfathers about everything." He praised the grandfathers of the Party but said that later-day Republicans will not trust youngsters—"they are afraid they have something up their sleeves."

CABINET MEMBERS TELL STORIES

There were times when members of the Cabinet relaxed and swapped stories. Wilson was the prize story-teller but he had good competition. Most of Wilson's stories in the early days were drawn from his university associations. In one—I do not recall how he brought it in, but probably when there were instances of brilliant repartee—he told how he once got even with Nicholas Murray Butler at a banquet in New York. The president of Columbia fired this shot at Wilson: "I envy the president of Princeton because he enjoys the sylvan shades and retirement of the country; his must be ineffable calm and physical repose." To this Wilson retorted, having reference to the large number of Jews at Butler's University: "We should commiserate with the distinguished colleague because he that watcheth over Israel neither slumbers nor sleeps."

One day a colleague said there were but eleven original jokes, all others being varieties of the eleven. I have regretted he was not asked to name them. Wilson did not agree and said that the Irish made new and original jokes every week. As proof he told this one, showing that he was master of a good Irish brogue:

"I was coming along a road and beyant the mill and forninst the bridge, there was a beautiful meadow. In the meadow sat a pretty girl milking a cow. As I walked along, down the meadow came a great big roaring bull, stamping the ground, switching his tail, snorting and charging. And I cried out to the girl: 'Girl, don't you see the bull?' And she never turned her head, nor was there even a glint in her eye. But all of a sudden, when the bull got nearer, he stopped stamping and switching his tail, and snorting, and down went his tail between his legs, and he trotted off like a little dog.

"Says I: 'Girl, whatever did that?'

"And then she looked up at me and there was a glint in her eye. And says she: 'Can't you make that I am milking his mother-in-law?'"

THE FIRST CABINET PHOTOGRAPH

President Wilson never liked to be photographed. I learned that during the campaign when, as chairman of the literary and publicity bureau, I tried to induce him to let me have many pictures to illustrate the campaign stories. I was not surprised, therefore, at his impatience at the first meeting of the Cabinet, "informal and unofficial," the day after the inauguration, when the photographers making a picture of the President and the new Cabinet, said, "Just one more, please." After much time had been given, the photographers were told that no more pictures could be taken. When they had left, the President told a story—a practice which continued to the very end of his administration. I wish some dictograph could have preserved his stories, every one pertinent. His story, anent the persistence of the photographers, ran like this:

> "There was a man who easily lost his temper and indulged in swearing. When he joined the church, he put a curb on his old besetting sin and had almost become victor over it until one day, while presiding over a heated convention, bitter denunciation of his rulings was made. With a mighty effort he restrained his hot temper until some opponents threw ancient eggs, which hit him square on the head. All his poise gone, he reached for his pistol and shouted: 'This damn Job business is going to last just two seconds longer.'"

Though there were many insistent demands for other Cabinet pictures, the President yielded only twice, once shortly before the war when the New York *Times* wished a picture of the members of the Cabinet standing and I was asked to obtain Wilson's consent. It required all my entreaties, plus those of other members of the Cabinet, to induce him to acquiesce. But for my persistence, that good picture, taken after several changes in the personnel, would not be in existence. It was even more difficult to induce him to permit a later photograph of the Cabinet after he had sufficiently recovered from an illness to preside at the meetings. He yielded only because unless he had done so there would have been no Cabinet picture including Alexander, Colby, Palmer, Payne, and Glass, who were appointed in his second term.

At the first meeting of the new Cabinet, Wilson and his associates did not seem to sense that the first big matters that commanded attention had to do with situations in Mexico and the Central American States and in Asia. Their thoughts were mainly on domestic problems and on how to advance the New Freedom which Wilson looked to as the chart of justice and the prevention of favoritism by government. In fact, he hardly touched upon foreign matters in his inaugural address, and though there were clouds on the international horizon, he awaited a study and survey before action. The same was true of the other members of the Cabinet, except Bryan, who was intent upon his treaties to prevent wars by arbitration and agreement before issues that might precipitate war got out of hand; but Bryan was not pressing consideration at the first meetings.

XIV

"DESERVING DEMOCRATS" DISTURBED

WASHINGTON WAS FULL OF what Bryan called "deserving Democrats" who had borne the heat and burden of the days of defeat and hoped to be called to positions of trust in the new administration. They were the captains and lieutenants who had kept the party organized in lean years and who were largely responsible for the nomination and election of Wilson. They wished to congratulate the new President and to apply for public positions. They had as much right, they correctly felt, to the smaller places as Democratic Cabinet officials had to the higher stations. Naturally "deserving Democrats," who wished to serve in the administration but were decried as "office-seekers" by men who had never done anything to secure the election of Wilson, wished to talk to their President.

WOULD SEE NO OFFICE ASPIRANT

At the first Cabinet meeting the President announced a new and radical policy, which was followed by a public statement. It was that he would see no applicant for office but would give audiences only to those who were invited by him to call. He told the Cabinet that he felt it his duty to devote himself unremittingly to the grave problems of national and international affairs, and he would, therefore, ask the members of the Cabinet to sift all applications, after which he would wish their recommendations. "I owe this to the people," he said, simply. He added:

"I will not decline to see them, but I cannot have my time taken up in that way. Besides, I am making it easy for every applicant to have his application considered by having him talk to the Cabinet official under whom he must serve if appointed. I am relying on you gentlemen of the Cabinet to sift out applications and bring me your recommendations. If it is a postoffice, Burleson will talk to the applicant and the members of Congress and will lay before me all the information, and instead of my statement's denying a full hearing, it aids applicants to secure the quickest possible consideration and action. Otherwise they would have to see both me and the Cabinet member."

Some members of the Cabinet questioned the wisdom of the new policy, saying that it would offend many good Democrats who were in the city and would chill their enthusiasm. "They want to see the President in person," said one, "and will feel a sense of denial of presenting their claims to the President whom they helped to nominate and worked to elect."

Postmaster General Burleson, who became the chief liaison officer between the President and Congress, made this declaration: "I shall present the name of no man for appointment who fought you." That wasn't Wilson's idea, and he replied, "All I desire is that the best-fitted men who favor progressive policies shall be selected for the places of trust. I do not wish the test to be whether they were for or against me." Burleson's original idea—to appoint for office only those who had favored Wilson's nomination at Baltimore—would have eliminated some members of his Cabinet. The only members of the original Cabinet who were at Baltimore working for Wilson's nomination were Bryan, McAdoo, Burleson, Daniels, and Wilson.

As time went on Burleson said that the Senate's right to confirm or reject made it impossible to appoint only original Wilson men even if it had been wise. In some States, notably in North Carolina, in the local appointments the Senators selected men regardless of their attitude before the Baltimore Convention, and most of the men appointed had not supported Wilson. In fact, most of the best places went to Underwood supporters, almost all of them efficient and loyal, but loyal chiefly to the Senators.

MY NORTH CAROLINA ATTITUDE

It was early in March that the matter of appointing officials in North Carolina came up. Even before the vacancy in the Collectorship in the Western North Carolina District, the State papers said that Senators Simmons and Overman would recommend for that position A. D. Watts, of Irdell. There was general and deep-seated opposition to Watts. He was regarded by the progressive element as only a shrewd machine politician. In the pre-convention campaign he had offended all the Wilson people by the use of money in hidden ways that would not bear the light. Mr. E. J. Justice and other North Carolina leaders came to Washington to protest against his appointment.

They saw McAdoo and President Wilson. The President, of course, had never heard of Watts and referred them to McAdoo. These friends thought I ought to go to Wilson and protest against the appointment. I was as much opposed to it as they were and resented the suggestion that one of the best positions in the State should be given to a man of Watts's reputation, particularly since he had been the head and front of the opposition to Wilson. I therefore undertook to try to induce Senators Simmons and Overman not to recommend him. I felt that if I should try to influence appointments in North Carolina, I would be at war with our members in the House and Senate; that I had a big enough job on my hands as Secretary of the Navy; and that I ought to leave recommendations for State offices to the members of Congress.

I took no such position with regard to appointments outside the State. I urged Secretary Bryan and President Wilson to appoint Governor Glenn as member of the Canadian Boundary Commission and Major E. J. Hale as Minister to Costa Rica. I also recommended to the Attorney General the appointment of Justice as Chief Counsel in the fight to insure the title of the Navy to Elk's Hill Petroleum Reserves, and I recommended the appointment of other North Carolinians to positions in Washington and the diplomatic service. I thought that Simmons and Overman ought to give the preference to Wilson supporters. They were not of that opinion.

When the Watts fight was on, Simmons came to see me about it at my request. I told him that, in my judgment and in that of many North Carolinians, Watts was not a suitable man to be appointed and that I had no doubt if I should go to the President and tell him what I knew about Watts, he would turn him down cold, but that I did not feel that it was proper for me to be in conflict with North Carolina Senators in a matter which had always been their prerogative and I was therefore appealing to him and would appeal to Overman to name some other than Watts as Collector.

Simmons said, "You wrong Watts. He is not nearly so bad or so unpopular as you think, and if you would let me show you the recommendations filed for him, you would see that he is overwhelmingly endorsed. Moreover, no State appointment has been made in the Wilson administration of my supporters in the Senate campaign, and my friends are wondering if they are proscribed from holding office and are asking me if I have any influence." He said that the opinion was forming in North Carolina that no active Simmons man need expect an appointment, and that he was compelled to try to meet the desires of his supporters by urging the appointment of some of his friends.

I suggested to him, as I later did to Overman, the appointment of W. C. Dowd, editor of the Charlotte *News,* who was not a candidate for the position but who was well qualified, highly regarded in the State, an ardent supporter of Simmons and Overman, and a leader in the North Carolina delegation in Baltimore that nominated Wilson and helped mightily in carrying his part of the State for Wilson. I told him the appointment of such a man would please the President and gratify all his supporters, and at the same time it would show all the Simmons and Overman men in North Carolina that they were not discriminated against by the administration. But I could not make any headway with him. He was determined to have Watts, and Overman joined in the recommendation. They secured the support of most of the House members. It was in this contest that the intimacy between Simmons and McAdoo began. I seriously contemplated going to the President and making an earnest protest, but refrained from doing so.

All Democratic Senators insisted upon their prerogative of naming State officials, but as to officials at Washington or in the foreign service they made no such insistence. When Wilson appointed Walter Hines Page, native of North Carolina but a resident of New York, as Ambassador to Great Britain, though Wilson did this without senatorial recommendation, Senators Simmons and Overman joined me in expressing gratification at the selection of the distinguished native of North Carolina.

POLICY AS TO APPOINTMENTS

Wilson was always irked by having to make appointments. When he was Governor of New Jersey, he delegated most of this work to his trusted associates, as he did in Washington.

After consultation with Bryan, the President selected most of the Ambassadors. He appointed the members of independent commissions and some of the lesser officials. As a rule, however, the men appointed were recommended by the Cabinet officers. In the Navy only a few times in the eight years did President Wilson suggest the designation of any officer for any post. While Wilson did not see applicants for office in person, he was keen to know that the men chosen measured up to his standards and had the requisite qualifications. A few days after the inauguration, he asked me to do him and Bryan "a great favor." He told me that Bryan had suggested Governor Osborne, of Wyoming, as Assistant Secretary of State, and that he thought the appointment would be a mistake to all concerned. "I have a high opinion of Mr. Osborne, but he has had no such experience as particularly fits him for diplomacy. If you can induce Mr. Bryan to let me appoint Mr. Osborne to some other position of equal or even higher rank, you will be serving me and Mr. Bryan. However, I will, of course, send in Mr. Osborne's name to the Senate if Mr. Bryan insists." Osborne and I were old friends, but I agreed with Wilson that he would serve better as Commissioner of the Land Office or Assistant Secretary of the Interior. I told Bryan so. His answer was, "It is too late. I have tendered the place to Governor Osborne and he has accepted." I am not sure, but at the time of his appointment I think Wilson, Bryan, and Osborne were under the impression that Osborne would be Acting Secretary in Bryan's absence, and that Osborne was disappointed when he learned that the Counsellor preceded the Assistant Secretary and that the Assistant Secretary's duties were mainly administrative. Osborne had an attractive wife who enjoyed the social life that fell to a high official of the State Department.

PERSONIFICATION OF IMPATIENCE

Wilson was the personification of impatience when long-winded men wasted his time, or repeated themselves. "That man insults my intelligence," he said to me one day early in the administration. "He called and stated very clearly what he had to say and in the course of twenty minutes repeated the same statement four times in somewhat different language. I cannot stand a man who thinks I am so dumb he must tell me a thing over and over."

One day, shortly after Wilson had been inaugurated, a friend and supporter of the administration told me that he had been unable to see the President except once—that Tumulty would not make an appointment for him though he had requested it several times. He asked me to arrange it. Upon my next visit to the White House I relayed the request. Wilson exploded, saying:

"No, I haven't the strength to see that gentleman again. Early in our administration he called and stated the matter uppermost in his mind and then talked and talked until I almost lost my mind. He has no terminal facilities. I have too many pressing duties to permit him to wear me out again by his incessant flow of talk. I look to you to find some way to save me from what would be too great an ordeal. He wishes the position of——an important place. I know he is honest and capable and you may tell him I will send his name to the Senate in a few days. That ought to satisfy him, but I simply cannot give him another chance to talk me to death."

The gentleman who lacked terminal facilities in conversation was appointed and filled the position with such ability that Wilson was proud of his administration. But the successful official never quite forgave the President for not giving him the opportunity he desired to talk matters over.

NEEDS SEA ROOM

Coming out of the President's office, I spoke of the matter to Tumulty, who often quietly bore the blame in protecting the President. Tumulty said, "Let me show you this note about a like case which the Governor will turn over to you," and he handed me this note to read:

"Dear Tumulty:
"I should like to see Mr—— but just now it does not seem possible because I know he is a gentleman who needs a good deal of sea-room. I am taking up his suggestions with the Secretary of the Navy.
                                                    "The President
                                                        "C. L. S."

At one meeting of the Cabinet, Wilson said that his policy of not seeing applicants for office had been put to a severe test. A gentleman called and the first thing he said was that he wished to secure appointment to a certain office, and began to tell why he should be named. Wilson never liked a man to boost himself. He said, "I referred him to my public statement that I would not discuss a public position with any applicant, referred him to Cabinet members, and terminated the interview almost before it was begun." That man doubtless retired saying:

"It is so soon that I am done for,
I wonder what I was begun for."

He soon learned that what he first thought was a rebuff was not that at all, for Wilson gave him the important post he desired.

More times than I can remember, Wilson would refer some insistent caller to me. Once he laughingly apologized for inflicting a bore on me by saying, "I was sure you would know how to handle him and keep him in a good humor." I told him that in that respect he reminded me of what Mark Twain said about Joseph R. Hawley, Connecticut Senator.

"How?" he asked.

Twain, introducing Hawley, said, "Gentlemen, General Hawley is a good man. He never turns a man away from his door empty-handed. He always gives him a letter of introduction to me."

In all his appointments, Wilson showed his high sense of obligation to public duty and regarded himself as a trustee of official positions for the public weal. One day I was urging him to appoint a mutual friend to a high position. Among other reasons I assigned was that the man in question had been active and influential in his support at the Baltimore Convention. The reference ruffled him. "I would give that man the shirt off my back because of my gratitude to him, but that office does not belong to me, and I would be recreant to my trust if I appointed him to it. You know and I know he is not qualified to fill it and I could not give it to him without doing a wrong to the public service. I cannot give what is not mine to give." Some months later the gentleman was appointed to another position, for which he was well qualified.

NO NEPOTISM PERMITTED

A few days before the extra session of Congress, which met April 8, 1913, I received a call from Senator Luke Lee, Senator from Tennessee, who was actively seeking to promote the election of Joseph R. Wilson, brother of the President and a member of the editorial staff of the Nashville *Banner,* as Secretary of the Senate and wished my coöperation. I was fond of Wilson, who had assisted me in the literary work of the campaign, and naturally would have been pleased to see the Senate select him for an important post. Shortly I learned that the older Senators resented the suggestion that they should name the President's brother rather than select a trusted official worthy of the promotion, Mr. James M. Baker, of South Carolina, who, in the administration of Franklin Roosevelt, was to become Minister to Siam. There was much publicity about the matter, to the embarrassment of the President. Soon the matter was dropped. It became well understood that the President would neither appoint nor permit the appointment of any person connected with him by blood or marriage. He held to the Jeffersonian doctrine that if any relative had ambition to serve the public he should seek a position within the gift of the voters and not an appointive position from his relative who happened to be in the White House.

Jefferson had truly said, in a letter to a relative who wished a presidential appointment, shortly after he entered the White House:

"The public will never be made to believe that an appointment of a relative is made on the ground of merit alone, uninfluenced by family views; nor can they ever see with approbation offices the disposal of which they entrust to their president for public purposes, divided out as family property."

Later an attempt was made to have Wilson's brother made Postmaster at Nashville. He was well qualified for either position suggested, no man more so. But nepotism was a sin which the President determined should not lie at his door, even though the recommendations of his brother from the people were overwhelming.

During the presidential campaign, in organizing the department of literature and publicity, I found that I needed additional assistance, and it occurred to me that Joseph Wilson would be deeply interested in the campaign and could find no place where he could exercise his "passion for anonymity"; so I wrote and asked him if he would like to come to New York to work in our bureau, where he could be in touch with every phase of the campaign, and help us prepare articles for the press. He accepted gladly at a compensation just enough to pay his expenses in New York. He greatly enjoyed the opportunity to lend a hand in his brother's election. He had great kindliness, a fine spirit, and good ability, but lacked the dynamic force of his more distinguished brother. I relied upon him for much research work, for he preferred service of that nature rather than the limelight. After the election he returned to his post in Nashville, and shortly found himself catapulted into the situation described above, which was embarrassing both to him and to the President.

Part Two

―――――――――――――――――――――

FOREIGN AFFAIRS

XV

END OF DOLLAR DIPLOMACY

FIVE DAYS AFTER he was inaugurated Wilson, who with Bryan had quickly assimilated the reports about unsettled conditions in the Central American States, read the Cabinet a statement outlining the policy toward those countries. This was no hasty action. One of the issues in the campaign had been around the Dollar Diplomacy of the Washington government whereby armed forces had been used to advance the fortunes of American investors—sometimes exploiters—in those smaller countries. It was resolved at once to do two things: First, to serve notice on all that we recognized no government in those countries unless it was based on the consent of the governed; and, second, that those dictators who started revolutions to line their pockets would not be recognized by the United States.

Wilson was between two fires—one the demand of American investors that he continue Dollar Diplomacy, and the other, dictators who seized control of the governments by force. He felt it imperative at once to give notice to both elements and all others of what they might expect. During the campaign I had sent out literature condemning Dollar Diplomacy and had talked with Bryan about our administration's putting an end to it. Therefore, though I realized it was not the easiest way, I rejoiced in Wilson's early announcement of his policy. I felt it was sound doctrine and should be declared at once. Houston wished to defer making it public until the statement could be shown to the most important South American diplomats. Bryan, the only member of the Cabinet who had been consulted, thought there should be no delay. Reports had been current that the restraining influences in those countries would be withdrawn by Wilson and there were indications of uprisings in several. Wilson decided to follow his own judgment and that of his Secretary of State, and his first important announcement touching foreign policies appeared in the press on March 12th. It was notice to the world that a firm hand was at the throttle.

THE SIX-POWER LOAN

The Wilson administration rejoiced to recognize the new Republic of China and hailed it as the forerunner of self-government by the people of the Orient. It assured Sun Yat-sen of sympathy and co-operation in setting up the Republic of China on a sound foundation. At the very threshold of Wilson's administration there was danger of putting the new Republic in chains to international bankers. On March 9, members of the big Morgan banking house called on Bryan to ascertain if the administration would carry out the Taft approval of the Six-Power Loan to the new Republic of China. Hold-over State Department officials sent Wilson memorandums favoring the participation. The important European powers had agreed to furnish the new Republic with money to pay its army and its other indebtedness, upon condition that the money should be disbursed by or under the direction of foreign governments. A group of American bankers wished to join in. One of the stipulations of those offering to make the loan was that if China should wish to borrow more money it could be borrowed only from those making the loan.

At Bryan's request a special meeting of the Cabinet was called (March 18, 1913) to discuss the loan. The discussion, which lasted over two hours, was opened by Bryan, who luminously stated his objection to the plan. He believed it would virtually put the international banking houses that furnished the money in a position to direct China's policy and further take away her initiative and freedom. McAdoo, Secretary of the Treasury, thought we could not agree to request the American bankers to subscribe to the loan, because it would be equivalent to asking bankers to take a hand in the control of China's affairs. Secretary Lane, who said he had made a long study of Chinese affairs, thought it would be a mistake to approve this old-time financiering since China had recently declared for new ways; that this country should not be a party to helping China upon the condition that it should be beholden to a group of bankers of the nations of the world. Secretary Redfield, however, feared that if we failed to approve the loan, it would be made by other nations, and America would lose in building up a large trade in China. My idea was that we ought to find some way for this government to help China coupled with the recognition of the Republic. I expressed the fear that the Republic would be one in

name only if it had to begin its existence with obligations to a syndi-
cate of international bankers; that by financing China the bankers
would obtain spheres of influence, and by so much expect to control
the development of independent China.

INTERNATIONAL BANKERS TURNED DOWN

The President expressed his conviction very clearly that we should
not request the group of bankers to make the loan. He thought a
better way could be found to help China. It was decided that the
President should draw up a statement giving the government's attitude, to be presented at the next meeting of the Cabinet, and this
was done. Wilson asserted that the condition of the loan would
"touch very nearly the administrative independence of China itself"
and that the governmental responsibility involved "might conceivably
go to the length of forcible interference." He declared participation
in the loan to be "obnoxious to the principles upon which the government of our people rests." He concluded by saying that ways would
be found to promote trade with China, but that we would continue
to stand for the Open Door—"the only door we care to enter." Some
critics called it "amateurish and sentimental," but Bryan correctly
gauged public sentiment in a letter to Wilson in which he said: "I
have yet to find the first man who dissents from your position on
the Chinese loan and I believe you have won the lasting gratitude of
China."

Huntington Wilson, Assistant Secretary of State, knowing he was
on the way out, resigned in a huff because, as he said, "I had no
reason to suppose that the fate of negotiations which had so long
had the studious attention of the foreign offices of six great powers
would be abruptly determined with such quite unnecessary haste
and in so unusual a manner." Like all Dollar Diplomats (and unfortunately many career officials have acted as if they were virtually
the agents of Big Business) he was shocked to see the government
free itself from the chains of the exploiters. But under Bryan the
State Department put an end to ordering Marines to land and by
force to collect debts for concessionaires. I recall that ten years ago
the son of an old friend, who had long been in the diplomatic service in the Dollar Diplomacy era, told me he was resigning. Asked
why—for "Few die and none resign"—he replied, "I am damn tired
of being a debt collector."

As I walked with Bryan back from the Cabinet meeting on the day the Six-Power Loan was vetoed, he was enthusiastic in praise of the wisdom of the President. "I love his audacity and his courage," he said with enthusiasm. I shared his feeling. Shortly thereafter Wilson was pleased to recognize the new Chinese Republic because he believed the democratic leaven was working in the Orient. I think our country was the first to recognize the government of the people that had come into being under Sun Yat-sen.

One reason I was happy at this recognition was that I had known Charles J. Soong, a young Chinaman educated in North Carolina.

This young Chinese lad, in a strange land, attracted the interest and confidence of a noble North Carolina philanthropist, General Julian S. Carr, of Durham, who sent him to Trinity College. After graduation he returned to China as an ordained Methodist preacher. His three daughters, all educated in the United States, married the three ablest public men in China. He was treasurer of the Sun Yat-sen organization and active for Sun Yat-sen when he was compelled to leave China and found refuge in Japan. Soong was the father of Madame Chiang Kai-shek, who is credited with having made her husband "the Christian general of China."

Recognition of the Republic of China was hailed as showing that Wilson had parted company with the policies hitherto governing at Washington of giving partnership to international bankers in affairs of the Far East and in Pan American countries. The administration thus formally ended the policy of Dollar Diplomacy.

XVI

DANGEROUSLY NEAR WAR WITH JAPAN

WE WERE NEAR WAR with Japan in May, 1913. On the day after the inauguration Ambassador Chinda, very much disturbed, laid a serious situation on the White House doorstep. Wilson and Bryan were greatly concerned at the serious demands the Japanese made. For weeks the situation occupied much of the attention of the Cabinet.

The passage in the early part of 1913 by the California Legislature of a law forbidding the Japanese to own or lease land in that State created such strained relations between Japan and the United States that many feared the long-predicted war between the two countries would ensue. Japan made very earnest representations to the government that this law was in violation of the treaty. Public meetings were held in Japan denouncing it and the Japanese in California were in an ugly mood. The people of Japan could not understand why the Federal government was not supreme in matters of this kind, for their emperor dominated their whole empire. They looked to Washington alone.

The Japanese Ambassador delivered a note in which Japan declared the California law was "obnoxious, discriminatory, unfair, unfriendly, and in violation of the treaty between the two countries." Wilson thought the Japanese statement "unfair." As a result, Bryan was to tell Chinda that the language was "objectionable" and explain that under our system the Federal government could not direct a State what it should do about its land laws. On May 16 Bryan brought to the Cabinet a reply to Japan's protest, which held that the California law was not contrary to the treaty; and in any case the courts would settle the question. "It never occurred to me that war could be possible between the two countries," said Wilson, "until I observed the manner of the Japanese Ambassador, who was very nervous and gave evidence that his country looked for war." The Japanese had acquiesced in our exclusion law, but California's action opened the old sore. Undoubtedly the Japanese were so aroused that their government officials could have carried them into war over what they regarded as a studied insult. The gravity of the situation was appreciated by the President and the Cabinet. Bryan had frequent discussions with the Japanese Ambassador, and when he had made what sounded like an ultimatum, the Japanese Ambassador asked: "Is this final, Mr. Secretary?"

Bryan answered in what became historic words: "Nothing is final between friends."

BRYAN GOES TO CALIFORNIA

While this matter was under discussion in the Cabinet the President turned to Bryan and asked if he would go to California to confer with the Governor of that State in a friendly way to see if some adjustment could not be made that would assuage the Japanese resentment. Wilson felt that if anybody could accomplish the desired end Bryan could and would. As we left the Cabinet, Bryan said to me:

"The President has asked me to undertake a task that gives little promise of success, but I am ready to try because even if it fails we will show Japan that the Federal government is doing everything it can to prevent a break. Our platform declared for the exclusion act. It will be regarded as inconsistent with our declaration, but unless we go the limit I fear the extent to which Japan will go. Wish me well, my friend, in what promises to be the most thankless task I ever undertook.

Therefore Bryan went to California, as a good soldier, after Governor Johnson agreed that he and legislators would confer with him. But it implied no hearty welcome. Nobody could have handled a delicate situation better than Bryan. His spirit was one of conference and exchange of views. He disarmed criticism by displaying no Big Stick. He sought a method of doing what Californians were set on doing, without singling out Japan, which was overwrought and whose people were talking militantly. In the end, while it did not satisfy the Japanese government, the law that Governor Johnson signed served to keep the dispute in diplomatic channels. The gesture of the Washington government in trying to adjust matters assuaged the war party in Japan and gave cooling time.

JOINT BOARD MOVES TOWARD WAR

While the President and the Secretary of State were seeking to make Japan understand that this country had no warlike intentions but was bent upon pacific policies, in May, 1913, one of the New York City papers carried under big headlines the sensational story that the Army and Navy were preparing for war with Japan and stated that the Joint Army and Navy Board had decided on the methods of conducting the war. This publication infuriated President Wilson. He felt outraged that a board composed of Army and Navy officers should take action and make it public without consultation with the Commander in Chief. The meeting of the Board as given publicity by the New York papers was held on May 13, 1913, and the following action was said to have been taken:

"At a meeting held this date (May 13, 1913) the Joint Board unanimously decided in consequence of urgent presentation made by the army member of the Board that it is a matter of the utmost military importance that the United States cruisers *Saratoga, Cincinnati, Albany, Rainbow* and *Helena* now on the Yangtze River be moved immediately to Manila to reinforce and co-operate with the Army there as well as to insure the safety of the vessels themselves.

"In view of existing conditions, the Joint Board recommends most strongly that the following disposition of the ships of the Pacific station be made at once: first, that six armored cruisers of the *West Virginia* class, five cruisers; four submarines and five destroyers be ordered to the Hawaiian Islands; that the *Oregon* and *Cheyenne* be ordered to Panama."

At the meeting Admiral Dewey asked what was the present status of the Japanese controversy. General Wood, who was the instigator of the action of the Board, said that the "Japanese notes were becoming more and more insistent" and that the Army had been moving supplies on the quiet to the Hawaiian and Philippine Islands. The New York papers said that the Army had made great preparations in the Philippines without the action of the Joint Board and that the Joint Board, upon the suggestion of Wood, had recommended Naval movements in the Far East. This publication was believed by the President and by me to have been made in order to force the hands of the Commander in Chief. At the same meeting the Board had recommended certain Army movements which had been approved by Secretary of War Garrison.

SECRETARY OF THE NAVY DISAPPROVES

When Admiral Fiske, Aide for Operations, presented the recommendations of the Joint Board to me and advised my approval of the action, I suggested to him that it was unprecedented for an Army officer to be initiating Naval activities, and that if there were to be any movement of Naval ships, it could not be done without the order of the Secretary of the Navy or the Commander in Chief. I also told him I thought nothing could be more injurious to peaceful negotiations than the movements recommended and that the Board had exeeded its functions because what it recommended might precipitate war.

"But Secretary of War Garrison has approved the prompt sending of Army forces, and the Navy should act quickly," said the Admiral.

"That is a matter for the President to decide," I answered. "Personally I think the Board has erred and I cannot approve the warlike recommendations. I have no criticism of the Secretary of War, but I will not be a party to such an ill-considered course taken without consultation with officials who are looking for a peaceful solution."

Admiral Fiske, who, like General Wood, was militant and really would like to have seen war with Japan, was not impressed by my position. I told him to inform the Joint Board that I disapproved the action and would take the matter up with the President.

HOT DEBATE IN THE CABINET

At the next meeting of the Cabinet, Garrison, Secretary of War, and I had quite a debate over the recommendations. He thought the Joint Board had acted wisely and, as a precautionary measure, it was the duty of the Army and Navy, unless we were willing to let Japan take the Philippine Islands, to strengthen the Army and Navy both in the Philippines and in Hawaii, thus serving notice on Japan that any hostile movement would be promptly met. Garrison was somewhat of the same mind as the imperialistic members of the Joint Board. He nearly always sided with the plans they mapped out for military preparation and action—this not because anybody on earth could influence him but because he looked at matters from the same standpoint as men like General Wood. I took the ground that it would be most unwise for any large movement of the Army or Navy in Far Eastern waters to take place while negotiations looking to a peaceful solution were pending. I said that it would be regarded by the Japanese as indicating we were preparing for war and that it would strengthen the hands of those Japanese who wanted war and would weaken the hands of those who, like our President and Secretary of State, hoped for peaceful adjustment. Moreover, I took the ground that if the Japanese were so minded, the very minute the ships (which were of an old type with guns of short range), left Chinese waters, it would be the easiest thing in the world for the Japanese to sink them before they could reach the Philippines. The President interrupted me by saying, "Yes, but they could not do so if we were good and ready." I agreed but said that time would be required. I also said that, even with this movement of ships and men which the Board recommended, we would still be unable to prevent the taking of the Philippines with our little force in the Far East, if the Japanese were determined to take them—we were so far from any base of supplies—and it would be a dangerous, provocative, and impotent gesture.

Bryan was more indignant if possible than the President at the action of the Joint Board and its publication. He declared that military officers were the last men to determine the policies of government, and said, "While we were discussing how to prevent a threatened war, these men were busying themselves with plans of how to get us in. It is time enough for the Army and Navy to make plans when the Commander in Chief calls upon them to do so."

Garrison urged that "we must take steps to protect and hold the Philippines at any cost." I replied that his remark was proof of our country's unwisdom in embarking upon a colonial and imperialistic policy when we took the Philippines by force, and added, "Just as a chain is only as strong as its weakest link, so no country is stronger than its remotest and weakest possession. The sooner we repair the wrong done under McKinley and give the Philippines their independence, the sooner we will return to real democracy and insure ourselves against the necessity—if it is necessary—to hold them in our possession."

Redfield disagreed, saying that while he was in Congress he had opposed the Democratic policy of giving the Philippine Islands independence—"they cannot govern themselves."

Wilson supported my position. Other members of the Cabinet joined in the discussion. At the end of the meeting the President said, "I would like for the Secretary of War and the Secretary of the Navy to meet me this afternoon at the White House when we can go over this matter at greater length." We met that afternoon and talked it over for a long time sitting in the garden of the White House grounds. Garrison was insistent that we should approve the action of the Joint Board; that he had approved so far as Army movements were concerned because he thought it was essential; that unless we did so we might find the Philippine Islands taken without a struggle and then we would regret that we had not been forehanded. He amplified this and insisted it was the only course for the government to take. I enlarged upon the reasons I had given in the Cabinet that morning and particularly stressed that any movement of ships or troops which was not large enough to make victory certain was worse than no movement; that if the Japanese situation was so critical that war was imminent, we ought to send our dreadnaughts over to the Philippines and have them ready to protect the smaller ships when they left the Chinese waters. Otherwise they would all be sunk if the Japanese were so minded, and the Board's action, was, in my judgment, from a diplomatic standpoint, provocative of war, and, from a military standpoint, both dangerous and impotent. The President, after hearing the discussion, directed us to make no movement in the matter recommended by the Joint Board until further directions.

WILSON DISSOLVES THE JOINT BOARD

In view of this discussion and his attitude in the matter, naturally Wilson had been greatly outraged when the publication of what the Board had recommended was printed. He directed the Secretary of War and the Secretary of the Navy to ascertain what officers had been responsible for the leak. He was ready to take summary action against them because he thought it was an attempt to forestall action by the Commander in Chief and because its publication was likely to foment bitter feeling in Japan. I suspected that Admiral Fiske had had a hand in this business of letting it get to the papers, and I think the President thought General Wood was not above it.

Directly, of course, they had not done so, but Wilson always believed and I was certain that one or both of these high-ranking officers had talked about the matter and that the information had therefore come from them whether directly inspired by them or not.

The very day that the publication was made—and of course nothing else was talked about in Washington—President Wilson directed Garrison and myself to order the members of the Joint Board to put an end to all meetings and not to assemble again until he directed them to meet. I gave this direction to Admiral Dewey who was the president of the Board. He was indignant that there had been a leak in the action of the Board. He showed no resentment at the President's order for the Joint Board not to function, and, while he had taken no part in the discussion when the resolution was passed, the meeting was presided over by him and I always thought that he sympathized with the President in feeling that those responsible for giving out the action had been untrue to him and to the Joint Board as well as to the Commander in Chief. From the moment the President directed the Joint Board to meet no more, it went into innocuous desuetude—that is to say, it was as if it did not exist—suspended between heaven and earth, and its members out of commission for more than two years.

In the early fall of 1915, when the European War necessarily caused the Army and Navy to be on their toes, in view of the possibility that we might be drawn into the war, I suggested to the President that he withdraw his veto and permit the Joint Army and Navy Board to resume their meetings and be ready to advise the Secretary of War and the Secretary of the Navy of conditions in Europe and of the necessary preparations which this country might be compelled to take. He agreed to this upon condition that we would see to it that there were no more leaks and that before any publication was made of any recommendations, he should have the right to examine them. The Board, therefore, resumed its meetings on October 16, 1915.

WAR WITH JAPAN AVERTED

Secretary Bryan acquainted the Japanese Ambassador with the President's feeling about the recommendations of the Joint Board and informed him it had not been approved by the Secretary of the Navy. The Japanese government was thereby assured that the administration had no thought of war and no intention of moving any of its ships in the Far East while negotiations for peace were pending. This assurance was given so promptly that the Japanese government was able to quiet superheated demonstrations in their country.

THE YELLOW PERIL

All that spring and summer when negotiations were going on growing out of the California land law, Admiral Fiske, Aide for Operations, was incessantly talking to me about the danger of war with Japan. He and Richmond Pearson Hobson, who was a member of the Naval Affairs Committee, were obsessed with the yellow peril. They sat up nights thinking how Japan was planning to make war on America and steal a march on us by taking the Philippine Islands and going on to Hawaii. Hobson made speeches about it, which the President regarded as in bad taste at a time when critical matters were at issue between two countries. Admiral Fiske, I think, fanned the fire with Hobson, and confined himself, so far as I knew, to trying to convince me that war with Japan was inevitable and that we ought to carry out the recommendations of the Joint Board. He was so obsessed by this plan that he took up much of my time with his arguments. One day while he was telling me of the imminence of the yellow peril, a Japanese photographer, who had taken an excellent picture of my two young sons in Navy uniform came by appointment into the office of the Secretary of the Navy to take my picture at my desk and a picture of the room. Before he came within earshot I said to the Admiral, "You are right. The yellow peril is on us. Here comes a Jap with a bomb. You had better get out." He was so serious and so confident that whatever he thought was right and so lacking in humor that he was shocked at my levity, but he retired while the photographer did his best.

XVII

McKINLEY LAID IT ON GOD

I HAD GONE to Washington hoping to see the Filipinos given their independence. The Baltimore Convention reaffirmed the position "thrice announced by the Democracy" "against" a policy of imperialism and colonial exploitation in the Philippines and favored "an immediate declaration of the nation's purpose to recognize the independence of the Philippine Islands as soon as a stable government can be established." Only two members of the Cabinet, Garrison and Redfield, dissented from the President's message, which took a long step—a message that the Filipino people hailed as "eloquent proof" of the new day. Personally, I thought Wilson did not go far enough.

Though I felt in 1898 that the United States could not be unconcerned over Spain's treatment of our nearest neighbors, the Cubans, I strongly opposed the purchase of the Philippine Islands and the cruel war we waged against the Filipinos after Dewey sailed away. I was in full accord with the pledge by the Democratic National Convention against the policy of imperialism which McKinley said he inaugurated by direction of the Almighty. Soon after Dewey's victory McKinley said: "Forcible annexation cannot be thought of; that, by our code of morality, would be criminal aggression." Why, then, did he conduct the bloody war for annexation? Let me quote McKinley's own words:

"The truth is I did not want the Philippines and when they came to us as a gift from God, I did not know what to do with them. I walked the floor of the White House night after night, until midnight, and I am not ashamed to tell you, gentlemen, that I went down on my knees and prayed to Almighty God for light and guidance more than one night. And one night it came to me that there was nothing left for us to do but take them all, and to educate the Filipinos and uplift and civilize and Christianize them, and by God's grace to do the very best we could by them as our fellowmen for whom Christ also died. And then I went to bed, and went to sleep and slept soundly."

While McKinley was praying, the Mark Hannas were ready to be preying.

BRYAN'S GREATEST MISTAKE

The greatest mistake Bryan ever made was in throwing the weight of his influence to secure the Treaty of Paris, by which we bought the Filipinos at so much a head. Gorman as leader of Democratic opposition and Hoar as leader of the Republican opponents had the treaty defeated when Bryan appeared in Washington and, with his influence, great at the time, persuaded seventeen Democrats to support McKinley and vote to ratify the treaty, in order, as he said, to end the war then raging in the Philippines. Even so, the treaty was ratified with only one vote to spare. Bryan was given the credit—or the blame?—of inducing seventeen Senators to vote for ratification of the treaty, which was ratified by the margin of one vote, thus saving William McKinley from a defeat akin to that which befell Woodrow Wilson two decades later. If Bryan had foreseen what would happen he would have taken the opposite course. The independence of the Philippines should have been given at that time. It remained for Franklin Roosevelt to promise full independence at the conclusion of World War II, and end the imperialism of William McKinley and Theodore Roosevelt.

"DAMN, DAMN, DAMN THE FILIPINOS"

I was invited on December 11, 1913, to deliver an address at the banquet of the Military Order of the Carabao, composed of Army and Naval officers who had served in the Philippines. I voiced my earnest desire to see the Filipinos given the independence which they had almost won when Dewey sailed into Manila Bay. I quoted Admiral Dewey as saying that the Filipinos were as capable of exercising suffrage as the Cubans. I believed the policy adopted for Cuba should be pursued in the Philippines. It was an anti-imperialistic speech and by inference a condemnation of the policy that had been pursued by our government contrary to the early pledge given.

The military as a whole believed in colonial expansion and wished Uncle Sam to emulate the example of Great Britain by "taking up the white man's burden"—a polite way of describing the exploitation of the weaker races. As an early opponent of the policy of imperialism as practiced in the Philippines and as one who had advocated letting the Filipinos govern their own country, I was not in sympathy with the prevailing opinion among military officers that we should keep these islands. My anti-imperialistic speech found little response, though of course the officers present paid the outward respect due to the Secretary of the Navy. During the dinner, the company was in a merry mood—prohibition was to come later—and some of the diners sang lustily and with much gusto the song, "Damn, Damn, Damn the Filipinos," the words of which were:

I

In the land of dopey dreams—Happy, peaceful Philippines,
Where the bolo man is hiding night and day
Insurrectos steal and lie where Americanos die;
There you hear the soldiers sing this evening lay.

CHORUS:
Damn, Damn, Damn the insurrectos [Filipinos],
Cross-eyed, kakiack ladrones!
Underneath the starry flag civilize them with a krag
And return us to our own beloved homes.

II

Underneath the nipa thatch, where the skinny chickens scratch—
Only refuge after hiking all day long.
When I lay me down to sleep, slithy lizards o'er me creep;
Then you hear the soldiers sing this evening song.

CHORUS:

III

Social customs there are few—
All the ladies smoke and chew
All the men do things the padres say are wrong
But the padres cut no ice for they live on fish and rice
When you hear the soldiers sing this evening song.

CHORUS:

OFFENSIVE TO BRYAN

That song was not the only evidence of disrespect for the known policy of the administration and its leaders. As particularly offensive to Secretary of State Bryan, who had said he wished to launch ships bearing such names as "Friendship," three miniature battleships were borne into the banquet hall bearing the names U. S. S. *Fellowship,* U. S. S. *Friendship,* and U. S. S. *Piffle*—a method of ridiculing an address made a short time before by Bryan in which he pictured metaphorical battleships which he said would be symbols of peace. The Carabaos revealed their delight at the take-off of Bryan and sprang to their feet to applaud the entrance of the battleships, particularly the U. S. S. *Piffle*.

Lack of sympathy for the plan to give the Filipinos their independence was further shown by a moving picture film, "Mr. Colonel and the Governor." It represented an "insurrecto" chased three years by a detachment of U. S. troops only after capture to have the district placed under his command as its governor.

Later at the feast an actor, posing as a Philippine assemblyman entered and announced that he "arrived in Washington to see Hon. William Jenny Bryan to ask him to make some different kind of haste in obtaining for my people their independence." "That honorable gentleman," continued the assemblyman, "so far I have not been able to find, and third assistant doorkeeper say he would not be back indefinitely." The comedy continued:

"Where I find him?" was next question I inquire.

"Mr. Honorable assistant he say, 'Search me.' This seemed too unnecessary. State Department, the way my people understand, is not responsible for lost articles.

"He tell me, howeverly, 'If you go to Chautauqua you might meet his whereabouts.'

"So I did.

"The honorable assistant doorkeeper make no intellectual reply to my next question, but took forth card printed full of words. This is what I read:

" 'Mauch Chunk. 6:30—"Juicing the Grape." '

" 'Hyattsville, 8:08—"Treaty-Making with One Hand." '

" 'Annapolis 10:50—"Battleships I Have Met." '

" 'Norfolk, 1:12—"Why I Need the Money." ' "

COULD NOT BE RESTRAINED

This spirit of contempt for the Filipinos and the song filled me with indignation and I communicated my feeling to Admiral Watson, who was president of the society. He was a mild-mannered gentleman whom I came to esteem very highly and to lean upon. Instead of leading the meeting he let it go its own way. In fact the great bulk of those in attendance were so vigorous in their denunciation of all ideas of Philippine independence that he perhaps could not have restrained them if he had tried. He expressed to me regret at the manifest opposition to the policy to which President Wilson and his party were known to be committed and was sorry at its manifestation, but that was all. He thought the feeling was not shared except by the younger and more vocal members of the party. I did not agree with him but did not think it wise to create a scene by giving expression to my resentment. I resolved that no future Carabao dinner would find me present.

WILSON ORDERS SERIOUS REPRIMAND

When President Wilson read the story of the meeting and sensed its spirit, he was in a state of righteous wrath. I never saw him quite so mad in my life. He asked me about it and I described it and told him that the paper had written it up correctly and that I refrained from publicly rebuking the spirit of the meeting because I thought best to pass it by than have a scene. He refused to pass it by and directed me to send for Watson and convey to him his indignation at the insubordination and insult which members of the Army and Navy had shown. He bade me tell the officers that their conduct was unworthy of their uniform, unworthy of their country, and to direct Watson to have nothing else to do with the Carabao society and if possible to disband the whole organization. He said he would not permit officers of the Army and Navy to be guilty of such wanton insult and outrage to the Filipinos or to show contempt for the policy of their country. I saw Admiral Watson and directed him, if the society could not be abolished, to decline to be president of it. I found the Admiral mortified at the conduct of his fellow officers. He followed the suggestion of the President and resigned his office. There was not another Carabao dinner held in Washington during Wilson's term of office.

The President sent an identical letter to the Secretary of War and the Secretary of the Navy, directing them to administer a "very serious reprimand," and declaring that the officers of the organization had "violated some of the most dignified and sacred traditions of the service." He added:

"I am told that the songs and other amusements of the evening were intended and regarded as fun. What are we to think of officers of the Army and Navy of the United States who think it is 'fun' to bring their official superiors into ridicule and the policies of the government which they are sworn to serve with unquestioning loyalty into contempt? If this is their idea of fun, what is their idea of duty? If they do not hold their loyalty above all silly effervescences of childish wit, what about their profession do they hold sacred?

"My purpose, therefore, in administering this reprimand is to recall the men who are responsible for this lowering of standards to their ideals; to remind them of the high conscience with which they ought to put duty above personal indulgence, and to think of themselves as responsible men and trusted soldiers even while they are among themselves as diners out."

The "rebuke" was delivered by both Secretaries.

APOLOGY IS OFFERED

A committee of the Carabao order wrote a letter expressing the "deepest regret" and added the members are "greatly distressed" that anything in its entertainment should be offensive to its invited guests. They characterized as absurd the public report that the performance was designed to show lack of sympathy for the administration's Philippine policy. There were many articles in the press—some serious and some humorous—about the dinner, the reprimand, and the apology. One writer suggested that the lines of "Damn, Damn, Damn the Filipinos" be changed to read:

> "Kiss, kiss, the little insurrectos,
> Soft-eyed, happy little host,
> Underneath the starry dome,
> In their lonely island home—
> Civilize the precious dears with tea and toast."

"HAIL, KING OF THE VIRGIN ISLANDS"

"Hail, your majesty, Josephus the First," was the greeting I received from Lane at a meeting of the Cabinet after we had bought the Virgin Islands and their government had been turned over to the Secretary of the Navy. He knew my serious objection to "taking" Hawaii, the Philippines, and Panama, and my opposition to the continued occupation of Santo Domingo and Haiti after the fear of German occupation had passed. He had before called me "The Emperor of Haiti" and "His Majesty, the Royal Ruler of Santo Domingo," when those islands were administered by the Navy. Lane was a liberal but was in sympathy with some of Theodore

Roosevelt's expansionist ideas and never agreed with Wilson's "watchful waiting" in Mexico, believing in the use of the Big Stick, though he had nothing in common with those Americans who wished to exploit other countries for their own enrichment. Taking over the Virgin Islands and all in the Caribbean, he doubtless thought, would give protection to the Panama Canal.

The first reference to obtaining the Virgin Islands by Uncle Sam is found in a declaration of the Republican platform in 1896. It stated that "by this purchase of the Danish West Indies, we should secure a proper and much needed Naval station in the West Indies." In 1903 President Theodore Roosevelt, believing Germany had avid eyes on the Virgin Islands, advocated the purchase of those islands as a part of the Panama Canal program. The General Board of the Navy said, "every additional acquisition, the greater the value as against aggression from European bases." It said that without a Naval base in St. Thomas, the Navy would not be able to maintain itself in Porto Rican affairs. We offered Denmark in 1903 the sum of $4,250,000 and Denmark demanded $5,000,000. Fifteen years later, in 1917, with the fear that the islands might fall into European hands, we paid $25,000,000 for them. The reasons for buying them were to prevent the possibility of their falling into the hands of the Germans and the belief that they would afford an ideal Naval base. No thought was given to the wishes of the residents of the islands.

DENMARK THREATENED

In his inside story of the purchase of the Virgin Islands, Lansing's papers published after his death disclose some parts of the negotiations in 1915, which he did not communicate to his Cabinet colleagues at the time. He shows that in the dickering for the purchase of the Islands, the Danish Minister asked Lansing whether, in case Denmark did not agree to make the sale, the United States would feel it necessary to take possession of them. Lansing says he made answer:

"I told the Minister that while I had not in mind such action at the present time ... that I could conceive of circumstances which would compel such an act on our part.

"He asked me what those circumstances were, and I replied that the possible consequence of absorption of Denmark by a great Power would create a situation which it would be difficult to meet other than by occupation of the islands, and such action would undoubtedly cause serious consequences.

"The other circumstance was that if Denmark voluntarily, or under coercion, transferred title to another European Power, which would seek to convert them into a naval base."

I am sure that, in the negotiation for the purchase of the Virgin Islands, Wilson was not informed of Lansing's imperialistic threat. He believed that the "acquisition of the Islands for defense purposes justified us" at a time when one of the warring European countries might seek to obtain them. I never heard—and I am sure his Cabinet colleagues never heard—of Lansing's threat to Denmark to seize the Islands.

GOVERNMENT BY THE NAVY

As soon as there was intimation that the Virgin Islands might be acquired, Lansing complained to the President that Naval officers had "shown activity in connection with them." He was told by Wilson: "You have a talk with the Secretary of the Navy about this. He will see at once what is involved, and will wish, I am sure, to coöperate with you in every way." The President added he was "sure that all his officers are doing now is to keep an eye on what is happening in and about the Islands, and to get as much useful information as possible—both very wise things to do, if wisely done."

The question was debated whether the War Department or the Navy should govern the Islands which were taken over on March 31, 1917. Lansing told me that he favored turning them over to my department because "from the view point of national defense the problems are essentially Naval." He wrote the President he was influenced in his recommendation because of "the marked efficiency shown by Naval officers in the conduct of affairs in Haiti and the Dominican Republic." I told Lansing that if the purchase was to obtain a Naval base, the Navy was the department to be given control, and the Navy would be glad to administer the trust. I appointed Admiral Oliver as first Governor. He was well versed in international law and had served as a legal adviser in neutrality questions after Wilson issued his proclamation of neutrality. I told Lansing we should look forward, when the war ended, to aiding the residents to set up an independent government of their own, our country wishing to retain permanently only a Naval base and prevent the

Islands' falling into the hands of any European power. In the meantime, I advised that while the Islands were administered by the Navy the officers must avoid any of the practices inherent in colonialism. The value of the Islands as a Naval base, as I learned later, had been overestimated, and soon the cost involved was so great that I feared we had bought a gold brick. Referring to the fact that rum was a chief product a friend advised: "Go into the manufacture of rum and you'll make enough money to pay the cost of administration." I could not see myself either as a king or as a manufacturer of rum.

After the war I found that the State Department wished no step taken looking toward future self-government of the Islands. The problems of Naval administration were many. When I discussed some of these with my nephew, whose sister had married a Naval surgeon assigned to duty on the Islands, he facetiously advised that we send Americans over and populate them. "The American population would increase rapidly," he added, "judging by the fact that my sister became the mother of twins and another child within two years."

WE PAID TOO MUCH

Long years afterward when I went to Mexico as Ambassador, I found an agreeable colleague in the diplomatic corps, Honorable Finn Lun, Minister from Denmark, who was born in the Virgin Islands. By way of badinage I rallied him upon Danish overreaching in taking advantage of Uncle Sam's extremity by making him pay $25,000,000 for the Islands in war days when Denmark had offered to take $5,000,000 fifteen years earlier. He replied by saying he was surprised at the moderation of his country, for if it had been a better bargainer it would have compelled us to pay $50,000,000. I asked him often in lighter vein how much he would charge to take the Islands back, seeing they had been a serious drain upon the Federal Treasury. As a matter of fact I have always believed Denmark was glad to unload the unprofitable Islands upon another country.

I never heard any real defense of spending $25,000,000 for the Virgin Islands. (Hoover called them "an effective poor-house"), until in 1940 German troops dominated Denmark. The argument advanced then was that if the Virgin Islands had been Danish, the

United States might have been confronted with the prospect of a German submarine base not far from the Panama Canal.

OVERSTAYED TIME IN HAITI

With war waging in Europe, there was fear that Germany might find bases for U-boats in Haiti and Santo Domingo, and Haiti was killing its presidents rapidly—seven from 1911 to 1915—most of them removed by violence, the last being dragged out of the French Legation and hacked to pieces. Anarchy prevailed. To prevent the possibility of an enemy's obtaining bases in these near-by islands, and protect the approaches to the Panama Canal, the Wilson administration felt that it must act. The job was turned over to the Navy. In August, 1915, I assigned Admiral Caperton and General Waller to the difficult task. General Smedley Butler was given the duty of restoring and preserving order. He performed his job in the most approved Marine fashion. The officers in charge of occupation built roads and made other improvements in Haiti and Santo Domingo and set a high standard of honest administration.

Though the Navy was the agency through which our government carried on, the decisions of policy were made by the State Department, sometimes with and sometimes without consultation or Naval approval. I thought some of their policies were tinged with imperialism and some of them were rather high-handed. The State Department hand-picked the President and General Butler was directed to inaugurate Phillipe Durtiguanave in place of Bobo.

Officially Butler reported, "I won't say we put him in. The State Department might object. Anyway he was put in."

The only way the ratification of the treaty and the Constitution of Haiti, "made in Washington," was brought about was under the militant Marine officer called by admiring Marines "Old Gimlet Eye." And even he could not have done it if he had not been Major General of the Gendarmerie of Haiti and backed by the Army and Navy of the United States.

It was a graphic story, told inimitably, that Smedley related to friends when he returned home—how he got the President to sign the paper dissolving the National Assembly and how there came about a virtual shotgun adoption of the Constitution. Afterwards, but not until Smedley had left Haiti, its President accused him of dissolving the national government by force and without authority.

Fortunately, Butler preserved the order of the dissolution signed by the President, but Haitians declared it was a forgery. My job in Haiti was to furnish the ships and Marines. They acted as policemen. The State Department directed the policy.

In vain I urged, when the Armistice was signed, that our forces should be withdrawn from both Haiti and Santo Domingo and their independence recognized. The Navy had done its job, even carrying out some repugnant policies. The World War over, and the fear ended that these islands would fall into the possession of some European government, with quiet restored, I could find no justification for further imposing our will upon the people of these islands. But Lansing's State Department, more or less imperialistic, did not agree, and Wilson was completely engrossed with fighting to secure the ratification of the League of Nations. I rejoiced later when a commission led the way to doing in Harding's administration what I urged should be done before the end of the Wilson administration.

XVIII

MEXICO—"WATCHFUL WAITING"

THE MOST PRESSING FOREIGN PROBLEM that confronted the Wilson
Administration on its threshold was raised by the murder of
Mexico's popular and idealist patriot, President Francisco I. Madero,
and Vice President Pino Suárez on February 22, 1913, and the
assumption of the presidency by Victoriano Huerta, commander of
the military forces. Huerta cabled President Taft: "I have over-
thrown the Government and henceforth peace and order will reign."
Taft declined to take any steps that might commit or embarrass
the President-elect. Henry Lane Wilson, Ambassador to Mexico,
congratulated Huerta, with whom he was in sympathy, and earnestly sought to secure his recognition, first by Taft and then by
Wilson.

Ambassador Wilson was a strong advocate of the Knox "Dollar
Diplomacy" and had actively abetted Huerta. He had refused to act
when, by coöperating with the Cuban Ambassador, he might have
saved Madero's life by acceding to the appeal of his wife to grant
him permission to be taken to Cuba on a ship provided by the
Cuban government. When President Madero and Vice President
Suárez were murdered, the Ambassador said he was "disposed to
accept the government's version of the affair"—that when being
transferred from prison to the penitentiary they had been shot because they were trying to escape—a story to which informed Mexicans gave no credence. He falsely informed Bryan that 90 per cent
of the people had accepted the Huerta regime, whereas the great
body of the people were in organized and determined revolt against
it. The Ambassador wrote Bryan on March 12, 1913, that "unless
the same type of government as was implanted here by General
Porfirio Díaz is again established, new revolutionary movements
will break forth and general unrest will be renewed"—that is, a
government under which the patrimony of fourteen million Mexicans had been given to favorites or bartered to foreigners. That
sentiment ended the Ambassador, President Wilson declaring: "My

passion is for the submerged 85 per cent of the Republic who are now struggling toward liberty."

President Wilson permitted that faithless official—spokesman of exploiters—to remain in office six months while he was seeking to inform himself of the true situation, confused by conflicting reports. To obtain this information before acting, he sent his personal friend and biographer, William Bayard Hale, to Mexico to make a first-hand study and report; and later he sent Governor Lind as his personal representative. Able attorneys and some personal and influential friends of Wilson, including his beloved schoolmate, honest and honorable Cleveland Dodge, and American investors in Mexico, particularly in oil, and others, urged a *de facto* recognition. Wilson seemed at one time inclined to accept their counsel. But not for long. Colonel House joined in urging Wilson to recognize Huerta. As House was sailing for Europe he was asked what would happen in his absence. He replied: "Nothing will be done while I am gone." He reckoned without appreciation of Wilson's fundamental devotion to the right of all people to select their own officials. This was not the first or last time House misread the mind of Wilson. He shortly sailed to England where he discussed the situation with Foreign Minister Sir Edward Grey. Partly as a result of House's misinterpretation of the President's attitude, his ineptness was followed by Grey's urging Wilson to recognize Huerta as the provisional head of the Mexican Government. Then, as thirty years later in the Roosevelt administration, the petroleum barons in both countries preferred a pliant or purchasable president in Mexico to one determined to observe the law which reserved all subsurface minerals and oils to the people of the country.

BRITAIN RECOGNIZES HUERTA

While Wilson and the Cabinet were seriously debating the policy to pursue in a most difficult situation, Great Britain gave its recognition to Huerta. The British recognized Huerta in a most marked manner by an autographed letter from the King. This was followed by naming Sir Lionel Carden as Minister to Mexico. He was not only an economic imperialist, but was anti-American and pro-oil. British recognition of Huerta was followed by similar action by Spain, China, Italy, Germany, Portugal, Belgium, Norway, Russia, and most Latin American countries.

The imperative question that commanded the serious thought of the Cabinet on May 23 was: Should Huerta be recognized? Wilson and Bryan had come to the firm conviction that it would be wrong from every consideration to recognize the usurper. They were confident that the masses of Mexicans were opposed to him. Garrison saw no way except recognition of Huerta, and Lane, who had been much in Mexico and thought he knew most about it, felt that if Huerta were not recognized Wilson should back some other Mexican for President. Houston said it would be "immoral to recognize Huerta," and I held a like view. The majority sentiment was against recognition. After long study and frequent discussion in the Cabinet, the President stated the conclusion he had reached: "I have to pause and remind myself that I am President of the United States and not of a small group of Americans with vested interests in Mexico."

JOHN LIND'S MISSION

Ex-Governor Lind, of Minnesota, was sent to Mexico to secure an agreement upon immediate cessation of fighting, security for a free election in which all should agree to take part, the consent of Huerta not to be a candidate, and the promise by all parties to abide by the result of the election and loyally support the officials chosen by the people. It was an ideal goal. If John Lind had possessed every art and talent and genius of all the diplomats of a century, he could not have secured the consent of Huerta to eliminate himself, or persuade Carranza or Villa to lay down their arms. The noble purpose failed, but John Lind, earnestly desirous of helping the people of Mexico and securing good relations between Mexico and the United States, did everything that a patriotic, upright, downright, forthright, honorable man could do. Lind's story of his experiences on that mission, in his autobiography, is proof of his ability and resourcefulness. One of the things that irritated Lind was that Lord Cowdray "controlled" the Huerta government. Lind believed "the differences between the contending factions would have been adjusted but for the encouragement Huerta received from European governments, which, he said had "supplied the means by which Huerta has attempted to force himself upon this country." Even Lord Bryce wrote Wilson, "Nothing can be done from outside to better Mexican conditions except at a dangerous cost to the benevolent neighbor." He said that Wilson's policy was an "impossible ideal." Even Homer nods!

MOBILE ADDRESS FORESHADOWS "GOOD NEIGHBOR POLICY"

As the time drew near for holding the Southern Commercial Congress at Mobile, Alabama, in October, 1913, its officers planned to make it a Pan American gathering and requested me to ask President Wilson to make the principal address. He accepted and invited me to accompany him. The stress of legislation, the charting of the new ship of state, and Wilson's absorption in grave problems had given me little opportunity, aside from Cabinet meetings, for personal talks with him. I was happy to have the companionship and intimate talks with my chief. We talked of men and measures as we sat in his compartment on the train, but mainly of the new Pan American policy of refusing recognition to military usurpers in Pan America, who by the use of force, sometimes paid for by American exploiters, kept these countries in the throes of internal warfare. He had not written his Mobile address, which was to be an historic one and which was awaited with interest all over Pan America. As we travelled in intimate companionship, the President began to think aloud, as was his wont. He loved to do that with a sympathetic friend. "In my Mobile address," he would say, "I have a mind to say" . . . and then he would make me the sole auditor of some of the best parts of what became a notable declaration. When he had finished, he asked me what I thought of this or that utterance.

In his audience at Mobile, October 2, 1913, were a number of Pan American diplomats who were eager to learn from his own lips the policy the new President would pursue toward their countries. They were more than satisfied—so thrilled that with the great audience they joined in applause that had reverberations all over the hemisphere. They were particularly gratified when he declared: "I want to take this occasion to say that the United States will never again seek one additional foot of territory by conquest," and stated that the Latin-American states "have had harder bargains driven with them in the matter of loans than any other people in the world," and "I rejoice in nothing so much as in the prospect that they will now be emancipated from these conditions." He added, as he unfolded the New Freedom he incarnated, "Human rights, national integrity, and opportunity as against material interest is the issue which we now have to face." Here was the foreshadowing of the Good Neighbor policy. I confess when it came my turn to speak, I could express only profound satisfaction that another Monroe had blazed the way for American solidarity based upon recognition of the equal sovereignty of all the countries, great and small. Wilson's speech foreshadowed his course in the then acute Mexican situation, which was to be a thorn in his side for many months.

"WATCHFUL WAITING"

John Lind, still in Mexico was urging a strong hand. Wilson, confident that Huerta could not hold out, committed himself to the policy of "Watchful Waiting." Lind visited Wilson at Pass Christian at Christmas in 1913 to confer with him. When Wilson returned to Washington he found a storm of criticism and ridicule of his policy of "watchful waiting." In the Cabinet Garrison and Lane were pronounced for more vigorous action. Bryan and Wilson and other members of the Cabinet understood what employment of force meant and were averse to its use.

In order to be rid of Huerta and end the revolution, Lane urged Wilson to select some strong man in Mexico, set him up as President, and get behind him. He insisted that only in this way could Huerta be driven from power. The idea possessed Lane so fully that one day, at a private luncheon he gave, he urged it forcibly to several of his colleagues. He advocated that we should counsel together as to the advice given the President. Bryan was not present. Lane stressed the necessity of selecting a man who could command the confidence of leading citizens of Mexico, and asked us to join in recommending to Wilson that Eduardo Iturbide, a relative of the former Emperor of that name, be selected as President of Mexico and supported by the American government. Lane's idea was that the foreign investors and diplomats and big business and the Catholic hierarchy would hail the selection of Iturbide. He said Iturbide was a clean man who knew the country, and that if he were known to have the backing of the United States, the Carranza, Villa, Zapata, and other revolutionists, sensing they could not win against the United States, would try to make terms with Iturbide, who was in Washington at the time, whether by arrangement or not, I do not know.

My reaction, like that of most Cabinet members present, was that the revolution in Mexico was deep-seated. The people would fight on until an entirely new character of government came in, with a

FROM CLEVELAND TO WILSON

Upper left, Hoke Smith, Secretary of the Interior, Senator. *Upper right,* Daniel C. Roper, U. S. Census official, Commissioner of Revenue under Wilson, leader in the 1916 campaign, Secretary of Commerce under Roosevelt. *Lower left,* Charles S. Hamlin, Massachusetts, Assistant Secretary of the Treasury under Cleveland, Wilson, and Roosevelt, chairman of the Federal Reserve Board. *Lower right,* Clifford K. Berryman, draughtsman in U. S. Patent Office under Cleveland, later cartoonist on the *Washington Star* and an institution in Washington.

NORTH CAROLINA LEADERS IN THE WILSON ADMINISTRATION

Upper left, Furnifold M. Simmons, chairman of Senate Finance Committee. *Upper right,* Lee S. Overman, chairman of the Senate Rules Committee and acting chairman of the Judiciary Committee. *Lower left,* Claude Kitchin, chairman of the House Ways and Means Committee. *Lower right,* Edward W. Pou, chairman of the House Rules Committee, who served in Congress from 1901 to 1933.

division of the great estates, a better system of labor laws, and an end of a policy under which 85 per cent of the people were illiterate and desperately poor while the natural resources were largely monopolized by foreigners. I had expressed that opinion several times in the Cabinet, and I so stated at the luncheon, adding that I did not think the President would or ought to try to name the Chief Executive of Mexico—that he had said the Mexicans had the right to determine what character of government they should have. I quoted Wilson's words: "It is none of my business and none of your business how long they take to determine it. The liberty, if they can get it, and God speed them in getting it—is theirs."

None of us thought the suggestion of putting in Iturbide as President of Mexico would find favor with Wilson. I told Lane that however worthy Señor Iturbide might be, the Mexican people had not forgotten the tyrannies of the old Iturbide, who, having himself illegally crowned Emperor, had betrayed and executed Mexican patriots. I added that the name Iturbide would not rally the men who were resolved to put out Huerta who was following Iturbide's tyrannies. If Lane ever presented this suggestion to the President I did not hear of it. Afterwards when I was entertained at the home of Eduardo Iturbide in Mexico City, I found him an agreeable gentleman, and my wife—a good judge—held Señora Iturbide in friendly esteem.

AN AMERICAN WISHES TO BE ENGLISHMAN

All these anxious days I was keeping Naval ships in Mexican waters for the protection of Americans. Several were on duty in the Panuco River at Tampico, the centre of the chief oil district. Admiral Mayo, in command, had ordered all except one to move into other Mexican waters, deeming one sufficient to bring out Americans or prevent injury to them. There was violent protest from a group of Americans against the withdrawal of any ships. A delegation of Americans living in Tampico came to Washington to ask the President to reverse the order, saying they were being left without the protection to which they were entitled. The President referred them to me, and they came over to the Navy Department. They had talked to the Washington correspondents and a crowd jammed the office of the Secretary of the Navy. The spokesman, in strident tones, demanded that more ships be ordered to Tampico for protection. I explained the other uses for the ships, and said that we had enough in Mexican waters to afford protection to Americans there or to bring home those who wished to return.

When I told the spokesman, who was indignant because a ship which had been moored in front of his property, had been ordered away to take Americans to a place of safety, he flew into a rage, and literally shouted: "And so you refuse to give protection to an American citizen. Up to this hour I have been proud of my citizenship but now I am ashamed of it. I wish to God I were an Englishman for that country protects the person and property of its citizens in any part of the world where they reside."

He continued to give vent to his indignation. When he had exhausted his tirade, I quietly asked: "How many years have you lived in Mexico?" I think he said twenty, "and all that time I have continued to be an American citizen and now am denied protection to which I am entitled." I informed him that it had cost the Navy many thousand dollars to keep that ship in front of his property and that the only way the Navy got the money to meet this expense was by taxation of its citizens, mainly through the income tax. I added: "Please show me your income tax receipt before you denounce the country of which you claim to be a citizen." He literally snorted his wrath, and declared "I will not stay here to be insulted!" and marched out of the Department.

MAYO DEMANDS APOLOGY AND SALUTE

When Admiral Fletcher was ordered to Mexican waters to await developments, I broke all Naval tradition by giving permission for his wife to go with him on the *Dolphin,* assigned for the use of the Secretary of the Navy. Some time afterwards that ship suddenly came into prominence through an incident that grew into an issue. At that time, when Mayo was in command of Naval ships in Mexico, the *Dolphin* was anchored in the Panuco River off Tampico. It was believed there was danger from the troops of either Huerta or Carranza, who were in that neighborhood. On the 9th day of April, 1914, Paymaster Conn of the *Dolphin* and seven unarmed men landed at the Iturbide Bridge with a whaleboat to get supplies which had been purchased for the ship. While engaged in loading the boat, the paymaster was arrested by an officer and a squad of men of Huerta's army. Two of the men were taken into custody. This, too, though the boat was carrying, both at her bow and stern, the flag of the United States. The officer was proceeding up the street with his prisoners when an officer of higher rank ordered him to face about and return to the landing and await orders. Within an hour and a half from the time of arrest, orders were received by the commander of the Huerta forces for the release of Americans, and General Zaragoza communicated his regrets through a subordinate officer. He said the Colonel who had ordered the arrest was ignorant of the laws of war and was simply carrying out instructions to allow no boats whatever at the warehouse dock.

Mayo sent an ultimatum to General Zaragoza demanding a more formal apology and a disavowal of the act, together with an assurance that the officer responsible for it receive severe punishment. He also demanded: "You publicly hoist the American flag in a prominent position on shore and salute it with twenty-one guns, which salute will be duly returned by this ship." A time limit of twenty-four hours was set for the salute to the flag. Huerta sent an expression of regret with assurance that the Colonel ordering the arrest would, if found guilty, be punished. He asked that the ultimatum be withdrawn.

Bryan, not satisfied with Huerta's note, insisted that the demands be complied with, but extended the time to April 13. Huerta refused to be moved. An unfounded report gained currency that a prominent oil official convinced Mayo that the Huertistas had conspired as to the course pursued toward the *Dolphin* and the subsequent course, to test whether Americans would accept a half-hearted apology for an affront instead of the customary salute. Mayo, doubtless on his own knowledge of conditions, reached the conclusion that unless he used the iron hand at the first wrong, the Huertistas would feel free to ignore American rights. He was not the man to be influenced by others. He had a mind and a will of his own, as well as courage. My estimate of Admiral Mayo was conveyed to him and the country he served honorably when he retired for age in 1920 in this telegram to him:

"It is a matter of congratulation that while under your command the United States fleet reached its highest efficiency and made its largest contribution in the World War. When we entered the war, largely due to your direction, the fleet was in its highest state of readiness. Your service abroad was not only recognized by your countrymen but by naval leaders of the allied nations, and contributed much toward hastening the adoption of measures which increased the allied offensive."

TO DISCREDIT WILSON ADMINISTRATION

When the news of the arrest and the ultimatum for the salute reached the Navy Department it seriously disturbed me. I felt strongly that, inasmuch as the Admiral was in easy reach of Washington by wireless and telegraph, he should not have issued an ultimatum without the authority of the government. He acted upon the old-time Naval practice which guided Perry in Japan and other Naval officers in foreign waters. Of necessity, without cable or wireless, a Naval officer is sometimes compelled to act upon his judgment, being unable to get directions from the Secretary of the Navy. But when the wireless and cable enable him to get into quick communication with his government, there is an indisposition on the part of some officers to surrender their diplomatic decisions. There is still adherence to a theory that "strength of the Naval forces determines diplomatic policy." That was the principle that was not questioned when the American ships at Tripoli and Tunis in 1805 determined the successes of treaty negotiations with those recalcitrant States. Like conditions prevailed when Commodore Kearny in the *Constellation* concluded the treaty inaugurating the open door with China. Mayo, versed in Naval history, followed the old-time precedent when he gave the time limit ultimatum at Tampico.

Certain Americans residing in Tampico later alleged falsely that Mayo had been ordered to abandon those citizens who needed protection because of the contemplated landing at Vera Cruz. Mayo in 1916 said:

> "It is a misrepresentation to say that American citizens in Tampico were deserted in an hour of imminent danger.... It is not true that American forces were compelled to seek refuge under the colors of a foreign flag. The fact that three thousand Americans were taken out of the city without loss of life or destruction of property is a result that speaks for itself."

This statement of Mayo was called forth by an organized propaganda to discredit the Wilson administration. As Mayo was an upstanding and honest officer, with no political bias, his statement was received as a complete refutation of the slanderous charges, and was accepted after the false charges had been exploited during the 1916 campaign. The American people can often be stampeded during a hot political campaign but not afterwards.

WILSON UPHOLDS MAYO

President Wilson was at White Sulphur Springs, with Mrs. Wilson, who was ill, when Mayo's demand reached Washington. I talked the matter over with Bryan. I found he thought that under the circumstances Huerta must be made to understand our determination to compel his abdication and that Huerta was capable of wishing to insult the flag and seeking to avoid personal responsibility. He communicated the incident to the President and in so doing made the comment: "I do not see that Mayo could have done otherwise." When Bryan's dispatch was received by Wilson, he was quoted as saying: "I have known for months that some such thing could happen—it was inevitable, in fact."

Huerta was making one proposal after another in the days following Mayo's demands in order to save his face. None were accepted. On Sunday night, Bryan, Garrison, and I were in conference long after one o'clock, keeping in touch with the President by long-distance telephone. We all felt that the various propositions Huerta was making through the American Embassy were intended to force some action that was tantamount to a recognition of his government, and to this we were opposed. I called upon the General Board of the Navy for an opinion and it strongly upheld Mayo's action. After communicating with the President, I directed Admiral Badger to arrange for the departure of all available ships at Hampton Roads, with a regiment of Marines, to Mexico. The State Department sent a sharp note to Huerta to impress him with "the very serious character of the present situation." The President was determined to uphold Mayo. No concessions were made.

I had never seen the President so disturbed. He told us that in his Sunday hike over the hills he had been oppressed with the thought that he might be the cause of the loss of lives of many young men. Would he be justified? Just before the Cabinet adjourned he said in as serious a way, as if he had been in the pulpit: "I hope those of you who believe in prayer will invoke divine guidance during the interval before our next meeting."

After the meeting, besieged by correspondents, Wilson told them it was "an issue between this government and a person calling himself the Provisional President of Mexico, whose right to call himself such we never have recognized in any way." And he added that it was "possible to deal with a dictator by the Navy without precipitating war."

After the Cabinet had decided that we should stand by Mayo's ultimatum, Wilson had a conference with leading members of the Senate Committee on Foreign Affairs. At the next meeting of the Cabinet, he reported his satisfactory talk with them. They were hot, ready to pass any law desired. "I'd make them salute the flag if we had to blow up the whole place," said Chilton. "If our flag is ever run up in Mexico it will never come down," said Borah, who added, "This is the beginning of the march of the United States to the Panama Canal." Wilson said he told the Senators he had a right to act without specific authority of Congress but that, as it was in session, he felt it would be best to ask specific authority.

In the Cabinet meeting Wilson cited the American bombardment of Greytown, Nicaragua, in 1854, as authority. Lodge had said that the President undoubtedly had the power to act to take possession of a port for the protection of American lives and property, without action by Congress, giving as precedent the Boxer Rebellion. All agreed that it was best to accept the President's suggestion and secure the specific authority. However, before doing so, seeing that Huerta was stalling for time, Wilson decided, on April 18, to issue an ultimatum of his own, in which Huerta was told that unless he announced his willingness to carry out Mayo's demand by 6:00 P.M. April 19, Wilson would lay the matter before Congress the next day, "with a view to taking such action as may be necessary to enforce the respect due the national flag."

Congress promptly voted approval to "the use of armed forces of the United States in such ways and to such extent as may be necessary to enforce its demands." In his address to Congress, Wilson had said, "There can be no thought of aggression," and he reiterated that "the people of Mexico are entitled to settle their own domestic affairs in their own way." Huerta stalled, making impossible conditions, and the salute was never returned.

NO MORE ULTIMATUMS

I found that in the State and Navy Departments I was almost alone in feeling that Mayo, when apologies were promptly offered, should have accepted them. President Wilson did not like the ultimatum at first—in fact, he was disturbed over the fact that Mayo's ultimatum had created a situation that might prove embarrassing. However, when a few days thereafter a Mexican censor withheld an official dispatch from the State Department to the American Embassy in Mexico, and other unfriendly acts were reported, the President put all these incidents together; and when he returned to Washington and discussed at a Cabinet meeting the course of action that should be pursued (he returned to Washington the day Mayo's time limit expired—April 13—with no salute), he said he felt that there was no course to pursue but to back up Mayo; that failure to do so would hearten Huerta and weaken our position. Bryan and the rest of the Cabinet agreed. I agreed, but expressed the opinion that no ultimatums should be sent by a Naval officer without the approval of the Commander in Chief when time permitted obtaining his views. Houston and some others of the Cabinet agreed with my position. "I do not think," Houston said, "that a military or Naval commander should have the right to take action which might lead nations into war without specific directions from the Chief Executive." The President had expressed that opinion, but felt that under the circumstances the only course left open was to enforce Mayo's demand. I agreed that we could not let Mayo down. However, I still strongly believed that Mayo should have accepted the apology of the Mexican Colonel, or should have cabled the full particulars with his recommendation and requested instructions. A long time after (September 15, 1916), when it would not be construed as a rebuke to Mayo, I changed U. S. Navy Regulations by inserting in Article 1648 the following:

"Due to the ease with which the Navy Department can be communicated with from all parts of the world, no commander in chief, division commander, or commanding officer, shall issue an ultimatum to the representative of any foreign Government, or demand the performance of any service from any such representative that must be executed within a limited time, without first communicating with the Navy Department, except in extreme cases where such action is necessary to save life."

NAVAL FORCE AT VERA CRUZ

While the flag incident was being discussed, there flared up a situation at Vera Cruz, much more serious, that put the Tampico salute issue in the background. Soon Vera Cruz was the centre of interest. On the night before the Navy ships were ordered to Vera Cruz, there was a conference at the White House of the President, the Secretary of State, the Secretary of War, and the Secretary of the Navy. News had poured in of the activity of the various revolutionary forces: under Villa in the north, Zapata around Cuernavaca to the Pacific Ocean, and Carranza in the east and northeast and near the Gulf. All of the revolutionary leaders were against Huerta but were not united. The threat of the destruction of the oil wells in the vicinity of Tampico gave concern to Garrison, and the military advisers saw no solution except in a declaration of war against Mexico. I think some wanted later to annex all the country to Panama to the domain of the United States. John Lind thought a serious show of force was the only thing that would bring Huerta to his senses. Once he advised taking all the sea-coast places on the Gulf. Wilson, Bryan, and I wished to get rid of Huerta without war, so that Mexicans, freed from the old feudalism, could work out the destiny of their country with their own chosen leaders. There was agreement that a strong Naval force should guard the eastern coast of Mexico, ready for any emergency. That was why Badger was ordered to move the fleet south.

HISTORIC CONFERENCE AT DEAD OF NIGHT

We adjourned late at night with serious forebodings. I was not, therefore, greatly surprised when some hours later, about 2:30 in the early morning of April 21, Private Secretary Tumulty called me on the White House telephone and informed me that Bryan had just received a serious message which he had communicated to the President. It was from Consul Canada at Vera Cruz to the effect that the German ship *Ypiranga* was approaching Vera Cruz loaded with 200 machine guns and 15,000,000 cartridges, and would arrive that morning about ten o'clock, consigned to Huerta. Consul Canada said there were thirty cars on the pier to load the munitions direct from the steamer and that trains with ten cars each would be sent out over the Mexican Railway as soon as loaded and there was plenty of coal and oil in the railroad yard. He added this significant statement: "The General in command states he will not fight but will leave with all soldiers and rolling stock tomorrow, tearing up the track behind him." Bryan said to me: "I have read the message to the President and have recommended that the Navy act to prevent the landing of arms."

It was at dead of night—all Washington sleeping quietly—and in telephone conversations Wilson, Bryan, and I were confronted with a situation demanding instant decision and action. When Bryan had advised that the Navy act to prevent landing, Wilson said: "Of course you understand, Mr. Bryan, what drastic action might mean in our relations to Mexico."

Bryan answered: "I thoroughly appreciate this, Mr. President, and fully considered it before telephoning." The President's voice showed his distress and hesitation.

"What do you think should be done, Daniels?" was the question the President addressed to me over the telephone.

I had no time for reflection. I replied: "I do not think that the munitions should be allowed to fall into Huerta's hands. I can wire Admiral Fletcher to take the customs house and prevent the shipment being landed. I think that is the proper course to pursue."

"Have you considered all the implications?" he asked.

I replied in the affirmative and said that if the munitions reached Huerta it would strengthen his hands, add to the loss of lives in Mexico, and the very arms nearing Mexico might be turned against American soldiers if Huerta's power were increased. It was this fear which controlled the decision. After further talk with Bryan the President called me again and said: "Daniels, give the order to Fletcher to take the customs house at Vera Cruz." Not a moment was lost and I dispatched this message immediately:

"Washington, D. C.
"April 21, 1914

"Fletcher,
"Vera Cruz, Mexico.
"Seize custom house. Do not permit war supplies to be delivered to Huerta government or to any other party.

"DANIELS"

The conclusion reached by the telephone conversation between the President, the Secretary of State, and the Secretary of the Navy, with only Private Secretary Tumulty as the witness, was not as casual as its relation might indicate. For months in Cabinet meetings, and in conferences with Wilson, Bryan, and Garrison, all together or separately, every phase of the situations that might arise had been under consideration. Plans had been made by the Navy for such eventuality, and Admiral Badger had his fleet in readiness, while Admirals Fletcher and Mayo in Mexican waters kept the Navy Secretary advised of every situation by radio.

NOT A MILITARY SECRET

We learned something as the result of that night's telephone conversation that was to be invaluable during the World War: It was that nothing can be kept secret that is discussed over the telephone. As I was walking up the steps of the Navy Department the next morning, I was joined by my friend Edward M. Hood of the Associated Press, who covered the Navy Department. Everybody called him "Eddie" as a term of affection.

"I hope you had a good night's rest," he began the conversation.

"I slept like a top," I replied.

"Did you have nothing to disturb your rest?" he asked, and before I could answer, he continued: "I know everything that was said over the telephone last night: what Bryan said to Wilson, what Wilson said to you, about your telegram to Fletcher. Has Fletcher taken the customs house at Vera Cruz? I have not printed anything about the important incident or repeated it to any soul. It would not be patriotic for me to use it until I have your permission."

I saw he knew what he was talking about, and only his soundness as an American had saved us from premature publication. Some journalists would have scored a "scoop" and not reflected upon the possible injury.

"How did you learn so much?" I asked.

"You must not ask a journalist the source of his secret information," he said, "for as a fellow-journalist you know I cannot disclose it."

How did Hood know what was said over the telephone? He could have gotten it only through a telephone operator. They are among the most trustworthy people in the world, but I had a reporter once who was kept informed of tips by a lady operator on anything that might give him a story. Did Hood get his information by such a route? Or how?

The result of this incident was that I recommended to the President that a special telephone line be installed by which he could talk with the Secretary of State, the Secretary of War, and the Secretary of the Navy in the confidence that nobody would listen in. It was done, and many conferences were held over that private wire in the crucial days of the World War. I could go in a little room adjoining my office, shut the door, and impart the most secret information to the President knowing that there would be no leak.

WILSON PROFOUNDLY DISTRESSED

The morning after the telephone conference and the critical decision, I was early at the Department after a sleepless and anxious night. I had a talk with Private Secretary Tumulty, who was as much shaken as I was over the situation. He said:

"After you and Bryan left the phone, and you had sent the fateful message, I found President Wilson was in a profound state of distress. 'What do you think of the action?' he asked. I told him that under the circumstances it seemed to me that there was no other course to take. 'It is too bad,' he responded, 'but we could not allow that cargo to land. The Huertistas intend to use these guns on our own boys. It is hard to take action of this kind. I have tried my utmost to keep us out of this mess, but we seem to be now on the brink of war, and there is no alternative.' His voice was husky. I saw by his words and his manner that he felt the deep solemnity of the situation he was handling while the people of America, whose spokesman he was, were quietly sleeping in their beds, unaware and unmindful of the grave import of the message which was already on its way to Vera Cruz."

I saw that Tumulty was as much disturbed as the President. He went on to say:

"I could not close my eyes. The telephone conversation and the thought of what lay ahead prevented sleep. I said to myself as, clad only in my pajamas, I sat alone reviewing the incidents of the night: 'I have been privileged to sit in while over the telephone three men, pacifists at heart, have gathered about a phone, and without hesitation agreed upon a course of action which may result in bringing two nations into war.' It seemed so strange and I reflected that those three men—Wilson, Bryan, and Daniels, had been criticised and lampooned throughout the country as being pacifists, taking this war-like action. I said to myself: 'Wilson, Bryan, and Daniels are pacifists no longer, but plain, simple men, bent upon discharging the duty they owe to their country and utterly disregarding their own personal feelings of antagonism to every phase of war.' "

During the conversation Tumulty asked: "Do you think the Huertistas will resist? Is it war?"

I told him that I both thought and hoped not, that the Naval force at Vera Cruz was so powerful that effective resistance would be impossible, and that we had reason to believe that the commander of Huerta's forces, General Maas, would not permit his men to get in range of our guns. I based my statement on what General Maas had some time before said to the American Consul at Vera Cruz. If there was no resistance, the Mexicans would be convinced that we were their friends, as was the fact except as to the Huertistas. I knew we were concerned only to help Mexicans escape from the Huerta attempt to perpetuate the Díaz rule of feudalism. Because of what General Maas had said to Consul Canada, there was foundation for Bryan's belief that the order to Fletcher would not result in bloodshed. I shared that hope, and I am sure the President did, for when the first news came that four Americans were killed and twenty wounded, it affected him as deeply as if it had touched his very own. "He was positively shaken," was the report of a correspondent who interviewed the President after the tragic news came. Before the news was received in the early evening (the resistance began at Vera Cruz at 11:30), Bryan and Garrison and Lansing and I were in conference with the President at the White House. At that time we fully expected that the landing would be effected without serious trouble.

When I went over to the White House that morning, I was subjected to a barrage of questions going and coming, and if I gave no news the journalists would print—"Today the Secretary of the Navy called at the White House and held a long conference with the President, and, while no information was given out, it is practically certain they discussed so-and-so"—the "so-and-so" being a matter that by its very nature was highly confidential.

VERA CRUZ CUSTOMS HOUSE TAKEN

My message to seize the customs house went swiftly and Fletcher acted with celerity. The *Ypiranga* was stopped outside by Fletcher. He seized the customs house without any attack by the Huerta forces. It seemed for a time that the action would be taken without resistance. General Maas had withdrawn the army from Vera Cruz, out of range of the guns of the American battleships, in accordance with his previous statement to the American Consul: "It would be suicide to us and invite the destruction of the city for me to attempt to prevent the landing." But the high-spirited young naval cadets in the naval barracks undertook the defense of the city, and a number lost their lives, the Navy Academy being destroyed. Something like two hundred young Mexican naval cadets had barricaded themselves in the massive stone structure built like a fort. It was not until the guns from the *Prairie* spoke destructively that the building was reduced. The cadets refused to surrender, going to their death in the belief that the Americans wished to conquer their country. Our sturdy sailors and marines, saddened at the sight, removed the wounded to first-aid stations and reverently laid the bodies of the dead Mexican cadets in the refectory, paying tribute to their deathless devotion to their country.

Encouraged by their act, and sharing their resentment at the action of General Maas in withdrawing the protection of the army from Vera Cruz, citizens from residences along the principal streets fired from upper chambers of the houses, killing a number of American sailors and marines. This precipitated a clash, which resulted in the death of 126 and the wounding of 195 Mexicans and 19 Americans killed and 71 wounded.

Admiral Badger arrived on April 22 with his powerful fleet. As soon as order was restored Fletcher issued a proclamation addressed to the Alcalde, Jefe Politico, and the citizens of Vera Cruz "enjoining upon all the inhabitants and property owners to prevent firing by individuals from the shelter of their houses." The desire was expressed that "the civil officials of Vera Cruz continue in the peaceful pursuit of their occupation." He said the Naval forces would "not interfere with the administration of the civil affairs of Vera Cruz more than is necessary for the purpose of maintaining a condition of law and order and to enforce sanitary conditions." Consul Canada found the Alcalde barricaded in his house, all other officers having fled with General Maas when he left the city.

TRIBUTE TO AMERICANS KILLED AT VERA CRUZ

The tragedy of the killings weighed heavily on Wilson. Later, when I asked him to go to New York and deliver a tribute to the Americans who were killed in the Vera Cruz landing, he said he would regard it as "a solemn and painful duty." In a sense we both felt responsibility and regret. He turned a deaf ear, and I rejoiced that he did so, to the fears of House, Grayson, and Tumulty that he might be in danger if he exposed himself in New York. There had been threatening letters which alarmed the secret service men. Wilson could not be deterred, saying with Calvinistic finality: "I am immortal until my time comes."

I can never forget that day. New York suspended all business as we rode behind the coffins of the nineteen dead men through streets jammed with hundred of thousands of silent and respectful people, to the Navy Yard. Each coffin was borne on a gun caisson, with sailors on either side and with Marines marching in the rear as sentinels of their dead comrades. Tolling bells of the churches and the funeral march added to the solemnity of a whole city, uncovered and silent. Mayor Mitchel paid a brief tribute as he laid wreaths on the coffins at the City Hall. Wilson's thoughts as we rode through New York were on the scene at Vera Cruz and the tragedy of it. He said in mournful tones that he hoped the sacrifice of their lives would save the lives of many others who might have fallen if the guns had reached Huerta, but the tragedy of it all rested on him as a pall. He had not written the address he was to make, but repeated to me a few of the ideas in his mind, emphasizing the reference toward the close which was most commented on in the press:

"I never went into battle; I never was under fire; but I fancy that there are some things just as hard to do as to go under fire. I fancy it is just as hard to do your duty when men are sneering at you as when they are shooting at you. When they shoot at you, they can take your natural life; when they sneer at you, they can wound your living heart."

The newspapers interpreted that sentence as referring to the volley of harsh pellets being thrown at him for his Mexican policy of "watchful waiting." And undoubtedly that was the correct interpretation, for it hurt his proud spirit, all the more because his policy had not at that time borne its fruit of the peace which was his goal.

At the Navy Yard, where there had gathered the relatives of the dead men and a great multitude of sympathetic men and women, I presided at the ceremony. My heart was full and sad. I had paid my tribute to the noble youths at the time of their death. It was for their Commander in Chief that day to voice the nation's tribute. I contented myself with calling the roll of the Republic's fallen heroes—whose names showed that some were of German, Irish, English, and Southern-European origin—and introducing the President.

The opening words of the Commander in Chief caught the approval of the multitude, particularly this immortal sentence:

"Here in the roster of the Navy—the list of the men, officers, and enlisted men and marines—men who have suddenly been lifted into a firmament of memory, where we will always see their names shine, not because they called upon us to admire them, but because they served us, without asking any questions and in the performance of a duty which is laid upon us as well as upon them."

I was thrilled to the core of my being as I, and all who heard him, involuntarily felt there were nineteen glorious stars added to the galaxy in the sky. I was glad he took occasion to define the country's attitude: "We have gone down to Mexico to serve mankind if we can find out the way. We do not want to fight the Mexicans. We want to serve the Mexicans if we can."

ADMIRAL FLETCHER A STATESMAN

Shortly after Fletcher had taken the customs house, he made it plain that America's only purpose in sending ships to Mexico was to prevent the munitions from falling into the hands of Huerta, and to oust the Huerta government. In this difficult task, in which he demonstrated that he had statesman-like qualities, Fletcher won the respect of all Americans, particularly those who had refugeed there from Mexico City, and of Mexicans who sensed his spirit of justice and respect for their rights, and he also won the commendation of President Wilson. In recognition of his ability, he was later named by me, after consultation with the President and with his approval, Commander in Chief of the fleet. Badger assumed com mand and continued this policy with wise administration until the Army of Occupation replaced the Navy.

Huerta, taking the position that the landing of American sailors at Vera Cruz was "understood as the initiation of war against Mexico," sent Chargé d'Affaires O'Shaughnessy his passports. With his family O'Shaughnessy reached Vera Cruz on a special train. Bryan directed the Spanish Minister to inform the Mexican authorities that "war has not been declared." But the break between the two Republics was complete.

Having prevented the munitions from reaching Huerta at Vera Cruz, I felt that when the ship sailed for United States ports the danger of munitions falling into his hands had been averted. The information I received was that on April 26 the agents of the Hamburg-American Line had been instructed to take the arms back to Germany.

The German Ambassador in Washington, when he learned that Admiral Fletcher had notified the *Ypiranga* not to leave the harbor at Vera Cruz with munitions of war consigned to General Huerta (the Admiral was complying with the spirit of his general orders, not to let the munitions fall into the hands of Huerta) called at the State Department and protested that as a state of war did not exist the Admiral had no authority to hold a German ship or control the disposition of the cargo. The lawyers of the State Department decided that the German contention was well founded, and the movements of the German ships could not be controlled by the United States. I felt a sense of bafflement at that decision. I could find no effective answer when the opponents of the administration based their criticism of the Vera Cruz landing on the ground that the Navy took the customs house at Vera Cruz for one of two reasons: (1) Either to enforce a salute of the flag, or (2) to prevent the landing of munitions from the German ship, and had obtained neither the salute of the flag nor prevented the munitions reaching Huerta. I felt a sense of frustration and indignation when I later learned that the *Ypiranga,* after leaving Vera Cruz and going to Mobile and New Orleans and landing refugees, had returned to

Upper left, Admiral Frank F. Fletcher, Commander-in-Chief of the U. S. Navy. Commanded Naval forces at Vera Cruz (Naval Records and Library). *Upper right,* Admiral Henry T. Mayo, Commander-in-Chief of the U. S. Fleet in World War, who demanded a salute from Huerta in Tampico (NR & L). *Below,* General John J. Pershing and General Smedley Butler. Pershing commanded the American forces in Mexico during the period of "Watchful Waiting." Butler was sent to Mexico City as a spy after the Navy landed at Vera Cruz.

Upper left, Carter Glass, chairman of House Committee, who led the fight for the Federal Reserve System. *Upper right,* Robert L. Owen, chairman of Senate Committee, led Senate fight for Federal Reserve System (Brown Brothers). *Lower left,* John H. Bankhead, Senator from Alabama (Brown Brothers). *Lower right,* Thomas S. Martin, of Virginia, president pro tem of Senate and chairman of Appropriations Committee (Brown Brothers).

Mexico, and the munitions in the latter part of May had been un-loaded at the port of Puerto Mexico, and presumably reached the Huerta forces. It was to the Navy like a blow on the head. Our chief incentive in seizing the customs house was to prevent the 200 machine guns and 15,000,000 cartridges from becoming available to the unspeakable Huerta. When, therefore, after we thought the small sacrifice of life was justified by the greater sacrifices that would have followed if these munitions should fall into the hands of Huerta's troops, diplomatic usage had been invoked, without my knowledge, and Germany had demanded and obtained the right to land them at another port, I felt a sinking of the heart. Of course, in all matters pertaining to diplomacy and international law, the State Department was supreme. I was impotent.

The attitude of the State Department, formed without consultation with the Navy, which I felt was not wise under the circumstances, was stated in the following memorandum concerning the *Ypiranga*:

"MEMORANDUM

"The Secretary of State called on His Excellency the German Ambassador at 7:15, April 21, 1914, to say that Admiral Fletcher had, today, through a misunderstanding exceeded his instructions and notified the captain of a German merchant ship not to leave the harbor of Vera Cruz with munitions of war consigned to or for General Huerta. Admiral Fletcher has been instructed to call upon the captain of the ship and present an apology and explanation.

"While the United States hopes that the munitions of war intended for General Huerta will be landed at the Vera Cruz custom house so that after landing the United States Government may detain them, still this Government does not claim the right—as a state of war does not exist—to interfere with the ship's departure or to exercise control over said munitions of war unless they are delivered at a wharf or custom house controlled by the United States. The Secretary of State, by direction of the President, offered through His Excellency the German Ambassador the apology and explanation which Admiral Fletcher was instructed to offer to the captain of the ship."

Shortly the Secretary of War suggested that, after conference with State Department officials, in accordance with an old custom, the Navy and the Marines should withdraw and turn over the occupation of Vera Cruz to the Army. That suggestion met the approval of the Chief of Naval Operations. I counselled against it, saying:

> "The situation at Vera Cruz has no precedent. Heretofore when sailors or marines have taken a city, it was regarded as an act of war, and it was held as a base for military operations. The President has said that we have no intention of waging a war against Mexico and our ships had no purpose in taking the customs house in Vera Cruz except to prevent the munitions from the *Ypiranga* falling into Huerta's hands. Huerta is a murderous usurper and for that reason recognition of his so-called government has been denied by the President. For the Army to relieve the Navy would be considered as an act of occupation and be regarded as in the nature of war. Therefore the wise thing is to regard our presence at Vera Cruz as a temporary act for two purposes only—to keep munitions out of the hands of Huertistas and to hasten the downfall of Huerta so that Mexicans can organize their own government."

My view was regarded as academic. The War Department insisted upon control. Naval officers agreed it was the usual course. The State Department agreed with the views of military leaders. I stood alone. General Funston was ordered to assume command and the Navy's responsibility was at an end.

THE ARMY OCCUPATION

The story of Funston's long stay, his care of American refugees, and the Army's good record has been told in Army history. Upon Funston's arrival the Navy withdrew, conscious that a delicate duty had been performed with the utmost consideration of the citizens of Vera Cruz and with no thought of war on Mexicans. However, many Mexicans, having in mind that in 1847 Naval ships took Vera Cruz as preliminary to General Scott's soldiers' marching inland and taking Mexico City, were convinced by Huerta that history was repeating itself. They were confirmed in this incorrect view when General Funston and his troops occupied the city, and even more so later when American soldiers entered Northern Mexico after Villa's raid. It was this fear and belief that hampered Wilson's friendly policy, and made many Mexicans fear that the United States contemplated another war like that of 1847.

With the taking over of the Vera Cruz situation by the Army I no longer had official direction of any phase of the administration's policy there. However, as a member of the Cabinet I sympathized with and gave active support to the policy when Pershing was sent "to get Villa." When Funston took over I ordered most of the ships back to their bases. Wilson wrote me in August:

"I confess I was worried about the news of the ships being taken away from Vera Cruz, but I quite understand. Things are by no means finally settled yet down there and we shall have to be very careful how we seem to give them a perfectly free hand ...

"I hope that you feel sure that Admiral Fletcher will do nothing on his own initiative and without orders. It is a great comfort and support to have you agree with me in what I am doing."

SCOTT THOUGHT WELL OF VILLA

For a time Wilson was troubled as to whether Carranza or Villa was the stronger north of Mexico City, and he sent General Hugh Scott to survey the situation and make report. I was interested in the good opinion that General Scott brought back of Villa. He expressed confidence in and admiration for Villa. Scott had been an Indian fighter and had won the friendship of the Indians. He spoke their language and helped them in every way in his power. They called him their best white friend. When Scott returned from Mexico I talked with him and found he believed that Villa had real ability as a general. At that time he thought Villa would control the North and, with Zapata's coöperation, would rout Huerta. He was not alone in that opinion. However, the time was to come when Villa's ruthlessness, his murderous raid on Columbus and other terrible acts, caused Scott to reverse his early belief that Villa might help stabilize Mexico.

GOOD OFFICES OF A. B. C.

When Argentina, Brazil, and Chile lent their good offices to find a solution of a troubled situation; when unlimited patience was required because of Carranza's lack of appreciation of the inestimable support Wilson had given to enable Mexico to build on better foundations after Huerta's expulsion; when coöperation of some in Mexico was lacking and hostility was felt at home in the difficult situations that were to recur during his whole term of office; and when Congressmen and others and the imperialists in the United

States were demanding that we take every foot of territory from the Rio Grande to the Panama Canal; when bitter denunciation of the policy of "watchful waiting" came, Wilson stood like a stone wall, thus giving defiance to the imperialists at home: "I shall fight every one of these men who are now seeking to exploit Mexico for their selfish ends. I shall do what I can to keep Mexico from their plunderings. There shall be no individual exploitation of Mexico if I can help it."

THE FIGHTING QUAKER

One of the most vital and dynamic officers at Vera Cruz was General Smedley Butler, who was ordered from Panama to join Admiral Fletcher when the *Ypiranga* was stopped. He was the Marine's prize "the-Marines-have-landed-and-have-the-situation-well-in-hand" officer. He had won distinction in the Boxer Rebellion and in half a dozen countries. He was a Quaker who, through the influence of his parents, remained "in meeting," though he could swear upon occasion like the celebrated men who made up the army in Flanders. He was known in the service as "The Fighting Quaker." When the *Maine* was blown up, the young Hicksite took off his Quaker coat and said, "Lie there until I help whip the dastards who blew up the *Maine*." He was sixteen years old, but he used the birthday of his older brother and enlisted as eighteen. When his father discovered that he had given a fictitious date of birth, the fine old Quaker said to his son: "If thee is determined to go, thee shalt go, but don't add another year to thy age, my son. Thy mother and I weren't married until 1879." Some years later, Butler told me of this incident, and I arranged as Secretary of the Navy to have his original date of enlistment changed so that the record was made to speak the truth.

Arrived at Vera Cruz, Butler found no outlet for his initiative and daring until one day Fletcher sent him to Mexico City as a spy. I never heard of this until after Smedley returned from Mexico, when he told it to me in his usual graphic fashion. He published the substance of it later.

"Admiral Fletcher, a sterling officer but no martinet," said Smedley, "told me that while officers had been directed not to go outside of Vera Cruz, he wished very much a correct description of the situation in Mexico City, how many soldiers there were, their equipment, etc., so that in the possible contingency of the Americans being ordered to Mexico City there would be on hand accurate information together with maps. He then said, "I wish you to go in citizen's clothes, without official orders, to take the risks without anybody's knowing you are going."

" 'You mean I am to go as a spy?' I asked the Admiral.

"He said it amounted practically to that because there was no other way the information could be obtained.

"I said, 'All right, Admiral, I will go.' "

Here is the way Butler related his experience on that singular mission:

"My wife's uncle, Sam Felton, had been president of the National Railways of Mexico, and because of that association the superintendent took me in his private car to Mexico City. I posed as an expert interested in public utilities and was introduced by Mrs. O'Shaughnessy, wife of the American Chargé d' Affaires, as Mr. Johnson. I obtained the confidence of one of Huerta's secret service men and led him to believe that I had come to Mexico as a secret service agent of the United States, looking for a dangerous criminal who was said to have enlisted in the Mexican Army. I showed him a fake photograph of my imaginary desperado. He took me with him to all the garrisons in my search for the criminal. This gave me opportunity to obtain essential information on the number and character of the Mexican troops and their munitions stores. I also put down in a book the names of all members of the American Colony and the place of their residence. One of the chief objects of my Mexican trip was to prepare a place of rescue for the Americans in Mexico City if they were in danger from the Mexican troops. I wanted to make a study of Chapultepec, believing that if American troops came to the city it would then be necessary first of all to take that vantage ground. But O'Shaughnessy said he could not abuse his diplomatic status to take me over that strategic place. One day, however, when we were riding together at the base of the hill, Huerta chanced to come up and paused to speak to O'Shaughnessy, who unwillingly introduced me to Huerta as an American who was writing a guide book. Huerta accompanied us to the summit of the hill. I was shown all through the palace, but I was not interested in the bed where the fated Empress Carlotta slept. I knew the palace had been built above an old fort and I wanted to examine the old fortifications. I knew if the Americans could get long range guns on those foundations, Mexico City would be at their mercy. When I had finished my examination, made maps, and become acquainted with the military secrets of the Huerta forces, I beat it back to Vera Cruz, putting my maps and data into the false bottom of my valise. On the train en route to Vera Cruz, I was afraid I would be discovered, and, if so, be shot as the spy I was. During the night two men got on the train at Jalapa, and I became convinced they were secret service men on my trail. When the train reached Vera Cruz I thought it prudent to slip out before entering the station. The trains run out on a Y and back into the station. When we reached the Y, I took my bag and clothes into the wash-room and got off the train before it switched back. I scrambled into my day clothes among the freight cars, made a hasty dash for the American Consulate, signaled to the flag ship for a boat. When I reached the water front, a gang of Mexicans pounced upon me and began searching my bag and nearly tore my clothes to pieces. However, the launch was near at hand. I jumped into the boat with my bag, and we moved off toward the flag ship. I was glad to get back, for I realized that for two weeks I had been sitting on a bag of dynamite."

BUTLER'S ACCOUNT OF THE LANDING AT VERA CRUZ

"Old Gimlet Eye," as his fellow Marines called Butler, thus tells of the fighting in Vera Cruz:

"I can never forget the morning we landed at Vera Cruz. Under command of General Lejeune, the best officer of the Marine Corps or any corps for that matter, the First Regiment of Marines came ashore in small boats from the transport *Havelock*. All day we fought like hell. By night all was quiet. At daylight we had marched up the street, peppered from the roofs by snipers. As some Mexicans were using the houses as fortresses, the Marines rushed from house to house, knocking on the doors, searching for those who had fired on us. Just as two of my men were smashing in one door, they were mysteriously shot in the stomach from below. The house was deserted, but from the angle of the bullets, the Mexicans were obviously under the floor. We poured a volley through the floor and then ripped up the boards. There were found two dead Mexicans dangling between cross beams. Our fire had caught them. The sailors who marched up the street were badly shot up, not only by the Mexicans, but, in at least one instance, by their own men. The Marines lost only two killed and five wounded. The Marine plan was to station a machine gunner at one end of the street as a look-out. We then advanced under cover, cutting our way through the adobe walls from one house to another with axes and picks. We drove everybody from the houses and then climbed up on the flat roofs to wipe out the snipers. Congress authorized the conferring of Medals of Honor to officers. I returned mine to the Navy Department, saying that I had done nothing to entitle me to that high decoration. It was returned with orders that I should wear it."

XIX

PANAMA CANAL—TOLLS AND "REGRETS"

ONE OF WILSON's early victories (bill passed June 11, 1914), and one which he secured over the opposition of the most influential leaders of the House, was the repeal of the provision in an act of Congress in the Taft administration exempting American coastwise vessels from paying the same tolls as British, German, or other ships passing through the Panama Canal. The platform on which Wilson was nominated approved the exemption, and Roosevelt's Progressive Party declared that the "Panama Canal, built and paid for by the American people, must be used primarily for their benefit." The Republican platform was silent. Hardly had Wilson been elected before Great Britain began to protest that the act violated the Hay-Pauncefote Treaty, which declared that "the canal shall be free and open to vessels of commerce and war to all nations on terms of equality." Shortly after Page reached London, he sensed Britain's insistence upon action for repeal. Bryan cabled July 19, 1913, that "the President is not prepared to take up the toll question and does not think it wise to enter upon the discussion of it while the tariff law is pending."

BRITISH ATTITUDE TOWARD HUERTA

The British at first were very strong for Huerta, whom they had recognized on March 13, 1913, and could not understand Wilson's attitude. Page, in London, sympathetic with Wilson's position, found no response there. Of the British view he wrote to Wilson: "They have a mania for order, sheer order for the sake of order and—of trade. They are stupefied by your concern about anything else in Mexico."

Later Wilson directed Page to tell Grey: "If General Huerta does not retire by force of circumstance, it will be the duty of the United States to use less peaceful means to put him out."

There was a belief in some quarters that the British were later influenced in withdrawing their recognition of Huerta by the expectation that if they stood with Wilson in his Mexican policy, he would secure the repeal of the exemption of tolls for American ships going through the Panama Canal. House saw Sir Edward Grey in London in July, 1913, and undoubtedly told him of Wilson's sincere conviction that the treaty must be respected, explaining why action should be deferred. As evidencing the feeling in Britain about exemption from tolls of American coastwise ships, Page had written in June, 1913: "The English government and the English people without regard to party—I hear it and feel it everywhere—are of one mind about this: they think we have acted dishonorably."

At that time Wilson was so engrossed with other matters that he did not ask Congress to repeal the exemption until March, 1914. Prior to that time—to be exact, November 14, 1913—by orders of the British Government, Sir Lionel Carden had the uncongenial duty of leading a procession of diplomats to General Huerta and advising him to yield to President Wilson's demands. The effect of this advice from diplomats who had early recognized Huerta convinced all that his days in office were numbered. Many people thought that this act by Britain was taken because it was believed Wilson could not win his fight to repeal the toll provision if Britain continued its recognition of Huerta. Page may have put that bug in Grey's ear. I think he did. One thing is certain: Wilson believed that exemption of tolls was in violation of a treaty we had made and that we were in honor bound to live up to our contract. He felt this so strongly that he declined to be bound by the declaration in the platform of the convention which nominated him. He made a winning fight over strong opposition.

Page had written in January, 1914, urging action on repeal of the tolls, saying, "In diplomacy, as in other contests, there must be give and take. It is our turn." He also told Wilson in another letter that repeal of the tolls would "put the English of all parties in the happiest possible mood towards you and whatever subsequent dealings may await us."

The opponents of repeal declared that Wilson's advocacy of repeal was the result of bargaining by which Britain would stand by Wilson in his Mexican policy in return for repeal of the Panama Canal Tolls Act. Wilson was incapable of making the trade suggested and Lord Grey emphatically denied in Parliament that there had been any trade, understanding, or agreement. Britain renounced recognition of Huerta in November, 1913. The Canal tolls repeal bill was introduced January 4, 1914. The United States did not vote repeal until Britain had withdrawn support from Huerta.

COLOMBIA GOT ITS $25,000,000

As a result of the "taking" of Panama from Colombia, without saying so much as by your leave, by Theodore Roosevelt, the Wilson administration was early faced with a claim from Colombia for payment of an indemnity of $25,000,000 for the high-handed seizing of the property upon which the Canal was constructed. There was bitter feeling in Colombia and other Pan American countries over the seizure of Panama and the refusal to make payment. Bryan, supported by Wilson, submitted a treaty expressing "regret" recommending the payment of $25,000,000. This aroused the ire of T. R. He said: "The payment of belated blackmail is an outrage on U. S. honor and a blow to the American interests"—and he used even more violent language. It was regarded by him as condemnation of the dubious methods he had employed, as it was. The result was that the treaty was shelved until Harding's administration paid Colombia $25,000,000 minus "regret." It would have been better if Colombia had earlier accepted Wilson's phraseology: "The Government of the United States sincerely desires that everything that may have marred or seemed to interrupt friendship between the United States and the Republic of Colombia should be cleared away and forgotten."

A DISHONEST MAN IN THE CABINET!

I was, as Secretary of the Navy, to agree with Taft that the Panama Canal would double the fighting power of the Navy and I looked forward to its completion with satisfaction. But I never dreamed I would have to put up a fight to use the American canal for the passage of American Naval ships without drawing on the Naval appropriation to pay tolls to use the Canal built largely to expedite movements of Navy ships from one ocean to another.

The U. S. Navy Collier *Jupiter,* as the record of the War Department shows, was the first Naval vessel to pass through the Panama Canal, which had been opened to commerce on August 15, 1914. It arrived at Balboa on October 8, 1914, on its way from the North

Pacific Ocean to Philadelphia. The ship's passage through the Canal was begun on the morning of October 10, and completed on October 12, lying over in Gatun Lake in the meantime to ascertain the effect of fresh water on its barnacles.

The bill for tolls covering the transit of the *Jupiter* through the Canal, amounting to $7,370.40, was sent by the Canal officials on the Isthmus to the War Department, which demanded payment by the Navy. I directed that the bill be returned to the War Department with the statement that the Navy denied the right of the War Department to charge tolls on Naval vessels and I would not pay the bill. The next day, Garrison, Secretary of War, expressed surprise at my "refusal to pay a just and lawful debt." He insisted that all ships must pay the tolls and that the law made no exceptions. For some time, there was a continuing demand for payment and a stern refusal to pay. When Garrison saw I was adamant, he brought the matter up at the meeting of the Cabinet, by saying: "Mr. President, I regret to inform you that one member of your Cabinet is dishonest and refuses to pay a just debt." Showing surprise at such a charge against a colleague, the President quizzically asked, "Only one?" and requested an explanation. Garrison replied, "I have caught only one with the goods on him. The dishonest man is the Secretary of the Navy. Under the law all ships that go through the Panama Canal must pay a fixed toll. Some days ago, the Navy Collier *Jupiter* went through the Canal. I sent a bill to the Secretary of the Navy for $7,370 for the tolls, but he has refused to make payment. I hate to expose him but I am charged with executing the law."

The President turned to me.

"Not guilty," I pleaded to Garrison's indictment. I argued that one of the chief reasons given for digging the Panama Canal was to double the efficiency of the Navy, by enabling the fighting ships to go quickly from one ocean to another, thus giving protection to the Pacific and Atlantic coasts. I recalled that in the Spanish-American war the need of the Canal was brought sharply to the attention of the country by the long time it took the *Oregon* to sail from the Pacific to the Caribbean to take part in the war. Nobody ever supposed that the Navy would have to pay tolls to pass through the Canal dug mainly to double Naval efficiency. I added that this would hamper Naval movements and advertise that our Navy would have no advantage over an enemy Navy.

Garrison interrupted: "The money all comes from the public treasury—it is taking money out of one pocket and putting it into another"—and he argued that the law fixing the tolls was specific and mandatory. I replied that if Garrison was right, it would require an undetermined increase of the Naval appropriation and would be establishing a principle which the Navy could not accept. Most members of the Cabinet agreed with me. The President said he would give consideration to the matter raised by the disagreement of the secretaries of the two armed branches. "In the meantime, I suggest they do not use submarines or big guns in their warfare," he added.

The next afternoon for over an hour at the White House, Garrison and I argued before the President our sharp difference. Though the President gave no decision, I sensed that he sided with me. Shortly thereafter, in order that there should be legal determination of the question which I had raised, and which had been debated in the Cabinet, the President requested the Attorney General to render a written opinion. That opinion sustained my contention and had the approval of the President. In an opinion rendered on June 3, 1915, the Attorney General held that the United States Government vessels not engaged in commercial operations, should not be required to pay tolls. When the opinion was rendered President Wilson wrote to the Secretary of War, saying:

> "I have an opinion from the Attorney General which is to the effect that vessels operated by the United States, including war ships, naval tenders, colliers, transports, hospital ships, and other vessels owned or chartered by the United States for transporting troops or supplies, are not required to pay tolls either under the provisions of the Panama Canal Act or of the Hay-Pounceforte treaty."

Secretary Garrison, then and then only, admitted that my contention was legal "but it is not just," he said, and returned the bill to the Isthmus for cancellation.

If I had followed the advice of some Naval officers, who, upon receipt of the bill, advised that the Navy had no recourse but to pay it, the question would probably never have been raised. Think of the increased Navy appropriations to pay the tolls on its fleets which now go freely through the Canal! I have never quite forgiven John Hay for agreeing to the Hay-Paunceforte treaty by which, though Uncle Sam paid every penny for the construction of the Panama Canal, British overreaching gave John Bull equal rights there without the expenditure of a penny. Wilson never approved Hay's free gift. He stressed only that national honor compelled our country to live up to the terms of the treaty we had ratified. But I could never have forgiven myself if I had not defeated the attempt to make Naval ships pay toll for going through the Canal built to double Naval power.

CANAL OPENING NOT CELEBRATED

Our government had planned to celebrate the opening of the Canal with a celebration befitting the importance of the greatest aid to world transportation in history. To that end invitations were prepared and all nations having navies were invited to send ships to show the might of sea power. The papers made much sport of Bryan and me because a clerk in the State Department had requested Switzerland, which had no Navy, to send ships to participate in the Naval parade. The sudden coming on of the World War about the time the Canal was completed compelled the calling off of the celebration, and there were no international formalities as the Canal went into use. The United States alone had completed what others had tried to do, thus defying what a king of Spain had declared was contrary to the will of God. When asked to join in the construction of a canal across Panama Isthmus at a time when Spain was a leading world power, the king had said he could not because it would be flying in the face of Providence. "In what way?" he was asked. He replied by saying the Bible had declared, "Those whom God hath joined together let not man put asunder."

I had made elaborate plans with Secretary Bryan for a formal opening of the Panama Canal and had talked with Colonel George W. Goethals, who was chairman of the commission which constructed the Canal, about the arrangements. Naturally, having won national gratitude by this unprecedented work of construction, Goethals looked forward to the formal world celebration of its incalculable value.

PANAMA CANAL SCANDAL RECALLED

As far back as the political campaign of 1908 I became convinced that, while President Roosevelt had no part in wrong-doing, there had been skulduggery in obtaining the so-called French concessions for the Canal. Information was conveyed to me at Democratic headquarters by Colonel John F. Stevens, member of the Isthmian Canal Commission, of corruption connected with the preliminary arrangements which, he said "would blow up the Republican Party and disclose the most scandalous piece of corruption in the history of the country." He told me there was dishonesty connected with the payment of $40,000,000 for the wreckage of the old DeLesseps enterprise, and gave the names of the prominent men who divided part of the $40,000,000 said to have been paid the French Government. He was unable to prove that the men he named got the rake-off because records were sealed in the archives of France. Stevens said he felt it was his duty to expose the corruption by those seeking to continue in power an administration which had not exposed the crooked men and punished those who got the loot. He was greatly disappointed when the full force of the Democratic Committee was not called into action to give the sordid facts to the public and expose what he called a "national scandal." He convinced me that "something was rotten in Denmark."

Very soon thereafter the New York *World* printed the story as it had been outlined to me by Stevens, with additional charges. The Roosevelt administration denounced the publication as false and prosecution was instituted against the *World* and Pulitzer, directed by Attorney General Bonaparte and District Attorney Henry L. Stimson. The indictment was brought under "An Act to Protect the Harbor Defenses from Malicious Injury and Other Purposes." It cost Pulitzer much money to keep out of jail for uncovering what he believed was a public crime. After long conflicts in the courts, the Supreme Court in an opinion by Chief Justice White dismissed the indictment against the *World* and Pulitzer, which was equivalent to a vindication.

Henry F. Pringle in his life of Theodore Roosevelt discloses facts that seem to bear out what Stevens told me in 1908. He says:

"Who, actually, were the owners of the more or less worthless French stock in the DeLesseps Company for which $40,000,000 was to be paid?" He answered his question by saying: "Cromwell denied ownership, as did Bunau-Varilla. The sum was paid to J. P. Morgan & Company, to be transmitted to mysterious stockholders, but to this day their identity is unknown." As Colombia was being spanked, "all the while Cromwell was earning the $800,000 fee he was to later claim. He wrote almost daily letters to Hay." Pringle adds: "To save the money of the unidentified stockholders, whose names he did not know, Roosevelt made ready to seize Panama. He was not deterred by possible bloodshed or by the fact that the United States would violate the fundamentals of international law."

In a private letter Roosevelt had bluntly said if the Panamanians had not revolted he would "have recommended to Congress to take possession of the Isthmus by force of arms," and he actually had written the first draft to this effect. Pringle says the revolt was "a farce," requiring "all the skill of Bunau-Varilla, Cromwell and other conspirators." The "faltering courage of Panama patriots had to be fortified by promises that the United States would, in spirit and probably actively, be behind them." As a matter of fact, the revolt did not begin in Panama; it began in the room of Mr. Bunau-Varilla, No. 1162, of the Waldorf Astoria Hotel in New York. Pringle says:

> "It deserves to be called the cradle of the Panama Republic. Mme. Bunau-Varilla, the Betsy Ross of Panama, secreted herself and stitched the flag of liberty. . . . Roosevelt acted with indecent haste in recognizing the new government set up under the Navy guns in Panama. . . . All the excess of patriotism, flag-waving, and excitement must not obscure the real reason for the Panama revolution—to preserve untouched the $40,000,000, of the new Panama Company, and to accelerate the construction of the canal across the isthmus."

HOW THEODORE ROOSEVELT "TOOK" THE CANAL

I was converted to the absolute necessity of constructing the Panama Canal when it required weeks for Captain Clark to bring the *Oregon* around the South American continent when it was sorely needed in the Caribbean during our war with Spain. In fact, I felt the need was so great that I almost, but not quite, forgave Theodore Roosevelt for "taking it while the Senate talked."

I had revolted at Roosevelt's declaration made to the students at the University of California on March 23, 1911, in which he said:

"I am interested in the Panama Canal because I started it. If I had followed traditional conservative methods, I should have submitted a dignified State paper of probably ten hundred pages to the Congress and debate would have been going on yet. But I took the Canal Zone, and let Congress debate, and while the debate goes on the canal does also."

If Kipling had been phrasing that declaration of contemptuous disregard of duty to weaker nations, he would have employed these lines of his creation to state the case briefly:

"An' what 'e thought 'e might require,
'E went an' took—the same as me!"

When Colombia protested that Panama territory had been taken by threatening force and disregard of its sovereignty, Roosevelt said, "We may have to give a lesson to those jack-rabbits some day." He referred to "these contemptible little creatures in Bogota," and in a letter to Hanna said, "It might be well to warn those jack-rabbits that great though our patience has been, it can be exhausted." Roosevelt also said, "The Colombians were entitled to precisely the amount of sympathy we extend to other inefficient bandits."

As an editor I had early followed the lead of Senator Morgan, the pioneer and militant advocate of constructing the Canal through Nicaragua and had talked to him about its value. He was long frustrated in his fight for the Canal, mainly because of the opposition of U. S. transcontinental railways. They saw diversion of traffic from rail to water. When the Spanish-American war emphasized the necessity for an Isthmus canal, Mark Hanna, who was opposed to any canal, managed to substitute Panama for Nicaragua, in the hope that Morgan would block it. This was regretted by Senator Morgan but his heart was more set on a canal than on any particular route.

When Roosevelt violated the sovereignty of Colombia, took the land through which the Canal was constructed, and set up, by threat of Naval strength, the new puppet country of Panama, I, in common with many Americans, believed we had sought a good end by ways contrary to all our professions of respecting the rights of small nations. I thought it was a violation of the principle of the Monroe Doctrine. And I wrote editorials denouncing the method employed as imperialistic and unworthy of a great republic.

Part Three

―――――――――――――

"THE NEW FREEDOM"

XX

NO LOBBY TAINT IN TARIFF LAW

SHORTLY AFTER his election, President Wilson announced that he would call a special session of Congress early in his administration to revise and reduce the tariff. At the Cabinet meeting on March 28 the President read his tariff message and asked for comment. The message was brief, clear, and strong. After reading it and emphasizing what he thought were the strong points, Wilson asked his associates for suggestions. He said:

> "Our party is now united for tariff reduction and we must secure a sound reduction measure now. There is division on monetary policies. My judgment is that we should take up one of these policies at a time and the tariff comes first. Our platform commits us to do it. That is why I called a special session. The sooner we dispose of the tariff the sooner we can take up other reforms."

There were few comments. The message was so admirable that I listened to its reading with a sense of thankfulness. One member of the Cabinet, praising the message (Lane, of California, I think) suggested that in view of the business situation it might be wise to move slowly in reduction. Wilson replied:

> "I have been deluged with advice by letter and otherwise that I ought to wait for a more convenient season before proceeding with tariff reduction. These suggestions remind me of a cartoon that appeared recently in a western paper. It had the picture of a man drawn in the stature of a giant, standing over me and saying: 'What do you mean by meaning what you said?'"

The President added that he must do as early as possible in the administration what he had promised before the election and support the cause which he had advocated all his life and which was a sacred pledge of the party.

Wilson believed that wisdom called for deep cuts and that it was better to cut quickly. He said he had talked with Underwood, who was ready to act promptly, and he had been assured by Simmons that as soon as the measure reached the Senate a real Democratic measure would be expedited. The member who had voiced caution did not press the suggestion. Wilson loved daring more than caution and declared he wished early to put into practise principles he had long entertained. He delivered the message to Congress in person and the message and the innovation were well received. The quick action lessened the opportunity of the special interests to organize effectively for log-rolling. But there were plenty of attempts to secure special favors. The Democratic caucus declared the tariff bill to be "a Democratic measure" and urged "its undivided support as a duty."

"WANTED SUGAR IN THEIRN"

I had little to do with the measure, except by contact with Senator Simmons, chairman of the Finance Committee of the Senate, and Representative Kitchin, of North Carolina, who were to have a large part in putting it through both branches of Congress. One day my fellow editor, Robert Ewing, of Louisiana, called to urge me to impress upon Wilson that Louisiana's life depended upon its tariff-protected sugar crop. I recalled that the Louisiana Democrats, or most of them, had refused to aid in tariff reduction, always demanding "sugar in theirn." I told Ewing that I wished no hurt to Louisiana growers, but that the time had come to give some consideration to the sugar consumers, who had been too heavily taxed. He had been an early and influential supporter of Wilson at Baltimore and thought that should give him some consideration. The Louisiana people received little comfort at the White House or from Democratic leaders in Congress. It was remembered that at previous sessions of Congress Louisiana had voted against all needed tariff reduction in exchange for sugar duties, and some of them had openly declared that Republicans were right on the tariff question. When the final vote came on the Underwood-Simmons tariff, both the Louisiana Senators joined the Republicans in voting against the measure. The result was that Congress reduced the sugar rates one fourth with promise that it be put on the free list later.

SIMMONS A TOWER OF STRENGTH

Wilson went to Washington feeling that the success of his administration depended largely upon having men in key positions in the Senate who were heartily in favor of progressive policies. Shortly after the inauguration, he told me he wanted to see the Senate organized with the important committees under the control of genuine liberals. He asked me: "How could I know that our policies would be supported by such men as Martin of Virginia, and Simmons of North Carolina, who are machine politicians with no sympathy for the things we are undertaking? The rule of seniority, in selecting chairmen of committees, is an anachronism and ought to be abolished and I would like to see it done now. I am strengthened in this desire because, in the organization of the Senate, seniority would give the chairmanship of the most important committees to reactionary Democrats."

He was very earnest about it and, at first, very determined. Simmons heard of his attitude, not through me, and came to see me about it. He asked me if it was true the President was opposed to his being elected chairman of the Finance Committee. I told him it was. He asked why. I told him the reason was because President Wilson knew he voted with the Republicans many times and had opposed practically the entire Democratic membership of the Senate on the reciprocity treaty. Wilson did not think he was sound on the tariff. I said that inasmuch as the first great measure Wilson would present to Congress was the revision of the tariff, drawn along Democratic lines, he wanted a chairman of the committee who held views in accordance with the declarations of the Baltimore platform and the President's inaugural address. Simmons said:

"You know, Daniels, that I have always been a strong party man and never failed to stand by the party declarations and party organization. The votes I cast, which you criticized at the time and which, I understand, the President does not approve, represented neither my attitude nor my convictions. The Republicans were making a high tariff bill and, as you know, there were many people in North Carolina, lumber men, textile manufacturers, and others, who felt that, inasmuch as protection was to be granted by the Republican Congress to industries in other parts of the country, the South ought to receive like treatment for its few industries and its lumber. Therefore, I voted for rates which would give them the same protection others were receiving."

He went on to say that he did not take that position because he believed in the policy, that, in fact, he was opposed to it, and wished to see the Democratic Congress enact a revenue tariff measure shorn of all special favors. He added that if he were not given the chairmanship of the committee to which he was entitled by seniority he would keep his campaign pledge and resign his seat in the Senate. But, he added, the seniority rule, long in practice, would remain, even if the President exerted his influence to make a change. As a devoted Democrat, anxious for his party to be harmonious and progressive, it would hurt him if the President fought his promotion but would not alter his determination to help to carry out the liberal policies of his party. He added: "You may say to the President that I am as desirous to pull up by the roots all favoritism in the new tariff measure as he is and I hope we can work together to that end."

I repeated to the President what Simmons had said and strongly advised that he make no fight on Simmons—that he would find him an honest man who could be relied upon—and that there was no man in the Senate who was more concerned for the success of the administration or would do more to advance its liberal program. He agreed, and there grew up a close association between the two. Wilson afterwards spoke to me of the dependability and ability of Simmons, upon whom he came to rely.

WILSON'S TRIBUTE TO KITCHIN

In writing the tariff bill in the House, Claude Kitchin, of North Carolina, next to Underwood, contributed most. He had mastered the question and was a militant foe of the favors which had so long made the tariff bill a covert for privilege. He was a born fighter and more than once was an opponent of Wilson's policies. Even so, Wilson had the highest opinion of Kitchin's sincerity and integrity. Private Secretary Tumulty relates this incident, showing Wilson's attitude toward those of opposing views with whom he discussed public matters:

"I recall a case in point. He was discussing the revenue situation with Representative Claude Kitchin of North Carolina, at a time when it was the subject of bitter controversy in the ranks of the Democratic party. The President and Mr. Kitchin held radically divergent views on this matter; the President sought to lead the party in one direction and Mr. Kitchin openly pursued an opposite course. I was present at this conference. No warm friendship existed between these two men; but there was never any evidence of hostility in the President's attitude toward Mr. Kitchin. He listened politely and with patience to every argument that Mr. Kitchin vigorously put forward to sustain his contention in the matter, and took without wincing the sledge-hammer blows often dealt by Mr. Kitchin. The President replied to Mr. Kitchin's arguments in an open, frank manner and invited him to the fullest possible discussion of the matter.

"I recall the conclusion of this interview, when it seemed that, having driven the President from point to point, Mr. Kitchin was the victor. There was no disappointment or chagrin evident in the President's manner as he faced Mr. Kitchin to accept his defeat. He met it in true sportsmanlike fashion. At the conclusion of Mr. Kitchin's argument the President literally threw up his hands and said, quietly, without showing a trace of disappointment:

'I surrender, Mr. Kitchin. You have beaten me. I shall inform my friends on the Hill that I was mistaken and shall instruct them, of course, to follow you in this matter.' "

BOYISH DREAMS REALIZED

I felt that the long-delayed achievement in just taxation had come when I joined fifty others at the White House to see the President sign the first good tariff law in half a century, one that had no taint of special privilege. "I have," said Wilson "had the accomplishment of something like this at heart since I was a boy and I know men standing around me can say the same thing." My mind went back to 1880, when, as a boy editor in Wilson, I took my stand with Roger Q. Mills and Vance against Randall and Ransom in the great tariff struggle, and I of course shared with Wilson the pleasure of seeing a youthful dream come true. The President praised Underwood and Simmons and wrote Simmons a warm letter of thanks. This gratified me, for I had assured the President of Simmons' support of tariff reductions. In fact, Simmons was so zealous that he caused reductions to be made in the House bill. At the ceremony of the signing, the veteran Senator Tillman said it was "the greatest tariff fight in the history of the United States Senate." The vote was close—44 to 37—not as big as a barn door, but enough; and, as a North Carolinian, I rejoiced that Senator Simmons and Claude Kitchin had helped Wilson win a great victory.

LOBBY DRIVEN FROM CAPITAL

When work began in reducing tariff schedules, the lobbyists descended upon Washington like the locusts in Egypt. Every hotel in Washington was crowded with them. The special interests had been in the habit of writing schedules for their own enrichment. They were not ready to surrender. Tom Pence, who had by that time become the President's chief eyes and ears for outside news, told me one night that the lobbyists were getting in their work. He thought they ought to be driven out of Washington. He had a list of many lobbyists, where they were staying, and which Congressmen they were approaching. I advised him to show it to Wilson. He did so. The President asked him to pursue the matter and complete the list. Within a few days he had the information in hand. Wilson made a public announcement of the pernicious influence of the lobby. On May 26 a lobby investigation was ordered, and the lobbyists hastened out of Washington like rats leaving a sinking ship.

The press hailed Wilson's action in "destroying an ancient industry and smoking out of corners a horde of vermin." One newspaper said his attitude towards the lobbyists was like the washing of the dog, adding, "The Fleas are entirely opposed to it. The dog does not like it much either, but will be more comfortable himself afterwards, and amazingly more agreeable as a member of the family."

OPPOSITION TO THE INCOME TAX

The big taxpayers at first hoped that they could prevent the levy of a tax on incomes. I had an argument about it with Colonel Robert M. Thompson, president of the Navy League, a Naval Academy graduate, who had resigned and made a fortune in business, but never lost his interest in the Navy. He had expected to be Secretary of the Navy in the Taft Cabinet, and most Naval officers hoped he would be named. He was a staunch advocate of a large Navy, second to that of Britain. We talked much in my first days about Naval preparedness. But he was strongly opposed to the income tax and several times talked to me about its unwisdom and wished me to urge President Wilson not to impose such a tax. Talking to me, who in the Cleveland administration had stood with Bryan and had helped get a plank in the platform demanding it! When he had finished his argument, I turned to him and asked, "Are you in favor of a large Navy?" "Certainly," he said. Above all things he thought we should have a large Navy. Then I said, "I see no way to have a large Navy without a large income tax," and I astounded him by saying, "If I had my way, I would levy an income tax on Mr. Frick, Mr. Carnegie, Mr. Morgan, Mr. Rockefeller, Mr. Mellon, Mr. Duke, Mr. Baker, and the ten other richest men in America— a tax large enough to let each one of them pay the cost of building a battleship or the equivalent in other fighting ships every year." I told him I thought one of the functions of the Navy was to protect the commerce of the world, and the very rich men and the industries they represented received the chief benefits from a strong Navy and they ought to pay for it. He disagreed vigorously and I think he thought me a hopeless radical.

Bryan had forced into the Wilson-Gorman Tariff of 1893 a provision for levying a tax on incomes. The Supreme Court said it was unconstitutional. Now Bryan, as Secretary of State, was to issue a proclamation that a constitutional amendment had been adopted, making constitutional the sort of provision he had secured in the tariff bill of 1893. In writing the Simmons-Underwood Tariff bill, the income tax provisions were drafted by Cordell Hull, who later became Secretary of State in the Franklin Roosevelt administration.

XXI

SETTING BUSINESS OF THE COUNTRY FREE

As HE SIGNED the new tariff law, Wilson had said that we would take "the second step in setting the business of the country free" by pressing the currency measure. It showed his "single track mind" was working. As far back as 1897, though he had opposed the free coinage of silver, Wilson had said that "nothing but currency reform can touch the cause of the present discontent." Later he had declared that "the great monopoly in this country is the money monopoly." He could not secure currency reform soon enough.

Lane urged a policy of delay; others were doubtful and spoke of "mutterings" of a silent panic in New York. Replying to Lane's plea for delay, Wilson said on June 12: "We shall never find the time more suited to what we wish to do, because whenever action is contemplated, the same obstructions will arise. A steady purpose and a just execution of it seems to me the only course open to us."

When informed at the Cabinet meeting that some party leaders in Congress wanted to postpone action until the next session, Wilson got hot under the collar and, turning to McAdoo, said: "Please say to the gentlemen on the Hill who urge a postponement of this matter that Washington weather, especially in these days, fully agrees with me and that unless final action is taken on this measure at this session I will immediately call Congress in extra session."

BRYAN URGES CHANGE IN BILL

The "second step" was to be a long and difficult road, with Carter Glass in the House, Senator Owen in the Senate, and Secretary McAdoo as the Big Three with whom Wilson coöperated. A bill was drawn up which Wilson tentatively accepted, permitting banks to issue money. It was contrary to the declaration of the Democratic Party in recent platforms. When Byran's friends in the House, led by Henry, of Texas, who had ardently supported Wilson's nomination, declared they could not support the measure with that feature, Bryan unbosomed himself to me. He said:

"I broke with Cleveland on the money question and for sixteen years our party platform has committed us to the principle
that the issue of money is a function of government and should
not be surrendered to banks. I am also opposed to that feature
of the measure which permits the bankers to name some members of the Federal Reserve Board. They ought all to be
appointed by the President and the government have both complete and undisputed authority over the issue of the government
notes and the personnel of the board."

I told him that in both respects he was right and that I was sure
if he presented his strong argument, plus the party declarations,
these two objectionable features would be deleted. He was fearful
that the President was committed to the bill as introduced.

"GOD ALMIGHTY HATES A QUITTER"

Earlier in the session, Glass had spoken doubtfully about success
when Henry and other House members were opposing the measure
and told Wilson he had a mind to resign. Wilson, who always held
with Manly that "God Almighty hates a quitter," replied—it was the
first time Glass ever heard Wilson use that expression—"Damn it,
don't resign, old fellow; outvote them." And that is what Glass did,
after he assented to Bryan's suggestions and had his powerful support. As a matter of fact, nothing could have induced Glass to quit.
His temper got the best of him and he spoke hastily. Like Wilson
he loved a scrap. With solid Republican and some Democratic opposition he had enough to make him get hot under the collar.

DIFFERENCES IRONED OUT

Bryan was in a mood to withdraw from the Cabinet if the provisions he opposed were insisted upon. Wilson and Bryan were
both troubled, for at heart they wished to reach the same goal. It
was largely through the good offices of Tumulty that conferences
between Bryan, Glass, Owen and McAdoo resulted in giving the
appointment of all members of the board to the President, eliminating banker selection of part of the members and confining the issue
of money to the government. This was one of many times that
Tumulty, by his tact and zeal for the success of the administration,
demonstrated the wisdom of his selection to the post.

When this adjustment had been made, Bryan, happy and smiling, said to the President after a meeting of the Cabinet: "Mr. President, we have settled our differences and you may rely upon me to remain with you to the end of the fight." Wilson was as gratified as Bryan. Glass accepted Bryan's views as to both points under discussion.

WILSON CONFOUNDS BANKERS

Relating how his conversion was accomplished, Glass told friends at the time what he afterwards stated in public. He said that at first he strongly believed, inasmuch as bankers were to subscribe for stock they ought to be represented on the board by members of their own selection. He was so convinced of the soundness of their request that he headed a committee of bankers to the White House to try to convert Wilson to their view. Glass and the bankers made their argument. "When we had finished, and I thought we had made a strong case," said Glass, "the President asked us: 'Will one of you gentlemen tell me in what civilized country of the earth there are important government boards of control on which private interests are represented?" Glass said, "There was a painful silence for the longest single moment I ever spent. Before it was broken, Wilson further inquired: 'Which of you gentlemen thinks the railroads should select members of the Interstate Commerce Commission?'"

Continuing, Glass said: "There could be no convincing reply to either question; so the discussion turned to other points of the currency bill; and, notwithstanding a desperate effort was made in the Senate to give the banks minority representation on the reserve board, the proposition did not prevail."

After Bryan wrote a letter urging passage of the measure, and the bill was approved by the Democratic caucus and passed the House, Glass, writing grateful appreciation to Bryan, said, "You have disappointed your enemies and pleased your friends, by standing firmly with the President for sound legislation in behalf of the American people."

But "Jordan is a hard road to travel." As the Senate had held up the tariff bill for months, so, during the long hot summer, a few Senators were fighting the measure by every weapon known to legislative ingenuity. The big bankers were pulling the strings and coming to Washington to direct the fight under cover.

WHIPPED TO A FRAZZLE

One day a young Naval officer came in to see me and said, "I have just come from the Army and Navy Club. I wonder why Messrs. (and he named four or five of the heads of the largest banks in the United States) are staying at the Army and Navy Club and receiving Senators." He said that these gentlemen were not registered and did not go out of the 'steenth floor of that building but men were coming and going to see them frequently. He added, "I think there is a hen on, but I don't know what it is." I knew this was the center of the organization of the big financiers to emasculate the bill or to defeat it. The next day I asked the young officer who frequented the club, to report to me who occupied these rooms, and the names of the men who visited them. I gave this information and their names to the President. The hot days were on, and the fight in the Senate was as heated as the temperature outside. After a while it became apparent to the big boys in New York that they could not defeat the measure. One of them finally called at the White House saying that he, and certain other bankers whose names stood highest in finance, had just arrived in the city and would like to talk with the President about the pending banking measure. Wilson refused to see them and sent them this message:

"I am on to you. I know that you have been in Washington for many days secretly trying to sabotage this bill. If you had sought an interview with me when you first came to Washington, I would have been glad to have talked with you and consider any suggestion you might wish to make to improve it, but you have exhausted every influence to kill it. Now I have got you whipped to a frazzle; therefore, there is no need for us to talk."

GLASS ANNIHILATES OPPONENTS

As Glass was the author of the original bill, he became its chief defender and advocate. I recall that he went to New York for a debate before a club composed mainly of opponents. When he finished an argument of surpassing power he had converted his hearers. They came to scoff and remained to pray. It stands out now—and was recognized then—as the greatest speech on finance New York had heard in a generation. It was annihilating to opponents. Glass woke next morning to find himself famous and his opponents confounded.

PROVINCIAL NEW YORKERS

Invited to speak at the Southern Society in New York I found I must reply to Martin Littleton who had made a vigorous onslaught on the measure, declaring it was aimed to destroy the financial strength of New York. I expressed surprise that Littleton, who had gone to the metropolis from the South, had become such a provincial New Yorker that he believed Jersey City was the extreme western confines of the American continent. I told him he reminded me of a story of a man who rented a skiff and went out into a river to fish. His boat turned over, and as he fell into the water he uttered terrified cries for help, spluttering in the endeavor to swim. Hearing the cries from the water, a Scotsman walking on the bank did not move to aid, but called out: "Hoot man, Stand up. The water where you are is only three feet deep." I compared myself to the Scotsman. I declared that an administration would be stupid to try to injure the greatness of New York, saying, "It could not end New York's lead in finance if it would and would not if it could."

It was two days before Christmas when Wilson signed the bill which had come out of the Senate after long and painful travail. It was hailed with rejoicing by its advocates. Opponents joined in accepting it as an improvement. How would it work? Wilson said to friends that it would bless the country as long as it was administered by its friends, but that it might fail of its object if controlled by those who wished to thwart it.

REED CLAIMS CREDIT

During the period when the Federal Reserve Act worked well, almost everybody claimed credit for its good provisions. Senator Jim Reed was a candidate for reëlection and I was asked to go to Missouri to speak in his behalf. During the currency fight Reed had fought Wilson at every step of the way and often with bitterness. I told the President of the invitation to go to Missouri, and asked his advice. "Do as you choose." That was all, and I went. Though wide apart on some measures, Reed and I were always friendly. Not until then had I appreciated Reed's effectiveness as a campaigner. "Let me speak first today," he said at Sedalia, "for I must catch a train to meet a distant appointment tonight." Of course I agreed. Such an adroit speech I have rarely heard. To hear him one would have supposed that he had disagreed with Wilson only on points looking to improving the measure, while in Washington he was regarded as a bitter opponent. He now declared it was the greatest measure Congress had passed in a decade and said he was proud of being able to coöperate with Wilson to give it to the country. It was news to me that he had "coöperated with Wilson," for he had tried to thwart Wilson's plans at almost every turn. I could but wonder at Reed's ability to get away with it. But he did, and I dared not break the news to Missouri voters of how deeply Wilson had resented his course at all stages of the fight.

HOUSE FAVORED ALDRICH PLAN

Aside from Wilson, to whom chief credit is due for the Federal Reserve system, Glass admits he is the author. Owen also admits a large part of the paternity. McAdoo ditto. Bryan saved it in days of peril. Several experts who helped have been given the credit. There was glory enough to go round.

It was not unexpected, however, when House, who was obsessed by the dream that without him nothing was made that was made in the Wilson era, came forward with the claim of credit for the measure. In his *Intimate Papers of Colonel House,* Seymour says that "it was in the currency question that he [House] took chief interest," and claims that he was "the unseen guardian angel of the bill." He quoted House as saying, "I advised the President that McAdoo and I whip the Glass measure into final shape, which he could endorse and take it to Owen as his own." About that time a publication was made attributing to House the statement that Glass had said he "knew nothing about finance," and had asked House's guidance. When I read Seymour's book and saw that statement, I knew Carter Glass would explode. And he did. In fact he wrote a book, a most illuminating story of the origin and passage of the Federal Reserve Act and its workings. In that book Glass not only denies he made the statements attributed to him, but says that so far from being "the guardian angel," House was actually in favor of the Aldrich plan and had no part in the drafting or the fight for passage of the measure. The Aldrich plan had been specifically denounced by the Democratic National Convention. Glass added, "When the currency bill was in shape to be translated into law Colonel House was 3,000 miles away. The impertinent assertion that he guided the measure is as offensive a fabrication as was ever penned on paper." Senator Owen, who piloted the bill through the Senate, says that "Colonel House had nothing to do with influencing my activities in connection with the federal reserve act." Glass showed that House was actually trying to get the President to follow the suggestions of Mr. Warburg, who was unalterably hostile to the principles of the measure.

Ever since the passage of the Federal Reserve Act, Glass has acted toward it as an old hen watches over her chickens, bristling when anybody wants to dot an "i" or cross a "t" of what he has regarded as the best piece of legislation in the history of the country, with the name of Carter Glass "blown in the bottle." And he deserved and received the plaudits of his countrymen for leadership in this greatest measure dealing with finance in a generation.

ANOTHER HOUSE OBSESSION

When I read how Carter Glass had exposed House's claim that he "whipped the Federal Reserve act into shape," for which House's biographer gave him credit, when, in fact, House had favored the Aldrich Act and was against the bill championed by Glass, I recalled that in *The Intimate Papers of Colonel House* there was a like unfounded claim of House's influencing the Navy's greatest building program. From his Diary, August 30, 1915, is taken a statement that I was at Gloucester and telephoned I "wanted to see" him and "we had a conference of an hour," and House added:

> "I urged him [Daniels] to ask for all that was necessary to make the Navy second only to that of Great Britain and easily superior to any other power. I told him it did not matter if it cost $300,000,000 or $400,000,000 for the country demanded it and it should be done. He promised he would go at it in that spirit."

That is the claim. What were the facts? Returning on the *Dolphin* with my wife and sons from Maine and New Hampshire, on a naval inspection trip, one of my sons begged, "Let's go into Gloucester for some fishing." We did so. I didn't know House was in a thousand miles of Gloucester and never dreamed of consulting him. Going ashore to get a newspaper, I was told that House had been in Gloucester that morning and was at his summer home nearby. My wife telephoned and asked House and Mrs. House to dine on the

Dolphin. The answer was that they had an engagement but House would call in the afternoon. He did. After tea we chatted for awhile. Incidentially, I told him I had been glad to get a letter from President Wilson at Cornish directing a study so that a program for a strong Navy could be presented to Congress and I had taken steps to get expert advice so as to present Wilson's recommendation that would give us "the most adequate Navy in the world." House commented that he thought Wilson was right, but that he believed we ought to try to build a Navy second only to that of Great Britain.

I never went to Gloucester to consult him, as would be inferred from his Diary; I never asked his advice; I never promised I would follow the advice he says he gave; and he never had any influence or part in the program Wilson had outlined a month before and which I recommended and Congress adopted. Instead of "promising" to follow his views, we secured a building program that would give us when completed incomparably the most powerful Navy in the world instead of the one "second to Great Britain" that he says he advised.

JOINT STOCK LAND BANKS

No one could have heard Wilson's message for currency legislation without noting that he was determined to help agriculture. Bryan had said in 1896: "Burn down your cities and leave our farms, and your cities will spring up again as if by magic; but destroy our farms and the grass will grow in the streets of every city in the country." Hoover probably borrowed that idea in 1932 when he talked about grass growing in the streets if Roosevelt were elected. Certainly, while Wilson never needed to borrow ideas, he voiced in 1913 the same thought:

"It is from the quiet interspaces of the open valleys and the free hillsides that we draw the sources of life and prosperity, from the farms and from the ranch, from the forest and the mine. Without these every street would be silent, every office deserted, every factory fallen into disrepair. And yet, the farmer does not stand on the same footing with the forester and miner in the market for credit."

It was to end that discrimination against the farmer that Wilson and McAdoo urged the creation of joint stock land banks, which were provided for in the Federal Farm Loan Act passed in 1916.

There was also provided a Federal Farm Loan Board to administer aid to farmers. Under this organization more than a billion dollars was loaned to farmers. Though McAdoo took the lead and had the direction of these agencies, Houston outlined plans for farm loan credits.

OUTLAWING PRIVATE MONOPOLY

After the victory in revising the tariff and the creation of the Federal Reserve system, Wilson's next step in putting the New Freedom into law was to find a way to end monopoly through the creation of the Federal Trade Commission and the passage of the Clayton Anti-Trust Act, which declared that "the labor of a human being is not a commodity or an article of commerce." But it was not easy. There was strong pressure brought to bear to take a breathing spell. At a meeting of the Cabinet in December, 1913, when Houston, replying to Bryan's suggestion that the party carry out its trust pledges, proposed that no legislation should follow until the currency system had gotten into perfect operation, Bryan said to Houston, "I agree with everything you say, but with nothing that you mean. There are only two times when the problem you raise, what to do about trusts, should not be touched—one is when business is good, the other when business is bad and ought not to be made worse."

Wilson was determined to go forward and secure anti-trust legislation. He not only urged effective legislation but in the summer of 1914 ordered the prosecution of the important monopolistic companies which had been begun but not pressed. He was particularly interested in pressing the prosecution of the transportation monopoly in New England, and engaged Thomas W. Gregory, afterwards Attorney General, to direct a proceeding to secure the dissolution of the unlawful monopoly of transportation facilities in New England; and he said he desired that "the criminal aspects of the case be laid before a grand jury." Some of Wilson's New England friends, even President Eliot of Harvard, wired Wilson that his attitude "shocked many friends and supporters." But that did not deter Wilson. Bryan, strongly supporting the President, insisted that "the party keep its promise on trusts as it was keeping those on currency." Wilson thus expressed his intention: "It is our purpose to destroy mo-

nopoly and maintain competition as the only effectual instrument
of business liberty."

Wilson was working to "make crime personal" and end monopoly
in a quicker and better way than by long-drawn-out litigation, often
defeated by executive interpretation, as when the tobacco and oil
men were found guilty of violating the Anti-trust Law and were
allowed to make a sham—a Wicker*sham*—settlement by a division
of their companies which helped no producer or consumer. Wilson wished the Federal Trade Commission to inform business
what it could and could not do under the law, believing that
most businessmen, with that knowledge, would carry on their
business without the hazard of uncertainty and prosecution. As his
purpose became known, Morgan, head of big business and some
others made a gesture of acquiescence in Wilson's plans by withdrawing as directors in interlocking companies. Had Morgan and
the others been converted and ready to accept the Wilson ideas?
Looking for light, but suspicious, Wilson wired to House to ascertain
the real feeling of big business leaders. As usual, House sided with
the interests and wired Wilson: "The action of Morgan and Co. has
created a profound impression and is thought to indicate that big
business is preparing to surrender unconditionally."

When Wilson's plan of dealing with trusts was under consideration in a Cabinet meeting, Wilson asked McReynolds and Garrison,
who were able black-letter lawyers, "Do you mean that business
should be in ignorance of the results of their acts and await a court
decision?" They answered that this was the approved practice in
the courts and no better methods could be devised. Wilson could not
agree with them. Replying to the objections of McReynolds and
Garrison, the President pointed out that sticklers for the ancient and
ineffective means of dealing with trusts got us nowhere in the fight
against monopoly.

Though McReynolds and Garrison thought the processes and
precedents should be followed, most members of the Cabinet felt that
Wilson and Bryan were right and that the only hope of stopping
monopoly was in the manner proposed. Attorney General McReynolds strongly believed that the old, slow and judicial method, which
had been pursued with the Standard Oil and the American Tobacco
companies, was the only process, whereas the President's idea was

that the Federal Trade Commission would investigate and determine whether corporations were carrying on their business in restraint of trade and give them the opportunity to adjust their business to legal methods before indictment or prosecution. He pointed out how long and tedious was the old way, and how it might work injustice to corporations indicted for violating anti-trust laws when they were not guilty. He wished a more prompt, a more direct method. He believed business would welcome the government's defining what they could do and could not do. The measure was fought bitterly by Morgan and other interests, who, as House blandly said, had "unconditionally surrendered." The Federal Trade Commission and the Clayton Anti-Trust Act were passed at the same session of Congress in the fall of 1914. But the breaking out of the war, together with other causes, prevented the development of the Commission along the lines intended by Wilson, and it has not measured up to what was expected of it by its originators.

Part Four

"A NAVY SECOND TO NONE"

XXII

NAVY DEPARTMENT STREAMLINED

I INHERITED an organization which my predecessor, Secretary Meyer, called the Council of Aides. They were the ears and eyes through which he directed Naval administration. When I took office these aides were: Admiral Bradley A. Fiske, Aide for Operations; Captain Templin M. Potts, Aide for Personnel; Captain A. G. Winterhalter, Aide for Matériel; and Admiral William F. Fullham, Aide for Inspection. In some respects I found this did not work well. Except in Operations, I preferred to deal directly with the bureau chiefs instead of having an aide as a go-between. In fact, from the beginning, I took up all personnel matters direct with Admiral Blue, Chief of the bureau that assigned officers to duty, and did not need an Aide for Personnel. The Aide for Inspection did not inspect, and when he went to sea, no one was appointed in his place. The Aide for Matériel was a very able man, who gave me good counsel, but when his time came to go to sea I dealt directly with the chiefs of the bureaus.

THE "SINGLE OAK" POLICY

I early determined that no officer should be promoted unless he had had long sea service, and I also established for the bureau chiefs, instead of an indeterminate assignment, a single term of four years. This was dubbed by Admiral McGowan the "Single Oak" policy, from the name of my home in a suburb of Washington, which was called "Single Oak." The Single Term—the "Single Oak"—policy brought new blood and new ideas into the department. Instead of the "fifth wheel" of acting through a Council of Aides, I dealt directly with the bureau chiefs and later established a Navy Council, patterned somewhat after the Cabinet, composed of the Secretary of the Navy, Assistant Secretary, the Chief of Operations, the Commandant of the Marine Corps, the Solicitor, and all the bureau chiefs. This Council met once every week, and all matters looking to official administration were given the joint consideration of all interested in carrying out Naval policies. It proved an excellent clearing house, and secured unity and coöperation.

The first bureau chief whose four-year term expired was head of the Bureau of Medicine and Surgery, Dr. Charles F. Stokes. He was eager to be reappointed and set every possible influence in motion to that end. He was quite an agreeable man who had made himself strong with the powers that be, and there were many people who recommended to me to continue him. They said he was the most efficient medical officer in the Navy. Wholly independent of his efficiency, I had made up my mind to adopt the one-term policy and so informed him. He thought he could change my mind or that his friends might do so. However, when his term expired I recommended the appointment of William C. Braisted as Surgeon General, calling him from the sea where he had been the Chief Surgeon of the Atlantic Fleet under Admiral Badger.

The organization of the Department was effected, after I had had time to get my bearings, by naming experienced and capable men as heads of the several bureaus. The organization thus effected was composed of the following officers: Victor Blue, as Chief of the Bureau of Navigation, a hero of the Spanish American War; David W. Taylor as Chief of Construction, perhaps the ablest naval constructor in the world, a graduate not only of the Naval Academy at Annapolis, but of the chief naval school in Britain; Admiral Robert S. Griffin, as Chief of Engineering, recognized as one of the ablest in his profession. To head the Bureau of Ordnance I named Admiral Joseph Strauss, a great ordnance officer and an able administrator, and when he went to sea, he was succeeded by Admiral Ralph Earle, who directed the greatest Naval enterprise of the World War, the laying of the mine barrage across the North Sea. Samuel McGowan was appointed as Paymaster General, and his practical vision in peace and war enabled the Navy not only to be ready with all necessary supplies but to purchase them in competitive markets and prevent profiteering. We were fortunate in having as head of the Bureau of Yards and Docks, F. R. Harris, an engineer of ability.

When I entered upon the duties of office, Captain Robert Lee Russell was Judge Advocate General. He had read law and wrote very long opinions on every case, with a citation of so many authorities that it would take a day to wade through them. When his term of office expired, I appointed Captain Ridley McLean to succeed him, but before appointing him I said, "Ridley, have you ever read law or do you know any law?" He said, "No." I said, "In that case I will make you Judge Advocate General. I want a man who will decide cases without such a wealth of authorities as will make me sit up all night to read his opinions." Some time after he had entered upon his duties, he went to a night school and studied law. Within a few months he was as long-winded and was quoting as many authorities as Russell. I sent for him one day and said, "Ridley, it is time for you to go to sea. I appointed you because you didn't know any law and would get at justice without lengthy citations, but you are writing as long and dull opinions as Russell. I will have to get me a new Judge Advocate General, and I am going to tell him that if he goes to a law school and writes long opinions I will send him to Guam."

SENATOR TILLMAN PROTESTS

In one of his calls at the Department, Senator Tillman, chairman of the Senate Naval Affairs Committee, urged me to name an excellent officer, Captain Richardson, of South Carolina, as bureau chief. I replied, "I have already named two South Carolinians as bureau chiefs—Blue and McGowan—and cannot give all the places to your State." I pointed out that there were forty-seven other States.

"Do you mean to say you will discriminate against South Carolina," he asked, "because it furnishes the Navy its best officers?" He added: "As to Blue, he was born in North Carolina." I answered, "Very well, if you disown him we will be proud to change the Navy Register and put him down as from North Carolina." He went up in the air at such a suggestion.

On another visit—this was before the World War—he said: "I wish you would require all officers on duty in the Navy Department to wear their uniform." I replied that as they preferred to wear civilian dress, I did not feel like making such an order, and asked why he advised it. He answered: "I want it done because now as I come into the Department I cannot tell the difference between an Admiral and a messenger." If Tillman had not been such an able advocate of a great Navy, his remark would have evoked criticism.

A PURELY AMERICAN SYSTEM

Admiral Fiske, Aide for Operations whom I inherited, was obsessed with the idea that the German system should be introduced into our Navy. He wished to make the Secretary a supernumerary and give virtually all the power of the office, except getting appropriations, to the Chief of Operations. "You work too hard," he would say, "signing so many letters and telegrams and reports. You should sign only the important decisions fixing general plans, and detail the Aide for Operations to sign all routine papers." He even told my wife I would break down my health if I did not turn over to others many of the things I did, which kept me at my desk ten to twelve hours a day. Urging my wife to induce me to slow down and turn over most of the mail I signed, the Admiral said, "Not even Napoleon could survive by imposing on himself tasks he could turn over to others." It was the first time she had heard me put in the Napoleon class and we often laughed at the Admiral's scheme of getting power into his own hands.

One day I said to him, after he had dinned the necessity of a system, patterned somewhat on that in Germany: "make me a chart indicating your idea of how the Navy Department should be organized." He was happy, thinking he had made a dent in my former opposition to the plans he had outlined. Shortly afterward he brought in a chart, drawn by an artist, which showed the Secretary of the Navy at the top, a Chief of Operations under him, with every other officer reporting to the Chief, who in turn was the only officer or official in the Department who could bring any matter to the attention of the Secretary. I told him I would look it over and give him my opinion the next day.

"What do you think of the diagram of naval organization?" the Admiral asked me the next morning.

"It is admirably drawn," I said. "Beautiful and as perfect a diagram as I ever saw."

The Admiral beamed. I continued: "The only objection I have is that in your chart you have put the Secretary of the Navy on the top of the Washington monument and denied him even telephonic communication with any officer or official in the Department except through Operations."

Finding that I would not abdicate the office of Secretary by approving his blue print, he with the coöperation of Richmond Pearson Hobson, and without my knowledge, sought to secure legislation which would make the Chief of Operations the head of the Navy and the Navy Department, leaving the Secretary little power except to draw his breath and draw his salary. In fact, a provision for transferring responsibility from the Secretary to the Chief of Operations was incorporated into a House bill by the committee, without my knowledge, the members not understanding it was against my desire.

When I learned of the plan to Prussianize the American Navy, I said to the chairman of the committee that if that provision remained in the bill it would be better to abolish the supernumerary office of the Secretary of the Navy, for no man worthy to fill the office would be willing to be a figurehead. "If the provision fathered by Fiske and Hobson is incorporated in the measure," I said, "I would be ashamed to draw the salary without duty or authority, and I would go home." As for myself, I told him I had discontinued the Council of Aides and wished a change in the organization which was incorporated in the legislation and which would create the office of Chief of Operations. The law as enacted provided that this official would be charged, under the direction of the Secretary of the Navy, with the operation of the fleet and with the preparation of and readiness of plans for its use in war.

FISKE TIRES

I almost sweat blood in selecting an Officer for Chief of Operations in the new set-up. I preferred to name an Admiral, though under the law a Captain could be appointed. I did not consider Fiske, since his consuming passion was to confer all power on the head of Operations. I determined to name an officer of practical judgment who believed in the American system. During Fiske's incumbency, and when I had grown weary of him, I told the following story at a meeting of the Navy Council, Fiske being present:

"I was over at Baltimore last night and heard Rev. Dr. Fiske tell a good story. He said he had not been in Baltimore long and his success depended upon interesting and holding congregations. 'And yet,' he said, 'I find myself insulted and flouted every time I turn a corner by a sign in large letters reading "Fiske Tires.'"

All laughed, even Admiral Fiske, when I told a story which all knew had a direct application. That is one of Franklin Roosevelt's prize stories.

WINSLOW ELIMINATED

My mind at first turned toward Admiral Winslow, who had been in line to be Commander in Chief of the fleet when Admiral Fletcher was selected. It was Fletcher's wisdom and sound judgment in the landing at Vera Cruz that so pleased the President that he characterized him as a "web-footed statesman." I went so far as to ask Winslow to come to Washington. His full name was Cameron MacRae Winslow. His mother was a native of North Carolina. His connection with my State early drew me to him. I was resolved to name no officer who believed the Chief of Operations ought to direct the Navy along the line outlined in the Fiske-Hobson plan. Winslow, the soul of frankness, told me he believed the Navy should be organized according to the German idea, with all officers and heads of bureaus reporting to and acting under the direction of the Chief of Operations. That eliminated him from consideration, much as I liked him.

WILSON'S WISE SUGGESTION

I was at sea as to a choice among the Admirals. While my mind was in debate, the President invited me to accompany him to New York, where he was to speak at the Associated Press luncheon. On the way over on the special car I told the President of the situation and my dilemma as to the appointment. He could always enlighten me by a direct question. He asked, "Why do you appoint an Admiral to the position, if there is not one available in sympathy with your wise policy? I would look for the best and soundest Captain and name him. Your field would be a larger one from which to choose." It did not take me long, after that lead, to decide upon Captain William S. Benson, then in command of the Philadelphia Navy Yard. I had visited that Yard twice and knew of his ability and sound judgment as well as his freedom from belief in bureaucracy and one-man control. In fact, he believed as I did in the American system, and later defended that system in an address at the Alumni Naval banquet at Annapolis, which brought criticism from those obsessed with the Prussian idea. In that address, after detailing how plans had been prepared, and telling of the perfect coöperation existing in the Navy Department, Admiral Benson had said:

"In my opinion the organization that exists is accomplishing in a purely American and business-like manner, all that could pos-

Upper left, Admiral Richard E. Byrd, pioneer aviator who later traversed the globe (NR & L). *Upper right*, Admiral John H. Towers, who was pilot when Secretary Daniels made his first flight in a Naval airship in 1913 (NR & L). *Below*, same type of plane as that in which first flight was made. With Towers was Ensign Chevalier.

CHIEFS OF BUREAUS IN NAVY DEPARTMENT

Upper left, Rear Admiral Robert S. Griffin, Chief of Bureau of Engineering (NR & L). *Upper right,* Rear Admiral David Watson Taylor, Chief of Bureau of Naval Construction (Harris & Ewing). *Lower left,* Rear Admiral William C. Braisted, Surgeon General (NR & L). *Lower right,* Admiral Samuel McGowan, Paymaster General (Harris & Ewing).

sibly be expected from the creation of a general staff, and is, I believe, doing this in a much more satisfactory way. It is folly to talk of or to advocate clothing a Chief of Staff or a Chief of Naval Operations with authority independent of the head of the Navy. Such independent authority would lead to confusion and would do great harm."

I appointed Benson to the important position which he filled with fidelity and ability before and during the World War and at Paris where he went as the President's Naval Adviser at the Peace Conference.

He was a deeply religious man, a devout Roman Catholic, and stood high among the leaders of the Knights of Columbus. He was a native of Georgia, and his mother was the first matriculate at Wesleyan Woman's College, a Methodist college. During his tour of duty at the Philadelphia Navy Yard some question had arisen that threatened a breach between Protestants and Catholics. He displayed a broad spirit of wisdom that had pleased me.

ASSISTANT TO THE SECRETARY

One day, just before the Cabinet meeting adjourned, President Wilson said to all the members that he was troubled—that Gilbert Close—"close by nature as well as name"—who had been his personal secretary at Princeton, had lost his position. "I have filled all the positions in the White House and have nothing I can offer him. If any of you gentlemen could make provision for him you would secure a competent man and make me thankful." I told the President that I would be glad to have Mr. Close as my assistant secretary. He was as warm in his thanks as if he had not been President of the United States with power to appoint many to office. Close proved as efficient and loyal as the President said he would be.

I offered the position of private secretary to Howard Banks, a North Carolina editor who had done excellent work on the Charlotte *Observer* and who was then editing a paper in Hickory. A little later, the position of assistant was offered to Frank Smith of New York. I had known him at Democratic headquarters, where the lady who became his wife after the election was one of the most capable assistants. This gave me, with civil service official John B. May, most efficient assistance. Later, when Banks resigned to become a member of the staff of the *Sunday School Times* (he was deeply religious)

I appointed Edward E. Britton of the staff of my paper, *The News and Observer*.

NEVER HEARD OF EACH OTHER

Shortly before the time came for the retirement of Admiral Southerland in the spring of 1913, I sent him telegraphic orders to move his ships on the West Coast to another port. It was a routine instruction. When he had turned over his command to his successor, the Admiral, a hearty and bluff old sailor man who had humor, called to see me at the Navy Department to pay his respects. I had never seen him. "Shortly after the fourth of March," he said, "my Aide gave me a telegram telling me to move my ships to another port. The telegram was signed 'Daniels.' I asked my Aide: 'Who is this Daniels giving me orders? I never heard of him.'"

And the Admiral laughed heartily, as did other officers who heard him, thinking he had one on me. "That is a singular coincidence, Admiral," I replied. "On the day it was decided to dispatch the order to the Admiral of the Pacific fleet, I turned to the Aide for Operations and asked, 'By the way, who is in command of that fleet?' He gave me your name, and I said: 'Strange isn't it, but I never heard of him.'"

He saw the point and we both agreed we had evened the score, when I continued, "Isn't it evidence, Admiral, of the bigness of our country when two such distinguished men as Southerland and Daniels never heard of each other until March, 1913?"

XXIII

"JOIN THE NAVY AND SEE THE WORLD"

THE POSITION in the Navy closest to the Secretary is the personnel officer, carrying the misnomer of Chief of the Bureau of Navigation. I sought a change so that it would be called Chief of Personnel. This was done later. That officer had nothing to do with navigation except to assign officers and men to duty, but because a century ago he had performed the functions of the Chief of Operations, the outworn name stuck for many years.

As men ranked with me above matériel I wished the closest contact with the officers and was always in close touch with the Bureau of Navigation, with whose head I could talk freely and who was in sympathy with the aims of the administration. Because he had won distinction in the Spanish-American war and because he was one of the few officers I knew before I went to Washington, I asked the President to appoint Victor Blue to head that bureau. He was born in North Carolina but was living in South Carolina when he went to the Naval Academy. I first met Blue when he went to Raleigh to speak at the unveiling of the statue of Ensign Worth Bagley. Like his predecessor, Philip Andrews, he was a younger officer than was usually named to head a bureau. Even then I was no worshipper of selection by seniority. I found him a man of wisdom and judgment and with a spirit of loyalty and helpfulness beyond compare. Not being acquainted with the inside workings of the Navy, I found his advice and coöperation valuable, but it is just to him to say I did not always take his advice. However, those men in the Navy, whose assignments were not to their liking, blamed it as much on Blue as on me when I had really directed the assignments. From the first I selected the officers of command rank and those for the places of most importance. Before the World War with wise foresight Blue had drawn up comprehensive plans creating the Naval Reserve, which proved invaluable when a large war expansion of the Navy was needed. He was a frank and wise counsellor. In the World War he commanded the dreadnaught U. S. S. *Texas* which was on duty with the British fleet in the North Sea. His son, Stuart, who was one of the first Naval officer casualities in 1943, and our boys were friends. The Navy named a destroyer *Blue* for the father and son who illustrated the best traditions of the service.

NO LANDLUBBER SAILORS

"I have been in the Navy two years," said an enlisted man to me one day when I was on a visit to the Navy Yard at Norfolk, "and I have never been outside of this place."

This was in answer to my question as to how he liked service in the Navy. I always made it a point to talk with the sailors when occasion offered. He proceeded to say that he had enlisted from Kansas and was induced to do so by seeing a poster carrying in big letters: "ENLIST IN THE NAVY AND SEE THE WORLD," and that if he had supposed he would be shut up in a Navy Yard he would never have left his home. "I want to go to sea," he said. "Can't you send me so I can see something of the world and learn navigation?"

Upon my return to Washington I called Blue in and asked him to let me know if what the young man had said at Norfolk was true in other cases. He said it was the purpose to send all the enlisted men to sea, but sometimes a situation existed where it had not been done.

"We will either see that everyone gets experience by going to sea," I said, "or we will tear down all our posters which say, "Enlist in the Navy and see the World."

CRUISE IN THE MEDITERRANEAN

I found when I became Secretary that the Congress had provided for 4,888 more enlisted men than had been secured to man the ships. I learned that not only were there not enough for the ships in commission, but that about one half of those in the service were not reënlisting. This made a serious situation and I set about to find ways to fill the quota, realizing that unless all authorized by law were enlisted, Congress would not grant the additional thousands that would be needed for the increased new construction. It was not long before 85 per cent were reënlisting. I set about studying how to make the Navy more attractive to ambitious young men. When the Chief of the Bureau of Navigation suggested the printing of more posters to increase enlistments, I said to Blue, and this was printed in all the papers, "The Navy must not induce men to join by false representation. If they are told that when they enlist in the Navy they will see the world, they must be given the opportunity promised. It costs no more to send the ships on a European tour than it does to go from Bar Harbor to the Carribbean and the Gulf."

I directed that a number of ships be made ready for a voyage to the Mediterranean and that all the men on duty on shore stations be assigned to this cruise. The Aide for Operations thought such a trip might disarrange some of the schedules for practice in the spring. "Let the ships go in the winter," I said, "and put on an intensive course of training during the trip to and from the Mediterranean. Sailors can be trained only by going to sea. Every one must have that experience."

The Bureau was instructed to check up on the assignments of the enlisted personnel and see that none were denied, or escaped, sea duty. As a manner of fact, some married men, desiring to be with their families, had sought and obtained duty ashore. But they could never be all-round efficient seamen any more than the few officers given berths ashore became competent to navigate a ship or be placed in charge of a division of ships.

I instructed Admiral Badger, Commander in Chief of the fleet, to make ready to take the fleet to the Mediterranean in the winter, so that the sailors could be trained in a sea voyage across the Atlantic and have the opportunity to see Rome and other historic cities of the countries bordering the Mediterranean.

The announcement of a winter cruise in the Mediterranean helped to increase enlistment so that it was not a great while before the full quota had been secured and the ships were fully manned—that is, fully manned according to the European idea of manning ships, but not in accordance with the idea of some officers who thought that every ship ought to have assigned to it at least a third more men than needed.

Shortly, 6,331 were enlisted and Congress authorized an increase of 22,981 men in Wilson's first term. Provision was made through an additional 831 midshipmen to the Naval Academy, and in other ways, to increase the number of officers. In addition, legislation was secured in 1916 for a Naval Reserve, which grew to 300,000 in the World War.

THE NAVY PIED PIPER

When better inducements were offered to enlisted men, the enlistments, which had
been very slow, soon filled the legal quota.

This winter cruise, the first real cruise of the fleet out of home waters since Roosevelt sent it around the world, attracted much attention in this country and abroad. In the summer and fall the officers and men were keen about it, making preparations. Though I had not then issued the order that every ship should be a school, I suggested to officers and men the advisability of reading up and studying Maury's charts and physical geography, the history of the countries bordering the Mediterranean, particularly the stories of ancient Greece and Rome and of Gibraltar. I suggested to the officers that in the interim of training in the summer and fall it would be well for them, after reading up on every point of interest which the sailors would see on the trip, to meet the men periodically and pass on to them the information gained from reading. This was done by some officers, and many of the seamen entered into the plan with enthusiasm. I was told that more books on Rome and Greece and the early history of the countries bordering the Mediterranean were read by sailors in those months than ever before, so that after they had passed through Gibraltar, many of them were familiar with the sea battles on that historic sea and with Roman and Grecian history.

The papers paid much attention to the cruise, and some of the European countries were suspicious. Chancellors began to inquire why the American fleet was going to Europe, as if there must be some ulterior purpose in such a cruise. I pointed out that, a few years before, Admiral Badger had gone with a few ships to England and to Germany and had been received by the King and the Kaiser with honor.

The cruise to the Mediterranean restored a waning morale; the officers and men had a great time. Visiting Rome, they were received by the Pope, and there were other highlights of the cruise. Admiral Badger, who had not been keen about it when the matter was first broached, came back enthusiastic about the training value of a trip, in which "seeing the world" was made a part of Navy enlistment.

On my first visit to Badger's home he showed me an autographed photograph given him by the Kaiser. Officers of the fleet told me the Kaiser greatly admired Badger and showed it in many ways, and well he might for Badger was an upstanding and outstanding American officer, hale, hearty and bluff, and with profound knowledge of seamanship and all that went to make a learned and success-

ful Naval officer. I do not know, but it was said that when the
Kaiser's U-boats began unrestricted ruthless warfare, the Admiral
took down the Kaiser's autographed portrait. I was not surprised, for
Badger was outraged at the savagery of the U-boat attacks.

XXIV

A SCHOOL ON EVERY SHIP

I SOON OBSERVED as I voyaged on the Naval ships, visited shore stations, and made trips of inspection, that sailors and marines had spare time which was not employed. I also learned that many of them were lacking in elementary education. Some did not even have knowledge of the three R's. When I visited the Training Station at Newport, Rhode Island, I learned that only nine enlisted men had been to college, ninety had gone to high school, but one hundred and fifty-six had little education. I was convinced by that visit and like situations I found at other stations, that every sailor and marine should not only have a chance to learn the fundamentals aboard ship, but also to learn a trade, and to win promotion by merit.

From time to time I discussed this matter with officers and with such of the enlisted men as I saw in my trips on the *Mayflower,* the *Dolphin,* and other ships. After much reflection and consultation with some officers in the Navy and Marine Corps, who shared my desire to give the sailors a better chance, I determined to strengthen the Navy as an educational institution, with schools on every ship. Of course, instructions had previously been given to the smartest men in practical engineering, gunnery, and the like, but none in the elementary subjects. Some of my aides thought my idea visionary.

In answer to the objection by a "sun downer" in the service: "You are not going to find men to coal a ship if you insist on making them study geography and arithmetic." I made answer:

"If you don't believe a man can coal a ship and shoot better or do any job better if educated, you ought to go to Massachusetts and tear down the statue of Horace Mann. When you have done that come back and talk to me. No American has the right to call himself that proud name who does not seek to educate and give large opportunities to every youth in the land."

I was speaking at Quantico one day with members of the Naval Affairs Committee, after we had visited schools for Marines. I

pointed out that in 1866, when it was found difficult to secure enlistments for the Army, Charles Sumner proposed a resolution that
at every Army post and garrison the officers should teach the men
the rudiments of education. To enforce his position, Sumner read a
letter from General Lew Wallace which gave an unanswerable
argument in favor of educating every fighting man. The letter so
impressed legislators that it was printed in the *Congressional Record*.
It is a classic. However, at that time there was wanting the sense of
democracy in the Army to take that step. It remained for the Navy
and Marine Corps in 1913 to adopt what Charles Sumner and Lew
Wallace proposed immediately after the war of the sixties.

COMPULSORY ATTENDANCE

There was opposition in the old cry, "It was never done in the
Navy." Opposition did not deter me, and I issued instructions that
schools should be open to every enlisted man and marine, that
attendance should be compulsory, and that young officers should do
the teaching, (General Order 53, issued October 1st, 1913.) The new
order was not received with enthusiasm. I followed it up with detailed instructions and a magazine article entitled: "The Navy's
Universities Afloat." I accompanied it with a statement that it
should be the foundation for opportunities for an enlisted man who
demonstrated ability to be advanced from seaman to Admiral. Some
of the young officers were not keen to teach the enlisted men, and
some of the officers objected to turning their ships into a schoolroom
for an hour each day. By that time it was known in the Navy that
"orders is orders" and most of the officers, those approving and those
disapproving, set about to establish and conduct the schools along
the lines laid down.

OPPOSITION AND RIDICULE

One day, going over to Baltimore, I fell in with a young Naval
officer whose father I had known. He voiced his opposition to
making the Navy a school and protested: "Mr. Secretary, I did not
join the Navy to become a schoolteacher."

"Maybe you didn't," I said, "but since the American people have
made a schoolteacher your Commander in Chief, you ought to regard
it as an honor."

Much fun was made of the attempt to make scholars out of sailors, and there were humorous cartoons, representing me putting an un-palatable pill marked "The Three R's" down the throat of a resisting sailor. One sailor wrote that he would be glad to go to school provided his instruction was confined to enable him to be a veteri-narian, thinking by that expression to ridicule education aboard ship. He forgot we had "horse marines" in the service.

COURSE OF INSTRUCTION OUTLINED

"How can I interest the sailors in history and geography?" I was asked by one young officer who was afraid that he could not hold the attention of the enlisted men. That question was asked at the time when American Naval ships were in Mexican waters. The revolution was on in Mexico and the whole country was thinking and talking about what was going on south of the Rio Grande. I answered by telling him to hang up a map of Mexico in his school-room, point out where our ships were stationed, and tell the men how the revolution started and what the President was trying to do for our Southern neighbor to help control their country for the bene-fit of the great body of Indians and mestizos who had never had a look-in as to their government. I added that, in teaching history, he should try to hitch instruction to something relating to what sailors were thinking about. For example, I said:

"Give the story of the Mexican war when American sailors went to Vera Cruz and General Scott's army captured Mexico City. Show the size of Mexico in 1845 and its size in 1915, and discuss frankly the two opinions about the action of the United States during Polk's administration. As Mexico is now uppermost in all minds, you will find teaching the geography and history of Mexico will catch and hold interest."

He and others tried it out and reported that there was not a dull moment while that subject was under discussion. Back in the head of each sailor was the thought that some day his ship might be ordered to Mexico and he was avid to know more about it.

The schools afloat and ashore and those for the Marines continued unabated, called off, of course during seasons of intensive practice. They stimulated ambition, and enabled some young seamen to ob-tain appointments to Annapolis; and when and if they left the Navy, their instruction qualified them for better positions in civilian life. As the years pass, I meet ex-sailors in all parts of the country doing well in civil life, who tell me that the training and schooling imparted in the Navy were invaluable to them.

COMMENDATION FROM MANY SOURCES

Commendation of making the Navy a school came from many sources at home and abroad. Shortly after a division of ships visited the Mediterranean, *L'Eclaire*, of Nice, had an article about the American sailors in which it commended their "good education and manners," and added: "Secretary Daniels when he ordered the cruise did more than he foresaw. He intended to educate crews, but he also educated us Frenchmen by showing us such splendid ships and men."

The value of schools was first impressed upon me in a conversation I had with Secretary of War Garrison upon his return from the Panama Canal. He said:

"I am just back from the Canal Zone and I learned something about your Marines which you probably do not know. Inspecting the men in the Army I also visited the Marine Barracks. There I saw a Marine officer—his name is Smedley Butler—teaching a school composed of Marines. They were on duty in a country where Spanish is spoken and Butler and other Marine officers were teaching them Spanish and they were keen to learn."

Secretary Garrison said that he had advised the Army officers to follow the example of Butler. Later, under the inspiring leadership of Generals Lejeune and Butler, the schools for Marines won high praise from both educators and men in the Corps.

WILSON TAKES A HAND

"I don't like these dinky little hats and the uniforms you make the sailors on your ships wear; why don't you change them?" was a question Lane asked one day at a Cabinet meeting when there were no weighty matters under discussion. Before I could reply, Wilson said:

"Let me answer that question, Mr. Secretary. I suspect Secretary Daniels refrains from making the change because he does not wish to invite the storm that broke on my head over what I thought was a small matter at Princeton. One day I ordered an old fence on the campus which was obstructing easy passage and which served no good purpose, removed. As soon as the work of tearing down began, telegrams poured in on me from alumni all over the country, the tenor of them all being: 'Why have you turned iconoclast? Who has given you permission to become a vandal by removing the wall erected by the immortal Witherspoon?' I capitulated. It wasn't worth a fight. The alumni, some of them fifty years out of the University, remembered some pleasant event in student days connected with that wall, and felt it was sacrilege to remove a stone. I guess Daniels felt it wasn't worthwhile to invite a torrential outpour of wrath by making a change in the ancient uniform."

The President may have been right, but ever since I left the Navy I have regretted I did not invite the storm by providing a uniform of dignity for the enlisted men.

PORT AND STARBOARD THROWN OVERBOARD

Early in April the Aide for Operations brought me an order to substitute "right" and "left" for "starboard" and "port." I hesitated to sign the order and said that I knew enough about the Navy's devotion to tradition and to old Naval lingo to cause me to hesitate to make an order that would throw into the discard the ancient "port" and "starboard." Sailors for so many years had used these terms that I doubted if any mere order of the Secretary of the Navy could eradicate their use, even though the words "right" and "left" were more easily understood and would be an improvement. The Aide told me that the matter of changing "starboard" and "port" to "right" and "left" had been under consideration by the General Board for a long time and that with only one dissenting vote the Board, headed by Admiral Dewey, had agreed upon the change. I told him I had been in office too short a time to pass upon it without more consideration. He urged it upon me, but I told him to leave the order and I would think about it before signing it. I kept it for some days and thought it over and spoke to two or three people about it. All the Naval officers I spoke to thought it was a good change, but I made up my mind to have a talk with Admiral Dewey before acting. He was president of the General Board, which was composed of what I called "Naval statesmen," in my addresses and reports. I expressed to him my doubt about changing the traditional words, so long used in the Navy. He said he had thought of the matter a long time and had held that feeling at first but that

Naval improvement ought not be impeded by an outworn tradition; that the Navy was getting so large and there were so many young men coming into it every year and they all had to be instructed in what "port" and "starboard" meant. But they all knew their right and left and it would be much easier to teach them what "right" and "left" meant than "starboard" and "port." After talking with him I decided to sign the order.

When I gave the announcement to the press, a storm of ridicule broke loose. Some of the papers said that a country editor had shown how little he knew about the Navy and its traditions by issuing an order to do away with an ancient and accepted tradition; that it would be resented and was a piece of meddling with Navy nomenclature by a civilian who knew nothing about the sea. The paragraphists and cartoonists took it up and for some weeks there was a tirade of criticism and ridicule and sarcasm. One editor, indeed, said:

"The country editor who is now in charge of the Navy, having abolished the ancient Navy terms of 'port' and 'starboard' and substituted 'right' and 'left' for them, will, no doubt, proceed to make other changes so that seamen will be deprived of their old-time Naval terms." He added: "We expect the next order to be to navigators that instead of using the directions always employed in the Navy they will be compelled to say, 'gee, haw, buck.'"

The poets also had lines about the change in nautical terms. Nixon Waterman wrote:

> Since "port" and "starboard" on our ships
>   Will be "right" and "left" hereafter,
> Landlubbers may avoid the slips
>   That have roused the sailors' laughter.
> And perhaps in another year or two
>   We'll be told that a steamship has a
> "Downstairs" and an "up" and a "basement," too,
>   And a front and back "piazza."

While all this ridicule was at its height, I declined to make any statement and said the order spoke for itself. In the fall of that year I took a number of Washington correspondents and Congressmen on a short expedition to witness target practice. Sitting on the quarter-

Nurse Columbia: YOU HAVE DONE VERY WELL, JOSEPHUS, BUT DON'T YOU THINK YOU'D BETTER PLAY WITH SOMETHING ELSE FOR A WHILE?

Harry Grant Dart. Copyright, *Life,* 1915

deck talking about different matters, one of the oldest of the newspaper correspondents said, "Mr. Secretary, I want to ask you a question. Why did you issue the order substituting 'right' and 'left' for 'starboard and 'port'?" I told him the story as related above and said that I was chiefly influenced to do so by the official recommendation reinforced by a private conversation with Admiral Dewey; that I had great faith in his judgment and the judgment of the General Board. Then the correspondent asked, "Why on earth, when the newspapers were lampooning and ridiculing you, didn't you say to the press that you made the order upon the recommendation of the General Board and the advice of Admiral Dewey. If you had done that, you would have at once silenced all criticism of you, and the country would have accepted Admiral Dewey's recommendation as perfect justification for your act." This gentleman, Richard V. Oulahan, chief of the New York *Times* Bureau in Washington, was a friend whom I had known many years, having first become acquainted with him when he accompanied Bryan, as I did, on his New England tour in 1896, and we had formed a friendship which endured. I said:

"Dick, the order would have had no value unless it had been signed by the Secretary of the Navy. I ought not to have signed it unless I was convinced it was right, and, having signed it, I did not believe in passing the buck. I was entitled to the credit, if any, because without my signature it would not have gone into effect, and I ought not to escape the criticism, if there was any, for making it an official decree. I have never believed in passing the buck and I do not intend to inaugurate my service as Secretary of the Navy by throwing upon officers who make recommendations the responsibility for my act."

CRITICISM

I made it a rule from the first never to reply to criticisms, but to content myself with clear statements of policies. There were no serious criticisms until I denied lush profiteering to the armor-plate, smokeless powder and other trusts which had been robbing Uncle Sam; until I thwarted the well-oiled long determination to exploit the Navy oil reserves; until I put an end to drinking on Navy ships and shore stations; introduced a measure (too small) of democracy and promotion by merit in the Navy; and refused to abdicate and let officers enamoured of Prussianism run the Navy.

"Why don't you reply to these unjust criticisms?", more than one friend asked. My answer was that the only complete reply would be "producing the goods," meaning such administration as would insure a Navy fit and ready for its job. In this attitude I was strengthened by Lincoln's words:

"I do the very best I know how—the very best I can; and I mean to keep doing so until the end. If the end brings me out all right, what is said against me won't amount to anything. If the end brings me out wrong, ten angels swearing I was right would make no difference."

LAUNDRY INSTALLED ON NAVY SHIPS

On an inspection trip at the Navy Yard in Brooklyn, I was received on board the *Texas* by Captain Grant. It was a hot and murky day and the Captain apologized for the looks of the ship. It was washday, and the sailors had hung their clothes to dry on the big guns and every other possible place. Soon they were black with an invasion of flies. I said to Captain Grant, "Why don't you install a modern laundry on the *Texas* and put an end to this antiquated method of washing and drying clothes?"

He replied that he had no authority to do it, that the Bureau of Construction had not arranged any place on a ship for a laundry and moreover he and other officers thought it was a good thing for the sailors to do their own laundry work; they had the time to do it and he saw no reason why the government should assume the expense of washing the clothes of the sailors; the officers had to pay for their own laundry and it was a good experience for the sailors to do their washing. I told him that I never had seen a man in my life, except a Chinaman, who wanted to do laundry work; that whether rightly or not, every man was born with the theory that the women ought to do the laundry work; and that sailors who did it felt that it was not in keeping with the duties for which they had enlisted; that the time they spent in washing the clothes ought to be occupied in going to school, learning more about gunnery and seamanship and the big jobs which would be required of them in case of trouble. I said to the Admiral, "I am inclined to make an order to install a modern laundry here to test it out and see whether it will work."

He was not very enthusiastic but he said, "If you do so, sir, I will undertake to make it work, if possible."

Upon my return to Washington, I sent for Admiral Taylor, Chief of the Bureau of Construction, and delivered myself of my feeling that it was an archaic custom to have washing done by eight hundred or a thousand men on a ship and that the time had come when this should be ended and a modern laundry installed, in which all the washing on board ship could be done. The Surgeon General gave it as his opinion that the flies attracted to the ship by laundering were unsanitary. And so the first laundry in the Navy was installed on the *Texas*. It gave great satisfaction to the sailors that they had been relieved of the weekly nuisance of having to wash their own clothes, and no more did one see the wet and flapping clothes hanging on the big guns. I gave orders then that all new ships should be constructed with a laundry, and gradually this innovation was introduced on all the large ships of the Navy.

It wasn't until later, however, that small laundries were installed on the destroyers. The men on these little craft still continued to wash their own clothes. Early in the war I assigned Commander Byron McCandliss, who had been my Aide and for whom I had a great personal regard, to go to Mare Island Navy Yard and superintend the completion of a destroyer, the *Caldwell*. He was to command it when completed. I knew he had driving energy and he was keen to get into the fight in European waters and that he would hurry up construction more rapidly than anybody else. He made a record in completing this ship and was given the title in the navy yard of "Captain Bing Bang." The Mare Island Navy Yard made the world's record in launching the destroyer *Ward*, called the "Liberty Destroyer No. 139"; its keel was laid March 4 and it was launched on June 1 and commissioned within seventy days after the keel was laid. This was later bettered at the great Victory Plant at Squantum, Massachusetts, where the *Reid* was finished and made ready for trial in forty-five and one half working days. In the pre-war days from twenty months to two years had been required to build a destroyer, but in war times Mare Island set a new pace never before equalled. Every day a new placard was put on the *Caldwell* in order to speed up the workers. Here is a sample:

"THIS DESTROYER IS NEEDED TO SINK HUN SUBMARINES.
LET ALL HANDS HELP SINK THEM."

Commander McCandliss had authority to do whatever was necessary to hasten construction, sending material by fast express whenever necessary. One day Admiral McKean, acting Chief of Operations, came into my office and handed me a telegram addressed to McCandliss saying, "Your application for authority to install a laundry on the *Caldwell* is denied."

I read it and asked to see the telegram from McCandliss to which this was a suggested answer. He gave it to me. In this telegram McCandliss had asked authority to install a laundry, saying it could be done easily without delaying construction of the ship and would be a great comfort and time-saver when the ship got into the war zone. I said to Admiral McKean, "I told McCandliss when we went out to Mare Island he had carte blanche to do any and every thing about the ship if he would get it out promptly. Write a new telegram and authorize him to install the laundry on his ship." McKean had long been with me in the Department and knew my early attitude toward laundries and was converted to the idea. He ran his hand in his pocket and pulled out a telegram he had written, saying: "I knew you would grant the request, and so here is a telegram authorizing its installation." I signed it and the *Caldwell's* crew had all their time to master their military duties without stopping to wash their clothes.

This was the history of the ending of an old-time custom and the emancipation of the enlisted men from having to act as washerwomen as well as gunners. They welcomed it because it not only relieved them of a disagreeable job but it put an end to the periodical invitation of flies to swarm over the ship, carrying with them filth and disease. And yet if a civilian had not cut across the grain and made the change, it is probable that the Naval officers would have continued until the crack of doom the traditional notion that it helps the sailor to be his own laundryman.

XXV

EDUCATING NAVAL OFFICERS

THE NAVAL ACADEMY at Annapolis was the pride of the Navy. The officers regarded it as its very heart, for it was in that institution that they received the inspiration and instruction which gave the institution international renown. I had visited it several times before I became Secretary of the Navy and knew of its thoroughness of instruction in all the technical branches of the education of the men who were to direct the operations of the Navy. Proud of its record and ambitious that it should be not only a great technical school, foremost in its training of officers, but also that the midshipmen should have a training of the same character as is given in liberal arts institutions, I recommended and Congress approved an increase in the number of midshipmen to be appointed to the Naval Academy, so that when the large new construction was completed there would be enough well trained officers to command the greater Navy.

I observed in my frequent visits to the Academy, with deep interest in its training, that while the graduates had been well trained in mathematics and vocational subjects, they lacked proficiency in history and English literature and, in general, in what is known as the humanities. Able to perform every practical duty of a Naval officer, they had received little training in speaking, and their general reading was not much more than is required in a high school. The plan in vogue was to order a good Naval officer, with no broad or liberal education, to be head of the Department of English. He was a master of the Naval profession, but not qualified to inspire in the midshipmen interest in history, in literature, or in elocution. I talked about the situation with scholars and Naval officers, and decided to name an able English scholar and writer, a civilian, as Head of the English Department. From the objections and criticisms which that plan received, one who heard the talk might have inferred that I contemplated using TNT to blow up the Naval Academy. "It has never been done"; it "is a reflection upon Naval officers who from the beginning have been heads of the Department"; it "will injure discipline"—these were a few of the objections voiced. I listened —in fact encouraged—officers to express their opinions. They never tried to convince me that the Naval officer assigned to head the department was a scholar or could inspire the midshipmen with ambition for a broad and liberal education.

I asked Dr. C. Alphonso Smith to become the head of the English Department at Annapolis. He had made a reputation as English teacher at the University of North Carolina and the University of Virginia, and as an author had written the best life of O. Henry. I told him he would not at first be welcomed; rather he would be regarded as an interloper; but he would have a free hand and my full and effective support. In fact I told him that he owed it as a duty to his country. He was made of good stuff and accepted. His wife also was a good sport. She was a native of my home city of Raleigh. It was no bed of roses. From the Superintendent down, his coming was opposed by Naval officers, both at the Academy and in the Navy Department at Washington. The officers at Annapolis received him with studied official courtesy. The residence set aside for the English head had been given to another officer before Dr. Smith arrived and he was told he would have to try to rent a house in Annapolis. When that came to my attention I gave an imperative order for the officer to vacate and for the civilian head of the English Department to be assigned the house in which the former head had lived. The next week Dr. Smith was told that he must pay for his heat and light, though it had been furnished his predecessor, who was a Naval officer. All of this was exasperating to me and embarrassing to the new head of the English Department. Explicit orders cleared up these annoyances. I told Dr. Smith:

"Do not let these annoyances disturb you. Nothing of the sort will occur again. I am confident that in a short time you and Mrs. Smith will be happy at Annapolis. You and I must remember how deeply embedded are Naval traditions. Naval officers regard the positions as heads of Departments as belonging to them by something like divine right. They think it is an invasion of an earned prerogative to introduce a civilian on equal terms. Can't you see their point of view, ingrained in the decades? Military men as a rule resist change, except in technical improvements, as something destructive of order and discipline. This is a part of their training. But when the innovation works well, they are quick to give the fullest coöperation. As soon as the boys throng your classes and you inspire them with the love of literature, as you will, the very men who resent a civilian coming as head of the Department will be your best supporters and friends."

He needed no such stimulus to be put on his mettle. It was not long before History and English were the favorite studies of midshipmen and the Superintendent and officers were proud of Dr. Smith and his department. He had the saving grace of humor and a fund of good stories. They open doors everywhere. Without this gift the new head would have found his road difficult. With it he made his way. I recall one story he loved to tell. In answer to a question he asked his class—why the Spanish Armada failed—one midshipman answered: "It was due to the lack of three ships—Seamanship, Marksmanship, and Leadership." Dr. Smith thought the answer excellent.

It should be said in justice to the very able Superintendent of the Naval Academy, Admiral Edward Eberle, one of the finest Naval officers that ever commanded a fleet, that though he had, in common with most of the other officers, opposed the innovation of a civilian head of one of the departments at Annapolis, he came to welcome the new arrangement. After Dr. Smith had stimulated the interest and admiration of the students, Admiral Eberle gave him every assistance.

EXPERT ADVICE OBTAINED

As a rule the members of the Board of Visitors at Annapolis had been made up of Congressmen and ex-graduates, who had no experience in educational methods. I named as members of the Board of Visitors college presidents from technical and literary institutions. They seriously undertook the duty and reported their findings and approval of the innovations to President Wilson, who received them at the White House. Naturally he had been with me in all my educational policies.

NO RESIGNATIONS ACCEPTED

One of the first policies announced by me was a reversal of a former one which had prevailed. This was that I would not accept resignations from graduates of the Naval Academy. Several Naval Academy graduates, who had been educated at the expense of the country, offered their resignations because they could secure positions in private business which would give them larger incomes. I declined to accept such resignations, saying it had cost the government more than $20,000 for their education; that the government had not spent this large sum of money to train them as Naval officers for their benefit but for the exclusive good of the Navy, and that to graduate them and then give them the additional instruction of a training on board ship would be to throw away the money spent on their education, so far as the taxpayers were concerned. I said I could not consent to such a waste of money, particularly since there was need in the Navy for all the trained officers and there was no source from which they could be obtained except from the Naval Academy. My refusal to accept resignations was commented on both favorably and adversely, and there was much discussion about it; but I found that Congress, and particularly the Naval Affairs Committee, which kept up fully with Naval matters, approved my decision. I told parents who came to see me that the time to settle whether the son was to be a Naval officer was when they solicited an appointment to the Naval Academy and that if they obtained the appointment in order to secure for their sons education for civilian pursuits at the government's expense, it was an imposition on the taxpayers and I could not consent to it.

HAZING ABOLISHED

Early in my administration there came from Annapolis reports that hazing had broken out again. It broke out periodically. I had taken the ground as a trustee of the University of North Carolina that the only way to stop hazing was by expelling with dishonor those who engaged in it and coöperating with the courts in punishing those guilty. I therefore sent to Annapolis a statement warning all the midshipmen that no clemency would be shown to any hazer and that every midshipman who indulged in hazing would, upon proof that he had thus violated the rules of the Academy and violated the laws of the country, be dismissed, and would not be permitted to reënter the Academy. This severe and new ruling was not very well received by many officers. They held, as did many civilians, that hazing was a boyish prank. Some said that it was necessary to reduce the "big-head" of egotistical youths and that dismissal was too severe a penalty for what they called a boyish prank. I told them that when a man took the oath as an officer of the United States Navy and was being fed and clothed and educated at the expense of the taxpayer, he occupied a very different position from that of the boy in college who paid all his expenses. I added that if they were not disciplined in the academy they would not be fit to discipline the men they would later command.

Afterwards, when there were dismissals, I found myself between two sets of opponents, first the Naval officers who resented a rule that put hazing in the same catalogue with criminal action, and second, with Senators and Representatives in Congress whose appointees had been convicted of hazing. A midshipman who had been appointed to Annapolis by my good friend Senator Stone, of Missouri, had been dismissed for hazing. Senator Stone was more vigorous than all the others in protesting at what he called my czarism and lack of appreciation of what a boy ought to be allowed to do. When I declined to change the order dismissing his constituent, he said, "I will appeal over you to the President of the United States. He has taught boys in college and will have more heart and a better sense of justice than you have."

WILSON STOOD FIRM

Of course, I said, I would give an "Aye, Aye, Sir" to any ruling of my superior officer. He went hot-footed and hot-tempered to the White House to see Wilson and fully expected to come back with an order to tell me to reinstate his midshipman. He did not come back at all. I knew what would happen in the White House, for I had had the foresight to confer with the President before making a public statement. He had given strong expression to his view that a midshipman was an officer of the Navy and that he must set an example in obeying the orders if he was fit later on to give orders. The next time I saw Senator Stone, he said, with a pleasant smile, "I do not know whose heart is the harder, yours or Woodrow Wilson's. You are both practicing cruelty which ought to be forbidden by the Constitution." Everyone in the Academy, midshipmen and all, knew that Senator Stone was going to try to use his rabbit-foot to put this young man back, and if he had been successful, hazers would have felt that they had full impunity. However, when Senator Stone failed—he was probably at that time the Senator closest to the President and well known to be an old friend of mine—the officers

LEADING ADVISERS TO THE SECRETARY OF THE NAVY

Upper left, Admiral Victor Blue, Chief of Navigation, who won honor in the Spanish American War. *Upper right,* Admiral Charles J. Badger, Commander-in-Chief of the Naval Fleet, successor to George Dewey as chairman of the General Board of the Navy. *Lower left,* Admiral A. G. Winterhalter, Aide for Matériel, Commander of the Asiatic Fleet. *Lower right,* Admiral Joseph Strauss, Chief of Bureau of Ordnance (Harris & Ewing).

Upper left, Admiral Edward W. Eberle, Superintendent of the Naval Academy. *Upper right,* Dr. C. Alphonso Smith, of North Carolina, first civilian to be appointed as head of the Department of English at the Naval Academy. *Below,* Secretary Daniels at his desk in the early days of his administration.

and the midshipmen at Annapolis understood that hazing would not be condoned and the practice was greatly diminished.

WILSON AT THE NAVAL ACADEMY

June week, 1914, was made notable at the Naval Academy by the presence of President Wilson, who delivered the address to the graduating midshipmen. He warned them against getting "the professional point of view" because "there is nothing narrower or more unserviceable than the professional point of view." He told them that they were "not serving a government," but were "serving a people." He urged them not "to be ready to fight merely at the drop of a hat or upon some slight punctilio", and said:

> "You are champions of your fellowmen.... We must strike out on new paths, and we must count upon you gentlemen to be explorers who will carry this spirit and spread this message over the seas and every part of the civilized world."

IMPROVING THE WAR COLLEGE

Early in June of 1913 I went up to Newport, R. I., to deliver an address at the Naval War College. In the course of my address on the effectiveness of sea power, I quoted a statement by former Secretary Herbert to the effect that the defeat of the Southern Confederacy was accomplished when the Federal Navy bottled up all the Southern ports, thus preventing the export of cotton to Europe—an export which, in the early years of the war, enabled the South to barter its cotton for medical supplies and other necessities for the military and civilian population. I adverted to the fact that brave and adventurous Confederate blockade runners kept North Carolina supplied until Fort Fisher fell. Cut off from outside trade, the South was strangled, just as a bird would die of strangulation confined in a bottle corked so that no air could get into it. Sea power had been the determining factor in that war as in many others.

This was my first visit to the Newport Naval Base. At night, as the guest of Admiral W. L. Rodgers, I sat up until long after midnight talking with Admirals Caperton, Sims, McKean, and other prominent Naval officers, the conversation largely turning on the best character of organization for making a Navy most efficient. Sims took the lead and was very positive in his views, pointing out defects in the present setup in a way that showed he had given the matter much consideration. He wanted an organization like the British Admiralty. As was characteristic of him, I was to learn later, he never admitted a doubt of the wisdom of his conclusions and paid very little attention to the views of others, unless they happened to be British. Even so, I saw that he had attractive qualities which drew young men to him.

THEY ALL TOOK WHITE ROCK

The morning after my address Admiral Caperton asked me if I would like to visit the Newport Library. Of course I said "Yes." I had not then been initiated into the mysteries of the Library with a big L. As we entered, I was conducted into a room in which a bar was fitted up in a manner that would do credit to any saloon. A barkeeper, with the regulation apron, stood behind the counter.

"What will you have, Mr. Secretary?" asked Admiral Caperton.

"White Rock," I said.

"And you?" he asked each of the half-dozen Admirals who had accompanied us to the Library.

"White Rock," everyone promptly answered and we every one lined up at the counter and drank that innocuous temperance drink to the astonishment of the barkeeper, who had never before served six non-alcoholic drinks to that number of Admirals. We then repaired to the Library. There were the morning papers and a few books, enough for the excuse to drop in for a bit of news and a chaser. I later learned that the officers had many good laughs when one of the number, who never failed to have his stiff drink before lunch, solemnly asked for White Rock. He said he would be damned if he would let other Admirals appear more temperate before the new Secretary than himself. Afterwards I was told that upon my departure, the other Admirals returned to the so-called Library for their favorite drink. Perhaps they took a stronger nip than usual to fortify themselves against the address they were to hear from the new Secretary a little later in the day.

FEW STUDENTS, MANY INSTRUCTORS

We resumed the conversation of the previous night, and to the pleasure of Admiral Rodgers, I turned the conversation to my surprise in finding less than a dozen officers taking the course prescribed at the War College. "Here are facilities and teachers for half a hundred and you have not a fifth that number. Why?" Admiral Rodgers explained that he had unsuccessfully sought to have more officers assigned for the course, but that the Bureau of Navigation claimed it could not spare them from service at sea, when, as a matter of fact, I had already learned there were too many on desk duty at Washington and at shore stations. I determined that we would either use the Naval War College or close it, for it was a waste to maintain an institution for teaching strategy and tactics and war history without matriculants.

Upon my return to Washington, I described the impossible situation to Admiral Blue, Chief of Navigation, who assigned officers to duty, and I decided that after a certain date no officer would be promoted unless he had graduated at the Naval War College. Blue persuaded me to postpone its execution until it was possible to give every officer the training. Of course, I had no intention of penalizing an officer who had wished to take the course but had been denied the privilege. There were some who boasted of being "practical," who had no desire to study, but not many. The failure to go to the War College was chiefly due to the lack of interest in its work by the Washington Naval administration. Admiral Blue was directed to send a large class at the beginning of the next course and in making assignments to see that captains and commanders had the opportunity to go before coming up for promotion so that within a brief period a certificate of efficiency from the War College would be a prerequisite to promotion.

I look back upon the change of attitude toward the War College as one of the best contributions I made to Naval efficiency in the first year of my incumbency in my position, and was gratified to find that all the forward-looking officers appreciated and approved the new policy. Instead of a haven of rest for a few, the War College became a real college with an increasing number of matriculants.

OLD STRATEGY MUST GO

From the beginning of the World War I had been eager that its lessons should be made use of for the improvement of our Navy. In an address at the opening of the War College in 1915, while Europe was plunged in war, I stressed this duty upon the officers and said:

"As you look abroad you see the foundations of old theories crumbling every day. Old tactics, old strategies, old theories of Naval warfare, which have stood unchallenged as almost axiomatic since the triremes of Carthage and Rome grappled in the Mediterranean, are disappearing over night. If war upon the land has reverted to the bayonet and the hand grenade, war upon the sea has leaped forward at a single stride and broken every shackle of ancient convention.

"We have seen the main fleet of the greatest sea nation in the world withdrawn from the seas to some secluded harbor without having fired a shot during the first years of the mighty conflict. We have seen battles begun at ranges believed to be impossible and ships disabled by shots from guns as yet invisible. We have been told that modern sea fights would be determined in the first ten minutes, and yet we have seen that it took six hours to decide one of the greatest ocean battles of the present war. We have seen ships of shallow draft used as fortresses to protect armies on the Belgian coast.

"We read only yesterday of the submarines gliding unchallenged past the impregnable fortress of Gibraltar and the guardian ships that watch the straits. We have seen fast cruisers raiding the coast and eluding their pursuers by the help of dirigibles hovering far above and warning, through the new miracle, wireless telegraphy, the ships beneath."

I then asked the officers, "With what weapon, by what strategy, shall we meet the terror of the submarine, the still unrevealed possibilities of the air ship?" and I said to the officers, "It is to you that your Secretary looks for the answer." I pledged myself to spare no effort "to assist in the onward march," and I called for "the most perfect plans and methods human wisdom can invent."

XXVI

DEMOCRACY IN THE NAVY

I HAD NOT LONG TO WAIT before learning that the most serious defect in the Navy was the lack of democracy. I, of course, strongly believed in discipline, in respect due to authority; I believed that an efficient Navy must have leadership that leads and intelligent and loyal followership. But I had no liking for the chasm that separated the officers from the enlisted men, upon whose united efforts Naval efficiency depends. Not long after taking office, I visited a Navy training base where the new recruits were given their first lesson. I invited Admiral Fullham to accompany me, knowing that he prided himself upon his ability to train and command both officers and enlisted men. I was to learn on that trip that he regarded officers as belonging to a superior caste, while the enlisted personnel lived in a different compartment. I had made a speech to the youths who were coming into the Navy—no draft then—voluntarily. I welcomed them into a service where they would have the high privilege of serving their country. Returning to Washington from the base, Admiral Fullham asked, "May I make a friendly suggestion?" I replied, "Certainly," and he said, "Today in your address to the enlisted men you called them 'Young gentlemen.' I would advise that you use some other term, as it might be misunderstood. It has never before been done in the Navy."

I suppressed my indignation at that evidence of snobbery, and quietly asked, "How should I have addressed them?"

He said that the usual way was to call them "My lads," or "Sailors," or "Enlisted men."

In the fall of 1913, when it was necessary to approve the plans for new Marine barracks at the Philadelphia Navy Yard, I directed the architect to make some changes. The amount of money available was limited, and the number of officers and men to be housed was at that time such that the money would not complete the buildings on the original plan. I ordered the plans altered and under this change officers and men were to be housed under one roof. This was another piece of iconoclasm that was not very acceptable. It was bringing officers and men too close together, some thought. But most of the Marine officers with whom I consulted thought it was a very good thing. It seemed to me that if officers and men could fight together, live in trenches, bivouac together at Haiti and Nicaragua, none of the ten commandments would be broken when they were housed under the same roof in the Navy Yard at Philadelphia.

ENLISTED MEN GO TO NAVAL ACADEMY

With enlisted men receiving instruction, my mind turned to opening avenues for advancement to those who were best qualified. There was a way provided, but it was so long and so difficult that very few men advanced from enlisted to officer rank. Now and then a superior man could make the grade, but very few did so, and there was not much encouragement to ambition. I became convinced that the method of securing officers lacked the democratic open door in a republic. I reached the conclusion that the chance to enter the Naval Academy for training should be open to all enlisted men, and that the brightest of them should, after a year's service in the ranks, be entitled to compete for appointment to the Naval Academy. This involved a radical change in the method, and required taking from every Senator and Representative in Congress the power to appoint youths of their own choice, without competition. However, I felt that if I proposed such a sweeping change, Congressmen would decline to give up that prized piece of patronage. I therefore recommended that each year as a beginning, not less than twenty-five enlisted men who, after serving a year's enlistment, passed the highest examination, should go to the Naval Academy on the same terms as the appointees of Congressmen.

This proposal struck a snag in the Senate. Some Naval officers, influenced by a sort of spirit of caste, objected. They persuaded Senator Weeks, of Massachusetts, who was a graduate of the Naval Academy, to defeat my proposition. The measure was in such parliamentary status that a single objection would kill it at that session of Congress. Senator Weeks told me I was making a mistake and he would make the objection which, under the circumstances, would be its death sentence. I could not move him at first. We were good friends and I used persuasion. He tried to convince me that I would be lowering the standard of Naval officers. There was an impasse.

I knew that Weeks owed his election to the support of the laboring men in Massachusetts, many of them Irish, who were ingrained in democracy, and usually voted the Democratic ticket. I therefore, with a smile on my face, asked the Senator, "How do you think it would look for the Boston papers to carry a story that the Navy Department wished to open a hitherto closed door for young sailors to win promotion but that Senator Weeks slammed the door in their faces?"

"By heavens, Daniels," he said, "you would not do a thing like that to me!" I answered:

> "Of course not but the plan I propose has passed the House, it is known to all the correspondents, many approve of it. If you make the fatal objection some correspondent, you may be sure, will report the fact, and ambitious youths who have no pull will resent your action, and your political opponents will score a point against you when you come up for reëlection."

We reached an understanding that if I would consent to limit the number he would not make the fatal objection. I agreed because I felt that if the principle of promotion from the ranks could once be adopted, the soundness of the plan would at a future time increase the number—as was done later, to one hundred. The day should come when every appointee will be required to serve a year as an enlisted seaman before he can go to the Naval Academy, and his selection should be based upon demonstrated fitness and aptitude.

OBEYS ORDER TO THE LIMIT

In the first graduating class after enlisted men were appointed, one of the number from California led the Academy in athletics and scholarship. I was at the Naval Academy when he graduated, and presented his commission. In the afternoon I sent for him to come to the Superintendent's home and congratulated him upon having done so well, thus demonstrating the wisdom of the new policy. I casually asked him what assignment he had received.

"I am sorry, Sir, but I have been instructed not to disclose my assignment."

That was the rule, and, in the presence of the Superintendent and the Chief of Navigation, who made the assignments to duty, he obeyed orders and declined to tell the Secretary of the Navy on what ship he would serve! That was obeying orders to the limit!

I followed the careers of these first Naval officers who came up from the ranks. They made good. One of them was Julian Bennett Noble, of California, who entered the Academy in 1915. On his first official practice with a machine gun he made 93 hits on 93 shots, a perfect record. The Captain of his ship wrote of his gunnery efficiency: "with the greatest admiration, and without whose help none of this would have been possible." His squadron in dive-bombing made the highest score ever made. His last shore duty was as special assistant to Charles Edison, Secretary of the Navy in Franklin Roosevelt's administration.

REFERENDUM ON UNIFORMS

The Navy is about the last place where you would expect to see a referendum in operation. I thought it wouldn't be bad if younger officers and the enlisted men were sometimes consulted instead of told to take orders—"theirs not to reason why."

What sort of uniform should officers of the Navy wear? Some of the younger men wished to do away with choker collars, which I thought, looking to comfort, ought to be changed. At that time all coats of officers were buttoned so tight around their necks that normal breathing was difficult, unless it had been endured so long that the necks had become more or less indurated. Some of the officers of commander and lower rank showed me that as soon as officers were off duty, they unbuckled the collar so that they could breathe and thus obtain comfort at the sacrifice of appearances. They suggested the adoption of a coat that called for a comfortable collar. I directed the Chief of the Bureau of Navigation to send out to all officers pictures of the uniform then in use and of the proposed open neck uniform, and give each one an opportunity to vote whether he wished a change. By an overwhelming majority, the result of the democratic referendum was for the more comfortable style. I therefore issued the necessary order.

As soon as Admiral Benson, Chief of Operations, and Admiral Mayo, Commander in Chief of the fleet, heard of the result of the voting, they were up in arms about it. They asked an interview and protested strongly against the issuance of the order to change the uniform. I listened to their protest, and then said, "You are too late. The question was submitted to all of the officers, and by a very large majority they showed by their votes that they favored a change. I feel bound, being a Democrat, both with a big *D* and a little *d*, to stand for majority rule."

They insisted that in a matter of that character the young officers knew little and ought not to be given as much voice as the older and more experienced officers. As they continued to urge that I overrule the majority vote, I said facetiously,

"Gentlemen, I have examined the vote, and find that all the young men with soft necks wish a change while most of the old officers whose necks have become indurated by long suffering in wearing the choking collar wish the old uniform. It looks to me that it is a case of the Rough Necks *vs* the Soft Necks. As there are more of the latter, the Rough Necks lose."

I repeated this to a young officer. He said, "The real reason the Admirals oppose the change is that now their stars are in evidence, being on the neck of the collar. In the new uniform the stars would be on the sleeve and not easily seen."

NO WHITE UNIFORMS IN PRODUCTION PLANTS

In my tours of inspection at the Navy Yards I observed that in the hot weather and in the grime and dust of the foundries and machine-shops and other plants where mechanics and workingmen were often so hot they would take off their shirts to work, the inspecting Navy officers wore immaculate white uniforms. This seemed incongruous to me. Here were men who were in charge of important mechanical work, where furnaces blazed and fires roared, and men were working under great pressure, and where it was impossible for a man to keep clean, wearing the sort of uniform that might have been expected at some official or social function.

"Why do you wear these white uniforms in this red-hot working place?" I asked the officer who was showing me about.

"Regulations," he said, "and it is absurd. I hate like the devil to do it, but I must obey orders."

"The regulations are changed," I said, "and tomorrow you may wear clothes suitable to the work in which you are engaged."

Most officers liked the change. Many years ago, when officers inspected wooden ships, the white duck uniform did not get dirty and was not so much out of place. The probabilities are that the incongruity of wearing such uniforms where workers were sweating over the blasts had not been called to the attention of my predecessors. A regulation in the Navy, like precedents in European countries, often becomes hoary with age because nobody thinks to change it or because there is a feeling that it would be sacrilege to drop an archaic custom.

Most of the young men in the Naval Academy, named by Congressmen, came from average homes and were trained in public schools, where the playgrounds constitute the purest democracy in the world. There the race is to the strong and the fleet, with no favors. Equality is the hallmark. And yet, so pervasive is the military tradition that a chasm separates Ensign and Admiral, and the gulf between officers and enlisted men is not often bridged. The same undemocratic practice was seen in the Army. It was borrowed from Europe, where, for generations, admission to officer status was impossible to a youth without title or money. I recall that early in the World War, a young lieutenant, sensing the separation between officers and enlisted men, asked if he could properly invite his brother, who was a private, to dine with him at the Army and Navy Club.

It did not take me long to learn that suggestions to bridge the chasm found little favor with some officers in both Navy and Army. Do Americans really believe in the equality upon which their republic was founded? I wish that question could be answered in the affirmative at Annapolis and West Point and in all military service.

I often showed my feeling by shaking hands with a sailor upon entering the barge, and inviting a private in the Marine Corps to dine with my son, who had enlisted as a private in the Marine Corps on the outbreak of war. One night at the table in our home, without design there sat together a young enlisted sailor (son of a North Carolina preacher), a private in the Marines (son of a Pennsylvania butcher), a Captain in the Navy, two ranking Admirals, and the Secretary of the Navy and his wife. And none thought of rank.

XXVII

PROMOTION BY MERIT AND SEA SERVICE

I LOOK BACK with satisfaction upon the adoption of the principle of promotion by demonstrated merit, and merit alone, which I caused to supplant promotion for length of service. There is no justification in the Navy or anywhere else, if the highest efficiency is to be obtained, of promotion by seniority or by any rule except that of demonstrated efficiency. I had not been long in office before I saw the need of supplanting the outmoded policy by which, if any officer kept sober, was prudent and meticulous in carrying out the regulations, and did not lose his ship, he was certain in the course of time to become an Admiral. This was independent of whether he had initiative, mastery of the lore of his profession, or that indefinable quality of leadership which inspires confidence that, in an emergency, he would demonstrate something of the stuff that made a John Paul Jones, a Farragut, or a Dewey. When assigning Admirals to important commands, I soon learned there were several officers of Admiral rank who were unavailable for commanding a division or a fleet, and were even lacking in the ability to be entrusted with important posts at shore bases. Such men ought never to be given the high rank. Recognizing that something should be done, Congress had authorized the setting up of what came to be known as the "Plucking Board." It operated to prevent the promotion of officers not deemed to have the high qualities of command. It was costly and cumbersome and gave great dissatisfaction. In conjunction with officers always alert for improvement, I recommended to Congress a system of Promotion by Merit and Merit Alone, which was approved by the Naval Affairs Committee and became a law.

On the morning that the papers carried my statement that I had recommended promotion by selection, thus junking the seniority ladder, I met General Crowder, one of the ablest Army officers on duty in Washington. "Do you think you can unhorse the hoary old traditional method of promotion by seniority in the Navy?" he asked.

"I am certain of it," I replied. "Before making the recommendation I talked with both the chairman and the ranking member of the Naval Affairs Committees. They believe a change is needed and will support the plan."

"I have not seen so great faith in Washington," he said. "You could as easily remove the dome from the capitol as to touch a hair of that entrenched system. If you succeed I will say the day of miracles has not passed." When, to his amazement the method of promotion was changed, General Crowder congratulated me, saying, "I never expected to live to see it. Henceforth I will believe in miracles."

There was some like skepticism among Navy officers in that group which, whenever any change in Naval tradition was proposed, would mourn that the country editor was going to ruin the Navy. Some told me that, and my answer was, "What, again?" I added that I had already, according to stand-patters, ruined it so many times that one more time wouldn't matter. But I always added: "The Navy is a tough old bird. It is so good that no Secretary could ruin it if he tried." I added that it was the pride of the country because forward-looking men in the service had not only not been afraid of change but had welcomed good innovations. The first promotions under the new plan elevated two or three of the ablest Captains to the two star rank above older men. While no system works perfectly because it must be operated by fallible human beings, and it caused some heartaches, it came to be recognized that it was based on the sound principle that the good of the service should be superior to individual ambition.

LONG SEA SERVICE REQUIRED

It was not long before the principle I had recommended to the President and he had approved, of granting no promotion to Naval officers who had not had adequate sea service, came up directly for action. In the usual order, a board was appointed to examine Captain T. M. Potts, Aide for Personnel, for promotion to the rank of Rear Admiral, and Commander Philip Andrews for the rank of Captain. I directed my aide to ascertain how much sea service these men had had in their grade and he reported "very little." Potts had been Chief of the Naval Intelligence Department and Aide For Personnel, and Andrews had been Chief of the Bureau of Navigation, on duty in Washington. The Board of Officers designated to pass upon the qualifications of these two officers recommended them for promotion. It was then up to me to determine whether the policy I had announced should be carried out. The issue was clear-cut. I had no alternative, when the report was presented to me, but to decline to approve it, and I directed that both these officers be given service at sea and their promotion held up until such time as they had shown by service in command of ships afloat that their long tour of duty on land had not lessened such capacity.

This action created something of a sensation in the Navy and in Washington, where both these officers had been popular, particularly in the circle of the Army and Navy Club and the social life of Washington. They had made many influential friends, particularly in the Navy League, which had been quite a power. Both of these officers felt outraged and began to bring every influence possible to bear upon me and upon the President to reverse the decision. Shortly the friends of Philip Andrews assured him, and his own good sense taught him, that a Naval officer's duty was to accept the decision of his superior officers. He accepted the situation and went to sea, determined to make good, which he did. Afterwards I had the pleasure of assigning him to very important duties, which he filled with great credit and distinction and later won the deserved promotion.

It was otherwise with Captain Potts. Shortly after it became known that the President had approved my recommendation not to promote Captain Potts to Rear Admiral, I received a call from Colonel Robert M. Thompson, head of the Navy League, who had kept in touch with the Naval officers, and had a genuine interest in Naval affairs. This interest, of course, was heightened because it gave him prominence in the country and in Naval circles. He had been very courteous to me. When I received him he launched into an earnest appeal for a reversal of the action refusing the Potts' promotion. I heard him not only one time but several times, but declined to change my position. He was very much put out. He had been accustomed to having his requests passed upon with approval by the Navy Department and thought he had done enough for the Navy to justify acquiescence in what he recommended. A principle, however, was involved and I could not, at his insistence or the insistence of Admiral Fiske and others of the Naval officers in Washington, change the policy. I had been careful not to involve Admiral Blue, Chief of Navigation, in this matter. He told me that my course would bring down on me condemnation from influential sources in the Navy, which, of course, I had known before I decided to take action.

The matter was much discussed in the press of the country, and the Potts supporters had the best of it with a number of important papers. The New York *Herald,* which had long given more attention to the Navy than any other paper and which had even then begun to be critical of President Wilson's policy and of mine, and its editor, who had had Naval training, took up the cudgels for Potts, as did other papers. The new policy was widely discussed. While the friends of Potts and what had been called the "far-from-the-blue-sea" Naval officers in Washington were critical, the bulk of the country approved the action. It had a salutary effect in deterring officers whose wives wished social prominence or who had other reasons, from desiring a long term of soft berths ashore. Nothing keyed up the morale of going to sea so much as that ruling. Captain Potts applied to me for reversal and thought I had been very badly advised. As a matter of fact, I took that course on my own initiative. I explained to him that there was no personal element in the matter at all, and that I would follow that course with respect to every promotion, as I had announced shortly after coming into office.

ARRIVED AT POTTS-DAM

When he could not move me, he appealed to the President to reverse my decision and prepared an elaborate document, undertaking to convince the President that I had done him a very great injustice and had not carried out the spirit of Naval procedure with reference to promotion. Of course, under the regulations, he could send no appeal to the President except through me. I received his appeal and took it over to the President at a meeting of the Cabinet on April 11. When it came my turn, in the regular order of Cabinet procedure, the President inquired: "Has the Secretary of the Navy any matter to bring before the Cabinet?"

"Yes, Mr. President," I replied. "I have here a written appeal from Captain Potts who wishes you to reverse my decision as to his promotion to the grade of Rear Admiral." The President was familiar with the case as I had talked with him about it, and he said: "Motion overruled. The decision of the Secretary of the Navy will stand in the Potts case."

Then he said, "That reminds me of an incident that occurred in a church meeting," and he related a story somewhat like this:

"At this church meeting, the whole discussion turned upon the action of a Mr. Potts—whether he had been right in some action or wrong. The discussion consumed the whole morning and was still the order of business when adjournment was had for lunch. When the body came together after luncheon, the moderator turned to the clerk (this must have been a Presbyterian Synod) and asked:

" 'At what point had we arrived when adjournment was had?'

"The clerk, who had grown utterly weary of the Potts discussion, replied: 'Potts-Dam!' "

THE CAPTAIN PLUCKED

I could not restrain a feeling of sympathy for Captain Potts. However, it had been his own fault that he had stayed on land so much, and I had given him a chance to go to sea and test whether land service had lessened his ability to command afloat. I gave him a good ship and he went to sea and won the regard of the officers and sailors. While he was yet at sea on the *Louisiana*, the Plucking Board met. There were not enough positions of Admiral to insure that every Captain should wear the two stars, and Congress had enacted that upon the recommendation of the Navy Department each year a board of officers should meet and select certain officers who would remain in the rank of Captain and never go up to the rank of Admiral. This Plucking Board was the nightmare of all Naval officers, who had lived all their lives in the expectation of wearing the stars. When this Board met, an official letter was written to the Secretary of the Navy asking the status of Potts, whether he was a Captain or whether he was an Admiral. If the latter, he would take the first vacancy in the Admiral ranks. If the former, he was in their jurisdiction and could be plucked if he was less qualified for promotion than others. Some Captain had to be plucked. I wrote officially that since the President had not approved the recommendation for promotion of Captain Potts and as the Senate had not confirmed the Board's recommendation, his status was that of Captain. There was no other answer to make. When the Plucking Board made its report, it put Captain Potts in the list of those plucked, which made it impossible for him to become an Admiral. This action, with which

I had nothing to do, of course increased the indignation in a small set in the Navy, and Thompson and others outside, who attributed to me Potts' failure to be promoted. Either he had to be plucked or some officer who had long sea service. Between plucking one who had enjoyed easy shore berths and plucking those who had been much at sea, the latter deserved first consideration. By that time it began to be pretty well understood that the new Secretary of the Navy was at the helm; that when he laid down a policy he would carry it out. The comparatively few officers who had desired shore billets began to make earnest appeals to go to sea. From that time shore billets were not desired by an officer until he had had adequate sea service. Captain Potts later retired. When the World War came on, he was called back to duty and served acceptably at a post at San Francisco. I met him there and found him doing his job capably, and our intercourse was free from any suggestion of the former difference.

POPULAR OFFICER PLUCKED

Not long after the Potts incident, a prominent officer in the Navy said to me one day, "Unless Captain Gibbons, head of the Naval Academy, goes to sea, he will be in danger of meeting the Potts fate. He has been Naval Attaché abroad and Superintendent of the Naval Academy a long time and he ought to go to sea."

I had come in close touch with Gibbons and had visited him at the Naval Academy. My wife and Mrs. Gibbons had become good friends. The next time I saw him, I told Gibbons that there was no desire whatever to have him retire from the superintendency of the Academy, which he was filling with satisfaction, but that some Naval officers had told me he was in danger of being plucked if he remained ashore much longer; that as Secretary of the Navy, I did not intend to permit any man to lose his chance of promotion by keeping him ashore against his will and I was ready to send him to sea at any time he desired such assignment. He was devoted to his duties at the Academy and his wife enjoyed the social end of it, and both were popular with instructors and midshipmen. He said he preferred to stay there. So he stayed on.

Some time later, Admiral Blue came into my office one day and said, "Captain Gibbons wishes to come over from Annapolis to see you." Of course I assented and when he came he told me he had been thinking seriously about the matter of going to sea and had reached the conclusion that my suggestion was a wise one and he would like to be relieved as Superintendent and be assigned to sea duty; that he wished to take no chance of a possible plucking, though he did not fear it would be done since his record was without a flaw. I sent for Blue and told him to give Gibbons a good assignment in command of a ship as soon as possible and he did so.

Gibbons had been at sea, however, only a comparatively brief time when the Plucking Board had its next meeting. They were face to face with plucking several Captains. There were not enough admiralships to go round, and when Blue brought me the report of the Plucking Board, he was white with regret that Gibbons' name was on the list. I was sorry also. In every respect except that he had been on shore an extra long time, his record was one hundred per cent. Blue hoped that something could be done. He thought the Board had made a mistake and personally I had such high opinion of Gibbons and liked him so much that I was greatly troubled because there was nothing that could be done. I had made the order and the President had approved it—that adequate sea service must stand first in promotion to the highest rank. The Board had taken that rule into consideration, had given first promotions to what was known as the "sea dogs," and Gibbons had fallen because, at his own request or acquiescence, he had elected to serve overlong in shore billets. It was a real tragedy and I felt it very deeply, and told him so, but I also told him when he spoke of bringing the matter to the President that the President strongly believed that the first requisite of an Admiral was that he had demonstrated by sea service his capacity to command a fleet and there was no hope. He was a very manly man and while humiliated and distressed, he held his head high and when the decision was against him, accepted it with a certain sort of stoicism that commanded respect.

NOT SO HIS WIFE

Mrs. Gibbons was a woman of strong will and great ambition for her husband. She was very wealthy. Gibbons had married late in life and his wife had greatly enjoyed the distinction of being the wife of the Naval Attaché in Europe and the Superintendent of the Naval Academy. In all the years she had looked forward to the time when she and her husband would ride behind a car or in a barge with the two stars as the insignia of high rank. When she saw this ambition could not be realized for her husband, it almost killed her. Her pride was hurt to the quick and she could not restrain her resentment. Hot anger possessed her. I profoundly sympathized with her and so did my wife. Months afterwards, I was her dinner partner at a dinner in Washington attended by a score or more prominent official and social leaders of the capital. For the moment I forgot her humiliation and passion. She was in gay humor at the dinner table (in Washington City at dinner parties the whole question of whether you have a good time or not is whether you draw an interesting partner), and we talked about many things in a light and breezy way. I do not recall how it came up, but upon some remark she made, I said by way of badinage:

"The truth is, Mrs. Gibbons, we are all savages. This thing we call civilization is nothing but veneering, and sometimes very thin veneering, and almost any one of us in a moment of outrage at some wrong done our loved ones will go back to savagery and kill with just as little regret as our ancestors in the German forest."

In this rather light vein, I pursued the subject, referring to people I had known who, educated and possessed of what we call culture, had gone back to the primitive, and I said: "You and I are like to do the same under sufficient provocation."

I then saw a light come into her eyes which had in it more fury than I had ever dreamed possible in any woman's eyes. What I had said or what she had thought brought back to her with poignancy the plucking of her husband, and I then understood something of her passionate hatred of those who had been responsible for his disappointment. Speaking rather in an undertone so that nobody could hear it but myself, and with hatred and bitterness in her voice, she said, "You are quite right, and the only reason I would not with my own hands tear and rend those miserable men who denied my husband what was his right is because he will not let me."

Then for ten minutes, with suppressed tone but with a violence in her voice which I cannot forget to my dying day, she proceeded to berate them with such denunciation as I have never heard any other woman employ. It was not so much her words as the letting out of long suppressed fury.

"If it were not for John Gibbons," she said, "I would kill them with my own hands," and as I looked at her sitting at this dinner table, almost an Amazon in build, dressed in the very latest Parisian style with sparkling diamonds, emeralds, and pearls galore, it seemed to me that all the civilization of the centuries had dropped from her and she sat there like a stark savage in the German forest. I have seen a few mothers like this when their children were in peril or wronged, more like tigresses than women, but she was the only woman I have ever seen who had that tiger-like view about a wrong done to her husband. I was transfixed with a sort of horror I have never escaped and with a sort of admiration for her passionate love and pride which had been hurt beyond healing as she exposed these bleeding wounds wholly unconscious that she did so.

When the passion had spent itself, she was almost limp. It had torn her as if some physical part had come out of her. Within a short time, such was her natural dominance of herself, it had passed, and without reference to it she turned to some topic of the day as if she were again a woman of the world, able to hold her head high anywhere with anybody. I was to see some other officers and their wives distressed and humiliated in somewhat like manner, but never comparable to this. I hope I shall never see it again.

BOARD OF SELECTION

Later I was to secure the repeal of the Plucking Board and the substitution of a Board of Selection, whose object was to secure the promotion of officers by recognition of superior ability rather than by seniority.

XXVIII

AVIATION AND MY FIRST AIR FLIGHT

G REAT EXCITEMENT PREVAILED in the Navy Department when I desired to make an examination of the plans of the *Pennsylvania* and officers reported that they had been stolen. The *Pennsylvania* was our largest dreadnaught, soon to be the flagship of the fleet, and the plans embraced new methods of fire control and other improvements which it was believed were not known to any other government. Every nook and corner was searched, but all in vain. The news of the theft got into the papers; detectives were set to work.

There were plenty of surmises. It was gravely charged that a certain noted actress, who had been in Washington, was paid by the Germans to filch the plans. How she managed to conceal herself in the Department and obtain the plans or what officer or clerk she vamped, were not revealed, but some people believed that the woman was at the bottom of it. "Look for the woman," said the French judge. Putting the blame on the woman is universal. Other conjectures connected the Japanese with the disappearance. The Yellow Peril stalked abroad.

While the papers and the officers were discussing the missing plans of the *Pennsylvania,* I had occasion to go to Annapolis for some function at the Naval Academy late in May. While there I took a flight over the Severn River in an airship. The next day Berryman had a cartoon in the Washington *Star* representing me in the clouds with long-distance glasses, and saying, "And not a sign of those missing plans." Another day he had a cartoon showing me as a tall man, wearing a dressing gown covered with anchors. I had a magnifying glass, looking for the *Pennsylvania* plans. Franklin Roosevelt was drawn as a short boy standing by me. I was saying "Ah Ha! A clue!" Roosevelt commented, "Marvelous!"

"Look at the Secretary up in the air!" cried a newsboy to my wife, who was watching the flight with Commander Castleman and Mrs. Gibbons on the steps of Bancroft Hall. They turned their eyes to the

C. K. Berryman, in the *Washington Star*

SEARCHING FOR THE PLANS OF THE PENNSYLVANIA

When there was a search for the missing plans of the *Pennsylvania,* Secretary Daniels was represented as saying, "A Clew!" and Assistant Secretary Roosevelt as thinking the discovery "Marvelous!"

heavens across the Severn where I was aloft in the airplane with Commander Towers, one of the earliest and most expert aviators in the Navy. I had not told my wife that I intended to make the flight and she was surprised to see me in the air. The plane was of the 1913 vintage, and it was necessary on a warm day to wear an overcoat and put cotton in the ears. We landed on the river. It was a fine experience and I returned to Washington more enthusiastic about the future of aviation. But I surely was under my lucky star, for flying was dangerous in the small machines. One week later Commander Towers went up in the same plane with Lieutenant Bellinger over the same course. Something went wrong and the ship fell into the Severn. Bellinger was killed, and Towers received injuries that kept him in the hospital for weeks. As soon as I heard of the accident I hurried to Annapolis to see him.

This first flight was made in May, 1913, in what was called "Flying Boat C-1." We traveled eight miles in eight minutes. As the airship passed the battleship, *Illinois,* the first salute of 19 guns to a flying Secretary of the Navy was given. In answer to a question of a reporter, when I returned to terra firma, I said: "It was delightful. I enjoyed the sensation thoroughly." This despite the fact that there was no protection from the impact of the wind.

Looking back to the smallness of the ship, I am not surprised at President Wilson's: "Did you want to get yourself killed?"

"Is it true, Daniels, that you went up in an airship at Annapolis yesterday?" President Wilson asked at the Cabinet meeting the day after my flight. I told him the report in the papers was true.

"Why on earth did you take such a risk with your life—do you want to get killed?" he asked in a way that showed his disapproval of my adventure. I replied, "I had to do it."

Wilson: "Who forced you?"

I answered that as Secretary of the Navy it was my duty to sign orders for Naval officers to fly and that I would not assign any man to any duty or order him to do anything I would not try myself. He had no come-back to that.

About that time Postmaster General Burleson came in. "Is it true, Josephus, that you went up in an airplane at Annapolis?" he asked. I told him it was.

"You are a fool," he said, "to risk your life." More in a spirit of

Secretary Daniels Takes a Flier

C. K. Berryman, in the *Washington Star*

IN THE CENTRAL BLUE

On May 21, 1913, at Annapolis, in a C-1, Secretary Daniels makes the first flight
in the air made by any Secretary of the Navy or Minister of the Marines.

badinage than of prophecy I replied, "Albert, before you get out of your present job you will be carrying the mail in airplanes."

"Now I know that you are not only a fool, but a damn fool," he replied.

Not many months after that conversation, I received an engraved invitation saying:

"The Postmaster General requests the Secretary of the Navy and Mrs. Daniels to be present in the mall south of the White House at the inauguration of the air mail route between Washington and New York."

President and Mrs. Wilson graced the occasion with their presence, and the picture in this volume taken of them has been pronounced the best picture of Woodrow Wilson and Edith Bolling Wilson.

At the next Cabinet meeting, recalling our former conversation, I asked Burleson, "Who is the damn fool now, Albert?"

At this inauguration of the first air route I was accompanied by my wife's mother, Mrs. Bagley. She had seen, at Asheboro, N. C., the mail carried on horseback and afterwards the stage-coach "fast mail" on the plank road when she was a girl. She had seen the first mail leave Asheboro by rail, and now she was witnessing the conquest of the air—four important advances in the delivery of the mail.

FROM OX-CART TO AIRPLANE

"Stop!" I cried out to the driver of a Navy Yard motor wagon on August 28, 1913, as I came out of the Navy Department to go to the Capitol to hear President Wilson speak on the Mexican situation. My car was nowhere to be seen and the time was short, and so I went up to the Capitol in state, seated on a Navy truck. That experience was added to one previously at Annapolis when, calling at the Naval Hospital to see Commander Towers after he was injured in an airplane flight, a heavy rain came up, and the only way I could get away in time to meet an appointment was to take a seat in the ambulance. When the ambulance drove up to the Superintendent's house, my wife and Mrs. Gibbons ran out fearing I was hurt.

I often reflect that in my time I have tried every method from ox-cart to airplane, including goat, muleback, horseback, buckboard, truck, ambulance, hearse; railroads—in every kind of accommodation, from a seat in a caboose to a private car—canoe, ocean steamer, sailing boat, submarine, yacht, dreadnaught, caissons, automobiles, the carriages of kings and presidents. There wasn't so much difference. The only requisite is that they get you there and carry you back. The chief difference is one of speed.

INTEREST IN NAVAL AVIATION

I was early interested in aviation and had asked Commander Towers to come to Washington to discuss the best way of making it a more effective arm of the Navy service. The death of Bellinger and the injury of Towers cast a gloom over aviation in the Navy and the Army, and there were those who believed that the risk to life was too great to make up for the advantages of flying. However, this was not the view of the aviators in the Navy. They realized that all progress costs blood, and the strategists and leaders in the Navy, instead of having their interest lessened, became even more interested in the development of Naval aviation. At Annapolis the Navy had four aviators and four unsatisfactory planes and no stations for training fliers. A Board of Aviation made plans for progress and long before we entered the war the aviation personnel numbered 200 under the direction of Rear Admiral Mark L. Bristol.

Congress increased the appropriations but even so the progress was slow. We obtained the first separate appropriation for aviation ever voted by Congress. The previous administration never spent over a hundred thousand dollars, and my first bill in the Wilson administration had in it three and a half million dollars.

The country and the world first learned the practical use of aircraft in the occupation of Vera Cruz when hydro-aeroplanes enabled the Admiral in command to know whether there was danger of assault from any quarter and to be sure an ambushed foe could not make an attack. Aircraft demonstrated that the day of surprises in war was ended. I gave such encouragement and assistance to Naval aviation as was possible and continued to do so during my whole term. I had the pleasure of seeing it win a high place in the World War.

DICK BYRD GETS HIS WINGS

In the early summer of 1913 Admiral Blue, of Navigation, said the ensign serving on the *Dolphin*, the yacht of the Secretary of the

Navy, would be due for another assignment and asked if I wished to name his successor. I answered in the negative, and then called Blue back and said, "When I was at the Brooklyn Navy Yard last Sunday I was attracted by a young ensign named Byrd. If he would like the assignment, give it to him, but write and tell him that it is open if he desires it; however, do not order him to the duty, unless he wishes it." He wrote young Byrd, who answered that he would be delighted to come and was gratified that I wished him on my ship. He added that he desired to do some postgraduate work at Washington and the assignment would be doubly gratifying.

And thereby hangs a story about a young man who was later to become a distinguished world explorer. The previous week, upon the completion of a Y.M.C.A. building at the Brooklyn Navy Yard, the $250,000 gift of Mrs. Helen Shepard (daughter of Jay Gould) and Mrs. Russell Sage, I went over to the dedication and was the guest of Mrs. Shepard. She was a gracious hostess, but I wondered how she would have felt toward me if she had read what I had written about her father in 1884, when my paper was charging that he was in a plot to steal the presidency from Grover Cleveland, and Robert VanWyck, afterwards Mayor of New York, was leading a crowd of angry Democrats in New York to his home to demand that the held-back returns be released. The charge was that Jay Gould, dominating the Western Union, was holding back the returns so that the vote of New York could be given to Blaine. This was not the only time nor the last time when, entertained by the scions of privilege, I was glad my country paper had not circulated in the metropolis.

Before the exercises in the new building, where I was to make the dedicatory address, Naval officers, Mrs. Shepard and Mrs. Sage and I went over the building, which was the last word in architecture and equipment. As an officer opened a door of one of the class rooms, it was observed that a young ensign was teaching a Sunday School class of sailors. The officer started to draw back, but I said we would like to attend the class. All of us went in and I motioned the ensign to continue as if we had not entered. He was visibly embarrassed but stuck to his text. Upon leaving I invited him—it was Richard E. Byrd, then "a youth to fortune and to fame unknown"—to join us at the dedicatory exercises. I did not stop to think that it was not according to protocol (if I knew the meaning of that word then or learned it in my diplomatic career, for certainly I paid little attention to its practice) to invite a young ensign to sit on the platform with the Secretary of the Navy, the Admiral of the fleet, other ranking officers, and the donors of the building. But "orders is orders," and he obeyed them. I had the opportunity to talk with him and instinctively felt that he had good stuff in him.

I felt strongly drawn to this young ensign, whose unassuming religion caused him to give his Sunday afternoons to teaching the Bible to newly enlisted men. It was his personality and his teaching the Bible class that prompted me to assign him to the *Dolphin*. This made him almost a member of our family for several years, and my wife always thought of him as one of her boys.

While serving on the battleship *Washington* at a San Domingo port, Byrd had been commended for an act of heroism in rescuing a sailor who had fallen overboard during a storm. That was the second like act performed by the young Virginian. I had a slight acquaintance with his father, begun at the Baltimore Convention. The Virginia Senators and most of the delegates were against Wilson, but Byrd's father stood almost alone for Wilson among the delegates from the State of Virginia, with the exception of the forthright Carter Glass, which was to have great pride that Wilson had restored Virginia's claim to being "the mother of Presidents."

FAILED OF PROMOTION

As time passed, Byrd came up for promotion, and the medical board reported that an injury to his ankle, which had been broken when he was a midshipman at Annapolis, had not healed, and this defect incapacitated him for standing watch and other duties required of a Naval officer. Since early boyhood Byrd's only ambition had been to be a Naval officer. To prepare for it he entered V.M.I. and had made a fine record at the Naval Academy and during his short service in the Navy. It was a death sentence to his one and only ambition that in early manhood he must retire. There was no help for it.

BECOMES AVIATOR

He turned to aviation, not then long out of its infancy. He had two reasons: First, in flying there was no requirement to stand long on his broken ankle; and second, he had the vision of the coming importance of the Navy that flies. One day he called at the Navy

Department, imparted to me his ambition, and said that if legislation could be enacted establishing an aviation bureau in the Department and he could be assigned to it, he believed it opened a real career and would help the Navy. I shared his belief in the value of aviation, wrote a letter to Chairman Padgett of the House Naval Affairs Committee recommending the necessary legislation, and gave it to Byrd to take to the committee.

My recommendation was favorably acted upon, and soon Byrd was installed in the Navy Department and demonstrated his ability as an administrator as well as an aviator. Some of the older officers did not like the innovation. They preferred that aviation "be kept in its place," as a branch of Operations. But I held that a Byrd must have an opportunity to help construct "an airy Navy" to battle in "the central blue." From that springboard, Byrd by his vision and courage mounted to fame. It has always been a happiness that I had the privilege at a crucial stage of his life to see the stuff of which he was made and open the door of opportunity to him. After his first historic achievement Congress gave him the rank and title of Admiral, thus making what he had done a great American Naval adventure. The discoverer of the North Pole, Commodore Peary, was, like Byrd, a product of the Navy.

XXIX

THE NAVY SECRETARY MAKES TIME

No MEMBERS of the Cabinet had seen the Navy in action at target practice—the most spectacular sight on sea or land. Shortly after the inauguration there was to be spring practice at Hampton Roads. My wife and I, Franklin and Mrs. Roosevelt, the daughters of the President, and most members of the Cabinet and their wives made up the party that sailed on the *Mayflower* and the *Dolphin* to the scene of the big-gun firing. When we arrived, Admiral Badger, Commander in Chief of the Atlantic Fleet, and his staff came on board, the nineteen-gun salute was fired, and the men in the party were taken on board the *Wyoming* to watch the target practice at close range. It was a new experience for all of us and we had to put cotton in our ears to be certain that the tremendous noise of the big guns did not injure our ear drums.

On the morning of our arrival at Hampton Roads, while we were at breakfast, the orderly came in, as is the Naval custom, and turned to me as the Commander in Chief of the Navy to make his morning report. He had been directed by the Captain of the ship to speak in such tones that all the company at the table could hear him, and to get off an old gag which had often stumped new Secretaries of the Navy unfamiliar with the ways of the sea. After he had made his formal report of the condition of the ship, he said:

"Mr. Secretary, it is eight o'clock.

"He expected me to look at my watch to see if he was right, as uninformed Secretaries had done many times, to their discomfort and to the great glee of the Navy personnel. To his surprise and to the surprise of the company, instead of doing that I said, in a commanding voice:

"Make it so."

I acted as if I were a Joshua who could make the sun and moon stand still. I had been tipped off by my Aide as to the history of this morning formula.

"What did the orderly say to you?" asked Mrs. Garrison, wife of the Secretary of War. I repeated the conversation. She was puzzled. I then explained to her that in the early seafaring days, when there were no clocks or watches on ships, the seamen sailed by the sun, and the ranking officer fixed the time that governed everything aboard ship. I added that nowhere did old customs and traditions persist as long as in the Navy. The "Make it so" was always employed when visitors were on board, to pique their curiosity. I then confessed to her—and all the guests at breakfast—that I had never heard of the power of the ranking officer on a ship to make time, until I became Secretary of the Navy.

Of course, with the introduction of clocks and watches, this ancient custom was no longer necessary, but in the Navy customs and traditions last much longer than the necessity for them, and so this old habit of making time goes on.

The civilians and particularly the ladies on board were very much interested when I, who had never heard of it until the night before, explained this custom and told them that while the Secretary of the Treasury might regulate the money, and the Secretary of War and other members of the Cabinet might have important functions, I, as Secretary of the Navy, was the only man who could look into the heavens and make time, and therefore my job was of more importance than theirs.

This trip to see target practice was my wife's first experience as hostess on shipboard, and she made everybody have a good time. Friendships were formed, on that voyage, with three officers who were afterwards to be important members of my staff in the Navy Department, Admiral Badger, Head of the General Board, Admiral Braisted, Surgeon General, and Admiral McGowan, Paymaster General.

XXX

LEARNING BY INSPECTION FROM COAST TO COAST

WHAT DOES the country editor know about the Navy?" some city paper asked when I was appointed.

"Why don't you reply to your critics?" a friendly journalist asked.

My answer was that when they said I knew little about the workings and technique of the Navy, they were telling the truth. "The only effective answer I can make is that I can learn about the Navy from a place in the Conning Tower." I knew that the way to learn was to leave my desk after experience in operating the Department, go to sea as often as I could, and make myself acquainted with every Navy Yard and every Naval base ashore. Therefore, in May, two months after I had been inducted into office, my wife and I and my Aide departed on a tour of inspection of Southern Navy Yards. There had been advocacy in Congress and in the Navy Department, to abolish all Navy Yards south of Norfolk. Should they be abolished? I wished to know at first hand how to answer that question properly. My predecessor had closed the Yard opposite New Orleans and recommended closing those at Charleston and at Key West.

The Charleston Yard was shaded by beautiful Carolina trees and shrubbery, and the Navy quarters were surrounded by a lovely garden. As we drove up to the Commandant's house, we heard for the first time, by a Navy band, the North Carolina State song. Admiral Helms had arranged it as a surprise, and it and the flowers overjoyed my wife. While I inspected every character of work going on and the equipment, my wife was happy in the social courtesies in an old town where old-time courtesy, with a capital C, flowered.

The Mayor of Charleston was a young Irish lawyer who did not belong to the old order. He had defeated a gentleman of the old school, and it rankled. Neither he nor his wife belonged to the exclusive country club. He had extended the freedom of the city to me and was the city's official host. Should he and his wife be invited to the club at the reception given the Secretary of the Navy and his wife? It was whispered that this question was debated behind the doors of social Charleston. I had said to my wife that I was minded, if the Mayor and his wife were snubbed, to be too busy to go. But the Mayor and his wife were invited, and the reception was worthy of old Charleston's reputation, as were the other social courtesies by a people who make an art—an indigenous art—of hospitality, with a flavour all its own. I have spelled "flavour" in the old-time way because that was the Charleston way—it seemed plebeian to leave out the "u."

EVERYTHING WHITE IN KEY WEST

"Everything is white here—I never saw anything like it!" said my wife as Admiral Reynolds welcomed us to the Key West Navy Yard. The land was white; all the one-story houses and ships were painted white; all the Naval officers were in white uniform; the sailors wore white; and the officials and police of the city were in white. It was our first sight of a tropical section, and it had delights for us. The Admiral was carrying on repairs of small ships on duty in the Gulf of Mexico and the Caribbean, with small appropriations, and the station was living under a near-death sentence. But it was important because of the strategic position of nearness to the lands and islands to the South. It was to become a base of essential value during the World War.

MY WIFE GETS A JOB

When my wife's brother, Ensign Worth Bagley, was killed at Cárdenas—the first and only Naval officer to fall in the Spanish-American war—his body was brought to Key West, and funeral services were held there. My wife sought out the officiating minister to express the family's appreciation for his kindness and his letters to her mother at that time. Visiting the Naval Cemetery, she found it neglected and, upon her return to Washington, reported its condition to the Surgeon General. He said, "I appoint you Director of all Naval Cemeteries," and she served in the keeping of these God's acres in a way worthy of the sepulchres of Navy heroes.

PENSACOLA TO BECOME AN AVIATION BASE

The Navy Yard at Pensacola was closed, but there was a keeper and I wished to see the Naval property. Even in its neglect it was beautiful. It had gone wild with Easter lilies and larkspur, and purple and white oleanders bloomed, while flowering trees and shrubs gave it color that particularly attracted my wife. The editor of the paper, Frank L. Mayes, Mr. Knowles, our host, and his wife and her mother, widow of Governor Ellis, the War Governor of North Carolina, and all the people showered gracious hospitality. I was interested in the groves of majestic trees. Their fitness for the construction of wooden ships had caused the location of a Navy Yard at Pensacola. The Navy owned a large tract of land covered with trees which were ideally fitted for ships when the Navy was composed of "wooden ships and iron men," to quote the saying of a worthy old tar who regretted that in his day the Navy "has now become composed of iron ships and wooden men." With the passing of the wooden ships, the glory of the shipbuilding yard at Pensacola passed away. The people felt that the Navy could and should find use for it.

Some years afterwards, when the Navy became air-minded, I gave directions for the utilization of the property as an aviation training base during the World War, where thousands of the best aviators in the Navy were trained. It is now one of the best Naval training bases in the world. I was happy to restore the Yard to a new use, one not dreamed of when at Pensacola the Navy was chiefly concerned to grow the kind of trees suitable for shipbuilding.

THE CHARM OF NEW ORLEANS

The hospitality of the people of New Orleans cannot be overstated. It was, if possible, heightened when it was known that the Secretary of the Navy had come to make a first-hand inspection of the Navy Yard, in order to determine whether it should remain as abandoned property or whether some use could be made of the Yard in the new policy of strengthening the Navy.

This was the last of the inspection trips to Yards south of Norfolk—yards which had been advertised as "political pork barrels." Some critics did not call the journey a "trip of inspection" but called it "a junket at the expense of the taxpayers at the request of politicians wasting public money expended in their State."

NORFOLK THE BEST YARD IN THE SOUTH

Between that long trip and my inspection trip to the West Coast, I visited the Norfolk Navy Yard and the Navy Hospital and enjoyed the hospitality of Mr. Barton Myers and others in that twin-city, where the people from the early days had been Navy-minded. Naturally, we felt at home in this neighbor city, for we North Caro-linians were fond of saying, "Norfolk is the finest North Carolina city in Virginia," having reference to the many Tar-heels who had made it their home and to its being the banking and business city for much of northeastern North Carolina. The Norfolk Navy Yard was the only Southern one which my predecessor wished to keep. I was glad to agree with him that it should be retained and ex-panded. During my term of office the Navy Yard was enlarged, and I converted it into a shipbuilding yard. Of course, it was not difficult to secure money for the enlargement of the Norfolk Navy Yard because Senator Swanson—afterwards Secretary of the Navy, in Franklin Roosevelt's administration—was chairman of the Naval Affairs Committee.

SEATTLE AND PUGET SOUND

July, 1913, was a month of events that had repercussions from Puget Sound to Washington City. I planned to visit the Navy yards and bases, all small, on the Pacific Coast to learn at first hand what new bases and additions to existing yards were required for con-templated Naval expansion on our Western coast. Accepting an invitation to speak at the annual Potlatch in Seattle before beginning the tour of inspection, my wife and I left Washington about the middle of July. The reception at Seattle was cordial, including a banquet at the Rainier Club, where, perfectly innocently, I made an apostrophe to Old Glory in my address, which started the fireworks. Shortly after my arrival I had a call from Mr. Blethen, editor of the leading paper in that city, apologizing for not attending a func-tion in my honor, saying that as I was an official guest of the city, he regretted, because of his regard for me, that he could attend none of the functions not being on speaking terms with Mayor Cottrell, who was a "blankety-blank radical and Communist." Though he was not a member of the Rainier Club, the Mayor had been invited and had a seat at the head table. He was a courteous host.

Stretched across and covering the entire ceiling of the banquet room was a magnificent American flag, the largest I had ever seen. It dominated the spacious hall, which was crowded with prominent citizens. During my address, after speaking of my purpose to increase the strength of the Navy on the Pacific, I essayed an apostrophe to the American flag, telling of the part played in its creation by Betsy Ross and John Adams and Thomas Jefferson, quoting a sentence from "Your flag and my flag." In the course of my remarks I said that it was the only flag for Americans, and added that I had read in the newspapers a few days ago how the Mayor of an Eastern city had halted a procession marching under a red flag, which was substituted for Old Glory. He told the marchers that "the only flag that should float over American citizens was the red, white, and blue." I closed by commending the Mayor and saying, "There is no place in any American community for the red flag."

I had hardly concluded that sentence when bedlam broke loose. Men rose from their seats applauding with such exuberance of enthusiasm as I had rarely heard when a great orator had moved his hearers to their depths. Nearly all the diners grasped a flag, a procession was formed, and they marched around the banquet hall cheering while the band played the Star Spangled Banner. I was carried along with the enthusiasm, and pinched myself to see if suddenly my poor prose had become "words that burn" and the afflatus of eloquence had descended on me. After a toast "to the President" the party broke up and I returned to the hotel wondering what electric spark I had touched off to produce such cheering and shouting.

FIRES BLAZED FIERCELY

I found out the next morning. The Seattle *Times*, published by the editor who told me he could not be present at any party where the "blankety-blank" Mayor was present, had a spread-head story on the banquet, and said that when I declared there was only one flag for Americans and that the red flag had no place in any procession I "pointed the index finger at the Mayor who had permitted and encouraged such use of the Red Flag to the exclusion of the American flag." As a matter of fact I had not pointed my index or any other finger at the Mayor. I did not know he had permitted the red flag to float over a procession, had never heard of the bitter political row in the city, and was as innocent as a newborn babe of designedly saying anything that could add to the political discussion going on in Seattle. To praise Old Glory and denounce what the red flag stood for seemed to me to be as natural and as unlikely to create a disturbance as if I had praised the Ten Commandments or the Declaration of Independence and disapproved Toryism or Sin. But the paper's account of the banquet lighted a fire whose flames blazed fiercely for days.

DID NOT OBJECT TO BALLINGER

I should state that on the afternoon of the Rainier Club banquet a member of the committee called at the hotel and asked me if I would enter any objection if Mr. Ballinger, former Secretary of the Interior, attended. He doubtless thought it possible that I might follow the example of Theodore Roosevelt, who refused to attend a dinner because he had denounced one of the guests. "Ballinger feels humiliated at the public criticism that forced his retirement from the Cabinet after the big Pinchot-Ballinger conflict over conservation policies," my caller said, "and has attended no public functions since his return home. Many of us here believe he is honest and was the victim of circumstances and would like to show him our feeling by inviting him to this banquet." He added that, of course, the invitation would not be extended if I objected. I was the guest of the city. I had accepted the tender of the banquet. I told the gentleman that it was not becoming in me to scan the list of the Seattle people who would attend and that an invitation to Mr. Ballinger would not offend or disturb me. Perhaps they had heard that in that bitter controversy I had taken strong grounds with Pinchot, and that my friend A. C. Shaw, of North Carolina, an official in the Interior Department, whose appointment I had secured in the Cleveland administration, had given me the inside of the story before it became public. Shaw would not be a party to what was done by Ballinger and resigned before his associates were removed or forced to resign. As a life-long conservationist I could have no sympathy with Ballinger's policy, for at that time it was necessary for me to oppose the organized effort to lease the Naval petroleum resources in California. However, it was not in my heart to add anything to his humiliation. Besides, what harm could it possibly do the Wilson administration that former Secretary of the Interior Ballinger should hear me expound its philosophy of the New Freedom?

SAILORS BURN I.W.W. BUILDING

The next night my Aide and my wife and I were invited to dine with Admiral and Mrs. Reynolds on the *West Virginia* in Puget Sound Harbor. During the dinner, after some confusion on deck which did not seem of importance to me at the time, an orderly came to the table speaking to the Admiral in a low voice. I did not hear what he said, but immediately the Admiral rose, asked to be excused, and went on deck. It was a long time before he returned. We learned then that some sailors from Navy ships had gone ashore and been charged with burning the plant of an organization known as I.W.W. which made use of red flags at their meetings. Before burning the building the sailors, soldiers, and others had torn up the I.W.W. literature. Blethen's Seattle paper practically approved the act as necessary to wipe out the unpatriotic organization that threatened true Americanism. So did others. The opposition charged that my speech was responsible for the incendiarism—that the sailors reading that their Commander in Chief condemned the red flag, naturally concluded that they would be carrying out his desires and the wish of the country if they wiped out the place which operated under the red flag. The I.W.W. officers demanded that the President remove me from office, saying they held my utterances as responsible for the sacking and destruction of their headquarters by the sailors moved by "artificialized psychology."

Asserting that the paper owned by Blethen was inciting rioting and endangering public peace, the Mayor sent officials to take charge of the paper's plant and prevent the publication of another issue. Naturally that created a city-wide furore. The editor procured an injunction from Judge Humphrey against the Mayor's action in attempting to destroy the freedom of the press and it looked for a time as if there would be bloody clashes.

I.W.W. ATTACK FEARED

My apostrophe to the flag was credited with responsibility for the succeeding lurid events. Telegrams were sent to President Wilson denouncing what I had said and done, demanding my recall to Washington and dismissal from the Cabinet. I ordered an investigation of the part the Naval men were alleged to have taken in the burning of the I. W. W. building. To keep my engagements, I left

Seattle, which was still seething so much that when I attended a big reception and dance that night, without my knowledge secret service men were assigned to my protection. For the next week as I visited cities on the west coast, and as far inland as Spokane, my wife commented on seeing the same two men on every train and at every hotel at which we stopped. She asked Commander Palmer, my Naval Aide, if he had seen them and he confided to her that the authorities, fearing an attack by I. W. W. zealots, had assigned them to accompany me during my Western trip. In all the cities, hardly had I registered and been assigned to my room before I received a call from labor leaders, or so-called leaders, who asked to talk with me about the occurrence at Seattle which had been widely circulated. Commander Palmer was suspicious of them, but as I was a known friend of organized labor I was glad to see them and found my explanations were well received. Naval officers and secret service men were distrustful of labor organizers, believing they were in league with the I.W.W., whereas I knew the American Federation of Labor had no sympathy with anarchistic practices.

Congress had made an appropriation for certain bases of doubtful wisdom in Puget Sound. I felt it my duty to visit them before authorizing the expenditure. The result of one visit (what a glorious trip that was on Puget Sound!) was the saving of a large sum of money.

BRIDGE AHEAD DESTROYED

One purpose of my visit to the west coast, in addition to inspecting Naval yards and Naval bases, was to visit coast cities in States whose Senators wished the government to establish Naval bases. I was invited to Portland and thence to Astoria. The Governor of Oregon, Oswald West, was our host and we formed a lasting friendship. En route, Governor West and my Aide woke me up in the middle of the night saying, "Dress as soon as you can. The bridge ahead of us has been burned and we must transfer across the chasm to another train." There was a voiced suspicion that the I.W.W. had set fire to the railroad bridge to get me, in retaliation for my denunciation of the Red Flag in Seattle. I attached no faith to that theory, and there was no evidence of it. I had never seen so steep a chasm. My wife was a good sport, and, aided by railroad men, we **were assisted down a rocky steep embankment of slippery rocks and** then climbed up an equally high and dangerous embankment. It seemed a miracle that the feat was accomplished, particularly since the night was very dark, the only light coming from a dingy railroad oil lamp. Later in the night it was necessary to transfer to another train. But we arrived in Portland in time for breakfast, to exchange greetings and to hurry to a special train for Astoria.

AT THE MOUTH OF THE COLUMBIA RIVER

It was our first view of the magnificent scenery along the Columbia River, whose scenic beauty is one of the world's loveliest. After visiting the waterfront and, along with every courtesy, being shown the possibilities and values of a Naval base at Astoria, and given historical and statistical data, we were invited to a barbecue in an elevated place where we could envision the future Naval base and view the Pacific. We learned that a barbecue in Oregon has a somewhat different meaning on the Pacific from that given it in the South. In North Carolina a barbecue is the pig or lamb roasted over a pit in the ground, with plenty of pepper sauce basted in as the animal is roasted over glowing coals in the pit. There is usually a large company invited to partake of the barbecue. In old times the best electioneering a candidate could do was to give a barbecue and invite all his constituents to partake of the roasted pig. I found in Astoria that the word barbecue is synonymous with the word picnic. The *pièce de resistance* at this barbecue was the largest salmon I had ever seen, served with all the delicacies of that section.

GILBRALTAR OF DEMOCRACY

During our trip through Oregon, Governor West wished us to drive through the apple section and arranged for us to leave the train and make a trip by automobile, catching the train at a town some fifty miles away. Even then the roads enabled us to outrun the train, for it had to stop at every station and take on fuel and water. At one point on the route, the Governor told us we were in a section almost solidly Democratic, an exception in rural Oregon. He said:

"At the close of the Civil War scores of families of Confederates from Missouri, who had been active in war, believing that 'woe to the conquered' would be meted out to them, set out in covered wagons, drove to this then sparsely populated section of Oregon, took up land, and became good citizens, and have regularly and constantly voted the Democratic ticket and denounced 'the Black Republican party.' Some of the older ones have never become reconstructed, but that is not true of their children, and this is still the Gibraltar of Democracy in rural Oregon."

Our auto was filled with Oregon apples and we feasted on them the balance of the trip.

At the Bremerton Navy Yard I sensed it had advantages which should be utilized on a larger scale, both for overhauling ships and for their construction. Plans for making it a great Navy Yard with ample facilities to meet the needs of the coming two-ocean Navy were undertaken. Its location made it ideal for the needs of the Navy in its larger duties to Alaska and all the Pacific. I found there a lady, the wife of a Naval officer from Ohio, whose father was named Josephus Daniels. Of course, I claimed her as a cousin.

IN SAN FRANCISCO HARBOR

At San Francisco we spent a portion of the day on Yerba Buena, called Goat Island, where recruits to the Navy were trained for service. It was midway between San Francisco and Oakland, a rocky island swept by the breezes of the Pacific and covered at times by the cold fogs that sweep over the bay. I found that the coal bill in this training station was very large and that the cold and fog did not give the best atmosphere for a training place for the young seamen.

I was taken by enthusiastic boosters to a dozen proposed sites suitable for a San Francisco Naval base, every one of which was under water. I had been brought up under a dictum, "Man can make anything but land." I had learned that at most of the Navy Yards land had been made, adjacent to the original site, by pumping out the water. In California they thought the best way to secure a Naval base was to pump out the water, for then they obtained a level site, whereas there was little level land shown us adjacent for the necessary deep water for the largest Naval craft. Better boosters I never saw or heard. I agreed to have engineers make surveys for the consideration of the Naval authorities, and looked forward to the great Naval development of San Francisco Bay as the essential for Naval activities in the Pacific. I found that the Golden Gate was truly golden as we voyaged in the late afternoon inspecting a number of sites.

NAVY YARD AT MARE ISLAND

From the Golden Gate I went to the Navy Yard at Mare Island, the oldest and most important of the Navy Yards on the Pacific. It was located at Vallejo when the Navy wished its bases to be as far from the ocean as possible for protection from attacks in case of war. There had been formal recommendations for the abandonment of the Navy Yard at that place and the construction of a new one in San Francisco Bay, where a greater depth of water could be obtained. The channel to Mare Island was not deemed by some officers sufficient for the big dreadnaughts under construction. I came to the conclusion, in view of the demand for large appropriations for needed fighting ships, not to follow the course of the Board, which had recommended the scrapping of the Mare Island Navy Yard, at least not until we could organize the contemplated two-ocean Navy.

In December, 1915, after President Wilson had paid me a visit at the Navy Department, I announced that one of the super-dreadnaughts would be built in the Mare Island Navy Yard. Senator Phelan wired the Navy Yard that the ship would be given the name *California*. The Vallejo *Times* the next day used red ink to print the announcement and approved the idea—"Build the *California* in California." The town took a holiday in celebration and the editor predicted that at the end of the war, one half of the fleet would be based on Pacific ports, a prediction which I made come true in 1920 when the United States for the first time had a two-ocean Navy. That paper also announced that on Sunday morning, "the Methodist preacher will talk Battleship."

During the World War we found the Mare Island Navy Yard indispensable, as has been true ever since, particularly since the Pearl Harbor Day of Infamy. I caused such enlargement of the Mare Island Navy Yard as fitted it for the construction of dreadnaughts, and other fighting craft.

My action greatly pleased the Representative in Congress from the Mare Island district, Honorable Charles F. Curry, who was diligent in the endeavor to show that, by dredging and by certain changes, the big ships could come into the Mare Island Yard and be repaired there. He was a faithful representative. We became real friends, and in the 1916 elections the quiet influence of the supporters of the enlargement facilities at Mare Island helped to overturn the regular

Republican majority and gave Wilson a record-breaking majority, contributing materially toward giving him the electoral vote of California.

RODMAN'S HEART'S DESIRE

I recall an incident in connection with Mare Island, in 1920. That was the only time I scored on witty Admiral Hugh Rodman. Franklin Roosevelt, before going to the Democratic National Convention at San Francisco, made an inspection trip at the Mare Island Navy Yard. The workmen and officers liked him so much that they arranged a dinner for him and Rodman and me at San Francisco during the Convention. In the course of his speech Admiral Rodman referred to the years he had spent at Mare Island when he was a young officer, dwelt upon its incomparable climate, fruits, etc., and said there was no place in the world where he would love so much to serve as at Mare Island. It, of course, won the enthusiastic approval of his hosts. During the applause, I said to Franklin, "As Rodman is so set on living at Mare Island, why not grant his heart's desire?" He approved. I arose and said that Mr. Roosevelt and I had listened to the Admiral's just praises of the delights of Mare Island and his yearning to go back, and we had not the heart to keep him elsewhere when he had the *animus revertendi*. I added, "Therefore, a telegram has just gone to Washington to detach Admiral Rodman from the command of the Pacific Fleet and assign him to duty as Commandant of the Mare Island Navy Yard."

The company roared. When silence was restored, Rodman asked: "Mr. Secretary, can't you take a joke?" and the people applauded more than ever. "You certainly got the best of Rodman, chief," said Roosevelt.

LOS ANGELES BECOMES A NAVAL BASE

Los Angeles gave us a characteristic California welcome. My wife and I agreed that the only difference between North Carolina and California hospitality was that California had more money and entertained on a more lavish scale. Some time before, Los Angeles, resolved to become the equal of San Francisco as a seaport town, annexed a strip of land extending from its suburbs to the ocean. Presto, change! Los Angeles ceased to be an inland city and became a seaport by the construction of an artificial harbor wherein great ships could lie at anchor. The officials escorted us through the strip and to the harbor and pointed out what they regarded as an ideal place for a Naval base. Later it was enlarged and is now an important Naval base in the increased activity in the Pacific. On a visit to Los Angeles in 1932, I spent the night on the U. S. S. *Arkansas* with my former Aide, Captain P. W. Foote, in the Los Angeles Harbor, which had become an important rendezvous for our Navy.

PRESENTED WITH THE PACIFIC OCEAN

At a banquet at Long Beach the Mayor said to me, "Mr. Secretary, I have the honor to make you a present—the most magnificent ever given to any marine minister—I present you with the Pacific Ocean," and he waved his hand toward that placid ocean. As I rose to reply he said, "I give it to you upon condition that you use it for real fighting ships to replace the old hulks the Navy has heretofore thought good enough for us." I accepted the Pacific Ocean with the condition annexed. Again the Mayor, taking a small package from his pocket and handing it to me, said, "You may wish to use your ocean today." I opened the package and held it up to the view of the diners. It was a bright red bathing suit the size of an envelope. It would be about the right size for the modern surf bather who goes in nearly nude.

EDITORIAL BANQUET

As I was the first editor, since Lincoln appointed Gideon Welles, to serve as Secretary of the Navy, the Press Club of Los Angeles backed by the owners of the rival and hostile editors of the prosperous newspapers, tendered me a banquet. The younger members put on stunts such as the Gridiron Club of Washington is famous for, good-naturedly ridiculing some of the policies I had inaugurated and giving happy skits and songs. I was told that for the first time in years rival editors of Los Angeles sat down together at a banquet. I had prepared my address before leaving Washington and followed it pretty closely, only prefacing it by courteous thanks for the cordial hospitality and the fraternal welcome by men of my profession. The substance of my address was that by its very nature a newspaper was a public servant, charged with public duties quite as much as were public service corporations. The difference was that railroads and telegraph and the like had their rates regulated by the State, whereas the press, guaranteed freedom by the Constitution, was expected under the doctrine of *noblesse oblige* to render its contribution without official regulation. I emphasized that such confidence in the press imposed a higher duty on journalists than did statutes. I added that, of course, newspapers, to carry on their public service, must have ample income from subscriptions and advertising to pay the costs, including fair salaries to men and women of talent to make their columns interesting and instructive. "But," I said, "they ought not to seek to make money like an industrial or business establishment." Particularly, I declared, the publishers should be careful not to profit pecuniarily by any public development which they had advocated. I instanced cases where unworthy publishers had secured municipal improvements in suburbs at public cost out of which the publishers enriched themselves. I declared that such publishers were a disgrace to the profession, and that, if such selfishness should spread, it might be necessary for governments to declare newspapers public service corporations, and regulate them as they did transportation and communication corporations. When I denounced publishers who became rich by using their columns for their own benefit I was interrupted by loud applause led by the reporters and younger men who had given the dinner. Their enthusiastic approval was a surprise, for I had regarded my suggestion of better newspapers under public service regulations as academic and employed only for emphasis. I wondered if the mantle of Demosthenes had suddenly descended upon me as the cheering and applause increased. When it ceased I finished my address. I received no applause or comment from the publishers, who did not even bid me good-night.

As I was leaving the banquet, the young journalist who had been the main actor in the skits and the leader in the applause, confided to me that the cause of the uproarious applause was that the evils I was denouncing ran rampant among certain Los Angeles publishers who had made money by the methods I had excoriated. The young writers rejoiced to hear their employers given the severe criticism they deserved. In vain did I assure him that I was not denouncing anybody and was unaware that Los Angeles publishers had enriched themselves by the reprehensible methods I had condemned. The youngsters expressed pleasure in the exposure of their chiefs by a member of the craft who held high official station. Naturally I scanned closely the columns of all the city papers next day to see how my speech and its reception were handled. The manuscript of my address had been furnished them in advance. There were good stories of the banquet, but the references which were applauded were cut out of my speech. None of the papers printed that part of the address or made any reference to it.

SAN DIEGO BECOMES BIG NAVY BASE

At San Diego our reception had a cordiality all its own. My wife said it was Southern. I told her it was American, with a mixture of Mexican and Southern as became this southernmost city of California. Its representative in Congress, "Bill" Ketner (he was affectionately called "Bill" by his associates in Congress as well as by his home folks) had talked to me in Washington of the advantages of San Diego as a Naval base, and the whole population was united to convince the new Secretary that San Diego was by far the best site for Naval bases on the Pacific. At that time we had only a fuelling supply base and a place for repairing small craft. It was not difficult to convince me of the advantages of San Diego, though the channel was not deemed ideal for the ingress and egress of the largest dreadnaughts. In fact, the captains of those great ships had hesitated in essaying such navigation. The citizens called them "timid mariners" and honored Captain William S. Benson because he had safely brought his dreadnaught (I think it was the *Utah*) at anchorage in the protected harbor. We were the guests of the grandson of President Grant, who owned the most modern hotel, and upon leaving San Diego for Los Angeles en route to Washington, we were the guests of John D. Spreckels on his yacht. It was a voyage so delightful it remains fixed in my own and my wife's lasting recollection. Mr. Spreckels owned the chief newspaper in San Diego and he boosted the place with persistence.

TRAINING STATION MOVED

As a result of that visit and my knowledge of the climate and the fact that San Diego was the nearest port on the Pacific to the Panama Canal, before my term of office expired there had been established at San Diego a Training Station for young sailors replacing the one on Goat Island in San Francisco Harbor where the fogs were not conducive to the best training; an aviation base on North Island, where during the World War it was largely expanded; a Marine Headquarters with training facilities for Marines; large supply buildings; repair shops; and in fact it has since become one of the greatest Naval bases in the country.

"Bill" Ketner urged that San Diego was the proper place for a Naval hospital and offered a free site.

NAVAL HOSPITAL BUILT IN BALBOA PARK

Upon my next visit to San Diego, "Bill" and the city fathers and leading citizens showed me half a dozen sites for a Naval hospital. All the time my heart was set on an elevation in Balboa Park for a Naval hospital, but the committee showed me every other possible location. I was not impressed with any of them. I finally said "Let us drive through Balboa Park." When we reached the eminence I had in my mind picked out for the hospital I asked "Bill" to stop so that we could stand upon the hill in Balboa Park and get a view of the Pacific Ocean and beautiful Point Loma in the distance. "If you will deed this site," I said to "Bill" and the committee, "I will recommend to Congress the erection of a modern hospital at San Diego." They were not eager to give that particular site. They conferred among themselves. It would be necessary to consult the city attorney and the city board, said the spokesman, before they could give me an answer. Riding back to the hotel, I told "Bill" that unless he could induce the city fathers to donate the site I had picked out the Navy would not be interested in the proposition. He and the other public-spirited citizens convinced them, and one of the best Naval hospitals in the country crowns that location, and convalescent sailors can sit on the lawns and look far beyond Point Loma and see the ships that ply up and down the Pacific.

SPANISH ARCHITECTURE

In the construction at San Diego all the buildings are in keeping with the Spanish architecture of Southern California and Mexico. When the plans of the first buildings were sketched, the architect followed somewhat the character of Navy buildings at Eastern Navy bases. "Tear them up," I said "and study the type of architecture that prevails in Southern California. It would be an architectural crime to adopt Newport, Rhode Island, or Norfolk architecture in Southern California." He saw the point and he and the other architects took pride in making all Naval buildings in San Diego of the type known as Spanish, admirably suited for the climate and in keeping with the style prevailing in the region.

SAN DIEGO A SECOND HOME

When I last visited San Diego, representing President Roosevelt at the opening of the Pacific Exposition, and made an unofficial inspection of all the Naval buildings, I felt a sense of gratification that I had been privileged to be Secretary of the Navy when San Diego was made an important Naval center. I have often said that I regarded San Diego as a second home. When my term of office expired, friends in that city offered to give me a house if I would spend my last years in San Diego. There was only one objection to accepting it—it was too far from Raleigh.

INSPECTION OF BASES IN NEW ENGLAND

In the summer of my first year in office, after inspection trips to Naval bases on the Pacific and in the South, I voyaged on the *Dolphin* with my wife and sons for an inspection trip to Naval bases in New England, visiting the Navy Yards at Boston, Portsmouth, New Hampshire, Naval plants and shipbuilding establishments at New London, and Bath, and the War College and torpedo plant at Newport, R. I., and coaling station at East Lamoine. Before leaving Washington, I accepted an invitation to speak on Flag Day at Boston and the celebration at Bunker Hill.

It was a magnificient sight on the Boston Common. There were thousands of sailors in their white uniforms, hundreds of Naval officers and patriotic citizens galore. After I had spoken on the significance of the flag, Admiral Usher, who was in command of the ships in Boston Harbor, rose and said, "You have now been listening to the official Secretary of the Navy. I wish to present to you the real Secretary of the Navy," and to my wife's great surprise and confusion, he led her to the front, where she received a great ovation.

I made a visit of inspection to the Boston Navy Yard and we were entertained by Admiral and Mrs. Coffman, and at night an enthusiastic Flag Day banquet was given in the Boston Hotel.

WITH T. R. AT BUNKER HILL

The next day we attended the Bunker Hill celebration and banquet at night. It was largely attended and the only speakers were ex-President Roosevelt and myself. He came in the middle of the dinner, having spoken at some other place before arriving, and we chatted together at the table. I had not seen him since he was in the White House. I had known him fairly well when he was Chairman of the Civil Service Commission and I was Chief Clerk in the Interior Department in Washington in the Cleveland administration. He was very cordial and courteous and had some pleasant things to say of my course as Secretary of the Navy—he had been greatly cheered by my advocating a larger Navy and told me that the beginning of the building of a larger Navy was in Cleveland's administration and that when he was President and wished to secure larger construction, he found that he depended chiefly upon Democratic members of the Naval Committee, most of whom were quite as strong for an effective Navy as he was. I remember he said, "I hear very good things about you from all sources, and Franklin Roosevelt tells me you are more than making good in a place in which I have long been tremendously interested. As you know, I once was Assistant Secretary of the Navy and have always taken a keen interest in everything about it."

COAL DEPOT ABOLISHED

I saw no need of a coal depot at East Lamoine, for our ships rarely went so far north. Sailing up that gloriously beautiful body of water, I almost envied the keeper of the station. I saw, however, that it was a waste of money. I was told that it had been established by Senator Hale, of Maine, who had always seen to it, while he was Chairman of the Naval Affairs Committee, that Maine got its share of what was going. Upon my return to Washington, I gave directions that this coaling station be closed, as it was of no practical value to the Navy.

ADDRESS AT WAR COLLEGE

At Newport I made the address, mentioned in a previous chapter, to the Naval officers at the summer conference at the Naval War College and spent the morning at the college and took some part,

Above, Flag Day Celebration, 1913, in front of War, State, and Navy Building. *From left to right,* William Jennings Bryan, Josephus Daniels, Woodrow Wilson, Henry Breckinridge, Assistant Secretary of War; William Phillips, Assistant Secretary of State; Franklin D. Roosevelt, Assistant Secretary of the Navy (Harris & Ewing). *Below,* Secretary of the Navy Daniels and Mrs. Daniels at a football game in New York on a rainy and snowy day.

ON U. S. S. FLAGSHIP *PENNSYLVANIA,* MAY, 1913

When Secretary Daniels and Assistant Secretary Roosevelt and members of the Cabinet and their wives witnessed target practice off Hampton Roads in 1913 under the direction of Admiral Charles J. Badger, Commander-in-Chief of the Fleet. *Left to right,* Josephus Daniels, Lindley Garrison, Secretary of War, W. C. Redfield, Secretary of Commerce, and Naval officers.

mostly a listening part, in the discussion of the problems which the Naval War College was considering. That day they were discussing what would happen if we had a war with Germany. They discussed plans which were elaborated as fully as if war had actually been declared and every move must be debated and decided upon. It was interesting to find that there was division of opinion as to tactics and strategy among Naval officers, and sometimes they deferred opinions until a future time that they might make a further study before determining upon a certain line of action.

ALL NAVY YARDS EQUIPPED

Upon my visit to the Navy Yards of the North Atlantic, I found that they had had to lay off skilled mechanics, that the investment was so large and the work so small that there was need of reduction or of doing something to make larger use of the plants. I gave out an interview in which I said that I would put it up to Congress that all the Navy Yards be equipped to build Navy craft as well as to repair them; that this would keep the Navy Yards busy all the year round and ought to enable the Navy to build its ships cheaper than they were built under private contract. This announcement of policy was far from being well received. In a conversation with Admiral Bowles, he inveighed strongly against it and said that experience would show that it was better to have ships built in private yards. He had left the Navy to become the head of the Fore River Ship-Building Plant, and naturally had become an advocate of private construction.

TO CONSTRUCT SUBMARINES

A board in my predecessor's time had recommended scrapping the Portsmouth, New Hampshire, Navy Yard. I wished to learn if that recommendation should be carried out. My visit convinced me that the investment was too large to be lost and that the wise thing to do was to give it the facilities for building new ships. It was so equipped, and its excellent submarines and other craft are on duty with the fleet. The Navy Prison located there—so I found—had almost as many Marines on guard duty as there were prisoners, and the most archaic prison practices prevailed. I believed we ought to mend, not break prisoners. I therefore persuaded Thomas Mott Osborne to accept a commission in the Naval Reserve and reform the system in operation. He accepted and made the Navy Prison as near a model one as was humanly possible. But some of the Old Timers mourned for "the good old days" of long terms without a ray of hope for youths, guilty mostly of offenses not criminal.

WHAT INSPECTION TAUGHT

Between these trips of inspection at points distant from Washington I had more than once made a visit of inspection at the Philadelphia Navy Yard and approved plans for its enlargement and for providing facilities to enable it to build dreadnaughts and other Naval craft and also planned enlargement of the Navy Yard at Brooklyn. In addition, I had visited all the Training Stations and planned for the expansion of the one at Great Lakes, where over a hundred thousand sailors were later trained in the days of the World War.

The inspection of these yards and a study of their operation convinced me that some were not being operated at the maximum of efficiency; that there was too much red tape, too many officers on duty who were doing military rather than industrial work and that there ought to be a change so that there would be a separation between the military duties necessary in a Navy Yard having marines and sailors and the actual mechanical operations of building and repairing ships. The more I saw of Navy Yard work, the more I became convinced that it was better to put Naval constructors or Naval engineers, trained in mechanics and in the handling of men and mechanical work, in direction of this production than to put it in charge of Naval officers whose training had been rather that of navigating and ordnance and the like. And later an order to this effect was issued, and we had industrial managers of the Navy Yards who reported direct to the Secretary of the Navy as to the industrial work in the Yards, whereas the Admiral or Captain in charge of the military matters reported through the Chief of Operations. This new plan, heartily approved by the Construction Corps and Engineering Corps, was vigorously opposed by not a few of the line officers, who wished to continue in full direction of everything that went on in a Navy Yard, even though their training and knowledge did not fit them for the best direction of the work of electricians and machinists and skilled workers. The new plan worked well wherever the industrial managers were able and competent and had tact and common sense and secured full coöperation. In fact, it worked

Uncle Sam: YOU MAY REMOVE THAT CAP, JOSEPHUS! YOUR REPORT SHOWS IMPROVEMENT AND
IT LOOKS AS THOUGH YOU WERE BEGINNING TO UNDERSTAND THE REQUIREMENTS OF YOUR JOB

Harry Grant Dart. Copyright, *Life*, 1915

"YOU MAY REMOVE THAT CAP, JOSEPHUS!"

much better than the old system, though most of the line officers resented it and were always agitating a return to the old system.

MUST LEAVE DESK

These inspection trips from Bremerton to Boston and from Key West to San Diego gave me first-hand knowledge which was invaluable. You cannot administer the far-flung Navy efficiently if you "stick to your desk and never go to sea." I had tried my wings in a flight in a Navy plane, taken trips on submarines and destroyers and dreadnaughts and every other type of Naval craft. And to the education of Josephus Daniels was added the personal contact with the men on the outposts. I learned how the Navy operated and appraised the qualities and capacity of its personnel. I was to repeat those trips from time to time as occasion offered, but my first year's education stood me in good stead during all my term of office.

XXXI

MARINES HAVE THE SITUATION IN HAND

I SOON FOUND that the Marines were a strong arm of national defense—the amphibious branch of the Navy, equally capable on land and sea. In every war "from the halls of Montezuma to the shores of Tripoli" and wherever Uncle Sam needs daring fighters and capable administration, he relies upon the Marines.

In the first month of my service, I learned that there had been an attempt to divorce the Marines from the Navy. Admiral Fullham, one of the aides, early sought to induce me to take the Marines off Navy ships, saying they had no place on modern fighting ships. When Theodore Roosevelt was President, Fullham got his ear and convinced him that Marines ought to be taken off. His argument was that in the early days of the British Navy when it was necessary to impress men into the service and they were unruly, the Marines had been introduced on the ships as policemen to keep the sailors in order, but, he said, the reason for this had passed, and with an enlisted personnel of a higher class no policemen were needed; the officers of the ship could attend to all matters of discipline and the presence of the Marines aboard ship was an irritant and ought not to be allowed except at certain critical times when landing parties were needed, and then it was very well to take along Marines. Even then, he thought the sailors could do the job as well. This argument convinced President Roosevelt, and with his impetuous manner of doing a bold thing, he ordered the Marines taken off the ships. This greatly offended the entire Marine Corps and a large element of the Naval officers. They believed Marines performed an excellent and important duty, a duty apart from that of the regular duty of enlisted men and that the situation worked so well, with Marines and sailors each doing their job, that Roosevelt had made a great mistake. It was a hot controversy in the Navy for some time. Worse than warm, it was bitter, with the result that after studying it more fully, Roosevelt reversed himself, and Marines were put back on board ship as aforetime.

Shortly, at a dinner party attended by a number of Admirals and Mr. Padgett, chairman of the Naval Affairs Committee, Fullham opened his batteries on me. Like Roosevelt, I was at first impressed by his argument, but the Admirals present took the other side of the question. I knew very little about it, and yet when the evening was over I understood the Marine situation better than I would have learned in the regular order. I took occasion afterwards to inform myself more fully, to invite the views of Naval officers and Marine officers, and I was later on to enlarge and strengthen the Marine Corps and to designate its head as a member of the General Board of the Navy—headed by Admiral Dewey—and composed of able men with long experience—which I called "The Board of Naval Statesmen." This Board was the Supreme Court of Naval policy.

WALLER OR BARNETT

When I went to Washington, the head of the Marine Corps was General Biddle, of the Philadelphia family. He was an agreeable gentleman but not noted for vigor and initiative. When he understood that under the Single Term policy he would not be reappointed, he sought and obtained retirement, to which he was entitled under the law, leaving me free to appoint his successor. It was a difficult matter to name the best man. The Virginia senators were urgent in pressing General Waller, member of a distinguished Virginia family, a brave man and an excellent officer. About that time Representative Jones, of Virginia, was pressing for a new policy in the Philippines. During the war in the Philippines, General Waller had been charged with cruelty, not personal cruelties but military harshness. He was of the old-type officer and, like most of them, believed the Filipinos were an inferior people. When I read the record, it seemed to me to be unwise to appoint as head of the Marine Corps an officer who was alleged to have needlessly caused the death of Philippine soldiers, though in the trial he had been acquitted. I did not pass upon whether he was deserving of the criticism he received at the time or whether he was better or worse than other officers of the Army and Navy on duty in the Philippines. After reading the record, I did not like his attitude, particularly in view of the fact that we wished to inaugurate a new policy looking to independence of the Philippines. The President wished to have a governor who would give the people a larger voice in the government of their own country. As we wished to remove all trace of what the Filipinos regarded as harsh treatment during our war in that country, it seemed to me better not to appoint an officer who had been under fire. The Virginia Senators went to see the President and urged the appointment of Waller after I had told them I would not recommend it. The more I looked into it, the more I felt the unwisdom of appointing Waller, and began to look about for a successor to General Biddle. In the light of experience, I have thought that Waller deserved the place. Except for my intense hostility to the war upon the Filipinos and my zeal that they be given the right of self-government, I would have favored him. I learned to have deep respect for his high qualities as a man and officer, and trusted him with important duties. He more than measured up to every assignment and duty.

BEST MARINE OFFICER

I became convinced that the best man in the Marine Corps was General John A. Lejeune, but his rank was rather low for the position. His fine qualities were later proven in the World War, when he commanded the 2nd Division in France. In 1942 the new Marine Training Base at New River, North Carolina, was named Lejeune in his honor.

Senator Weeks, among others, brought to my attention the name of General George Barnett. He was not as vigorous or able a man as General Waller. He was not as able and learned a soldier as General Lejeune, but he had a good record, and he was appointed. I found him capable and agreeable, ready to carry out any policy the President or Secretary inaugurated. He got along well with his officers and men, shortly called General Lejeune to be his chief assistant, and had his department well organized. It made a fine record.

ECONOMY WITH A BIG E

Devotion to economy was not universal in either the Navy or the Marines, but a shining example of efficiency and economy was General Cyrus S. Radford, who made the Marines the best-dressed, at the least cost, of all the military men in the service. It was at his suggestion that the Charleston Navy Yard was equipped to manufacture uniforms for the Marines, greatly to the delight of Senator

Tillman, chairman of the Naval Affairs Committee. In this instance, the word economy was found outside of the dictionary.

ROASTED BY GOVERNOR BLEASE

Should the Marine Training Base at Port Royal be continued? That was a question debated in the Navy and in Congress. Senator Tillman, chairman of the Naval Affairs Committee, being a South Carolinian, had defeated the attempt to close it. As I had to make a decision, I made a trip of inspection in 1913. As nearly always, my wife accompanied me. We were entertained by the Commandant, Captain Hatch, and his wife. They had a charming little daughter, called by everybody "Peachy," who walked into my wife's heart. Afterwards, during the World War when the moral conditions at Philadelphia were bad and action was demanded by the Navy to make them cleaner, I sent Captain Hatch to Philadelphia to undertake the job. He handled it admirably and showed he was one of the best officers of the Marine Corps.

Port Royal had originally been a Naval station in the days when the Naval bases could be located where very deep water was not required—not more than twelve feet; but with the building of larger ships, Port Royal Naval Station was no longer suitable and had been converted into Marine barracks. I had heard before going there that one of the serious objections to continuing the Port Royal base was that at the very entrance to the station there had congregated in little shacks lewd women and bootleggers, who solicited every Marine coming and going. When I examined this place, I found it was utterly sodden and disreputable, a menace to the morals and proper instruction and training of young Marines. I directed Captain Hatch to telephone to the Sheriff of the county to come over. Together we visited disreputable quarters adjoining the Marine barracks and agreed that they were disgraceful. I told the Sheriff that there were strong influences at work to close Port Royal and move the Marines to the base at Philadelphia and that this attempt at removal might succeed if conditions were not improved. I did not tell him I would recommend the removal unless it was done, but I told him that neither Senator Tillman nor I could stand against removal if its advocates told of the bad situation. I told him that, as Secretary of the Navy, I would not be justified in sending men to be trained for service in the Marine Corps if they were subjected to

Upper left, General George Barnett, Major General Commandant U. S. Marine Corps (NR & L, U. S. Marine Corps). *Upper right,* General John Lejeune, Commandant of U. S. Marine Corps, Commandant Quantico Marine Base (USMC). *Lower left,* General Smedley Butler, dynamic Marine called "Old Gimlet Eye" (NR & L, USMC). *Lower right,* General Cyrus Radford, who made the Marines the best dressed and equipped men in the armed services, and got a hundred cents out of every dollar (from painting by George Gibbs).

Upper left, J. C. McReynolds, Attorney General in Wilson's Cabinet, 1913-1914, and Associate Justice of the U. S. Supreme Court. *Upper right,* Thomas W. Gregory, Attorney General in Wilson's Cabinet, 1914-1918. *Lower left,* John H. Clarke, Associate Justice of the U. S. Supreme Court (Harris & Ewing). *Lower right,* Louis D. Brandeis, Associate Justice of the U. S. Supreme Court (Brown Brothers).

these temptations and sordid immoral surroundings. He promised to take the matter up and see that the situation was so cleaned up that I would be justified in saying to Congress that the former bad conditions had been removed.

In pursuance of this he took the matter up with Governor Blease. Before I returned to Washington, Blease came out with a blast in the papers denouncing me and saying that I was assuming to dictate to the officials of South Carolina how they should perform their duties, by giving them the ultimatum that unless they obeyed my orders I would close the Marine Base at Port Royal. I never read a more bitter diatribe or more vicious one. I paid no attention to it except to give to the press of South Carolina exactly what I had said to the Sheriff. Port Royal was cleaned up, and the Marine base remained.

XXXII

BUILDING "THE MOST ADEQUATE NAVY IN THE WORLD"

WHEN I BECAME Secretary of the Navy I found that the General Board had said, "Considering displacement of ships built, the United States advanced from third to second place in 1907, and dropped to third in 1911." The previous administration had carried out the plan, as President Theodore Roosevelt said in his message to Congress, of "building each year at least one first class battleship." His goal was to "keep the Navy at its present strength." No headway was made in Naval strength under the Taft administration. In those days presidents undoubtedly fell in with the sentiment of the country, which did not wish to pay for a large Navy. In the Wilson administration in its first two years appropriations were secured for five dreadnaughts, and steps were taken in 1913 toward the goal of "a Navy second to none." Admiral McKean declared in 1916 as to building fighting ships, "We have made more real progress in the last two years than in any previous five-year period in the Navy."

TWO-BATTLESHIP PROGRAM

My first statement to the press, early in March, was that I would advocate a two-battleship program and other increases in Naval strength. In the previous year Congress had appropriated for only one dreadnaught. While that measure was pending in 1912 I had, as a private citizen, gone to Washington to urge Congressman Kitchin and Robert N. Page, and other North Carolina Representatives (E. W. Pou already favored two) and Senators to give their support to two. Therefore as Secretary of the Navy I was carrying out a policy I had supported as an editor. Navy officers were gratified when it was announced that I had decided to include in my estimates money for the construction of two dreadnaughts and a corresponding number of destroyers, with other recommendations that would, in the course of a few years, give the United States a Navy second to none.

THREE-YEAR BUILDING PROGRAM

The building went on steadily on the two-battleship ratio—until 1915, when President Wilson wrote me (July 21) from Cornish that he had given "a great deal of thought, as I am sure you have also, to the matter of a wise and adequate Naval program to be presented to Congress." He said, "First we must have professional advice for a Navy in order to stand upon an equality with the most practicable." He added that upon his return to Washington he would "take this important matter up with you at your earliest convenience." I had a conference with Admiral Dewey and Admiral Badger of the General Board, and asked them to draw up a program covering a period of five years that would give us a Navy second to none. By the time Wilson returned to Washington, a comprehensive program had been formulated including the first important authorization of airplanes. I approved and took it to the President. He was pleased with it and urged it upon Congress. The Naval Committee decided to authorize the whole program of construction to be completed within three years. It went through both houses. Thus one act of Congress authorized construction that would give the United States the most powerful Navy in the World. It was the largest construction program in times of peace ever authorized by any country in the history of the world. No time was lost in making contracts to private builders and allocating construction to Navy yards. Shortly, the Navy had practically every shipbuilding plant working on the program with all their facilities. When later the Shipping Board sought to secure the building of ships, it found that all facilities were already working on Navy ships and the Board had to rush the construction of Hog Island and other plants.

The new construction program authorized the construction of ten battleships, six battle-cruisers, ten scout-cruisers, fifty destroyers, fifteen fleet submarines, eighty-five coast submarines, four gunboats, one hospital ship, two ammunition ships, two fuel-oil ships, and one repair ship.

In his address to Congress urging this large program, the President had said on December 7, 1915:

"If this full program should be carried out, we should have built or building in 1921, according to the estimates of survival and standards of classification followed by the General Board

C. K. Berryman, in the *Washington Star*

WILSON AS PREPAREDNESS DOCTOR.

The President directs the Army and Navy nurses to make their charges able to uphold national policy and guarantee national defense.

of the Department, an effective Navy consisting of twenty-seven battleships, of the first line, six battle-cruisers, twenty-five battle-ships of the second line, ten armored cruisers, thirteen scout-cruisers, five first-class cruisers, three second-class cruisers, ten third-class cruisers, one hundred and eight destroyers, eighteen fleet submarines, one hundred and fifty-seven coast submarines, six monitors, twenty gunboats, four supply ships, fifteen fuel ships, four transports, three tenders to torpedo vessels, eight vessels of special types, and two ammunition ships. This would be a Navy fitted to our needs and worthy of our traditions."

At St. Louis, in his swing around the circle, on February 3, 1916, Wilson made a statement that caused people to sit up and think. He said:

"Have you ever let your imagination dwell upon the enormous stretch of coast from the Canal to Alaska,—from the Canal to the northern corner of Maine? There is no other Navy in the world that has to cover so great an area of defense as the American Navy, and it ought in my judgment to be incomparably the greatest Navy in the world."

When told by Walter Lippmann that the statement was injudicious, Wilson changed it to be "incomparably the most adequate Navy in the world." There wasn't really any difference. At the first meeting of the Cabinet after Wilson's return, Burleson told him of his surprise at favoring such a big Navy and asked if the papers had quoted him correctly. "Yes," said Wilson, "and that was the soundest utterance I made on the trip and the policy that the country should adopt."

NAMING DESTROYERS CAUSES SAMPSON-SCHLEY FIGHT TO FLARE UP

The Navy personnel has long thoughts and long memories. I was soon to learn that old feuds were only smothered. Unaware of the bitterness remaining from the old Sampson-Schley controversy, I, without dreaming where I was going, plunged headlong into its smouldering fires. As the new Navy-building program authorized by Congress got under way, it became my duty to give names to a number of fast destroyers—then and now the most serviceable Navy fighting ships. According to custom they were to have the names of Naval heroes. I decided to name the first two *Sampson* and *Schley*, for two of the Naval leaders in the Spanish-American war. In my innocence of old antagonisms, that brought on severe criticism.

In this old controversy and long-drawn-out trial, my paper had sided with the Schley partisans and had praised Dewey for his testimony, free from bias, which offended the powerful Sampson group. Of course I knew nothing about the merits of the case except what I read in the papers, and regarded both Sampson and Schley as heroes who had added glory to the Navy. I had printed with approval Mr. Dooley's analysis, which still rankled in the hearts of Sampson's admirers. Right or wrong, it is a classic of its kind. Mr. Dooley wrote thus:

An' now it's Schley's turn. I knew it was comin' to Schley an' here it comes. You used to think he was a gran' man, that whin ol' Cevera come out iv the harbor at Sandago he called out 'Come on, boys', and plunged into th' Spanish fleet and rejooced it to scrap-iron. That's what ye thought, an' that's what I thought, an' we were wrong. We were wrong, Hinnesy. I've been r-readin' a thrue history iv th' campaign by wan iv the' gr-r-reast historyians now employed as a clerk in th' supply stores iv th' Brooklyn navy yard. Like mesilf, he's a fireside vethran iv the war. He's a mimber of th' Martin Dooley Post No. 1, Definders of th' Hearth. He's the boy f'r ye. If iver he beats his sugar scoop into a soord, ye'll think ol' Farragut was a lady cook on a lumber barge. Says th' historyian: Th' conduck iv Schley durin' the Campaign was such as to bring th' bright blush iv shame to ivry man on the pay-roll iv our beloved counthrye....

So they've arristed Schley. As soon as th' book come out th' Sicrety if th' Navy issued a warrant ag'in him, chargin' him with victhry an' he's gon' to have to stand thrile f'r it. I don't know what th' punishment is, but 'tis somethin' hard f'r the offinse is onus'l. They're sure to bounce him an' maybe they'll give his job to Cevera. As far as I can see, Hinnesy, an' I cud see as far as me fellow vethran Mackay an' some one hundherd miles farther, Emannel is the on'y wan that come out of the battle with honor. Whin Schley was thryin' to give up the ship, or was alongside it on a stagin' makin' dents in t' armorplate with a pickaxe, Sampson was off writin' letters to himself an' Bob Ivans was locked in a connin'-tower with a life-priserver buckled around his waist. Noble ol' Cevera done nawthin' to disgrace his flag. He los' his ships and his men an' his biler an' iverything except his ripytation. He saved that, he bein' a good swimmer an' not bein' an officer iv the United States Navy.

"I should think Schley'd thry an' prove an allybi," Mr. Hennessy suggested pleasantly.

"He cain't," said Mr. Dooley. "His friend Sampson's got that."

Undoubtedly Sampson was one of the ablest and best-educated and statesmanlike of Naval officers, whose service was worthy of the highest traditions of the Navy and whose courage was equal to his statesmanship. I recognized that, but neither Winslow nor the others of his fervid friends could forgive placing him in the class with Schley, particularly after the bitterness of the trial.

Shortly after the papers carried the announcement that two sister destroyers had been named *Sampson* and *Schley,* I had a call from one of my earliest friends among the high ranking officers, Admiral Cameron MacRae Winslow, of North Carolina stock. He said with long-pent-up feeling, "You have made a serious mistake and done a great wrong to the Navy." I replied that, on the contrary, I had honored two brilliant and courageous officers who had brought distinction to the Navy. He replied, "But you have dishonored the great officer Sampson by giving the same honor to Schley, who did not deserve the equal honor with Sampson, if he deserved any honor at all." That was the frank statement of what the Sampson partisans thought of my perfectly innocent intention of recognizing the great place he had won in the Navy. But the Sampson partisans resented his being coupled with Schley.

Some writers agreed with Admiral Winslow and sought to relight the flames of an old controversy. But, aside from the shipmates and friends of the principals, there was no response. The American people had put both these fine officers on their list of Naval heroes and did not propose to reopen an old controversy. With these heroic names the destroyers carried on the tradition of the officers whose names they bore.

INEFFICIENCY OF SUBMARINES

It was not until the German U-boats came so near to winning the World War in the days before Wilson led in "shutting up the hornets in their nest," that the submarine was regarded as a great weapon of offense. They held a secondary place in the United States Navy.

I was not long in learning the defects of our submarines. Examining the reports of the manoeuvres in the spring of 1913, I observed that at critical times, when there was dependence upon their efficiency, the submarine failed to function well. I ordered an investigation, which disclosed the fact that the submarines either had not been properly constructed or were not properly operated, or both. The more I looked into the submarine question, the more I found we were depending more or less upon a broken stick. Nobody in particular seemed responsible for passing upon the efficiency, up-keep, and performance of these modern craft. Rarely a week passed without reports that a submarine was lagging in performance. When this was brought to the attention of the builders, they passed the buck to Naval officers and said it was due to lack of efficiency in operation and care. The officers passed the buck back to the contractors and said the submarines were not properly built.

ADMIRAL GRANT IN CHARGE

I had come in pretty close touch with Admiral Grant while he was in command of a dreadnaught, and had faith in his vigor and ability. I therefore detached him from other duty and put him in control of the submarines, directing him to compel the contractors to live up to their guarantee and to ascertain where the trouble was and remedy it. This was a rather drastic method because some of the officers thought that the submarine, being a part of each division, should be cared for by the Admiral in command. I found that the method theretofore employed had fallen down and that we must have some able officer who knew how, and give him the authority to put the submarine on the same basis of efficiency as destroyers and battleships. It was a difficult task. Admiral Grant entered upon it with his usual vigor and was assisted by Captain Sterling, but in that year I had to forfeit two contracts made with the Lake Torpedo Boat Company and to require the Electric Boat Company to put their boats in proper shape. I ascertained that when these boats were on trial they functioned well enough to be passed and accepted, but that they were accepted and paid for by the Navy without a long enough test to insure efficient performance. The meaning of this was that, having accepted them, it was up to the Navy to continue to tinker on them in an effort to make them perform. This cost money and in the main gave unsatisfactory service. I may say that the lack of efficiency of the submarines in the first summer of my term of office gave me more trouble than anything else. I felt relieved when I turned it over to Admiral Grant, but neither then nor afterwards during my entire term in the Navy were submarines entirely satisfactory, though by the most strenuous efforts there was marked improvement before the World War.

WANTED EXCLUSIVE CONTRACT

Before the World War, at the Portsmouth (N. H.) Navy Yard provision was made so that the Navy itself could build submarines. I thought that the only way to compel the two private submarine builders to make the best submarines at a reasonable price was to demonstrate that they could be built in a Navy Yard. This succeeded both as to cost and as to quality. One of the troubles was that the Lake Torpedo Company, headed by Mr. Simon Lake, who had been really the inventor of the modern submarine, got into financial difficulty. He was a genius in devising submarines but not a success as a business man, and found it difficult to complete the ships on contract time. Later in my administration when we were having trouble with the submarines and before we entered the war, there was necessity for contracting for a large number and the Electric Boat Company made the hardest sort of a drive to secure the contract for all the submarines the Navy needed. They knew of the financial difficulties of the Lake Company, and knew they had failed in several instances to furnish ships that met every requirement. Therefore, they asked that the Electric Company to be given the exclusive contract for building submarines for the Navy.

At that time, the Electric Boat Company was headed by Mr. Corse, a prominent banker of New York. He came down to see me several times about getting the contract for all the submarines. I pointed out to him that, while it was true the Lake Torpedo Company had not aways built boats on contract time, the same thing was true of his company and it seemed to me to be a good policy to divide the contracts between the only two companies that could build submarines, seeing that neither lived up to their contract, rather than to give his company a monopoly of Navy work, at least, until we could build them in Navy Yards. Later Mr. Corse retained as his representative Mr. McAdoo, brother of the Secretary of the Treasury, to represent him in the Navy Department in securing contracts. McAdoo was a very agreeable man and, of course, I received him with courtesy. He took the matter up with Admiral Griffin and Admiral Taylor, Chief of Engineering and Construction, and sought to persuade them to recommend that all the contracts be awarded to the Electric Boat Company. I told McAdoo frankly that my own opinion and that of the two Admirals was that it would be a mistake to give all the contracts to any one company and that it was better to keep the Lake Torpedo Company in the business by nursing it along, because the head of the company knew much about submarines and was doing his best, rather than to put all our eggs in one basket, particularly at a time when we wished to build every submarine possible. I added that we had enough contracts to keep both yards busy and that the company he represented had been almost as unsatisfactory as the Lake Torpedo Company.

MCADOO TAKES A HAND

While this discussion was going on, I visited the plants of both companies and sought to find out where the trouble was. The Electric Boat Company had two corporations, one that furnished the motive power and the other that built the boat, and like all holding companies, they wished, I thought, to make profit coming and going. My purpose as frankly outlined to McAdoo and to Corse, to give contracts to both companies, was stoutly resisted. They brought all the pressure possible to bear to secure the whole contract. One day as the Cabinet was adjourning, President Wilson said,

"I wish the Secretary of the Navy to remain a few minutes after Cabinet adjourns."

I did so and he asked me about the status of the contracts for building submarines and told me that Secretary McAdoo had spoken to him about it having reached the conclusion that the only way to secure satisfactory submarines was to give the contract to a certain Boat Company—the President did not remember the name of the company—about which Secretary McAdoo had spoken to him. He said McAdoo feared I was making a mistake in giving contracts to a company which was not financially able to fulfill its contracts. It was the only time the President ever spoke to me about any matter of this kind. At first, I was disposed to take exception to McAdoo's going to the President about a matter in my Department, but in a moment I saw that was a wrong point of view to take. I understood that McAdoo's brother, retained by the Electric Company, had been able to convince Secretary McAdoo that the good of the Navy required excluding the Lake Company from getting any contracts. I thereupon explained to the President the whole situation and told him if the Electric Boat Company had lived up to its obligations, if its ships fully met the high tests, and if their boats had always functioned well, they might with some reason come to the Navy Department and ask to be given the exclusive contract, but that in my judgment and that of my technical advisers, it would be fatal to end all competition. I also told him if the Electric Company had not functioned well as they ought to under competition, I saw no hope of improvement if we turned over to them the building of all the boats. I convinced him that the Navy ought not to be confined to one company when that company's performance had fallen short of efficiency.

The President concluded the interview by saying he knew nothing about it and had only brought the matter up because somebody had convinced McAdoo that a mistake was about to be made. He said that, of course, my statement showed I had taken the right course and he fully approved it. I never spoke to McAdoo about this matter nor he to me. McAdoo, of course, having married the President's daughter, had his ear and undoubtedly his brother had convinced him that the plan he was advocating was best for the government. Upon reflection I made allowance for a brother's influence with a brother and did not permit the matter in any way to break up the very pleasant relations between McAdoo and myself. It convinced me, however, more than ever that people related to government officials by blood or marriage ought to have no part in trying to secure government contracts. Here was a perfectly honorable and high-minded and able Secretary of the Treasury going to the most disinterested and honest of presidents urging something which he believed was right; and yet the Secretary's judgment had been influenced by his brother, who, though an engineer by profession, was not an expert in submarine building. Blood is the most powerful influence in the world, and helping a kinsman warps judgment more than any other motive.

TRIP IN A SUBMARINE

By the time the World War came on, our submarines had been much improved but never to my mind were one hundred per cent as good as they ought to have been. When the U-boat warfare was at its height, I marvelled that the Germans had been able to perfect submarines to carry on as they did. Upon my first visit to the Navy Yard at Norfolk in the spring of 1913 in pursuance of my intention to know everything possible about the Navy, I had gone down in a submarine and had taken a spin to Hampton Roads. The sub functioned perfectly but, after a brief trip I was glad enough to come to the surface. After that I had a greater respect and admiration for the men of the Navy in the submarine service and advocated the measure in Congress which would give them increased pay when on active submarine duty. I regarded it as extra hazardous, but the daring youngsters in the Navy were as keen for submarine duty as later the more venturesome were attracted to the air service.

ADMIRALS AND PIRATES

When I named a destroyer *Burns* in honor of Otway Burns, a privateer of North Carolina, who sank many ships in the War of 1812, Admiral Badger said, "Mr. Secretary, I find no Naval hero named Burns." I acquainted him with the exploits of Burns and said, "You know that some Naval officers regarded privateers as not far removed from pirates." I added, "In those days, the difference between an Admiral and a pirate was in the twilight zone, and since my association with Admirals, I don't think there has been much change in a century." He thought it a good joke.

CONGRESSIONAL LEADERS FOR AN ENLARGED NAVY

Upper left, Benjamin Tillman, chairman of Senate Naval Affairs Committee, 1913-1916. *Upper right,* Claude A. Swanson, chairman of same committee, 1916-1921, who piloted through the Senate the greatest Naval construction bill in history. *Lower left,* Lemuel P. Padgett, chairman of the House Committee, 1913-1919, who did the same in the House. *Lower right,* Thomas S. Butler, of Pennsylvania, chairman of the House Naval Affairs Committee, 1919-1921, champion of Big Navy.

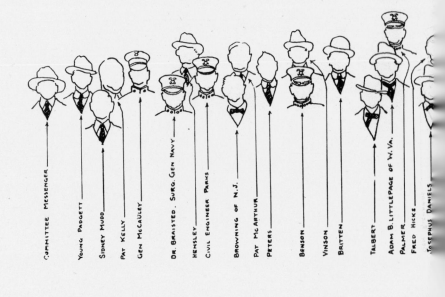

COMMITTEE MESSENGER

YOUNG PADGETT

SIDNEY MUDD

PAT KELLY

GEN MCCAULEY

DR. BRAISTED, SURG. GEN NAVY

HENSLEY

CIVIL ENGINEER PARKS

BROWNING OF N.J.

PAT MCARTHUR

PETERS

BENSON

VINSON

BRITTEN

TALBERT

ADAM B. LITTLEPAGE OF W. VA.

PALMER

FRED HICKS

JOSEPHUS DANIELS

THE NAVAL AFFAIRS COMMITTEE AND NAVY OFFICIALS IN 1915

when the committee approved the recommendation of the Wilson administration for the largest construction of Navy ships in peace time in the history of the world.

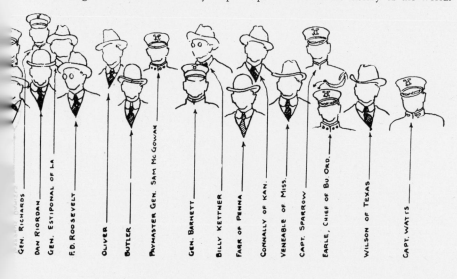

GEN. RICHARDS — DAN RIORDAN — GEN. ESTIPONAL OF LA — F.D. ROOSEVELT — OLIVER — BUTLER — PAYMASTER GEN. SAM McGOWAN — GEN. BARNETT — BILLY KETTNER — FARR OF PENNA — CONNALLY OF KAN. — VENEABLE OF MISS. — CAPT. SPARROW — EARLE, CHIEF OF BU. ORD. — WILSON OF TEXAS — CAPT. WATTS

IN FIGHT FOR THE NAVAL OIL RESERVE

Upper left, J. Crawford Biggs, chairman of Wilson pre-election caucus in North Carolina, Assistant Attorney General of the U. S., argued and won Naval Oil Reserve Case in Supreme Court. *Upper right,* E. J. Justice, Assistant Attorney General of the U. S., who made possible the preservation of the Naval Oil Reserve in California. *Lower left,* John Barton Payne, who as Secretary of the Interior gave decision that saved Naval Oil Reserve (Brown Brothers). *Lower right,* Admiral H. A. Stuart, adviser in the Navy on Naval Oil Reserves.

XXXIII

CONGRESS ALWAYS COÖPERATIVE

I N 1913 the strength of navies was measured in dreadnaughts. I asked Congress for two, with the complement of other ships. Congress gave the authorization. It approved every recommendation of the Navy in my first year, and this was true at every session during my eight years' administration. I never had to suffer being turned down by the Naval Affairs Committee or Congress. There was unanimity in the Committee, which was composed almost equally of Democrats and Republicans. This was quite as true later, when the Republicans controlled the Committee. The one exception was that the Republican Committee turned down my earnest plea to complete the Three Year Program after the Armistice. The Chairman asked me, "Now that the war is over, why a strong Navy?" I told him that we must either go into the League of Nations or have incomparably the strongest Navy in the world. Again, after the Senate had declined to let us take our seat at Geneva, I stressed that this crime made it imperative to complete the construction of dreadnaughts and battle cruisers which had been held up during the war. But, believing that even with the United States out, there would be no more wars, they reduced Naval construction.

COÖPERATING CHAIRMEN

I acted on the presumption that the members of Congress, charged with responsible duties with respect to the Navy, were as much interested as I was. I sought their advice before I made my recommendations—that is to say, I would always see the chairman of the committee and the ranking member of the opposition party, and lay before them the major projects I had in mind and ask their frank opinions. I was very fortunate in the early days of my administration in that the two chairmen of the Naval Affairs Committee had served long on the committees and were deeply interested in the Navy. They became not only wise counsellors but warm personal friends, zealous that the Naval administration should be a credit to the country and ready at all times to take up the cudgels in support of the Navy Department. The Honorable Lemuel P. Padgett, of Tennessee, chairman of the House Naval Affairs Committee, had a grasp of practical matters which was invaluable. He knew as much about the Navy as any Naval officer. Offhand, he knew the expenditures for every kind of service, the range and calibre of the guns, what the electrical equipment ought to cost and how long it should last, and was keenly interested in any project for increasing speed or power, was deeply concerned with the personnel and came to talk the lingo of the sea. He came from a State laved by neither ocean, and when he first came to Congress he was as ignorant, so he told me, of all nomenclature and inside workings of the Navy as I was when I became Secretary of the Navy, but he mastered it all and I found his judgment of the greatest value. He was conservative, too, and economical, but was always a little advance of the temper of Congress and the spirit of the country, so that as we made progress steadily if not rapidly, I found him forward-looking and conservatively progressive.

I was equally fortunate in that Senator Tillman, of South Carolina, was chairman of the Committee in the Senate. We had long been friends, having served together on the National Democratic Executive Committee. Our States, lying side by side, had similar interests, and he was deeply concerned that the United States should have a strong and efficient Navy. Some people thought his interest was heightened by the fact that he had secured the enlargement of the Navy Yard at Charleston, South Carolina, and had compelled Congress to continue it when the former Secretary of the Navy wished to close it. He had expressed in his blunt fashion in a previous Congress his position when he said, "If there is any pork to be distributed, South Carolina must have its share," and he held up the Navy bill until the Navy Yard at Charleston had been given adequate work along with that of other Navy Yards. He regarded the Navy Yard at Charleston as one of his pets and was always keen to secure more work for it.

Upon the death of Senator Tillman, he was succeeded in the chairmanship by Senator Swanson of Virginia. The country owed much to his constructive leadership in strengthening the Navy in every way; and because of his knowledge of the Navy and his devotion to it, he was appointed Secretary of the Navy by Franklin Roosevelt and held that position until his death.

CLOSE COÖPERATION APPROVED

These cordial relations were emphasized by the lack of sympathy of the Military Committee with the Secretary of War. The chairman and secretary were non coöperative, so much so that once Woodrow Wilson, when the Military Committee of the House and Secretary Garrison were at cross purposes, asked members of the Committee to come to the White House. After they had threshed out the matter at issue, Wilson said, "I find that the Naval Committee is so zealous to strengthen the Navy, that the members and Secretary Daniels work together in perfect harmony and accomplish important results. I wish you would find the recipe and pull together with the Secretary of War."

This experience in dealing with members of Congress convinced me that if the executive and legislative agencies of government would believe in each other and practise Woodrow Wilson's plan of common council, there would be fewer clashes and a better government.

ROUND TABLE CONFERENCES

Ninety per cent of the "passing the buck" between "the Hill" and executive departments would not exist if responsible executives and legislators would sit around a table and discuss policies and programs in the early stages. Agreement would follow and friction be eliminated. But "who will bell the cat"? It is too late after the executive has sent down a "must" and Congressmen have replied, "We will not take orders." It was largely due to the coöperation of the executive and legislative branches of government that the Navy was powerful and in the highest state of efficiency when it was called into action upon the declaration of war in April, 1917.

XXXIV

BITTER MEDICINE FOR THE NAVY LEAGUE

THE NAVY LEAGUE, which made its goal "the second largest Navy" thereby conceding lasting primacy to Britain, was, when I went to Washington, militantly urging a strong Navy. I joined hands with them but told the leaders that, while we could not build a greater Navy soon, the goal of the United States must ultimately be a Navy second to none. I was invited early to speak at their banquet and to make known the attitude of the new administration. We worked together—Colonel Robert M. Thompson, a Naval Academy graduate, its president, being a Big Navy advocate. As time went on, the leaders of the League became anti-administration, opposing neutrality and other Wilson policies. I found that Congress paid little attention to the League and that its influence was not in proportion to its claims. However, there was never any break until its leaders, who became more against the Wilson policies than for a strong Navy—showed it in its true colors. Then came war to the knife.

In August, 1915, the dominant officials of the League sent out in the name of the League a statement charging that the investigation of the Mare Island explosion had been blocked at the demand of labor leaders. In view of what I called "treasonable action by the League toward the government and a gross slander of patriotic workers in the Navy Yard," in a vigorous letter to Thompson I demanded that he and other officers of the League resign from what had come to be an unpatriotic organization. In a sarcastic letter, in which he sought to minimize the wrong done by the slander, issued on August 16, Thompson replied saying he would be a good sport and would resign as president of the League if I would resign as Secretary of the Navy. Two days thereafter I issued an order excluding all officers and representatives of the Navy League from ships or Naval reservations. I followed that up by directing patriotic women not to send gifts through the Navy League and recognizing an organization for that purpose headed by Mrs. E. T. Stotesbury, of

Philadelphia, who resigned from the League and gave herself wholly to the patriotic work.

In October I gave endorsement to the plan of H. P. Davison, head of the Red Cross, for forming Naval auxiliaries in all local Red Cross chapters and appointing sixteen members of the Woman's Advisory Committee on Naval Auxiliaries. This provided a plan for the knitting of sweaters, through the Red Cross, without the need of accepting the service of the Navy League, which had wished to be designated as the exclusive agency for such gifts to sailors. The League had broadcast that my refusal to accept gifts from the Navy League was a denial to enlisted men of sweaters, etc., which they needed, and it appointed a committee to ask President Wilson to lift the ban I had placed on League officers. Wilson did not lift the ban and through the Red Cross and Mrs. Stotesbury's organization and Naval Auxiliaries there was no lack of gifts to Naval personnel.

The workmen of Navy Yards wired approval of my action in the Mare Island situation and pledged loyalty. The report of the explosion at Mare Island Navy Yard proved that the Navy League charges were without the slightest foundation. Two weeks went by without a word from Colonel Thompson. His sporting proposition fell like a dud, and members of the League showed indignation at the gratuitous slander of patriotic workmen, which had been inspired by a desire to injure the Navy in its conduct of the war. But after two weeks had gone by and public condemnation was apparent, Thompson gave out a statement that the Navy League Bulletin reflecting upon the loyalty of the workmen of the Mare Island Navy Yard had been issued without his knowledge. A few days later a bulletin was issued by the Navy League accepting the Mare Island report and withdrawing its charges.

Nothing but the order of exclusion of members of the League from Naval ships and Naval bases and exposing the slanders of Naval workers secured the withdrawal. The League was convicted in the forum of public opinion of a gross libel upon good men. Its apology came grudgingly, and never during my term of office was it reinstated in public favor. I was to the end the object of its hatred. I consoled myself that I had protected the good name of the service and exposed machinations that were unpatriotic if not traitorous, by some Navy League leaders.

I could not have done anything that would have cut deeper than to deny to any officer of the League the opportunity to put his foot on a Naval ship or on a Naval shore station. They loved that association, and they basked in the prestige they derived from it. I knew the medicine for those gentlemen and administered it. They cried out more loudly than a boy given a dose of castor oil. The Treasurer of the League, brother-in-law of Pierpont Morgan, called at the Navy Department to intercede. I told him that all the League had to do was to withdraw its traitorous statement and make apologies. He deprecated the act but had no authority. The order stood, being suspended only so that former graduates of the Naval Academy could attend June week exercises at Annapolis. I told them that as a matter of fact instead of helping the Navy, the Navy League had become a hindrance and a danger, and that the best thing it could do would be to disband or reform. It had degenerated into a coterie of men who assumed to direct Presidents and Secretaries. Capable public officials need no self-appointed wet nurses. The Navy was never helped by the League, but often hurt by its assumptions and loud demonstrations of its value, though in its membership there were many patriotic men and women animated solely by devotion to the Navy. Many of them sided with me, but the leaders never forgave me.

LEAGUE SCARED HOOVER

Nearly every President who has not been a rubber stamp for the Navy League has received its criticism. Hoover failed to strengthen the Navy as he should have done but did not deserve the assumption of the League that it had the right to dictate Naval policy.

XXXV

PROFITEERS WAVING THE FLAG

I WENT TO WASHINGTON imbued with the intention of putting into operation the economy in public administration I had always advocated. Nothing is less desired in some circles in Washington than economy, and the sure road to criticism is to demand a dollar's worth for every dollar expended. Most Army and Navy officials are keen for efficiency, but few know how to spell Economy, although some do. The official who is a liberal spender is regarded as "a broad-minded statesman." If he insists upon close examination and rigid economy, he is "a niggardly politician." I soon found that, while Naval personnel would stand for no graft, many had little interest in "government economically administered," and I could not count on full coöperation in that policy.

HE WAS ANGRY

One morning in December, 1913, a few days after my first annual report had been printed, a fine looking gentleman, evidently laboring under excitement and suppressed anger, Colonel E. G. Buckner, an official of the Du Pont Powder Company (it had not extended into other fields then on a large scale) literally strode into my office. Without any preliminaries or good mornings he addressed me in a loud voice to this effect:

"I was never so astonished in my life as when my ship reached my country, before I landed to read in your annual report, which my secretary brought me, your misrepresentation of my company. I was so outraged at what you said that I came in haste to Washington to express my indignation and to call upon you to withdraw your statement that our company is a trust and had charged the Navy excessive prices for smokeless powder. It is a slander based upon false information given you."

"You are mistaken. I am not the author of the statement," I replied, "that your company is 'the powder trust.'"

"But here it is in your report," he said, showing the place he had marked. "Do you deny you made that statement?"

I told him I was the author of the report and assumed responsibility for everything in it, but, I added, "I am not the author of that charge. I was only quoting the opinion of the Supreme Court of the United States. If you have any grievance against anybody it is the members of that Honorable Court."

He was not mollified but departed not quite so belligerent.

Animated by belief that the Navy ought to get a dollar's worth of munitions for every dollar expended, I made a study of prices paid and found that money could be saved by the manufacture of munitions in Navy plants instead of buying from profit-making concerns, some of which, with little or no competition, were charging excessive prices. Smokeless powder was the next worst offender after armor-plate. It was easy to save money on both.

NAVY MAKES SMOKELESS POWDER

The Navy had constructed a small plant at Indian Head, where it was making some smokeless powder. Before the plant was in operation the Du Pont Company charged the Navy one dollar a pound. When the Navy began producing, the Du Pont Company reduced its price to sixty cents. The enlarged Navy plant made smokeless powder for thirty-eight cents a pound, and in the first three years of my administration we saved $1,169,000 over the price the private company had formerly charged. I wished to enlarge the plant and make all the smokeless powder needed.

The success of the Navy in saving much money by the manufacture of smokeless powder in its own plants caused the War Industries Board during the war to cancel a War Department contract with the Du Pont Company to manufacture a million pounds a day. This would have given the Du Pont Company a profit of over sixty million dollars. Following the Navy example, the Board built its own plants. The cost of government manufacture was reduced from eighty to forty-three cents.

MONEY WAS SAVED ON MUNITIONS

In order to secure satisfactory Naval mines and to obtain the type approved by the ordnance department, I made a contract paying royalty to the Vickers Company of England so that the Navy could manufacture them. We saved $145 on each by manufacturing them instead of buying them abroad. In addition, employment was given to American workers.

I learned that there was a time when our Navy purchased torpedoes in Europe. Later we were dependent upon private manufacture in America. In 1914, at my request, Congress appropriated money to enlarge the Navy's facilities for manufacturing torpedoes, and we manufactured 400 per year at $1,100 less for each torpedo than when purchased from private companies. A saving of $400,000 a year was thus effected, with the additional benefit of keeping for the exclusive use of our Navy every new process discovered.

As further reason that the government itself should manufacture what it needed in munitions, I found that when the Navy needed ten 14-inch guns it asked for bids from the private companies and from the government plant operated by the Army. The Army's price enabled the Navy to save $18,000 on each gun. The lowest offer by private concerns was $79,000 whereas the Army's bid was $61,000.

COMPETITION REQUIRED

Within three months after I became Secretary I became convinced that every Navy Yard should be equipped so that some could build ships of every kind. I did not believe that the Navy should be dependent upon the few concerns that built for profit, and I thought that competition between government and private yards would result in better ships as well as in economy. This departure from the old plan of giving all contracts to a few companies received criticism from the stockholders of the shipbuilding companies and from those who did not wish Uncle Sam to undertake anything that private capital could do. However, the President and Congress agreed, and every yard was able, before I left office, to build ships—Philadelphia, New York, Norfolk, and Mare Island to build dreadnaughts, and the others to turn out smaller vessels. Private builders found they must compete to get orders, and Navy Yards understood they must do as well or better than outside concerns. Other things being equal, it was wise to keep any new devices for the Navy's exclusive use.

DUPLICATION ENDED

Not long after I came into office, there were presented to me directions for advertising for the construction of Marine barracks at

Panama. Congress had authorized an appropriation for this construction and we had quite a number of Marines on Panama. I made some study of the situation in Panama and asked the question why there should be permanent Marine barracks on the Isthmus, seeing that Panama Canal and the Panama Railroad and all Panama affairs were under the direction of the Army, which kept soldiers in barracks in Panama. I told General Biddle, Commandant of the Marine Corps, that I could see no use in spending money to build barracks for Marines at Panama; that it was mere duplication; and, that the only possible need of Marines there would be in case of trouble, when they would be landed from ships. I talked to aides about it and with Secretary of War Garrison. He said it was perfectly all right with the Army, for us to build, but he could see no necessity for two military agencies ashore at Panama. Therefore, much against the advice of the Commandant of the Marine Corps, I directed that the matter be held in abeyance until I could take the matter up with Congress. I advised that the appropriation for building Marine barracks at Panama be turned into the Treasury as there was no need for such expenditure.

MARINES WERE AMPHIBIOUS

This was not the only expensive and unwise duplication. The amphibious Marines worked nights and Sunday to increase their enrollment and widen their sphere of activity, while the Army was jealous of any encroachment upon what had been regarded as its peculiar field of operation. Amphibious warfare was then a Marine function, the Marines being equally efficient on the sea and on the land. And not only this, but they were also getting ready to operate in a new medium and conquer the air.

ECONOMY PLEDGE KEPT

The Wilson administration having been elected on a pledge of economy, it seemed to me that it was its duty in this and every way possible to cut down expenses. Naturally, every branch of service in Washington wished to expand, and my annulling the building at Panama was not very popular with the head officers of the Marine Corps, but I found later that both these actions were warmly approved by the Naval Affairs Committee in Congress. It opened the way for that coöperation which existed nearly all the time between the Secretary of the Navy and the Congress.

OPPOSED NAVY YACHTS

Early in the summer also, having in mind the desire to reduce every expense possible so that no money would be spent in the Navy except for essential needs, I caused a statement to be made showing the cost of operation of the *Mayflower* and the *Dolphin*. For many years the *Mayflower* had been kept in Washington as a personal yacht of the President and there was also kept a smaller yacht called the *Sylph*. I found that in the first months of his term Wilson had never used either. The *Dolphin* was kept in Washington for the use of the Secretary of the Navy, and, except for week-end trips, going to target practice, carrying distinguished visitors to Mount Vernon, and a trip to the New England Coast for inspection of Navy Yards, which I could have done by rail many times cheaper, I had rarely used the *Dolphin*. The report of the cost of maintaining these ships and a considerable crew which was busy only a few weeks in the year was larger than I had supposed. I made a statement of the expenses and took it over to the White House to President Wilson and suggested that the way to economize was to begin with ourselves, and if we voluntarily gave up the two yachts provided for the President and the Secretary of the Navy, it would enable us not only to save hundreds of thousands of dollars but would stimulate economy in every other department of government. He looked over the figures but said he would hesitate to change a policy which had long been in operation without time for further consideration and said he would take it up later.

"DOLPHIN" AT TAMPICO

The next year, however, the situation in Mexico became so acute and the need for small craft so keenly felt, that I ordered the *Dolphin* to active duty in Mexican waters. Its draft enabled it to go into harbors where the battleships could not enter and it was at the service of Admiral Fletcher and later of Admiral Badger in our long and tedious operations in Mexico. Later, when the World War came, the *Dolphin* was sent to the Caribbean and Gulf of Mexico. The *Dolphin* was really in active use as a fighting or patrol ship until after the end of the World War, so that I succeeded in carrying out, so far as the *Dolphin* was concerned, the economy I had earlier suggested.

PROFITEERS WAVING THE FLAG

In June of 1914 I came in for some severe criticism from the self-appointed one-hundred-per-cent Americans because I would not give a contract for material for flags at a price fixed by a combination of the U. S. Bunting Company and the N. E. Bunting Company. Having combined the companies which were bidding on making the American flag and bunting for the flags, these companies made a high bid without competition. I told them that while it would cause me the deepest regret to have to buy bunting for the American flag in a foreign country, if they insisted upon holding us up by an extortionate price based upon the favoring tariff rates given to American industries by Congress, I would not hesitate to open the competition to the makers of bunting everywhere in the world. I told them that they were violating the spirit if not the letter of the Sherman Anti-Trust Law and, while waving the American flag, they were violating every principle for which that flag stood. There was considerable criticism in a portion of the press at my suggestion that bunting manufactured abroad could be used in the American flag, but there was also commendation for my refusal to let the flag be used for extortion against the American people. It was not very long before the manufacturers, who could not stand before the American people as profiteering in the flag, modified their bid so that it was not necessary to go abroad to buy bunting.

NAVY HOLDS ON TO ITS LAND

Every day as I signed the mail, an Aide would explain the subject matter of the letters that had been written. If I approved, I would sign. If not, I would discuss the subject and often instruct the Aide to write a different answer. Much of this was more or less routine but essential, if the Secretary was to keep in touch with what was going on in the Navy. On my second day Admiral Fiske brought me a letter to sign, which was an order for the insertion of an advertisement in a Boston paper to sell a portion of the land on which the Naval Hospital at Chelsea was located. I asked, "What does this mean? Why is this land being sold?"

Fiske replied, "This is purely routine. Secretary Meyer signed orders a short time before he went out of office for the sale of this land and this is merely your authorization for an advertisement in the paper setting the date of the sale."

I asked, "Can this land be sold unless I order this advertisement inserted?"

He said this was purely routine. I insisted on knowing why the land was to be sold. I learned that Mr. Roberts, important member of the Naval Affairs Committee of the House, who lived at Chelsea, was back of the movement to sell the land. The Chamber of Commerce of Chelsea, wishing to secure more industries, desired to sell to people who would build factories on a part of the waterfront land belonging to the Naval hospital.

I had, just the year before, taken a strong stand, as trustee of the University of North Carolina, against the sale or long leasing of any land belonging to the University. That institution had previously sold off some of its most valuable land and had later bought it back at a price far in excess of what had been received at its sale. It had also given long leases to professors of the University on which they had built residences, and, when these professors resigned, the land went into the hands of other people who had no connection with the University.

It was probably that experience which prompted my questioning the wisdom of selling the Naval land. I told Admiral Fiske I would not advertise it and it would not be sold. My objection was that land around a university, a Naval yard or hospital, particularly the latter, ought not to be adjacent to business or factories. He insisted that the sale had been settled by the former Secretary and that it was good policy to carry it out.

The next day I received a call from Congressman Roberts, who expressed astonishment that I had held up the sale. He explained that Chelsea had grown to a point where its industry would stagnate unless this land could be obtained; that it was the only land in Chelsea that was suited for its industrial expansion, which the Chamber of Commerce desired. He said he had informed the Chamber of Commerce that everything had been arranged and it would put him in a very embarrassing position if it was not carried through. A few nights after that, my wife and I were at a dinner party. I was the dinner partner of Mrs. Roberts, the wife of the Congressman from Chelsea. We had scarcely been introduced before she opened up on the Chelsea matter and wanted to know why I was checking the growth of Chelsea. This was my first contact with the social lobby. Naturally, living there, she could see no reason for my action. She said there was already too much land at the hospital and that it would not be hurt at all by this sale. I had calls also from Senators Lodge and Weeks of Massachusetts who, when Roberts had informed them of my action, had been approached by the Chamber of Commerce of Chelsea to see that the sale was not prevented. I promised them that I would take no action whatever until some later day when I would go to Chelsea, and that after looking over the property, I would then act, taking into consideration all they had said.

It was late in the spring before I had the opportunity to go to Chelsea. No man was ever received with so much courtesy. The Mayor, Congressman Roberts, and others, were all on hand. We went over the property. They explained to me how and why they regarded this land as essential to Chelsea's growth. I saw very quickly that it would deny the sick men of the Navy an adequate park on the waterfront during their convalescence. When I returned to Washington I revoked the order and the land on the hospital grounds at Chelsea was not sold.

Not only was economy practiced, but time was taken by the forelock to provide war essentials at the saving of money. Here are some examples: Foreseeing the need of tin, the Navy bought a two years' supply from Singapore, sodium nitrate from Chile, and hemp from Manila. By utilizing colliers to bring these war essentials to the United States $100,000 was saved, while by using colliers to carry coal to Guam and the Philippines and other like economies, $800,000 was saved.

XXXVI

ARMOR-PLATE MONOPOLY BROKEN

N OT LONG AFTER I became Secretary of the Navy, it became necessary to ask for bids for the armor-plate on the new battleship
Arizona. I had been making some study of the cost of armor-plate
and had observed that my predecessor in giving the contract for the
two battleships in his administration had divided the order equally
among the only three companies in America making armor-plate.
I had also learned from ex-Secretary Herbert of his trouble with the
armor-plate people who had furnished defective armor-plate, and I
had learned that one of the companies manufacturing armor-plate
had sold it cheaper to Russia than to the United States. In 1894 the
Bethlehem Company sold armor-plate to Russia at $249 per ton and
charged the United States Navy $616.14 per ton. In 1911 they sold
to Italy at $395 and charged Uncle Sam $420. Later they sold to
Japan at $406.35 and to the United States at prices ranging from
$440 to $540 a ton. I directed the Chief of the Bureau of Ordnance
to advertise for bids for armor-plate for the new battleship.

IDENTICAL BIDS

When the bids came in from the three companies, they were each
in the identical sum to a cent—$454 per ton—and the chief officer of
each company filed an oath that in making the bid for his company
he had not had any conference or talk with any other producer of
armor-plate. I could not reconcile this oath with the fact that the
bids were identical. Therefore, I telegraphed the responsible officer
of each company to come to Washington on a given day. When they
arrived, they were ushered into my office together and given seats
side by side on a sofa. Sitting at my desk opposite them, I turned to
them and said:

"Gentlemen, I have asked you to come here to discuss the bids for
armor-plate. I have observed that although the law requires you to
make affidavit that you have neither conferred nor agreed before

making your bids, they are as alike as three black-eyed peas. Perhaps you can explain this."

Then I turned to the representative of the Carnegie Company and asked, "Did you have any communication with the representative of the Midvale or Bethlehem Company before you made this bid?"

"I did not," he said. I asked the same question of the other two and they made the same reply. I then read to them the law forbidding any discussion or collusion between bidders and they said they were advertent to that law and had lived up to it.

MENTAL TELEPATHY

Whereupon I said:

"This recalls an incident in North Carolina many years ago. I had a friend, a young artist who hoped to make reputation as a portrait painter. He was a fine young man of talent. His wife also was a lady of talent, but they were so poor that they pursued their artistic ambitions upon very little sustenance. Shortly after they were married, a relative of the artist's wife, feeling that she needed training to become a portrait painter, gave her the money to go to Paris to take lessons. The husband remained in Raleigh in his little studio, working always with enthusiasm and fine spirit and confidence. In those days he painted my portrait, and the portrait of my wife and young daughter, which I have always preserved, not so much because they are fine works of art, as because he put so much of his affection and ambition in them.

"About a month after his wife had gone to Paris, I met this friend one day and said, 'Good morning, Randall. When did you hear from your wife and how is she?' 'She is very well,' he said, 'I have just heard from her.' It chanced that as I was going every day to my office I passed by his studio. After the customary greetings—for we were very good friends and I had a genuine affection for him, increased because I felt that his ambition would not be realized—I would ask, 'When did you hear from your wife?' He would always reply 'I have just heard from her. She is very well.'

"One day I said to him, after he made this reply 'Does she write every day?' He said, 'No.' 'Does she telegraph?' He answered, 'You know we are too poor to send cables,' and so I asked, 'How on earth is it you hear from her every day if she does not write or cable?' With a far-away look in his eyes he asked, 'Don't you understand? Mental telepathy.' It was a rather new word to me. I had read about it but had never run into any person who believed in it or had had any experience with it. I said, 'No, I don't understand.' 'I will explain it to you,' he said. 'Before my wife left Raleigh, we arranged that every day at a certain hour we would send each other a mental telegram. At that hour she goes to her room in Paris and I go to my room in Raleigh and we open our windows and exchange messages and I can communicate with her just as well while she is in Paris as if we were together in Raleigh. Don't you understand?' I told him I did not and I could not see how it was possible. He looked at me with some sympathy for my lack of understanding and said, 'Well, we have exchanged messages every day and feel as near together as if we were in the same house.' "

After telling this story, I turned to these three representatives of Carnegie, Midvale, and Bethlehem Steel Companies and said:

"Gentlemen, until today when you indicated that you reached the exact figures in your bidding by mental telepathy and not by personal conferences, I have thought that mental telepathy was a figment of the imagination and I had never quite appreciated my friend Randall's living in a telepathic atmosphere, but now I see he was not daft, as I thought then, but very wise. If you three gentlemen, representing different companies, living in different towns, can by mental telepathy make identical bids on armor-plate, he could exchange messages with his wife across the sea. You have converted me, a confirmed skeptic, to mental telepathy."

DESTRUCTION OF COMPETITION

They smiled and insisted they had never had any conferences. Then they told me that if there was no competition, it was due to the policy of the Navy Department as practiced by my predecessor. "At a former bidding," said one of them, the representative from Midvale, "our company made a bid much lower than the other two companies, but Secretary Meyer sent for us and compelled each company to take one-third of the contract at the price of the lowest bidder. If there is no competition, it is not our fault but the fault of the Navy Department." They said the Navy was the only buyer of armor-plate and the Department had said it wished to keep all three of them employed and therefore intended to give each one one-third of the work, and it was with that knowledge that they had declined to enter into real competition. "We knew," one of them said, "no matter who bid the lowest, the Navy Department, if it followed its former policies, would give each one of the companies one-third of the work and the incentive for competition was destroyed by your Department."

It was a destruction which, I think, was very agreeable to them and I have no doubt that Secretary Meyer, in making that ruling, was following the desires of the companies. They knew that if competition was destroyed they would make larger profits in the long run and each one would keep its plants busy. I told the gentlemen that I should follow the law requiring competitive bidding and would accept none of the bids, and that competition would be the rule of the Navy Department from then on. I saw that so far as armor-plate manufactured by private companies was concerned, it was another case of "All Gaul is divided into three parts," and I soon made up my mind that the only protection the government could have was to build an armor plant of its own so that, unless the private companies would do this work at a fair price, the government would be able to make all its own armor-plate. I told these gentlemen that the Navy would not accept armor-plate bids unless the steel companies would show cost of production figures to justify the prices. As a result of the rejection of these bids, though the government was still at the mercy of the armor-plate people, and would be until it was able to put into operation a plant of its own, the Navy effected, in that one instance alone, a saving of five hundred thousand dollars on the armor-plate for one battleship.

STEEL MEN WAGE BIG FIGHT

I took this matter up with the President, who was indignant. I told him the story of mental telepathy, at which he laughed heartily and expressed his resentment that such rich companies favored by the government should wish to hold it up in prices. I told him it was my purpose to ask Congress to authorize the Navy to construct a government plant of its own to make armor-plate and shells, pointing out that the same people who made armor-plate made shells and that I apprehended we would have the same trouble about bids for shells as we had had for armor-plate. He approved the idea and I announced that I would ask Congress to provide enough money to build an armor-plate factory.

This request of Congress resulted in a battle royal between the Secretary of the Navy and the armor-plate people. It was preceded by a campaign of advertising under the direction of Charles M. Schwab, head of the Bethlehem Steel Works. This company, and other companies probably joining in, inserted large advertisements in practically all the big newspapers in America, antagonizing the recommendation of the Department and seeking to show that it would work injury to the taxpayers and would not result in any saving to the government. These advertisements were attractively gotten up, widely published, and in some parts of the country, notably in Pennsylvania, where the armor-plate factories were located, some of the papers followed these advertisements with vicious denunciation of the Department for advocating the government's undertaking to make its own armor-plate. They declared that it was an attack upon private industry and would destroy the value of plants in private hands which had been built at the request of the Navy Department, and that it would cost more to manufacture armor-plate in a government plant than in the private plants.

ARGUMENT FOR ARMOR-PLATE PLANT

The Naval Affairs Committee held hearings on the bill for the armor-plate plant. In addition to the argument that building a plant would save millions of dollars I advanced as another reason that if the government, in manufacturing armor-plate, discovered new processes, their value would inure only to the government, whereas that if new processes were discovered in the private manufacture, these secrets would be available to any government which wished to buy armor-plate from them. Along that line I stated that in the previous year the Navy had been compelled to bring suit to prevent a private company's making torpedoes from using our secret processes in contracts for a foreign government. That disclosed the dangers to which the Navy was subjected in permitting the manufacture of armor-plate to be exclusively in the hands of private concerns. Experience had demonstrated that profits weigh more with munition makers than guarantee of American Naval superiority. I cited instances of other contracts where money had been saved or would be saved if the Navy manufactured at least part of its munitions and other needs, so that it could escape excessive prices from private manufacturers.

PROFITS AND PEACE

After the hearings the Committee favorably reported the bill for the Navy to build an armor-plate plant. There was quite a sharp exchange of views between Senator Penrose, of Pennsylvania, who was always the spokesman of the steel companies, and myself. Schwab was present and other armor-plate manufacturers. Representatives of the Carnegie Works said that they had gone into the manufacture of armor-plate with the desire to help the government; that they had no desire to do so, but that when Whitney was Secretary of the Navy, no concern in America could manufacture armor-plate and Whitney did not wish America to be dependent upon British manufacturers for its armor-plate. So Whitney had sent for Carnegie and had requested him to manufacture armor-plate, promising that if he would do so the Navy would give him the orders for all the armor-plate it used.

Later I had a talk with Carnegie, who confirmed this statement. He said:

"I never did want to make it, it was contrary to my desire. We had all the work we could do manufacturing steel products for peace. I hated to make war material, but what was I to do when my government, through its Secretary of the Navy, called upon me to do something which he felt was essential to relieve the American government from dependency upon Britain for a prime necessity in the construction of dreadnaughts? I yielded."

Carnegie said he had no interest whatever in the controversy and only made the statement to me because he thought I would like to know the history of it. It was in the same conversation with Carnegie—one of the few I held with that interesting, delightful man, as shrewd as he was possessed of a naïve vanity, a self-esteem which was so open and so free from the usual offensiveness of vanity that you really liked it—that we talked of many things, particularly about the importance of ending war, in which he was greatly interested. At that time he had retired from business and was giving his chief thought to promoting peace. It was the passion of his life, and he expressed the hope that America would quit building dreadnaughts and lead the world in scrapping its navies and bringing about peace. When I told a Naval officer of Carnegie's sincere desire for peace, this officer cynically remarked that Carnegie never showed any zeal for peace as long as he could make armor-plate or shells for the government at a great profit and was converted to peace only when he retired from business. This remark did Carnegie injustice because after he retired, I think he was sincere in his zeal and would have given everything he had to advance the cause of peace. Carnegie's gifts of large sums to build the Pan-American Building in Washington and to erect buildings at The Hague for peace gatherings, and his warm friendship for Bryan, which was mainly due to their common interest in peace, showed his consecration to the cause of peace. He fondly believed he had done much to promote it, and he woke up in his old age to find that his dream of peace had been shattered with the German Army's invasion of Belgium in 1914. I think it hurried his end.

CARNEGIE TELLS OF HIS FLASHES

"How do you account for your great success in life," I asked Carnegie in that conversation, "when you reflect that you came to this country a poor boy and have now become one of the world's richest men? What enabled you to win this great success?" He looked about him cannily, his eyes sparkling and he chuckled and said with a sort of infantile smile of self-appreciation: "I owe it all to my flashes."

I was mystified and said, "I do not understand. What do you mean by flashes?"

"All my life," he replied, "I woke up early in the morning and always there came into my mind with the waking a flash telling me what to do that day, and if I followed those matin flashes, I always succeeded and they directed me so plainly in the line I ought to go to win success that I always followed them."

"You mean," I said, "that you have heavenly visions and like the man in the scripture you were not disobedient to your visions."

"Call it that if you like, or call it flashes, but it was the following of those silent admonitions and directions which brought me the success you say I have achieved."

I unfolded to him my earnest hope that during my term of office we would be able to bring about some understanding with the big navy-building nations of the world by which navies would no longer be provocative of war but would be maintained only to hold in order any imperialistic nations showing Napoleonic desires to control the world. He seemed gratified that the Secretary of the Navy should hold this point of view. We had other exchange of opinions and he sent me an occasional message fraught with the hope that the peace we favored might come in our day.

ADVERTISING PROPAGANDA

To come back to the fight over my plan to win congressional direction and appropriation for building an armor-plate plant, after the rather spirited hearings before the Naval Affairs Committee, in which I had to take the laboring oar for the plant and meet the objections of the armor-plate manufacturers and others, one day at the conclusion of the hearings I said to Schwab, "I think I owe you an apology or explanation."

"What for?" he asked, very much surprised.

I replied, "I picked up a copy of my paper, *The Raleigh News and Observer*, this morning and I saw glaring from one of the pages a big advertisement which you had inserted in that as well as other papers opposing the erection of an armor-plate plant. I hardly think," I said, "that it is ethical for me to take your money and then fight you." It amused him very much and he often afterwards made reference to it.

MONOPOLY OF WORST TYPE

The debate in the Senate on Senator Tillman's bill to authorize the Navy to build an armor-plate plant, drew the line sharply between those who stood for the big interests fattening on government favors and those who were hostile to seeing the taxpayers mulcted by profiteers. The Democrats and Progressives stood for the measure. The Old Guard Republicans fought it bitterly. Senator Tillman characteristically stated the attitude of the opponents in this sentence: "The armor-plate plants constitute a monopoly of the worst type. They are now in a position to force the government, in the language of the highwayman, to 'stand and deliver.' "

He quoted an official announcement of the Bethlehem Steel Company that if the government dared to exercise its right to build its own factory, Bethlehem Steel would raise its price $200 per ton on armor-plate. Referring to that threat, the *Manufacturer's Record*, said, "The Government would be pusillanimous in the extreme if it did not meet it by building an armor-plate plant. It cannot permit itself to be brow-beaten."

SWANSON'S MASTERLY ARGUMENT

Senator Swanson, later Chairman of the Naval Affairs Committee and Secretary of the Navy in the Roosevelt administration, took the laboring oar for the bill. After a review of the monopolistic practices of the armor-plate manufacturers, he showed that the government itself, in the years prior to 1913, "did everything it could to prevent competition between the three companies and to encourage them to enter into a combination and destroy all competition." However, in 1906, when there was competition, the price dropped from $439 per ton to $346. "If the competitive price had continued, the government would have saved $21,706,200." He added:

"In the first bid submitted to Secretary Daniels the three companies engaged in the manufacture of armor-plate were identical to the penny and similar to the bids previously submitted to the outgoing administration. The magic spell which has for sixteen years protected them with unerring foresight and the harmonious agreement which distinguished this combination had not been dissipated. Secretary Daniels promptly rejected all of the bids and vigorously protested against the system, and by his earnest and energetic efforts reduced the price of the armor-plate for the battleship *Arizona* and other ships. By refusing to submit to the demands of this combination he has saved the government on the armor-plate purchased by him $1,110,-084. This is an indication of what an efficient and vigorous Secretary, looking after the interests of the government, can save on one item in a very short time. The passage of this bill will mark the end of the domination of the notorious Armor-Plate Trust which for more than sixteen years has levied immense exactions upon the government. The extent to which this country is at the mercy of this combination is illustrated by the statement that if the pending bill becomes a law they will charge a price of $200 per ton in excess of what is now being charged. In the two years that would be required to erect the plant, these manufacturers would have it in their power to extort $12,000,-000 in excess of the prices paid at the present time."

Swanson estimated that the government could save $9,810,000 in five years by making its armor-plate, almost enough to pay for the plant. Swanson made the telling argument also that if the government made its armor-plate it would alone be in possession of any new processes it discovered, whereas the private manufacturers will not disclose to the government any secrets but rather think the government should give them all its secrets. He pointed out that the Navy was manufacturing smokeless powder in its own enlarged plant at 38 cents a pound, whereas it had been compelled to pay private manufacturers at prices ranging from 58 cents to 69 cents a pound, thus in three years saving the taxpayers a million and a half dollars. It had been successful in manufacturing mines, torpedoes, guns, and ships. It saved $180,000 in the manufacture of guns and $400,000 a year in manufacturing torpedoes.

GOVERNMENT SHOULD MANUFACTURE

Senator Hitchcock said the time has come for the sovereignty of the United States to assert itself and make for itself the armor which it requires. Senator Cummins declared: "I shall vote for it because it is my profoundest convictions that the manufacture of armor-plate for battleships is a governmental function. I hope the private enterprises will be entirely eliminated. I shall vote for it because it is my hope that profit may be taken out of war."

Senator Martine said: "I am in favor of an armor-plate factory and many other government owned utilities." In like vein, Senator Works, of California, declared: "The Government should manufacture not only its armor-plate but the arms and munitions that are used. I do not believe that anything that is manufactured for the purpose of killing human beings should be left to the speculation of profit." Senator Gronna asserted his creed thus: "I believe the government should manufacture not only armor-plate but all the munitions of war."

ADMITS ROBBING UNCLE SAM

Senator Jim Reed had collected all the advertisements which Schwab had inserted in the newspapers against the government plant and read them to the Senate as an exhibit of the attempt of the makers of armor-plate to work up public sentiment against a wise public policy proposed by the Secretary of the Navy in the interest not only of the taxpayers, but also to free the Navy from profiteers and insure the best armor-plate at the lowest cost. When Penrose sought to have the advertisements printed as a Senate Public Document, Reed objected to permitting the Bethlehem Steel Company to frank its paid propaganda. He said: "If the Steel Company wishes to print its defense or its argument, let it do so out of some of its own profits it has been making by charging the government, for twenty-nine years, prices which it now says it is ready to cut to a very large degree—a plain, bald confession that it has been despoiling and robbing this government for the past twenty-nine years." He was referring to the offer of the armor-plate manufacturers made only to defeat the bill, to reduce the price of armor plate to $395 as compared to the former price of $425. Reed said that offer of reduction was made in spite of the fact that material and the cost of production were higher than in twenty-nine years, and repeated, "It is its absolute admission that for twenty-nine years it has robbed the government." He quoted a report of the Naval Affairs Committee of 1894, which declared that the U. S. Steel Corporation making armor-plate had been guilty of "making false reports, doctoring of specimens, plugging of plates, fraudulent re-treating of test plates and 'jockeying' of the testing machines, and that its representatives had been guilty of "frauds, disregard of truth and dishonesty." The testimony of their officials "renders them unworthy of confidence," said the Committee report. A more terrible drubbing has rarely been administered in the Senate than was delivered by Reed of Missouri, whose climax was the familiar quotation, loudly applauded by the galleries:

> "How sweet the watch dog's honest bark
> Loud baying when we draw near home."

The conviction in the Cleveland administration of Schwab and others for palming off defective armor-plate and the assessment of a fine (too small) for the endangering of the life of men in the Navy were recalled in the newspapers as the debate raged in the Senate.

ONLY REACTIONARIES VOTED "NO"

Under the skillful piloting of Swanson the amendments aimed at the heart of the bill were defeated and the appropriation for the government plant passed by the House, won by a vote of 58 to 23.

C. K. Berryman, in the *Washington Star*

MANY CITIES BID FOR LOCATION

Having secured Congressional approval for the building of a government armor-plate plant, Secretary Daniels asked for bids from cities which wished the location of the plant.

The only votes cast against it were by the reactionary Republicans from the East. As soon as the President signed the bill—and it gave him great satisfaction as another step in the realization of the New Freedom—I appointed a commission headed by Admiral Fletcher to receive offers from cities that desired to secure the location of this plant. The General Board of the Navy, whose advice was asked as to the proper surroundings for the plant, recommended, in order that it might be protected from any possible foreign enemy, that it be built not nearer than one hundred miles from the seashore. This, of course, put an end to the suggestion that the plant be built either at Philadelphia or in Tidewater Virginia. After examining all proposed sites in a dozen or more places, the committee recommended the location of the plant at Charleston, West Virginia, and it was built there. However, the delay in designs and appropriations, and the dislocation due to the World War prevented its early completion.

With America's entrance into the World War, all Naval building was centered upon the construction of destroyers and small ships, so that the armor-plate plant at Charleston was not ready to build armor-plate or make shells during the War. With the end of the War, work was pressed on the Charleston armor-plate plant and the government saved much money by making shells there. With the outgoing of the Wilson administration, however, the Pennsylvania influence came back to dominance, and there was more desire to give work to the private armor-plate manufacturers than to realize upon the investment of an armor-plate plant, and it was not completed.

FIVE REASONS

Years afterward, when I was urging the election of John Davis as President, I visited the uncompleted plant at Charleston, West Virginia, and saw the blighting of the dream of a great armor-plate plant. Asked why my successors had failed to carry out the direction of Congress, I declared that there were just five reasons: Senator Penrose, Senator Oliver, the Carnegie, Bethlehem, and Midvale Steel officers, and told the Charlestonians that those five had more influence than the people and the Congress. They had virtually repealed the law directing the construction of the government plant. Monopoly won when it put Harding in the White House.

XXXVII

LABOR GETS MAGNA CARTA

LABOR OBTAINED its Magna Carta in the Wilson administration. The President was most fortunate in his Secretary of Labor, who was the first occupant of that new Cabinet position—William B. Wilson. He was a rare man, as modest as he was wise. He had come to America as a lad from Scotland, gone into the mines of Pennsylvania as a boy in the days when labor was treated as a commodity. Once a striker when his union rebelled against the hard conditions and low pay, he had risen, by sheer ability, to a position as labor leader. When labor sought to unhorse feudalistic practices, he was elected to Congress—a sort of "petition in boots" for recognition of men who toil. He saw that if labor was ever to come into its own, it must have a place, not only in Congress where laws are made but in the Cabinet where governmental policies are shaped. He championed and secured the passage of the act which created a new Cabinet position—Secretary of Labor—and, as the first incumbent, he organized it upon lines that have made it an increasingly important arm of government.

He was the only man considered for the post when Wilson began cabinet-making. He had secured the creation of the post when Republicans seemed entrenched in power and had no thought that he was creating a position for himself. With the vision of the type of administrator who would give justice to labor he early became one of the influential Pennsylvania Democrats who made possible the nomination of Wilson.

Pennsylvania Democrats—there were hundreds of thousands. They lived in a State where no political recognition or reward could be expected, but in all the lean years they held the rudder true. They came into their own with Wilson's election, with two Cabinet members, and two Ambassadors among the positions they filled with honor to themselves and the administration.

Secretary Wilson was an associate of Samuel Gompers, who like Wilson rose from a child laborer to be the most distinguished and able labor statesman which organized labor has produced. These two men served in the Council of National Defense in the World War and were Wilson's strong right arm in peace and in war.

RELATIONS WITH WORKERS

A short time after I reached Washington, while conferring with labor leaders at the Navy Yard, I met Mr. Carroll, a machinist who unfolded to me what a close tab labor organizations keep on public officials. He said:

"When the papers carried the announcement that you were to be the new Secretary of the Navy I was directed to go to Raleigh and study your record, particularly as it related to labor organization. I remained there several days incog and found out more about you than you know about yourself. I talked to your political enemies—and you have some stout ones—and with your friends—and you have good ones,—associated with your employees and found that to a man they believed in you. My report upon returning was that your record from the standpoint of labor, as an employe and as a journalist, had won the approval and admiration of labor leaders and workers in your city and state."

One thing he had not ascertained on his visit which doubtless affected my feeling of brotherhood with Naval and other workers. This was that my father was a ship carpenter, had learned his trade at Washington, N. C., where wooden ships were built to ply between that port and the West Indies, and had perfected himself in the shipbuilding craft by working for a period as shipbuilder in Rhode Island. Without being untrue to his memory I could not be indifferent to the advancement of labor.

NAVY BIG EMPLOYER

I was soon to learn that the Secretary of the Navy is one of the biggest employers of labor in the country and that he has an opportunity to set an example of fair-dealing and justice to all other employers. I found that all Naval officers were not sympathetic with the standpoint of labor, that some lacked tact in dealing with the mechanics and others, but that in most Navy yards the relations between officers and the men whose skill was employed in fashioning and repairing ships was all that could be desired.

The direction of the Navy Yard employees devolved, in the division of duties, on Assistant Secretary Roosevelt, but policies were made by us in consultation and executed by him. His experience in dealing with organized labor had been slight, but I soon found that our minds ran along the same channel, and labor understood that in the Navy it could always get a hearing and fair treatment. In the first year of my term I visited every Navy Yard and shipbuilding plant, coming in contact with officers who directed the work and with machinists and other skilled workers, and soon the whole Navy personnel, officers and enlisted men, and the men upon whose skill the Navy relied, understood that at the Department they were sure of receiving the consideration to which they were entitled and just compensation and appreciation.

DESERVED RECOGNITION

During the war, when the strain was severe and demands upon them called for all that was in them, the Navy Yard personnel of mechanics and other workers was as patriotic and self-sacrificing as the men who commanded the ships and manned the guns. They received no Navy Cross or other such awards as were conferred upon the fighting forces, but I recommended that those who had served with distinction should be given the recognition by honors to which they were entitled. They deserved it, and medals of recognition should have been awarded them.

LABOR'S APPRECIATION

Nothing in my Naval career brought me more satisfaction than the action taken by the Navy Yard personnel in resolutions of regard and regret when my term of office expired. Among these evidences was a ship's clock which had been on my desk for eight years and which had been purchased by the mechanics at the Philadelphia Navy Yard and sent to me at my home in Raleigh a few weeks after my retirement. It contained this inscription:

"The Clock of the Secretary of the Navy,
Which Marked the Minutes of the Great War.
To HONORABLE JOSEPHUS DANIELS,
Secretary of the Navy—1913-1921.
In Recognition of his Accomplishments
Which the American Navy Will Ever Hold
in Grateful Memory.
Presented by the Men of the Philadelphia
Navy Yard Who Served Under Him.
April 16, 1921."

CORDIAL RELATIONSHIP

In Baker, in the War Department, labor had an understanding and just employer. In his association with labor leaders there was a friendliness that opened the way for frank interchange of views.

"If you had your way, Mr. Alifas, what would be the working hours and days you would prescribe for Army and Navy armories and yards and plants?" asked Secretary Baker, when we were talking to the representative of the machinists and workers in Washington about wages and hours. The government had an eight-hour day with a half day for Saturday. Mr. Alifas had been the faithful spokesman of the workers in the War and Navy Departments and had sometimes made requests which neither the Secretary of War nor the Secretary of the Navy could grant. In a friendly conversation, following a request for shorter hours or larger pay (I've forgotten which), Alifas, with a smile indicative of his lack of seriousness, said, "Well, if I had my way I would let the workmen all knock off Friday at noon and not return to work until Monday morning."

Answering in the same spirit, Secretary Baker said, "Now, Mr. Alifas, you are too moderate. You should be asking for a six-hour day, half holiday on Friday, a full holiday Saturdays and half holiday on Monday. You know after the Friday, Saturday, and Sunday without work, it would be asking too much to expect men to return to work until Monday afternoon."

We all three laughed. I relate this as one of many incidents showing the relationship between labor leaders and the heads of the War and Navy Departments.

XXXVIII

EIGHT-YEAR FIGHT TO PRESERVE THE NAVY
OIL RESERVES

ALMOST FROM THE DAY I became Secretary of the Navy, March 6, 1913, until the close of my service, March 7, 1921, the conflict over Naval oil reserves was on. The previous Congress had authorized the construction of one dreadnaught, which was named the *Nevada*. Up to that time, while destroyers had been constructed as oil burners, every capital ship obtained motive power from coal. Should the Navy make the *Nevada* an oil burner? That question was in debate by the construction and engineering officers. There was little, if any, disagreement as to the superiority of oil in every particular. It would give a wider steaming radius, it was cleaner, and required a smaller personnel. The debate raged over whether it would be safe to make the ship an oil burner seeing that in some quarters there was fear that the oil supply might not be such as to justify relying upon it.

I believed that the first thing to know before making a decision was to ascertain whether the probable oil supply of the country would justify changing from coal to oil. I said, "The geologists in the Interior Department ought to be able to answer that question." Having been Chief Clerk of the Interior Department in the Cleveland administration, and being a friend of Dr. Charles D. Wollcott, Director of the Geological Survey, and Dr. David T. Day, an expert on oil in the early days of the increased production, I knew the government had an agency well qualified to aid the Navy to reach a wise decision. A letter was therefore prepared and sent to the Secretary of the Interior requesting expert advice as to whether, looking ahead twenty years—that was then deemed to be the life of a dreadnaught—the Navy would be safe in making the *Nevada* an oil burner. Soon Secretary Lane advised that it would be safe to rely upon a sufficient supply of oil for twenty years. Therefore the order was given to make the new dreadnaught the first oil burner in any Navy.

I then made inquiry why the Navy did not obtain the oil needed from the Naval oil reserves, which President Taft had set aside for the exclusive use of the Navy in California. I said, "I recall that Theodore Roosevelt and Gifford Pinchot began a policy of conservation of forests and minerals on public lands, and this step was followed by President Taft in setting aside public lands as petroleum reserves in California, but I have never heard anything about them since." The Aide for Matériel, Captain Winterhalter, said that the whole Naval reserve was in litigation but he did not know its status. I examined the cost of oil, and, after some investigation, came to the conclusion that the oil companies were charging what we believed to be an excessive price. This was due not only to the price that the producers received for the crude oil but also to the high price charged for refining by the Standard Oil Company. I made my first recommendation of many as to the Navy's oil policy by advocating a government refinery to escape the exaction of the oil companies.

SNAIL-LIKE PACE

I took up the matter of the petroleum reserves with Attorney General McReynolds and asked him about the status of the litigation. He said:

"Judging from the snail-like pace of attorneys who are employed by the government in this litigation, I do not suppose it will be ended in a generation. I think it will be necessary to put in charge of the government suits a lawyer who has brains and courage and who would go out to California with the vigor to fight. Do you know such a man? If you will find him, I will appoint him, but he must be an able lawyer and a man with tenacity to contest with the large retinue of lawyers who are appearing for those claiming the Naval oil reserves."

Without hesitating a minute, I answered, "I know a man who fills your description exactly. He is the Honorable E. J. Justice, of North Carolina, ex-Speaker of the House, and one of the ablest lawyers in the country. He has youth and ability, and nothing pleases him better than to be in a fight for a righteous cause."

"Telegraph him to come to Washington. I would like to talk with him," said McReynolds.

Consistent with my intention not to initiate appointments for North Carolina but to let all such be sponsored by our North Carolina Congressmen, I took the matter up with Senator Overman, acting chairman of the Judiciary Committee. He went to see the Attorney General and recommended the appointment of Mr. Justice. The Senator was glad to do this on every ground. The fact that Justice was a potential candidate for his toga increased his interest in the appointment. Within a few days Justice was in Washington, had a satisfactory interview with the Attorney General and the Secretary of the Navy, and was soon on his way to California to take up in the courts and otherwise the long and difficult task of rescuing the oil reserves from the squatters. When Taft set aside this reserve, there were contentions that a part of it had already been entered under the Public Land Laws. Congress by subsequent action gave title to those who had complied with the Land Laws. Others entered upon the land without any color of title, but they were in possession, drilling for oil, and refused to recognize the validity of Taft's order. It was a long time by the slow processes of the courts before the validity of Taft's order was affirmed. I assigned Lieutenant Commander Landis, an expert in oil matters, to assist Justice.

A man less tenacious and patient than Justice would have imitated his predecessors and let the matter drift on in court year after year, but Justice was no such lawyer. He had been accustomed to hard battles against powerful interests and had been accustomed to ferreting out things that were covered. I recalled, when I recommended him, how in litigation over the freight and passenger rate contest in North Carolina, he and the Honorable F. A. Woodard, representing the State in that litigation, had uncovered large expenditures made by the Southern Railroad to newspapers in payment for their editorial support—among others to the Raleigh *Times*, then owned by John C. Drewry, State Senator from Wake County, a paper which had received large sums of money ostensibly for advertising that never appeared in the paper but really for financing the candidacy of the Senator, who, in any contest, personally and through his paper took the side of the railroad rather than the people. Fighting the oil people called for more astuteness than Justice had found necessary to fight the entrenched interests in North Carolina, but he was equal to the task; and patiently and with almost the ability of a Sherlock Holmes he laid the foundations which resulted in upholding the claims of the Navy to the oil reserve and ousting the fraudulent claimants. I have known no lawyer with a clearer mind and keener intellect, combined with zeal for justice and with the spirit of a crusader. Subsequent events proved he needed all these qualities. I did not fully realize that he was undertaking a mission in which he would have to fight hundreds of hungry claimants for the oil reserves and a host of the most resourceful lawyers retained in the desperate determination to secure the rich oil fields to which their clients had no just claim.

SOME HONEST, SOME DISHONEST

Among the claimants there were some who, entering upon the lands, discovered oil before the withdrawal order of September 27, 1909, and had some equities. They were given title to the land upon which they had made discovery. There were others who had bought claims which they believed were legal—innocent purchasers for value. The former had protection under the Pickett Act. But those who had bought lands from those who were, in fact, squatters in defiance of law, stood in the shoes of those from whom they had purchased land or shares of stock and had no standing in law. There were many of the latter who, having made purchases without sufficient investigation of the rights of the vendor, urged that as they had committed no fraud, they ought to be allowed to lease the land which they thought they owned, having paid good money for it. One such company included honorable citizens of Massachusetts who had made their purchases in good faith. They enlisted the interest of Senator Lodge, who came to see me in their behalf and urged that they be protected in any legislation enacted. When I explained to him that they had been fleeced by squatters who had entered upon the land after President Taft's withdrawal order, and that if their claims were allowed it would take part of the petroleum reserve from the Navy, the Senator declined to press the claims of his constituents, asking only that they be treated as well as others in like situation. In this, as always, Lodge's devotion to the Navy was apparent, even if he occasionally urged special consideration of an officer because of family reasons. Other classes of claimants were hi-jacks, speculators, men who made no "diligent prosecution" as the law required to discover oil, but were in the game in the gambling spirit which permeated many oil sections. Some of these had even entered the lands after the Supreme Court had declared the original Taft withdrawal order legal and valid.

Justice, after mastering the law and the decisions made prior to his assignment, undertook to meet the serious situation in a practical way. In cases in court, where delay caused the loss of oil by seepage or otherwise, he secured receivers who would recover oil that would otherwise be lost alike to the Navy and claimants, and impounded the oil or the money derived from its sale, to be awarded to the winner in the courts. Most of the people in the oil region were in sympathy with the claimants. The reason was that if they won, they would take the oil out of the ground and develop the region, give employment which would increase local business. If the Navy won, the oil would be locked up in the ground to be drawn upon at some future time. That did not please those whose attitude was "neither Posterity nor the Navy has done anything for us; why should we deny ourselves in order to help Posterity and the Navy?"

DUMMY ENTRIES

Those who claimed under dummy entries were the worst of all. They were often crooks, or to use a term that later came to be a favorite designation, "racketeers." Justice told me this incident which he unravelled by Sherlock Holmes methods: A certain company laid claim to a particularly good section in the Naval reserves which it had bought from a number of men who, they said, had actually entered upon the land and by diligent prosecution had made discoveries. The claim was duly recorded with the names signed on applications in the manner prescribed by law. Justice set out to locate these original entry-men. Nobody thereabout knew them. They could not be located. But he was the sort of man who never gave up. Finally he ran upon their scent. After patient investigation, the men who had signed the application to enter the naval reserve land were located in the stockyard district of Chicago. An agent was dispatched to interrogate them. All who could be located, when shown the petition and asked "Is that your signature?" replied in the affirmative. They admitted they had signed the paper. Each one said: "I thought I was signing a petition for a primary election in my district in Chicago." It was such frauds that made the recovery of the petroleum reserves most difficult.

In addition, there were legal questions and legal traps galore. Into none of the latter did Justice fall. While in the midst of the litigation in which he had made marked progress and shown his great ability and resourcefulness, he was stricken with a fatal disease and fell on sleep at the post of duty. But he worked until the last with resolve to wrest the oil reserve from those who had entered upon the oil lands in defiance of law. He indeed gave his life in what proved to be the first victory for the Federal government in a conflict lasting from Taft's withdrawal order in 1910 until the Supreme Court of the United States in 1919 restored the reserves to the Navy.

JUDGE BIGGS WON DECISION

After the death of Justice, the Honorable J. Crawford Biggs, of Raleigh, Solicitor General of the United States in the Roosevelt administration, was retained by the government. Like Justice, he was more than a match in the courts for the lawyers who had made a lifetime business of mastering oil laws and who had the advantage of the widespread feeling that the oil in the Naval reserves belonged to the people of the West and that Uncle Sam and his Navy were trying to tie up what should be utilized for the present generation. With the same vigor displayed by Justice, he amassed evidence amounting to hundreds of pages, arguing the cases in the lower courts. When the matter came up on appeal to the Supreme Court of the United States, he made a masterly and convincing argument. His contention was confirmed by the Supreme Court, which upheld the title of the Navy.

NO APPEAL ALLOWED

Not long after the Department of Justice had appointed Justice as its representative in the Naval petroleum litigation, it came to my attention that the Honolulu Oil Company had pending before the Commissioner of the General Land Office a claim for patents to oil land in the very heart of the Naval petroleum reserve. It had applied for a patent to seventeen locations in No. 2 of the California oil reserves. The Navy department fought the clear-listing of the lands claimed. After conferences with the Attorney General, an assistant was directed to defend the Navy's right in the hearing before the Commissioner of the General Land Office. After examining the claims, Attorney General Gregory told me that in his opinion the oil company had not a scintilla of legal right to the lands. I asked the Secretary of the Interior for a hearing. It was granted. A representative of the Department of Justice presented what I regarded as an unanswerable argument with irrefutable evidence showing there was no justification for the claim filed by the Honolulu Oil Company. However, to my great surprise, a few moments before the Cabinet meeting some time later, Secretary Lane said to me, "I have been going carefully over the Honolulu Oil Company case and I am afraid you are going to lose. The Commissioner has approved thirteen of the claims of the Honolulu Oil Company and denied four. I see nothing to do but to affirm the finding of the Commissioner of the Land Office."

That stunned me. After talking the matter over, I said, "If, after going more fully into the matter, you feel that you must uphold the decision of the Land Commissioner, I wish you to note an appeal of the Navy Department."

That request showed how little I knew about the land law and how it operated as to claims for oil land. Secretary Lane replied, "The law allows no appeal. The decision of the Secretary of the Interior is final."

I was even more stunned and had a fear of defeat for all the conservation policies as they related to preserving a petroleum reserve for the Navy.

"At least I will request you to withhold your decisions until I can confer with the Attorney General and we can talk with you again."

"Certainly," said Lane, "and I will be glad if you can show me how I can decide with you, but as I see it now, the Honolulu Oil Company has made out a good case."

At the close of the session of the Cabinet I took the matter up with the Attorney General and told him of the disquieting remark of the Secretary of the Interior. He agreed that we should go over the matter with Lane. He said he was convinced that the Navy's claim was sound by all the law and the precedents which he had examined. He confided to me that he believed Lane had made up his mind and that nothing he could say would alter his decision. "However," he added, "you make an engagement with Lane and I will go with you any time."

PRESIDENT INTERESTED

I went back to the Navy Department greatly disturbed. My heart was set upon preserving the petroleum reserve for the Navy, and I had told Lane I would be compelled to oppose his plan of leasing public lands unless he excepted the petroleum reserve from its operations. If the Honolulu claim stood, the reserve would suffer a severe loss. After reflecting upon the full meaning of an adverse decision by the Secretary of the Interior, with no appeal, I decided to lay the whole matter before President Wilson. I had previously talked with him on the general matter and had found he was deeply interested in preserving the oil reserves. I had not discussed the Honolulu case with him. I therefore went to the White House and went over with him in detail the whole history of the setting aside of the petroleum reserve, the multiplication of illegal entries, the long-standing litigation, and the vital value of the oil in that portion of the reserve which the Land Office had decided to award to the Honolulu Oil Company. The President listened intently, plied me with questions as was his habit to bring out every aspect of any subject brought to his attention. At the conclusion of the conversation, in which I had said that it was embarrassing to me to discuss a difference with a fellow Cabinet member, one whom I regarded highly, and that I had done so only after exhausting every other resource to save the Naval Oil Reserve. Wilson's conclusion was in these words:

"I will tell you what to do, Daniels. At the next meeting of the Cabinet, when I turn in the regular order and ask the Secretary of the Navy to bring up any matter he has for consideration, you relate the situation to the Cabinet as you have unfolded it to me. After you have finished, I will call upon Lane to state the situation as he sees it, and I will then ask the Attorney General to give his opinion as to the legal question involved. By that means we may acquaint our associates with a situation which concerns the government as a whole rather than any one or two departments."

In compliance with the President's suggestion, at the next meeting of the Cabinet, I made a statement of the importance of retaining the lands claimed by the Honolulu Oil Company for the Navy, both because of their inherent value and because if they were awarded to the company, it would be able to drain oil in adjacent lands set aside for the Navy. At the conclusion of statements by Secretary Lane, Attorney General Gregory and myself, President Wilson turned to Lane and said: "Please, Mr. Secretary, do not make any decision on this case until we can have another conference." Weeks passed and Lane suggested to me that the inaction was embarrassing.

I proposed that he and Gregory and I take the matter up with the President. We discussed it at the White House for an hour or more. Wilson was evidently impressed with our argument, but did not like to direct Lane to make a judicial decision. Therefore he said to him, "Mr. Secretary, do not decide this case until we can confer again." The Honolulu case hung on for months and months. Lane grew impatient. He told the interested parties that he was ready to act, but had been directed to hold his decision in abeyance by the President. In the meantime Attorney General Gregory resigned. However, he did not lose his interest in the Honolulu case. A short time before Lane resigned as Secretary of the Interior, Gregory called at the Navy Department, and said: "Lane is so confident he is right in the Honolulu case that he is apt to take it up and decide it before he goes out of office; and unless you are ready to lose your oil, you had better go over to the White House and see 'the old man' (that's what between ourselves we called Wilson in terms of affection) and tell him that he should again direct Mr. Lane not to act on the case. Gregory had come to distrust Lane. He said Lane was resigning from the Cabinet to take a position at a very large salary with an oil company. That turned out to be true. I told Gregory that though Lane believed the Commissioner's decision was right and that he ought to approve it, he would not take any action before going out of office. Gregory was unconvinced, and as he departed he said, "Unless Wilson sends Lane a written order, I think he will give the decision that your oil reserve belongs to the Honolulu Oil Company." Later that afternoon I went over to the White House and told President Wilson what Gregory had said. He again wrote Lane not to act on the Honolulu Oil Company case without instructions from him. Always Gregory believed that without such an order, Lane would have adjudicated the case before his resignation took effect. I did not agree with him, but resolved to take no chance.

PAYNE UPHOLDS NAVY

A few days later John Barton Payne, who was appointed to succeed Lane, took the oath. I requested him to give a hearing on the appeal from the Commissioner of the Land Office. Before that, President Wilson had ordered that the Honolulu case be reheard. Testimony was again taken before the local land officers, who advised against the issuance of patents, but their decision was reversed by the Commissioner of the General Land Office. In reviewing his decision, Payne reversed it and denied the application (June, 1920) on the ground contended all along by the Secretary of the Navy and Attorney General Gregory that the company was not diligently prosecuting the work leading to the discovery of oil and gas in any of the locations involved. The Honolulu Company gave notice of application for a rehearing in accordance with the practice of the Land Office. But it was not pressed, and later developments showed why the appeal was not prosecuted during the remaining months of the Wilson administration.

NO TAKING OUT OF OIL

The Navy had won its long fight to preserve Naval Oil Reserve No. 2, but it would have lost if it had not been for Wilson's clear understanding of the facts and the law and his firm insistence that the mistaken view of the General Land Office should not deprive the Navy of its legal ownership of an important part of the Naval Oil Reserve.

On December 10, 1920, a representative of the Honolulu Oil Company called at the Navy Department and said that if they could be given a lease on all the lands they had claimed, they would surrender all their claims. Their application was denied. "The reserve must be kept intact and the oil kept in the ground. The Navy has won its fight," I said, "and there will be no taking out of oil."

The representative then said (and it looks as if he knew what would happen), "If the new administration reverses the decision of Secretary Payne, the Navy will lose all its oil."

I quote the following from my diary of that date:

"I told Mr. Ward that I must act on the assumption that the incoming administration would protect the Naval Oil Reserves. But I would have a newspaper and would keep in touch, and if the Honolulu Oil Company went before the Interior Department and got the oil, I would make the truth known to the public."

THE FIGHT AGAINST LEASING RESERVES

In our frequent conversations about the petroleum reserves Lane always maintained the same position that was later the policy of the Harding administration, when all oil matters were turned over to the Secretary of the Interior with such calamitous results. I said to Lane, "I have no desire whatever to entrench upon your powers with reference to land or oil matters except when lands set aside for the exclusive use of the Navy are involved. In such cases, as trustee for the rights of the Navy, I feel it to be my duty to fight to the last ditch for their preservation unimpaired."

It was for that reason that the Navy Department fought the incorporation of petroleum reserve lands in the General Leasing measure which was Secretary Lane's chief recommendation to Congress in the early days of the Wilson administration. The administration was in favor of leasing public lands along the line of Secretary Lane's recommendation. I urged upon Lane the wisdom of not including the Naval petroleum reserves in the leasing act. He insisted upon its inclusion. I went before the Committee on Public Lands and argued that the petroleum reserve lands having been withdrawn for the Navy, they were not properly subject either to entry or to leasing. Unable to secure the exclusion of these lands from the measure by the committee, only one way was open. That was to prevent the passage of Lane's leasing measure. Senator Tillman and Representative Padgett, respectively chairmen of the Naval Committee of the Senate and of the House, agreed to object to the bill unamended when it reached the stage in the closing days of Congress that such objection would prevent its passage. On two nights, in the closing hours of the Congress, I remained on watch in the Senate and Assistant Secretary Roosevelt in the House to call the attention of these two chairmen if the leasing measure should be brought up. "I have so many measures to look after, and must be out of the Chamber so much," said Senator Tillman, "that you must stay here on the all-night watch to call my attention when the necessary objection must be made." That was also the attitude of Chairmen Padgett in the House. So Roosevelt and I remained constantly on guard at the Capitol until the time came for Congress to adjourn.

At the night session of Congress, the naval petroleum reserves were exempted, and the measure became a law, the control of the oil reserves being vested in the Secretary of the Navy. We had won a hard battle in the face of the organized opposition of the claimants, who, seeing they would lose their fight for ownership, were fighting to take the oil from the Navy by securing a lease. The Navy was fighting not only against claims it regarded as illegal, but also to hold the oil in the ground as a future reserve in time of need.

TEAPOT DOME

I urged upon Secretary Lane the use of all diligence to secure new oil reserves for the Navy. At one time he thought such lands could be obtained from the Indians in Oklahoma in a way to serve the advantage of both the Navy and the Indians. That hope failed. Later Lane was to recommend the oil area known as Teapot Dome and President Wilson signed the order (April 15, 1915) setting it aside "for the exclusive use of the Navy." It contained 2,481 acres of government land and was declared by experts of the Interior Department to contain rich deposits of oil. Lane told me, knowing my interest in petroleum reserves, that Teapot Dome would make up for any losses or drainage of the reserves in California.

"Eureka!" said Lane to me as we entered the Cabinet room bearing the proclamation for the President's signature to Teapot Dome. He had previously told me that his experts believed the search for oil on government lands had been rewarded and they assured him that Teapot Dome would exactly meet the Navy's requirement. He said, happy as I was to add to Naval reserves, "Your California oil reserves are so surrounded by sections owned by others that parts of them can be drained, and you may lose some of this to contesting claimants. This Wyoming field is situated so that drainage will be negligible and you can keep your oil in the ground until kingdom come, and that's exactly what you want."

The seven-year fight to retain and hold the reserves intact, with gratitude to Lane for finding another source in Teapot Dome, made me confident that the Navy would be independent of private companies for oil—which is now called munitions—in any day of need. However, before my term of office expired, I was to learn that oil men, avid for the Naval reserves, had their eyes on getting the oil out of Teapot Dome, and would stop at nothing, as the Teapot Dome scandal demonstrated in the Harding administration.

DEMOCRAT DENIED LEASE

In the latter part of November, 1920, when my term of office as Secretary of the Navy was nearing its close, my friend George Creel requested me to see some "good friends, sterling Democrats, from my old home, Denver, who wish to discuss with you a proposition to lease oil reserves in Teapot Dome." I told him I would, of course, be glad to see any of his friends but there would not be the leasing of a single oil deposit in the Naval reserves. They called the next day, Mr. Leo Stack and another gentleman whose name I do not recall. They said they were "independent oil men" and would pay larger royalties than had prevailed in leasing contracts. Courteously but positively, I said:

"It cannot be done."

"Do you think that oil can be kept in the ground?" asked the Denver man.

"No, I don't think so," was the answer. "I *know* it can and will be kept there as a reserve."

"Those of us who wish to lease Teapot Dome," he said, "are Democrats. We will pay a bigger royalty than anybody else, and other things being equal the Democrats should be given the preference."

He was told that there was no politics in Naval administration, and that under no circumstances would the Naval oil reserve be either operated or leased. Before leaving, Mr. Stack said, "The oil men will not permit this oil to remain in the ground. If this administration does not let its political friends take it out, the incoming Republican administration will turn it over to their favorites before frost falls in 1921."

I told him that "Republicans and Democrats alike stand for the Navy. There may be, as you say, rascally Republicans who would like to exploit these reserves for their own profit, but I have confidence that the incoming Republican Administration will be as diligent to protect those reserves as the Democratic Administration has been. No man of any party would dare to let the Naval reserves be exploited or depleted."

CONFIDENCE MISPLACED

Events within a few months proved that my confidence in the incoming Republican Administration was misplaced. I learned afterwards that Doheny was interested with Stack. He evidently had told Stack of his pull with Albert Fall if Stack, representing himself and his associates as deserving Democrats, failed to get a lease from the outgoing Democratic administration.

FALL GIVES THE RESERVE OIL

When Fall became Secretary of the Interior, the Honolulu Company's appeal was pending. No time was lost in securing action by which the policy of the Wilson administration was reversed, Fall filed an opinion in which he asserted that if the question was before him as a new one, he would grant the patents to Honolulu Oil Company, but that, inasmuch as his predecessor had ruled otherwise, he would not disturb that decision. However, though denying the appeal to uphold the decision of the Comissioner of the General Land Office, Fall directed that leases of the 3,000 acres of the reserve be granted to the Honolulu Oil Company. Under the law, he had authority to lease only producing wells. The Honolulu Oil Company leases covered tracts of land. The Leasing Act authorized the President to grant leases of claims within which producing wells had been leased. No producing wells had been leased in the land claims of the Honolulu Oil Company. The President neither signed the leases nor authorized them. There is no written evidence that Harding had any knowledge of the leases. Fall awarded them without any authority of law, thus illegally undoing all that had been done to preserve that reserve for the exclusive use of the Navy.

XXXIX

MISFIT SHIPS SOLD TO GREECE

THE BIGGEST CHECK I ever received, and I was told it was the biggest single payment to the Treasury Department, was for $12,535,275.96. It was in payment for the purchase of two U. S. battleships by the government of Greece. In the spring of 1914 I was approached by Fred J. Gauntlett and asked if the Navy would sell the *Idaho* and the *Mississippi*. He was connected with the Newport Shipbuilding Company and knew those two ships did not correspond with the other dreadnaughts—were misfits in the fleet. The accepted explanations of constructing undersized battleships was that the elder Senator Hale, who was not above using his position as chairman of the Naval Affairs Committee to secure contracts for his friends, had secured a provision in the Appropriation Act to enable his favorites, who could not build standard dreadnaughts, to get the contract to build ships smaller than the standard. Gideon Welles, who was Lincoln's Secretary of the Navy, in his diary characterized Hale as "lazy, noisy; a harlequin and demagogue," a "Senatorial buffoon," who lacked "appreciation or fidelity," who is "neither honest nor sincere," and added, "I will waste no time on a man like Hale."

NAVY ORPHANS

The *Idaho* and the *Mississippi* were perfectly good ships but were called "Navy orphans." These ships had a displacement of 13,000 tons and were placed in commission in 1908. I asked Mr. Gauntlett whom he represented. He said the Greek government lacked fighting ships and wished to buy those two ships for protection in case any of its neighbors should declare war against them. He brought the Greek Minister, M. Vouros, to the Navy Department to talk over the matter, and P. D. Tsukalos, Commander of the Royal Hellenic Navy, who had been sent to Washington by his government as special representative in the matter. It was plain that the Minister and the Commander were eager to secure the ships and as early as possible. I frankly told them that the Navy would be glad to sell the ships because they were of a type smaller than our Navy needed, and that if they would make an offer I would recommend their sale to the President and Congress, but I doubted that Congress would authorize the sale to a foreign country. Admiral Taylor, Chief of Construction, and the would-be purchasers agreed upon an acceptable price. President Wilson was agreeable. I talked to Senators Tillman and Lodge, and Representatives Padgett and Butler, leaders in Naval legislation. They approved, and a bill was passed by Congress authorizing the sale in the Naval Appropriation Act of June 30, 1914. Eight days thereafter the transaction was completed. In the negotiation I sensed that Greece was nervous about conditions and feared war with Turkey, and Mr. Gauntlett confirmed my feeling. I expected when the bill came before Congress there would be a vigorous protest from Turkey, but the authorization came so quickly and the sale followed so soon that no protest came to me before the money had been paid and I had, by direction of President Wilson, executed a bill of sale to Mr. Gauntlett. The *Idaho* was in Villefranche, France, and the *Mississippi* was turned over at Newport News, Virginia. When incorporated in the Greek Navy they were christened *Kilkis* and *Lemnos*.

The sale of ships as good as new to go into the Navy of a foreign government and the passing of a bill of such a large amount made the news of the deal quite an event, and a function was made of the passing of the big check in the office of the Secretary of the Navy, who was surrounded by Assistant Secretary of the Navy Franklin Roosevelt, Navy Admirals on duty at the Department, and others. A picture was taken upon the delivery of the check. Before the transaction could be completed, I had to secure the coöperation of the Secretary of the Treasury, and my recollection is that McAdoo would not accept the check until the full amount ($12,535,275.96) in gold was deposited with the Treasury.

As throwing additional light on the sale of these ships, Mr. Gauntlett writes me that early in 1914 he approached me in reference to selling the *Oregon* and other ships and that I told him that, on account of the sentiment of the American people, I would not consent to any other nation's owning the *Oregon*. As a member of the "Safety of Life at Sea" Conference in London, he met members of the Greek Embassy in the British Capital, who wished to obtain the

Rivadeira and the *Moreno,* built in the United States. They could not be purchased and Mr. Gauntlett adds:

"I then suggested it might be possible to get the *Idaho* and *Mississippi* as they were misfits in our navy but particularly suitable for operations in the Mediterranean.

"The Ambassador communicated with Mr. Venezuelos who was then in Paris arranging a loan and I was asked to return at once to negotiate the sale if possible. I returned at once and started the negotiations with the result you are familiar with.

"During all the negotiations great stress was laid on the necessity of prompt action, as the vessels must be delivered prior to the delivery of the new fleet to the Turks, and this was stressed both in Washington and London, and it was no secret that Turkey proposed to annihilate the Greeks just as soon as their new vessels were delivered.

"It was also interesting to note that the Turks sent a special Plenipotentiary to Washington to prevent the sale, and when the matter was before Congress he wrote a personal and confidential letter to each member of both houses urging a negative vote on the amendment."

TURKEY PROTESTED

The records of the State Department show that on June 3, 1914, the Turkish Embassy at Washington asked to be informed regarding the proposed sale of the *Idaho* and the *Mississippi*, and Lansing, then Counsellor, gave information of the transaction. No subsequent communication in the nature of a protest from the Turkish Embassy at Washington has been found.

The records further reveal, however, that on June 1, 1914, Ambassador Morgenthau telegraphed to the Department that the Turkish Minister of the Marine had stated to him that the Turkish Government should be entitled to an equal opportunity with Greece to buy cruisers and should be allowed to compete for the same. Secretary Bryan replied (June 4) that the Turkish Ambassador at Washington had been informed of the situation. On June 26, Ambassador Morgenthau telegraphed that the Turkish Grand Vizier urged that the delivery of the ships to Greece should not be made until battleships under construction in England for Turkey should be delivered. No reply appears to have been made to the telegram. In a despatch (July 7) Ambassador Morgenthau reported further interviews with the Turkish Grand Vizier, the Minister of Marine, and the Minister of the Interior, all of whom had expressed their great disappointment at the sale of the *Idaho* and the *Mississippi* to Greece. It seems reasonable to conclude that the possession of the *Idaho* and the *Mississippi* by Greece prevented the outbreak of war between Turkey and Greece.

Mr. Morgenthau reported that he had an agitated visitor early in June, Djemal Pasha, the Turkish Minister of Marine, who, wildly gesticulating, begged and implored the Ambassador to intervene against the sale of the ships to Greece, offering to pay more than Greece would pay. He urged that if the sale could not be prevented, it be delayed until a dreadnaught Turkey was having built in England was commissioned. War was imminent between Turkey and Greece, and Mr. Morgenthau reports that the German Ambassador to Turkey entered the picture and asked Morgenthau to cable the President and urge him not to permit Greece to get these ships. Evidently at that time the Germans were confident that when they entered the war, Turkey would be their ally.

XL

INTOXICANTS BANNED IN THE NAVY

FROM TIME OUT OF MIND grog was served to sailors, and decades ago there was a common saying, "drunk as a sailor." When John Branch, of North Carolina, was Secretary of the Navy under Jackson, he ended the age-old practice of serving grog, and Secretary Dobbin, of North Carolina, promoted temperance. McKinley's Secretary of the Navy, John D. Long, issued an order prohibiting the sale or issue to enlisted men of alcoholic liquors on ships or at shore stations. But, though enlisted men were forbidden even a glass of beer, the officers made merry as they indulged their appetite. Enlisted men were ordered to bring intoxicants on board and serve officers, though if they brought a bottle of beer for themselves they were punished for violating the regulations. Convinced, after a year's reflection, that the cause of both temperance and democracy demanded it, I issued the following order:

"General Order No. 99.   "Navy Department
                                   "Washington, D. C., June 1, 1914.
        "CHANGE IN ARTICLE 627, NAVAL INSTRUCTION (99)
    "On July 1, 1914, article 827, Naval Instructions, will be annulled, and in its stead the following will be substituted:
    "The use or introduction for drinking purposes of alcoholic liquors on board any naval vessel, or within any navy yard or station, is strictly prohibited, and commanding officers will be held directly responsible for the enforcement of this order.
                                   "JOSEPHUS DANIELS,
                                   "Secretary of the Navy."

That order, coming as a surprise, created more than a sensation. On the morning when it appeared, Admiral Fiske, Aide for Operations, white with resentment, asked me if the order in the morning paper was correct. I answered in the affirmative. He said that Naval regulations prescribed that general orders should be prepared in the Operations department. "Yes," I said, "when ordered by the Secretary, but not when he chooses to write the order himself." The next

Sunday Fiske spent the afternoon trying to persuade me to alter or annul the order. When I declined, he asked, "Is there no way by which it may be revoked?" I replied: "Yes, there are two ways: (1) For me to die. (2) For the President to remove me from office." It was good night for him, for he saw I was very healthy and he knew the President held me in high regard.

ORDER APPROVED

When the press representatives called on the day the order was issued, they asked many questions, among them: "Did the President approve the order?" I answered that nobody spoke for the President. They hot-footed over to the Executive Office and asked Tumulty if the President approved.

"Never heard of it," Tumulty replied. "It is Daniels's own idea and nobody here even heard about it until it appeared in the paper this morning." Therefore Wilson was publicly absolved from any responsibility. As a matter of fact, however, unknown to Tumulty, when I had drawn the order after conference with the Surgeon General and nobody else in the Navy, I had taken it over to the White House, read it to President Wilson, and explained the reason why I felt impelled to issue it. He listened and said that if I thought it was a wise order I should issue it. With his sanction I gave it to the press that night. If it was unpopular, the burden should fall upon me alone and the President should be shielded. It is the business of a Cabinet officer never to pass the buck to the chief executive. He should take the responsibility. In this case, the initiative and action were mine. I felt that was all the more proper since Wilson would be a candidate in 1916 and I knew that the wets would denounce the step and might vent their resentment against him. I could not permit that. Never until 1921 was it known that I had acted with the President's knowledge and approval.

When the chorus of criticism became loud, I gave out a statement justifying the policy, and quoting statements against the use of intoxicants by Navy men—one by the Kaiser, who had said that in war "that nation which consumes the least alcohol wins," and one by Admiral Beresford of the British Navy: "I drink no wine, spirits and beer, not because they do me harm, not because I think it wrong to drink, but simply because I am more ready for any work imposed upon me, day or night; always fresh, cheery and in good temper."

SECRETARY LONG'S ORDER

I received commendation from former Secretary John D. Long, who wrote:

"Secretary Daniels' order is the natural sequence of my own prohibiting liquors for enlisted men in the Navy. That was as far as we could go at that time, but in due season it became apparent that enlisted men could not be prohibited from the use of intoxicating liquors and at the same time officers associated with them and in command of them permitted their use."

He declared also that it promoted temperance, and added: "With such an evil as intemperance, the Government should lead in its suppression."

The order issued by Secretary Long—General Order No. 508—was as follows:

"After mature deliberation, the department has decided that it is for the best interest of the service that the sale or issue to enlisted men of malt and other alcoholic liquors on board ships of the Navy or within the limits of Naval stations be prohibited.

"Thereafter, upon the receipt of this order, commanding officers and commandants are forbidden to allow any malt or other alcoholic liquors to be sold or issued to enlisted men, either on board ship or within the limits of Navy Yards, naval stations, or marine barracks, except in the Medical Department."

JOHN D. LONG—*Secretary*

WHY THE ORDER WAS ISSUED

Why was the order issued at the time that I signed it? That question was often asked. One day a gentleman of Quaker stock from Pennsylvania called to see me and earnestly urged the restoration of his nephew who had been dismissed from the Navy for drunkenness. He was shown the record and I pointed out that the young man had repeatedly been drunk in public and had brought disgrace on the Navy. The gentleman replied:

"I do not doubt he was drunk, but it was entirely the fault of the Navy. Before going to the Naval Academy the young man had never touched intoxicants. His officers drank, some of them too much. If he had not joined the wine mess he would have been called a 'sissy.' He had to drink to be an acceptable associate of fellow officers. The Navy taught him that it was narrow-minded if he turned down his glass. He followed your system. Now that your Navy has ruined him your Navy kicks him out and puts a stigma on him."

He was in dead earnest. I had no answer. His indictment was severe but true. After he left I could not rid myself of his righteous indignation. I saw that the Navy practice had wrecked his nephew's life. The more I reflected upon my responsibility and that of my predecessors, the clearer it came that it was my duty that such temptation should not assail young men whose parents trusted the Navy to train them for service. That was the immediate reason why the wine mess was abolished in the Navy.

PEN AND PICTURE RIDICULE

A storm of opposition and ridicule raged. The cartoonists drew pictures of Mumm's Extra Dry walking the plank and paragraphers and wits had a new theme. The cartoonists in particular had the time of their lives. More than a hundred cartoons appeared in April. My wife, a good sport, wrote to the artists, asking for the original of the best, and hung them in our study. When they learned that the sharp darts and caricatures did not get under my skin, some felt they had fallen short on their campaign. Under a particularly effective cartoon by Rogers were the words:

Don't Fail to See

JOSEPHUS

in his

Great

Soda Fountain Scene

Or the Piffle

Beats

Pinafore

The *Tribune's* cartoon had Sir Josephus, Admiral of the U.S.S. *Grapejuice Pinafore,* prancing about the fountain deck and singing:

When I was a lad I pondered some
On the horrible effects of the Demon Rum;
I scorned to dally with the dread highball,
And I never saw a bottle of champagne at all.
I kept away from guzzling men,
And now I am the ruler of the U. S. N.

FIELD DAY IN THE NAVY

Aunt Josie Daniels: AFTER YOU THROW OVERBOARD ALL THEM DECANTERS AND WINEGLASSES
YOU CAN SET THE CREW TO POLISHIN' THE SHIP'S HAND-MIRRORS AND SCENT BOTTLES——
"AYE, AYE, MUM!"

Writing of his call on an American cruiser at Tampico in 1914, Frederick Palmer said:

"We found the ward-room officers making a sad ceremony of packing up the mess wine glasses. In future the toast to sweethearts and wives with the time-honored joking corollary: "May they never meet," would be drunk with water—for that day Secretary of the Navy Daniels' prohibition order went into effect."

The liquor advertisers joined the chorus, one inserting an advertisement like this:

W's whiskey popular in The Clubs
The Army
Not the Navy

AFTER "PINAFORE"

Among the cleverest skits was one by F. H. Warren in the New York *World*, a parody on *Pinafore*. It was entitled:

THE DRINK-NOUGHT OF THE USN

or

THE LAD THAT LOVED A TODDY

The company enters singing the chorus:

We sail the ocean blue, and our ship is sober, very
We are as dry and sober too, as the Naval Secretary,
Highballs whistle full o'er the Army
We stand by H2O,
When at anchor we ride (this is on the side)
Ashore we often go.

Enter Little Buttercup with basket on her arm singing as she offers her wares. Enter Sir Josephus who sings:

When I was a lad I served a term
As office attendant to a hydrant firm.
I drank the water and I coiled the hose,
And I polished all the brasses on the nozzles nose
And I polished up the nozzles so carefully
That now I am the ruler of the whole Navy.

As I grew up, as boys will do,
I stuck to water as the only brew
And I spurned all liquors as I watched the fall
Of many who were riddled by the Scotch highball.
And I spurned all liquor so faithfully
That now I am cabineting with WJB.

Now, sailors all, do you stir the spoon
Or kick the sawdust in a back saloon?
Is your taste still fettered to the good old grape?
Just clip this little morsel from my new red tape
Stick close to water and never drink a drop
Or you never will be ruler of the Navy shop.

There drifted from overseas a story that some American Naval officers, who never liked the Wine Mess Order, gathered in cafes and sang:

"Josephus Daniels is a goose,
If he thinks he can induce
Us to drink his damn grape juice!
"(CHORUS) Away! Away! With sword and
    drum,
Here we come, full of rum,
Looking for something to put on the bum!"

A short time before, Governor Glynn had asked an appropriation to provide a silver service for the *New York,* which drew forth this comment:

"The big thing in a battleship is a punch-bowl. Of what use is a punch-bowl when there is no punch? There is no 'punch' in grapejuice. We had better make the punch-bowl a pickle-dish. Daniels has put the 'bit' in prohibition."

WHAT MR. DOOLEY SAID

Finley Peter Dunne—the celebrated "Mr. Dooley"—took his fling at General Order No. 99 and he and Hennessy discussed it at such length that their observation filled a whole column in The New York *Times* and other papers. In part here are the comments:

"I see," said Mr. Dooley, "that me frind Josephus Daniels has decided not to go aboord a man iv war again."
"Does it make him seasick?" asked Mr. Hennessy.

"Iv coorse it does that," said Mr. Dooley. "Ivry sicrety iv the navy is seasick ex-officyo, as Hogan says. That is how ye distinguish thim fr'm other officers iv th' navy. Ye can always tell a sicrety iv th' navy aboord ship be his stovepipe hat, his indiff'rence to human s'ciety, his appealin' glances tords th' shore, an' his complexion, which shades off fr'm a light green to a lively yellow. . . .

"The prisint sicrety if th' navy wud not quail, no matter how th' ship squirmed undher him. He is a brave man. He's been th' iditor iv a pa-aper in North Caroliny f'r manny years, an' anny wan who's done it knows that it takes more skill an' courage to manoover a newspaper in the south thin to sail a battleship through Hell Gate. . . .

"What's he done? He's dealt a staggerin' blow at wan iv th' oldest thraditions iv th' navy, that's what he's done. He has dashed th' wine cup fr'm th' lips iv th' boys that pace th' quarther deck. He has ordhered that hincefoorth an' f'river no officer iv th' navy can blot up anny spirichous, ferminted, or otherwise improvin' dhrink abbord ship except on a doctor's perscription. I hear that among th' spicifications in th' new superdhreadnought is wan f'r a prescription bar an' beer pump f'r th' doctor's quarters."

EDITORIAL OPPOSITION

Some of the paper treated the matter more seriously, as this editorial in the New York *World* shows:

"It is not reformatory. It is revolutionary. It is a shameful reflection upon a noble profession. We send our officers to sea chaperoned like school-girls. . . . This use of military discipline as a cloak for sumptuary despotism is so intolerable that Secretary Daniels should be allowed no time in sobering up after his temperance debauch."

Philip R. Dillon answered the *World's* repeated severe condemnation by writing:

"Obviously Secretary Daniels will have the overwhelming sentiment of the citizens of the country at his back. We have just read that Lloyd George, backed by the common citizens of England, is in the mood to democratize the army of England. It is a bad time for any American naval officers to assert that they by reason of superior class are entitled to more and better food and whiskey, gin, wine, and beer than those clear-headed, bright-eyed men before the mast. The joke is not all on Daniels. He is in close touch with the 40,000 enlisted men in the Navy, and finally with the common sense of the American people."

A correspondent of the *World* said, "Daniels will go into history with Tiberius and is on a par with Caligula, who built a bridge from his palace to the capitol that he might be next-door neighbor to Jupiter. He is like Mayor Gaynor, who assumed the role of Justinian."

Another paper said: "At one swoop larboard, starboard, and sideboard have been jettisoned."

A correspondent asked the *World*: "If officers are permitted to have drinks served while aboard ship, why not let the able seamen have the same right? Where do you stand on special privilege?" There was no reply.

As the high light of the propaganda against the order, *Life* issued a special issue called "The Josephus Daniels Issue." In cartoons I was dressed up as an old spinster only a few degrees removed from idiocy, and there were scores of pictures and special articles full of ricidule. It filled the entire edition with scintillating (sin-till-late) products of writers and artists, many of them quite clever, so much so that I preserved a copy of that issue. *Life* kept up its barbed darts until the United States entered the World War and the Navy was ready for the great service rendered. *Life*, showing it was a good sport, had the justice to retract its long campaign against me in an article, "Wherein we Apologize," paying high tribute to the Secretary of the Navy's devotion to preparedness and efficiency.

DOCTORS APPROVE

While the distillers, brewers, cartoonists, and others were denouncing the order, medical journals and physicians and temperance forces gave commendation. The *American Medical Journal*, in a long article commending the order, closed with these words:

"Entirely aside from the moral or sentimental reasons, and considered simply as a scientific regulation in the interest of efficiency, this order will recommend itself to the vast majority of the American people."

Surgeon General Braisted of the Navy, who helped me draft the order, said: "Except in certain cases the use of alcohol is harmful and its abuse disastrous." The great General Gorgas, Surgeon General of the Army, while refraining from discussing an order in another department of government, said:

"Every man would be better off without alcoholic drinks. I used claret wine at meals for several years, but found it was doing me harm and stopped it some years ago."

In addition to approval from physicians, many civic organizations, health bodies, women all over the country, and religious bodies passed resolutions endorsing the order. In Congress the predicted opposition never materialized. In fact, Senator Tillman, chairman of the Naval Affairs Committee, voiced the prevailing sentiment when he said:

"I am not a prohibitionist but I approve the order and I say if Secretary Daniels can keep liquor out of the Navy it will be a good thing. It ought to be kept out of the Army too. I recognize that there is too much drinking in the Army and Navy, especially among officers. The greatest difficulty about the order will be its enforcement."

NOT DISTURBED

When the denunciation reached its crescendo, with wits and half-wits and nit-wits, humorists and near-humorists, distillers and cocktail shakers, Naval officers who resented being fed out of the same spoon in the matter of drink with the enlisted men, shouting their hard words in falsetto and all other ways, I was not disturbed in the least as to the wisdom of what I had done. My only fear was that the opponents of prohibition, especially in New Jersey where they were influential in politics, might visit their displeasure on the President, who was a resident of that State, and organize opposition to him because his administration was placing condemnation on intoxicants by the Naval arm of the military service. But as that did not disturb the President (and he was reëlected in 1916) why should I worry?

At the Democratic National Convention at Houston which nominated Governor Alfred E. Smith, I was informed by Carter Glass that Woodrow Wilson told him he was opposed to the repeal of the Eighteenth Amendment. This was in 1928.

PROTECTS PROPERTY AND LIVES

Not long after the order was issued, Colonel Thompson, head of the Navy League, asked me to speak at the annual banquet in New York. I knew leaders of the League had joined the anvil chorus of disapproval of my order, and I answered: "I will do so, and discuss the Wine Mess Order, if that is what you'd like to hear." He didn't, but he wished the Secretary of the Navy to attend the banquet and assented. In the course of my address, after declaring that "there is no body of men more temperate, clear-headed in the world than our Naval officers," I said:

"Of all the trades, there are probably no finer or more sober or more intelligent, more self-controlled men than our railroad engineers. Upon their sobriety, upon their clear-headedness, upon their capacity to govern themselves depend daily the lives of millions of our citizens. Your life today, tomorrow, or whenever you leave this city, will for a greater or less time lie in the hollow of the engineer's hand. Many of the railroads have established club houses for their engineers, where they may read, meet and pass away time between runs. What say you, gentlemen, with railroad tickets in your pockets, to a proposition that the railroads should issue an order that their engineers off duty at their club houses should be allowed to establish a wine mess of their own? Would the fact that 99 percent or 999 out of 1,000 of these men would take no advantage of such an order and would go to their work the next morning with eyes just as clear and hands just as steady as they were the night before—would that fact do away with the possibility of the one-hundredth man or one-thousandth man moving the wrong lever at a critical moment or sleepily overlooking the danger signal? Would you not demand an order abolishing such an arrangement? Yet, this is precisely a fair comparison. The wreck of a great battleship, the loss of a critical battle, and the honor of your country may easily hinge upon one of many men in the varied and complex duties which these great masses of intricate machinery called battleships have created. Would you take any chances with the engineers of your train? Why then would you seriously ask me to take chances with those who direct the movements of your ships?"

ORDER IS ENFORCED

Fear was expressed by Senator Tillman that the order might not be enforced. When at a press conference I was asked what I would do in such a situation, I answered: "Naval officers always obey orders, whether they like them or not. That is the essence of Naval honor and Naval efficiency."

The fear that the order would not be enforced, never troubled me. A few days after it had been made public, Admiral Mayo, Commander in Chief of the fleet, calling on me, reported that when he first read the order he didn't like it, but he added, using an old Naval expression, "I am a captain's man, and I sent for my steward and directed him to remove the supply of alcoholic beverages I had laid in the day before for the guests I would be entertaining." "But," said the steward, "you only put the supply in yesterday." Mayo replied: "It is the duty of an officer of the Navy to obey orders of superior officers. Take them back to the shop where they were purchased." The steward obeyed orders but the vendor refused to refund all the money Mayo had paid him.

NAVAL OFFICERS APPROVE

The example of the Commander in Chief became known throughout the entire Navy and was followed. If there was any failure to enforce General Order No. 99, I never heard of it. A long time after, Mayo said to me:

"When your Wine Mess Order came to me, I didn't like it at all. I felt it would convey a wrong impression to the public on the habits of Naval officers. But I wish to tell you after a year has passed that I would not have it repealed.

"I have had rare opportunity to observe the feeling of officers. My own opinion is that the Wine Mess Order is the wisest thing you have done as Secretary, and if its future were committed today to the officers of the fleet, the Wine Mess Order would never be restored."

There were officers who were irritated—not many—because drinking while on duty was not allowed. They were silenced when, after the Wine Mess Order had been in operation two years, George Dewey, the Admiral of the Navy, asked what he thought of it, said:

"A good thing. There was some feeling about it at first because the papers made fun of it, and there was also an attempt to make it appear that Secretary Daniels was charging officers with intemperance. I think that feeling has disappeared completely. Every railroad, every great corporation, has long had an ironclad rule forbidding men to drink while on duty. Isn't a ship as important as a locomotive?"

Attempts were made to induce my successors to restore the wine mess on Naval ships, but with no success. The rule stands that no intoxicants are permitted to be served on any ship in the American Navy.

FIGHT BETTER WITHOUT GROG

There were some officers in the Navy and in the Army, too, who thought a "nip" helped men and said serving grog would make them fight better. They evidently were not advertent to Cooper's account of an incident in connection with the battle between the U.S.S. *Constitution* and the *Levant* and the *Cyane* on February 20, 1810. He wrote of it:

"The manner in which Captain Stewart handled his ship on this occasion excited much admiration among nautical men, it being an unusual thing for a single vessel to engage two enemies and escape being raked. So far from this occurring to the *Constitution* she actually raked both her opponents, and the manner in which she backed and filled in the smoke, forcing her opponents down to leeward when they were endeavoring to cross her stern or forefoot, is among the most brilliant maneuvering in naval annals."

An incident on the *Constitution* which was brought to the attention of the occupants of Captain Stewart's cabin after the battle showed the character and determination of the crew. While Captain Stewart was in conversation with one of the British commanders, a midshipman came from the deck to say that the officer of the deck wished to know if the men could have their grog. As the grog was to have been served before the time of the engagement, Captain Stewart asked in surprise, 'The men have had their grog already, haven't they?'

" 'No, sir,' replied the midshipman. 'It was mixed ready for serving just before the battle began, but the forecastle men and other older soldiers of the crew said they didn't want any Dutch courage on board, and capsized the grog tub into the lee scuppers.'"

NO WINE FOR DIPLOMATS

Perhaps no matter was more discussed in Washington and in the country and in fact in nations over the seas than the announcement that Bryan, the new Secretary of State, would not serve wine or other intoxicants at the official dinners, which by custom had always been given by the Secretary of State to the Diplomatic Corps. It was a radical innovation. Time out of mind, it had been regarded as essential that wine should be served even by Secretaries of State who themselves were total abstainers, when they entertained the Diplomatic Corps. Europeans and South Americans felt, as did many in this country, that a State function with no wine was stale, flat, and unprofitable. When it became known that Bryan, because of his convictions for prohibition would omit the wines, it created almost as much discussion as if he had resigned from the Cabinet, maybe more. Some of the American papers said it was an affront to the members of the Diplomatic Corps and would be resented by them and by their country; that it showed a provincial spirit out of harmony with broad diplomacy, and, whatever Bryan's own personal habit or views were, he was an officer of the government now and he should follow long-time precedents in this and all other countries. There was much adverse criticism in and out of the press, and even in Cabinet circles some of the members were disposed to join in this sneer at Bryan because he insisted that as an officer he was not called upon to do anything contrary to his convictions.

Some time before, when he had talked to me about the invitation Wilson gave him to become Secretary of State, he told me he had said to the President that he could not accept if it would require him to serve intoxicants at dinners given by him as Secretary of State. He told me that the President regarded that as inconsequential and said that was a matter for him to determine himself and was within his own province, and would not be at all embarrassing to the administration. Wilson himself in the White House, as had his predecessors before national prohibition went into effect, served wines at White House functions; but the attempt to induce him to intimate to Bryan that he should do likewise had no effect. Mr. and Mrs. Bryan were long-time total abstainers and prohibitionists. They felt that serving wine at diplomatic dinners would belie Bryan's oft-repeated statement that men in public life ought to set an example for the people of the nation.

I talked with several of the diplomats of big countries about it, and they referred to the criticism in this country and others as a tempest in a teapot. Ambassador Jusserand of France told me that it was his habit to pour water into his wine and take a little every day at dinner, but he said he resented the thought or any suggestion that diplomats would be embarrassed or troubled because Mr. Bryan did not serve them wine. He resented the implication that ambassadors and ministers from other countries could not enjoy themselves without intoxicants. That was the view of the older and wiser of the Diplomatic Corps in Washington, but some of the younger men joined with the Americans, though they did it privately, in criticism of Bryan.

BRYAN AND T. R. COMMENDED

Asked about my view of the matter by newspaper correspondents, I told them I heartily approved of Bryan's course; that while I had never said anything about it, I had never at home or in Washington served any intoxicants at any dinners in my home and I did not propose to do so; and I had never found that any Naval officer or other guest enjoyed himself less because of its absence. I had not at that time issued my Wine Mess Order which was to create so much comment. In the same statement in which I approved Bryan's policy, which was widely published, I took occasion to commend Theodore Roosevelt for bringing a libel suit against a Michigan editor who had charged him with drunkenness. I said that these two incidents, the Secretary of State having no wine at diplomatic dinners, and the ex-President regarding the charge of excessive drinking as a reflection upon his character, would do much to strengthen the cause of temperance in America; that the time had been when no public man would have regarded it as a libel to say that some officer on some occasion had drunk to excess, and that no Secretary of State would have dared to depart from the long-standing custom. I expressed the view that the example of these two distinguished and popular men ought to be followed by all men in public life, and, whether it was done or not, these two outstanding incidents would largely influence public opinion and help in the crusade toward ending the legalized drink traffic and evil.

BOUQUETS THAT SURPRISED

Election returns showed that the people rebuked the Republican Campaign Textbook.

SQUARING OURSELVES

James J. Montague, one of the most popular columnists in the Wilson era, sometimes wrote poetry as well as prose. He joined the critics on the Wine Mess Order and the teaching of sailors when it was inaugurated. Later he wrote this poem, when Uncle Sam entered the World War, recanting his early criticism and approving the policies derided, as the Navy showed it was fit and ready:

SQUARING OURSELVES

How they howled about Josephus every time a sailor
    man
Found an unresponsive barkeep when he went to rush
    the can!
How they growled about Josephus when commanders
    got the news
That the Admiral had orders for a dry and boozeless
    cruise!
Even such a wild teetotaller as the temperate T. R.
Shouted from a thousand housetops that Josephus
    went too far.
From all quarters of the nation excellent, well-meaning
    folk,
Said in letters to the papers that Josephus was a joke.

Poets chuckled (we among them) in all sorts of jibing
    verse
When Josephus said that seamen might be brave, and
    still not curse.
Never on the rolling ocean had men navigated ships
Be the weather fine or dirty, without oaths upon their
    lips.
Even Dr. Lyman Abbott had to pause and breathe a
    prayer
For a man who said that sailors had not simply GOT
    to swear!
And there swept across the nation, North and South
    and East and West
The unanimous conclusion that Josephus was a jest.

But when Congress started peering into things that had
    to do

With the arming of the warship and the comfort of
    the crew,
When grave statesmen asked him questions as to this
    and as to that
It was noticed that Josephus answered right straight
    off the bat.
For his drinkless, curseless navy—every unit—thanks
    to him,
From the dreadnoughts to the cutters, is in first-class
    fighting trim.
Now at last the pitying jesters (we among them) see
    a light,
For the fact has dawned upon us that Josephus is all
    right!

LINCOLN'S SECRETARY OF THE NAVY APPROVES

During the Civil War, Captain Joshua N. Rowe, of the U.S.S.
St. Louis, refused to contribute to the Wine Mess Fund and was virtually ostracized by his brother officers. He appealed to Secretary
of the Navy Gideon Welles, who wrote him:

"I wish to commend the stand you have taken in regard to
the payment into the Wine Fund. You have done right. I am
proud that there is an officer in our Navy who will stick to his
principles in spite of opposition and disapproval. Furthermore,
all those on board who have shown you discourtesy will
cordially apologize."

XLI

A PARTNER OF CUPID

Oᴺᴇ ᴍᴏʀɴɪɴɢ a modest and good-looking young woman called at the Navy Department and related a story of her unhappiness which moved me to an action that brought joy to two young people. She was Mrs. J. E. Austin. While the ship on which Midshipman Austin was attached was in Pearl Harbor, Hawaii, he was married to the young lady, a case of genuine love on both sides. It seems that the officer lost sight of—and the young lady had never heard of—the Naval regulation forbidding the marriage of a midshipman under pain of dismissal from the Navy. "The Captain was invited to the marriage," Austin told me later, "and the executive officer was present at the ceremony. Neither of them warned me that I would lose my officer status if I married. It was later that the blow fell."

I never saw a more dejected couple. He loved the Naval service, for which he had been trained, and was unfitted for civil duties. His only hope was for reinstatement. Without it, the future looked blank to both of them. I promised to do all I could to secure his reinstatement, wrote a letter recommending special legislation to restore him, after an examination of his record at Annapolis and in the service showed that he had stood high in his studies and in efficiency. The papers made much of the story, and cartoons appeared representing me as the partner of Cupid. Congress showed that it had a heart and passed the act reinstating the young man, and I had the pleasure of congratulating Mr. and Mrs. Austin, who called at the Navy Department to express their joyous thanks. "The older officers are right in advising young men not to marry until they have had their first sea duty," President Wilson said, "but there is no reason why good advice should become a law."

COMMANDED FIRST ARMED GUARD

Early in 1914 Midshipman Knauss, wishing to be married, requested a transfer to the *Mayflower* so that his honeymoon might not be interfered with when his ship went to sea. Some of the older officers thought I would be making officers soft and lessen their efficiency by such consideration. Within a year the newly wed Knauss couple were the proud parents of twins. Did the consideration lessen Knauss' efficiency? When the time came that it was decided to put armed guards on ships sailing through the U-boat infested zone to Europe, Lieutenant Knauss was chosen to head the first armed guard on that important and perilous duty. He was ready and proved himself possessing the best stuff of the Navy. Upon his return from his first trip across, I was eager to learn the details of this new departure, which had been under critical fire when adopted, and I invited him to dinner. Of course it wasn't quite the thing for the Secretary of the Navy to do, according to an old caste system.

ENGLISH PHOBIA

At the dinner Knauss told me of his experiences and added a story showing that British nerves were on edge. "Shortly after I reached London," he said, "I observed that I was under surveillance, a secret service man following me everywhere, even eating at my table. It irritated me when I learned that because of my German-sounding name I was suspect in England. I, trusted by my government to protect ships from German submarines, was treated as if I could not be trusted."

I asked him what he did. He said that he told the official responsible for the indignity that he would not stand for being watched because he had a German-sounding name. He added; "My Dutch ancestors were fighting for American independence against the British in the Revolutionary War, and men of my blood have fought in every war in which the United States has been engaged, and I resent the intimation that I am to be watched in England." His hot protest and vigorous proof of his Americanism brought apologies and an end of an intolerable situation. At that time English phobia caused all persons to be suspect whose name had a German tinge, even, as Knauss told them, American Dutch, who had a large share in bringing about American independence when the British employed Hessians to fight against the Pennsylvania Dutch under Washington. I was glad I had made it easy for Knauss to marry. America cannot have too many of his name and patriotism.

RANG MARRIAGE BELLS

My "partnership with Cupid," advertised in a Berryman cartoon, was begun when, about Christmas in 1913, I transferred two young officers from the *Dolphin* to the *Mayflower* in order that they might be married during the Christmas holidays. They had planned their marriages before the *Dolphin*, which, like the *Mayflower*, had its home port at the Washington Navy Yard, had been ordered to sea duty. When this order was issued, the matrimonial plans of the two officers went awry. In order that the marriage bells might ring according to plans, the transfers of the officers were made to the President's ship, which would not be going to sea during their honeymoons.

I was in full accord with the spirit of the Navy discouraging officers from marriage until after their Midshipman long cruise, but did not feel it right to exercise the drastic power of expulsion to carry that idea into effect; and, after my experience with the Austins, I abrogated the penalty. It was both a beautiful and a sad sight to see the marriages in the Chapel at Annapolis June week— joyous to see how happy the bride and groom were at the realization of their dream, and sad in the early separation when the Midshipman had to say good-bye almost at the beginning of the honeymoon to take his baptism in the separation which makes Naval service a sacrifice of home pleasures.

"OPEN DOOR" POLICY

I could never endure the un-American spirit of caste which prevails too largely in the Navy. One day, not long after I had assumed office, my secretary said that a young sailor, on leave from his ship, wished to see me. He told me his ship was at the Philadelphia Navy Yard for overhauling and would be there months and had recently returned from a cruise of six months. He had secured three days leave and had come to Washington to see me. His story was that his wife in a town in Ohio was to be a mother in a few weeks, that he had asked leave to be with her at the time of her confinement, that it had been denied, that she was not strong and the separation and her condition had made her ill. His story was a

"I DO NOT BELIEVE THAT MEN SHOULD BE REFUSED THE RIGHT TO OBEY THE DICTATES OF LOVE BY RED TAPE REGULATIONS.

JOSEPHUS DANIELS
SECRETARY OF THE NAVY

C. K. Berryman, in the *Washington Star*

SECRETARY DANIELS IN THE ROLE OF CUPID

straight one, and I gave direction that leave be granted the sailor. After the sailor had gone, happy at the thought of being with his young wife, my secretary told me that the Aide for Operations had started to enter my office and on the threshold had seen the sailor talking to me. "How did he get into the office of the Secretary of the Navy, a thing unheard of?" he demanded of the private secretary. He was told that the young man had called and I had directed that he be admitted. "You should have refused to take his request to the Secretary and have sent him to the Bureau of Navigation," said the Admiral, showing hot disapproval that an ordinary sailor could prefer a request directly to the Secretary.

"I am here to serve the Secretary and carry out his wishes," answered my private secretary.

SAILOR GOES HOME TO GREET BABY

This recalls an incident that happened long afterwards, in fact in 1932, at Portland, Oregon, where I had gone to address the National Convention of the American Legion. On the night of the Colonial Ball, at which I was expected, I had gone to dine with my old-time friend, Revenue Collector Miller, at his hotel. The chauffeur assigned to me had been on steady duty day and night for several days. When he left me at Mr. Miller's hotel, I told him he could take a night off, that I would call a taxi when I was ready to go to the ball. However, when the time came, neither Mr. Miller nor the hotel proprietor could obtain a taxi for love or money. We went on the sidewalk where a lady dressed like Martha Washington, and other ladies, were standing waiting for a taxi. The manager said, "The first taxi is engaged for them and you could probably have a seat with them." I sidled up to Martha, a lovely lady from Maine, and asked if I might attach myself to her party, explaining the taxi shortage. She graciously assented. Her maiden aunt looked daggers at me. But there was no first taxi, either for her or anyone else. We waited half an hour as cars full of people dashed by. It looked as if she were all dressed up for the ball and could not get there, and I was on the point of giving it up when a nice-looking young man walked up to the little party and, addressing the lady, said, "How are you, Martha?" He then turned and addressed me as "George." Of course the party snickered at what they regarded as his freshness.

Without my knowing it, Mr. Miller asked the young man if he

knew whom he was addressing so familiarly as "George." He said
he did not. Miller told him he was speaking to Mr. Daniels, who
was Secretary of the Navy during the World War. "My God!" he
said. "You don't say so! I'd rather see him than any man in the
whole world." He then informed me that he had served in the Navy,
going into the war zone in Europe, and had wished for years to
see me to express his gratitude for the greatest favor ever done him
by any man. To the little group and to me he told this story:

"Upon the return of my ship from Europe, I asked the officers
of the ship for leave to go home to be present when my first
baby was born. I was told that orders were for us to be sent
south on a ship leaving in two days and that no leave could be
granted any of the crew until that duty had been performed. I
appealed unsuccessfully to the Captain. I was nearly wild. In
my desperation I sent you a telegram, stating the circumstances,
and begging permission to go home for my wife's confinement.
My buddy told me I was throwing away my money, that the
Secretary of the Navy would never see the message, and if he did
he would refer me to the Captain. I told him if it ever reached
Uncle Josephus [the name which the sailors called me] he had
a heart and would help. When I got back to the ship that night,
I was told that my application for leave had been granted by
orders from Washington. Can't you imagine my joy?"

He had told his story more graphically and feelingly than I can
convey it, and as we listened to his story all the group seemed to see
the whole situation—the wife anxious while he was in the war zone
and waiting with joy when his ship would dock—and the tragedy
of separation. I was watery about the eyes and Martha and the other
ladies had been similarly affected by his simple and frank story.

"My wife is here," he said, "and our little boy. She would love to
tell you how much she owes you."

I told him I would be glad to see her and her thanks filled my
heart full of gratitude that I had been privileged to confer a blessing
on her and her Navy husband, and young son.

As this scene was being enacted on the sidewalk of a crowded city,
overflowing with Legionnaires, the automobiles thundered by and
Martha felt distressed lest she would never get to the ball. Someone
told the young ex-sailor of our inability to secure a car to reach the
ball.

"You don't mean to say that the war-time Secretary of the Navy cannot get a car in this city?" he remarked, and in a tone of command said: "Wait here, I'll have a car." He walked into the middle of the street and as a large private car rolled up, he held up his hand and in tones of authority ordered it to stop. The owner, who was driving it, came to a halt. "The war-time Secretary of the Navy is unable to secure transportation to the Legion ball. I want you to do your country a service and yourself a service by taking him to the ball." The gentleman assented, and Martha and I and two other ladies piled in. My friend and his wife and boy waved to us, and soon Martha was happy as the belle of the ball. Her aunt, who had been very cold to me, warmed up over the story of my young friend and the fact that it was only through me that she could get transportation to the scene of the festivities. I should add that the car was over-crowded and Martha sat on my lap. She wasn't heavy and she was good-looking.

CULTIVATED CLOSE CONTACT

These incidents are not told to convey the idea that officers of the Navy are inconsiderate of the men who serve under them. The contrary is true of most of them, for to my knowledge officers have sacrificed their own leaves to grant leave to sailors under the circumstances mentioned. In these two cases, the officers probably had orders from their superiors which they felt obliged to carry out, or they may have been the exceptions who lacked consideration and kindness of heart. There are a few such men in all callings, in civil life as in the Navy. My experiences, however, have shown me that they are few in number.

I often wished while Secretary of the Navy that I could get in closer contact with all who made up the personnel so as to do more to make the career of the youngest as happy as conditions made possible. It is a hard service at best and is no place for coddling, and yet too often there seems a gulf fixed between the head of the service and the newly enlisted who need to feel that they are regarded as fellow humans by their superiors.

XLII

FIRST STEPS TAKEN FOR PEACE

THE MOST IMPORTANT proposal in my first annual report came at its conclusion. After making recommendations for appropriations for strengthening the Navy and outlining plans for educational and welfare work, I discussed what was then being talked about in all Navy circles in the world. Winston Churchill, First Lord of the British Admiralty, had recently made an address, directed chiefly to Germany, calling for a naval holiday. As in all his utterances, he spoke with brilliancy and vigor. He pointed out the tremendous burden laid upon the taxpayers of all countries by competitive navy building, particularly in Germany and Britain, and made the offer that the British people would quit building for a year if the German people would cease naval construction for a like period. As he expressed it, the proposal sounded very fair, and it was warmly applauded in Britain and in other nations. Germany, which had but lately entered upon the policy of big naval construction and was determined to be as strong on the sea as England, took the suggestion of a naval holiday as approval of a perpetual continuation of British supremacy on the sea. At that time the British Navy was twice as large as that of Germany. The Germans were building feverishly and at heavy cost. The British fixed policy was that it must have twice as much strength in its Naval units as any other nation. Churchill pointed out that a holiday for a year would not change the relative status of any nation, and would save millions of dollars. He held out the hope that within the year there might be agreements which would lessen if not end competitive naval construction. The fly in that ointment, as Germany looked at it, was that the British Navy was to continue twice as strong as the German Navy, and that, instead of being a generous offer on the part of Churchill as it had been acclaimed in his own country, it was, in effect, an attempt to induce Germany to acquiesce in British supremacy. Therefore German Big Navy people jeered at it and refused to accept it.

Churchill did not continue long as First Lord of the Admiralty after the failure of the Dardanelles enterprise, but in World War II, when Germany, under Hitler, was seeking to dominate the world, Churchill, who had vainly warned his country of the danger, was called to be the Prime Minister of Britain and to lead his country in the most difficult days of its whole existence. His photograph today differs greatly from that of 1919, reproduced in this volume, and shows that time and responsibility have left their traces.

REACTION OF THE UNITED STATES TO CHURCHILL'S PROPOSAL

In the United States Churchill's proposal was not well received, though there was a desire to end naval competitive building. In my discussion of Churchill's proposition, which had not been limited to Germany, I took the ground that no naval holiday would meet the situation; that what was needed was to put an end to competitive building by the naval nations. I declared that this could not be brought about by any one or two nations—that no nation of itself could settle the policy of the size of navies, but that there ought to be held a council of nations having large navies and they ought to discuss and agree upon, not a holiday, but a permanent policy which would look to an end of competition which was both hurtful to the pocketbooks of the taxpayers and in the end might be provocative of war.

PROPOSAL DELAYED FOR BRYAN'S TREATIES

This suggestion met with much popular favor and at a meeting of the Cabinet I discussed the matter and requested the President to invite each nation having a strong navy to appoint commissioners or delegates who, with their own naval statesmen, would consider the best plan to end competitive building of fighting ships. The President and members of the Cabinet were in hearty accord with this idea. Bryan of course strongly favored it in principle, but he had brought forward the draft of his peace treaties, providing that no nation would go to war without giving a nine-months period of discussion before a shot was fired. At that time the peace treaties, providing what Bryan called "cooling time," were regarded as a forward movement toward peace. Bryan argued that nations, like individuals, generally fought while their blood was up and that if time were given for their anger to subside, most of the causes for fighting would be adjusted by conciliation and arbitration, and this would go far toward ending war.

Wilson had approved the peace treaties and had made them a part of the New Freedom program. The world took kindly to Bryan's plan, and I strongly favored it. He now suggested and urged that I would defer asking for a naval conference to end competitive building until after his treaties had been sent to the various nations and had been acted upon. He believed that was the first step to take in the program looking to peace, which in the early days of Wilson's administration dominated the thought of the President and most of his Cabinet. Bryan's suggestion was concurred in by all of us, and it was agreed tentatively that my proposition should be held in abeyance until the Bryan treaties were ratified. This took some time. However, in what would in former days have been regarded as an incredibly short time, the Bryan treaties were ratified by almost every nation in the world. Bryan was elated, and all of us felt that a long step forward had been taken. However, there was a cloud in the sky, not then larger than a man's hand. Japan and Germany, while speaking in friendly terms about the treaties, were slow about taking them up, and as a matter of fact, when the World War broke, neither Germany nor Japan had ratified them.

With these two nations, more militaristic than any others, outside the organization of nations who pledged themselves not to go to war until after months of attempt to settle their differences by peaceful methods, it was seen that these two links in the chain weakened it very much. There were many Americans who believed that Japan was only looking for an opportunity to strike in the Philippines or in Hawaii, that it was building a great navy and strengthening its army for conflict with the United States, and that all Europe went to bed at night with a gun under its pillow feeling that Germany would precipitate a European war. When, therefore, these two nations dilly-dallied about ratifying the Bryan treaties—and as a matter of fact never did ratify them—it was regarded as something sinister and dangerous.

So far as Germany was concerned, when the war of 1914 broke out, people then understod why Germany had refused to bind itself to wait nine months or any other period of time before it should let its guns thunder in what proved to be the worst war the world had hitherto known. Inasmuch as the Bryan treaties had not been ratified by these two nations when Germany invaded Belgium, the time never came when my proposition of a conference of the navy building nations could be called. The World War put an end to that and many other fine dreams of the Wilson administration.

TO CALL A CONFERENCE

However, I never lost sight of the fact that as soon as the war was over, a naval conference of the nations should be called. Later on, when we had induced Congress, upon my recommendations made in 1915, to adopt a large naval construction program to be completed within three years—the biggest construction of naval vessels ever authorized by any nation in peace times—in coöperation with Representative Hensley of Missouri and other peace-loving men, there was incorporated in this mammoth appropriation bill a provision that at some suitable time, not later than the end of the war then in progress, the President should call a conference of the navy-building nations with a view to putting an end to competitive construction of fighting ships, with the further provision that if the keels had not been laid of any of the ships authorized in that bill, they should not be constructed. The thought was that we were building this large number of ships to give us strength upon the sea if needed, but if other nations would agree to cut down their program, the United States would not complete this large number of naval units. That peace resolution, in the heart of the biggest provision for naval construction ever known, gave it strength in Congress. The peace men believed it was the open door for reductions, and the Strong Navy people were for it because it was taking a long step toward that equality afloat which they believed was necessary for the United States Navy. This declaration in the Navy bill for a conference to reduce the strength of navies was the first official declaration of its kind. Later, after Wilson returned from Paris and was on his swing around the circle in the West urging the ratification of the Versailles Treaty, he referred to the fact that the authority for ending big navies and the spirit of that portion of the treaty was found in the Naval Appropriation bill of 1916, "the last place," he said, "where we would have looked for it."

GERMANY AND JAPAN

When Germany and Japan postponed consideration of the Bryan treaty—and postponement was a practical rejection—it is strange we did not sense the significance of it and see in Germany's refusal that it then entertained the intention to do, at some future time, what it did when, in the summer of 1914, it shocked the world by entering Belgium. Nor did we then envision the "Day of Infamy," when Japan secretly attacked Pearl Harbor on December 7, 1941.

XLIII

THE MERCHANT MARINE

WILSON CLEARLY UNDERSTOOD the place of the Merchant Marine in advancing the commerce of the country and as an auxiliary of the Navy in time of war. He was fully in sympathy with Mahan's warning years before, when that apostle of sea power warned: "the United States may have a rude awakening of those who have abandoned their share of the common birthplace of all the people—the sea." Mahan's creed was: "The security of military communication entails that of the nation's commerce," and, "A nation's sea-borne trade is the life blood of its power, the assurer of its greatness, the preserver of its comfort," and, "Commercial enterprise is never so secure, or so untrammeled as under its own flag." It was in the light of this doctrine that, after provision had been made for an increase of Naval strength and the revision of the tariff and the reform of the currency, Wilson called upon Congress for the creation of the United States Shipping Board to construct ships for carrying American goods to all parts of the world. There was bitter opposition. The big business interests wished, instead of the government's building and operating its own ships, that subsidies should be voted to private shipping companies.

Next to my zeal for strengthening the Navy and lifting agriculture into prosperity, my chief interest was to see the restoration of the almost vanished Merchant Marine. Most of our commerce was carried in foreign bottoms. Perhaps my interest was born of my knowledge that in the town of my birth, Washington, North Carolina, water-borne commerce had been carried in home-owned ships built in the State before the Civil War.

In 1913 the South was burdened with high freight rates. Most North Carolina products—cotton and tobacco—when sent abroad went in ships under foreign flags. The Republicans had let the Merchant Marine languish along with the Navy. I was happy therefore when Wilson declared in the campaign that it was ridiculous to build the Panama Canal and have "no ships to send through it." Perhaps the hardest fought of all the battles was that for a government-owned Merchant Marine. J. P. Morgan told McAdoo that "government's entrance into the field would be considered a menace." He wanted the government to give subsidies to private interests. Wilson opposed subsidies, saying: "They amount to this, that money taken from the taxpayers is given into private hands to be used for private profits without regard to the regulations of the service or the study of the interest of the public in general."

Wilson's foresight was never better illustrated than in fighting to secure a Merchant Marine in 1914. The Republicans, led by Root and Lodge, bitterly fought the shipping bill. It was while that conflict was occupying the Senate that Wilson went to Indianapolis to speak on Jackson Day. He had always been an admirer of Jackson, and in that speech he donned the militant armor of Old Hickory and made a fighting speech that breathed the spirit of the Hermitage. Referring to the filibustering of Republican Senators against the bill he said: "The Republican party is still a covert and refuge for those who want to consult their grandfathers about everything." The Senate justified Wilson's excoriation. It sat fifty-five hours on a stretch, one Senator holding the floor for thirteen hours. Seven Democratic Senators, led by Clark, of Arkansas, joined the Republicans to prevent action. "The members of that ill-omened coalition must bear the whole responsibility," Wilson said, "for infinite damage to the business of the United States. They have fastened the control of the selfish shipping interests on the country and the prospect is not a little sinister." Wilson girded up his loins for a great fight at the next session of Congress, when he won.

Secretary McAdoo, always resourceful, had originated the bill for the Merchant Marine. Some of his colleagues objected because they said the government ought not to go into business. He pointed out that water-shipping rates had gone up so high that a shipowner could pay for the cost of a ship in a few voyages. Even so, private capital could not be induced to build ships. The plan was a corporation which, though government-owned, would be operated like the Panama railroad, which was successfully operated by the War Department. President Wilson, who was to put his whole strength behind it, said in a Cabinet meeting that he knew it would be opposed by the big interests, who would denounce it as "socialistic."

"We will have a hard fight to get it through Congress," Wilson said. "We certainly shall," said McAdoo. "Well, then," said the President, "let's fight." He never dodged a fight for a good cause.

I suggested that instead of a Shipping Board, as a new agency, the construction of the ships be turned over to the Navy. "We have the best construction force for sea-craft in the world," I said, "and we have Navy Yards, more than are needed for building fighting ships, and the ships could be built quicker and better than by any newly created agency."

Senator Simmons, of North Carolina, who led for an American Merchant Marine, referring afterwards to the error in postponing the shipping bill, pointed out that if the bill had become a law when introduced in 1914, at the time of the Senate filibuster, the country would have saved millions of dollars. He said: "Ships could have been bought in the late summer of 1914 at forty dollars per ton, while two years later they could hardly be purchased for five times that amount. In 1914 we could have bought almost at our own figures hundreds of the interned vessels of Germany in America."

When the first measure had been filibustered to death, and before the next session of Congress, McAdoo said that Senators had shown such spleen against him, he believed the best thing to do was to create a Shipping Board which should have the Secretary of the Navy as chairman.

SECRETARY OF THE NAVY NAMED CHAIRMAN

The measure, redrafted, passed the House with the Secretary of the Navy as head of the Board. However, when it reached the Senate, there was objection to having any Cabinet officer on the Board—that would be making it subject to administration politics, opponents said. They declared what was needed was an independent board of experienced shippers. In those days, when there was no Big Navy building program, if the building of a Merchant Marine had been entrusted to the Navy it would have been a certain guarantee there would be no political angle.

In 1914 I had wanted the Navy to build the Merchant Ships. Eighteen months later, with Big Navy construction, I was glad to be relieved of the task. I thanked my lucky star that the Senate relieved the Navy of a difficult, almost impossible, job. The measure passed only seven months before we entered the war.

IT WAS DOUBLE-HEADED

There was a serious defect in the set-up. It provided a double-headed arrangement, and was organized with General George W. Goethals, who had won fame as the builder of the Panama Canal, as chairman of the Emergency Fleet Corporation, and William Denman as head of the Shipping Board. Denman was an able admiralty lawyer of California. Two better men, or two more strong-headed individualists, never lived. They were, under the terms of the act, compelled to coöperate and each was a soloist. When Theodore Roosevelt started to dig the Panama Canal, he wanted Goethals given the power to do it alone. Finding the law required him to appoint a board, he named as the other members only those who would agree to vote "Aye" on every proposition favored by Goethals. Naturally, Goethals wished a like free hand in shipbuilding. But Denman was no man to say "Aye" when his convictions were "No." From the beginning there was friction. Goethals did not care about the cost of the building of ships any more than he counted dollars when he was building the Panama Canal. He was honest, an able autocrat. Denman believed in strict supervision of expenditures, in competitive bidding and other sound business policies. The difference which widened the breach was in buying steel plates. Goethals made a contract to pay a certain figure, about 50 per cent higher than the Navy was paying for the same plates. Denman refused to sign on the dotted line until he could investigate. He called to see me and I showed him the price the Navy was paying. He went up in the air and said he would never agree to pay the steel corporation a higher price than they were charging the Navy. There were other sharp disagreements. It was a tragedy that two men were put in double harness who could pull only in single harness. Neither of them would yield an inch. It got so bad that Wilson had to request both of them to resign so that the work could go forward.

HURLEY DID A GREAT JOB

The President then appointed Edward F. Hurley, of Illniois, as the head of the Shipping Board. He was a successful business man of ability and driving power, and did as great a job as conditions would permit. A few days after he was appointed, Hurley came over to the Navy Department and said he needed my help.

"I will help you in any way in my power," I answered. He said he wished me to release Admiral F. R. Harris, Chief of the Bureau of Yards and Docks, so that he could be made head of the Emergency Fleet Corporation. My reply was: "I will stick to my promise to help, but before complying I must tell you that I think you would make a mistake to name Admiral Harris."

"I think you are wrong," he said. "He is the very man for the place."

"I know him better than you do," I said. "If you wish a man to build big dry docks there is no better man than Harris, but he knows nothing about building ships. You ought to have the best naval constructor in the country. I can let you have one, but Harris is not the man you need. If you insist, I will give him leave to go, but I strongly advise against his appointment to that place."

I had named Harris at the earnest solicitation of Senator Tillman and Assistant Secretary Roosevelt, and in fitness for that job had made no mistake. But he soon needed a hat several times the size of his head, and I foresaw that in an independent place he would not prove a success. However, nothing would do except that Hurley must have Harris, and he was named and sent over to Philadelphia to start important work. Within a week or two, my telephone rang. Hurley was on the other end of the line. His voice showed excitement. He wanted to know, if he came over right away, if he could see me. "Of course," I answered.

He was at white heat when he arrived. "You must take Harris back," he blurted out.

"What's the trouble?" I asked.

"My God!" he answered, "You had better ask, 'What is not the trouble with that man.'" He proceeded to enlighten me by saying that Harris had gone over to Philadelphia and without consultation rented a large office building at a fabulous rental, had named a personal press agent at a big salary, a secretary and others at outrageous salaries, and was running him crazy. "I cannot stand him a day longer," he said, as he concluded his long recital. "You must order him back to the Navy." I told him I would order him back to duty in the Navy, but that he could not come back as Chief of the Bureau because I had already offered the place to Admiral Parks. "But I will provide a good position for him to keep you from going crazy," I said.

That afternoon, debonair and confident as usual, Admiral Harris called. He proceeded to tell me that he had made a big mistake to go with Hurley. "He is impossible to work with and I am ready to return as Chief of the Bureau of Yards and Docks." He went pale when I told him that Admiral Parks was on his way from Honolulu to fill that position. Having offered it to him and he having accepted, I could not recall the appointment. He saw the hopelessness of it. I told him I would put him in charge of the work of the Norfolk Navy District, where he would have important duties. He was soon back and carrying on with vigor and ability—but minus a press agent.

SCHWAB ENTERS THE PICTURE

Sometime before we entered the war, I received a call from Charles M. Schwab, head of the Bethlehem Steel Company, and had come to know him pretty well after our run-in about the government Armor-Plate plant, which he had tried to defeat. He had been refused permission by the Council of National Defense of which I was a member—this before we entered the war—to use steel to build a large number of ships for the British. Like myself he carried no resentment and we had gotten along together famously. During a pleasant chat he told me that he had made more money than he needed and more than he wanted. "I never want to make another dollar in my life," he said. "The only thing I wish to do for the balance of my life is to serve my country and do it without reward." He was very earnest in this dedication of himself. He may have seen a suspicion of doubt in my eyes, for he asked, "Don't you believe me?" I was not quite sure that a money maker like Schwab didn't want "to make another dollar," but I answered that it was heartening to see men of his position willing to serve their country at home with their great ability, as patriotic boys were ready to do on the sea and on the land.

Soon thereafter, Hurley asked Schwab to become head of the Emergency Fleet Corporation, and he threw into the work an ability and enthusiasm which stimulated every worker from top to bottom to do his very best. He feasted and feted the men and women at Hog Island; he leased the biggest theatre in Philadelphia and gave them fine parties, of course at Uncle Sam's expense. He invited me to attend one and give a pep talk. It was a wonderful meeting gotten up by a remarkable man. Later experiences convinced me that he had deceived himself when he said that he never wished "to make another dollar."

ATTENDED BY A JINX

From the first it seemed that some jinx attended the Shipping Board. Some of the ablest and best men in America headed it and the Emergency Fleet Corporation for a time, but almost from the first there were jars within, and under some administrators there was waste of money. However, under whip and spur the Emergency Fleet Corporation built ships at record-breaking speed which were invaluable. I asked myself in March, 1933, when President Roosevelt wished me to become Chairman of the Shipping Board and work out plans for a better Merchant Marine, whether the fact that it had always been a jinx and had failed in the Harding-Coolidge-Hoover administrations, unconsciously influenced my declination of the position. The reason I gave the President, and it was the true reason, was that all independent boards ought to be administered under a member of the Cabinet and I recommended that it be placed under the Secretary of Commerce. He followed that course and it was administered under Secretary Roper until the exigencies of war caused change in policy. I do not believe there should be any independent bureau in Washington, but that all should be directed by a Cabinet officer and thus have a place in Cabinet councils. I found the independent agencies and bureaus and boards in the Wilson administration were as a rule too expensive and lacked cohesion with administration policies. When urged by Redfield to appoint a board for some particular service, Wilson declined, saying with a smile, "I will create no more boards. I find most of them are long, wooden, and narrow."

Part Five

RESIGNATIONS AND ELECTIONS

XLIV

"THE WEST IS THE HEART OF THE COUNTRY": ELECTION OF 1914

P OLITICS, which had taken second place while the New Freedom legislation was being enacted, most of it over Republican opposition, came to the fore in 1914.* The Republicans hoped that the tariff barons and their dupes, mad over tariff reductions; the financial interests, resentful over the Federal Reserve system; the shipping interests wishing subsidies, determined not to permit a government merchant marine; and other dissatisfied elements would enable them to elect a Congress that would undo the reform legislation. The Democratic slogan was: "WAR IN THE EAST! PEACE IN THE WEST! THANK GOD FOR WILSON!" It was a battle royal.

Wilson told the members of the Cabinet it was up to them to carry the accomplishments of the administration to the people. With Bryan speaking from coast to coast as the chief defender and with most of us and other liberals on the stump in October, every voter heard the record proclaimed and defended. The unprecedented majority in 1912 was reduced, the Democrats losing 63 seats in the House. They retained a majority of 27 in the House and held their ten majority in the Senate. There was no break in the Solid South. The losses were in the East where the moneyed interests were entrenched. The West stood with Wilson, presaging the even greater support they would give him when they insured his reëlection in 1916. Wilson's comment on the result was: "After all, the West is the heart of the country."

The result was a vote of confidence in the administration and approval of the New Freedom legislation. It was also a test of Wilson's popularity. Before the voting George Harvey, no friend of Wilson and a foe and bitter critic of most members of the Cabinet had said:

* The outbreak of war in Europe in August, 1914, is discussed later in other connections.

"The return of a Democratic majority, however greatly reduced, would signalize the most striking personal triumph of any President since Andrew Jackson overwhelmed the opposition in 1832. Now, as then, the issue is not a party but a personality."

BOSSES AND TOGAS

In one campaign Roger Sullivan was the Democratic nominee for Senator in Illinois. In the early part of the year, while I was enroute to Peoria, Sullivan joined me and asked what I thought of his becoming a candidate. I told him that while it was easy for a Republican machine politician to be elected, it would be wisest for him not to be a candidate. I had sincere regard for him born of his support of Wilson at Baltimore. But I had a hunch he could not win and so advised. However, tendered influential Republican support, he entered the race.

Bryan and other liberals took the stump against him, alleging that he had gotten rich by promoting policies desired by the utility companies. I was asked to go to Illinois to speak in his behalf. "Use your own judgment," was Wilson's answer when I asked his advice. I spoke in other states, not wishing to debate with Bryan when he was charging Sullivan with using his political position to enrich himself. I was never quite satisfied with my action and when the most reactionary of Republican reactionaries was elected I censured myself for not getting into the fray for Sullivan. He might—probably would not—have approved legislation clipping the wings of public service corporations, but on all other matters he would have been a strong supporter of the administration. He was a fellow member of the National Democratic Committee.

My belief that Democratic machine bosses could not win in elections was proved later in Indiana when Tom Taggart, after filling a short term by appointment in the Senate, was defeated in a vote by the people.

XLV

BRYAN'S RESIGNATION

THE FIRST BREAK in the Cabinet came on June 8, 1915, when Bryan tendered his resignation as Secretary of State. It created the greatest sensation in Washington since Blaine's resignation as Secretary of State in Harrison's Cabinet in order to become a candidate against his chief for the presidential nomination. I could feel its reverberations in the Minneapolis Convention when I was present as a reporter. Some writers thought Bryan was resigning for a like reason and was making ready to enter the contest for the nomination in 1916. Nothing was further from the truth.

On the afternoon before I knew of the resignation, Bryan sent me word he wished to ride out to my home with me, as Mrs. Bryan was receiving with my wife at an afternoon tea. I invited my friend, and Bryan's friend and supporter, the Honorable E. J. Justice, to accompany us. Bryan was wholly unlike himself and scarcely talked at all. He looked as if he had lost sleep. I knew he had been under great stress and worry over the exchange of notes with Germany—going through a Gethsemane. As he and Mrs. Bryan left our house, he asked me to come and take breakfast with him the following morning, saying, "I must see you early upon a most important matter."

When I arrived, Bryan, looking as if he had slept none the night before, said, "Read these letters," and handed me a copy of his letter of resignation and Wilson's letter of acceptance. It was like a bolt out of the blue. It struck me between the eyes. As I finished the reading, I said to him, "I do not think, in view of our long friendship, you ought to have taken this course without talking to me about it."

"My reason for not talking to you about it," he replied, "was that I felt impelled to take this course and I feared it might embarrass you. You have a great work to do here, and under no circumstances would I wish you to be involved in any action I am compelled to take. You must stay in the Cabinet. The President will need you. As for me, I cannot do otherwise."

BRYAN THOUGHT IT MEANT WAR

Bryan added, "I am convinced that the note as written will involve us in war with Germany.* It is a reversal of our established policy. It ignores the principle of the thirty treaties into which we have entered with thirty nations. It is the old system."

The die had been cast before I saw him. His resignation had been accepted. Argument was useless. His mind had come to the immovable conviction that duty to conscience compelled him to retire from the Cabinet. He had come into the Cabinet, not for the gratification of ambition for office, but solely in the furtherance of his desire to be in a place where his passion for peace might find implements wherewith to work.

FAITHFUL TO COVENANT

As I left him I recalled that two days before he entered the Cabinet he had spoken in Raleigh and had said: "There will be no war while I am Secretary of State." He had made the same pledge on a hundred platforms. I knew he regarded the pledge as in the nature of a holy covenant. Wilson and Bryan had prevented war with both Mexico and Japan when war clouds hovered. Now, if war must come with Germany—and he believed Wilson's policy could not avert it (and it did not, nothing could), he could not fail his conscience, or those who had followed him, by signing a demand that might bring war. I did not believe the note would inevitably lead to war. It was signed in July, 1915, and we were not at war with Germany until April, 1917—nearly two years. Many other things beside the note coöperated to bring us into the conflict. I believed then that Bryan should remain in the Cabinet. He and Wilson saw eye to eye in wishing peace. His successor was of quite a different mould. He wanted war but did not avow it at the time. Bryan could not have changed the policy of the government, but the State Department would not have tended toward the old Big Stick policy as it did in other years, and as it did when Lansing controlled its policy.

Bryan had negotiated treaties not to go to war until there had been "cooling time," and he thought that, though Germany and Japan

---

* Wilson had written the note to Germany, following the sinking of the *Lusitania* on May 7, 1915, in which Wilson demanded that Germany give up her "ruthless" submarine campaign, or else she would be held to strict accountability.

SECRETARY DANIELS AND HIS ADVISORY COUNCIL

Left to right, Major General George Barnett, USMC, Captain Wm. C. Watts, USN, Assistant Secretary Franklin D. Roosevelt, Rear Admirals S. McGowan, Robert S. Griffin, and D. W. Taylor, Vice Admiral William Shepherd Benson, Rear Admiral Earle, Commander Sparrow, Rear Admirals Charles W. Parks, Leigh C. Palmer, William C. Braisted. *Seated,* Secretary Daniels.

Upper left, Senator James A. Reed, who made a vigorous fight for the armor plate plant and routed Senator Boies Penrose (*right*), who championed the armor plate trust (both from Brown Brothers). *Below,* "Daniels Day" in Charleston, West Virginia. Breaking ground for the Government Armor Plate and Projectile plants, August 30, 1917. Governor McCorkle is seated. The Mayor and Secretary Daniels are standing. Mrs. Daniels is in rear seat.

were the only two important nations which had not signed these treaties, Germany had accepted "in principle," and he believed we should again offer her the opportunity to sign. Neither Wilson nor the Cabinet believed that Germany would enter into such treaty and if it should do so, did not think it would regard any treaty as more than a "scrap of paper."

BRYAN'S TRAVAIL

Bryan did not reach his decision to lay down office without travail. His wife, a real partner, lover, and wise counsellor, later told of his vigils—how "his sleep became broken, lying awake three and four hours at a time, tossing, jotting down memoranda." "He had signed the first note, he said, because it was the opening statement of our position, but the second note placed the power to declare war in another nation." She added:

"Saturday morning I saw something had to be done. He must get out of town for Sunday. I telephoned an old friend, Senator Blair Lee, asking if we might go to Silver Spring Saturday night after dinner and stay until Sunday afternoon. His response was quick and cordial. Mr. Bryan consented to go and twilight found us listening to the good-night song of birds. We retired early—were in bed eleven hours, of which Mr. Bryan slept four. The next morning Senator Lee took Mr. Bryan—more heavy-eyed than ever—out for a long walk. They were gone two hours and a half. He then took a nap of about an hour, ate dinner, and took another long walk. We hoped by this exercise to get him so weary physically that he would sleep. He gave Senator Lee his view upon the note, but did not tell him he thought of resigning. As we went home, in desperation I went to Dr. Kelly, who gave him a harmless powder to make him sleep. This I gave to him and he slept at last.

"On Monday Mr. Bryan went to the White House. His interview with the President lasted about an hour and was conducted with calmness and earnestness. Mr. Wilson would not yield a point nor would Mr. Bryan. That night the resignation was sent and accepted."

His understanding wife's story of these days of travail shows that Bryan was torn as truly to the depth of his being as was Martin Luther "when he set himself to find salvation." The German fasted and scourged himself in accordance with medieval ideas. Bryan's conflict was as terrible. It began with the first note to Europe. It continued until he had felt in his soul, as he resigned, "I cannot do otherwise."

WILSON'S ATTITUDE

Nobody in the Cabinet knew of Bryan's contemplated step except McAdoo, who tried to dissuade him. Bryan said, "I spoke to nobody about my resignation before offering it except McAdoo, and I talked with him about it because of his relation to the President." McAdoo told Bryan, "This will destroy you," to which Bryan replied, "I believe you are right; I think this will destroy me; but whether it does or not, I must do my duty according to my conscience, and if I am destroyed it is, after all, merely the sacrifice that one must make to serve God and his country."

Bryan would have remained in the Cabinet if Wilson had consented to shape the note to Germany in accordance with Bryan's views. But, there happened what always occurs when an irresistible force comes in conflict with an immovable object. The two Presbyterian elders could not surrender convictions. So they separated in mutual respect.

That afternoon, having an engagement with the President, I said to him that I wished I had known of Bryan's purpose, for I would have exhausted every effort to cause him to "abide in the ship."

"I wish to heaven you had," was his answer with the sincerity characteristic of him.

In no case did Wilson ever request a member of his Cabinet or other official to withdraw a resignation once submitted. I am sure he hated to lose a member of his official family, but he would ask none to remain who needed to be persuaded. He regarded Cabinet team-work as essential, and unless every member could in good conscience work with the others, it was better that the member not in accord should give place to one who was in hearty agreement upon vital policies.

EVENTS LEADING UP TO THE BREAK

For a week the Cabinet had met with the President often, sitting throughout the days in exhaustive consideration of the response that was to be made to Germany's unsatisfactory answer to the President's protests. Wilson had on the preceding Tuesday presented the first draft of the note. There had been changes. A word had been stricken out and another inserted. The President insisted upon holding Germany to "strictest accountability" and the recognition of the right of neutral citizens to traverse the seas on unarmed ships of whatever flag. Germany had stiffened unexpectedly, and the sternness of the President's note was thus fraught with the gravest possibilities.

On Saturday the meeting was brief, with the Cabinet in almost full agreement, barring the protest of Bryan, who gave no indication of his determination to leave the Cabinet.

Monday afternoon the Cabinet was again assembled. The finished note was presented to the members by the President. Bryan asked that he be allowed to take it home with him, and he left immediately, carrying the note in his hand. He was stormed by upwards of fifty reporters, but made his way through the throng, smiling broadly. He waved the note at them and shook his head. He had nothing to say. Later in the evening he returned the note to the President.

SEPARATION REGRETTED BY COLLEAGUES

When the Cabinet next assembled to consider the final draft of the note to Germany, the seat of the Secretary of State on the President's right was vacant. The President's face was grim and unsmiling, and he said as he took his seat: "Mr. Bryan has resigned as Secretary of State. The resignation was brought to me twenty minutes ago to become effective the moment this note is put on the cables to Germany. I have, with regret, accepted. Mr. Bryan feels a delicacy in attending this meeting."

To the majority of the members of the cabinet it was a complete surprise. Bryan had left the Cabinet meeting when it adjourned at six o'clock the preceding evening. He had insisted that the note be modified, but had given no intimation that his protest would go to the length of resignation. Unanimously the Cabinet suggested that he be asked to attend, and the President sent for him. He was affectionately greeted. All felt regret at the separation. At its conclusion most of the members accepted Bryan's invitation to lunch. In a private dining room heart opened to heart. To his colleagues Bryan unbosomed himself with deep feeling. Unable to suppress the emotion which almost shook his frame, he said in substance:

"Gentlemen: This is our last meeting together. I have valued our association and friendship. I have had to take the course I have chosen. The President has had one view. I have had a different one. I do not censure him for thinking and acting as he thinks best. I have had to act as I have thought best. I cannot go along with him in this note. I think it makes for war. The President still hopes for peace and I pray, as earnestly as he, that Germany may do nothing to aggravate further the situation. Because it is the duty of the patriot to support his government with all his heart in time of war, he has a right in time of peace to try to prevent war. I shall live up to a patriot's duty if war comes—until that time I shall do what I can to save my country from its horror.

"I believe that I can do more on the outside to prevent war than I can on the inside. I think I can help the President more on the outside. I can work to direct public opinion so it will not exert pressure for extreme action which the President does not want. We both want the same thing—peace."

Bryan's eyes were not the only ones dimmed with tears in that quiet room.

Impulsively and emotionally and sincerely Lane said: "You are the most real Christian I know," and others shared that sentiment.

Controlling himself after this expression of admiration by his old associate, Bryan added: "I must act according to my conscience. As I leave the Cabinet I go out in the dark, though I have many friends who would die for me. The President has the prestige and the power on his side."

BRYAN'S PUBLIC STATEMENT

Many asked, "What caused the resignation of Bryan from the Cabinet?" Here is his public statement made on the day he resigned, June 9, 1915:

"The two points on which we differ, each conscientious in his convictions, are: First, as to the suggestion of an investigation by an international commission, and, second, as to warning Americans against travelling on belligerent vessels."

He had said in his letter that "the prevention of war" was "the cause nearest my heart" and he believed the note Wilson had written to Germany would eventuate in war. Wilson believed he must

WILLIAM JENNINGS BRYAN

Secretary of State in the Wilson administration. In his hand he is holding one of the treaties of peace which were negotiated in his administration. From a painting by Irving R. Wiles, made while Bryan was Secretary of State. Portrait in State Department in Washington.

BRYAN'S CROWNING ACHIEVEMENT

Signing the first of thirty peace treaties, September 15, 1914. *Seated, left to right:* Mrs. William Jennings Bryan; Señor Don Juan Riaño Y Gayangos, Chamberlain to His Majesty the King of Spain, Ambassador E. and P.; Mr. J. J. Jusserand, of France, Ambassador E. and P.; William Jennings Bryan; Sir Cecil Arthur Spring-Rice, of Great Britain, Ambassador E. and P.; and Mr. Kai Fu Shah, of China, E. E. and M. P. *Standing:* Members of the Cabinet and other officials. Reproduced from *The Memoirs of William Jennings Bryan* by permission of the publisher, The John C. Winston Company.

assert the right of Americans to travel on the seas in their legitimate pursuits and that the killing of non-combatants by the U-boats could not be overlooked. If such policy led to war, he felt then as he said later in his war message:

"There is one choice we cannot make, we are incapable of making; we will not choose the path of submission and suffer the most sacred rights of our nation and our people to be ignored or violated. The wrongs against which we now array ourselves are no common wrongs: they cut to the very roots of human life.

In his letter of resignation Bryan said:

"Obedient to your sense of duty and actuated by the highest motives, you have prepared for transmission on to the German Government a note in which I cannot join without violating what I deem to be an obligation to my country, and the issue involved is of such moment that to remain a member of the Cabinet would be as unfair to you as it would be to the cause which is nearest my heart, namely, the prevention of war."

In a statement, given to the press the day after his resignation, Bryan explained his action more fully:

"My reason for resigning is clearly stated in my letter of resignation—namely, that I may employ as a private citizen the means which the President does not feel at liberty to employ. I honor him for doing what he believes to be right, and I am sure that he desires, as I do, to find a peaceful solution to the problem which has been created by the action of the submarines."

WHY WILSON ACCEPTED

The President was as frank in his letter accepting Mr. Bryan's resignation as the Secretary of State had been in tendering it. He accepted "only because you insist upon its acceptance," and did so "with a feeling of personal sorrow." He said he more than regretted the separation—"I deplore it." He declared, "Our objects are the same and we ought to pursue them together," and he added what is one of the finest expressions of friendship on record:

"Our two years of close association have been very delightful to me. Our judgments have accorded in practically every matter of official duty and of public policy until now; your support of the work and purposes of the Administration has been generous and loyal beyond praise; your devotion to the duties of your office and your eagerness to take advantage of every opportunity for service offered has been an example to the rest of us; you have earned our affectionate admiration and friendship. Even now we are not separated in the object we seek, but only in the method by which we seek it."

DID BRYAN EVER GIVE REAL REASON?

Washington, always skeptical of official statements, believed that other than the published reasons contributed to the resignation. Those who thought that Bryan would bring trouble to the administration and that he and Wilson would not team up, shook their heads and said, "I told you so." This, in spite of the fact that Wilson and Bryan had seen eye to eye on every measure of the New Freedom and had worked together with growing mutual esteem. Others said, "Bryan is going out to build his fences to run against Wilson next year." That was disproved in 1916 when Bryan gave Wilson enthusiastic support, and his speeches all over the West had a large part in giving the electoral vote to Wilson.

"Bryan is resentful because Wilson sent House abroad as his personal representative to contact the heads of European governments instead of depending on the State Department," was frequently whispered; but House had long been a friend of Bryan and had advised Bryan's appointment as Secretary of State—though it was believed he tried to ship Bryan off to the position of Ambassador to Russia. House was profuse in his protestations of friendship, and Bryan accepted these assurances at face value, though some of his friends doubted, and it was proved later that House joined others in trying to undermine Bryan.

The resignation of Bryan was more than a loss to Wilson. The President needed Bryan's devotion to peace and his noble patriotism. His successor had no consecration to peace or to democracy.

Leaving the Cabinet, Bryan set to work on the "outside" to "do more to prevent war than I can on the inside." He addressed large gatherings from New York to San Francisco, approving every attempt made by the administration to seek an understanding that would bring peace in Europe and keep his country out of war. Undoubtedly his zeal for peace was partly responsible for the refusal of the people to go into war as long as there was hope of doing so without the surrender of rights which the great majority of the country in those months held dearer than peace. When war was finally declared, though the saddest man in the world, Bryan wired Wilson volunteering his services in any capacity, adding: "The quickest way to peace is to go straight through supporting the Government in all it undertakes, no matter how long the war lasts or how much it costs."

XLVI

LANSING SUCCEEDS BRYAN

W HAT DO YOU THINK of our new Secretary of State?" was the question Postmaster General Burleson asked me on the morning of the announcement. I answered, "I do not like it. Lansing is a good international lawyer and a fine gentleman. He obtained nearly all his practice in the State Department and in service on government commissions from his Republican father-in-law, ex-Secretary of State Foster. He is wholly unknown in the country except as a son-in-law of Foster and a beneficiary of Republican favors. I suppose he is a Democrat by inheritance, but if he has ever turned his hand over to strengthen the party I never heard of it, and if all Democrats were of his type, Taft instead of Wilson would be President. His appointment will add no strength to the administration or the party. He lives in the District of Columbia and is unknown outside a small circle of Washington city lawyers."

"You are all wrong," replied Burleson. "Woodrow Wilson is going to be his own Secretary of State. Lansing is the very man he wants—a good lawyer, without outstanding personality, who will be able to carry on the regular duties of the office and be perfectly willing for the 'Old Man' to be the real Secretary of State."

None of the members of the Cabinet were consulted about Bryan's successor, but McAdoo had asked Houston to go with him to the White House to discuss Bryan's contemplated resignation. Here is Houston's account of the interview:

"The President asked us to think of a man for Bryan's successor, saying that he had canvassed the field and could not hit upon a satisfactory outside man. He said that Colonel House would be a good man, but that his health probably would not permit him to take the place and that his appointment would make Texas loom large. He remarked that Lansing would not do, that he was not a big enough man, did not have enough imagination, and would not sufficiently vigorously combat or question his views, and was lacking in initiative. I agreed with him and said that I thought Lansing was useful where he was but that he would be of no real assistance to him in the position of Secretary of State."

When later Houston read in the paper that Lansing had been selected, he said:

"Lansing will be the President's Private Secretary for Foreign Affairs. He will not be of much more assistance than he would have been as an expert in the Department, with the growing burdens. I do not see how the President can stand the strain. He will have to do all the thinking and planning. What a pity he could not get a man like Ex-Secretary Olney."

If Wilson had consulted his Cabinet, he would have found that most of them would have favored Newton Baker or Frank Polk.

DISCIPLE OF ROOT

When Wilson became President, Lansing, recognizing his own size, aspired to be Assistant Secretary of State. That official was the Social Secretary of the government, who sees that all the forms are properly complied with and nothing happens to mar the pleasure of visiting diplomats and other distinguished officials. Lansing was more than that, as he demonstrated in his wordy and disingenuous state papers. His promotion to Counsellor for the State Department came when John Bassett Moore resigned.

I had known of the objection to Lansing when he was appointed Counsellor. The charge was that he had been guilty of "improper conduct" in connection with "Ward-Chinese claim." When Bryan and Wilson talked over the charges, the President suggested that Root, who had been Secretary of State, be consulted. Root had recommended Lansing, who wrote thanking him (March 4, 1913) saying: "As to your personal interest in my behalf when the President had my name under consideration as Counsellor, you know how deeply I feel. It was an evidence of friendship which I shall never forget." In response to a letter from Lansing's father-in-law, John W. Foster, acquainting him with the charges, Root answered that Lansing's action was honorable and the charges did him injustice. Root undoubtedly spoke truly, for, however one might differ with Lansing, all who were associated with him regarded him as upright and honorable.

I had sensed that he was not in sympathy with Wilson's policies, but rather held to the old diplomacy that encouraged exploitation of small countries by American industrial captains. Later, his record proved this. When the Russian Mission was named, it was Lansing who first suggested the appointment of Root to head the Commission. I believed Lansing shared the Root-Foster Big Stick and Dollar Diplomacy policy, which had guided the State Department from the early days up to 1913 in most of the years except now and then when Andrew Jackson or Grover Cleveland or other militant executives were in the White House. The record of the State Department under Lansing justified my doubt of the wisdom of his appointment, for it showed that in almost every policy his mind ran along in harmony with that of J. Pierpont Morgan and others in Big Business. It was not that Lansing was told what to do. He was above that. He just naturally believed that the strong ought to rule. He was a disciple of Root. It followed that those newspapers which were the spokesmen of privilege approved Lansing, while they were critical of Wilson and Bryan.

WHY LANSING WAS NAMED

Upon the resignation of Bryan (June 9, 1915) the President authorized Robert Lansing, then Counsellor, to act as Secretary of State *ad interim* until a successor was appointed. Fourteen days later Lansing was named. He promptly signed the note Bryan believed would be a long step toward involving the United States in the World War. Lansing had no hesitation and had no such feeling about possible participation in war as dominated his predecessor. "The President told me," said Lansing afterwards, "that he appointed me because he had become convinced by our intercourse that we were of the same mind concerning international matters." Wilson was to ascertain later, particularly in Paris, that Lansing's mind ran along with the old diplomatic practices foreign to Wilson's hostility to the Big Stick and Dollar Diplomacy, which Lansing in some instances sought to restore.

In the early days as Secretary of State Lansing wrote notes and changed them at Wilson's direction until his colleagues thought for a time that their minds ran together. He seemed eager to follow Wilson's ideas and to do so with gladness. In all Cabinet meetings he was so deferential to the President's policies that none of his colleagues regarded him as holding other views. With respect to the notes on the Declaration of London, the insistence that Britain should not infringe on American rights on the sea, and like matters which were pressed vigorously in notes to England, it was not known until much later that the most vigorous notes demanding that Britain refrain from interfering with our shipments to neutral countries were written by the forthright and able Texan, Cone Johnson, Solicitor of the State Department. In all the Cabinet discussions over the Orders in Council and the notes to Britain, Lansing, after reading the prepared note, would lapse into silence while other members debated the matter. When he answered questions, he upheld the vigorous demands on Britain in the written note. To most of us his arguments for the preservation of sea-borne commerce seemed genuine. His colleagues at first thought he was giving expression to his sincere convictions.

WARLIKE NOTE NOT APPROVED

When the *Sussex* was sunk in March, 1916, there was a long discussion in the Cabinet on April 4 over the course to pursue. Lansing declared that the time had come "to quit writing notes" and "for action." There was a difference of opinion in the Cabinet, the President not being as ready for war as Lansing and some others. The warlike note drawn up by Lansing was not sent, but a somewhat modified note was approved. It gave notice to Germany that "unless the Imperial German Government should now immediately declare its intention to abandon its present practice of submarine warfare and return to a scrupulous observance of the practice clearly prescribed by the law of nations, the Government of the United States can have no choice but to sever diplomatic relations with the German government altogether." Lansing wanted to close the door at once. Considering the previous vigorous notes to Britain over freedom of the seas and defense of neutrality and against entrance into the war and trying to avert it, I could not then reconcile Lansing's belligerency with his previous attitude.

The position of the President in keeping the door open was approved by the Cabinet. I took the ground that, aside from other questions, if Wilson brought on war with Germany except after exhausting every possible means to avert it, the country would rise up against him in the 1916 election.

LANSING WANTED WAR

Lansing's opinion was that war with Germany, declared after the *Sussex* sinking, would insure Wilson's election. Later he wrote: "If this country had been at war with Germany when the ballots were cast in 1916, President Wilson would have been overwhelmingly elected." The facts refute this, for it is undoubtedly true that the situation behind the slogan "he kept us out of war" was largely responsible for the 1916 victory.

Before his warlike expression at the time of the *Sussex* note, Lansing, according to a memorandum dated July 11, 1915, published after his death, in an "Outline of Policies" said he was shaping things to bring the country into war on Britain's side, adding: "I have come to this conviction with the greatest reluctance and with an earnest desire to avoid it."

REAL POSITION SUBMERGED IN VERBOSITY

It was not until the publication of *War Memoirs of Robert Lansing* printed after his death, that his colleagues learned that from the first of the notes he prepared before the United States entered the war, Lansing was pro-British while Wilson disapproved the course of Page and House in following the lead of Lord Grey rather than the President of the United States. In that book, printed in 1935, Lansing makes known his hitherto unrevealed attitude saying:

"I did all I could to prolong the disputes [with Great Britain] by preparing, or having prepared, long and detailed replies and introducing technical and controversial matters, in the hope that before the extended exchange of arguments came to an end something would happen to change the current of American public opinion or to make the American people perceive that German absolutism was a menace to their liberties and to democratic institutions everywhere."

Again he said:

"In dealing with the British Government there was always in my mind the conviction that we would ultimately become an ally of Great Britain and that it would not do, therefore, to let our controversies reach a point where diplomatic controversies give place to action. . . ."

"Short and emphatic notes were dangerous. Everything was submerged in verbosity.... It was done with a deliberate purpose. It insured continuance of controversies and left questions unsettled, which was necessary in order to leave this country free to act and even act illegally when it entered the war."

As Lansing's words show, this "was done with deliberate purpose" and continued in the hope that "German action," ruthless submarine warfare, would justify the United States' going into war with the allies.

BRYAN AND LANSING CONTRASTED

The two heads of the State Department were as unlike as two men could be. Bryan was a politician who believed in the people, a statesman whose vision and advocacy made more changes in the Constitution than had been incorporated since Reconstruction, an eloquent orator, a crusader for righteousness and justice for the underprivileged and an apostle of peace. He came to the office with no more experience in diplomacy than Daniel Webster or Henry Clay. He was not a trained international lawyer and was not versed in protocol and the like. He had a passion for peace and secured treaties with thirty nations not to go to war without "cooling time." He was happiest in dealing with the problems involved in the reorganization of the Republic of China, in preventing war with Japan, and in working for cordial relations with the Pan-American States, with recognition of their rights and without sending troops into weak nations to help American exploiters. He was frank and open, and he loved companionship and discourse with his fellows.

Lansing was trained to the law, an authority on international law, a devotee of tradition, technique, and precedents. He was capable, industrious, meticulous, metallic, and mousy. His personal and official integrity were above reproach. He had the point of view of the old-time career diplomat. Never taking part in politics, he looked from afar upon the great struggles on tariff and currency. He never went into the arena to venture all for a cause. If left to him, we would have had war with Mexico and continued the Big Stick Policy, but he would have countenanced no act contrary to old-fashioned diplomatic ethics. When he began as a subordinate, Wilson regarded him as an able official, skilled in drafting diplomatic notes to carry out the policies of the chief executive. Lansing grew to think himself a great statesman and diplomat. At Paris, to the surprise and distress of Wilson, he sought to wreck Wilson's League of Nations, which he knew to be the heart's desire of his chief, although Wilson had lifted him out of obscurity and trusted and leaned upon him.

And both were Presbyterian elders whose private lives were above reproach.

PAGE THOUGHT LANSING ANTI-BRITISH

Not only did Lansing conceal his true feeling from the President and his Cabinet colleagues and the American people in 1915-16 but Ambassador Page at London, who was pro-British when Wilson and the American people were neutral, regarded the notes signed "Lansing" as calculated to prevent coöperation between the two English-speaking nations. At that time the notes to Britain expressed the resentment of the great body of the American people because our cotton, intended for neutral countries, was taken into British ports. Southern Senators pressed for vigorous protests. On the other side of the ocean and wishing the United States to get into the war, Page was not in harmony with the policy of his government. He voiced his deep feeling in a letter he wrote to the President on October 15, 1914, completely taking the British side. He said:

> "The present controversy [over American rights to freedom of the seas] seems here, where we are all close to the struggle, academic. . . . I recommend most earnestly that we shall substantially accept the new Order in Council, or acquiesce in it, and reserve whatever rights we have. I recommend prompt information be sent to the British Government of such action. I should like to inform Grey that this is our decision."

In the course of letters to House about that time, Page was very critical of Lansing. In a letter to House, October 22, 1914, Page said:

> "Lansing's method is the trouble. He hates Great Britain to start with, as if she were a criminal and an opponent. That's the best way I know to cause trouble to American shipping and to bring back the good old days of mutual hatred and distrust for a generation or two. If that isn't playing into the hands of the Germans, what would be? And where's the 'neutrality' of this kind of action? . . . If Lansing again brings up the Declara-

tion of London—after four flat rejections—I shall resign. I will not be the instrument of a perfectly gratuitous and ineffective insult to this patient and fair and friendly government and people who have done us so many kindnesses and never an injury but Carden, and who sincerely try now to meet our wishes. It would be too asinine an act ever to merit forgiveness or ever to be forgotten. It would grieve Sir Edward more than anything except this war. It would knock the management of foreign affairs by this administration into the region of sheer idiocy. I'm afraid any peace talk from us, as it is, would merely be whistling down the wind.... If Lansing isn't stopped we've needlessly thrown away our great chance to be of some service to this world gone mad. Why doesn't the President see Spring-Rice? Why don't you take him to see him?"

In his *Life and Letters of Walter Hines Page*, Hendrick voices Page's appraisement of Lansing,

"His methods were tactless, the phrasing of his notes lacked deftness and courtesy, his literary style was crude and irritating; but Mr. Lansing was not anti-British, he was not pro-German; he was nothing more nor less than a lawyer. The protection of American rights at sea was to him simply a 'case' in which he had been retained as counsel for the plaintiff. It was his duty to scan the law-books, to look up the precedents, to examine facts, and to prepare briefs that would be unassailable from a technical standpoint. To Mr. Lansing the European conflict was the opportunity of a life-time. He had spent thirty years studying the intricate problems that now became his daily companions. His mind revelled in such minute details as ultimate destination, the continuous voyage as applied to conditional contraband, the searching of cargoes on the high seas, belligerent trading through neutral ports, war zones, orders in council, and all the other jargon of maritime rights in time of war. These topics engrossed him as completely as the extension of democracy and the significance of British-American cooperation engrossed all the thoughts of Page and Grey."

BRITISH AMBASSADOR CONFUSED

Page was not the only Ambassador who accepted Lansing's attitude on the basis of his written notes. For a time Britain's Ambassador Spring-Rice had a rather poor opinion, as shown by the following, which he wrote to Stephen Gwyn:

"Mr. Lansing, the counsellor, is a lawyer accustomed to conduct matters of smaller importance like claims commissions. He finds himself suddenly in charge at a moment when very much may hinge on his personal action. You will see the difficulty of negotiating with a subordinate who has the lawyer's instinct to make good his case."

And yet a little later on, we find Lansing, after writing a severe note, conferring with Spring-Rice about modifying it so that Britain would understand it was a mere "slap on the wrist" and not intended to be accepted seriously.

XLVII

GARRISON RESIGNS AND IS SUCCEEDED
BY BAKER

THE SECOND CHANGE in the Cabinet came with the resignation of
Secretary of War Garrison, in January, 1916. He virtually gave
an ultimatum to the President when he demanded that the House
Military Committee enact measures with reference to the Army
which the committee had declared they would never accept. From
the first Garrison felt disposed to accept fully and press the views
of his chief of staff and boards composed of high ranking officers.
He told me that as civilian secretaries we should defer to the views
of our military advisers. "On technical questions, yes," I replied.
"On policies, no." He opposed the President's views when the Army
and Navy board wished to send ships and troops to the Far East
during the California trouble over ownership of land by the Japanese. He was wholly out of sympathy with Wilson in his Mexican
policy. He did not favor Philippine independence. He would have
taken Mexico or recognized Huerta. He was for a great standing
Army. And he was forthright and determined in his position. He
had no spirit of compromise. When there came an impasse between
him and the House Military Committee, he called on Wilson to
force the Congress to adopt the War Department's views. Wilson
told him: "I do not share your opinion that the members of the
House who are charged with the duty of dealing with military
affairs are ignorant of them or of the military necessities of the
nation."

Garrison pressed the program of the Army board. He was insistent that the House members should be spanked and made to
accept the project to increase the regular Army to 142,000 men and
organize a new "contingent Army" of 400,000 men. Wilson wished
to seek accord with Congress. When he declined to have a conflict with Congress and "sign here" on Garrison's proposal, Garrison resigned in a letter which pleased the militarists. Wilson
accepted it. At the same time Henry Breckinridge wrote a "Me too"

letter and resigned as Assistant Secretary. These resignations created a sensation, coming with such suddenness that they astonished the people.

Garrison and I were billed to speak at a patriotic gathering that afternoon. I had spoken and the company waited in vain for Garrison. When he did not come, the chairman of the meeting telephoned to the War Department. The news came that Garrison had resigned and would not speak. The meeting broke up as if a bomb had exploded. That night the Vice President and others were dining at my home, and we sent out to buy an "extra" and for the first time learned his reasons. Nothing else was talked about for days. The morning after the resignation I met Ollie James, Senator from Kentucky.

"Have you heard the sad news about Henry Breckinridge?" he asked. I had not.

"He is suffering from a terrible cold. It was caused by the fact that he hung his head out the window all night expecting to hear the newsboys shout 'Henry Breckinridge has resigned as Assistant Secretary of War and the Government is in peril.'"

Breckinridge became a severe critic of Wilson and was quoted by Lodge against Wilson in their sharp differences. Our friendly relations were unchanged. My wife's brother, Ensign Worth Bagley, who was killed at Cárdenas, and Breckinridge's brother, Ensign Cabell Breckinridge, who lost his life in a gale in the Caribbean just before the war with Spain, were roommates and devoted friends. That friendship extended to both families.

SCANDAL IN CABINET

General Hugh L. Scott, Chief of Staff, who was greatly admired and liked by President Wilson, succeeded to the administration of the War Department. His wife was an equal partner. One day before Garrison's successor was appointed, at a meeting of the Cabinet ladies, Mrs. Scott whispered: "Ladies, have you heard of the latest scandal in Cabinet circles?"

They all pricked up their ears and asked particulars of the scandal. Even political leaders and their wives listen to gossip. "The wife of one member of the Cabinet," she said, "is living with three men and it is terrible." There was a general laugh when she said she was living with the Secretary of War, the Assistant Secretary of

War, and the Chief of Staff of the Army, for her husband filled all three positions until Newton D. Baker was appointed Secretary of War.

AN INDIVIDUALIST

Garrison went out of office with the support of the military forces, that portion of the press most critical of the President, and a large sector of the American people, who, believing we could not keep out of the war, pressed for the immediate formation of a great Army. When we did enter the war less than a year later, they were confirmed in their opinion that Garrison was right, and he was always confident that his recommendations were wise. In fact, he had a certain engaging sincerity about him that gave him strength. His attitude about any matter on which he had formed an opinion was: "I am glad if anybody can convince me I am wrong, but I am damn sure nobody lives that can do it." He said of himself once, showing how well he understood his limitations, "I am an individualist and am not cut out for coöperative effort. I let you go your way and I will go my way." He simply could not coöperate and did not try. He reached conclusions quickly when he had examined the evidence, for he had a nimble and scintillating mind. When he had reached a conclusion—it was generally right, but sometimes wrong—nothing could budge him from his position. He loved to argue and discuss hypothetical cases, and often he wearied the President in Cabinet meetings by his legalistic arguments. He loved the clash of mind. Except when in the mood, Wilson was not fond of talking. He never liked debating. He liked to hear the views of Cabinet members, but long arguments were not to his liking. They irked him. On the contrary, argument was Garrison's delight. Sometimes, with cool courtesy, the President would change the subject when Garrison was just getting ready for an enjoyable mental joust. This often got on the President's nerves. Moreover, Garrison had no sympathy with the President's idealistic and humanitarian views. He became a quick convert to Army opinion and out-Wooded Wood on militaristic beliefs. He had long been on the bench and had taken delight both in the clashing of wit between the lawyers and in his ability to render a quick decision when they had concluded. He regarded the humanities that meant so much to Wilson and Bryan as meaningless. He was what Wilson called a "legalist" who believed in the old order in government and in economics. As clean as a hound's tooth, honest, frank, outspoken, he was cut out for a judge, and it irked him to be compelled to deal with Congressmen and to make concessions in policies that he believed were right. I had many "run-ins" with him, for I did not think an Admiral or General was always right, and, except on technical subjects, did not always accept their recommendations. Garrison's logic was in substance: "They have given their life to the study of war and preparation for war. I have given mine to the study and administration of law. Every man to his own profession. I will follow my military advisers' recommendations and I will interpret the law." Upon almost every subject that came before the Cabinet he liked to be heard, and often he would take up two-thirds of the time of the discussion at a meeting of the Cabinet.

Garrison laid down his portfolio as quietly as he had assumed it and enjoyed a large practice until a stroke compelled his retirement. When his deep conviction put him in disagreement with the President, he recognized the right of his chief to govern. He therefore, in an able presentation of his views, which did not convince the President, said he must resign so as not to cause "the slightest embarrassment." This was "a great surprise to Wilson," who said "the whole matter is under debate and all the influences that work for clarity and for agreement ought to be available." Garrison was never heard to comment upon Wilson's administration. He set a good example of retiring, when he retired with dignity and grace.

After he was partially paralyzed and cared for by a nurse, my wife, a dear friend of Mrs. Garrison, and I spent some days with him in Florida. He was the same delightful gentleman, full of stories and anecdotes, with affection for his old colleagues and expressions of admiration for our old chief. If I could possess what Wilson critically called a "legalistic mind," I would wish one as clear and honest as that possessed by my dear friend, Lindley Garrison. If I could be a conservative, which God forbid, I would like to be one like forthright and honest Garrison.

BAKER SUCCEEDS GARRISON

The appointment of Newton D. Baker as Secretary of War to succeed Garrison was known by me before the position had been tendered him by the President. On March 5, 1916, the President sent

Upper left, Lindley Garrison, Secretary of War in Wilson's Cabinet until he resigned in 1916. *Upper right,* Newton D. Baker who succeeded Garrison as Secretary of War. *Lower left,* Cordell Hull, author of Federal income tax law of 1913 and of Federal estate and inheritance tax law of 1916, who served nearly twenty years on the House Ways and Means Committee (Harris & Ewing). *Lower right,* Robert Lansing, Counselor for State Department who succeeded Bryan as Secretary of State.

NAVY CONSULTING BOARD IN THE OFFICE OF THE
SECRETARY OF THE NAVY

In the group are Secretary Josephus Daniels, Assistant Secretary Franklin D. Roosevelt, Thomas A. Edison, President of the Navy Consulting Board, William L.
Saunders, Chairman, Admiral W. S. Benson, Chief of Operations, and other members
of the Navy Consulting Board and the Chiefs of Divisions of the Navy Department.

TRANSMITTING THE FIRST NAVAL ORDER EVER SENT BY
WIRELESS TELEPHONE, MAY 16, 1916

The group at the desk of the Secretary of the Navy, taken in the Navy Department,
are, *left to right,* J. J. Carty, Mr. Sherardi, Mr. Porter, Mr. Stevens, Secretary
Daniels, Mr. Buehler, Mr. U. N. Bethell, Mr. Kingsbury, Mr. F. H. Bethell.

me a code message from the *Mayflower* asking me to send, in Navy code, the following telegram:

Washington, D. C.
March 5, 1916

Honorable Newton D. Baker
Cleveland
Ohio

Would you accept Secretaryship of War? Earnestly hope that you can see your way to do so. It would greatly strengthen my hand.

(signed)   w. w.

BAKER SUCCEEDS GARRISON

Ever since I had been thrilled by Baker's matchless eloquence in the Baltimore Convention, I had hoped for closer association with him. I regretted that his obligations as Mayor of Cleveland had prevented his acceptance of the Secretaryship of the Interior in the original Wilson Cabinet and was glad that he was now being offered the War Secretaryship. I sent him a telegram in the open which only he would understand. I wired:

"My wife and I and her sister, Belle, send love. We hope to see you and Mrs. Baker in Washington very soon for a long stay."

Mrs. Baker and my wife's sister, Belle, had been friends and classmates at Wilson College in Pennsylvania, and early in the administration Baker and his wife had come to Washington as our guests at the first Cabinet Dinner in honor of the President.

Baker had been among the earliest supporters of Wilson for President, and their minds ran very much along the same channels. Intellectually they were of the same mould, thinking clearly and writing with a beauty and force all their own. He and Garrison were as unlike as two honest, upstanding men could be. Both were able lawyers. Garrison had served on the bench but had never been in active politics. He was, as Wilson said, "legalistic" and paid homage to precedent and tradition. Baker, like Wilson, believed that the law was a living thing and that it should be interpreted in the light of meeting the economic needs of a changing world. Garrison would ask, "What has been decided?" Baker would ask, "What should be the decision in the light of the public welfare?"

MILITANT PROGRESSIVE

Baker had come up in the Tom Johnson school, a disciple and friend of that great early militant progressive, who blazed the way for many reforms as Mayor of Cleveland and member of Congress. Succeeding Johnson as Mayor, he carried on with ability but without the dynamic force of Johnson. In those days, Cleveland set the pace for a new type of city government, free from the domination of city bosses in league with public service corporation financiers.

CLOSE TO WILSON

Baker had been heralded as a pacifist and he was as great a lover of peace as Wilson, both being diligent in preparedness if war should come. He had a passion for peace. In all the months after he came into the Cabinet, when against heavy odds Wilson was maintaining neutrality, he had no stronger supporter than Baker. Later, in the Cabinet, when McAdoo and Lane were pressing for entry into the war against Germany, Baker shared Wilson's determination to stay out of the war as long as it could be done honorably.

Wilson often designated Baker to be spokesman at important gatherings and conventions. I recall that at the National Democratic Convention in St. Louis in 1916, Baker had taken out with him the President's draft of planks in the platform and was in frequent touch with the White House to keep Wilson advised. He had a hand in drafting that platform and in keeping out of it declarations which he and Wilson and the rest of us thought might not make the proper appeal to the electorate.

CLOSE COMRADES

As the war clouds gathered, my association with Baker became closer and more intimate. Together we broke down the barriers that very often denied that perfect coördination between the two military branches of the service which ought always to exist, and which unfortunately did not exist at Pearl Harbor in 1941.

At one time, when I suggested to Garrison a policy of coöperation between the Army and Navy that would be economical and strengthen the national defense, Garrison, who prided himself on not being influenced by the thought or action of others, answered my suggestion of united effort by saying, "I don't care a damn about the Navy and you don't care a damn about the Army. You run your machine and I'll run mine." The attitude of Baker was as different as possible. He and I were yoke fellows in everything and stimulated the perfect working together of the Army and Navy, which made them invincible in the World War. I recall that early in the war I told Baker that we had a regiment of Marines organized, armed and fully equipped ready to go to the battle fields of Europe immediately. There was no enthusiasm among the Army officers for incorporating the Marines into the Army as I suggested. Baker was quick to say that he would welcome them and made provision so that they became an integral part of the Second Division, which won glory in France.

When bitter critics assailed Baker and tried to make the people believe that his pacifism endangered military strength, Wilson wrote of Baker, "He is one of the most genuine and gifted men I know, and I am sure that the better he is known the more he will be trusted, loved, and admired."

XLVIII

WILSON'S SECOND MARRIAGE DOES NOT
DEFEAT HIM

O<small>NE AFTERNOON</small> in the early fall of 1915, Albert Burleson, Post-master General and Political Generalissimo of the Wilson administration, called at the Navy Department by appointment to discuss what he had said over the telephone was "a very important matter." He waited until after 4:30, when all the clerks had gone home, so that the conversation or conference (everything in Washington is a "conference") would be both secret and undisturbed.

"What do you think," my colleague began, "of the gossip that the President is deeply interested in Mrs. Galt?"

I told him there was no need for surmise, and added that in my judgment, before Christmas "we will have another Boss."

"Are you certain of it?" he asked.

"Just as certain as that you are sitting in that chair. No, nobody has told me anything. In this matter I am not in the President's confidence. He has not asked my advice or consent or so much as intimated that he contemplates taking such a course. But the sails are set, and I predict that by New Year's Day Mrs. Edith Galt will change her name to Mrs. Woodrow Wilson."

"It is exactly because I feared such might be in contemplation that I have come to see you," Burleson said.

"Why to see me?" I asked.

He then told me of how scores, yes, hundreds of prominent Democrats all over the country had been coming to see him and writing him letters, and they all believed that victory the next year was impossible if the President remarried before the election. He gave the names of Senators, members of the House of Representatives, members of the national committee, chairmen of State committees, influential editors whose support was essential to secure victory, and said: "It is unanimous, if the President remarries before November, 1916, we might as well give up the fight right now."

I ventured to suggest that it was not as bad as that, agreeing that in a close election the effect might be injurious, seeing the sentiment was as strong as he had pictured it. "Something should be done," he declared, "to secure postponement." He was in the depths. "What do you suggest?" I asked him.

"That is exactly what I have come to see you about," he said. "A few days ago," he continued, "in your absence from the city, we had a little conference about the matter." He told who was in the conference—pretty big men in the Democratic party, they were, and influential, too. "We unanimously agreed," he said, "that someone should go to the President, lay the whole matter before him, tell him it is the unanimous view that remarriage before the election would result in his defeat. We also agreed it should be borne in on him that not only is the success of his party at stake, but that a Republican victory would result in the repeal of his splendid measures and shut the door in the face of other measures on which his heart is set."

I saw there was danger to victory in the step which I was sure the President contemplated, and said so. My colleague went on: "The women vote in many States. We cannot hope to win without their support. They are coming our way. They believe in Wilson's human and humane policies. I believe we have a chance of getting a great preponderance of their votes. They are not tied to party as the men are. We should do nothing to check the movement of the votes of women to Wilson. The suggestion of the President's remarriage has already threatened to cost him their support. If he remarries, we will lose nearly all of it. That spells defeat."

Then came the shock of my life. Burleson had been moving to his dénouement, and the climax came when he said: "At the conference we all decided that you were the man to go to see the President, acquaint him with the situation and urge him to think of the party's success and not to jeopardize victory for next year."

As soon as I could catch my breath I quietly and with what calmness I could summon, inquired why I had been honored with the carrying out of this delicate mission. Only I don't think I said "honored." But I concealed my real feeling, knowing that the gentleman who had called was my friend. If there had not been abundant proof of his friendship, I should have been inclined to doubt it. His devotion to the party and his belief that the President was the one hope of success alone had animated him. "We discussed at some length," he went on to say, "the question of who was the best man to go to see the President and decided upon you because we know that his relations with you are those of warm friendship as well as of official ties, and" (he praised me too highly) "you have the tact to do it in the best way." And he added, "Your wife and Mrs. Ellen Wilson, both staunch Presbyterians, are closer than the wives of any other Cabinet officers."

It is not necessary to quote the words I employed in declining the proffered distinction of being Minister Plenipotentiary and Ambassador Extraordinary to the President of the United States. Very few offices have come my way. None with such high title and confidential duties had before been offered. Before giving a reply to the tender of the place of honor, I firmly applied my hands to be certain I was safe in the chair set apart for the Secretary of the Navy. That job was secure. I never did believe in one man's having too many offices or titles. Confidentially, just "between us girls," I had never aspired to so exalted a place as Secretary of the Navy. Having been called to that by President Wilson I did not feel inclined to exchange it for the difficult and, perhaps, dangerous high and exalted position of Minister Plentipotentiary and Envoy Extraordinary to the Court of Cupid on a mission in which neither my heart nor my head was enlisted and in the performance of which my official head might suffer decapitation.

Many times in my life I have rushed in where "angels fear to tread" to serve a friend or a cause. But that day, and only that day (was I like Caesar?) when the ambassadorship was thrice presented to me on the Lupercal, I thrice declined to climb "where fame's proud temple shines afar"—or didn't. Wilson was not warned.

They were married before Christmas and two things followed: (1) Wilson was reëlected, proving that political prognosticators are not always right; and (2) they lived happily together and Mrs. Wilson's charm and sound wisdom made her greatly beloved and admired.

Mrs. Wilson undoubtedly sensed what Burleson feared, and in the early days at Cornish (1915) she set herself against a wedding before the election. If I had carried to her Burleson's message, "Wait until after the election," at that time, it would have accorded with her opinion. But an appeal for postponement would have found no echo in Wilson's heart. He would probably have shown me the gate.

Wilson's need of love and companionship soon made her realize that she "could and would go to the end of the world with or for him." When he told her in the fall of 1915 that he did not have the right to ask her to "share the load that is almost breaking my back," she could resist no longer. She put her arms around his neck (right in the automobile in Rock Creek Park, with the secret service man and the chauffeur in the front seat), and said, "Well, if you won't ask me, I will volunteer, and be ready to be mustered in as soon as can be." In those war days, even lovers used military terms. The secret service man and the chauffeur politely kept their eyes on the Washington monument, which loomed in the distance. There is no record that the President used the selective draft—not then a law—but undoubtedly the spirit of the draft was invoked. That high day when love lighted the way was September 3, 1915. Three months later they were married.

Instead of the marriage's affecting the election unfavorably, there was proof once more that all the world loves a lover. In the months before the election, Edith Bolling Wilson gave cheer to the White House, and the American people learned her poise and charm and wisdom. When the people went to the polls they cast a ballot for Wilson to remain President and for Edith Bolling to continue as his partner and strength and mentor. The "volunteer" proved a noble soldier in the days before the war clouds broke, a brave comrade in war, a wise counsellor in difficult days, and a ministering angel when illness placed the great casualty of the war out of commission.

Burleson and I and all the rest of the politicians who had been tempted to advise where advice is never wanted, lived to be thankful that the people were wiser than the politicians, and that Woodrow Wilson's life was blessed with a strong love that strengthened him and gave radiance to his life to the last.

XLIX

THE WOMAN-SUFFRAGISTS BOMBARD WILSON

FOR MANY YEARS, even before I entered the Wilson cabinet, I believed in woman suffrage. President Wilson once asked me why I was so strong for giving women the ballot "I have two reasons that are convincing," I replied. "What are they?" he asked. "My mother and my wife," I said. "The first had the highest wisdom and soundest judgment of any inhabitant in the town where she lived and the most influence when she chose to exert it, and you know my wife and know how well qualified she is." I added, "Perhaps I am influenced by Emerson's advice: "Attach yourself to an unpopular righteous cause."

That conversation took place shortly before the Democratic National Convention in 1916 when the President was renominated. Wilson was still standing "with reluctant feet." He had suggested a platform declaration that looked to action by the States. I pointed out that the States already could act and some of them had granted suffrage to the women, and that it should be uniform in all the States. He was slow to favor suffrage and he dictated the plank in 1916 which read:

"We recommend the extension of the franchise to the women of the country by the States upon the same terms as to men."

Even that moderate declaration called for the vigorous denunciation of Governor Ferguson, of Texas, who wished the Convention to go on record against its extension. Later, after he had been impeached, the only method of seeking half vindication was for Ferguson to bring out his wife as candidate and secure her election so that, by proxy, although he was not eligible for office, he really exercised the duties of chief magistrate of a State which had formerly declared he was disqualified for election to public office. If those of us who believed in suffrage had not succeeded in securing the passage of the suffrage amendment to the Federal Constitution over his opposition, Ferguson's wife could not have been elected.

If the war had not absorbed attention, that evasive position might have cost Wilson votes, but the militant woman-suffragists were in accord with his "Keep us out of war" attitude, so that the straddle platform did not affect the result. The women, feeling they had scored a point, bided their time.

CONVERTED BY MRS. CATT

I had given little thought to woman suffrage prior to 1912. In North Carolina little or nothing was heard of the agitation that the great women leaders were making in other States. In the closing days of the Cleveland administration I chanced to be in Washington when Mrs. Carrie Chapman Catt was billed to speak on woman suffrage.

"Let's go and hear what the pussy cat will say," I remarked to a friend.

"I don't like her name," he said, "and moreover I do not care to hear a woman who wants to ape men."

The hall was small and crowded, and I had to stand in the rear. I went out of curiosity, perhaps to scoff, and was converted and always remained a real convert. Mrs. Catt spoke so logically, so clearly, and was so free from emotion that I could neither answer nor resist her arguments. Some time afterward I witnessed a woman suffrage parade on Fifth Avenue. In a spirit of badinage I wrote my wife: "I am now on the side of woman suffrage. Reason: Every woman in the parade wore a hat that cost only 39 cents. If that sort of hat will come to be universally worn when women get the ballot, husbands will save a lot of money." Upon my return home my wife asked me how the women in the parade looked. I said, "Fine." She banteringly replied, "I'll bet they looked like 39 cents." It was a long time before she was a convert, and she never did declare for it until she heard Mrs. Anna Howard Shaw, whose eloquence and personal charm and reasoning power captivated her. "I got religion when she spoke," she often said afterwards. We were both converted to the suffrage for women by the eloquence of great women—she by Anna Howard Shaw and I by Carrie Chapman Catt.

In 1920 my wife was appointed by President Wilson as the delegate to represent the United States at the World Woman's Suffrage Conference at Geneva, and later was active in the cause both in Washington and in North Carolina.

The first Cabinet discussion touching women and the vote was in the spring of 1914. Protest had been made against Civil Service clerks taking part in woman-suffrage parades. There was heat between those who favored it and those who held that such action violated Civil Service rules and regulations. The President sought advice of some members of his Cabinet. Of course I advised him to give them the privilege—in fact, thought they should be encouraged in every proper way.

McAdoo agreed with me and was always an ardent suffragist. He had pioneered in Equal Rights to Women long before; after he had built the tunnel under the river in New York in 1907, he employed them as ticket sellers. The superintendent said, "We can secure the service of women at a much lower rate than we pay men." McAdoo said, "Employ the women, but we must pay them the same as we pay men." He added, "I want the road run with economy but not at the expense of justice."

Wilson asked Lane to give his views in writing. "I think," wrote Lane, "that I am a prejudiced partisan in this matter for I believe that women should have the right to agitate for suffrage." He said he believed they were going to get it, "and that it would be particularly unwise for the administration to create the impression that it was attempting to block the movement," and he added this sound observation: "What Civil Service clerks may do outside of the government offices is none of our business, so long as they do nothing toward breaking it down as a merit service, do not discredit the service, or render themselves unfit for it."

Wilson wrote to Chairman J. A. McIlhenny: "We ought to be as liberal as possible in the matter and I respectfully suggest a ruling like this:

"If the employees in a department conform to the regulations of the Civil Service governing such action, there is no reason why they should not join a suffrage society or take part in the work organized by such a society."

The advocates of the ballot gave Wilson many an uncomfortable hour. They moved in on Washington, and on the day before his inauguration staged a spectacular parade on Pennsylvania Avenue. Some became bitter because he did not at once father their cause, but the wiser ones were courteously insistent and persistent and lived to see him their champion. In his earlier years Wilson had opposed it, but its advocacy by his daughters softened him. And led by Dr. Anna Howard Shaw, the suffragists camped on the White House doorsteps until he was won to their cause. In November, 1913, they began to mobilize, and a delegation of seventy-three by "a good-humored show of force," invaded the executive office. The most Wilson promised was to give the subject "earnest consideration."

Dr. Shaw was not satisfied; she returned to the White House and told the President to his face that he was "dodging the issue." She secured his promise to approve a special committee of the House. But the suffragists never gave him any escape from their peaceful, and sometimes warlike, attitude. He once said that he might have to join hands with them lest their continual coming should leave him little time for what he regarded as more pressing matters.

The most winning and persistent advocate of suffrage camped in Washington was Helen Gardner, a rare personage. Wilson conceived a sincere admiration for her and rated her ability so high that he appointed her a member of the Civil Service Commission.

It was not until women did such yeoman service in the World War that Wilson was fully converted. He then made a strong argument for woman suffrage in an address in the Senate Chamber, but, unfortunately, the Senate delayed approval until Wilson went out of office.

L

WILSON WINS IN 1916 BY THE SKIN OF HIS TEETH

THE CAMPAIGN of 1916 was closely contested. Fortunately, it was directed by Vance McCormick, of Pennsylvania, who declined two posts in Wilson's Cabinet but was always ready to respond unselfishly to any call for patriotic service. He had a large part in the nomination of Wilson, who esteemed him as a brother. They do not make better men. When some Democrats lacked hope, McCormick had faith in victory, but, win or lose, he kept the rudder true. He and his associates snatched victory out of the jaws of defeat. Most rich Democrats held back, and McCormick's campaign chest was often nearly empty while the Republicans had no lack for campaign oil.

When the good news came from California, it was seen that Wilson had 277 electoral votes to Hughes' 254. He had polled 9,127,695 votes, nearly three million more than he received in 1912, and a majority of 594,188 over Hughes.

The campaign started with confidence on the part of the Republicans, which was heightened by the desertion of the Progressive Party by Theodore Roosevelt; Elihu Root's attacking what he called Wilson's "bankrupt diplomacy"; Lodge's proclaiming Wilson's administration as "the worst in history except Buchanan's"; and Democratic division over the question of neutrality. There was no contest in either party. Hughes was the choice of the Republicans, and at the Democratic Convention at St. Louis the old ticket, with approval of the record of the administration, had no opposition.

The Democratic Convention was thrilled and cheered by oratory which inspired hope of victory. Rarely has any keynote speech stirred the pulses as did that by Governor Martin H. Glynn, temporary chairman and a true American, with Irish fire and true patriotism. He captured the multitude by his first sentence and held them enrapt until the end with such bursts of eloquence as have rarely moved convention-goers. Its spirit gave impetus to the slogan, "He kept us out of war," which was to attract many voters to the support of the ticket. Of Wilson's peace policy Glynn said:

"This policy may not satisfy those who revel in destruction and find pleasure in despair. It may not satisfy the fire-eater or the swashbuckler. This policy does satisfy the mothers of the land, at whose hearth and fireside no jingoist war has placed an empty chair.... It does satisfy the fathers of this land and the sons of this land who will fight for our flag, and die for our flag."

McGlynn never finished that sentence. The crowd, roused to the highest pitch of enthusiasm, cried out: "Say it again!" Glynn replied: "All right, I will"—and went on:

"When Reason primes the rifle, when Honor draws the sword, when Justice breathes a blessing on the standards they uphold...."

In like vein Senator Ollie James, Permanent Chairman, stirred the great gathering with this burst of oratory:

"Without orphaning a single American child, without widowing a single American mother, without firing a single gun, without shedding a single drop of blood, Wilson wrung from the most militant spirit that ever brooded above battlefield an acknowledgment of American rights and an agreement to American demands."

Then came the matchless Bryan, hailed with old-time fervor: "I have differed with our President on some of the methods employed, but I join the American people in thanking God that we have a President who does not want this nation plunged into this war." There was, on the part of some Eastern supporters of Wilson, fear that Bryan might defeat the desired harmony and they did not wish him to speak. I had talked with him in the early days of the Convention, and my wife and Mrs. Bryan were much together. I knew his spirit and rejoiced that again he confounded his critics. His eloquence and Glynn's and James's reached the heights—a trinity rarely equalled.

"HE KEPT US OUT OF WAR"

After these demonstrations showing the deep feeling against taking part in the war, nothing could have prevented the adoption of the platform declaration which praised Wilson's "splendid diplomatic victories preserving the vital interests of our Government and its citizens," ending with the climax, "and kept us out of war." These last words were not in the text which Secretary Baker, commissioned by Wilson to represent him, carried to St. Louis. Wilson's planks recognized the hurdles and possibility of war. It pledged adherence to policies that would sacrifice no American rights even if that involved war. But the slogan came out of the hearts of most American people, hoping and believing then that the Germans would heed Wilson's wise counsel.

FEW CAMPAIGN SPEECHES

Wilson made few campaign speeches upon his progressive policies. While Theodore Roosevelt, having thrown the Progressive Party overboard, was declaring that no man could vote for Wilson "without moral degradation," many Progressives came out for Wilson and in the election most of those in the West voted for him. Hughes began his campaign ineptly by an attack on a minor official, and Republican leaders thought to win by denouncing Burleson, Baker, and myself. I was particularly the object of attack because I had committed three offenses—defeated the armor-plate trust, put liquor out of the Navy, and prevented the oil companies gobbling up the Navy oil reserves. That trinity brought down on my head the concerted denunciation of those big interests.

DEPENDENCE UPON INDEPENDENTS

I early saw that Wilson must receive a large portion of the independent vote to win. There were two men who loomed large in the public, with whom I had come into friendly relations—Edison, president of the Navy Civilian Consulting Board, and Ford, then at the zenith of his fame. They were not Democrats but were independent in politics. I knew their support of Wilson would induce many voters to follow where they led. They were close friends. I had obtained Edison's aid in Naval research and Ford's in building ships for the Navy. I knew they both admired Wilson, and when I suggested that each write a letter favoring his election they were glad to do so. These endorsements proved big vote-getters. In all my speeches through the West, I emphasized that the foremost inventor and the foremost industrialist—Edison and Ford—not belonging to the Democratic Party—were leading the way to continuing good government and upholding true Americanism.

In his letter advocating Wilson's nomination, Edison caught the ear of the country in this sentence: "They say Wilson has blundered. Perhaps he has, but I notice that he usually blunders forward."

SEEKING CAMPAIGN FUNDS

In October I was making speeches in Indiana. One day I received a telegram from Vance McCormick, Democratic chairman, urging me to come to national headquarters at once on a matter of vital importance in the campaign. He added, "Senator Owen will fill all your dates." Of course, in true Naval parlance, I wired, "Aye, Aye, Sir," and reached New York the next morning. Going to Democratic headquarters, I found McCormick, Morgenthau, Roper, and Woolley expecting me. As I went into the chairman's office, after cordial greetings, I asked, "What is the vital matter which caused you to summon me from the campaign to headquarters?" His answer was that the committee was in desperate need of money to meet the expenses of the campaign. He said the Republicans were spending money without limit and that the Democratic fund was about exhausted; in fact, there was not enough money in the treasury to pay the bills. Morgenthau confirmed this and said he did not see how we could go on unless we could secure some large contributions.

"Why on earth did you summon me? I have no money. I have already contributed all I can and I do not know where I can get any," I said.

Whereupon McCormick told me he had asked Edison and Ford, who had publicly declared their support of Wilson, to come to headquarters for a conference, and each one of them had replied saying that he was not a politician and not interested in campaigns. They said they had no affiliation with the Democratic Party and knew few Democratic leaders, but each one said he would come to New York for a conference, provided "Josephus Daniels will be present at the conference." McCormick then said, "That is why we wired you. Edison and Ford are to be here this morning, and we want you to get Ford to make a large campaign contribution. It seems to be the only source available in our need and you are the only man who will have any influence with them." Of course, I was very happy to do anything in my power that would help in the campaign.

A little later Edison and Ford arrived at the hotel agreed upon, to take lunch with McCormick and myself. Edison and Ford received me with evidences of cordial friendship and we four sat down to luncheon. I was advised by McCormick I must broach the matter to Ford and get him to make a large contribution.

A KICKING MATCH

I do not suppose anything so strange ever occurred at a luncheon in New York, or elsewhere. We sat down at a round table and a splendid lunch was served. After the first course, Edison, pointing to a large chandelier, with many globes, in the middle of the room, said, "Henry, I'll bet anything you want to bet that I can kick that globe off that chandelier." It hung high toward the ceiling. Ford said he would take the bet. Edison rose, pushed the table to one side of the room, took his stand in the center and with his eye fixed on the globe, made the highest kick I have ever seen a man make and smashed the globe into smithereens. He then said, "Henry, let's see what you can do." The automobile manufacturer took careful aim but his foot missed the chandelier by a fraction of an inch. Edison had won and for the balance of the meal or until the ice-cream was served, Edison was crowing over Ford, "You are a younger man than I am, but I can out-kick you." He seemed prouder of that high kick then if he had invented a means of ending the U-Boat warfare.

All this time McCormick was on pins and needles waiting for me to open the subject and get Ford to write a big check. It was hard to get Edison and Ford down to earth. McCormick gave me a kick under the table as if to say, "Proceed." I thereupon told Edison and Ford that I had just returned from a campaign trip in the West where I had spoken in a number of States and that they would be gratified to know that the part of my speech, which secured the best response from the audiences, was when I quoted their endorsement of the President's policy and were supporting him for reëlection. I said: "Your support will get Wilson more votes than any other one thing." Ford expressed pleasure that the campaign was going well. I do not think Edison heard me, but he sensed what I was saying. I then turned to Ford and said that while the outlook was good in the Western States it was not going so well in the Eastern states, that the Republicans had an unlimited campaign fund, and that we sorely needed money to present our cause to the voters.

I made a direct appeal to him to follow up his endorsement with a contribution that would enable us to reach the voters. McCormick almost fainted when Ford replied, "All this campaign spending is the bunk. I wouldn't give a dollar to any campaign committee."

At this moment I wished for some spirits of ammonia to keep McCormick from fainting, and I needed a stimulant myself. It looked as if my trip from Indiana and McCormick's plans were to go awry. I replied to Ford:

> "I think you are quite right, Mr. Ford. Most money spent in campaigns is the 'bunk.' It is often used for corrupt purposes, to buy influence and to buy votes. Wilson would not wish to be elected by any such method. I assure you that not one dollar you give will be used for any purpose except for legitimate publicity, which both you and Mr. Edison would approve."

I sensed that McCormick thought I was giving up when I said "You are quite right, Mr. Ford," but I continued to appeal to him to help us make known to the readers of the newspapers the reasons he and Mr. Edison had given why Wilson should be elected. I told him that he had doubtless observed that the Republicans were getting their argument through the papers in big advertisements and that we lacked the money to reach them. That seemed to be the dead end. However, just as we were taking our coffee, Ford said, "I will not give a cent to the campaign fund. I sincerely hope that Wilson will be elected, and in my own way I will see that the reasons why he ought to be elected are presented in the papers of large circulation in the pivotal states." I added that was all we wanted—to get our message across—and if he would do it in his own way, it would have a better effect than if done by a party committee. He did not say how he would do it, when he would do it, or through what channels, but I was convinced that we might expect even better results from him than a large check would have brought about.

Saying good-bye to Edison and Ford, we returned to Democratic headquarters, where the committee members were awaiting our report. When we told them the result of the conference and what Ford had said, their hopes were dashed, and one of them said, "Ford will not do anything. He was just talking that way to get out of giving you any money." He thought the jig was up. With the campaign money box empty it was a disappointed gathering when

I said goodbye and went back to stump speaking. My faith in Ford was well founded. In a little while there appeared in a number of the big papers of wide circulation full-page articles signed "Henry Ford," advocating the election of Wilson. He had kicked higher than Edison.

Not only did Edison and Ford support Wilson but the third member of that immortal trio, John Burroughs, also urged the voters to keep him in the White House. He closed a letter to me on October 16: "Here is to the success of Wilson in the coming election. I hope I will be here to go camping with you and Mr. Edison and Ford next summer."

SOURCES OF SUPPORT

Campaigning in the West, I soon sensed that organized labor was generally enthusiastic for Wilson's reëlection, particularly the railroad men. His leadership in securing the enactment of the Adamson law had won them. At not a few of my meetings the presiding officer was a railroad man who had been a Republican.

In the early days of the campaign the Germans were decidedly cold, but detached. It was plain that some had been attracted by "He kept us out of war," but were waiting to see what Hughes would say. Above all else, they wished no war with their fatherland. It was not until Hughes pursued a pussy-foot policy and Theodore Roosevelt let loose his invectives against Wilson because he had not gone into the war against Germany, that the trend of the German vote from Ohio to the Pacific set in toward Wilson. It was not so much pro-Wilson as it was pro-peace and anti-T. R. and Hughes.

When election day came, the Wilson sweep was made possible because he held a considerable portion of the Progressive vote of 1912, resentful that T. R. had deserted his supporters and gone back to the Old Guard; labor was grateful for its Magna Carta; a big German contingent had decided Wilson was safer than Hughes backed by T. R.; and the slogan, "He kept us out of war," attracted many.

ENEMY COUNTRY

The situation in the East was different. The War sentiment and pro-ally leanings were stronger; Big Business was resentful because Wilson had turned a deaf ear to them in setting up the Federal

Reserve and in supporting the Adamson eight-hour measure; and Tammany was cool to the White House occupant and ready to rebuke McAdoo's attempt to build up an anti-Tammany Democratic organization in New York. A portion of the Irish element, violently hostile to Great Britain, were against Wilson, as were also Germans angered by Wilson's notes to the Kaiser, and by his speech of acceptance at Shadow Lawn, in which he had declared with emphasis: "I neither seek the favor nor fear the displeasure of that small alien element among us which puts loyalty to any foreign power before loyalty to the United States."

NO DISLOYAL VOTE WANTED

As the campaign progressed the hyphen-vote was seen to be so important that local politicians angled for it. An incident occurred shortly before the election that caused Democratic politicians anxiety. Jeremiah O'Leary, who staked all in the hope of an independent Ireland and thought the Irish ready to do anything to secure a free Ireland while Britain was in the stress of war with Germany, gave to the press a telegram he had sent to Wilson in the name of the "American Truth Society," charging him with "truckling to the British Empire" and in offensive terms declaring opposition to Wilson's election.

Wilson did not hesitate a moment in making an answer which stirred the whole country at a time when Hughes was charged with using language to conceal his position, if he had any. Wilson gave his answer to the wings of the lightning by telegraph: "I would feel deeply mortified," he said, "to have you or anybody like you vote for me. Since you have access to many disloyal Americans and I have not, I will ask you to convey this message to them."

The effect of that courageous declaration was electrical. It showed that Wilson would risk all rather than compromise with hyphenates. It stiffened the backbone of Americans who put America first, particularly in the West. The East had already been sewed up for Hughes, but the whole country showed admiration for a candidate who rang clear when others were trying to win by pleasing the hyphenates. Many believed that clarion note turned the tide and insured Wilson's election; however, some doubted it. "It is glorious and brilliant," said a Democratic politician to me, "but it is not war. It will stampede the German and Irish vote against Wilson and will gain him commendation where it will do him no good." It is not easy to determine the controlling factor in a close election. One thing is certain: The American people love a fighter and courage evokes their admiration.

ALWAYS AGAINST HYPHENATES

Wilson's epic telegram to O'Leary was not the first time he had spoken out strongly against hyphenated Americans. On May 16, 1914, a statue of John Barry, whose friends claim that he was "the father of the American Navy," was unveiled in Washington on Franklin Square. I was asked to make an address, following one by President Wilson. After paying high tribute to Barry who, he said, "illustrates for me all the splendid strength which we brought into this country by the magnet of freedom," Wilson gave his first condemnation of "hyphenism," which he was to denounce vigorously in war days and after, saying:

> "John Barry was an Irishman, but his heart crossed the Atlantic with him. He did not leave it in Ireland. . . . Some Americans need hyphens in their names because only part of them has come over; but when the whole man has come over, heart and thought and all, the hyphen drops of its own weight out of his name. This man was not an Irish-American; he was an Irishman who became an American. I venture to say if he voted he voted with regard to the questions as they looked on this side of the water and not as they affected the other side; and that is my infallible test of a genuine American, that when he votes or when he acts or when he fights, his heart and his thought are centered nowhere but in the emotions and the purposes and the policies of the United States."

At the conclusion of my warm tribute to Barry, I congratulated the great crowd that we had Naval heroes in our own generation, worthy to wear the mantle of John Barry, and in a tribute from my heart, I presented Admiral George Dewey, as "a Naval hero and Naval statesman of whom all America is proud." The enthusiastic reception given him warmed the Admiral's heart.

A STIMULATING CAMPAIGN

When early in the campaign I reported to Democratic headquarters that Wilson would carry the West, Vance McCormick,

Democratic chairman, told me that when my message of cheer and optimism was read by the pessimistic leaders in New York, most of them agreed with the politician who said, "Josephus is carried away by his own eloquence and thinks because his hearers applaud his speeches, the Kansas Republicans are turning Democrats." It was a stimulating campaign. I recall that one day in Kansas I made an early morning speech to an enthusiastic gathering, made up largely of railroad men at Parsons, Kansas, and spoke at a different hour at some town several times in the day, closing with a city meeting at night. Rushing from place to place, I would be embarrassed after speaking ten minutes at my last place because I would not remember whether I had told my favorite story to the people I was addressing or had told it at the last town where I had spoken. I was in deadly fear that I would repeat myself to my hearers.

After completing my dates in the West, I rushed to Newport, Rhode Island, to make the closing speech in the campaign for my friend, Peter Gerry, a Big Navy man, whose reëlection was in jeopardy. My frequent visits to the Naval base and enlarged torpedo bases there had put me in close touch with the Rhode Island voters. They turned out in full force to hear me and when the election returns came in, Newport voters insured the reëlection of Gerry, though Wilson lost the State. Leaving Newport immediately after speaking at night, I had a few minutes at home in Washington, and hastened to Wadesboro, North Carolina to make the closing speech of the campaign in Anson County, and that night closed the campaign in the city of Winston-Salem, where the Republicans were strong and confident. For several years before and after that campaign I was invited to make the closing campaign speech in that city. In concluding my speech I told my neighbors of my tour through the West, and predicted that the country would be astounded at the number of Western States, usually Republican, that would give their electoral votes to Wilson, thus insuring his reëlection. The Democrats, in touch with the trend to Hughes in New York, had almost lost hope. My confident prediction of victory created the greatest enthusiasm. After my speech, leaders asked: "Do you really mean it? Will Wilson carry the West?" My answer was: "Most of it is in the bag. He is as sure, for example, to carry Kansas as North Carolina." When my predictions came true, I basked for a time in the glory of a prophet.

DARK ELECTION NIGHT

In spite of my optimism about what the West would do, election night found me receiving the election returns in *The News and Observer* office in Raleigh with deep anxiety. Before nine o'clock, the New York *Times* and the New York *World* conceded the election of Hughes. That seemed to end it, and the crowds in the street melted away. I confessed to some friends, who sorrowed with me, that "Raleigh looks very good and I will be happy to come back home."

Shortly before midnight, when I was to take the train for Washington, the managing editor of the paper, holding sheafs of telegrams in his hand showing that Hughes had carried everything east of Ohio, that Wilson was running ahead in Ohio and Kansas, and Hughes was leading in Indiana, asked me: "We must go to press for the first edition in a few minutes. What do you suggest for the headlines?" I recalled that California was voting three hours after the polls closed in New York. I asked for a pencil and wrote down: "It Looks Like Hughes; But Wait Till You Hear From the West."

LIGHT COMES WITH THE MORNING

Soon I was asleep in my Pullman, with the sinking feeling that Wilson had probably lost. Leaving the train, I was met by my wife, who had the morning paper. "Wilson has carried California and most of the West and is elected," she joyfully said. I could hardly believe it. But there it was in black and white. "I went home early, last night," she said. "At nine o'clock Burleson, who had invited me to the Post Office Department, gave up, put out the lights, reached for his umbrella, and we all went home without hope. I awoke to find the sun shining, with cheering news."

COULD NOT STEAL CALIFORNIA

But it was several days before California's vote was counted, and the country was on its nerves. Lane said to fellow Cabinet members: "Unless somebody can prevent the stealing of the vote in Los Angeles, they'll swindle Wilson there as they did me when I ran for Governor. There was no doubt that the election thieves in Los Angeles stole the election then. They will do it again unless prompt and effective action is taken." Chairman McCormick and leaders had already gotten busy, as had Democratic leaders in California. If there was a plan to steal the election, it was thwarted. How? Some years afterwards, when I was in Los Angeles, I saw much of Meredith P. Snyder, Mayor of the city. He was a native of North Carolina, and had gone to California as a young man. He married the daughter of Senator Ross, of Kansas, who put his life in jeopardy and found political death by voting against a verdict of "guilty" in the impeachment proceedings against Andrew Johnson. Snyder was a Democrat, and the previous year, on a Citizens Reform ticket, had been elected Mayor. He told me of the tragic hours that followed the election. He said:

> "I did not close my eyes until the result of the election was declared. Shortly after the polls closed, I ordered that every ballot-box be sealed and stationed policemen in every booth with orders to shoot any man who should lay the weight of his hands on the ballot-box. With associates I went from booth to booth all night. We kept vigilant watch, and a staunch Democrat was assigned as watcher at every booth. Nothing was left undone to see that there was no tampering. I knew that the fate of the presidency for the next four years would be settled in these boxes, and I staked my life that the votes should be counted as cast."

He succeeded, with the backing of a militant Democracy ready to do anything necessary to have the vote counted as cast. There were no "visiting statesmen" or need of them. The California Democrats believed they had won and the "Spirit of the Forty-Niners" animated them. Any man, tempted to tamper with the returns, knew that it would be his last act in this world.

WHAT CARRIED CALIFORNIA

Many influences, of course, contributed to Wilson's carrying California. The failure of Hughes to call on Hiram Johnson was given a determining effect out of proportion to its importance. I was one of the few Democrats in Washington who had confidence that Wilson would receive the electoral vote of California. I based my optimism on my knowledge of the changed political situation in San Diego, Los Angeles, and the Vallejo (Mare Island Navy Yard) district. Early in my administration I had visited the Pacific coast, as told in an earlier chapter. Up to that time, except when Theodore

Roosevelt sent the fleet around the world (incidentally to let Japan take notice), the people on the Pacific coast had been treated by the Navy Department as red-headed step-children. They had no good Naval bases, the officers preferred manœuvres on the Atlantic Coast where their families lived or at summer resorts, and the Eastern section alone had Naval protection.

As a result of my visiting all the bases on the Pacific, the Navy yards from San Diego to Bremerton were expanded in readiness for the time when the fleet of the American Navy would be as strong in the Pacific as in the Atlantic. I made known to the people on the West Coast my intentions of providing the best facilities on that coast.

Naturally, having felt themselves neglected by the Navy for many years, the people on the Pacific Coast appreciated the first recognition given them and welcomed a day when they could fittingly show their appreciation in an impressive way. Their opportunity came in 1916 when by giving the electoral votes of California and Washington they could show their gratitude. The election returns showed that Wilson carried every part of both states where Naval expansion had been made or was in the making. Except for the big change in the vote in San Diego, Los Angeles, and Mare Island districts, Wilson would have lost California. The change from Republican to Democratic votes was revolutionary in the districts most affected by the new Naval policy.

THE CALMEST MAN

In the exciting and hectic days before the result was known, Wilson was outwardly the calmest man in America. Playing golf while McCormick and the rest of us were sweating blood, he went on the links for a golf game. Answering a friend, "How is your game?" Wilson replied, "Grayson has me three down, but I don't care. I am four States up on yesterday's election."

I learned the strange story of how President Wilson and his family were marooned in their home on the Jersey coast, without knowing how the election was going, when it was told to me by Mrs. Wilson years afterwards. As is well known, Wilson did not believe in campaigning from the White House. Realizing that he would be busy in the campaign and would have to make a number of speeches he took a cottage at Spring Lake in New Jersey and received visitors there and made speeches from that place. A few days before the election, the telegraph company volunteered to put in a special wire to his house. The President declined. He lived up to his principle never to accept favors. On election day and night, he was surrounded by his daughters and Mr. Sayre, Mrs. Wilson's mother and sisters, Dr. and Mrs. Cary Grayson, and Mr. Joseph P. Tumulty. As election day closed, the family party played games and tried to find diversion while waiting for the news of the result of the election. Nobody telephoned, and up to nine o'clock the Wilson family was as completely shut off from the world as if they had been on a desert island. It was nine o'clock when the telephone rang. Margaret, very tense, hastened to the telephone. From the other end of the line a friend of hers in New York, with a far-reaching voice that could be heard all over the large room where Wilson and his family were sitting, said, "Miss Margaret, I am calling you up to condole with you."

"What do you mean?" asked Margaret.

"The New York *Times* has conceded the election of Hughes," was the answer.

"It is not true," in tones of excitement and disbelief, answered Margaret.

"But all the papers have given up and so has the Democratic Committee," was the answer.

"I do not care who gives up," said Margaret. "It isn't true and I do not care who gives up. I know it isn't true."

Her confidence was not shared by the other members of the little group. No other news came and none of the party made calls. Dr. Grayson and Secretary Tumulty had gone out to obtain news and promised to telephone. Not a word came from them. So the only news that reached Spring Lake was the call to Margaret. Shortly after she finished telephoning, the President said, "I am going to bed." Mrs. Wilson ordered milk and ginger ale and orange juice to be brought up as was the habit before retiring. "And when it came," she put in, "none of us could swallow."

The President went to bed and in fifteen minutes he was sleeping as soundly as if the result meant little to him.

Later in the night, there came a telephone message saying Chairman Vance McCormick had not given up and expected good news from the West. Margaret wanted to wake her father. Mrs. Wilson tip-toed to his room and found him sleeping soundly and vetoed the suggestion of arousing him. The next morning and the whole day passed without a message about the result of the election reaching the President or any member of his family. They did not talk about it.

Mr. Fine and another friend of the President from Princeton had called up the day before the election and said they would like to call the day after the election. They were invited to luncheon. Shortly after noon they arrived and at the luncheon no mention was made by either of them or by the President or any of his family about the result of the election. At the end of the luncheon, Mrs. Wilson and the other ladies, thinking the visitors wished to talk with the President about Princeton matters, withdrew. The conversation lagged. Finally the President asked the visitors what was on their mind. It turned out that they had made the engagement expecting to offer congratulations. As it looked as if Hughes was elected, and Wilson had no news, they were embarrassed and did not stay long.

On the morning after the election while the President was shaving, Margaret knocked on his door and said, "Father, the New York *Times* has issued an extra saying the election is in doubt, with indication of a Wilson victory." Without stopping shaving, Wilson replied, "Tell that to the Marines." Tumulty says that, when he and Margaret told him the news of his election, the President said he had just begun to feel the reaction of defeat.

In the afternoon, still without a word about the result from anyone, the President and Mrs. Wilson left Spring Lake to go by train to the place where the *Mayflower* was waiting to take them to Massachusetts to attend the baptising of the Sayre baby. Still they had no news. As they entered the train, a lady rushed up to Mrs. Wilson and gave her a large bunch of violets and congratulated her upon the result of the election. That was all, and it was ten o'clock Wednesday night before the President had the news that he had carried California and was reëlected.

That is one of the strangest stories of how a presidential candidate, near both New York and Philadelphia, in the very center of the news nerve, remained in total ignorance of how the voters had deposited their ballots for a whole night and day and part of another night. I could not have believed this possible if I had not afterwards heard from members of the family the strange story of how the family was virtually cut off from the world. The President was ready to accept defeat as Lincoln had been in 1864. Lincoln had made plans of what his course should be if he had been defeated.

Both Wilson and Hughes spent election night sleeping soundly, Wilson resigned to defeat and Hughes rocked to slumber believing he had been elected. A story current at the time, which gave pleasure to Democrats, was the following:

A little after midnight a newspaper man called to tell Hughes that California was in doubt.

"The President cannot be disturbed," announced young Charles Hughes, Jr.

The newspaper man persisted.

"You will have to come back in the morning; the President cannot be disturbed," said the son.

"Well, when he wakes up, just tell him that he isn't President," the reporter replied.

IF DEFEATED, WHAT?

President Wilson, seeing the possibility of defeat, had written a letter to Lansing, and not long after the election Secretary Lansing confidentially imparted to his colleagues this story that seemed too strange to be true:

"After voting at Watertown, I reached New York City on election day, and met Under-Secretary Frank L. Polk, who gave me a letter, which he said President Wilson had instructed him to deliver to me. It was enclosed in a wax-sealed envelope, addressed in the President's handwriting and marked 'Most Confidential,' to be opened by no one except myself. The letter had been personally typed by Mr. Wilson. In substance the letter said that during the four months that would elapse after the election, if Mr. Hughes should be the choice, crises might arise which would have to be met by the President who would be called upon to act in the ensuing years. He said that if the people at the polls repudiated his policies, he could not successfully conduct governmental affairs. He felt, therefore, that if defeated the welfare of the country would be advanced if he should relinquish the office to the man who had been elected. Inasmuch as there was no method provided by the Constitution for such an emergency, he had decided that shortly after the election, he

would ask me to resign as Secretary of State and would name
Mr. Hughes as my successor. He would resign as chief executive
and ask Mr. Marshall to resign the office of Vice President.
Then, under the law, Mr. Hughes would at once succeed to the
presidency for the intervening four months and in the following March enter upon his four-year term."

Mr. Lansing, so far as I know, never showed this letter to any
person. He regarded the "most confidential" letter as "the best evidence of Wilson's patriotism and loyalty to the people, believing
Wilson's decision to be made as a public duty rather than as a
personal sacrifice."

THE 1916 CAMPAIGN

Upper left, Vance McCormick, chairman of the Democratic National Committee in 1916, who three times declined a portfolio in Wilson's Cabinet. *Upper right,* Martin H. Glynn, Governor of New York, keynoter at the Democratic National Convention in 1916. *Lower left,* Meredith P. Snyder, Mayor of Los Angeles, whose vigilance prevented any tampering with the election returns. *Lower right,* Henry Morgenthau, chairman of the Finance Committee in 1912-16. Ambassador to Turkey.

KEYNOTE SPEECH AT THE 1916 CONVENTION

Governor Martin H. Glynn, of New York, keynoter and Temporary Chairman of the Democratic National Convention in 1916, whose eloquence brought the delegates to their feet with the slogan, "He Kept Us Out of War."

Part Six

PORTRAITS

LI

ELLEN AXSON WILSON AND THE WHITE HOUSE

IT REQUIRED only a few days after the Wilsons entered it for the White House to have the feel of being a home presided over by a homemaker who understood its real relation to the republic. My wife and I—naturally thinking it the best—felt that it irradiated what people below the Potomac call "Southern hospitality," a quality that has a flavor all its own. But there was no sectionalism in it, for the Wilsons had tasted and accepted the fine hospitality of New England and the Middle States, through their long residence in Connecticut, Pennsylvania, and New Jersey. The Wilsons— the President particularly—emphasized that, aside from public functions, the White House was the private home of the family of the chief executive and they were entitled to the same privacy as any citizen in his own home. But that goal was impossible of realization, though Wilson never ceased to resent what he called the intrusion of the public in the home life of his family.

Mrs. Wilson and her three daughters gave a radiance to the White House. Two of the girls, Jessie, who married Francis Sayre, and Eleanor, who married Secretary of the Treasury McAdoo, had their weddings in the White House, the first to occur in the presidential family since the marriage of Alice Roosevelt to Nicholas Longworth. Margaret never married. I always called them the Three Graces.

No President owed more to the wife of his youth than Woodrow Wilson owed to Ellen Axson. They were both products of the Presbyterian manse, with like traditions and upbringing. Her talent turned to art, and some of her paintings found place along with those of the best of her contemporaries. Wilson's early aspiration was to master the science of government and to teach it to the students in his classroom, to give the result of his studies in treatises which were adopted as textbooks, with the hope which he rarely admitted to himself, that he might be called in public office to put in practise the theories he had expounded. His wife shared this latter dream, fostered it, and gave it momentum, and was the more ambitious of

the two. With wifely self-effacement she never lost her perfect faith
in his star. She kept up with every detail of the campaign for
the nomination. The news of the cordial reception in Raleigh in
1911 cheered her. On June 2, Mrs. Wilson, discussing his speaking
and plans, wrote him: "What a tremendous ovation you had in
Raleigh!" Her daughter (Mrs. McAdoo) had been a student at St.
Mary's in Raleigh and Mrs. Howe (sister of Wilson) was then
living in Raleigh and doubtless sent her the papers and wrote of
Raleigh's enthusiasm.

She unconsciously drew the pen-picture of herself after she had
been in the White House two years, as if she had a premonition of
the short span of life in store for her. It was in a letter to her friend,
Mrs. Hoyt: "I wonder how anyone who reaches middle age can
bear it, if she cannot feel on looking back, that, whatever mistakes
she may have made, she has on the whole lived for others and not
for herself."

Her husband leaned upon her in all things, having learned to
trust her wisdom. He recognized her clear mind and paid tribute
to her judgment, saying once, "When I was going to make a speech
and would read it to her she would usually suggest some one
change—an idea. And do you know it was just that passage which
made the strongest impression in the whole speech. She was a
friendly critic."

NOT SLAVES TO PROTOCOL

"Sit down and behave yourself." These were the words used by
President Wilson, putting his hands on my shoulders and pressing
me down on the sofa from which I had hastily risen. It was the
night of the first big reception in the White House, after the Wilsons had become the occupants. My wife and I, who were to be in
the receiving line, had arrived early, and had been shown into the
Library on the second floor. President Wilson and house guests
from Princeton were the only occupants of the room. He greeted us,
and we stood on either side of the fireplace, I talking with the wife
of his teacher friend from Princeton, and the President and my wife
talking on the opposite side. After a few minutes, the lady took a
seat on a near-by sofa and I followed suit, while my wife and the
President were standing. My wife knew it was an unwritten rule
that no one should sit down while the President was standing. She

could not tell me of my *faux pas.* In order to attract my attention, she clicked her heels together. At once, I came to a standing position, as did the lady. The President heard the click of the heels, saw the "come hither" look on my wife's face, and took in the situation, as the occupants of the sofa suddenly stood up. He quickly strode across the fireplace, and putting his hands on my shoulders, pressed me back to a sitting position on the sofa, saying: "Sit down, and behave yourself" and told my wife that when he occupied the White House he wished no adherence to an old rule of empires.

My wife knew the unwritten rule of protocols that it was *lèse majesté* for anyone to be seated while the king or the chief executive was standing. Not many years before when a lady had transgressed that rule, an aide of a former President had ordered her to stand, telling her that it was not showing the right respect to the President for anyone to take a seat until he was seated. My wife did not wish her country-editor husband to violate an unwritten law of the White House.

One day, later, Wilson made a public statement perhaps suggested by that incident. He said:

> "I shall not say whether it is unwise, simple or grave, but certain precedents have been established that in certain companies the President must leave the room first and people must give way to him. They must not sit down when he is standing up.
> "It is a very uncomfortable thing to have to think of all the other people every time I get up and sit down and all that sort of thing. So that when I have guests in my own house and the public is shut out, I adjourn being President and take leave to be a gentleman. If they draw back and insist upon my doing something first, I firmly decline."

Under the Wilsons the White House, except at official dinners or formal occasions, was very much like a home. The President and Mrs. Wilson observed the proprieties but refused to be the slaves to a rigid protocol. Insistence upon traditions borrowed from royalty irked them. Wilson refused to follow such undemocratic customs. His wife always preceded him. He said, "I was a gentleman before I became President."

I had never met Mrs. Wilson until my wife and I, along with other members of the national committee, went to see the presidential nominee at Sea Girt to plan the conduct of the campaign. However, during the pre-convention days, I had received several messages, one saying that the two papers that she read with most pleasure were *The News and Observer* and the Trenton *Times*, which were ardent advocates of Wilson's nomination. In that first visit a lasting and affectionate friendship was begun. The only word to describe the relationship between my wife and Mrs. Wilson was *simpática*—the best word in any language to express perfect understanding and oneness. These two women, who were to be closely associated in official and social Washington, had a common background and faith—Southern to the core, Presbyterian in religion, full of friendliness, goodness to and understanding of the Negro, and that something called charm—indefinable as it rests upon a woman who possesses it as a crown of glory.

A GOOD POLITICIAN

It was during the 1912 campaign that I came to agree with Private Secretary Tumulty that Mrs. Wilson was a better politician than the Governor. During the long-drawn-out Baltimore Convention, when Wilson was almost on the point of letting McCombs withdraw his name after Clark received a majority, it was Mrs. Wilson who furnished the faith and sticking quality. Talking to Governor Fort about the suggestion of withdrawal, Wilson said, "Mrs. Wilson thinks I should stay in. She says I've nothing to lose." Fort agreed and Wilson said, "Well, I believe I shall."

Almost every week in that campaign I went to Sea Girt to consult Wilson (he did not resign as Governor of New Jersey until a few days before his inauguration as President) about some phase of the campaign, and always I was admitted to the family gathering and Mrs. Wilson and the daughters joined in the conversation. I would ask the Governor what he thought of this or that matter about the conduct of the campaign, and he would turn to his wife and inquire, in a voice with a perfect blending of love and confidence in her judgment, "What do you think of that, Ellen?" And her view, clearly stated, was often accepted by both of us. She kept up with every incident and move and I came to lean upon her wisdom as much as did Wilson. I found our minds clicked oftener than did mine and the candidate's. You always attribute wisdom to one who agrees with you. But she spoke her own mind, agreeing or not agreeing. She sensed, with both woman's intuition and her knowledge of politics, situations better than either of the men participants. Though always behind the scenes, she knew the political situations and outlined them with grasp and judgment. And Wilson often followed her suggestions, made with all wifely deference. And she was generally right.

Only once in those campaign days did I distrust her advice. I yielded to it, but unwilling. In preparing the Democratic textbook, I picked out what I thought was an excellent likeness of Governor Wilson for the front page and sent a sample to Sea Girt for approval. Very soon I received a different photograph from Mrs. Wilson, saying that it was desired that it be used on all the literature sent out. It was ten years younger than Wilson and there was not a line in it—a calm and beautiful face. I protested that the campaign picture should show strength and power and fight, and that the people would be more attracted to a candidate not too good looking. In vain. Mrs. Wilson loved that picture. I gave orders, because Mrs. Wilson would have no other, that it should be the official picture and it went on the cover of the textbook, and other literature. But it wasn't a "go," and later, unbeknownst to Mrs. Wilson, a picture with more vigor and less beauty, and more like the candidate, was substituted.

Mrs. Wilson ran true to wifely form in sending a youthful picture of the candidate for President. In my long experience as an editor, I learned that whenever I requested the wife of a candidate or public official to furnish a photograph of her husband, she almost invariably sent one a dozen or a score years younger than he actually was at that time. Frequently she sent a picture taken of him when she fell in love with him, or in the honeymoon period, when she saw him through orange blossoms. I recall that when I wired to the wife of a candidate for Judge in North Carolina for a photograph, she sent one taken on their bridal tour when his hair was abundant and he was clean shaven. At the time of his candidacy he was so bald his head looked like a billiard ball and he had a flowing gray mustache. If I had printed the picture sent by the wife, the voters would not have recognized him. Mrs. Wilson's heart controlled her judgment in the matter of the photograph.

DECIDED AGAINST AN INAUGURAL BALL

After the election I went to Princeton for a conference with the President-elect and talked with him and Mrs. Wilson. There was much in the papers about the inauguration and the inaugural ball. Mrs. Wilson had never attended one and said she did not know what the inaugural ball was like. I had been in Washington and had looked in on the inaugural ball when Cleveland was inaugurated in 1893 and described it to her as well as I could. My description made it a rather glamorous and spectacular affair. Outside the official guests it was attended only by those who paid for tickets, the money going to pay the expenses of the ball and other inauguration expenditures. It had become somewhat commercialized. "Do you think," she asked, "that there ought to be an inaugural ball when Woodrow is inaugurated?"

"As an old-fashioned Methodist who never danced in his life, I am not competent to advise," I replied. "I do not like the idea, particularly as it is commercialized. I ought to say that it has so long been a custom at inaugurations that many people look forward to it and would be greatly disappointed if that brilliant evening entertainment were omitted. More than that, all the dressmakers and shopkeepers who will make money providing gowns, etc., for the ball would resent it if it is not held."

Mrs. Wilson saw that side of it, but she looked to the inauguration as a solemn consecration, and, after some further talk, she said: "I cannot bear to think of Woodrow's inauguration (she used the word as if it was his consecration and that was how she regarded it) being attended with a ball in which all sorts of people would engage in these modern dances which I do not like."

I knew from her manner as well as her words that she felt Woodrow, as she always called him even after he was President, was going to Washington on a sacred mission and that she had already in her mind vetoed the inaugural ball. It was the veto of the daughter of a Presbyterian parson rather than the President-elect, but he shared her views and denied the gaiety of an inaugural ball in Washington in 1913. I did not know then, but learned afterward, that as soon as she knew Woodrow had been elected, she made known to him that she placed me first in her Cabinet choices. Indeed one biographer of Wilson said that my designation was largely due to Mrs. Wilson.

"PORTRAITS"

Upper left, Mrs. Thomas R. Marshall, wife of the Vice-President (Brown Brothers). *Upper right,* Ellen Axson Wilson, wife of the President. *Lower left,* Admiral Cary T. Grayson, physician to Presidents Theodore Roosevelt, William Howard Taft, and Woodrow Wilson. *Lower right,* Thomas R. Marshall, Vice-President of the U. S.

THOMAS A. EDISON, PRESIDENT OF THE NAVY CONSULTING BOARD,
AND JOSEPHUS DANIELS

Taken at the home of Mr. Edison in Orange, N. J., in 1916.

I clearly recall my conversation with Mrs. Wilson on the afternoon of the new President's first personal message to Congress. She beamed her pride, and said in gay mood: "Woodrow's delivering his message to Congress in person is the kind of thing that Theodore Roosevelt would have liked to do—in fact would have done if he had thought of it."

"I would like to show that dinners and other social functions can be both beautiful and simple," Mrs. Wilson said, as she was taking up her duties as the hostess of the White House. One other expression characteristic of the South, whose virtues she incarnated, and by which her life was governed, was this: "We do not care enough for the relationships of the home. What the Romans meant by piety, was not just a thing based on congeniality; it was something in the blood that held whether people found their fathers and mothers queer nor not." In the White House as in her other homes, relatives came first and were welcome guests. The Wilson home was in spirit like that described: "Relatives came to make a visit and stayed all winter." And such kin-visiting was typically Southern in her youth and continued all her life.

Mrs. Wilson's social duties did not lessen her passion for beauty in her surroundings. As in her Princeton home, of which she was the architect and the planner of her garden, she set herself in Washington to remodel and beautify the White House grounds, planning the marble pool of clear water set in the thick grass amidst the roses. The two gardens to the south of the White House were too conventional for her and she loved doing them over. She sent for enough roses from her own garden, "Prospect," at Princeton to make a lovely spot. Like the beautiful garden in Princeton, the White House garden when completed was her own creation. Her deft hands were seen in the interior arrangement of the White House. She thought it "ugly" and set about making it have the charm of a real home. She was happiest when she could hang the President's portrait on the walls beside those of his predecessors. Perhaps her letter to the President's college chum and close friend discloses her artistic appreciation and her devotion to her husband more clearly than does any other expression. She wrote:

"We are all perfectly delighted that the portrait is to be at the White House, and it is impossible for us to say how much we appreciate what you and Mrs. McCormick have done! I am *very* glad for Mr. Thomas, too, for he put his whole heart and soul into the work. He is a real enthusiast about Mr. Wilson, so that the work was certainly done sympathetically. I am glad that the picture will be shown in England, it will serve as a corrective of the innumerable caricatures of him, (some so intended, others not) with which the press is flooded. The interest in him in England and Scotland is very great, and they ought to know how he looks."

WARS AGAINST SLUMS

But her woman's civic interest carried her beyond the White House and its grounds. As an art student in New York before her marriage, Ellen Axson had interested herself in settlement work among the slums on the lower west side, as a like call to her daughter Jessie sent her into settlement work before her marriage. Soon Mrs. Wilson was troubled as she observed the squalor of the alleys in Washington. She grasped the fact that many of the 96,000 Negroes, a third of the population, were living in unsanitary houses, and sought to bring about an improvement in living conditions. She initiated a bill for better houses and took Congressmen into the dark alleys to show them the pressing need of action. She felt the conditions where Negroes lived were a disgrace to the national capital and with other good women she set about effecting improvement. Within three weeks after reaching Washington she joined a movement headed by Mrs. Archibald Hopkins to clean up the slums. She appealed to Secretary Bryan—always zealous in bettering conditions for the underprivileged—to make an address at a public meeting she called, to arouse public sentiment over the opposition of vested property interests. The Commoner responded, and funds to prosecute the campaign were obtained and the ground work was laid for the greatly accelerated slum clearance which later had the active support of President and Mrs. Franklin Roosevelt. In her characteristic way, she was modest about her part in the reform, writing: "Do you remember Wordsworth's Simon Lee? I think of that line:

"'Alas! the gratitude of men hath oftener left me mourning.'"

TOOK TOLL OF HER STRENGTH

Mrs. Wilson entered the White House a tired woman. The bitter feeling aroused over her husband's resolve to make Princeton "a democratic institution" had laid its heavy hand upon her. Once when I was remarking upon the breaking of ties and the hate that followed political conflicts, she said: "They are as nothing to the feuds and depths of separation and bitterness that changed the whole atmosphere of Princeton in the conflicts through which I have passed." Truly they had been searing to her. The stress of the campaign had taken toll of her strength, for she followed every step with absorption and counsel. But nobody in Washington suspected that her health had been undermined, and not even those nearest suspected it until the end was near when she suffered a fall in the White House. Even afterwards her strength of will was magnificent. A cousin, Miss Helen Woodrow Bones who lived at the White House, gives this instance of her strong self control:

"As the time for Nell's wedding approached, her mother made herself well for the time being. It was pure will. She would be well for her daughter's wedding. Her high color (which some people believed she got out of a box) made her look so well that we were fooled by it, but when she no longer needed to pretend, she sank back into the illness that ended her life. She knew she was dying. I know that now. One day when a number of us were sitting in her room someone asked to see the dress she had worn at the wedding, and she smiled up at the things and said, half to herself: 'Too bad that I shall never wear them again.' We all exclaimed, but she knew."

SHE WAS TOO WONDERFUL

When Miss Bones suggested that a biography of Mrs. Wilson be written, the President said: "No one could write Ellen's biography without sounding fulsome. She was too wonderful." Miss Bones, who knew her intimately, told me:

"I, who have never considered any human being perfect, have to confess I am unable to name one fault in Ellen Wilson, unless her adoration of her husband and her children may be called a fault. She seemed almost stern when questions of right and wrong were involved. She was always doing for others, utterly unselfish and generous and kind. And so forgiving, except when her husband was attacked. I recall an incident that is most illustrative: There were threats against Wilson's life if he attended the funeral of the Marines whose bodies had been brought back after being killed in Vera Cruz. The day before he was to go with you to New York, as we were going out of the dining room after lunch, Mr. Tumulty hurried in looking sick with anxiety. He begged the President not to go to the funeral, and told us of the threats that had been made. As the President insisted that he would go, Tumulty turned to Mrs. Wilson and begged her to use her influence. She laid her hand on the President's shoulder and said very gently: 'A soldier's wife has no right to interfere with his duty,' and she smiled. If she was frightened she didn't show it, and no one who heard her doubted her sincerity."

That was Ellen Axson Wilson. She would sacrifice anything, dare anything, for the husband she admired up to the very hour of her death (August 12, 1914) when the dark clouds of war and his personal sorrow shut out the sun from his horizon. In the days when her life was ebbing out, he sat by her bedside and wrote down in shorthand notes the tender of good offices to the warring nations.

THE ABIDING INFLUENCE

An illuminating incident when Wilson was ill, showing the abiding influence of Ellen Axson on his life is thus told by his daughter Eleanor (Mrs. W. G. McAdoo):

"As my father lay ill on Lincoln's great carved bed, I closed the book I was reading to him, as he was apparently asleep. Suddenly he opened his eyes and, with the happy smile of the old days, he spoke softly saying: 'I was back on the island at Muskoka. Do you remember our picnics there, and your mother reading poetry under the pines? I wish I could hear her voice. . . . I owe everything to your mother. You know that, don't you?' . . . I said: 'I wish I could have her touch on my children.' He answered: 'You can—tell them about her. That is enough.'"

As the recollections of the departed wife of his youth dominated his thinking in his last days, so the thought of her husband was uppermost with his wife as she faced the sunset of life and the sunrise of eternity. Perhaps her last spoken words were to Dr. Cary Grayson, whom she loved almost as she would love a son: "Promise me that you will take good care of my husband."

LIGHT OF THE WHITE HOUSE

For nineteen months she was the gracious lady of the White House, the first lady of the South to preside since 1848, following

Mrs. James K. Polk, an alumna of the old Moravian College at Salem, North Carolina. In the months before her death in August, 1914, after a long illness, she was the light of the home she had made out of the stately White House, the model national hostess, the inspirer of good works, the incarnation of devotion to family and friends, the guide, lover, and partner of the husband of her youth, who was beset with the gravest problems that had ever confronted a chief executive.

"I never dreamed such loneliness and desolation of heart possible," Wilson wrote to a friend after he had returned from the funeral in her old beloved Rome, Georgia.

LII

EDISON JOINS THE NAVY

EARLY IN JULY, 1915, Edward Marshall, a well-known feature writer whose friendship I prized, visited Edison and in the story in the New York *Times* of his interview with "the wizard of Menlo Park," quoted him as saying that he would not devote his inventive genius to warlike service "except at the call of my country." Engrossed as the Navy was at that time in preparedness for any eventuality, that statement challenged my attention and that of others in the Navy Department. I decided to apply the voluntary selective draft and induce Edison to turn his genius into channels to improve Naval technique. A short time before, several scientists from France, concerned with helping to promote better war efficiency, spent some weeks in Washington with Naval experts. Upon returning to their country they called at the Navy Department to say good-bye. As they were leaving I told them the men directing the fighting on the sea looked to men of their knowledge to devise ways to check the U-boat menace. In a few minutes they returned and said they had come back to say that while they hoped to help, they did not wish the fighting branch to depend on their research and discovery. They were prompted by their modesty and the knowledge that, in that war, force to the utmost would be the determining factor. However, I knew and so did able men in the Navy, that our dependence for modern weapons rested upon civilian inventors and scientists as well as upon Naval personnel. As a matter of fact, while most of the improvements had originated with those who navigated the ships, the debt of the Navy and the Army as well was due to such civilians as Sperry for the gyroscope, to Gatling for the first machine gun, to the Wrights for pioneering the fighting ships that fly, and to others who had no connection with the armed forces.

ENLISTING EDISON

Seeing that the Allies had been unable to devise effective weapons against the U-boats and our Naval officers could suggest no better ways, I seized upon the sentence in Edison's interview that only "at the call of my country" would he turn his efforts to war weapons. As Secretary of the Navy (for I had no acquaintance with him), I wrote him a letter asking him to render the Navy and the country "a very great service," telling him that "one of the imperative needs of the Navy is machinery and facilities for utilizing the natural inventive genius of Americans to meet the new conditions of warfare as shown abroad," and saying that it was the intention of the Navy Department to establish a Department of Invention and Development, to which all ideas and suggestions, either from the service or civilian inventors, could be referred for determination. He was told that its success would depend upon the ability to have "some man whose inventive genius is recognized by the whole world" to head such service and the letter added: "You are recognized as the one man above all others who can turn dreams into realities and who has at his command, in addition to his own wonderful mind, the finest facilities in the world for such work." He was told also that there were no funds and "I unfortunately have nothing to offer you but the thanks of the Navy and I think the country at large." The letter went on to say:

"We are confronted with a new and terrible engine of warfare in the submarine, to consider only one of the big things which I have in mind; and I feel sure that with the practical knowledge of the officers of the Navy, with a department composed of the keenest and most inventive minds that we can gather together, and with your own wonderful brain to aid us, the United States will be able as in the past to meet this new danger with new devices that will assure peace to our country by their effectiveness."

He was also told, "If you are not able for any reason to do this I will frankly hesitate to undertake the matter at all."

THE NAVY CONSULTING BOARD

What was the response? Immediately Edison expressed his readiness by sending Miller Reese Hutchison, then associated with him, to Washington, and I later went to Orange to talk over the details. "You will need more than a few men to undertake this gigantic task," he said. "You will need to enlist the scientific and engineering and inventive organizations." Instead of picking out here and there a few men to constitute the Navy Consulting Board, "who would represent themselves alone," Edison displayed his genius by suggesting that heads of eleven of the largest engineering societies in the United States be asked each, as president of the organization, to select two of its members to serve on the Navy Consulting Board. This wise suggestion was at once acted upon, and I wrote: "The judgment of your members as to who is most qualified among you to serve on this Board will be far better than my own." All the societies promptly named their representatives, and within a few weeks the organization was effected in Washington with Edison at the head, and the twenty-two eminent members had the cordial support of all their organizations, embracing the foremost scientific men in America. This was due solely to the vision and wisdom of Edison.

The story of the patriotic devotion of these distinguished men has been told in Lloyd Scott's book, a record that shows every member deserved the honor given to those who do things "beyond the call of duty." At first, they paid their own expenses, giving much of their time without pay. They did not even get the "dollar a year" compensation. It was not a war organization. It was called into being in 1915, long before America entered the World War, and it gave to Naval problems study and research and investigation before the stress of war laid the imperative hand upon all Americans.

Simon Lake wrote in his book *The Creation*, that "the civilian board of advisers to the Navy of the present Secretary of the Navy, Mr. Josephus Daniels, I consider one of the greatest achievements of the Wilson Administration."

In 1893 Mr. Lake offered to put his talent and knowledge at the service of the Navy, but it lacked the vision to accept the tender. If Naval experts and Mr. Lake had worked together, they would have perfected a submarine boat that would have made America the leader in undersea craft.

The Board, as organized at Edison's suggestion, was composed of Thomas A. Edison, president; William L. Saunders, chairman; Benjamin B. Thayer, vice-chairman; Thomas Robins, secretary; Lawrence Addicks, Bion J. Arnold, Dr. L. H. Baekeland, D. W. Brunton, Howard E. Coffin, Alfred Craven, W. L. R. Emmett, Peter Cooper Hewitt, A. M. Hunt, M. R. Hutchison, B. G. Lamme, Hudson Maxim, Spencer Miller, J. W. Richards, A. L. Riker, M. B.

Sellers, Elmer A. Sperry, Frank J. Sprague, A. G. Webster, W. R. Whitney, and R. S. Woodward. Admiral William Strother Smith was named as special representative of the Navy Department. All bureau chiefs and other Naval experts worked in coöperation with the Board.

The foundation of industrial preparedness was laid in the inventory of manufacturing plants in the country and how they could be adapted to making parts of munitions. Howard E. Coffin was the moving spirit in this and expressed its value in this sentence:

"Twentieth-century warfare demands that the blood of the soldiers must be mingled with from three to five parts of the sweat of the men in the factories, mills, mines, and fields of the nation in arms."

Walter S. Gifford, later Director of the Council of National Defense, undertook the survey of industry in 1915, and it was of incalculable value in making ready for war.

RECEIVED BY WILSON

On October 6, I asked the President to receive the Edison Board. He was enthusiastic about the creation of that Board and gave them a cordial welcome, expressing gratitude for the coöperation they were giving in preparedness. Speaking to them, after I had presented the members separately, Wilson in the course of a brief talk said:

"I think the whole nation is convinced that we ought to be prepared, not for war, but for defense, and very adequately prepared, and that the preparation for defense is not merely a technical matter, that it is a matter in which we must have the best minds and knowledge of the country, outside the official service of the government, as well as inside."

So far as I know this was the original use of the phrase "best minds," which was to be invoked many times later and was to be ridiculed when Harding employed it.

RED TAPE HUMBUGGERY

Gold braid and Naval etiquette and regular hours bored Edison. When he was interested in an experiment he forgot to eat or sleep. He expected Naval officers to do likewise. One day, when he was irritated at what he called "red tape humbuggery," he asked me how I could stand the frummery. Another day, in irritation over the failure of some officer to give him credit for the notable service he performed during the war, he declared: "I made about twenty-five inventions during the war, all perfectly good ones, and they pigeonholed every one of them. Naval officers resent any interference by civilians. The fellows are a close corporation." At times, it called for all the diplomacy I could command to keep the wizard from exploding when there was delay in furnishing him everything he wanted. But although Edison did not like red tape, he loved the Navy and made large contributions to it, and his name became inseparably connected with it when President Roosevelt appointed his son Charles Edison Secretary of the Navy.

INITIATING NEW WAYS

I count it among the high privileges of my life to have known Edison and to have had association with that remarkable man. I use the word "remarkable" of his personal side, for the moment setting aside the wonderful contributions his genius made to mankind in his day and for all time. His personality was as winning as his inventions were revolutionary in the physical world, where he said: "Let there be light and there was light." He loved folks—all sorts of folks. He loved to talk with them and had deep interest in his fellowmen. The distinctive thing about him was his keenness to examine what made the world go round in every department, to take the works out and look at them, but greater than that was his urge to initiate new ways, to improve what had been going along in ways that could be accelerated.

GOES IN SUBMARINE

There sprang up in our exchange of visits a rare friendship between our families. Edison was very deaf, and when I talked to him his assistant, M. R. Hutchison, used the telegraph signals. But my wife's sweet and carrying voice reached him so that they could converse without a second party. With great pride, while we were spending the week-end as the guests of Mr. and Mrs. Edison, he showed us on a pedestal a square foot of copper. Some years before, he told me that after he had made some experiments in which he had used copper, he had ejaculated: "If I had a square foot of copper I would want nothing else in the world." This statement being published, the copper producers sent the square foot. "So you see," he said, "according to my expressed wish I have the only thing in the world I wanted and I ought to be perfectly happy."

Edison had never been in a submarine when it submerged. He wanted to know how it worked. So we ate a hurried lunch and hurried over to the Brooklyn Navy Yard where his request was gratified. First he examined it as it was anchored on the water. Then it was submerged. He was so engrossed in the examination of every part that he forgot all about time and would have remained all day and night if the officers had not signalled for the ship to come to the top.

FIRST TALKING MOVIES

On one of our visits to the Edison's, my wife and I were permitted to see a preview of the first talking movie picture I had ever heard about. Edison confided to us that he was experimenting with a talking movie and would put on a private exhibition for us. The story had a Southern setting. It represented the love-making of a Federal soldier in the South in 1865 and the daughter of a Confederate soldier whose mother hadn't quit hating all Yankees. The Southern family violently objected to the marriage. It was a gripping picture. It seemed miraculous that the characters in the moving picture could be heard to talk and sing. Edison said he had not yet achieved perfect synchronization, but was sure it would soon be perfected and take the place of the silent pictures then on the screen. I do not know whether Edison got the credit for inventing the talking picture, but my wife and I were thrilled at the miraculous picture. I recalled that, though Graham Bell got the telephone patent, Edison had perfected a telephone about the same time. There was no limit to his inventive mind.

BILLION DOLLAR WIFE

"I do not know how much Dannels is worth [he always called me Dannels] but whatever the amount in dollars, he has a billion dollar wife," Edison said to Hutchison after we had visited the Edisons at their Orange home.

"A MODERN OLYMPIAN"

If asked to appraise Edison and his contribution, I would quote the following from Mary Childs Nerney in her book, *A Modern Olympian*:

"More than any other person Edison shaped and focused the forces of lineage. He was a great man and perhaps the greatest inventor of all times. Among industrial leaders he ranked a giant. An individualist, he hewed out a career possible only in America and in an America that is forever past. He was, moreover, one of those rare beings the world calls genius. But above everything he was human, delightfully, charmingly, naïvely and utterly human."

NAVY DIRECTS WIRELESS

The coming of the World War stimulated the inventive genius of men in and out of the Navy. It was discovered that some of the wireless stations in New Jersey were conducting German propaganda, and the Navy was instructed by the President to take them over. All wireless was put under Navy control, and soon Navy wireless girdled the globe, and all Navy men had pride in that it was entrusted with this new and important and near-miraculous communication. I felt that it would have been wise if it had been continued under Navy direction in peace as well as in war.

INVENTIVE GENIUS STIMULATED

When I became Secretary of the Navy, the mystery of wireless, but recently introduced, greatly intrigued me. I recall the awe with which it filled me when I first read about its introduction. Even now it seems to me to be the miracle of miracles. In America, before the World War, the chief authority on wireless was Admiral Bullard, whom I had known when he was a teacher at the Naval Academy.

"What do you know about wireless?" I asked him one day.

"Nothing at all," he answered. "I know that certain things will produce certain results, but as to the why of it I am ignorant."

Toward the close of my term I congratulated Admiral Bullard upon the achievements accomplished in a few years. He said:

TWO HUMAN DYNAMOS, BENJAMIN R. TILLMAN
AND THOMAS A. EDISON

Above, left to right, Admiral Huse, Mrs. Josephus Daniels, Josephus Daniels, Thomas A. Edison, Mrs. Edison, and Admiral Usher. *Below,* In the White House Grounds upon the occasion of the first mail carried by air. *Left to right,* President Wilson, Secretary Daniels, and Mrs. Edith Bolling Wilson.

"But for your faith and enthusiasm and complete coöperation, the large results could not have been attained. From the day we talked wireless in 1913, we who are called experts have relied upon your help and your zeal has been a stimulus to all of us."

The Navy and the world also owe gratitude to the vision, wisdom, and technical ability of Admiral S. C. Hooper who, as an authority at home and in world conferences did much towards advancing the wireless to its present value in war and peace.

TALKING TO A SHIP AT SEA

Arrangements having been made with the American Telephone Company to bring the Navy Department into such close touch with distant ships and stations as the exigencies of war might demand, I held the first wireless conversation with a ship at sea on May 6, 1916. Promptly at 4:00 P.M. in my office at Washington I lifted the receiver on my desk and was connected with Captain Lloyd H. Chandler, who was on the bridge of the *New Hampshire* at Hampton Roads.

I asked, "Is that you, Captain Chandler?"

"This is Captain Chandler."

"Where are you?" I asked.

"On the bridge of the U.S.S. *New Hampshire* at Hampton Roads."

I continued: "It is interesting that the first conversation with a warship at sea should be between the Secretary and the son of a former Secretary. It is interesting, also, that the first conversation is with the *New Hampshire*, of which you are the captain, and incidentally that she bears the name of the State from which you come."

"Thank you, sir," replied Chandler.

After some further conversation, I said: "I will be in my office in the Navy Department at ten o'clock tomorrow morning. I will ring you up then and have another conversation. I can hear you as well as if you were in Washington, Captain Chandler. It will not be long before the Secretary of the Navy will be able to sit in his office and communicate with vessels of the Navy all over the world by wireless telephone."

The next morning, after calling Chandler as I had promised, I said, "You will never be happy again, Captain Chandler."

"Why not?" he asked.

"You know the old saying by Naval officers—'I am never happy except when my ship is at sea where neither my wife nor the Secretary of the Navy can give me orders.'"

I then told him to stand by for a few minutes. I had asked my Aide to get Mrs. Chandler on the phone, and I called to her: "Is that you Mrs. Chandler?" The reply being in the affirmative, I told her that her husband wanted to speak to her.

"But he's at sea, Mr. Secretary," she said. "He left Hampton Roads yesterday on the *New Hampshire*."

"Yes, I know," I replied, "but miracles are happening these days. He is calling you now."

After they had conversed she called me back and said she thought I was playing a joke on her when I told her she could sit in her home in Washington and talk to her husband at sea. "It quite thrilled me," she said. "Wonders will never cease." I repeated to her what I had said to her husband that with this new discovery, happiness for Naval officers was at an end because they could not be free from directions from their two bosses. I was as much thrilled as Mrs. Chandler.

Admirals Benson and Badger and other officers in the Department talked with Chandler. The next day on the *New Hampshire*, cruising fifty miles at sea, Chandler talked to the Commandant of the Navy Yard at Mare Island, California.

More than seventy guests were present in the Navy Department when this new and direct communication was inaugurated, including officers of the American Telephone and Telegraph Company, U. N. Bethel, Vice President, and J. J. Carty, Chief Engineer, who made addresses. I expressed the thanks of the Navy, saying, "This is indisputable proof that whether American business men are acting as individuals or as corporations, their hearts respond readily and unreservedly to the call of their country, and they are planning to serve their country in ways hitherto unknown." Mr. Carty said: "There is no Navy in the world which has the power of the United States Navy to mobilize instantly its resources through such a system of communications."

FURTHER NAVY RESEARCH; HELIUM FOR AIRPLANES

The inflammability of the gas used in airplanes was responsible for the accidents and consequent reduction of usefulness of the new airplanes introduced in the Navy. "Is there not some safe substitute?" I asked Admiral Griffin, able head of the Engineering Bureau, saying that the best research men should be called upon to see if such substitute could not be obtained at a cost justifying its use. He said there had been reports of the presence of such a substitute found in Kansas, but not in sufficient quantities to be useful. The value of such substitute was deemed so great that the Navy Department began experiments in securing helium from the gas of the Petrolia field in Texas. Scientists believed that helium could be obtained by a new and original process and that the cost would not be prohibitive. Two plants were constructed at Fort Worth, Texas, where there was produced a substance, camouflaged as "argon," the term used to designate helium, to be used by the Army and the Navy. The conduct of the experiments and production were under the control of the Navy, a compliment to the efficiency of its experts.

The Navy was able to produce helium in increasing quantities. It was so precious that not a drop of it could be taken out of the country except by permission of the Secretary of the Interior. No other country possessed it. Some years ago, sensing the need of helium to prevent the inflammability of planes, Germany made a request to purchase some of it. There was no war then, but as I had fathered the building of the first helium plant in 1916 I rejoiced when Secretary Ickes gave an emphatic "No," while others with less foresight were willing to let Germany have a supply. Later our own need was great and we wished the supply larger.

A NAVY LABORATORY

Early Edison suggested there ought to be a Navy laboratory, where civilian and Naval experts could perfect their discoveries and inventions. Such a laboratory was built near Washington on the Potomac and has more than justified whatever it has cost. I do not know the name it bears, but it ought to be called the Edison Naval Laboratory.

Among the many contributions it has made is radar, which has worked something of a revolution. Unfortunately, instead of keeping it as the exclusive property of the government, it, like other Navy discoveries, has been turned over to private capital for manufacture for profit. That unwise course should cease.

LIII

FRIENDSHIP WITH ADMIRAL DEWEY

A FEW DAYS AFTER I became Secretary I had a call from the Naval Aide of Admiral Dewey, who conveyed the message that the Admiral wished me to name an hour when he could call to pay his respects. There was no other Admiral, and Dewey's title was "The Admiral of the Navy." He was always referred to as "the Admiral." All others so called were in fact only Rear Admirals. To Dewey's Aide I replied, "Please convey my compliments to the Admiral and say to him that I cannot consent for him to call on me. It is my desire and pleasure to do myself the honor to call on the man I recognize as the real head of the Navy."

I was told that the message pleased the Admiral. The next morning I called, being received by him and all the members of the General Board. The Admiral rose and insisted that I take his seat at the head of the table. I declined, insisting upon his occupying his own seat while I sat at his right. Some of the Naval problems were briefly discussed, and in a few minutes the other members of the Board withdrew, leaving me alone with the Admiral. He opened the conversation by saying that he was appointed to the Navy under the administration of Franklin Pierce, a Democrat, from his native State, and that the Secretary of the Navy at that time was James C. Dobbin, of North Carolina, "one of the ablest Secretaries in the history of the Navy." He went on to say, "I have, as every Naval officer should, refrained from taking any part in politics, loyal to the Commander in Chief, but in principle I am a Democrat." I could see that he was happy that a member of the Democratic Party was Secretary as he was serving his last years in the Navy, to which he had long given the full measure of devotion.

FOUNDATION OF FRIENDSHIP

The foundation of an intimate friendship I will always cherish had its beginning in a way I little imagined. Not long after Dewey returned from Manila, the hero of heroes, American admirers, after showing him every honor that could be bestowed, presented him with a house in Washington City. Shortly afterwards, when he was married, chivalric sailor that he was, he presented the house to his bride. He acted in the belief that the American people would applaud his act, for who could object when it gave such happiness to the Admiral to transfer the gift to his wife? It is difficult to understand the flood of denunciation which followed. Papers which had given him rank with Nelson and Farragut poured out their vials of wrath upon the head of the brave man they had been hailing as the country's noblest hero. It was true that Dewey's wife was rich, but that was no justification for what seemed a conspiracy of propagandists to berate Dewey and withdraw the admiration given him so enthusiastically. It astonished and stunned him. Not to the day of his death could he understand why a people who had almost worshipped him could treat him so. It cut him to the quick. It was the only incident in his life that gave him trouble. It was proof of what Mr. Dooley said of the ingratitude of republics: "Triumphal arches created in honor of heroes should be made of brick," said Mr. Dooley to Hennessy shortly after the criticisms of Dewey's chivalrous act. Hennessy wished to know why. "Because," said Mr. Dooley "so they can tear it down and hurl them at the hero when they get tired of worshipping at his shrine—these Americans are queer people."

I was editing the Raleigh *News and Observer* when Dewey on May 1, 1898, sailed into Manila Bay in the early morning, and when, to be precise, at 5:40, his ships were within two and a half miles off shore, Dewey turned to Captain Gridley and gave the first and only permissive Naval command recorded in history: "You may fire when you are ready, Gridley." That order resulted in victory and the wresting from Spain of its rich territories in the Pacific and the Atlantic. Dewey's victory thrilled me, and I conceived deep admiration for him. Later, when the tirade of criticisms followed his presentation of the house to his bride, I took occasion editorially to denounce in *The News and Observer* those guilty of trying to undermine the high place he had won by foresightedness and courage. I did not suppose Dewey had seen the editorial.

DEWEY SAYS NAVY BETTER THAN EVER

Rarely did the Admiral of the Navy offer any suggestion or make any recommendations except in his full and wise official recommendations during the four years of delightful association. But in every way he gave me helpful support with many evidences of friendship. In days when a few officers were critical, I was strengthened by his whole-hearted support. This confidence was made public in a letter written by Admiral Dewey in May, 1915, when President Wilson made an address in which he expressed full confidence in the Navy and the Secretary of the Navy at a dinner given to the officers of the Atlantic fleet in New York. At that time some of the critics of the Navy were filling the papers with charges of deterioration of the fleet. Admiral Dewey's letter was complete refutation of their charges. Regretting that he could not be present, and expressing his appreciation for the magnificent welcome received from the people upon the occasion of the return of the *Olympic* to Seattle in 1899, Admiral Dewey said that "the country should continue its wise policy of increasing the size of our Navy until it is strong enough to meet on equal terms the Navy of the strongest probable adversary." The Admiral also said in the letter:

"The people of New York have just cause for pride in the fleet now assembled in their harbor. Not only is it composed of the finest and most efficient warships that we have ever had, but it is not excelled, except in size, by the fleets of any nation in the world. As President of the General Board for the last fifteen years, I can say with absolute confidence that the efficiency of the fleet has steadily progressed, and has never been so high as it is today."

At a dinner given to the officers of the fleet, I set forth clearly the purpose of creating a greater Navy, saying: "Our Navy is good; it is not good enough. The Navy is strong; it is not strong enough. We will make it stronger so that by our very strength we may be able to demand the right to live at peace with all the world."

OPPOSES GENERAL STAFF

In an interview with George Creel printed August 20, 1916, in the New York *World*, Admiral Dewey was asked: "What is all this clamor about the Navy needing a General Staff? "I don't know," the Admiral replied. "I have tried to pin them down, but not one has ever been able to make clear just what it was that he wanted. Down in their hearts I suppose they want a small, select body to have entire charge of the Navy. Well, they'll never get it and should not get it. I can conceive of no greater madness than to put the Navy in the hands of a Naval group."

Mr. Creel, in view of criticisms of my administration, asked the Admiral: "Has Secretary Daniels demoralized the Navy?" His answer was "Bosh!" "The exclamation was one of disgust and indignation," said Mr. Creel, who quoted the Admiral as going into detail and adding that never in his knowledge had the matériel and personnel been so efficient.

The Navy League, in its propaganda for increasing the Navy, stressed the goal as "the second strongest." Admirals Dewey, Badger and Benson joined with me in urging a Navy equal in every way to the strongest that sailed the seas. "The second strongest" was regarded by Dewey as an admission that some other nation had a right to superiority.

When the Gridley monument was unveiled in Erie, Pennsylvania, I accepted an invitation to deliver the address. Of necessity, I could not speak of the courage and patriotism of Gridley without also telling the story of Dewey at Manila, for Dewey and Gridley were imperishably linked together. A short time after the address, Mrs. Dewey rode out to our home, "Single Oak," and told my wife that she and the Admiral had been so touched by what I had said at Erie that she wished to give me a present, a beautiful silver ink-stand. Before my wife could thank her, Mrs. Dewey said, "My dear, in this world you know men always get the best of everything, but I was determined in this instance to break that old rule, and so I have brought you a present." It was a handsome silver vase engraved "M.D." (for Mildred Dewey) to "A.D." (Adelaide Daniels). "Between them M.D. and A.D. count for something," she said in the affectionate manner she always showed toward my wife.

WHEN THE ADMIRAL LOST HIS TEMPER

In all the years of intimate and official association I had never seen anything about Dewey but courtesy, kindness, and an equable temper. I was therefore wholly unprepared to hear him give way to such a torrent of swear words as both astonished and shocked me.

ADMIRAL GEORGE DEWEY

President of the General Board of the Navy, hero of Manila Bay,
and foremost Naval statesman.

MEMBERS OF THE COUNCIL OF NATIONAL DEFENSE
AND THE ADVISORY COMMISSION

Seated, left to right, David F. Houston, Josephus Daniels, Newton D. Baker, Chairman of the Council; Franklin K. Lane, William B. Wilson. *Standing, left to right,* Grosvenor B. Clarkson (Secretary), Julius Rosenwald, Bernard M. Baruch, Daniel Willard, Dr. Franklin H. Martin, Hollis Godfrey, Howard E. Coffin, Walter S. Gifford (Director). Taken in the office of the Secretary of War.

He thought he had provocation and had nursed his wrath until it dominated him. One afternoon, after office hours, about a year or more before his death, my Aide informed me that Admiral Dewey had called to see me. His mission was to give high commendation of Admiral Samuel McGowan, whose name was under consideration as Paymaster General of the Navy. I knew he held McGowan in genuine affection. I informed him that his commendation confirmed my opinion of McGowan and I would recommend him to the President.

As the Admiral was rising to leave, Admiral Benson, Chief of Operations, came into the room. I saw a baleful light come into Dewey's eyes as Admiral Benson advanced and held out his hand in salutation. The Admiral drew back, the blood rushing to his face, and with a look of passionate indignation, he said in bitter tones: "How dare you to offer to speak to me, you damned hypocrite and snake who has been seeking to undermine me, you blankety-blank God damned blankety-blank." That denunciation in language that astonished me continued to pour from the Admiral's lips as he turned his contemptuous look on Admiral Benson. It was for me a terrible moment. I moved toward Admiral Benson and said, "For God's sake, say nothing, leave it all to me." That was asking too much of a proud-spirited man who had been denounced as every sort of a hypocrite and knave. He could not keep silent under the accusation. I do not recall his exact words. With indignation, and evidently trying to restrain himself, Admiral Benson expressed his astonishment at the Admiral's denunciations and told him that some enemy had spoken falsely of him. He denied emphatically that he was capable of trying to undermine the Admiral, saying that he had always regarded him as an inspiring Naval leader and had always been glad to follow where he led. This did not soften Dewey's wrath. Indeed he was more inflamed, warning Benson not to add falsehood to treachery. I literally begged Benson to make no answer, but to return to his office and trust me in the situation. As he retired he said to the Admiral that when he learned the truth he would regret he had spoken thus to his warm admirer. Dewey hurled after him bitter denunciation, and at once, in spite of my entreaty to remain, abruptly left the office by another door and walked down to his car, not waiting for the elevator.

After Admiral Dewey had departed, I sent for Admiral Benson.

I congratulated him that, in the face of severe provocation, he had acted as well as he had. He said that he had never been so astonished at anything in his life, for he had done nothing or said nothing that justified the suspicion of the Admiral. He said he thought he knew who had sown the seed. It developed that an officer who never liked Benson had poisoned Dewey's mind by telling him that Benson was scheming to secure appointment as President of the General Board for himself, thus ousting Dewey on the ground that he was too old to carry on. I was indignant at such attempt to make a breach between Dewey and Benson. Satisfied that there was not the least foundation for the story whispered to Admiral Dewey, I determined to try to mollify the Admiral. Whether to attempt it while he was still angry after his passionate outbreak, or wait until another day, I found it hard to determine.

DEWEY KISSED SECRETARY

When my wife called for me as usual late in the afternoon, I had made up my mind. After acquainting her with something of what was to me a real tragedy, I told her that I must see the Admiral at once. It was our habit to drop in at the Dewey home for a brief visit on our way home. The Admiral had recovered his equanimity. As we entered, we noted that the Admiral and Mrs. Dewey were listening to a familiar song on the phonograph. When it was finished, I talked with him about the incident, told him that the President and the Secretary of the Navy would not think of anything except that he should remain as head of the General Board in active service as long as he lived, and that he should have known that no change could be made except by us, even if some lesser man should deem himself qualified to step into his shoes. I proceeded to say that somebody had misrepresented the attitude of Admiral Benson who was incapable either of hypocrisy or lack of loyalty to him. He listened and said little except that he knew no conspiracy would win as long as I was Secretary. When I was leaving, he put his arms around my shoulders, and turning to his wife and mine so that they could hear, said, "You are a dear good boy," and accompanied me to the elevator, and as we said good-bye, he embraced and kissed me, greatly to my surprise. It was the first time any man has kissed me. It was his method of expressing his appreciation for what I had done and his affection which was and is so dear to me that I have cherished it as a sort of lasting blessing.

DEWEY LOSES TEMPER AGAIN

Admiral Brownson told me a story showing how Admiral Dewey lost his temper on another occasion. He said:

"I went to see Dewey in a rage because a doctor had been put in charge of a hospital ship. As Commander in Chief I was outraged that a medical man who knew nothing about navigation had been put in charge of a ship in my fleet and expressed myself in lurid language. 'Be calm,' Dewey counselled. 'Don't get excited, but be moderate.' We talked on for some time. I don't know how it came about; but before we had finished Dewey, forgetting his counsel to me, said: 'By God, if I could get my hands on the man who abused my wife I'd break his neck.'"

Dewey held no resentment toward any individual except those who had cruelly wounded his wife by bitter criticism when he deeded to her the house given by the people upon his return from Manila.

BOTH WORLD WARS ENVISIONED

I never talked with the Admiral much about the Battle of Manila, or his problems in the Philippines until I was preparing my address for the unveiling of the Gridley monument. He has written that glorious page of history but to hear him recall that epic was an education in Naval warfare and diplomacy, for he demonstrated his skill in both at Manila. He feared the Germans would do exactly what they did in the World War. He was convinced of danger from that country and cited a conversation he had with Admiral Von Goetzen at Manila in 1898. Here are the exact words of the German Admiral:

"About fifteen years from now my country will start a great war. She will be in Paris in about two months after the commencement of hostilities. Her move on Paris will be but a step to her real object—the crushing of England.... Some months after we finish our work in Europe we will take New York and probably Washington and hold them for some time. We will put your country in its place with reference to Germany.

"We do not propose to take any of your territory, but we do

intend to take a billion or so of your dollars from New York and other places. The Monroe Doctrine will be taken charge of by us, as we will then have to put you in your place, and we will take charge of South America as we wish to.... Don't forget this—about fifteen years from now remember it, and it will interest you."

When the Admiral recalled that statement, after giving me some data for my tribute to Gridley, I confess now that in that quiet room surrounded by Dewey's trophies, I did not think it possible that the prediction of the German Admiral would come true in sixteen years. He missed it by only one year. Did Dewey expect to see that prophecy and threat come true in his lifetime? I do not know, but he devoted his life after Manila to preparedness, in case. And he lived to see Germany begin the war with the ambitious designs seen in 1914-18. He did not live to see Armistice Day, but he never doubted the victory of his country.

DEWEY'S SEVENTY-NINTH BIRTHDAY

The last birthday before the passing of Admiral Dewey was celebrated quietly. A delegation of Naval officers and the Secretary of the Navy called to present their affectionate greetings and good wishes. As his friends were leaving, the Admiral said, "I appreciate your coming; I hope I will be here next year. I have that incurable disease which John Hay called 'anno domini.' Well, we all have it."

During the call, I read to the Admiral an extract from a log— December 26, 1866—of an old shipmate of the Admiral. The shipmate who sent me the log was First Assistant Engineer, Henry Brown U.S.N., on the *Colorado* just after the Civil War, at the time Dewey was First Lieutenant. I read from the log:

"Mr. Dewey, our First Lieutenant, as well as captain in the absence of Captain Wyman, succeeded in making all on board happy and contented (Christmas, 1866). He made each man a present of a bottle of wine, or in that proportion from the Slush Fund. Dinner was served for 700 men.

"The ship was in a manner given to the crew. Throughout the whole day all was perfect order with the exception of here and there a loud voice from one who had probably taken more than his allotted share. Mr. Dewey will certainly be long remembered for his endeavor to make the crew comfortable."

The Admiral showed pleasure in having the old days recalled to him and was very happy.

After reading the log and commenting on it, I said that it showed the interest in the welfare of the men of the Navy on the part of Admiral Dewey when he was a young officer, and that attitude had been characteristic of him during his long career. Dewey said, "I remember that day very well. It was in Port Mahón. The captain was in the country. I went in to play backgammon with Admiral Goldsborough, which we did for an hour every evening. While I was in the cabin with him, he said, 'Mr. Dewey, your men seem to have had a happy time today. What was all the cheering about?' I said, 'They gave you nine cheers.' 'They did' he replied, 'and I was much delighted. It was a happy ship, gentlemen.'"

BURIED IN ARLINGTON

Early in the New Year the Admiral was confined to his room and died while I was on a brief visit to Raleigh. I hastened back to Washington to pay tribute and to join in the distinguished honors paid him when he was buried in Arlington in January, 1917.

A short time after his death, for his widow leaned on me and my wife, Mrs. Dewey evinced her affection more after the passing of the Admiral because she knew of the strong ties that existed between us and her husband. At her request, I went to see Secretary of War Baker to ask that she be permitted to erect a sarcophagus on the eminence in Arlington where he was buried. There was a regulation of the War Department limiting the height of any monument, and she wished her memorial to be imposing. She also wished to have assurance that when she died she would be buried by his side in Arlington. Both requests were granted. For many hours Mrs. Dewey and my wife and myself and Admiral McGowan pored over plans for a suitable memorial. One, with the four stars of an Admiral on a field of blue glass, was selected. Mrs. Dewey found sad satisfaction in every detail of its construction. Often we drove out to Arlington as the work progressed and when it was completed she seemed lost. Never very strong, withdrawn in solitude and sorrow, she did not live long. To the regret of his shipmates and friends, who felt that his body should always rest in Arlington with those of his shipmates and comrades, she was persuaded to permit the removal of the Admiral's body from Arlington.

One day long afterwards, talking with Admirals Badger and Rodman, we expressed regret that the body of Admiral Dewey had been removed from Arlington. I offered to join them in becoming body-snatchers and taking it back to the place of first interment. The only thing that deterred us was our deep respect for Mrs. Dewey. There was gossip in Washington that Bishop Freeman had, in her days of illness, overpersuaded her to consent to the removal to the Washington Cathedral, of which the Admiral had been a trustee. Admiral Rodman quoted some lines written about it, which ran something like this:

> "There was an old Bishop named Freeman
> At body snatching a demon
> He got a President
> As a permanent resident
> And now he has our first able seaman."

When I talked to Bishop Freeman about this matter he corrected the gossip, saying that he acted at the request of Mrs. Dewey. All the same I told the Bishop that it seemed to the Navy that Arlington was the most suitable place of interment for the great Naval hero.

MONUMENT TO DEWEY

I did not wish to go out of office without assurances of a worthy memorial to Admiral Dewey. I quote from my Diary of December 17:

"Yesterday, in my hearings before the House Naval Affairs Committee, I recommended that a commission be appointed to prepare plans for erecting a suitable memorial to the late Admiral Dewey, and that it be worthy of the great Admiral.

"Mrs. Dewey had told me that the Admiral would not feel that it would be a suitable distinction to name a destroyer the *Dewey*. Seeing that hundreds of destroyers had been constructed and named for heroes who were not world figures, I urged that some memorial in keeping with the magnitude of Dewey's achievement should commemorate his great service. I stressed that Dewey had become more than a distinguished Admiral: he was in a real sense an institution in Washington, an exemplar of patriotism and naval prowess."

ADMIRAL DEWEY'S TRIBUTE

Shortly after Admiral Dewey's death the General Assembly of North Carolina passed resolutions of respect embodying a statement made in March, 1913, about Honorable James C. Dobbin of Fayetteville who was Secretary of the Navy when Dewey entered the Naval Academy. A copy of this resolution was sent to Mrs. Dewey. She acknowledged it in the following letter to Overman, who had the resolutions and Mrs. Dewey's letter printed in the *Congressional Record:*

1601 K STREET, *February 10, 1917.*

HON. LEE S. OVERMAN,
    United States Senator from North Carolina.

DEAR SENATOR: I am sending you a copy of the resolutions adopted by the General Assembly of North Carolina expressing the appreciation of the people of that Commonwealth of the services rendered to his country by my husband, George Dewey, the Admiral of the Navy.

I am grateful for this tribute kindly sent by the secretary of state of North Carolina. My husband had a warm spot in his heart for North Carolinians, particularly for Hon. James C. Dobbin, who was Secretary of the Navy when he entered the Naval Academy, and for the present Secretary of the Navy, Hon. Josephus Daniels, under whose administration he rendered his last service to the Navy and to his country.

In the following letter written in 1913 the Admiral expressed his estimate of Mr. Dobbin as Secretary of the Navy:

"ADMIRAL OF THE NAVY,
    "Navy Department, March 12, 1913.

"DEAR MR. SECRETARY: Referring to our conversation of this morning, it gives me pleasure to restate what I said at that time, that I was appointed an acting midshipman in the Navy in September, 1854, by the Hon. J. C. Dobbin, Secretary of the Navy, a resident of North Carolina. During his administration of the Navy Department we built 18 of the finest ships of their class that there were in the world: Six frigates of the *Wabash* class, six sloops of the *Hartford* class, and six third-class sloops of the *Iroquois* class. In my opinion, Mr. Dobbin was one of the ablest Secretaries of the Navy the country ever had.

"Faithfully, yours,   "GEORGE DEWEY."

"SECRETARY OF THE NAVY,
    "Navy Department, Washington, D. C."

I wish you, and the people of the country also, to know that my husband felt for the present Secretary of the Navy, Hon. Josephus Daniels, a sincere affection. Only a short time ago the admiral said, "I have been in the Navy 62 years, and have served under many Secretaries of the Navy, but Secretary Daniels is the best Secretary we have ever had, and has done more for the Navy than any other. I am amazed by his knowledge of technical matters. He has studied profoundly, and his opinion is founded on close observation."

Will you express my profound thanks to the General Assembly of North Carolina? I am, Senator,

Very truly,   MILDRED McLEAN DEWEY.

The affection between the Admiral and Mrs. Dewey was beautiful, and her admiration of him and pride in him knew no bounds. She loved to talk to me about him. In the days following his death, my wife, Mrs. Dewey and I would sometimes sit in the early twilight listening to his favorite songs and hymns on the victrola, always closing with the song that he loved best in his last days, "The loved ones are looking this way." We recalled that there would be tears in his eyes as the sentiment suggested by the words of the song carried him back in memory to those he had known long since "and lost a while." After he had passed on, as we sat quietly and listened to words that had so touched his heart, our own hearts were moved to what seemed like communion with the departed. For the Admiral was a deeply religious man, as are most men who go down to the sea in ships—this is true even if they sometimes do swear.

With the end of the Wilson administration, our furniture packed to go to our old home, in Raleigh, Mrs. Dewey insisted upon our coming to her house as her guests in the last week of our official life in Washington. We all lived over the days of association with the great sailor. The beloved and lonely widow of "The Admiral of the Navy" presented me with the silver shaving cup she had given to the Admiral a year before and which he had used every day. "I know if the Admiral could speak he would say that above all men he wished you to possess this cup which he prized."

LIV

ADMIRAL GRAYSON, PHYSICIAN AND FRIEND

WILL YOU BE KIND ENOUGH to tell me whether there is anything I can properly and legitimately do to set forward Cary T. Grayson's chances of promotion?" That was the question President Wilson asked me in a letter dated July 2, 1915. It was written from Cornish, where the President was spending the hot season. The suggestion made in that letter caused one of Wilson's most stubborn contests with Senators. It was, I think, the only time he was charged with favoritism during his two terms. When the name of Lieutenant Commander Cary T. Grayson, Surgeon, U. S. N., was sent to the Senate for confirmation as Rear Admiral in the Medical Corps of the Navy, Washington literally buzzed with gossip that "Wilson is passing over older and abler men to give the four stars to a younger officer because of personal friendship." In view of what followed, Wilson's letter is interesting.

"THE WHITE HOUSE
 "WASHINGTON

"CORNISH, N. H.,
 "July 2, 1915.

"My dear Daniels:
 "Will you be kind enough to tell me whether there is anything I can properly and legitimately do to set forward Cary T. Grayson's chances of promotion? I mean any such thing as, for example, ordering him to an examination, or facilitating the process by which he may qualify.
 "I need not say that he has not spoken to me about this and that the question has arisen in my own mind merely out of the desire to reward an uncommonly faithful and serviceable man. It would embarrass him if I were to do anything irregular and I myself would not desire to do anything of that kind, but I thought that it was possible that I might legitimately increase his opportunities in some way that would be above criticism.
 "Always

"Affectionately yours,
 /s/ "WOODROW WILSON"

"Hon. Josephus Daniels,
 "Secretary of the Navy."

It was the only letter Wilson wrote to the Navy Department relative to the promotion of a Naval officer. It got him into a hard fight for a time. Me too. However, it brought deserved promotion to a skillful surgeon, and it all turned out so well as to vindicate Wilson's action.

If there was the suggestion of personal desire to advance Dr. Grayson it had grown out of knowledge of his fitness as much as from a desire to favor a friend. Wilson had never seen Grayson until the night of his inauguration. I doubt if he had ever heard of him. The sister of the President, Mrs. Howe, had sustained a slight injury. "What shall I do for a doctor here in Washington, E. P.?" asked Wilson of his old college mate, Dr. E. P. Davis, of Philadelphia, who had come to the inauguration. First aid had been administered by Dr. Davis, who said to the President: "The Navy surgeons have a fine reputation. Send for Dr. Grayson."

Cary T. Grayson had been the surgeon at the White House during the Taft administration and had been an Assistant Surgeon there during the Theodore Roosevelt administration when Dr. Rixey was the White House physician. As President Taft was leaving the White House, he affectionately laid his hand on Grayson's shoulder and said to President Wilson. "Here is an excellent fellow that I hope you will get to know. I regret to say that he is a Democrat and a Virginian, but that is a matter that cannot be helped."

Not long after Wilson came to the White House, he said one day to Grayson, "I have had several requests from parties on behalf of surgeons to be assigned to duty at the White House. You have made no application. Why not?"

The answer Grayson made pleased the President. He replied, "I do not think it in good taste."

Not long thereafter when I was lunching at the White House with the President and his family, Wilson turned to me and said, "Mr. Secretary, there is one part of the Navy I must ask you to let me have. I want you to let me appropriate this part," laying his hand upon the arm of Grayson as he said it. He added: "I wish this part of the Navy for my very own."

"I see that when you want the best, you know that you must come to the Navy," was my answer.

That was the way Grayson was notified of the official designation that he was to be regularly detailed as the President's physician.

DOCTOR BECOMES ADMIRAL

Wilson made it a rule to leave matters of promotion in the Army and the Navy and the assignment to duty of military officers to the Secretary of War and the Secretary of the Navy. Not even in the matter of details to the White House did he issue any orders. Of course in selecting officers who were to be his aides, the secretaries conferred with him. In nearly every instance he preferred that the secretary should make the designation.

The Personnel Navy bill of 1915 for the first time gave the rank of Rear Admiral to officers in the Medical Corps. Congress left the method of how the promotion should be made to the Navy Department with no legislative provision as to the method of selection. When the time came to recommend the two surgeons who should be the first to receive rank and title of Rear Admiral, Dr. W. C. Braisted, Surgeon General of the Navy, with the rank of Captain, and Lieutenant Commander Grayson were recommended by me. Upon his return from Cornish, President Wilson was assured that he had the full legal power to designate the two Admirals. I told him that in point of ability and standing in the medical profession the two men who had shown themselves best qualified were Dr. Braisted and Dr. Grayson. In the case of Dr. Braisted the promotion was regular. If appointed, he would pass from Captain to Rear Admiral without jumping over any grade. His relative standing would call for no criticism even from those who believed all promotions should be controlled by length of service. Moreover he had come to the position of Surgeon General after successful assignment as Surgeon of the Atlantic fleet, and his subsequent record in war preparation brought him the highest commendation.

In the case of Dr. Grayson, if the former old rule of promotion by seniority should be applied, of course Grayson could not be named. By authority of Congress, the Navy Department had abolished promotion by seniority in all grades of the service. Congress had in fact put its foot down on promotions by seniority.

PROMOTION PROTESTED

I recommended that the promotion of surgeons and other staff officers be by merit, initiative, and ability, regardless of length of service. However, when the name of Grayson was sent to the Senate, the friends of some excellent surgeons, older in point of service, felt that the younger man had been given the promotion because of the President's personal regard for him, and that it was contrary to the rule that ought to prevail in promotions. They protested vigorously against the older men's "being jumped over," as they put it.

The last thing that Wilson wished to do was to practice favoritism. It was contrary to his convictions. The fact that his appointment of Grayson might be regarded as giving a distinction or honor to a close friend troubled him. The question was the subject of several discussions between the President and the Secretary of the Navy. The President was assured that, while there would be opposition and disappointment, the Naval service as a whole, except those wedded to seniority, would regard Grayson's promotion as worthy of the best traditions of the service. My prediction that there would be a flare-up came when some of the leading newspapers of the country declared it was "pure favoritism."

WITHIN THE LAW

The fight for confirmation was a long and rocky one. It looked doubtful for a time to everybody except Wilson. It was January 18, 1917, that the President sent to the Senate the nomination of Grayson as Medical Director with the rank of Rear Admiral. On the same day the names of five other staff officers went to the Senate for confirmation with the rank of Rear Admiral. In not one of the five cases was the rule of seniority followed, though one, Admiral Taylor, was the senior in his staff. But he was not selected for that reason. He was recommended because he was the ablest man in that corps in the Navy and, for that matter, in any other corps. If he had been ten years younger and it had been necessary to jump him over scores of others, his name would have gone in. The Senate promptly confirmed Taylor. His nomination fitted in with the old seniority rule as well as the rule of merit. On January 23 I issued a statement saying that before the President appointed the new Rear Admiral, the Judge Advocate General of the Navy gave an opinion, concurred in by the Attorney General, that it rested entirely within the discretion of the President to select the staff officers whom he deemed best fitted for advancement. The statement said that while in the line the Navy promotions were to be made by a special board, no method for advancement of staff officers was provided. The statement concluded:

"The fact that an officer selected for advancement to the rank of Rear Admiral happens to be in a junior grade does not deprive the President of his constitutional power to make such advancement, but merely necessitates as a preliminary step that the officer be promoted to the higher grade which has the rank of Rear Admiral attached. Such promotion can be made only after the officer has fully demonstrated his qualifications, as required by law, which requirement has been observed in the case of staff officers recently nominated for promotion."

FIGHTING THE PRESIDENT

The Senators, who were placing their opposition to Grayson on the ground that he was "jumped over" many of his superiors in rank, confirmed the other staff officers, who had been promoted by merit instead of seniority. The further fight was to rebuke Wilson for promoting his physician. The Republican Senators, led by Lodge and Weeks—always the senior Senator could be counted on to oppose what Wilson wanted—began a filibuster against confirmation. These tactics were pursued until March 4. They thought they had the President defeated. They had no objection to Grayson. It was Wilson they were gunning for. But they reckoned without knowing the kind of man they must meet in combat. On March 6, he sent Grayson's name back to the Senate. The Senators saw that Wilson had enlisted for the war. He was fighting for a principle that constituted the right of the executive as Commander in Chief of the Navy to nominate to vacancies. The Senate could withhold confirmation if the officer nominated was unworthy, but in the absence of law, the Senate could not control the executive's right to nominate the officer he believed best qualified. In that, as in almost every other case, Wilson won in his combat with the Senate.

HE WON HIS PLACE

Grayson was no accident. He had won his place. Long before Wilson was in politics, Grayson had been called as Assistant Surgeon to the White House in Roosevelt's day. T. R. dearly loved his horseback rides, and he picked out Grayson as riding companion. He sat on a horse—all country boys in the South could ride well almost as soon as they could walk—as if he had been born there. Roosevelt ordered Army officers to ride a given number of miles in a given time to keep themselves "fit." He was the sort of man who would not order another man to do what he would not do himself. He gave a thriller when he made his famous horseback ride from Washington to Warrenton and back in a cold sleety rain that froze as it fell. It was young Dr. Grayson who was his companion. When the papers played up Roosevelt's feat, the name of the young physician was not printed. Upon leaving the White House, Roosevelt gave high recommendation of Grayson to Mr. and Mrs. Taft. The physician won the heart of Mrs. Taft, in her delicate health, by his sympathetic devotion.

There was no foundation for the flippant statement of one critic who said, alluding to the close friendship between the second Mrs. Wilson and Dr. and Mrs. Grayson, "Most men got their four stars from participation in war, but Grayson's came from the boudoir."

If any sentiment controlled the President in his insistence upon the confirmation of Grayson it was the recollection of the first Mrs. Wilson's friendship for him and her grateful appreciation of his goodness in her long illness. Her last words to Dr. Grayson were: "Take good care of Woodrow. Promise me." He was true to that promise to the very end.

Admiral Grayson was not only an excellent physician and a wise administrator; he was a man of fine poise, sound judgment, and broad wisdom. His affection and admiration for Wilson, and his loyalty to him are beyond appraisement. He was the soul of frankness, and when his advice was asked—and it often was—it represented both sincerity and knowledge. Moreover, he was a good judge of men. As a Navy man he felt free to give me his experiences and opinions of men around the President. Nobody fooled Grayson; for example, when writers were making House a miracle man, Grayson said to me, "House is a Me-Too Man"—and he was, until he became infected with Paris-itis, a disease that gave some Americans an undue sense of their importance.

Years afterwards President Roosevelt, familiar with Grayson's ability as an executive, made him the head of the Red Cross, and he ably administered that great organization until his untimely death.

LV

WILSON AND TWO VIRGINIANS

THERE WAS HARDLY any man in the country, outside his Princeton classmates, for whom Wilson had higher admiration than for Edwin A. Alderman, president of the University of Virginia. When the trustees of the University decided to depart from Jefferson's idea of a rotating chairman of the Faculty and elect a president, Wilson was approached with a view to making him the first president of an institution which was proud of his having studied law there. At the time Wilson could not make a change, and he suggested Alderman, who was elected. Early in his administration when Alderman was at Saranac Lake, temporarily out of harness because of a throat affection, Wilson said to me, "How I wish Alderman were well. He would make a great Ambassador at the Court of St. James's."

While he was at Saranac, Alderman wrote often to the President about matters in which both were interested. Sometimes he let me read them. He and Wilson were alike masters of style. One day I received a letter from Alderman in which he asked me to see Wilson and tell him that he would be everlastingly grateful if he would appoint his brother-in-law, Mr. Anderson, Postmaster at Wilmington. Anderson had held the position in the Cleveland administration and wished to be named again. Alderman said that he hated to make the request and be importunate, but that the appointment was very near his heart. When I informed Wilson of Alderman's letter and read him a part of it, I saw he was as keen to grant the request as Alderman was to obtain the place for his kinsman. Wishing to act in harmony with Congressman Godwin of that district, he said to me, "I wish you would see Godwin, and tell him that I would regard it as a great personal favor if he would recommend Alderman's brother-in-law to the Postmaster General."

Of course I was glad to be the intermediary. When I saw the Congressman I began the conversation by saying, "Godwin, how many applicants are there for Postmaster at Wilmington?"

He answered that he was about to turn gray trying to decide which one to recommend. "I must disappoint a dozen," he added. I then told him I had a plan to relieve him of all difficulty and responsibility. He asked me to explain. I then read him part of Alderman's letter, told him I was conveying President Wilson's earnest request that he would recommend Anderson. "You will be doing something very agreeable to the President," I said, "and you can tell all the other applicants that, of course, you could not do otherwise than accede to the President's wishes. You will be killing several birds with one stone and not make any enemies." He saw the point, made the recommendation, and when he next called at the White House, Wilson expressed his deep appreciation.

As the time of the Baltimore Convention drew near, the matter of the winning presentation of Wilson's name was deemed so important that I asked Alderman, who was born in Wilmington, North Carolina, where Wilson spent part of his boyhood, to second Wilson's nomination. I felt sure he would be happy to do so and was certain no one could do it in a more eloquent and convincing manner. I was surprised when, in response to the request, Alderman said:

"Old man, there is nothing on earth I would rather do. I profoundly believe in Wilson. The man and the hour have met. I share your admiration for him. However, I cannot yield to my heart's desire. There are others who can present his fitness as well as I. There is a compelling reason, not personal but based upon my duty to the University, why I must deny myself the most coveted opportunity of my life. But, gee, how I would like to do it! I hope and pray he may be the next occupant of the White House.

"You ask my why I must decline? I will tell you. From the day I went to Charlottesville to take the presidency of Jefferson's University, Senator Martin has been my neighbor, my friend, my counsellor, my support in everything I have undertaken. You know that, following Jefferson's ideal, the University had never had a president. Powerful friends of the institution did not like the innovation. Moreover, influential men did not relish the idea of any other than a Virginian to be its head. The appropriations for the University were wholly inadequate. It was my task to justify the selection of a president and of an outsider, and to secure an increase in income. Martin with his powerful influence has been my strong right arm. I owe him so much that I simply cannot do what you ask. His dislike of Wilson is a passion. He would never forgive me if I spoke for Wilson. Why he hates Wilson with such bitterness is beyond my comprehension, but it is a fact I cannot ignore."

Alderman then told me that at his table at the University, when Wilson was his guest, a verbal combat between Wilson and Martin reached such heights of passionate ferocity as he never imagined could dominate two such leaders. He had to intervene and change the subject.

If the sense of obligation to Martin denied Alderman the privilege of seconding Wilson's nomination at Baltimore, there came a time when, in a most distinguished way, he delivered an immortal eulogy of Wilson at a joint session of Congress after Wilson's death. It will live in American annals among the masterpieces of eloquence, along with Blaine's eulogy of Garfield. It is the American counterpart of the tribute of Pericles to the heroes of the Peloponnesian wars.

A deep chasm of views separated Wilson and Martin. The Senator was ordinarily suave and courteous, but he lost control of himself when Wilson's name was mentioned. He was a machine politician, who owed his rise to his manipulation of politics for the benefit of railroads and monopolistic corporations, which furnished the oil for his machine. Wilson was the antithesis of all his beliefs and practices. Martin sensed that Wilson, if elected, would do to all machine politicians what he had done to Senator Jim Smith, whom he unhorsed in New Jersey. Therefore, in the philosophy of Martin, it was essential to destroy Wilson before he destroyed the gods which Martin worshipped. As was to be expected, Martin threw nearly the whole vote of Virginia against Wilson's nomination. I recall that during the long balloting I stopped to talk to my friend, Senator Claude Swanson and urge him to come to the support of Wilson, the Virginia-born candidate. I said to him: "Never before did I desire to be a Virginian even for a day. I'd like to be a delegate from the Old Dominion to vote to restore the ancient prestige of the Commonwealth as the mother of Presidents and put a Virginian in the White House." But Martin had most of the delegates sewed up against Wilson and held them until it was plain that Wilson would win.

I was not surprised, therefore, in December, 1912, shortly after his election, when Wilson was visiting his birthplace, Staunton, Virginia, on the anniversary of his birth, he gave mortal offense to Martin and other machine politicians, in his address. He let it be known he understood the political situation in Virginia, saying "Virginia showed no great enthusiasm for my nomination," and after outlining his policies and saying he would put on "war paint" for "good hard fighting" against privilege, Wilson added—and it was believed he was serving notice on Martin and his Virginia machine:

"I could pick out some gentlemen, not confined to one State, gentlemen likely to be associated with the Government of the United States, who have not had it dawn upon their intelligence what its government is set up to do. There are men who will have to be mastered in order that they shall be made the instruments of justice and mercy.

". . . . There are certain gentlemen—I dare say one is present tonight—who have frankly told me that there was a time when they were afraid of me. . . . But these gentlemen now say to me that in view of things that I have said since I was nominated—which are exactly the same things that I said before I was nominated—they are no longer afraid of me. By which I draw this simple conclusion, that they did not read the things that I said before I was nominated, and that after I was nominated it became worth their while really to find out what I did actually say. . . .

"The trouble with some gentlemen was that they had ceased to believe in the Virginia Bill of Rights. . . ."

Martin and his associates were deeply offended, regarding the statement as notice that they had to be "mastered" and "made the instruments" for carrying out the New Freedom, whose creed they detested. Virginia papers regretted that Wilson should "unnecessarily antagonize the Virginia leaders." Martin, though voting for most of Wilson's measures of "justice and mercy," never forgave him.

The first time I ever heard of Martin was in 1895. One morning early in that year my good friend Henry St. George Tucker, Congressman from the Lexington, Virginia, district, called at the Interior Department where I was Chief Clerk. He was mad all through and could not conceal his indignation and humiliation that "Virginia had disgraced itself by defeating Fitzhugh Lee and electing Tom Martin, whose use of corporation money in the election of legislators had caused Virginia to bow its head in shame. I have just returned from Richmond where I saw a United States Senatorship put on the block and sold." He added that the railroads and other corporations had put up the money that compassed Lee's defeat.

Martin was astute, capable, agreeable, and he controlled Virginia politically from his election in 1895 until the day of his death. As long as he lived, Carter Glass could not realize his senatorial ambition. It was the very irony of fate, so the Martin machine thought, that by an accident of politics Virginia had a Governor at the time of Martin's death who gave Martin's toga to Glass, his long-time political foe. One great source of Martin's strange hold on Virginia's politics was that he had as backers the big corporations and also, through an alliance with Bishop Cannon, the Anti-Saloon organization when it was powerful.

Unless Martin had possessed some finer qualities than Henry St. George Tucker attributed to him when he defeated Fitzhugh Lee for the Senate, he could not have won the friendship of Alderman or held the place of leadership in Virginia given him until his death. But this does not say that he was not a product of machine politics, which was married, as nearly always, to corporations desiring public favors.

Martin's dislike of Wilson was increased when, announcing his support of Wilson in the Baltimore Convention, Bryan introduced a resolution denouncing Thomas F. Ryan, a close friend and supporter of Martin, who had caused Ryan to be elected as a delegate. It was not lessened when he had to swallow the bitter medicine of casting Virginia's vote for Wilson who was nearing the goal of the nomination. Martin was a soldier, never guilty of mutiny, keeping in mind party regularity and fearing his own fate and that of his well-oiled machine.

In spite of Martin's dislike of Wilson, he supported nearly all of the President's policies. I never heard his bitterness break out but once. At the request of Wilson, when vital appropriations for the war were being held up in the Senate Appropriations Committee, of which Martin was chairman, I went to his committee room to convey Wilson's urging for prompt and favorable action. The formal hearing by a subcommittee over, Martin asked me to remain. When we were alone he broke into a fury of passionate abuse of Wilson, the like of which I had never heard, accompanied by a volley of profanity which both astonished and shocked me. I had always found him a soft-spoken man of quiet manner. He was beside himself with uncontrollable rage. He denounced Wilson's extravagance and poured out so much vindictiveness that I simply waited until his fury spent itself. And then I quietly asked him: "What answer must I take to the

President? Are you going to appropriate promptly the money necessary to carry on the war?" Still in white anger he answered:

"O, hell, yes. Every cent of it, and it is because I have got to do it that I am so damn mad. Wilson sends requests that are unreasonable. I am opposed to them, but I am under duress. If I oppose Wilson, his clacquers in Virginia all cry out, "Tom Martin is a reactionary," and hound me. Yes, you tell Wilson I'll vote every damned dollar he wants, and expedite the passage of the measure, but I must tell somebody what a bitter pill it is to be held up by the man in the White House. You and the rest are hypnotized by this schoolmaster. I am distrusted because I was opposed to his nomination and so Swanson and I will vote for every damn thing he proposes to show the Wilson men of Virginia that they would be foolish to want to retire us from the Senate in order to support the policies of the President. You may say we will support Wilson better than his most perfervid admirers, but it makes us damn mad to have to do it."

Upon my return to the White House, I informed the President that Senator Martin not only would support the bill but would expedite its passage. He was as good as his word. But I never conveyed any intimation of Martin's evidence of hate and his bitter words. Wilson said: "Please convey to the Senator my appreciation." If he had known of Martin's denunciation and hatred, he might have felt like saying: "Tell Martin I thank him—damn him."

I never talked with Martin again and did not know whether his feeling against Wilson had softened until, having gone to the Senate, September 30, to hear Wilson urge the submission of the Woman Suffrage Amendment, as I was leaving the Chamber I met Martin, who was hot with indignation at the President's bringing up woman suffrage in the stress of war and trying to persuade Senators that such action would help win the war. "It is ridiculous and an insult to senatorial intelligence," said Martin. He was always glad to oppose the President when he could safely do so.

One fact, evidently known to Martin in addition to his ingrained feeling that it was bad to have a school teacher using the rod, was that when Wilson was elected he was resolved to put only progressives on guard (it's a pity he ever varied from that course), and in so far as he could, to secure progressives in the direction of legislation in Congress. The one Senator he at first most wished to see denied leadership was Martin. But the Senate, committed irrevocably to the great god of Promotion by Seniority in Service, and resenting executive direction, made Martin chairman of the important Committee on Appropriations and also elevated him to be president *pro tem* of that body. Though he didn't like Wilson and though as a standpatter he did not approve many of Wilson's policies, and personally did not like the most progressive ones, Martin piloted some of the most important Wilson measures through the Senate. It went against the grain, but as "a regular of regulars" he followed the lead of the chosen party leader as he expected Democrats in Virginia to "follow your leader, meaning me."

Wilson later referred to the fact that the conservative Senators like Martin could be depended upon once they were committed to the party policy, even better than the men of more progressive learnings. He attributed it to the fact that they regarded politics as similar to a military organization in which superior officers must be obeyed. He said to me, "If once you get the machine men committed to a program, they can be relied upon to carry it out better than liberals, because they understand there must be discipline and obedience in the organization."

LVI

AMBASSADOR BRYCE AND EX-SECRETARY
CHANDLER

M Y FIRST FOREIGN VISITOR, when I became Secretary of the Navy, was James Bryce, the distinguished British Ambassador. Some time before, Bryce had delivered the annual address at the North Carolina Literary and Historical Society at my home city. It was my pleasure to spend most of the day in his company. I had been interested in his writings on American politics and government. On that day in Raleigh, I was more than fascinated by the man. He seemed an encyclopaedia, as indeed he was, with the charm of the simplicity of greatness. It interested him that our State Capital bore the name of the illustrious English explorer, and he told me stories about Raleigh which I had never heard. He was keen to know more about Flora MacDonald and the thousands of Scots who settled on Cape Fear after the Battle of Culloden. He wanted to hear the story of Virginia Dare, the first white child born in America, and to learn about her birthplace on Roanoke Island. He was interested in stories of local color and in the relation of the two races in the South.

Shortly after he had accepted the invitation to make the address in Raleigh, I had written and asked him to send me a copy of his address in advance of delivery. I was interested when he told me in Raleigh that before coming to America he had never furnished an address for the press in advance of delivery. He said:

"In our small country the telegraphic report of a speech delivered at night reaches all the papers so quickly that it can appear in every paper the next morning. I did not conceive it was different in the United States until I learned that when I spoke in Portland, Maine, and had a message which I wished to reach all your people, not a word of it appeared the next morning in any newspaper in Portland, Oregon, or in any other city on the Pacific Coast. I, therefore, found it necessary to prepare my addresses and give them to the press before delivering them. It has its disadvantages, for often I find that I am led by the surrounding conditions or some new happening to change my prepared address."

Mr. Bryce also told me that he did not dictate his addresses. "I write them with my own hand," he said. "When you dictate you use too many words, whereas when you use the pen you employ fewer, you erase and change so as to select the word that best expresses your meaning."

I felt flattered that the great Ambassador should wish to renew the brief acquaintance. Washington had added attractions because my wife and I came in cordial relations with Ambassador Bryce and his wife. Later, during the World War, I had several letters from him to the effect that he earnestly hoped my country would join with democratic nations to prevent the sway of imperialism in the world, and he sent me a happy message in April, 1917, when the United States entered the war. When we were in London in 1919, my wife and I were happy to renew the acquaintance with the Bryces.

EX-SECRETARY OF THE NAVY CHANDLER

A few days after I entered upon my duties in Washington my Aide told me that ex-Secretary Chandler, one of my predecessors, wished to call to pay his respects. I fixed an hour for the following day and that night said to my wife that I had an engagement to see a man the next day who was the greatest thief in America. "Who can that be?" she asked. I answered that it was William E. Chandler, who in 1876 had robbed Samuel J. Tilden of four years in the White House after the people had elected him.

I recalled that as a fourteen-year-old boy in the politically-minded village of Wilson, North Carolina, I made it a point to spend part of my time out of school in the office of the Wilson *Advance*. Its editor, Colonel Henry G. Williams, ate, slept, and drank politics. From boyhood he had given himself wholly to the advancement of the Democratic Party in trying days. He knew the game and the players, from the township to Washington, and was long the closest friend of Senator Matthew W. Ransom. It was the day after the election. We had gone to bed on election night confident, after New York, New Jersey, Indiana, and Connecticut had voted for Tilden, that he was the next President. In that village, where every white man was a Democrat, the people had fireworks and a jubilee to rejoice that Tilden had been elected President and that Vance had been elected Governor. The "John W. Dunham cannon" made the welkin ring.

The next day I stood on the outskirts of the crowd, anxious for later news.

"Is it certain Tilden is elected?" asked Asa Hill, a farmer who had ridden to town to get the news.

"Yes," replied Colonel Henry G., "but there is a blankety-blank thief who has set about to steal the presidency."

I had never forgotten that remark. Colonel Henry G. was a sort of political source of information, who honored a fourteen-year-old boy by explaining politics and newspapers to him.

When I was to meet "that blankety-blank thief Bill Chandler," over the lapse of two score years, the words of Colonel Henry G. came back vividly to me and I could almost hear his voice of bitterness as he spoke. In all the intervening years, without ever having seen him, William E. Chandler incarnated for me the worst of political haters of the South. Soon I was to find the truth of the words of Charles Lamb that "if you know a man you cannot hate him."

Mr. Chandler was at that time (1913) an old man, somewhat feeble, as I observed when he crossed the large room occupied by the Secretary of the Navy. I received him with the official courtesy due to a man who had long held high stations. I found that his mind was clear and strong and he talked from a wealth of knowledge of the country and of the Navy. His interest in the Navy had not abated and he gave me an insight into its workings and growth that I later found valuable. He invited me to call to see him, saying that his strength did not permit him to get out often, and his visit of courtesy to me was the first he had made for weeks. He talked entertainingly of his association with Senator Vance, of North Carolina, at whose feet I had sat and learned true democracy. He told of how he and Vance and Tillman had coöperated to secure legislation to curb railroad domination, and how later he had been the victim of railroad opposition in his State. I recalled how about the same time Vance had engaged in controversy with railroad magnates in North Carolina, and how they sought in vain to break his hold on the support of the people.

OFFERS FRIENDLY AID

When my newspaper plant was burned, ex-Secretary Chandler offered me the plans of his plant in Concord, New Hampshire, where he owned a newspaper, and in other ways showed me friendship. I found he possessed many fine qualities, and we had much in common, in spite of differences in politics and the fact that from early youth I had regarded him as "the man who robbed Tilden of the office of President." Our association convinced me that Charles Lamb was right. I have had many other like evidences in my intercourse with public men whom I had not previously known and who were ogres only in the bitterness of political difference.

FORMER SECRETARY GAVE GOOD ADVICE

During his visit Mr. Chandler out of his experience gave me good advice. Later I regretted I had not followed it. "May an old man who is retired make a suggestion so that you will avoid the mistake I made when I was Secretary of the Navy?" he asked. I told him I would thank him. He then said, "Do not keep in the Department or in key positions any officers appointed or assigned to duty by your predecessor. They will feel they owe you nothing and few of them will be loyal to your policies. Select new men who will feel they are a part of your administration and help make it succeed." He added he had suffered because he unwisely kept in position men selected by his predecessor. I did not at once take his advice, to my regret; but as soon as I became well seated I called to positions men of ability who were keen to advance policies adopted and upon whose loyalty and support I could rely.

LVII

RUN-INS WITH SENATOR LODGE

Senator Henry Cabot Lodge was a staunch supporter of all policies to strengthen the Navy before the World War and upheld and defended its conduct of the war. The ranking member of the Naval Affairs Committee, he never permitted politics to influence his actions in matters affecting the Navy. I had, however, several run-ins with him over the assignment to duty of a Marine officer which demonstrated that he let his heart influence him more than his colleagues thought possible.

Early in my administration I made it a rule that no officer should have a long assignment of duty in Washington. Having ordered several desk officers to sea, I issued like orders giving duty to Marine officers at posts not in or near the national capital. But in one case I ran up against an obstacle that proved insurmountable. The story illustrates how deep-seated is senatorial pull and how Senators seek to aid their friends and relatives even in assignments in the Army and the Navy.

A PERMANENT FIXTURE

Colonel Charles McCauley, whose father had been Major General Commanding of the Marine Corps, had gone into the service as a field clerk while his father was in command of the Marines, and he had remained in the service ever since, in the Quartermasters Corps Department. He had been promoted step by step until he was then second in rank in the Quartermasters Department, of which General Denny was the head. He had been in Washington practically all his life. As a young man he was a favorite in society, the picture of sartorial elegance. As a matter of fact, he had never, since he was a young man, been out on the field, and he was regarded in Washington as more of a club and social leader than as having any great efficiency in the Marine Corps. This does not mean that he did not do his job well or that afterwards, when he came to be head of the Quartermasters Corps Department, he did not see that his department functioned well. He was very agreeable, always obeyed orders, but somehow or other he had enjoyed a pull all these years that gave him the soft place in Washington. I determined that the policy of not permitting any officer to stay in Washington for a long period demanded that he be given an assignment away from the capital, and so I gave orders for him to be detached from duties at headquarters of the Marine Corps in Washington and assigned to duty in San Francisco. That order created a sensation. Washington society and Washington clubs were aghast. They thought McCauley's pull was such that the Washington monument would fall down sooner than McCauley would be ordered out of Washington.

ROOSEVELT'S IMPISH LOOK

I remember that the day after the order became public Franklin Roosevelt, Assistant Secretary, came in and expressed great surprise that McCauley had been ordered away, and he laughingly said that nobody believed it could be done. He added, "You are up against it. You will find more pressure will be brought on you to keep McCauley in Washington than you ever imagined."

"Has Charlie McCauley gone?" inquired Franklin Roosevelt the next morning. He was evidently acquainted with the appeals of Lodge and Tillman and Swanson.

"No," I answered, "but he will go on the date of the order."

"I will believe it when I see him on the train," he said. He may have known more than he revealed.

Afterwards he said, with an impish grin, as he poked his nose into my office, "I told you I did not believe either you or the President or God could get Charlie McCauley out of Washington."

I had been hoist with a petard prepared by the law I had urged. When I acted, I was not familiar with the influences that were around McCauley and I paid little attention to Franklin Roosevelt's prediction. I had assigned an officer to come to Washington to take McCauley's place and given directions that McCauley should leave and be on duty at San Francisco within thirty days. And then the big guns came into action. From more sources than I can remember came people urging that the order be revoked. If I believed all that was told me by some of McCauley's friends, it appeared that the Marine Corps would cease to function unless McCauley should be in the national capital. This made me feel it all the more necessary to see that the order was carried out. I had a notion then, and have never lost it, that no man is indispensable. Old Andrew Jackson was right when, having removed an officer of the government and being told that the duties could not be carried on except by that man, Old Hickory said, "Abolish the office then, because if he should die, the government would go on the rocks."

"YOU HAVE RAISED HELL"

Pleas for McCauley's retention in Washington did not have any effect. I did not know the secret of his pull until some days later when Senator Tillman, chairman of the Naval Affairs Committee, came to see me. He said, "You have certainly raised hell. Why did you dig up so many snakes by ordering McCauley to San Francisco? Didn't you know that you would incur the lasting hostility of Senator Lodge if you touched McCauley?"

I told him I did not know Lodge had any interest in McCauley, and Tillman said, "Well, he has, and he has asked me to make an appointment with you for some time after office hours so that he could talk with you about it. He is deeply stirred. He rarely makes any requests, and I have come to ask you to make the appointment and do what Lodge asks. In the main I think you are right about these officers hanging around Washington all the time, but it is more important to you and to the Navy to have Senator Lodge on your side than to be so damned consistent in any rules or plans or policies."

I told him I would be very glad to see Senator Lodge that afternoon at five o'clock. In the meantime Senator Swanson, who was an influential Democrat on the Naval Affairs Committee, telephoned me that Lodge had spoken to him about the matter and that he earnestly hoped that I would grant Lodge's request; that it was comparatively a small matter and Lodge had done so much for the Navy and was ready to coöperate so fully that I ought to respect his wishes. I then began to see how serious it was.

LODGE SHOWS HE HAS A HEART

I shall never forget the conference that afternoon with Lodge. He was frank and sincere. He said he had hesitated to come to see me about the matter; that he rarely preferred any requests to a Cabinet officer with reference to any assignment of duty; that he quite approved the general policy that I had inaugurated, particularly as to men who were to command ships, though he did not see how it would be helpful with reference to men in the Quartermasters Corps or Staff Corps. However, that was a matter which he would not urge. He then told me of his interest in McCauley. He said, "You may not know, but Colonel McCauley married Mrs. Davis, who came to see me yesterday with tears in her eyes and made such an appeal to me that I could not resist it. My son, who is dead, married Mrs. Davis' daughter." Lodge was very much attached to her and, without dwelling upon it, he let me see how deeply the death of his son had touched him and how near to him was his widow and her mother. He told me that Mrs. McCauley was a very sick woman under the care of specialists in Washington and that removal from Washington where she could have the daily attention of these specialists would be very serious and on that account he had come in not to ask me to change any policy but to postpone McCauley's order to go to San Francisco for a year or until Mrs. McCauley's health was improved, when she could go without risk.

He took a half hour to tell me all this, and he was so sincere in his friendship for Mrs. McCauley and laid all his cards on the table so frankly that I was greatly tempted at once to do what he wished done. However, consistent with what I had promised myself, I told him I appreciated his call; that what he had said made a great impression on me and that I would take the matter under consideration and let him know later and I wished to assure him that if I could find a way to do it consistently, I would be pleased to grant his request.

The more I thought about it, the more I felt that the whole policy I had inaugurated would break down if an officer who had been in Washington a quarter of a century or more and had been ordered to duty away from Washington did not go to that assignment. I heard afterwards that people were betting in Washington clubs whether I would stick to my order or give in as others before me had done. The more I thought about it, the more I felt it my duty to refuse to change McCauley's orders. Senator Tillman in the meantime again insisted that it was good policy to please Lodge; that it meant more than I knew. Having reached the conclusion that it could not be true that only one doctor in America could treat Mrs. McCauley, and knowing that there were eminent specialists in San Francisco, I informed Senator Tillman that I could not change the order and wrote Senator

Lodge expressing my deep appreciation of his interest and my sincere regret that a sense of duty forbade granting his request.

But I was defeated. In a day or two General Denny tendered his resignation as Chief of the Quartermasters Department. I signed the acceptance without appreciating that I was thereby elevating McCauley to the vacancy. I did not then know, and nobody advised me, that McCauley automatically took Denny's place and that under the law passed by Congress the Quartermaster General's place of duty must always be the city of Washington. With Denny's resignation and McCauley's automatic promotion, there was no way to send McCauley out of Washington.

Denny resigned, as he said to his friends, in order to become connected with an important real estate firm in Washington, where he could earn more money. It was generally supposed by those on the inside in Washington that this position had been procured for Denny by McCauley or his friends. It was even supposed that he had been given a large guarantee by this concern and that McCauley's friends were behind it in order to secure McCauley's promotion and keep him in Washington. The morning after this coup had been accomplished and I had been defeated, Franklin Roosevelt came in laughing and said, "Chief, I told you so. There is not enough power in heaven or earth to get McCauley out of Washington."

I did not know how it happened, but it happened. Not many weeks thereafter I picked up the paper one morning and was shocked to read in the headlines that Denny had fallen from the second story of his home and had been killed in the fall. There were those in Washington who did not hesitate to say quietly that, after he had retired from his position as Quartermaster General, he found he was unsuited for the business he had entered; that he was very unhappy and dissatisfied and that it was not at all improbable that in his depression he had committed suicide. Of course there was no evidence of this and all the attendant circumstances indicated that it was an accident, but the impression persisted with some people who believed Denny had taken this way to end his life because he was unhappy.

LODGE SHOWED NO RESENTMENT

I supposed from what Tillman had said that my refusal to grant Lodge's request would cause such resentment that it would affect his attitude toward me and the Navy Department, but it never did.

Whether the fact that I had been circumvented and McCauley stayed in Washington had anything to do with assuaging his disappointment, there is no way of telling. I never spoke of the matter to him again nor did he to me, but always until the end of my term of office, though upon one or two occasions in public addresses he joined hands with his son-in-law, Mr. "Gussie" Gardner, as he was called, in his criticism of the Navy, Lodge was always courteous and helpful. In fact, there was no member of the Naval Affairs Committee outside Tillman and Swanson who gave me such cordial support and showed such intimate knowledge of the Navy and sympathy with all the policies for strengthening it as Lodge. I came to lean upon him, and in all the important matters that came before Congress, I counselled with him, Tillman, and Swanson. He seemed to appreciate consideration shown him, and later on during the World War, when I was assailed in the Senate by Penrose and Brandegee and other Republican Senators, it was Lodge who came to my defense and declared that "the Secretary of the Navy has done everything humanly possible in preparation of the Navy and in its administration." This was all the more remarkable, too, because he was very bitter in his antagonism to Wilson, hated him sincerely, and was hated quite as deeply by Wilson in return. There was never anything I wished him to do that he did not do for the Navy and do it efficiently—this not because of any personal reason but because he was deeply interested in the Navy. He knew much about it, probably more than any other man in Congress, was very proud of its history and very keen in promoting its advancement. He married the daughter of an Admiral of the Navy, was himself fond of the sea, had written much about Navy matters, and had the keenest and deepest interest in it. When the position of Secretary of the Navy was created as a separate department, President John Adams tendered the position to George Cabot, saying he was "eminently qualified." The nomination was confirmed and the commission forwarded, and Adams warmly urged acceptance of the post. His great grandson, Senator Lodge in his *Life and Letters of George Cabot,* says, "The position was declined because of honest belief in his own unfitness, combined with his dislike of publicity and great natural indolence." Lodge believed his ancestor was "well suited and might have rendered important services." He was right, for the Cabots had long loved the sea.

AGAIN WANTED FAVOR FOR MCCAULEY

About the time of the beginning of the World War, I again had occasion to do something which I thought would bring down upon me the personal antagonism of Lodge. After the Naval Bill had passed the House and reached the Senate, a paragraph was inserted in it, seemingly very unimportant, to the effect that any duty performed by any person in the Marine Corps service—or words to that effect—as a civilian clerk should be counted as military service. I had not noticed this until the bill was under consideration by the Senate Committee. I asked Swanson what it meant. He said: "We put that in to please Lodge. McCauley wanted that to go in so as to give him a length of service so that if he desired he might retire earlier than he otherwise could retire." This was as flagrant a piece of favoritism as ever found its way into Naval legislation. I told Swanson I could not acquiesce in that piece of favoritism, that it was wrong to count clerical service as military duty. He said: "It will affect nobody but McCauley. Lodge is intent on having it in the bill. It is a small matter. You had better not offend Lodge. He will appreciate it greatly, and I put it in at his earnest request. If it goes out he will be sore about it."

However, when the bill went back to the House, I took it up with Chairman Padgett of the Naval Affairs Committee and pointed out what it meant. I added that I had always opposed special legislation for any individual and I urged that the House eliminate it; that I did not wish to have any publication or public discussion about it but unless the Committee would omit it, I would feel called upon to write a letter and make it public, saying this was a piece of legislation which ought to be entitled "An Act to Give Colonel McCauley Something To Which He Is Not Entitled." Mr. Padgett agreed with me that it was indefensible and it was taken out of the bill by the House without any public discussion. In fact, its proponents had hoped it would slip through and did not wish to be put on the spot by explaining that it was a piece of pork for Lodge. This incident showed me how far Lodge would go to do something desired by the mother of his dead son's wife. I do not think she could have asked anything of him that he would not have done. A request from her, which brought back his devotion to his son, seemed to be a command and seemed to dull his sense of public duty. It illustrated also that a man who remains long in public life in Washington is apt to overlook the public interest for the private good, particularly when that private good touches anybody connected with him by blood or marriage. I never discussed this matter with Lodge nor he with me, and if he was offended he never showed it.

THREE TIMES AND OUT

There was to be one more contest between Lodge and me—if I might call it a contest when we did not come in personal touch about the matter—with reference to McCauley. He was Quartermaster General during the World War and his department functioned efficiently. When the war was over, a provision was inserted in the Navy Affairs bill in recognition of their service in the war to promote the Major General Commanding of the Marine Corps and other officers at headquarters to the rank of Major General. It had the approval of Chairman Padgett of the Naval Affairs Committee in the House and of Chairman Swanson of the Naval Affairs Committee in the Senate, and, of course, of Lodge, because he was always ready to do anything for McCauley. Before I knew anything about this matter, the leading members of the Naval Affairs Committee had committed themselves to it.

The Marine Corps officers had done a fine job. They were entitled to commendation and recognition, but I could not see making any of them who had never been in action Major General. It seemed to me that the Corps was too small. The head of the Marine Corps, General Barnett, had done his job well, but he had not been in action during the war. None of the officers who were to be so signally honored had taken active part in Europe and it seemed a recognition too great to give to men whose duties had not been in the field. I took strong ground against these promotions even opposing the views of my good friends. They were not given the high rank to which they aspired. I insisted that all promotions to highest rank go to those who had been on the firing line in France.

LODGE'S SON-IN-LAW

The most vicious assailant of the Naval administration in Congress was Senator Lodge's son-in-law, A. P. (Gussie) Gardner. Unlike Lodge, whose devotion to the Navy made him helpful to the Naval administration, Gardner was a blatant and bitter critic. He was

C. K. Berryman, in the *Washington Star*

"LISTEN WHILE I WARBLE"

Congressman Gardner compelled to listen while Secretary Daniels sings the
answers to questions he has answered before.

obsessed with the opinion that Naval target practice showed that the
sailors could not hit the mark. He bombarded me with demands that
all the scores, which had always been kept secret, should be made
public, and when they were not disclosed, he denounced the Secretary of the Navy for being a party to Naval inefficiency in gunnery
and fired questions at me every week for a long time.

During a campaign in Maine when I was speaking in the interests
of the Democratic candidates, Gardner preceded me by one day in an
appointment in a Maine town. I arrived in the night, and when I
read the paper the next morning, I saw that in his address he had
devoted himself mainly to me, and the paper contained a score of
questions which he claimed he had asked me and I had failed to
answer. He said, "When Secretary Daniels speaks tomorrow night,
make him answer these questions," and the questions were published
in full in the morning paper.

It was a good advertisement for my speaking date and brought me
a great crowd in a Republican town. I related that I had answered
all these questions of Gardner by telephone, telegraph, special delivery, and every other known means of communication, but he could
not seem to understand the direct answers, and therefore, I said,
having tried ever other means with the Congressman, I saw no way
to enlighten him unless I should sing the answers to him. That reply
of singing the answers caught the eye of Cartoonist Berryman of
the Washington *Star*, who drew a cartoon of Gardner at his desk in
the House, while I stood behind him holding a book of songs entitled "As I Have Said Before," and saying, "Listen while I warble."

The questions Gardner asked as to actual scores in target practice
were regarded as military secrets, but I requested Admirals Fletcher
and Benson to give the score to the Congressional Naval Committee.
Fletcher testified: "Scores recorded in the last target practice were
higher than ever before."

LVIII

McREYNOLDS, BRANDEIS, AND CLARKE

WILSON MADE three appointments to the Supreme Court bench. When he came to make his first appointment in 1914, there were two aspirants in the Cabinet—McReynolds and Lane—for the appointment, but neither spoke of it to me and I am sure neither made effort to influence the President's decision. If Wilson had possessed the power to look into the future, I am sure he would not have "kicked McReynolds upstairs," as it was said he did. He had named McReynolds Attorney General because McReynolds had refused to go along with Wickersham, who refused to pray judgment when the tobacco trust was convicted. I shared Wilson's early expectancy that McReynolds would be a legal "trust-buster." It soon developed that any tendency in that direction had almost exhausted itself in the prosecution of the tobacco trust. McReynolds had been brought up in a school of strict construction and in the belief that *stare decisis* came from God. He was as honest and courageous as he was reactionary.

If Lane was disappointed, he never gave evidence of it. Years afterwards, when he and Wilson differed widely and he resigned to accept a position with a big oil company, some of Lane's critics said he never forgave Wilson for overlooking the appointment of a progressive of his type and appointing a reactionary like McReynolds. But I do not think Lane was capable of harboring such resentment. Lane thought—and correctly—that Burleson was at least in part responsible for his not being called to the coveted position. In two letters he wrote to his wife shortly after the McReynolds' appointment, there is evidence that he was disappointed. Neither letter indicated resentment toward Wilson. In the first he wrote:

"Neither the President nor myself alluded to the late lamented oversight on his part, and on meeting the members of the Supreme Court I did not find that through the omission of appointing me on said court the members thereof felt that a great national loss had been suffered. No one, in fact, throughout the evening alluded to this miscarriage of Wilson."

In the other letter he showed resentment toward Burleson:

"I loitered for a few minutes behind the line [at the President's reception] and then betook me to the President's library, where I spent most of the evening hearing the Postmaster General tell of the great burden that it was to have Congress on his hands. Bernard Shaw writes of the Superman, and so does, I believe, the crazy philospher of Germany. I was convinced last night that I had met one in the flesh."

"I DID IT," CLAIMED BURLESON

If Burleson could have looked over Lane's shoulder as he wrote, it would have made him happier at having favored McReynolds. About a year before he died, while my wife and I were visiting Mr. and Mrs. Burleson in Austin, the Texan told me, "I was responsible for the appointment of McReynolds," and proceeded to detail the steps he took to influence it. I said:

"Albert, that was one time you gave Wilson bad advice. While I have the same respect for the honesty of McReynolds that you have, history has shown, what I sensed at the time, that McReynolds was congenitally unable to favor the progressive policies Wilson incarnated. He was sound on the tariff, he did a monumental job in convicting the tobacco trust, and is free from influence from any quarter, but on the bench he has shown that the tides of liberalism have never reached him. He has sought by most technical and archaic reasoning to scuttle every piece of needed New Deal legislation. He is the most reactionary justice on the bench."

He agreed that McReynolds was conservative but was glad he had been appointed instead of Lane. If I had been consulted, as between the two, I would have favored Lane because, while we had differed widely and were sometimes dangerously near an impasse over Naval oil reserves, which threatened but never produced a breach in friendship, I knew that Lane in most things was a progressive, even if a backslider when it came to oil conservation for the Navy. His decisions on the bench would have upheld the New Freedom legislation, whereas McReynolds had no sympathy with any of it. I am sure that, while always respecting McReynolds' intellectual honesty,

Wilson lived to regret he had placed a man on the bench with a mind not open to the need of judicial growth and not willing to uphold humanitarian legislation, as were Holmes and Brandeis. Time proved my hunch was right. There were no regrets in the White House, when, after his vigorous dissents in New Deal legislation, McReynolds resigned, and Roosevelt embraced the opportunity to appoint a man whose mind ran nearly along with his way of thinking. McReynolds found himself in a hopeless minority, and, unable to cast off his devotion to old convictions, he gave up in despair that "the good old times" (which never were) were gone forever. He was the last defender of the Has Been.

THE WORST THING THAT EVER HAPPENED TO HIM

McReynolds never married. Was that what made him a standpatter who was wedded to early training in the profession at a time when the great gods Precedent and Tradition ruled? Rallying him for his bachelor estate when his colleagues mistakenly thought he had lost his heart to one of the loveliest daughters of the Cabinet circle, McReynolds, who had a sense of humor all his own, said:

"I am like the man thrown from a high bridge into a swamp. While he was lying prone and helpless hoping for first aid, a keen reporter found him and insisted on interviewing him, propounding many questions about how the accident occurred and about his life history, ready for an obituary if he should die—questions which in his agony he found difficult to answer. To the last question the reporter asked: 'Are you married?' The man replied: 'No, this is the worst thing that ever happened to me.' "

FIGHT OVER CONFIRMATION OF BRANDEIS

The ablest Jew in America in my generation was Louis D. Brandeis, a native of Kentucky, who became a leader of the bar in Boston. He first won prominence as counsel for the public or for labor in questions relating to public utilities and hours of labor and the cheapening of life insurance. He became the ablest expert on railroad rates and was in opposition to all monopolistic practices. He backed up every statement or position with such an array of facts and logic as to make his positions impregnable. He was one reformer who knew the bottom facts of every industry or corporation or situation touched by his position. He became *the* authority. As a result, labor and all progressive movements looked to him for light and leading, whereas the exploiters feared him. Long before I knew him and came under his personal charm, I had followed his royal fight against Privilege. I was familiar with the fact that he had stood with Glavis and Pinchot against the plundering of government national resources in the Ballinger scandal, precursor of the Teapot Dome oil reserve steal.

"They may deny me the right to name their greatest man in the Cabinet," said Wilson to a friend, when the Democratic leaders of Massachusetts made vigorous objections to Brandeis as Secretary of Commerce, "but they likewise deny New England a seat in the Cabinet." That was near the end of Wilson's Cabinet-making and he substituted Redfield for Brandeis, having relied upon Redfield during the campaign as tariff adviser. But if the politicians could keep Brandeis, who had been rather independent in politics, out of the Cabinet, they could not keep him off the Supreme Court bench.

WILSON KNEW HIS MAN

In January, 1916, President Wilson nominated Brandeis as Associate Justice. Wilson knew his man. Their minds ran together. Wilson knew that Brandeis had said, "In the last century our democracy has deepened. Coincidentally, there has been a shifting of our longing from legal justice to social justice." When Wilson was a candidate in 1912, Brandeis showed he knew Wilson, for he had said, "Wilson understands the dangers incident to the control of our industries and finance. He sees that true democracy and social justice are not attainable unless the power of the few be curbed, and our democracy become industrial as well as political."

Brandeis's appointment was a blow full in the face for the forces of Privilege. He was not a conformist. He had fought and defeated the privileged classes and drawn blood. He was a Jew. He was a radical. It would never do for such a man to go on the conservative Supreme Court. The nomination aroused class and purse and racial antagonism of the most bitter character. The Tory Brahmins were up in arms against a Hebrew who had exposed their fattening on the public. They organized opposition. President Lowell, of Harvard, Senators Lodge and Weeks, and that portion of the bar of Boston which stood for the status quo were shocked at such profanation of the highest tribunal. They sent out an SOS call in their fight to prevent confirmation.

THEY INJURED THEIR REPUTATIONS

It was answered, and six able former presidents of the American Bar Association—William H. Taft, Simeon E. Baldwin, Francis Rawle, Joseph H. Choate, Elihu Root, and Moorfield Storey—appended their names to a statement that "taking into view the reputation, character, and professional career of Mr. Louis D. Brandeis, he is not a fit person to be a member of the Supreme Court of the United States." That declaration did not add to the reputation of these ex-presidents of the Bar Association. As an offset to these declarations, former Chief Justice Fuller was quoted as having said that Brandeis was the ablest man who ever appeared before the Supreme Court in his day, adding, "Also, he is absolutely fearless in the discharge of his duties." The President wrote a letter urging the confirmation. It culminated with the sentence, "This friend of justice and of man will ornament the high court of which we are all so justly proud."

ELIOT AND POUND RANG TRUE

Though Massachusetts Senators and others waged a bitter fight against Brandeis, the broad-minded men of Harvard, headed by former President Eliot and Roscoe Pound, urged his confirmation. Pound wrote: "To have one of such a stamp on the bench of our highest court at this time is a happy augury for the law," and New England's grand old man, Dr. Eliot, rang true. He wrote: "I have known Mr. Brandeis forty years and believe that I understand his capacities and character," adding: "Under present circumstances I believe that the rejection by the Senate of his nomination to the Supreme Court would be a grave misfortune for the whole legal profession, the court, all American business and the country."

That delightful conservative, ex-President Taft, responded with an adverse opinion, as did "Tray, Blanch, and Sweetheart, see, they bark at me." But opposition was not confined to the Republican Party. Within the Cabinet there was opposition that found no public expression. Democratic lawyers who believed in the divine right of monopoly were astounded, and Democrats who didn't like innovations and new styles in Supreme Court Justices joined their "regrets that President Wilson had named a radical."

HOW ABOUT OVERMAN?

One day while this sabotage of a good man was going on, I received a message from President Wilson to come to the White House. He referred to the organized opposition to Brandeis. The Republican Senators were nearly solid in opposition and some Democrats had joined them. "I am informed that our friend Overman, of North Carolina, the acting chairman of the Judiciary Committee, which is considering the nomination, is hostile," he said. "I wish you would see him and get him active for confirmation." I told the President not to worry about Overman—that he was so conservative the nomination had shocked him—and he had said to me he wished the President would withdraw the nomination—but that when the roll was called his vote would go to Brandeis. Wilson urged me to make sure of my prediction.

I called to see the Senator; in fact we had several conversations, and in every one he voiced his feeling that the President had made a mistake. I combated his view and said that it was the best nomination that could have been made. One day Senator Chilton, chairman of the subcommittee to report on the nomination, called at the Navy Department and said Overman was against confirmation. "Has he said he would vote against Brandeis?" I asked. He answered, "Everything but that. He talks against it in the cloakroom. Unless something can be done to change him I fear he will vote against us." I told him that though Overman did not approve Brandeis, at the proper time he would vote for him. "He is regular," I said. "He has not voted against any nomination of the President yet and he will not. I have known Overman many years. He never crosses a bridge until he gets to it. When the time comes and the Democratic roll in the Senate is called, he will vote 'aye.' He is more liberal than he talks."

WILSON WINS OVERMAN

The fight went on, and action was delayed. At the same time there was opposition to the confirmation of George Rublee on the Federal Trade Commission. A short time before the vote was to be taken on the Brandeis appointment, President Wilson went to Charlotte, North Carolina, to speak on May Twentieth, the big day in North Carolina, when its people celebrate the signing of the Mecklenburg Declaration of Independence on May 20, 1775, over a year before Jefferson's Declaration was signed. He invited Overman and me to go with him. On the morning of the twentieth, before I had dressed Overman came to me on the train and said, "Joe, I wish you would see Wilson and induce him to go out on the platform and make a brief speech to the people of Salisbury." He told me that he had made the request and Wilson had said he had no voice for rear-end speaking and must save himself for the Charlotte meeting. "I could not budge him," Overman continued. "You must get him to do it. If I cannot induce the President to speak in my home town the people there will be disappointed and blame me." I promised to do all I could.

I hastened dressing and went to see Wilson. "We will be in Salisbury in half an hour," I said, "the home of Overman, and he wants you to say a few words to his neighbors." Wilson said "Yes, I know, but I have told Overman I cannot do any rear-end speaking." I adverted to the approaching vote on the Brandeis confirmation, for which Overman's vote was indispensable, and urged that what Overman asked was a very small thing comparatively.

"You think my speaking at Salisbury will cinch Overman's vote?" he asked.

"Maybe not," I said, "but your refusal to respond to his natural request would not help in the confirmation."

He saw the importance of pleasing Overman. "Tell him, please, to come to the car just before we reach Salisbury, and I will be glad to greet his townspeople."

When the train stopped at Salisbury, Overman—handsome, distinguished-looking and smiling—presented President Wilson to his home people in a happy brief speech. Wilson said in part:

"I told Senator Overman that I was loaded with only one cartridge this morning, which was to be exploded at Charlotte; but I am very glad indeed to give you my cordial greetings and to say how glad I am to find myself in Senator Overman's home town. You have reason to be proud of your Senator, and I am very glad to give him the tribute of my praises, and if he will permit me to add it, of my friendship."

Then, without "naming any names," gave his opinion in vigorous Anglo-Saxon of certain reactionaries in America who blocked the road to progress. As he proceeded, it was clear he was roasting the men who were opposed to the confirmation of Brandeis and Rublee and consigning them to a hot region. He warmed up in his denunciation of the men who controlled the Republican Party, saying, "They are looking backward, not forward." The people applauded enthusiastically. And as the train pulled out for Charlotte, Wilson and Overman stood side by side waving their hats to the cheering people.

"What do you think now?" Wilson asked with a twinkle of triumph in his eye, as we were seated in the train. "Did I pull it off all right? Do you think Overman's vote is cinched?"

"There is no doubt about what he will do," I said. "There has never been any question in my own mind about his vote, but he will go back to Washington and advocate instead of merely voting 'aye.'"

At Charlotte Wilson spoke eighteen minutes. The keynote of his speech was:

> "We have come down here to celebrate an historical episode, but we have not done it because we are looking backward: We have done it merely in order to give ourselves the excuse to get together and feel the thrill of being Americans, and in an age when it is worth while being Americans."

LONGEST INTRODUCTORY SPEECH

The Mayor, Thomas L. Kirkpatrick, quite an orator, occupied over twenty minutes in making the introduction and did not stop then until the murmuring of the crowd admonished him that the people had come to hear the President of the United States and not the Mayor of Charlotte. It was a good speech. The only thing wrong about it was its length. I think the long introduction irked Wilson so much that he deliberately cut short his speech to let the people, all standing, see that he had more consideration for them than their Mayor. They were so surprised when he quit that they did not move for some seconds. They wanted more. Wilson almost always had a way of stopping when his hearers wished he would go on. I told him that I thought he had caught that idea from the advice of Samuel Weller who said: "Samuel, my son, when you are writing a letter to your sweetheart, always stop when she is wishing to have a few more of them sweet words."

At the luncheon that followed, a gentleman sitting next to the Mayor asked me, "You introduce the President sometimes when he is going to speak, do you not?" I replied in the affirmative.

"What sort of introductory speech do you make?"

I answered "The President of the United States."

"Is that all?" the gentleman asked.

"Isn't that enough—a mouthful?" I answered.

I feared—or did I hope—my good friend the Mayor, if he heard, would catch the hint that all introductions of distinguished speakers should be brief. If the speaker is distinguished he needs no praise. If he isn't, he ought not to be asked to speak. In Mexico the introduction of a speaker is dispensed with and much time is saved.

BRANDEIS CONFIRMED

Two days after we returned to Washington, Senator Chilton, meeting me at the White House, asked, "What did you and Wilson do to Overman on the Charlotte trip? He came back a strong advocate of the confirmation of Brandeis and he will be confirmed shortly." The committee acted favorably by the vote 10 to 8. By vote of 47 to 22 the Senate confirmed the nomination. No regular Republican voted for him; only one Democrat voted "no," and three progressive Republicans—La Follette, Norris, and Poindexter—voted "aye."

Events proved I had made a correct diagnosis. The fight against Brandeis went on, but, while never enthusiastic for him and hesitating to go contrary to the request of both Massachusetts Senators, Overman made it known he would vote for confirmation. Brandeis was confirmed and Overman came to see the wrong position of Taft, Lodge, Weeks, and others. The record of Brandeis on the bench set new high standards for a court which needed the infusion of forward-looking members.

GAVE WILSON ADVICE

Although while on the bench Brandeis abstained from any participation in politics or in legislation, Wilson often wished the benefit of his counsel in matters on which he was an authority. Not once but a number of times discussing humanitarian or progressive policies, he would say to me: "I wish you would go to see our friend Brandeis, acquaint him with the problem and get his reaction." Brandeis knew he was talking to the President through me, but I learned much in the conversations, which often took a wide range.

· The last conversation I had with him—it was while I was Ambassador to Mexico—he was annoyed by the lobbyists who infested Washington and were getting rich by using their political influence. "Can't you advise X and Y (mentioning two lawyers he thought were well-known to me) to go home? They ought not be selling their influence."

CLARKE A REAL PATRIOT

When the next vacancy came Wilson named a great liberal, John H. Clarke, of Ohio, neighbor and friend of Newton Baker, whose friendship I also cherished. When his appointee felt constrained to resign, Wilson wrote Clarke:

"Like thousands of other liberals throughout the country, I have been counting on the influence of you and Justice Brandeis to restrain the Court in some measure from the extreme reactionary course which it seems inclined to follow. . . .

"The most obvious and immediate danger to which we are exposed is that the courts will more and more outrage the common people's sense of justice and cause a revulsion against judicial authority which may seriously disturb the equilibrium of our institutions, and I see nothing which can save us from this danger if the Supreme Court is to repudiate liberal courses of thought and action."

Clarke had profound faith that the law is a growth and that Supreme Court Justices had no right to impose their views on legislation. He welcomed the broader humanitarian laws and made an ideal judge. I have never fully forgiven him for resigning his position in 1922 to follow the gleam of lasting peace so as to be free to devote his entire time to cultivating public opinion in favor of the League of Nations. He became head of the organization to uphold that covenant. He had previously served as United States District Judge. I had sensed his rare quality when we both spoke at a banquet in Cleveland, and was happy to welcome him to the circle of sincere Wilsonians when he came to Washington. No Sir Galahad was ever inspired by nobler chivalric consecration to a holy cause than was Justice Clarke to the League of Nations. But the cards were stacked against the League in the Senate, where one-third of its members were afflicted with provincialism and devotion to the great God Protection. And neither the eloquence of Wilson nor the knightliness of Clarke could stem the isolationist tide.

LIX

MARSHALL AND THE VICE-PRESIDENCY

W HOM DO YOU FAVOR for Vice President?" a reporter asked me
at Baltimore the day before the Convention. "A man big
enough to be President," I replied. "The time has come to stop nominating politicians like Arthur as appeasement to a defeated faction,
or a Hobart or an English or a Morton, who were supposed to put up
a big campaign fund. We should do what the Democrats did when
they nominated Cleveland and Hendricks."

My comment was widely discussed and approved. The Convention
considered only heavyweights and named the most popular Governors in the country to occupy the two highest offices within the
gift of the people.

Though Indiana entered its Governor, Thomas R. Marshall, as a
candidate for President, he was never a serious contender, receiving
only the vote of his State. As a matter of fact Committeeman Thomas
Taggart, long the most powerful politician in Indiana, from the first
expected only that Marshall's candidacy for the presidency would
give him such prominence as would enable him to land the second
place on the ticket. It turned out as he expected. But Marshall hoped
to land the first place. Why? He believed the hot contest between
Clark, Wilson, and Underwood would eliminate all three and he
would be the beneficiary. Before the Convention met Marshall wrote
to Colonel Sam Tate, of North Carolina, that the leading candidates
"may induce Democrats to nominate a dark horse and my enemies
will tell you that I am the blackest one you ever saw."

NO VICE-PRESIDENTIAL TRADE

There was a report, which is accepted as correct by Marshall's
biographer, Charles Marion Thomas, that a trade was made between
William F. McCombs, manager for Wilson, and Tom Taggart and
Roger Sullivan late Saturday night, all sitting in their pajamas, whereby if Illinois and Indiana would throw their votes to Wilson for President, the Wilson supporters would support Marshall as his running

mate. There are four reasons why I do not believe there was a trade: (1) Wilson had virtually repudiated McCombs as authorized to speak for him when McCombs threw up the sponge and advised Wilson to withdraw; (2) Wilson would countenance no trade; (3) No such suggestion was mentioned in the various meetings of Wilson's leaders; (4) After Wilson was nominated, the nomination was virtually offered to Bryan, Champ Clark, and Oscar Underwood, all declining. The leaders for the nomination on the first ballot were Marshall who had 389 votes; Governor John Burke of North Dakota, 304⅔; and Senator Chamberlain, of Oregon, 157. Bryan supported Burke, and I also at first personally favored his nomination. I did not know Marshall. I was to learn later of his successful war on stock watering and his war on monopoly during his term as Governor. He refused to buy school desks from a trust. He prevented the Chesapeake and Ohio Railroad's watering its stock by thirty million dollars, saying the proposed financing was merely "a melon to cut on Wall Street." He declared he was going to see to it that the Wall Street crowd "got nothing but the wind." As such courageous acts became known, Marshall grew in popular estimation.

Burke came from a small State and Indiana was a large one and pivotal. Bryan was not favorable to Marshall, because, for one reason, when the Nebraskan had appealed to all presidential candidates to oppose the selection of Parker as temporary chairman, Marshall had refused and wired: "Parker came to Indiana in 1908 to advocate your election and mine. I do not see how his selection as temporary chairman will result in a reactionary plank in 1912." In the test vote for temporary chairman Indiana cast 21 votes for Parker and 8 for Bryan. The answer of Burke to Bryan's telegram was an explicit acceptance of the challenge offered by the Wall Street crowd. That made it impossible for Burke to get any votes from New York. When appealed to, Wilson declined to name a preference. Ray Stannard Baker quotes Burleson as saying, when he telephoned Wilson that the Convention was tending toward Marshall, "but Marshall is a small calibre man." However, when Burleson urged Marshall, Wilson acquiesced. McAdoo says in his *Crowded Years* that he advised Wilson to accept Marshall "more from the standpoint of political availability and geographical location than anything else." He adds: "With Wilson's permission I advised Wilson's friends that the nomination of Marshall would be acceptable to Wilson."

When informed of Marshall's nomination, Wilson gave out this statement: "Governor Marshall bears the highest reputation both as an executive and as a Democrat, and I feel honored by having him as a running mate. He is, as I am happy to say, a valued personal friend of mine as well as a fellow Democrat," and Marshall telegraphed Wilson: "To the length of my ability and influence I purpose to work for your election."

His biographer says Marshall told his friends before the Convention he would not accept if nominated for Vice President, the salary being too small for a Washington residence, and added:

> "Marshall was at his home with his wife and Meredith Nicholson when the question reached him for decision. Mrs. Marshall wanted to go to Washington instead of returning to Columbia City. Her tears and Nicholson's reasoning swayed Marshall, who promised to accept the nomination if the Convention chose him."

Inasmuch as the Republicans were trying to popularize the untrue slogan "As goes Maine in September, so goes the country in November," Wilson agreed with the national committee that it was best for him not to speak in Maine. Marshall volunteered to do so, and the big increase in the Democratic vote in September was regarded by the country as indicating a Democratic victory for Wilson and Marshall. His speaking in the campaign from Maine to California was marked by freshness, originality, and charm. His home State gave the ticket a majority of 120,000, largely because of confidence in Marshall and pride in its Governor.

When Marshall in his refreshing inaugural address (March 4, 1913), both gay and serious, urged that the forcible seizure of the Panama Canal be corrected, the Senate saw that it had a downright and forthright Vice President who did not feel he was "condemned to silence."

NOT A CONSERVATIVE

Marshall began his term believed by Bryan to be a conservative. He refused to be classified. He was a Democrat without affix, suffix, or prefix. He worried the liberals because he opposed woman suffrage, the child labor law, and like legislation. He was censured by the drys because he said "no decent Democrat" could favor the prohibition amendment." The conservatives—or perhaps I should call them by a truer designation 'the reactionaries'—roasted him because he favored the La Follette Seaman's Act and for weeks denounced him because in a Jefferson Day address in New York, April 13, 1913, he had made these declarations, near Wall Street:

"I have come to beard the lion in his den, the Douglas in his hall. Current opinion, justly or unjustly, holds that the welfare of the country depends not a little upon the conduct of certain men in this city of New York. If the tendency of certain men to accumulate vast fortunes is not curbed, America may face socialism or paternalism.... These individuals should go slow or the State may see fit to revoke the statute which made it possible for their fortunes to be handed down to their children, until some reckless descendant shall have dissipated it. The right to inherit and devise are not constitutional rights but privileges given to citizens."

That address brought down upon Marshall's head bitter denunciation by newspapers and others. He was accused of advocating property confiscation, "inciting class hatred," "appealing to the predatory poor," and was called a "demagogue." In a series of severe denunciations, the New York *Times* urged that he "give his fancy a period of repose," and the *Herald* advocated "a silencer for Mr. Marshall of the wild and woolly." Colonel Watterson came to the Vice President's defense saying, "the Vice President had no more thought of stirring up class hatred than the senior Senator from New York [Root] had last December when, addressing the Chamber of Commerce, he told them that "half the world believes them a lot of thieves."

The next year, in an address at Wabash College, the Vice President followed up his New York address by saying:

"In 1850 the proportion of the annual wealth created in this country by the joint efforts of labor and capital was one-fourth to labor and three-fourths to capital. Sixty years later the proportion had changed to less than one-fifth to labor and four-fifths to capital. This disproportion to my mind has much to do with the present discontent."

WISHED TO KEEP OUT OF WAR

The Vice President was in accord with and advanced the policies of the administration up to the days when the country debated whether it would go into the war. He was loyal to administration programs which he furthered in every possible way. His vote in case of a tie was on the side of policies advancing the New Freedom. This is not to say he was always in harmony with Wilson's policies, and he was always open and frank, whether in agreement or disagreement, from the beginning to the end of the administration. Marshall was opposed to involvement in the European war and did not hesitate to say so, even after Wilson had decided to recommend a declaration of war. He was caustic at times in his criticism of those urging our participation. He held no pro-British and no anti-German attitude. He wished the United States to let Europe fight it out without our participation and loved to quote the advice of Washington and Jefferson. When a violent denunciation of Germany flamed in the papers, he was criticized because of former high praises of German-American citizens and because shortly before we entered the war he had said: "There are too many men in the United States crying for war who would not enlist unless they could get a position of selling goods to the commissary department and who do not consider the awful seriousness of war." However, when our country entered the war, no man was more loyal. He made an address, in September, 1918, dedicating the Altar of Liberty in Madison Square, New York City, which expressed his serious conviction. In the course of it he said:

> "I came here partly to make an apology, an apology for my attitude during almost two and a half years of that fateful conflict, an apology that a God-fearing man in the twentieth century of civilization could have dreamed that any nation, any people or any man could be neutral when right was fighting with wrong."

That illustrated the spirit of the man. He hated war but he loved right more than he hated anything, and the ruthlessness of Germany and its undertaking to make the Kaiser lord of the seven seas aroused his indignation and stirred his patriotism. He stimulated his countrymen to patriotism and sacrifice as the war progressed and soon won the commendation of papers which in the earlier days had been critical because they lacked understanding of his democracy.

The Vice President rarely sought to influence action by the administration. I recall, however, that when an armor-plate plant was to be constructed by the Navy, Marshall was very insistent upon its being located in Evansville, Indiana. I told him that I had appointed a committee of Naval officers to examine all sites and they would visit

Evansville. He didn't like that and urged me to designate Evansville. He appealed to Wilson, who told me that he "would have been glad to agree to the recommendation of the Vice President but the recommendation of the Naval Board should not be overruled."

In Washington society the Vice President is the prize figure in the formal dinners which are popular in the national capital. The President accepts no invitation to dine out except once a year with each member of the Cabinet. Coming for the first time to the nation's capital from a small Indiana city, the Marshalls soon became the toast of Washington society. During the illness of the chief executive, with dignified simplicity they did the honors when titled visitors came to the capital.

The devotion of the Marshalls was beautiful. They were never separated twenty-four hours during their married life. He would accept no invitation to any place that did not include Mrs. Marshall. They were childless, but, becoming interested in a lovely child, Mrs. Marshall persuaded her husband and they adopted the child, who soon became the light in their home. It is not too much to say that when death removed the child all Washington sorrowed with the Marshalls in their grief.

A FLAG FOR THE VICE PRESIDENT

The Vice President acted for the President on a number of occasions. One of the most important was to officiate at the formal dedication of the Panama Pacific International Exposition. As I could not go, I designated Assistant Secretary Franklin D. Roosevelt to accompany the Vice President in doing the honors. Up to that time though all other high officials had a special flag, such emblem had not been designed for the Vice President. I caused a special Vice President's flag to be provided—and Roosevelt and I decided that the emblem be an American eagle on a white square and that it should be displayed on Naval vessels whenever the Vice President was on board. It was designed for Vice President Marshall and is permanent. Acting together as representatives of the President and the Secretary of the Navy at the Exposition, the Marshalls and the Roosevelts formed a mutual attachment.

NOT CONSULTED ENOUGH

There is no doubt that Marshall was aggrieved because Wilson rarely consulted him about policies or gave him advance information of what was to be proposed. And that feeling was justified because the coöperation of the Vice President is of great value in securing legislation. On one occasion when Wilson requested me to see the Vice President to secure his coöperation, Marshall showed his feeling by coldly answering, "I have your orders, sir." If Wilson had consulted him in advance, the chasm which at times existed between them could have been bridged. Even so, there never was a time when Marshall's assistance was needed to carry out an administration policy that he did not measure up to all expectations of loyalty.

AUTHOR OF QUAINT SAYINGS

A record of Marshall's quaint sayings and humor would fill a volume. When people were seriously debating international and domestic issues, Marshall brought them to earth by discounting the remedies proposed by those of solemn mien, saying, "What this country needs is a good five-cent cigar." Marshall's favorite story on himself was:

"I was seated in a smoking car in Indiana thinking about a campaign speech I was to make that night, when a large man slumped down in the seat beside me and remarked, 'Mighty bad day for business,' as he observed the rain falling in sheets.

" 'I asked the man: 'What's your line?' 'Automobile accessories,' he replied. 'What's yours?'

"Quickly reflecting I was out making campaign speeches, I replied, 'My line is selling dope.'

" 'I thought they wouldn't let you sell that stuff,' my seat partner commented.

" 'But,' I remarked, 'I have a special arrangement with the administration for a short time.'

"My sad reflection was that an Indiana Vice President was not recognized in his own State."

Many a smile was caused by the publication of a letter from Marshall to the President, in which he signed himself "Your only vice." He had a habit of jokingly making light of his office, saying, in the days of Wilson's perfect health, that his chief duty was "to sleep

while Senators droned and inquire about the health of the President."
When Coolidge was chosen to succeed him, Marshall telegraphed:
"Please accept my sincere sympathy."

WILSON'S GOING TO PARIS

There was no law against Wilson's going as head of the American
delegation to the Peace Conference. Marshall had two grievances:
(1) That he had not been consulted before Wilson made known his
decision publicly; (2) That when Wilson decided upon leaving the
country for an indefinite period, the duties of the office did not de-
volve upon the Vice President for the time being. No President had
before gone outside the country during his incumbency except when
Taft greeted Díaz over the line at El Paso or when one stepped across
the Canadian border. Many deemed Wilson's action as violating a
settled tradition. He did not consult the members of his Cabinet. In
an address at the Governors' Conference, Lane approved it and the
others—I among the number—felt that only Wilson could secure a
League of Nations. When Lansing learned of Wilson's intention, he
urged him not to go. Lansing knew that if Wilson went the Secretary
of State would not hold the important place in the conference which
he coveted.

Marshall was urged to assume the duties of the presidency when
Wilson stepped aboard ship. Former Republican Attorney General
Wickersham thought it would be legal for Marshall to take charge
the minute Wilson's ship was beyond the three-mile limit. Replying
to specific questions from the New York *Times,* Marshall said:

> "I shall not of my own volition assume President Wilson's
> office if he goes to the Peace Conference. If Congress should by
> resolution direct me to assume the duties of the office, I would not
> commit myself unless or until Congress acts.
> "If, as had been suggested, the court should mandamus me to
> exercise the duties of the office I would obey."

When Wilson took heed of the turmoil his going created, he called
on Marshall in order to compensate for any unintentional neglect
and to explain what he regarded as imperative reasons for his going
to the Peace Conference. He asked Marshall to perform certain duties
and asked him to preside at Cabinet meetings, but kept the reins of
government in his own hands. Marshall agreed to Wilson's requests,
saying at the first Cabinet meeting over which he presided: "I am

here and am acting in an unofficial and informal way over your meetings out of deference to your desires and those of the President." He caused a smile when he said, "In view of differing opinions of constitutional questions that have arisen, I have asked Abe Martin [Hoosier humorist and philosopher] and Abe has given it as his considered opinion that Wilson had given up the office but was drawing the salary."

NO PROHIBITION REPEAL

The Cabinet meetings and their associations won to Vice President Marshall increased regard and respect from the members of the Cabinet. He mingled humor with wisdom at Cabinet meetings and parried jests and thrusts. I recall one remark that was characteristic: While Wilson was in Paris some of his friends in the United States wrote and urged him to issue a proclamation annulling prohibition passed during the war. I never knew who, without consulting the Cabinet, advised such a proclamation sent from Paris. Wilson very properly referred the suggestion to the Vice President and the members of the Cabinet. Marshall and most members of the Cabinet strongly advised against the suggested proclamation. Soldiers were under arms in Germany to see that the terms of the armistice were carried out and full demobilization of the Army and Navy had not been ordered. We held that war prohibition should remain until complete demobilization and the conclusion of the Peace Conference. Burleson earnestly favored immediate annullment, to which Marshall said: "I understand that it is the sense of the body, in which I concur, that the President be advised not to issue a proclamation now and that I so advise him." Burleson said, "Please add that I dissent." With a gleam in his eye Marshall laughingly said: "It will be unnecessary to include that in the cable. Wilson knows your attitude without hearing from Washington."

In a short time Marshall ceased to attend the Cabinet meetings, saying he did not think the Vice President "ought to be in a confidential relationship with the legislative and executive departments." I did not agree with him and felt that he should continue to preside.

ATTITUDE ON LEAGUE OF NATIONS

There was a wide difference in the attitude of Wilson and Marshall as the League of Nations debate grew into weeks. Marshall favored accepting reservations which he thought necessary to save it. Wilson thought the reservations proposed would be "a dishonorable compromise" and wrote Senator Hitchcock, who was leading the fight for the ratification without any change except explanatory clauses (November 19): "In my opinion the resolution in that form (embodying the reservations) does not provide for ratification but rather for rejection. . . . I trust that all true friends of the Treaty will refuse to support the Lodge resolution."

MOSES SAID WILSON WAS DISQUALIFIED

From the time Wilson was stricken, Marshall often complained to friends, me and others, that he had to depend for his information about the President's condition upon what he read in the papers. He often expressed his feeling that he was entitled to more consideration. Once he went to the White House and was informed by Mrs. Wilson that her husband was too ill to see him. Senator George H. Moses, assuming absent treatment of Wilson, said he had suffered "a cerebral lesion" and that he was "disqualified" in the terms of the Constitution. Friends of Wilson after that called Senator Moses "Old Doc Moses." Leading Republican Senators informed Marshall that he could have the support of the Republican majority if he assumed the presidency and advised him to do so, but he turned a deaf ear, saying to Mrs. Marshall, "I could throw this country into civil war, but I won't."

When doctors feared Wilson's death was near, on October 2, J. Fred Essay was requested to tell the Vice President confidentially that Wilson had suffered a second stroke. Marshall sat speechless, making no response to the information, not even looking up. During the long weeks the White House knew that certain Senators believed that Marshall ought to 'assume the duties of President, holding that Wilson was "incapacitated" to exercise the duties of the office.

MARSHALL AND THE PRESIDENCY

I will always believe Marshall held the opinion that Wilson ought to have turned over presidential duties to him while the President was in Paris, and that when he was ill and for a portion of his time "incapacitated" for carrying on his duties, Marshall should have exercized presidential functions. That belief was strengthened by reading his biography by Charles Marion Thomas, who, among other things indicating Marshall's feeling, says:

> "Wilson was not a President who evaded responsibility by permitting bills to become laws without his signature. He customarily either signed or vetoed bills, yet twenty-eight bills became laws without his signature between September 30 and November 18, 1919."

Mr. Thomas adds: "Congressmen carefully scanned Wilson's signatures, which did not seem natural, and some persons suspected that the President's hand had been guided, but that was an unfounded suspicion." It was printed that on October 2, when Wilson was believed to be *in extremis*, Dr. Francis Dercum told Mrs. Wilson she must keep all matters away from him that would excite his interest, and she replied: "Then, had he not better resign? Let Mr. Marshall succeed him to the presidency, and he himself get that complete rest that is so vital to his life." One reason Marshall did not become President is in the reply of Dr. Dercum (concurred in by other physicians): "No," he said, "for Mr. Wilson to resign would have a bad effect on the country, and a serious effect on our patient. He has staked his life and made his promise to the world to do all in his power to get the Treaty ratified and make the League of Nations complete. If he resigns, the greatest incentive to recovery is gone; and as his mind is clear as crystal he can do more with even a maimed body than anyone else."

Sometime later the Vice President said to me: "The most serious hour in my life was when the news was flashed to Atlanta, where I was speaking, that President Wilson was dead." He continued:

> "I was about to speak to a large audience, November 23, 1919, when a gentleman came into the auditorium and whispered that a message had just come that the President was dead. It dazed me. In a moment I asked that 'Nearer My God To Thee' be sung, and Mrs. Marshall and I went to our hotel. For minutes, it seemed hours, I meditated upon the grave duties that would devolve upon me and prayed for wisdom to guide me. In a short time I was relieved of the greatest burden when I was informed that the message was not correct and that the highest official position would not come to me. In the period when I saw myself in the White House, there was no sense of elation, but rather the contrary. I was stunned, first by grief for my dead chieftain

and second by the awful responsibility that would fall upon me. I was resolved to do my duty, but I can truly say that I dreaded the task."

In his *Recollections*, writing of the weeks when Wilson was very ill, Marshall says: "Those were not pleasant months for me...I hoped that he might acquire his wanted health. I was afraid to ask about it, for fear some censorious soul would accuse me of a longing for his place."

To his secretary, Mark Thistlethwaite, who, when Wilson was very ill, undertook to convince Marshall that he should make ready to assume the presidency, the Vice President said in his characteristic way: "I am not going to seize the place and then have Wilson— recovered—come around and say, 'get off, you usurper.' "

In 1920 Marshall was more than a receptive candidate for the presidential nomination. Indiana formally presented his name. He never received more than 36 votes but hoped the contest between McAdoo, Palmer, Smith, and Cox might bring the honor to him as he was well regarded by all. He said to a friend, "If I am nominated I can beat Harding."

SET A GOOD EXAMPLE

When his term expired, Marshall declined to accept a large retainer to represent a big oil firm as general counsel and remain in Washington. He declined, saying to a friend in Indiana, "I knew I was not worth that much to any firm; so I thought I had better just come back to Indiana." His example, alas, has not been followed by men of high station, some of whom put their influence on the block for sale to the highest bidder. His only positions after his retirement, March 4, 1921, was as member of the Lincoln Memorial Commission and, by Harding's appointment, he became a member of the Federal Coal Commission. It paid a good salary and he needed it. For his *Recollections* he received later $50,000 and lesser sums for other writings.

The Vice President was in demand at chautauquas and lyceums and added to his income by lectures and addresses. He mingled sparkling wit and sound philosophy in so original a manner as to delight all who heard him. After the Republican victory in 1920, as I was preparing to return home, I was offered contracts to speak at chautauquas in the summer and in lyceum courses in the winter. I was offered my choice of a fixed fee or a commission. I asked advice from the Vice President. "Don't hesitate a minute in deciding," he said. "Take a fixed fee. You know that you are certain to get a specified amount no matter what the weather or counter-attractions that cut down attendance. Only Bryan can afford to depend on commission—The folks just come in droves to hear the Commoner."

I took his advice and sold almost enough hot air—for once I was a profiteer getting more than it was worth—to build a home in Raleigh.

The test of a man's proper conception of his place in the scheme of things is his ability to laugh at himself. Marshall measured up to that appraisal. He had many stories in which he figured, not always as the hero. He often humorously described Indiana as a State which produced second-class statesmen and vice presidents. But America knew that in Marshall that State had furnished a real statesman of patriotism, ability, originality and devotion to the public weal. Marshall added distinction to a great office often underrated, and died in Washington, June 1, 1925. And it was observed, as he passed into the other world, that he was reading the Bible, which was open at the Fourth Chapter of Mark's Gospel.

Part Seven

PREPARATION AND NEUTRALITY

LX

FIGHTING FOR PEACE THROUGH NEUTRALITY

HARDLY HAD the reverberations of the first guns in Belgium died away before the propaganda for Uncle Sam to fight with the Allies began. Honorable Charles J. Bonaparte (member of the distinguished Bonaparte family of France) who had been Attorney General and Secretary of the Navy in Theodore Roosevelt's Cabinet, wrote his old chief: "I hear mutterings on every side that 'if this thing goes too far' the United States will come to England's rescue, partly because 'blood is thicker than water' but largely for the sake of civilization in general."

Many declarations, upholding Germany, came from American citizens of German blood. In the main, fearing the United States might go to the aid of the Allies, German-Americans and their sympathizers, along with opponents of America's entering the war, upheld the doctrine of neutrality.

The general opinion in the United States in the early days was that the war "would not last long." The Dallas *News* said, in August, 1914, that it would be over "long before the cotton season is." The Detroit *News* thought "the war must be brief because Europe cannot possibly sustain prolonged warfare on so destructive a scale," and that was the prevailing opinion of people and press. My paper, *The Raleigh News and Observer,* which said, "our sympathies are with Servia," was "fearful the war might last for years," and declared that the Kaiser was mostly to blame for the conflagration.

The proclamation of neutrality, which Wilson read to the members of his Cabinet, who heartily seconded it even if two or three members were not personally neutral, was issued in August, 1914, and was as follows:

"We are true friends of all the nations of the world, because we threaten none, covet the possessions of none, desire the overthrow of none. Our friendship can be accepted, and is accepted, without reservation because it is offered in a spirit and for a purpose which no one can even question or suspect. Therein lies our greatness. We are the champions of peace and of concord."

Showing his true neutral spirit, on August 19, fifteen days after the invasion of Belgium, which shocked him as it did others, Wilson issued this appeal: "Every man who really loves America will act and speak in the spirit of true neutrality, which is the spirit of impartiality and fairness and friendliness to all concerned." While sharing the feeling of indignation against the wrongs to Belgium, Wilson on September 16 told the members of a Belgian Commission who asked him to redress their wrongs: "It would be inconsistent with the neutral position of any nation which like this, has no part in the conflict." Seven days later Theodore Roosevelt, in an article in *The Outlook*, writing of the Belgian Commission's visit, said, "It is certainly eminently desirable that we should remain entirely neutral," and added:

"Of course, it would be folly to jump into the gulf ourselves to no good purpose; and very probably nothing we could have done would have helped Belgium. We have not the smallest responsibility for what has befallen her. . . . Of course, if there is any meaning in the words 'right' and 'wrong' in international affairs, the act was wrong. . . . I think, at any rate I hope, I have rendered it plain that I am not now criticizing, I am not passing judgment, one way or the other, upon Germany's action. I admire and respect the German people. I am proud of the German blood in my veins. When a nation feels that the issue of a contest in which, for whatever reason, it finds itself engaged, will be national life or death, it is inevitable that it should so act as to save itself from death and to perpetuate life."

There was hardly any division of sentiment. Lodge wrote that he favored "the observance of strict neutrality," though later he was to write that it "was perfectly unsound." The fact that the militant Theodore Roosevelt, in the early days of the war, seconded Wilson's neutral statement, is the best proof that neutrality was then favored by the overwhelming majority of the American people. No suggestion in Congress was made of participation in the war, and if it had been proposed, the people would have risen up almost *en masse* against it. Theodore Roosevelt afterwards became the most explosive opponent of the neutrality he upheld in 1914, and the most bitter critic of Wilson. The truth is that there were few consistent public men in the country in those hectic days.

HOUSE'S FUTILE PEACE TRIP

Wilson was fearful that what did break out in 1914 might occur, for, unknown to anybody in America except a few people—I know of no others who knew of it in America outside the members of the Cabinet—in the early part of 1914 he entrusted House with a secret mission to European countries. Wilson said to me one day that if the United States and England and France and Germany would agree not to make war themselves and not to permit other nations to go to war, these big nations had it in their power to make war an anachronism. It was with this idea in his mind that he sent House to Europe. When House unfolded the President's suggestion that these four big nations agree to prevent war—this was only a few months before war actually broke out in Europe—neither Ambassador Page nor the Premier of England thought that the suggestion required immediate attention. England was lulled to sleep. Germany had sent to England as its Ambassador a very fine gentleman whose friendship for England was so well known that nobody suspected him of failure to do everything in his power to prevent war between these nations. It was a part of German strategy thus to close the eyes of the English Government to danger of war with Germany, though there were not wanting men like Winston Churchill and men in the War Office and in the Admiralty who continued to try to make Asquith and Lloyd George understand that Germany's rapid building of a big navy, its strengthening of its army, the connecting of the North Sea with the Baltic, its canalization, and the building of giant ships like the *Leviathan* to be used as transports, were all in preparation for the mammoth struggle to ensue. House was able to make no headway in England, though the authorities told him that his ideas were good and that they would see him at a more convenient season.

In France House was given little more, if any, consideration. French leaders were busy with politics. They had felt for twenty years that a war with Germany was possible but it seemed no more imminent in June, 1914, than it had in any previous year.

THE YELLOW PERIL

When House reached Germany, he found it difficult to get access to the Emperor, and when he finally did, the Emperor unfolded to him in his town-meeting-hall style of speaking that there was no danger of war in Europe. Said he, in substance,

"I have been on the throne for many years and the fact that my army is invincible has guaranteed the peace of Europe. That is what Germany's great military establishment means—peace— and as long as we have this mighty instrument of power, there will be no war in Europe."

He asked House to convey to the President his conviction that the white nations of the earth ought to keep their eyes on the yellow races. He thought Japan and other Asiatics were preparing for war. He pointed out that in numbers they were far superior to the white races and that the war of the future would be a contest between the white and yellow races. He seemed obsessed by the yellow peril and quoted Napoleon as having that fear, saying, "China will one day be a lion. Let the lion sleep."

And so, of course, Wilson's dream of an agreement between these four nations to prevent war, a precursor of his idea at Versailles, came to naught.

HOUSE NO FRIEND TO BRYAN

The consummation of Wilson's plan to effect an agreement with the rulers of Britain, Germany, and France to prevent war—for the purpose of which he sent House to Europe early in 1914—was the thing nearest to the heart of Bryan also. The dispatching of a private citizen with a roving unofficial commission to survey the conditions in Europe was not in accord with the best traditions, and the results were of no value. If Bryan did not like the idea, he expressed no dissent. House's unofficial mission was to put the President in possession of the inside information that a private citizen known to have the confidence of his government might obtain. If any ambassador objected, it is not recorded, though, until he learned that House was as pro-British as he was, Page didn't like House's activities.

All the same, it was a mistake for a President to send a private citizen to do what officials of the State Department were supposed to do—I mean, without a commission. If House had been named as Assistant Secretary or Ambassador it would have been different. Should not a President be authorized to have one or two members of his Cabinet without portfolio to be eyes and ears? That is a moot question.

Other Presidents, as well as Wilson, have sent close personal friends abroad to make surveys. House had no official status. Unknown to Bryan, it was not long before House was secretly anything but his friend. In August, 1914, he suggested to the President that "you do not let Mr. Bryan make any overtures to any powers involved in the European crisis." Later he repeated the advice "to keep Bryan out of any statements made," and Page advised against any peace meetings in America. In September House suggested to the President that there was "no danger of anyone on the outside injecting himself into it [negotiations abroad] unless Mr. Bryan does something on his own initiative," which caused Ray Stannard Baker, in his life of Wilson to make this significant comment: "Rank outsider—the Secretary of State!" Baker thus sums up the result of House's mission to Europe: "It is significant that House travelled about Europe for two years, finger on lips, in an atmosphere of mysterious conferences and secret codes, with no result whatever."

TOOK TIME BY THE FORELOCK

Before the formal declaration of war in Europe, Wilson and Bryan, in keeping with their earnest desire to arbitrate, were offering the good offices of the government to avert the threatened war. On July 28 Bryan cabled Page asking if our good offices "under Article 3 of the Hague Convention would be acceptable?" Page and House, each on his own, discouraged the suggestion. Page cabled, "There is not the slightest chance," and House advised twice: "Do not let Mr. Bryan make any overtures." The Cabinet was at one with Wilson and Bryan. Ignoring the advices of House and Page, the President cabled tendering his "good offices." He next asked the nations to conform to the Declaration of London. Britain declined. Wilson urged the Senate to ratify the Bryan "cooling off" treaties. Eighteen were ratified in one day. On August 20 Page made the imperialistic suggestion that England, Germany, and France be invited to join us in "cleaning up house," to which Wilson gave no answer. House also dreamed of our joining an international "balance of power," and Page urged "the tightest sort of an alliance, offensive and defensive, between Britain, colonies and all, and the United States."

Wilson felt so deeply that neutrality must be preserved that he asked McAdoo "to have a conference with Lansing and with Daniels to effect very definite arrangements for coöperation between the three departments in these matters." And he sent messages to the diplomatic corps "not to express any unneutral feelings, either by word of mouth, or by letter, and not even to the State Department."

WILSON'S INSTRUCTIONS DILUTED

In August, 1914, House, according to his later papers, wrote to Wilson: "Germany's success would ultimately mean trouble to us," and Lansing wrote a memorandum of like import. Bryan disapproved and wrote to Wilson: "Our attitude being that of absolute neutrality, it is not wise, in my judgment." Wilson stood with Bryan in spite of the later fusillades of Theodore Roosevelt and Choate and others and the early House-Lansing desire to destroy neutrality and take sides with the Allies. As evidence of Wilson's refusal to be influenced by them, Wilson said in a Cabinet meeting that he had informed Ambassador Spring-Rice that if Prussian military prowess overcame the Allies, it might be necessary for the United States to "give up its present ideals and devote all its energies to defense, which would mean the end of its present system of government." He also related a conversation with others to the effect that if Britain should deny American rights he would be forced to hold it to "strict accountability."

Wilson was continuously urging Britain to join a council for peace, and he wrote Grey that British statesmen would "take a great responsibility upon themselves if they hesitate or delay." When Grey did not accept Wilson's plan for mediation, the President again directed House to stress the peace plan with Grey, and said, "If Britain postpones, we must insist to the limit upon the rights of the United States and upon such freedom of the seas as international law already justifies her in insisting on as against Great Britain, with the same plain speaking and firmness that she has used against Germany." He demanded: "The choice must be made immediately." Wilson sought to word all his proposals in "a way that would be very hard for the Allies to reject as well as the Germans." House diluted the President's directions, and more than intimated that we were ready to join England "if it was fighting for the emancipation of Europe."

Ray Stannard Baker says: "Wilson felt that House's mind worked just as his own did. That was a fatal mistake in Wilson's policy." He also wrote: "It is unfortunate that America during these months should have had representatives in England who were as completely committed to the Allied cause as Page and House."

In March (1915), when House was being hypnotized by Grey in London, Wilson cabled him: "If the impression were to be created in Berlin that you were to come only when the British Government thought it the opportune time for you to come, you might be regarded when you reached there as their spokesman rather than mine."

In the early part of 1915 Ray Stannard Baker pointed out: "We find Page, our most important representative in the firing line actually taking the part of our chief diplomatic opponent, playing the game of the British; and Colonel House, wandering anxiously about Europe seeking peace, being used by the Allies as a pawn in their deliberate and most effective policy of delay."

Page, though not wishing House to return to England, gave no support to the President's plan, and was later called home to "get in touch with American sentiment." Grey told Parliament, "It is no time to talk peace," and Page wrote that some English paper said that "any Englishman who talks peace ought to be shot." Wilson still held the vision of peace. He did not know that House and Lansing were undermining his position and were as pro-British as Page, though not open and frank.

PAGE'S MISSION A DISAPPOINTMENT

In August, 1916, in the heat of the national campaign, Walter Page, Ambassador to Great Britain, came home to try to soften the feeling caused by British actions against our commerce. Wilson did not wish to see him, and Page, after a greeting, cooled his heels outside the White House gates. When Wilson saw him, the Ambassador was told that the causes of the war was "England's having the earth and Germany wanting it." Page had, since the sinking of the *Lusitania*, wanted the United States to enter the war on the side of Britain and came to urge Wilson to take that course. Wilson, determined to keep out of the war if honorably possible, refused to listen to Page's pleas and defense of Britain's policies. Wilson said about that time: "It is very difficult to be friends with Great Britain without doing whatever she wants us to do."

It was not until near the end of September that Page was able to talk at length with Wilson. It was only then when Page wrote he had "a most important and confidential message for you from the British

Government" that Wilson invited Page to visit him. They were personal friends, but Page's defense of the British policy did not impress Wilson. The President wished an armistice looking to peace, but Britain would have none of it. And Page went back a saddened man. His extreme partisanship for British policies made Wilson feel as he said of House once, that Page was "Edward Grey's representative, not mine."

Page returned to London with a sense of the futility of his mission. He had irritated Wilson by his partisanship for British policies and his criticism of his country's earnest desire to uphold national honor without going into war. As he sailed, Page was resolved to resign in disgust. He did not realize that Wilson, exhausting every resource to secure peace without resort to war, never contemplated surrendering the rights of his country and when Germany violated its promise and returned to submarine ruthlessness, he would be stronger for using "force without limit" to uphold the American freedom of the seas than many who had earlier been clamoring for war.

It was on that trip to Washington that Page in one part of his memorandum said:

"I sat at luncheon (at a hotel) with Lansing, Secretary of State; Lane, Secretary of the Interior; Gregory, Attorney General; Baker, Secretary of War; Daniels, Secretary of the Navy; and Sharp, Ambassador to France; and all the talk was jocular or semi-jocular, and personal—mere cheap chaff. Not a question was asked either of the Ambassador to France or of the Ambassador to Great Britain about the war or about our foreign relations. The war wasn't mentioned. Sharp and I might have come from Bungtown or Jonesville and not from France and England. We were not encouraged to talk—the local personal joke held the time and conversation."

Of course, none of the Cabinet members knew of this indictment until it was printed in the early 1920's in Hendrick's *Life and Letters of Walter Hines Page*. It was a caricature of the Cabinet members, made in ignorance of the justifiable reason for the lack of serious discussion. Meeting Houston shortly after its publication, I found he felt aggrieved—so did all the rest of us—that Cabinet members should have been pictured in such a light. Houston said:

"You know, as we were going to luncheon with Page and Sharp, a secret service man called us aside and told us that he had learned that Austrians would wait on us at the luncheon—that he suspected they were spies—and advised that we say nothing at the luncheon about matters relating to the war or diplomacy because the waiters might be in the employ of the German Embassy. Asked why these spies had not been arrested, the secret service officer said they were keeping them under surveillance but had not yet been able to get evidence to justify arrest.

"Instead of printing Page's pen picture of our supposed indifference to the great questions, it would have been a very easy matter to have obtained the true information from any member of the Cabinet. Instead of that Page's story of the lunch put us in the light of ignorance or indifference to the great matter in which we were profoundly interested and absorbed.

"During Page's visit I had long talks with him about the situation in England and solicited his views and so did you and other members of the Cabinet."

Page's memorandum and Hendrick's story of the visit showed Page in a critical attitude towards Wilson and all others who were not so pro-British that they preferred going into the war on her side to using every endeavor to secure peace without America's sending its youth into the trenches. Page wrote House (July 21, 1915): "It is a curious thing to say, but the only solution I see is another *Lusitania* outrage which would force war."

The difference between Page on the one hand and House and Lansing on the other was this: Wilson and Page had been close friends from college days and there was complete candor between them. The relations between Wilson and the others were based on public service without personal background. Wilson never knew House until the Texan followed other Texans in supporting him for the nomination and gained his confidence to a degree that is one of the mysteries not yet solved. He never knew Lansing until he appointed him to office. He had lifted them into high places believing in their loyalty. Page thought England was entirely right and Germany entirely wrong and told Wilson so. House and Lansing held the like view, but in the main concealed it from Wilson, who relied on House because he mistakenly thought that they were tuned in on the same wave length.

TWO PARTISAN ADMIRALS

Not long after Wilson's proclamation of neutrality, I felt called upon to draw the attention of two distinguished retired Admirals to the fact that the order of their Commander in Chief to be neutral applied to them as well as to the active officers of the Navy. Admiral Chadwick was very pro-German as indicated by his letter to Henry White from which these extracts are taken:

> "The attitude of our press so fills me with wrath that were I free to do so, I would take the stump against their infernal silliness. The more I study the subject, the more I see that England is the true devil in the whole business. . . .
>
> "It sorely vexes my soul that America should have so fully failed as to England. We shall pay dearly if England is triumphant. We shall be tied to her chariot wheels just as she purposes to tie Germany. . . . I am firmly convinced that *our* interest lies in a German victory."

Admiral Mahan, the most distinguished of American retired Admirals, was quite as strongly partisan for Britain. Long before the war he had written books showing his admiration and partiality for Brittain's policy and advocated a similar one for the United States in his classic *Sea Power*. His convictions were strongly set forth in various letters. He deprecated my order of August 6, 1914, directing all officers of the Navy, whether active or retired, to refrain from public comment of any kind about the war in Europe, and to observe in spirit and in letter the neutrality proclamation of the Commander in Chief. That order greatly disturbed the pro-British Admiral Mahan, who criticized me severely and did not refrain in spirit and in conversation from his desire to see the United States from the beginning an ally of Great Britain. The neutrality proclamation was equally resented by Admiral Chadwick, who was so pro-German that he actually believed what was wholly untrue, to wit, as he wrote in a letter to Henry White in June, 1915: "An odd thing is the fact that (so far as I know) at least three fourths of the officers of the Army and Navy have throughout favored the German side." In this view, the Admiral was as wrong as a man could be. The truth was that at the time he wrote to my knowledge nearly all the officers of the Navy were strictly officially and personally neutral, though of course, all the time men like Mahan were pro-British, while Chadwick and a few others were pro-German, Admiral Chadwick incorrectly included on the pro-German side such officers as Admiral Fiske, Aide for Operations, who admired the German system of administration so much that he wished the American Navy to adopt it, but did not follow Chadwick in taking sides.

Wilson was incensed by the evidences of partisanship by Mahan and Chadwick and directed that I send a second letter and a reprimand if they were guilty of further statements. They refrained from public statements but nobody could have cooled their partisanship or prevented their writing letters.

IT'S A LONG WAY TO TIPPERARY

In the winter of 1914, when the President was using every effort to secure adherence to the policy of neutrality, a small incident obtained undue proportions in the press. One morning the papers carried an item that the Commandant of the Naval Training Station at Newport, Rhode Island, had forbidden the enlisted men in training to sing "Tipperary." It seems that he felt they were singing it in a way to indicate resentment to the neutrality program and doing it boisterously. When the press correspondents came to see me the morning of December 5, 1914, they called my attention to a dispatch from Newport saying that the order of the Commandant had been resented by the sailors who had the right to sing whatever they pleased. They asked me what I was going to do about it.

My reply was that I had no official report from Captain Welles; that he was an officer of experience and judgment; and that it was not a matter for the Secretary to take up in the absence of any request from Newport. There might have been something in the manner of the singing, I said, or in the spirit that did not appear in cold type. Having confidence in the wisdom and good sense of Captain Welles, I had no disposition to make any ruling about what he had done. This gave the cartoonists an opportunity to pillory me. One of the brightest of them pictured me as an old-time Puritan, dressed in black, with a black hat, and carrying an umbrella, yanking out an American sailor from a lunch counter for eating English mustard, and another at a restaurant for eating German cooking; driving a sailor away for petting a Russian wolfhound, and forbidding another sailor to smoke Turkish cigarettes, and driving away a sailor who, in the day of long dresses, was looking at a girl wearing a French heel. This ridicule of the policy

NEUTRALITY!

Nelson Harding, in the *Brooklyn Daily Eagle*

RIDICULING SECRETARY'S NEUTRALITY ORDER

Cartoonist pictures Secretary Daniels as carrying neutrality to a ridiculous
extreme.

of neutrality was taken up by some of the Canadian papers which from the first wished to involve the United States on the side of England and resented the policy of neutrality.

Every official who was truly neutral had to meet the outrageous propaganda that he sympathized with Germany. I observed strictly the President's neutrality proclamation. It was denounced by the element that regarded everyone as pro-German who did not early advocate entering the war on the side of the Allies. One day, after a critical cartoon had appeared, there came to me open in the mail a black iron cross, having a linen mailing tag. It was addressed thus:

Honorable Wilhelm Josephus Daniels
Secretary of the Navy

On one side was a white band on which was written: "It's a long way to Tipperary." On the other side was another little tag inscribed "Made in Germany."

President Wilson was incensed by these criticisms. A guest of the White House at that time, Mrs. Crawford H. Toy, writes thus of his irritation:

"I have never seen the President angry before. I never want to see him angry again. His fist came down on the table:

" 'Daniels did not give the order that 'Tipperary' should not be sung in the Navy. He is surrounded by a network of conspiracy and lies. His enemies are determined to ruin him. I can't be sure who they are yet, but when I do get them—God help them.' "

An examination of the Navy register showed a large number of officers of German lineage with German names. They were among the ablest and most patriotic Americans, with no sympathy for the Kaiser. And yet in the perfervid hate of all things German in the country, there were a few officers and many civilians who urged me not to give any important assignment to any officer with a German name. It was a war craze to which I gave no heed. My answer was to detail Captain Taussig to command the first division of destroyers sent to fight the U-boats overseas, and to place Admiral Winterhalter in command of the Far East fleet. His father emigrated to the United States shortly before the War of the Sixties, and, as soon as he became naturalized, volunteered in the Federal Army. I trusted patriotic officers with German antecedents as I did all other honorable officers of the Navy. That trust was fully justified by their devotion to Old Glory.

TWO MASTER GOALS

Wilson in his adherence to neutrality through thirty-two long and troublesome months was moved by two considerations:

1. He wished his country to escape the tragedies inherent in war.

2. He thought that by not becoming a participant in a struggle with which he said his country "was not directly concerned," he could make or find a way to induce the combatants to unite in making an honorable and durable peace. He even then had the vision of a League of Nations which he regarded as "the pearl of great price."

To these two master goals he fully consecrated himself and never doubted they would be achieved until Germany repudiated its pledge and gave notice of the resumption of unrestricted U-boat killing of Americans travelling on the high seas on lawful missions.

Wilson's heart's desire—and he sought its attainment without deviation in the long period of neutrality—was, as he said after learning of the fate of the *Lusitania:* "My earnest hope and fervent prayer has been that America could withhold herself and at the right time offer herself as the only mediating influence to bring about peace." And every day was "the right time" for him, though he was thwarted by trusted agents who, without Wilson's knowledge, were not in sympathy with his hope and prayer; and by British and French belief that German defeat was their only hope; and by Germany's ruthlessness. But neither the lack of loyalty to the trust reposed in them, nor opposition, nor denunciation, nor the storm of ridicule on both sides of the Atlantic swerved him from his high resolve to use neutrality as the ladder to attain lasting world peace. "We are not trying," he said, "to keep out of trouble; we are trying to preserve the foundations upon which peace can be rebuilt."

NEUTRALITY A SLIPPERY ROAD

Upholding neutrality became increasingly difficult in view of the conflicting tides and currents. On one day Wilson would be infuriated by Britain's attacks upon our trade rights and seizure of our mails. At other—often and many—times Wilson was so outraged at the brutal conduct of Germany that he felt moved to favor war in answer to the murderous attacks upon American ships on lawful missions on the high seas.

As the days went by, neutrality became a slippery road. "These are indeed deep waters," Wilson said, and one day, thinking aloud to me, he said: "In one breath the people demand that I keep the country out of war. In the next breath they demand I do not surrender our rights. They talk of me as though I was a God. Any little German lieutenant can put us into war at any time by some calculated outrage."

Torn between German U-boat ruthlessness and British injury to our commerce with neutral countries, Wilson used the period of neutrality diligently to find a way to end the war and to insure a warless world. He was often misjudged, the pro-war advocates blaming him for lack of courage and the pacifists denouncing him for a course they said would lead to war. It was in the days of these cross-currents of public opinion that Wilson had to steer between Scylla and Charybdis. It called for the skill of an experienced navigator—a demand sometimes that tested his leadership almost to the breaking point.

DEMAND OF COTTON GROWERS

Cotton growers, denied old-time markets in Europe, demanded access to them, and North Carolinians urged my coöperation, which caused me to take the matter up with the President and the Secretary of State and urge the administration to demand an end of British action as to shipments of cotton and tobacco. Replying to the appeal of a constituent, Honorable Claude Kitchin, Democratic floor leader wrote:

"I believe that the President is going to show a firm hand finally, but thus far he has not 'spoken out in meeting' to her as resolutely and as clearly as I had hoped. We are in a position to force Great Britain to just and rightful terms and we ought to do it."

When Representative E. Y. Webb, chairman of the Committee on the Judiciary of the House of Representatives, wrote to Kitchin that it was "high time for our government to issue a note of protest to England against her unlawful blockade and unlawful seizures of our commerce," Kitchin sent a prompt response:

"I am certainly gratified to know of your strong position in favor of a big protest to Great Britain. You can count on my cooperation with you to the fullest extent. I will have to go to Washington one day next week and I am going to talk with some of the Administration folks about the matter."

THE SUNRISE CONFERENCE

At a time when the U-boat sinkings had aroused Wilson's hot wrath, certain House leaders, hearing that Wilson was bent on demanding war against Germany, asked for a conference "as soon as possible." And the much-talked-of Sunrise Conference was held at the White House on February 25, 1916, with Speaker Clark, Floor Leader Kitchin, Chairman of the Foreign Relations Committee Flood, and the President present. In his book on Claude Kitchin, written after Kitchin's death, Professor Arnett quotes Kitchin as believing Wilson was anxious to go to war with Germany immediately. In 1921 Kitchin affirmed that in that talk Wilson was bent on war and that he and Clark and Flood combated his purpose vigorously. Kitchin told me about the conference shortly afterwards and said Wilson ought to be prevented from his warlike policy. He said that Wilson's whole manner was that if Germany continued its course war would come and it might be a good thing and hasten peace. Kitchin was the soul of truth and so were Clark and Wilson. They inferred from his indignation that he was belligerent, but at that time he was resisting to the limit the many who were trying to hurry the country into war, including some of his official family.

I told Kitchin that Wilson's attitude was exactly opposite and that he was combating the views of members of his Cabinet who wanted a declaration of war. I said that when Britain had carried American ships into its ports and injured our trade with neutral nations of Europe, Wilson had denounced the action so vehemently that his hearers might have inferred he wanted to go to war with Britain. And at another time, when U-boats were guilty of ruthlessness, I had heard Wilson storm at the outrage with such denunciation that a hearer might think he wanted to go to war with Germany. He must have been in that mood at the Sunrise Conference. Between such denunciations, all well deserved, he was spending himself to secure peace and was being assailed because he was "too proud to fight." When his resentment at wrongs flared, I am sure that if the perpetrators had been present, they would have felt, as Kitchin did, that Wilson was in a fighting mood.

Kitchin left no written statement and neither did Clark, but their recollections were in accord. When the papers printed a story along the line of Kitchin's impression of Wilson's attitude, Flood, who was at the Sunrise Conference said:

"I have heard the President say nothing to indicate that war with Germany might not be a bad thing for this country or that he desired war. On the contrary, the President told me that he was working night and day to keep this nation out of war."

When the report that Wilson had talked war at the conference got out, Wilson made a public statement that he "had not made any utterance to which any such meaning could be attached." Clark and Kitchin had opposed the repeal of the Panama Canal toll act, and their relations with Wilson were not the most cordial.

HOT DEBATE IN CABINET

After Germany's pledge in the *Sussex* note, in which Germany met Wilson's demands as to U-boat sinkings (May 4, 1916), Wilson's energies were devoted to peace, even a "peace without victory." He did not give up his ardent hope and sincere effort for peace until the resumption of unrestricted submarine sinkings on February 1, 1917. Up to that hour, in spite of a growing sentiment for war, Wilson resolutely devoted every energy toward securing an end of the holocaust. I recall his words in a meeting of the Cabinet in January, 1917. A colleague said: "People are demanding that we go to war against Germany and are accusing the administration of cowardice." Wilson flared up. I never saw him look more like a righteous prophet. In tense tones he replied: "I do not care what they say about us as long as we are seeking our goal without loss of life." He reviewed with great eloquence and deep sincerity the long and perilous journey since the fires of war flamed. He concluded with a condemnation of those who were unwilling to test every avenue to peace if thereby war could be honorably avoided. At that time McAdoo and Lane and Houston and Redfield were openly belligerent. The rest of us, except Lansing, held the same hope and desire as was incarnated in Wilson.

WHY WILSON OPPOSED WAR

That afternoon I had an engagement to see the President at the White House. Before entering upon the business in hand, Wilson laid his hand affectionately on my shoulder and said:

"I was very glad you spoke out so clearly in the Cabinet meeting this morning when some of our brethren were trying to drive us into war. It may be—I fear so—there will be no other course. If the German pledge is broken there will be no escape, but I am resolved to keep out if possible. There are two reasons why I am resolved to keep our country out of this war if possible:

"1. If we go to war thousands of young men will lose their lives. I could not sleep with myself if I do not go to the extreme limit to prevent such mourning in American homes.

"2. Every reform we have won since 1912 will be lost. We have got new tariff, currency, shipping and trust legislation. These new policies are not thoroughly set. They will be imperilled or lost if we go to war. We will be dependent in war upon steel, oil, aluminum, ships, and war materials. They are controlled by Big Business. Undoubtedly many captains of industry will be patriotic and serve their country, but when the war is over those whose privileges we have uprooted or started to uproot will gain control of government and neither you nor I will live to see government returned to the people. Big Business will be in the saddle. More than that—Free Speech and the other rights will be endangered. War is autocratic."

In the critical days before the German Ambassador was given his walking papers, Secretary Lansing read a note at a Cabinet meeting which contained the words: "The Imperial German Government *demands*." Cabinet members showed indignation at the use of the word "demands." Wilson directed the Secretary of State to return the communication, pointing out the objectionable word. It was returned later with "requests" substituted for "demands."

LEAGUE TO ENFORCE PEACE

I can never forget the historic address Wilson made at the banquet of the League to Enforce Peace in Washington (May 27, 1916). Two thousand patriotic Americans, headed by ex-President Taft gave it distinction, but Wilson's inspiring address high-lighted the event, with Lodge as a close second in advocacy of a world organization to end war. Looking back, it is evident that Wilson was outlining the Covenant of Peace that emerged from Versailles. In his address Lodge went even further than Wilson in declaring for the League to Enforce Peace, in the course of which he said: "I do not believe that when Washington warned us against entangling alliances he meant for one moment that we should not join with the other civilized nations of the world if a method could be found to diminish war and encourage peace." But when the method was found,—and the only method—Lodge sneered at "Wilson's League," compassed its rejection, and thereby assumed large responsibility for World War II, which would have been averted if we had followed Wilson.

Shortly thereafter, I spoke in Philadelphia at a League to Enforce Peace where I found the same zeal for world organization. Governor Bickett, of North Carolina, stirred all by his eloquence.

MANDATE FROM THE PEOPLE

Wilson hoped that because of his reëlection (1916) he "could not only suggest peace," but could "demand it." He regarded it as a mandate from the people. He told House to inform Grey that he and others looked upon "the continuation of the war through another winter with the utmost distaste and misgiving." He suggested to House (still thinking House spoke his mind) that he wished no softening of pressure on Britain by the intervention of Page, and even suggested that "Page no longer represents the feeling and point of view of the United States," not realizing that House was in accord with Page.

On the 25th of November, Wilson drafted his matured plans for peace. As Wilson was making ready to send his note, a peace proposal came from Germany which was repudiated by all the allied countries. But Wilson still persisted.

WORKING FOR PEACE

On December 18, 1916, Wilson made his final formal plea for peace in a note to the Powers asking them to state frankly their views as to the terms upon which war might be ended and the peace guaranteed. He did not offer mediation but hoped that this note would lead to an interchange of views and to a conference in which he would be "happy to serve or even to take the initiative." The olive branch was received with scorn by German leaders, who believed their submarines to be invincible. In England it was received with a sense of resentment. News from London was that "the King wept" when he read Wilson's suggestion, and the London *Post* said it was "reminiscent of the attitude of the antique gods." Neither side would disclose its terms, but rather acted as if Wilson were "meddling." He would not give up even then, but on January 22 delivered his famous "Peace Without Victory" address, in which he appealed to "the peoples of the world who have as yet had no place or opportunity to speak their real hearts out concerning the death and ruin they see to have come already upon the persons and the homes they hold dear."

A torrent of bitter criticism followed, led by Theodore Roosevelt and Lodge. After long discussion, the Senate adopted a resolution approving that part of Wilson's note which requested the terms upon which peace might be discussed. The debate foreshadowed the Senate's later rejection of the League of Nations.

In all his noble aspirations, Wilson had no coöperation from Lansing and House. Along with Page, they wished for war. But Wilson stood unmoved in his efforts for peace until Germany announced that, beginning February 1, 1917, it would resume unrestricted submarine warfare. Wilson then went to Congress and informed that body that diplomatic relations with Germany were severed. Even then he was still hoping against hope, saying:

> "I refuse to believe that it is the intention of the German authorities to do in fact what they have warned us they will feel at liberty to do. Only actual overt acts on their part can make me believe it even now."

Influences beyond mortal control were carrying us into war. Wilson resolved not to take the final plunge if it could be avoided.

GERMANY'S GRIEVANCE

Germany was bitter because munitions were flowing freely to the Allies from United States industrial plants, and demanded an embargo on munitions of war. Bryan replied that there is no power in the Executive to prevent the sale of ammunition to belligerents and no restriction had been placed on neutrals by international law or statute. Any country was at liberty to buy munitions in the United States. Britain could do so freely because of its strong Navy while Germany could not because of Britain's sea power. That was Germany's chief grievance, and that country continued to argue that this gave aid to Britain. If so, it was because of conditions outside the control of this country. When the United States declined to surrender its doctrine of freedom of the seas, the German U-boats increased their ruthless sinking of American shipping.

LIFE SUPERIOR TO THINGS

The difference between the wrongs inflicted by Germany and by Britain on the United States was that Germany's policy resulted in the death of Americans, while the British wrongs affected merchandise. Germany would kill human beings while Britain killed commerce. In the final wind-up, human life was regarded as more sacred than trade.

WILSON'S UNALTERABLE POSITION

Perhaps the clearest statement of Wilson's unalterable purpose, pursued consistently in the many months when he was seeking to obtain it by negotiation without recourse to war, was in a letter to Senator Stone, Chairman of the Finance Committee, who warned against "plunging the nation into the vortex of this World War." After expressing the hope that the Central Powers would keep their promises, he said that if the promises made to him were violated,

> "We should, it seems to me, have in honor no choice as to what our course should be. For my own part, I cannot consent to any abridgment of the rights of our country in this respect. The honor and self respect of the nation are involved. We want peace and shall preserve it at any cost but the loss of honor.... If, in this instance, we allowed expediency to take the place of principle, the door would inevitably be opened to still further concessions. Once accept a single abatement of right and many other limitations would follow."

LXI

THE COUNCIL OF NATIONAL DEFENSE

A S A MEASURE of preparedness Congress in August, 1916, had made provision for the creation of the Council of National Defense for the purposes its name implies, and created with it a National Advisory Commission. It had large powers; for example, it could "place orders for war material directly with any source of supply," and could commandeer plants. Naturally as the Secretary of War, Newton D. Baker was its Chairman, and Josephus Daniels, Secretary of the Navy, its ranking member. This gave perfect coördination with the Army, the Navy, and national industry. The Council was constituted with this membership:

MEMBERS: Newton D. Baker, Secretary of War, Chairman; Josephus Daniels, Secretary of the Navy; Franklin K. Lane, Secretary of the Interior; David F. Houston, Secretary of Agriculture; William C. Redfield, Secretary of Commerce; William B. Wilson, Secretary of Labor.

ADVISORY COMMISSION: Daniel Willard, Chairman; Bernard M. Baruch, Julius Rosenwald, Dr. Franklin H. Martin, Hollis Godfrey, Howard E. Coffin, Samuel Gompers.

DIRECTOR: Walter S. Gifford; Secretary, Grosvenor B. Clarkson.

Politics played no part in the organization. The Advisory Commission was said to contain three Democrats and three Republicans. It worked harmoniously and efficiently, calling into being, with the approval of the President, the numerous agencies that were essential for efficient war service, originating and carrying out plans that secured national participation in war at every point.

A STRANGE ACCUSATION

At an early joint session a strange accusation was made against the three officials directing war operations: the President of the United States, Commander in Chief; Newton Baker, Secretary of War, directing the forces on land, and Josephus Daniels, directing Naval activities, and against Secretary Wilson and Mr. Gompers. This

accusation is thus quoted by Dr. Franklin Martin in his autobiography:

> "Messrs. Secretaries of War, Navy, Labor and Mr. Gompers: It
> is asserted that you four, together with President Wilson, are
> avowed pacificists. As we are here to prepare for war, how can
> you, as pacificists, consistently lead us?"

That question, originating with enemies of the administration and
propounded by men who had been requested by us to help prepare
for war, was, to say the least, gratuitous, if not insulting. I felt my
temper rising at the imputation that those of us who wished to keep
the country out of war were not worthy to prepare for war and conduct it if the storm broke. I watched Newton Baker, Secretary of
War, who was presiding. If his temper was ruffled he did not show
it but quietly, after lighting his pipe, replied:

> "I am, and so is Secretary Daniels and President Wilson,
> opposed to war, as are a large majority of the American people.
> This hatred of war and desire to escape it does not stand in the
> way of leaving nothing undone to discourage the thought of war
> by would-be enemies or making the most adequate preparations
> for war if it is eventually forced upon us. We hope to dissuade
> other countries from waging war against us by the most thorough
> preparedness if reason fails. In any event...."

Continuing the relation of a remarkable conversation, after quoting
Baker's statement in condensed form, Martin continues:

> "Then the Secretary of the Navy, Josephus Daniels, hesi-
> tatingly, his strong emotions not so well controlled as those of
> the Secretary of War, confessed that he was morally, spiritually
> and economically opposed to the practise of settling differences,
> individual or national, by physical encounter or warfare. He
> hoped, even yet, that we would not be drawn into the existing
> conflict. If destroyers of peace manifest themselves, our Navy
> must repel them to the utmost limit of our resources.
> "Secretary Wilson said war was an abomination. When hosts
> of men become unmanageable they must be treated as we treat
> other elements of nature, they must be subdued. To subdue them
> we must be prepared.
> "Mr. Gompers was disinclined to discuss the contingency of
> war, and shrank, apparently, even from admitting that it was

TOO LARGE FOR HIS BREECHES

Critics, regarding Bryan and Daniels as pacifists, ridiculed their supposed pacifism by representing them as tailors, giving the Army and Navy suits that did not fit.

possible so much talk of war would tend to break down the resistance of a peace-loving people. He had no doubt, however, as to our job: we must prepare to defend ourselves and our nation if aggressions thrust the necessity upon us."

After recording the implication that lovers of peace were not the best men to prepare for war, and the above statements, Martin adds for himself and his associates of the Advisory Commission:

"We gathered comfort from these revelations for they reflected the strength of character of each of our associates, and convinced us that these men, occupying responsible positions, were already determined to bend every effort to fortify the departments they controlled to meet the sternest realities. Struck by the cordiality of each member of the Council, I immediately felt that the newcomers were distinctly welcomed. Particularly was I impressed by the much-discussed Mr. Daniels."

As the perfect coöperation progressed, under the exigencies of war service, all political and other differences were quickly submerged and one day Willard said to Martin:

"This is a strange life. If any one had told me that my personal antagonism toward Samuel Gompers would change within one week to ardent admiration and real affection, I would have pronounced that individual a fit candidate for an insane asylum."

The Council was fortunate in securing Walter S. Gifford as director. He came into the important position because when the Naval Consulting Board (often called the Edison Board) was called into being by me in 1915, Gifford, who was loaned by the American Telephone and Telegraph Company, of which he later became the president, did a remarkable piece of work in making an inventory of all industrial plants in the country and ascertaining to what production of war materials they could be converted. For example, he ascertained quickly that the manufacturers of sewing machines could convert their plants to the manufacture of parts of mines, and before war was declared the Navy had—thanks to Gifford and his capable assistants—a perfect inventory of places which in short order could be converted into factories for the manufacture of articles or parts of articles needed for the conduct of war.

Grosvenor Clarkson became secretary and carried on when Gifford returned to his duties as president of the American Telephone and Telegraph Company after the Armistice.

Dr. Martin also records that Gompers buried his face in his hands and burst into tears. I do not recall this. "Suddenly," says Martin, "he threw his head back and broke forth: 'By God's help I can no longer stand it. I must yield. War to suppress crime is justifiable; my boys, many of them already straining at the leash, will follow me.'"

This questioning whether the President and the officials who had worked with him in the hope of averting war and garnering peace after the carnage were the proper men to direct preparations and the execution of plans for the great struggle ahead, was not a propitious start, to say the least. Dr. Martin was new in Washington. He did not know that from the breaking out of war in Europe, Wilson had led in strengthening the Navy as the first arm for war, or that Baker and I had put munition plants and shipbuilding plants and every concern that could make war materials, on an overtime basis, and that Baker had in his desk a selective draft ready to put into effect. Baker and I and the officers had worked night and day to make ready, while critics were seeking partisan advantage. The good doctor was right in saying my emotions stirred me. He would have been nearer the truth if he had said I showed indignation, seeing what the Navy had done without blowing horns— "and that is the best thing about it," Lodge testified. I was hot under the collar because a civilian we had called in to help in the great work should suggest the unfitness of the men who had selected him and his colleagues as advisers.

Dr. Martin had been reading the hammering of the administration in the Chicago papers and had not examined into their animus. Neither Washington nor Lincoln nor McKinley nor Wilson wished war. But they waged war more efficiently than men who glorified war. The victory showed that Dr. Martin had accepted unfriendly propaganda. When he learned the truth, he became the strongest friend and supporter of the President, the Secretary of War, and the Secretary of the Navy. He rendered distinguished service, particularly in organizing the medical profession for the great work that brought new glory to the disciples of Aesculapius.

LXII

PREPARING FOR WAR

ON THE DAY before Wilson gave to Congress his message breaking relations with Germany, the Cabinet had held a long session. All the members had read the German note and were ready to follow their chief. As he entered the Cabinet room, all rose to greet him as a mark of honor and as comrades in the grim days they felt were ahead. The President was grave and serious. The feeling was that the destiny of one hundred million people—perhaps the whole world—lay in the decision of that hour. The President read the note aloud so that all could hear and then invited comment from the members of his official family. All were agreed as to the course, though presenting different suggestions as to the means. The unanimous verdict was that relations with Germany must be severed. The session lasted through several hours of grave discussion of the declaration and the preparation to meet the expected eventuality of war. Most of the time was devoted to what steps each department, particularly the Army and the Navy, should take. That night I sent this message to every ship and station:

> Six Alnav-a—In view of the present international situation, take every precaution to protect Government plants and vessels.
>
> DANIELS

PRECAUTION AGAINST PROPAGANDA

The February days were anxious and tense. Previously the Navy had taken over wireless stations, some of which had in peace times been operated by Germans. That move was necessary to prevent their use for German propaganda and for communication from German officials to their agents in the United States. There were pacifist Americans who believed if they could communicate with the Kaiser they might induce him to withdraw his U-boat ultimatum and seek peace. They assumed they could have more influence than officials. It was reported that they hoped to send messages which they regarded as harmless through wireless stations operated by the Navy. Fearing this possible outside attempt to negotiate, President Wilson sent me the following note written on his own typewriter:

"8 February, 1917

"THE WHITE HOUSE
"WASHINGTON

"My dear Daniels:

"So many people who want to run our foreign affairs for us are trying to communicate with the German Government that it has occurred to me that they might try to employ the wireless stations, which are under the control of your Department. I hope that you will very carefully guard against that and issue very strict and definite orders about it. There is extreme danger in everything of that kind. Impressions are apt to be made which will be so misleading as to make war more rather than less likely, by leading the German authorities to a wholly wrong impression,—especially as they know that no messages go through that we do not officially let through.

"I hasten this over to you, because it is a matter which I had omitted to cover in our conferences.

"Faithfully yours,
"WOODROW WILSON"

"The Secretary of the Navy"

READY TO VINDICATE RIGHTS

Ardently clinging to a peace spar in the deep waters had not permitted Wilson to lose sight of his pledge to be ready to "vindicate our right to liberty, and justice and an unmolested life." He had closed his address to Congress with a prayer from the very center of his being: "God grant we may not be challenged to defend them by acts of wilful injustice." Just as Wilson was announcing the severance of relations, the news came that the *Housatonic* had been sunk in European waters.

At three o'clock that afternoon the President, the Secretary of War, and Secretary of the Navy were in conference at the White House. The President was concerned about the safety of government property. There was cause for anxiety, for there were thousands of aliens who could not be legally interned until war was declared. Some might resort to violence to cripple the government's preparation for war. That night I sent orders directing all vessels to report their readiness for war. All Navy yards and Army posts were closed, all communi-

C. K. Berryman, in the *Washington Star*

COMMENDED BY UNCLE SAM

A report of the greatest Naval construction in the history of any country in
peace time.

cations placed on a war basis, a coast patrol was established, and guards at the strategic Panama Canal were strengthened by orders from the Secretary of War.

Monday afternoon, consulting with officers on plans and orders, Wilson appeared unexpectedly in my office. I reviewed with him the details, informed him of all the things that been done, and asked his directions as to further steps. I had long ago learned that he was a better Naval strategist than any Admiral. As we finished this review, the President suggested that we go over to the War Department to confer with Secretary Baker. He knew that both arms of the military service must work in perfect unison. We discussed steps for readiness for any eventuality. Men concerned him as much as weapons. He wanted to know about officers for the most important commands. He advised that if there were any in key positions not equal to the tremendous tasks ahead, they should be replaced.

ARMING MERCHANT SHIPS

With the sinking of the schooner *Lyman M. Law* on February 12, the Cabinet discussed the immediate steps to be taken. Wilson had long resisted the pressure to arm merchant ships. In a stormy Cabinet meeting on February 23, Houston, Lane, and McAdoo insisted upon immediate action. Wilson said, "You are trying to push us into war." He was irritated when Lane inquired whether it was true that German authorities had stripped the wives of American consuls to "search for writings on their flesh." Lansing had no such reports, and Wilson regarded this as a suggestion that we should work up a propaganda of hatred against Germany. He said that Lane was appealing to the Code Duello. It was not these urgings by Cabinet members but the German attitude that caused Wilson to go before Congress and ask for the authority to arm merchant ships.

In the Cabinet meeting the President asked: "Daniels, has the Navy the gunners and the guns for this job?"

"We can arm them as fast as the ships are ready," I replied.

The sentiment was unanimous for arming them, but the question was debated whether, in the absence of congressional authority, the President had the right to do so. Wilson believed that he had that authority but wished the power of Congress behind him—to be employed at the proper time.

Therefore, on February 26, in an address to a joint session of Congress, he requested authority to "supply our merchant ships with defensive arms, should that become necessary, and with the means of using them, and to employ any other instrumentalities or methods that may be necessary and adequate to protect our ships and our people in their legitimate and peaceful pursuits on the sea." The House gave approval by a vote of 403 to 14, but a filibuster in the Senate in the closing days by a handful of Senators, called by Wilson the "little group of willful men," prevented a vote. The Congress expired without giving the requested authority. All the Senators but five signed a statement that they would have voted for the resolution but for the filibuster.

"MEN'S HEARTS WAIT UPON US"

In the last hours of Wilson's first term there could be heard in the White House the echoes of the bitterness of the Senate filibuster; the sounds of the machines fashioning munitions for the Army and Navy; and from across the Atlantic, the jubilation of Frenchmen and Britishers rejoicing in deliverance from losing the war. Even above the thundering of the guns, the lightning of the artillery, and the whirring of "the airy navies in the central blue," Wilson still hoped—even against hope—that Germany would hold back from its threat of ruthless undersea warfare.

Conscious that he had left no stone unturned to induce the warring nations to find a better way than war to settle their differences—even 'peace without victory'—and thankful if the worst came that the blood of no American mother's fighting son would be on his head, Wilson stood ready, with courage and fortitude, to face whatever the future held in store. He was resolved not to permit any abridgment of the inherent right of his countrymen to sail the seas on lawful missions or to lose the vision of a warless world. He was strengthened by the patriotic and united support of his once divided America.

In that period before neutrality was giving place to war, Wilson sensed that the hearts of the people beat in unison with his own, and that they were responding to the spirit of his challenge when he first entered upon his duties as chief executive:

"This is a day of dedication," he said in his inaugural address (March 4, 1913) "Here muster the forces of humanity. Men's hearts wait upon us; men's lives hang in the balance. I summon all honest men, all patriotic, all forward-looking men to my side. God helping me, I will not fail them, if they will but counsel and sustain me."

Wilson did not fail them. And the American people did not fail to counsel and sustain him in the grim days of war that faced the country in the spring of 1917.

INDEX

INDEX

A.B.C. Powers, and the Mexican situation, 203

Abell, Ed S., 40

Adams, John, 535

Addicks, Lawrence, 492

Agriculture, and the Wilson administration, 94-95

Air mail, inauguration of, 292

Alderman, Edwin A., and Wilson, 519 ff.

Alexander, Joshua W., 144

Alifas, Mr. spokesman for workmen in War and Navy departments, 367

American Federation of Labor, 306

American Legion, National Convention of in Portland, Ore., J. D. addresses, 408

American Medical Journal, commends Wine Mess Order, 394

American Telephone and Telegraph Company, 497, 498, 590

Andrews, Philip, and new Navy promotion regulations, 280 ff. *passim;* mentioned, 247

Annapolis. *See* Naval Academy.

Apex, N. C., 39

Armor-plate monopoly, and the U. S. Navy, 351 ff.

Armor-plate Plant, government, 354 ff.; cartoon of, 362; building of prevented by World War and Republicans, 363

Army, U. S., takes over Vera Cruz situation, 202 ff.

Arnett, A. M., on Claude Kitchin, 580

Arnold, Bion J., 492

Asheville, N. C., opposed Wilson in 1912, 37; offers Wilson summer home, 94, 96

Asquith, Herbert H., blind to Germany's designs in 1914, 567

Astoria, Ore., J. D., visits, 306, 307

Austin, Midshipman and Mrs. J. E., story of, 404

Avery, Judge A. C., characterized, 43, 44 n.

Aviation, Naval, J. D.'s, early interest in, 288 ff.; Bureau of established in Navy Department, 296; Board of, 293

Aycock, Charles B., for Wilson in 1912, 36

BADGER, Charles J., ordered to guard eastern coast of Mexico, 192; at Vera Cruz, 197, 199; and the Kaiser's photograph, 251; in first wireless conversation with ship at sea, 498; mentioned, 194, 240, 297, 298, 327, 347, 504, 510

Badger, George E., former Secretary of Navy, 113

Baekeland, L. H., 492

Bagley, Mrs. Adelaide Worth, at inauguration of air mail, 292

Bagley, David Worth, 122

Bagley, Ensign Worth, 122, 247, 300

Bailey, Josiah, for Wilson in 1912, 40, 41

Baker, James M., 152-53

Baker, Newton D., relations of with Labor, 367; succeeds Garrison as Secretary of War, 448 ff.; characterized, 450, 451; at 1916 Convention, 462; and Council of National Defense, 586 ff. *passim;* mentioned, 54, 437

Baker, Ray Stannard, on Wilson's nomination, 48; characterization of Wilson's Cabinet by, 113; quotes Burleson on Marshall, 551; on House's mission to Europe, 569; on Wilson-House relationship, 570-71

Baldwin, Simeon, opposed Brandeis for Supreme Court, 544

Ball, Thomas H., 48, 57

Ballinger, Richard A., 304

Baltimore Convention, full account of, 49 ff.; fight for temporary chairman of, 49 ff.; Bryan explodes a bomb, 54 ff.; nominates Wilson, 62

Baltimore *Evening Sun,* 46

Baltimore *Sun,* on Bryan, 58; supports Wilson, 62

"Baltimore Transformation, The," cartoon, 56

Bankhead, John H., Sr., leader of Underwood forces in 1912, 36; as manager for Underwood invited to leave N. C. on eve of Democratic Convention, 41-42; characterized, 43

Bankhead, John H., son of John H. Bankhead, Sr., 43

Bankhead, Tallulah, 43

Bankhead, William B., 43

Banks, Howard, 245

Barbecue, in Ore. and N. C., 307

Barnett, George, appointed head of Marine Corps, 323

Barry, John, 468

Bart (Charles L. Bartholomew), cartoon by, 56

Bartlett, Ralph T., 120

Baruch, Bernard M., sketch of, 87; on Council of National Defense, 586